The

Theology of Plato

Proclus

Translated by
Thomas Taylor

Published by
The Prometheus Trust

Volume VIII

of

The Thomas Taylor Series

The Prometheus Trust

194 The Butts, Frome,
Somerset BA11 4AG, UK.

A registered charity,
number 299648.

The Theology of Plato

This Edition published in 1995.
Reprinted 1999.

ISBN 1 898910 07 3

First Edition published in 1816.

British Library Cataloguing-in-Publication Data.
A catalogue record for this book is
available from the British Library.

Printed in England by Antony Rowe, Chippenham, Wiltshire.

The Prometheus Trust was founded in 1986 in order to help reintroduce to educational establishments those true First Principles which have been the basis of all the world's lasting civilisations. These Principles were given their clearest expression in the West by Plato and those great ones who either provided his grounding in Truth or continued and expanded his beautiful exposition of reality. It is for this reason that the Trust is now making available the whole of the published works of Thomas Taylor, the 'English Platonist', whose philosophical understanding of the principles enshrined in the writings of Plato, Proclus, Plotinus and others is unparalleled in recent times.

The Prometheus Trust would like to thank all those who have contributed to the work involved in the Thomas Taylor Series. We are especially indebted to members of **The Platonic Guild** and would recommend this organisation to all those who wish to make a study of this pure philosophy in order to establish the virtuous life.

The Prometheus Trust is a registered educational charity number 299648. All enquiries should be addressed to: Mr T J Addey, Chairman, The Prometheus Trust, Huan House, 17 Rossiters Hill, Frome, Somerset, BA11 4AL.

The address of The Platonic Guild is: The Old Shop, Lamyatt, Nr Shepton Mallet, Somerset, BA4 6NP

CONTENTS

Preface to the Thomas Taylor Series iii

Thomas Taylor v

Introduction to *The Theology of Plato* vii

Notes on the text x

The contents of the chapters of the seven books xiii

Taylor's Introduction to *The Theology of Plato* 1

Book I 51

Book II 126

Book III 173

Book IV 235

Book V 303

Book VI 394

Book VII 466

Additional Notes 638

References to the writings of Plato 695

Preface to the Thomas Taylor Series

This series makes available all the writings of Thomas Taylor for the first time since his death in 1835. There are several general purposes for the presentation of this series; these are as follows:

Firstly, Thomas Taylor's translations and original writings represent the most comprehensive philosophical re-expression in the English language of the wisdom of European antiquity. Taylor not only understood the *philosophy* of the Platonic tradition but also revered its *religion*. His works draw upon the fragments which survive from the earliest Orphic and Pythagorean mystery schools, through Plato and Aristotle's pure philosophy, and onwards to the later Platonists who were the final flowering of the Classical civilisation. As such, Taylor's work as a whole, when studied patiently, will awaken the mind to reasonable and intuitive truth.

Secondly, it is obvious that while our educational system and institutions have grown out of the Platonic world-view, the clarity of the original vision has been gravely distorted by materialism. Therefore there is an urgent need for a purging of the damaging false opinions now so prevalent in the very institutions which should be leading enquiring minds to the intelligible beauty. The precision and purity of Thomas Taylor's writings will undoubtedly act as such a purgative.

Thirdly, that as the short-comings of the various so-called philosophies of recent centuries are exposed, a re-appraisal of the ancient philosophy prematurely rejected will need to be made. The reasons for this rejection lie in the pressures of the history of past centuries and millennia: In the fullness of time, no doubt, the exploration of empiricists, materialists and reductionists down the dead-end paths of philosophy will be seen as a dialectical testing of the negation of truth and will thus serve a better end than they themselves could imagine. Nevertheless the immediate philosophical inheritance of the twenty-first century is one that is narrow-minded and barren. A new beginning must be made: the depth and breadth of Taylor's writings (a result of a labour of truly Herculean proportions) make them an ideal foundation for a genuine philosophical education. It is to be devoutly hoped that in the not-too-distant future a system of training will be properly established on the principles expounded by the true philosophers of the ancient West, which complement and confirm the teachings of the East. Such a system will lead to a beholding of the highest truths and, ultimately, to the contemplation of Beauty itself. To those who in the future so labour, this series is especially dedicated.

Fourthly, it was almost certainly the wish of Thomas Taylor that a uniform edition of all his writings be published. After his death, his literary executor and friend, Isaac Preston Cory, arranged that his library should be auctioned by Sothebys and the final lot offered at this auction was that of the copyright of all Taylor's writings: the catalogue, which bears the marks of someone who knew Thomas Taylor well, states "The reason of the entire copy-right of all the works being offered for public competition altogether, is, to enable the purchaser to publish his works in a uniform manner....." The copyright was, unfortunately, never bought and the wish has remained, until now, unfulfilled. This series is, then, a small mark of gratitude for his selfless service to Wisdom and to those who love Wisdom.

Aside from these general purposes there are important academic reasons for the presentation of this series: it is of especial interest because Taylor's was the first complete translation into English of Plato and Aristotle along with the major part of the surviving works of the later Platonists. Taylor himself writes from within the so-called neoPlatonic tradition and this further adds to the academic value of his works. There is at present a revival of interest in the later Platonists, whose texts have become the subject of attention of certain leading authorities in the history of philosophy, to such an extent that all the available texts are being collected together, and critically examined and translated. The texts upon which Taylor worked were even more incomplete and full of errors than those which are now available. Where he came across these difficulties, Taylor rectified errors in the original Greek and filled lacunas in the text by conjecturing what, in his view, should have been there. Modern textual evidence points to the fact that he was very largely correct in these conjectures and this, in turn, bears witness to his profound understanding of the philosophy to which he devoted his life. As an aid to academic studies the series will include line and page numbering, such as Stephanus and Bekker, wherever appropriate. The wording of Taylor's books is kept except where there are obvious errors - all of which will be noted.

THOMAS TAYLOR

Born 15 May 1758, London; died 1 November 1835, London.

THOMAS TAYLOR the Platonist was certainly the most extraordinary and admirable philosophic character of modern times. He was the first English translator of the whole of Plato's works, of the whole of Aristotle, and of the majority of the works of Plotinus, Porphyry, Proclus, Iamblichus and the other later Platonists. In his own age he was the subject of the irrational and barbed criticism of pseudo-intellectual popular critics, who failed to perceive that although they may have known more Greek, Taylor knew more Plato. His intuitive appreciation of both the truth and the grandeur of Platonic thought, coupled with its living day-to-day practice, enabled him to undertake and complete a remarkable body of work. When one inspects such a collection of translations and original works, it seems extraordinary that these were the fruits of one self-taught man, labouring under the triple burdens of ill-health, financial insufficiency, and negative criticism for most of his exceptional life. His translations and commentaries were the chief source of Greek philosophy to the writers and poets of the Romantic movement, including Blake, Shelley and Wordsworth. In America his works provided the firm foundation for the Transcendentalist movement of R W Emerson and Bronson Alcott; his name was held in higher esteem here than ever it enjoyed in his native England. His living espousal of both the intellectual and religious disciplines of the ancient wisdom, coupled with his philosophical observations on the limitations of Christianity, earned him the mocking title of the "English Pagan". No doubt he would have accepted this as just praise. Taylor's motto, written by himself, was:

> "No servile scribe am I, nor e'er shall be,
> My sire is Mind, whose sons are always free."

His motto is at once both a dedication to the pursuit of Truth, and a rebuttal to his hireling bigoted critics, whose folly he dismisses in these vigorous verses - again, written by himself:

> "Vent'rous I tread in paths untrod before,
> And depths immense, and dazzling heights explore;
> Anxious from Error's night to point the way

> That leads to Wisdom's everlasting day;
> To check my flight in vain blind Folly tries,
> For, Heav'n my friend, I conquer as I rise."

Thomas Taylor was not only a scholar of a high order, but also an ardent philosopher in spirit and in energy. His love of wisdom dominated every last element of his life and developed an insight into the esoteric meaning of Greek philosophy that has never been equalled nor approached by any scholar of modern times. There may be 'easier' or more readily accessible translations of the sacred works of the Platonic tradition, but there are none more consistently reliable nor more replete with that profound understanding which comes from elevation of mind and inspiration alone.

Thomas Taylor was in truth "an exile straying from the orb of Light," and his epitaph, written by himself, sums up the dedication and course of his life:

> "Health, strength, and ease, and manhood's active age,
> Freely I gave to Plato's sacred page.
> With Truth's pure joys, with Fame my days were crown'd
> Tho' Fortune adverse on my labours frown'd."†

Thomas Taylor dedicated his works to the 'sacred majesty of Truth' - a great and noble cause for a great and noble soul.

---

† The three verses quoted can be found in Thomas Moore-Johnson's *Life of Thomas Taylor* which appeared in the journal *The Platonist*.

THE THEOLOGY

OF PLATO

INTRODUCTION

By The Prometheus Trust

The following work is one of the most profound and sacred products that an inspired human intellect has ever produced. Though little known, the importance of this magnificent exposition of theology, at once both Platonic and universal, can never be overstated, as it is an extraordinary and lucid blend of pure philosophy, religion, and science, in all of which the divine Proclus was an adept. Earlier volumes in this series have shown that the mythology of the Greeks is neither a collection of fantasy tales, nor merely a form of anthropomorphic or cosmic symbolism and allegory, but that it is a body of images replete with the most spiritual and arcane truths which defy commonplace modes of expression. Plato concealed very well his personal teaching and theological interpretation of this mythology, and it was the work of Proclus, the Platonic Successor, to bring to consummation the evolving revelation of Plato's theology as the last great Platonist to chair the philosophic school in Athens. As Proclus himself says on page 1 of this work: "But I particularly think that the mystic doctrine respecting divine concerns, which is purely established on a sacred foundation, and which perpetually subsists with the Gods themselves, became thence apparent to such as are capable of enjoying it for a time, through one man (Plato), whom I should not err in calling the primary leader and hierophant of those true mysteries, into which souls separated from terrestrial places are initiated, and of those entire and stable visions, which those participate who genuinely embrace a happy and blessed life. But this philosophy shone forth at first from him so venerably and arcanely, as if established in sacred temples, and within their adyta, and being unknown to many who have entered into these holy places, in certain orderly periods of time, proceeded as much as was possible for it into light, through certain true priests, and who embraced a life corresponding to the tradition of such mystic concerns. It appears likewise to me, that the whole place became splendid, and that illuminations of divine spectacles every where presented themselves to the view."

The Theology of Plato is an essentially religious work, and ranks with the very best of the sacred teachings of all nations. It is, in reality, a monumental and near perfect attempt to express in a manner accessible to the reasoning mind, the universal order of all things. As such, Proclus' masterpiece is pan-cosmic in its scope, illuminating the principles which produce, vivify, and perfect the whole of Being, Life, Intellect, Soul, Nature, and Body, as well as their parts; whilst suspending all of these from one exempt and superessential Unity, called The One and The Good, from which all things can be seen as proceeding, and to which all things desire to return. This is the simple pattern Proclus adopts throughout the whole of *The Theology of Plato*.

The absence of a scientific theology in the Christian religion, and in others, produces an inexplicable gap or vacuum between the one God (upon which all religions agree) and his ultimate creations. But if man, and therefore the universe, is made in the image of God; and if all living things effect to generate offspring similar to themselves, this one God must be more prolific and perfect in the generation of similars than any and all of his creations, and these offspring will be legitimately named Gods. Thus the vacuum is filled through the progressive generations of divinity, producing and permeating every sphere of existence, life, and intelligence. Yet the exempt transcendency of The One is referred to continuously in this Theology; and Thomas Taylor points this out in gentle caution: "It must not be supposed, that the Gods are nothing more than so many attributes of the First Cause; for if this were the case, the First God would be multitude, but the one must always be prior to the many. But the Gods, though they are profoundly united with their ineffable cause, are at the same time self-perfect essences; for the First Cause is prior to self-perfection. Hence, as the First Cause is superessential, all the Gods, from their union through the summits or blossoms of their natures with this incomprehensible God, will be likewise superessential; in the same manner as trees from being rooted in the earth are all of them earthly in an eminent degree. And as in this instance the earth itself is essentially distinct from the trees which it contains, so the highest God is transcendently distinct from the multitude of Gods which he ineffably comprehends."

This is the only English translation of *The Theology of Plato*; and as such, we owe an inestimable debt of gratitude to Thomas Taylor for leaving to all future generations a great key to the understanding of the nature of the Gods, the cosmos, and the nature and destiny of man. No other translation could so accurately and beautifully express the intentions of the original's author, unless the translator not only profoundly understood this Theology, but also believed it in the depth of his soul - both of which Thomas Taylor possessed to a very high degree. The seventh Book, which Thomas Taylor added to supply the want of the original, completes the total sweep of this Platonic Theology, and no editions of this work would be complete or useful without it.

The Prometheus Trust is delighted to present *The Six Books of Proclus On The Theology of Plato* to the general public for the first time since 1816. It is indeed a most sacred theology dealing with the most profound of ideas, written by Proclus to be an aid and a vision for all mankind. His own words, in the beginning of his Commentary on The Parmenides, sum up his view of the Platonic Philosophy and Theology: "FOR, WITH RESPECT TO THIS TYPE OF PHILOSOPHY, I SHOULD SAY, THAT IT CAME TO MEN FOR THE BENEFIT OF TERRESTRIAL SOULS; THAT IT MIGHT BE INSTEAD OF STATUES, INSTEAD OF TEMPLES, INSTEAD OF THE WHOLE OF SACRED INSTITUTIONS, AND THE LEADER OF SAFETY BOTH TO THE MEN THAT NOW ARE, AND TO THOSE THAT SHALL EXIST HEREAFTER."

It is in this spirit that this work is now presented.

Changes to the original text

i. Where Taylor had *the one, the one itself, the good* or *the good itself* this edition gives these names capital initials; this to distinguish them as the highest names the Platonists gave to God. Other principles have been left in lower case.

ii. A few very obvious grammatical errors and archaic spellings have been corrected; wherever there is any doubt as to the validity of possible errors the original has been followed.

iii. We have followed Taylor's explicit method of printing Greek characters without accents or breathings (see his defence of his Greek at the end of his *The Fable of Cupid and Psyche* and also his reference to this in the Introduction of *Proclus' Commentary on Euclid*).

iv. Some references to works quoted are added, and some original references are given more precise indicators.

v. There are two minor changes to the text, as detailed in footnotes.

vi. Page numbers in references: Taylor normally quotes page numbers to his own works whenever he refers to texts he had already published and these we have kept (*i.e.* they refer to the original publications' numbering). However, in cases where works have been republished in this Thomas Taylor Series we have changed these page numbers so that they refer to the numbering within the Series; see over for a full list of these works.

* * *

The three quotes in the Trust's introduction are from Chapter I of Book I of this work; from a footnote from Taylor's translation of Sallust *On the Gods and the World* (TTS. vol. IV, page 5); and from Proclus' *Commentary on the Parmenides* (Book I, 618.)

The Thomas Taylor Series

Volume I - *Proclus' Elements of Theology*

Volume II - *Select Works of Porphyry*

Abstinence from Animal Food; Auxiliaries to the Perception of Intelligibles; Concerning Homer's Cave of the Nymphs; Taylor on the Wanderings of Ulysses.

Volume III - *Collected Writings of Plotinus*

Twenty-seven treatises, being all the writings of Plotinus translated by Taylor.

Volume IV - *Collected Writings on the Gods & the World*

Sallust On the Gods and the World; The Sentences of Demophilus; Ocellus on the Nature of the Universe; Taurus and Proclus on the Eternity of the World; Maternus on the Thema Mundi; The Emperor Julian's Orations to the Mother of Gods and to the Sovereign Sun; Synesius on Providence; Taylor's essays on the Mythology and the Theology of the Greeks.

Volume V - *Hymns and Initiations*

The Hymns of Orpheus together with all the published hymns translated or written by Taylor; Taylor's essay on Orpheus.

Volume VI - *The Dissertations of Maximus Tyrius*

Forty-one treatises from the middle Platonist, and an essay from Taylor - The Triumph of the Wise Man over Fortune.

Volume VII - *Mysteries and Oracles*

A Collection of Chaldean Oracles; Essays on the Eleusinian and Bacchic Mysteries; The History of the Restoration of the Platonic Theology; An essay on A Platonic Demonstration of the Immortality of the Soul.

Volume IX - *The Works of Plato I*

General Introduction, Life of Plato, First Alcibiades, Republic

Volume X - *The Works of Plato II*
Laws, Epinomis, Timæus, Critias.

Volume XI - *The Works of Plato III*
Parmenides, Sophista, Phædrus, Greater Hippias, Banquet.

Volume XII - *The Works of Plato IV*
Theætetus, Politicus, Minos, Apology of Socrates, Crito, Phædo, Gorgias, Philebus, Second Alcibiades.

Volume XIII - *The Works of Plato V*
Euthyphro, Meno, Protagoras, Theages, Laches, Lysis, Charmides, Lesser Hippias, Euthydemus, Hipparchus, Rivals, Menexenus, Clitopho, Io, Cratylus, Epistles.

Volume XIV - *Apuleius' Golden Ass and Other Philosophical Writings*
The Golden Ass (or Metamorphosis), On the Dæmon of Socrates, On the Philosophy of Plato.

Volumes XV & XVI - *Proclus' Commentary on the Timæus of Plato*
The Five Books of this Commentary, with additional notes and short index.

Volume XVII - *Iamblichus on the Mysteries and Life of Pythagoras*
Iamblichus On the Mysteries of the Egyptians, Chaldeans, and Assyrians; Iamblichus' Life of Pythagoras; Fragments of the Ethical Writings of Certain Pythagoreans; Political Fragments of Archytas, Charondas, Zaleucus, and other Ancient Pythagoreans.

Volume XVIII - *Collected Essays and Fragments of Proclus*
Life of Proclus (Marinus); On Providence, Fate and That which is within our Power; Ten Doubts concerning Providence; On the Subsistence of Evil; Fragments of Proclus; Seven Hymns (Taylor).

Contents of the Chapters of the Seven Books

Book I

Chapter I 51

The preface, in which the scope of the treatise is unfolded, together with the praise of Plato himself, and of those that received the philosophy from him.

Chapter II 53

What the mode of the discussion is in the present treatise, and what preparation of the auditors of it is previously necessary.

Chapter III 55

What a theologist is according to Plato, whence he begins, as far as to what hypostases he ascends, and according to what power of the soul he particularly energizes.

Chapter IV 59

The theological types or forms according to all which Plato disposes the doctrine concerning the Gods.

Chapter V 62

What the dialogues are from which the theology of Plato may especially be assumed; and to what orders of Gods each of these dialogues refers us.

Chapter VI 64

An objection against collecting the Platonic theology from many dialogues, in consequence of its being partial, and distributed into minute parts.

Chapter VII 67

A solution of the before mentioned objection, referring to one dialogue, the *Parmenides*, the whole truth concerning the Gods according to Plato.

Chapter VIII 68

An enumeration of the different opinions concerning the *Parmenides*, and a division of the objections to them.

Chapter IX 69

A confutation of those who assert that the *Parmenides* is a logical dialogue, and who admit that the discussion in it is argumentative, proceeding through subjects of opinion.

Chapter X 72

How far they are right who assert that the hypotheses of the *Parmenides* are concerning the principles of things, and what is to be added to what they say from the doctrine of our preceptor [Syrianus.]

Chapter XI 76

Many demonstrations concerning the conclusions of the second hypothesis, and of the division of it according to the divine orders.

Chapter XII 82

The intention of the hypotheses, demonstrating their connexion with each other, and their consent with the things themselves.†

Chapter XIII 84

What the common rules concerning the Gods are, which Plato delivers in the *Laws*. And also concerning the hyparxis of the Gods, their providence, and their immutable perfection.

Chapter XIV 90

How the hyparxis of the Gods is delivered in the *Laws*, and through what media the discourse recurs to the truly existing Gods. How the providence of the Gods is demonstrated in the *Laws*, and what the mode of their providence is according to Plato.‡

Chapter XV 96

Through what arguments in the same treatise [the *Laws*] it is demonstrated that the Gods provide [for all things,] immutably.

Chapter XVI 98

What the axioms are concerning the Gods which are delivered in the *Republic*, and what order they have with respect to each other.

Chapter XVII 99

What the goodness of the Gods is, and how they are said to be the cause of all good; and that evil according to every hypostasis is itself adorned and arranged by the Gods.

Chapter XVIII 103

What the immutability is of the Gods; where also it is shown what their self-sufficiency, and firm impassivity are; and how we are to understand their possessing an invariable sameness of subsistence.

Chapter XIX 106

What the simplicity is of the Gods; and how that which is simple in them appears to be various in secondary natures.

---

† The 12th chapter is not marked in the original; but it begins conformably to my translation.

‡ The 15th chapter also is not marked in the original; and is comprehended in my translation in the 14th chapter. Perhaps it should begin at the words, "If therefore the Gods produce all things," on p. 91.

Chapter XX 108

What the truth is of the Gods; and whence falsehood is introduced in the participation of the Gods by secondary natures.

Chapter XXI 110

From the axioms in the *Phædrus* concerning every thing divine [it follows] that every thing divine is beautiful, wise, and good.

Chapter XXII 111

A discussion of the dogmas concerning the goodness [of the Gods,] and an investigation of the elements of the good in the *Philebus*.

Chapter XXIII 113

What the wisdom of the Gods is, and what elements of it may be assumed from Plato.

Chapter XXIV 114

Concerning divine beauty, and the elements of it, as delivered by Plato.

Chapter XXV 116

What the triad is which is conjoined with the good, the wise, and the beautiful, and what auxiliaries to the theory of it, Plato affords us.[†]

Chapter XXVI 118

Concerning the axioms delivered in the *Phædo*,[‡] respecting an invisible nature. What the divine nature is. What the immortal, and the intelligible[§] are; and what order these possess with reference to each other.

Chapter XXVII 121

What the uniform and indissoluble are, and how sameness of subsistence [and the unbegotten are] to be assumed in divine natures.

Chapter XXVIII 123

How paternal, and how maternal causes are to be assumed in the Gods.

Chapter XXIX 124

Concerning divine names, and the rectitude of them as delivered in the *Cratylus*.

[†] Such is the title in the Greek, which is obviously erroneous. For the proper title is, "What that is which unites us to *The Good*; and that it is divine faith." What is said indeed in the Greek to be the contents of this, belong to the preceding chapter.

[‡] For εν φαιδρῳ it is necessary to read εν παιδωνι.

[§] In the Greek το μονοειδες *the uniform*, but it should evidently be το νοητον, *the intelligible*.

Book Two

Chapter I 126

A method leading to the superessential principle of all things, according to the intellectual conception of *The One* and the multitude.

Chapter II 133

A second method unfolding the hypostasis of *The One*, and demonstrating it to be exempt from all corporeal and incorporeal essences.

Chapter III 139

Many arguments in confirmation of the same thing, and evincing the irreprehensible hypothesis of *The One*.

Chapter IV 145

A confutation of those who say that the first principle is not according to Plato above intellect, and demonstrations from the *Republic*, the *Sophista*, the *Philebus*, and the *Parmenides*, of the superessential hypostasis[†] of *The One*.

Chapter V 149

What the modes are of ascent to *The One* according to Plato; and that the modes are two, through analogy, and through negations. Likewise, where Plato treats of each of these, and through what cause.

Chapter VI 150

By what, and by how many names Plato unfolds the ineffable principle, and why he unfolds it by such and by so many names. And how these names accord with the modes of ascent to it.

Chapter VII 153

What assertions are in the *Republic* concerning the first principle, through its analogy to the sun; where also it is shown, how it is celebrated as the good, and as the most splendid of being. How the sun is the offspring of the good; and that according to each order of divine natures, there is a monad analogous to the first principle. And how the first principle is the cause of all beings, and is itself prior to power and energy.

Chapter VIII 158

What Plato in his Epistle to Dionysius says the first king is. And admonitions, that the first God is discussed in that Epistle.

Chapter IX 161

What the three conceptions are which are delivered [in that Epistle] concerning the first king. How all things are about him. How all things are for his sake.

[†] For υποθεσεως I read υποστασεως.

How he is the cause of all beautiful things. What the order is of these conceptions. And from what hypotheses they are assumed.

Chapter X 164

How in the first hypothesis of the *Parmenides*, Plato delivers the doctrine concerning *The One*, employing for this purpose negations. And on what account the negations are such and so many.

Chapter XI 166

How it is necessary to enter on the theory concerning *The One*, through negations. And what disposition of the soul is most adapted to discussions of this kind.

Chapter XII 167

A celebration of *The One*, demonstrating through negative conclusions that it is exempt from all the orders of beings, according to the order delivered in the *Parmenides*.

Book Three

In this work the first four chapters of the Greek are gathered into one (the first); the fifth and sixth into the second; the seventh and eighth form the third chapter; thus the original ninth is here the fourth, the tenth is the fifth and so on. The original chapter numbers are given in brackets.

Chapter I 173

(i) That after the discussion in common of the one principle of things, it is requisite to treat of the divine orders, and to show how many they are, and how they are divided from each other.
(ii) That the multitude of unities according to which the Gods have their hypostasis, subsists after *The One*.
(iii) How many the particulars are which ought to be demonstrated previous to the discovery of the multitude of the divine orders, and an uninterrupted narration of the doctrine of these.
(iv) That all the unities are participable. And that there is only one *truly* superessential one; but that all the other unities are participated by essences.

Chapter II 180

(v) That the participations of the unities which are nearer to *The One*, proceed into more simple hypostases; but the participations of those that are remote from *The One*, proceed into more composite hypostases.
(vi) What the natures are which participate of the divine unities, and what the order of them is with respect to each other. And that being indeed, is the most ancient of these; life, the second; intellect, the third; soul, the fourth; and body, the last. And that there are also as many orders of the divine unities.

Chapter III 188

(vii) A resumption of the doctrine concerning *The One*, and a discussion of the biformed principles posterior to *The One*.

(viii) What the two principles are of all things posterior to *The One*; how Socrates in the *Philebus* calls them bound and infinity; and of what things they are the causes† to beings.

Chapter IV 192

(ix) What the third thing is which is produced from the two principles. Why Socrates in the *Philebus* calls it that which is mixed. That it is nothing else than that which is primary being.‡ And how this proceeds from the two principles, and from *The One*.

Chapter V 196

(x) How from images also, it may be inferred, that the first thing which subsists from bound and infinity is being. How this may be demonstrated. And how bound and infinity are twofold; one order of these subsisting in being, but the other existing prior to being.

Chapter VI 197

(xi) What the triad is, which Socrates in the *Philebus* says is inherent in every thing that is mixed.

Chapter VII 199

(xii) Concerning the first intelligible triad in common; and how the second triad proceeds analogous to this.§

Chapter VIII 199

(xiii) What the second intelligible triad is. A more accurate account of it, as subsisting from that which predominates, from that which is participated, and from that which characterizes the mixture.

Chapter IX 201

(xiv) What the third intelligible triad is; what that is which predominates, and is participated in this. And at the end, a discourse in common concerning the distinction of the three triads.

Chapter X 204

(xv) How the intelligible triads are delivered in the *Timæus*. And many admonitions concerning animal itself, [evincing] that it has the third order of intelligence.

---

† For ουσιαι it is necessary to read αιτιαι.

‡ For εν, it is necessary to read ον.

§ It appears from this account of the contents of the 12th chapter, that a considerable part is wanting in the original; because nothing is said in it about the manner in which the second triad proceeds analogous to the first.

Chapter XI 205

(xvi) Many demonstrations that eternity subsists according to the middle order of intelligibles.

Chapter XII 207

(xvii) That the one in which eternity abides is the summit of intelligibles.

Chapter XIII 208

(xviii) Concerning all the intelligible orders in common, according to the doctrine of Timæus. And a more accurate account of the peculiarities in the intelligible triads.

Chapter XIV 211

(xix) Concerning intelligible forms, and the doctrine unfolding the peculiarity of them. How likewise they are four, and from what causes they subsist.

Chapter XV 213

(xx) That also from what is said in the *Sophista*, it is possible to discover the three intelligible orders; *viz.* in that part of the *Sophista*, in which it is shown what *the one being*, what *whole*, and what *all* are.

Chapter XVI 217

(xxi) A summary account of what has been said concerning the intelligible triads. And admonitions from Plato that it is possible to divide them into father, power and intellect.

Chapter XVII 221

(xxii) How in the *Phædrus* it is said that every thing divine is beautiful, wise, and good. What triple elements of each of these Plato delivers. And how from these it is possible to accede to the union and separation of the intelligible triads.

Chapter XVIII 222

(xxiii) How Parmenides delivers the multitude of Gods in the second hypothesis. And how we should discourse about each order of them, employing for this purpose the conclusions of that hypothesis.

Chapter XIX 224

(xxiv) What the first intelligible triad is according to Parmenides. Whence he begins, and how far he proceeds, teaching concerning it.

Chapter XX 225

(xxv) What the second intelligible triad is. And how it is delivered by Parmenides in continuity with the triad prior to it. And how far he produces the discourse concerning it.

Chapter XXI 227

(xxvi) What the third intelligible triad is. And how Parmenides unfolds it through the third conclusion.

Chapter XXII 229

(xxvii) Concerning the three conclusions in common, through which the three orders of intelligibles are characterized. And how through these it is possible to dissolve the most difficult of theological doubts.

Chapter XXIII 233

(xxviii) A celebration of the intelligible Gods, unfolding at the same time the union of intelligibles themselves with the good, and their exempt hyparxis.

Book Four

Chapter I 235

What the peculiarity is of the intelligible and intellectual Gods. How they illuminate imparticipable life, and are in conformity with the intelligible Gods.

Chapter II 237

How the intelligible and intellectual Gods subsist from the intelligible Gods. And how they communicate with the intelligible Gods.

Chapter III 239

What the division is of the intelligible and intellectual Gods according to triads. And what the difference is of these triads with respect to the intelligible triads.

Chapter IV 242

How Socrates in the *Phædrus* leads us to this order of Gods.

Chapter V 243

That it is not proper to understand the Heaven, and celestial circulation [celebrated in the *Phædrus*] as pertaining to sensibles; and many admonitions from the Platonic words themselves, that these are to be referred to the first order of Heaven.

Chapter VI 245

That the supercelestial place is not simply intelligible; but demonstrations from what is delivered about it [in the *Phædrus*,] that it is allotted an intelligible order as in intellectuals.

Chapter VII 246

That the subcelestial arch is the boundary of the intelligible and intellectual Gods, evinced from the peculiarities of it.

Chapter VIII 247

Why Plato characterizes this order of Gods from the middle which it contains, and delivers the names of the extremes according to the habitude of this middle.

Chapter IX 248

That Plato delivers the same mode of ascent to the intelligible, as is delivered by initiators into the mysteries.

Chapter X 251

What the supercelestial place is. How it proceeds from the first intelligibles. How it is supreme in intellectuals. And how Plato demonstrates its prolific power.

Chapter XI 253

How Plato has indicated the unknown peculiarity of the summit of intelligibles and intellectuals, and why he celebrates it at one and the same time affirmatively and negatively.

Chapter XII 255

What the negations are of the supercelestial place. That they are produced from the divine orders. What kind of negations also designate the uncoloured, what, the unfigured, and what, the privation of contact.

Chapter XIII 257

What the things are which Plato affirms of the supercelestial place, and from what intelligible peculiarities, he ascribes to it affirmative signs.

Chapter XIV 258

What the three deities of the virtues, *viz.* science, temperance, and justice, are in the supercelestial place; what order they have with respect to each other; and what perfection each of them imparts to the Gods.

Chapter XV 259

What the plain of Truth, and what the meadow are. What the unical form of intelligible nutriment is. What the twofold nutriment of the Gods is which is distributed from this intelligible food.

Chapter XVI 261

Many admonitions that the supercelestial place is triadic. And what the signs are of the three hypostases in it.

Chapter XVII 263

Who Adrastia is. What the sacred law of Adrastia is. That she ranks in the supercelestial place. And on what account she does so.

Chapter XVIII 264

A summary account of what is said about the supercelestial place, unfolding the peculiarities of it.

Chapter XIX 265

Demonstrations that the connectedly-containing order is in the intelligible and intellectual Gods. And that it is necessary there should be three connective causes of wholes.

Chapter XX 268

That according to Plato the celestial circulation is the same with the connective order.

Chapter XXI 269

How we obtain auxiliaries from what is said by Plato of the triadic division in the connective deity. And why he especially venerates the union in this triad.

Chapter XXII 272

What the theology in the *Cratylus* is concerning Heaven. And how it is possible to collect from it by a reasoning process the middle of the intelligible and intellectual Gods.

Chapter XXIII 274

That the most divinely-inspired of the interpreters have defined the subcelestial arch to be a certain peculiar order. And that our preceptor has unfolded it in the most perfect manner.

Chapter XXIV 275

Many admonitions that the peculiarity of the subcelestial arch is perfective, from what Plato has delivered concerning it, and from the souls that are elevated to it.

Chapter XXV 277

What the triadic division is of the perfective order, which Plato has delivered in the subcelestial arch.

Chapter XXVI 279

What the elevation is of souls separate from bodies to the intelligible and intellectual triads. What the most blessed *telete* is. What *muesis*, and *epopteia* are. What the entire, simple, and unmoved visions are. And what the end is of all this elevation.

Chapter XXVII 280

How Plato unfolds in the *Parmenides*, from intelligibles the intelligible and intellectual orders. And what that which is common, and that which is different are, in the theology concerning these.

Chapter XXVIII 281

How the intelligible and intellectual number proceeds from intelligibles. And in what it differs from intelligible multitude.

Chapter XXIX 283

How divine number adorns all beings. And what the powers in it are which are symbolically delivered from the division of number.

Chapter XXX 287

How Parmenides has delivered the feminine and generative peculiarity [of first number] in what he says concerning number.

Chapter XXXI 289

How we may discover in what is delivered concerning number, the triadic division of the summit of intelligibles and intellectuals.

Chapter XXXII 291

Whether it is proper to place number prior to animal itself, or in animal itself, or posterior to it.

Chapter XXXIII 292

Whence Parmenides begins to speak about number. How far he proceeds in what he says about it. And how he unfolds the different orders in it.

Chapter XXXIV 293

What the unknown is in divine numbers. What the generative is in them. And admonitions of these things from what is elsewhere said by Plato concerning numbers.

Chapter XXXV 295

How Parmenides delivers the middle order of intelligibles and intellectuals through *The One*, *whole*, and *finite*. And what the peculiarities are of these.

Chapter XXXVI 298

Whence Parmenides begins to speak about this order. And how far he proceeds in what he says about it. How he likewise unfolds the three monads in it conformably to what is said in the *Phædrus* concerning them.

Chapter XXXVII 299

How Parmenides delivers the third order of intelligibles and intellectuals. And how he unfolds the perfective peculiarity, and the triadic division of it.

Chapter XXXVIII 300

An Admonition what the union is of the three intelligible and intellectual triads, from the conclusions of Parmenides.

Chapter XXXIX 301

How many theological dogmas we may assume, through the order of the conclusions delivered by Parmenides in his discourse concerning the intelligible and intellectual Gods.

Book Five

Chapter I 303

How the intellectual orders proceed from the intelligible and intellectual Gods. And according to what peculiarities they subsist.

Chapter II 305

What the division is of the intellectual Gods. And the progression according to hebdomads in this order of Gods.

Chapter III 308

Who the three intellectual fathers are according to Plato. What the three undefiled monads are. And who the seventh deity is, that is co-arranged with the two triads.

Chapter IV 311

How from the writings of Plato, the procession of the intellectual Gods into seven hebdomads may be collected by a reasoning process.

Chapter V 312

Who the mighty Saturn is, according to the theology in the *Cratylus*. And how he is in a certain respect intelligible, and in a certain respect intellectual. In which also, the dogmas are discussed concerning the union of intellect with the intelligible, and its separation from it.

Chapter VI 314

What the kingdom of Saturn is. In what manner it is delivered by Plato in the *Politicus*. And of what it is the cause to the world, to the mundane Gods, and to partial souls.

Chapter VII 315

What the Saturnian life of souls is. And what peculiarities of this circulation the Elean Guest delivers.

Chapter VIII 317

How souls are said to be nourished by intelligibles. And what the difference is of the nutriment derived from different intelligibles.

Chapter IX 318

What the orders are which mighty Saturn causes to preside over wholes. In which also, who the Saturnian intellect is that is delivered in the *Gorgias* is unfolded.

Chapter X 320

How this God [Saturn] is peculiarly called by theologists insenescible, or free from old age. And how Plato has delivered this peculiarity of him.

Chapter XI 321

Who the vivific Goddess is. How she is the collector of the Saturnian and Jovian kingdoms. And what orders she possesses conjoined with both these kingdoms.

Chapter XII 324

Who the third father in intellectuals is. How he proceeds from the causes prior to him. And that he is the demiurgus of the universe.

Chapter XIII 326

Demonstrations that the whole demiurgus of the universe, is the third father of the intellectual Gods.

Chapter XIV 327

An answer to those who say that there are three demiurgi according to Plato, demonstrating through many arguments that the demiurgic monad is arranged prior to the [demiurgic] triad, in the third order of intellectuals.

Chapter XV 330

That Timæus especially delivers the peculiarity of the demiurgus, by calling him intellect. And that this pertains to the third of the intellectual fathers.

Chapter XVI 332

How according to another method it is requisite to discover the peculiarity of the demiurgus. And how the demiurgus is called in the *Timæus* effector and father. In which also, it is clearly shown, where the paternal, where the paternal and at the same time effective, where the effective and paternal, and where the effective only are, according to Plato. And in short, in what effector and father differ.

Chapter XVII 337

How following Timæus, according to a third method, we may purify our conceptions concerning the demiurgic monad.

Chapter XVIII 339

A theological explanation of the speech of the demiurgus in the *Timæus*, distinctly evolving our conceptions about the demiurgic energy.

Chapter XIX 344

What the second speech of the demiurgus is to divisible souls. In what it differs from the former. And how in this all the measures of the life of souls are defined.

Chapter XX 345

A summary of all that is said about the demiurgus, following the doctrine of Timæus.

Chapter XXI 348

Admonitions from what is said in the *Cratylus*, that Plato attributes fabrication to Jupiter.

Chapter XXII 349

Admonitions from what is said in the *Cratylus* of the fabrication of Jupiter. In which also the concord is demonstrated of the theology from names, with the arrangement of the demiurgus in the *Timæus*.

Chapter XXIII 352

Admonitions of the fabrication of Jupiter from what is demonstrated in the *Philebus*. In which it is shown, what the royal soul, and the royal intellect are.

Chapter XXIV 355

Demonstrations of the same thing, from what is said in the *Protagoras* about political science.

Chapter XXV 357

An argument showing that Jupiter is the demiurgus and father of the universe[†] according to Plato, from what is said in the *Politicus* concerning the twofold circulation [of the universe.]

Chapter XXVI 361

Admonitions of the same things, from what is said in the *Laws* concerning analogy, viz. that it is the judgment of Jupiter.

Chapter XXVII 362

How Jupiter subsists according to cause in animal itself, and how animal itself is in Jupiter.

Chapter XXVIII 364

How Timæus attributes to the demiurgus the unknown and ineffable.

Chapter XXIX 366

What Timæus thinks fit to denominate animal itself, and is of the opinion that it may be known, but leaves the demiurgus unknown and ineffable.

Chapter XXX 368

Concerning the Crater in the *Timæus*, a theology teaching what the genera are that are mingled in it, and how it is the cause of the essence of souls.

Chapter XXXI 371

That the Crater in the *Timæus* is fontal. And admonitions from the writings of Plato, concerning the principle and fountain of souls.

Chapter XXXII 373

That the three vivific fountains co-arranged with the demiurgus, may be assumed from what is said in the *Timæus*, viz. the fountain of souls, the fountain of the virtues, and the fountain of natures.

[†] For πλατωνος, it is necessary to read παντος.

Chapter XXXIII 376

Admonitions concerning the undefiled Gods; that there are such Gods according to Plato; and what the peculiarity is of their essence.

Chapter XXXIV 377

More manifest demonstrations of the hypostasis of the undefiled Gods, according to Plato.

Chapter XXXV 380

Admonitions through many arguments how it is proper to denominate the undefiled Gods according to Plato. In which also, the union of them, what their separation, and what their peculiarity are, is delivered.

Chapter XXXVI 382

How from what is mystically asserted by Plato, auxiliaries may be obtained, concerning the seventh monad of intellectuals.

Chapter XXXVII 384

How Plato delivers in the *Parmenides* the summit of the intellectual Gods.[†]

Chapter XXXVIII 387

How Parmenides unfolds the middle order of the intellectual breadth, and through what signs.

Chapter XXXIX 390

How Parmenides defines the third order of intellectuals, and through what peculiarities.

(Chapter XL - see footnote;

A common theory of the intellectual hebdomad, from the conclusions of Parmenides.)

Book Six

Chapter I 394

That the ruling order of the Gods is in continuity with the intellectual Gods. And that the division into fountains and principles may be assumed from the writings of Plato, through the theory about souls.

[†] The contents of chapter thirty-seven in the original erroneously form the conclusion of the contents of chapter thirty-six. And instead of ως την ακροτητα, it is therefore necessary to read πως την ακροτητα. Hence what are marked as χεφ. λς, and χεφ. λη and χεφ. λθ should be marked χεφ. λη, χεφ. λθ, and χεφ μ. It will be found also that chapter forty is wanting.

Chapter II 395

How the ruling Gods proceed. And that the supermundane peculiarity pertains to these Gods alone.

Chapter III 399

What the peculiarity is of the ruling Gods. That the assimilative is especially characteristic of them. And how the causes of assimilation are antecedently assumed in the demiurgus; and how in the intelligible paradigm.

Chapter IV 404

What the powers are of the assimilative Gods. What their energies. And how many goods are imparted by them to the world, and to all mundane natures.

Chapter V 407

What the divisions are of the assimilative Gods. And that the greatest part of the discourse about them is concerning the middle orders in them.

Chapter VI 408

Many demonstrations, that both according to Plato and other theologists, there is one demiurgus prior to the three demiurgi.

Chapter VII 411

That Jupiter is twofold; one indeed, being prior to the three sons of Saturn, [but the other being one of them.] And how the three proceed from Saturn, and the one Jupiter.

Chapter VIII 413

That according to Plato also, the demiurgic monad subsists prior to the three sons of Saturn. Demonstrations of this from what is said in the *Politicus*, and in the *Laws*.

Chapter IX 417

More Manifest admonitions of the same things from what is said in the *Gorgias*, and in the *Cratylus*.

Chapter X 420

Who the three demiurgi are, and what order they have with reference to each other. Likewise what their progressions are, and their divisions about the world.

Chapter XI 421

What the vivific triad is among the Gods. And whence we may derive auxiliaries from the writings of Plato concerning the union and division of this triad.

Chapter XII 427

What the convertive triad of the ruling Gods is; and what the monad which it contains. In which also, the union of Apollo with the sun is demonstrated; and it is shown, how from what is said about Apollo we may be led to the theory of the solar orders.

Chapter XIII 432

What the undefiled order is of the ruling Gods. And how from the writings of Plato conceptions about it may be obtained.

Chapter XIV 434

How Parmenides forms his conclusions about the ruling Gods, in continuity with the demiurgic order. And that he characterizes the whole order of them, through similitude and dissimilitude.

Chapter XV 437

What the supermundane and at the same time mundane genus of Gods is. And how through their own medium they preserve the continuity of the Gods that proceed from the demiurgus.

Chapter XVI 439

How the liberated Gods are characterized. And how from their liberated peculiarity they are exempt from the universe, and co-arranged with the mundane Gods.

Chapter XVII 442

What the common powers, and what the common energies are of the liberated Gods, according with the essence that has been delivered of them.

Chapter XVIII 446

Concerning the twelve leaders or rulers mentioned in the *Phædrus*, and that they have a liberated order.

Chapter XIX 448

Many and clearer demonstrations that the great leader Jupiter, and all the dodecad of leaders, are liberated.

Chapter XX 451

An explanation from precedaneous causes whence the number of the dodecad in the liberated Gods is derived.

Chapter XXI 452

What the division of the liberated leaders is into two monads and one decad. And what the one division of them is.

Chapter XXII 454

The theology concerning each of the twelve Gods, unfolding the peculiarities of them from the subjects of their government.

Chapter XXIII 456

Concerning the mother of the Fates mentioned in the *Republic*. Likewise concerning the triad of the Fates. What orders they have with reference to each other. What powers of them are delivered through divine symbols. What their energies are. And how Plato characterizes the liberated peculiarity.

Chapter XXIV 462

How Parmenides forms his conclusions concerning the liberated Gods immediately after the assimilative Gods. And how he characterizes the order of them by *touching* and *not touching*.

Book Seven

Chapter I 466

On the mundane Gods in general, the source of their progression, their orders, powers, and spheres.

Chapter II 467

On the divisions, and allotments of the mundane Gods.

Chapter III 471

That the mundane do not differ from the supermundane Gods in habitudes to bodies, etc. That the providence of the Gods is not circumscribed by place. That it pervades all things, and like the light of the sun, fills whatever is capable of receiving it.

Chapter IV 474

After what manner the visible celestial orbs are Gods. That a celestial body is eminently allied to the incorporeal essence of the Gods. That the visible are connected with the intelligible Gods. And that the perfectly incorporeal are united to the sensible Gods, through the essence of each being characterized by *The One*.

Chapter V 477

The nature of the mundane Gods unfolded from the speech of the Demiurgus to them, in the *Timæus*. And what the whole conception of the speech is according to Proclus.

Chapter VI 481

What the demiurgus effects in the multitude of mundane Gods by the first words of his speech. That the words of the Demiurgus are addressed to the composite from soul and animal, viz. to the animal which is divine and partakes of soul. The meaning of the words, "Of whom I am the demiurgus and father," etc.

Chapter VII ... 485

The meaning of the words unfolded in the speech of the Demiurgus, "Every thing therefore which is bound is dissoluble, but to be willing to dissolve that which is beautifully harmonized and well compared, is the province of an ill nature."

Chapter VIII ... 489

The following part of the speech of the Demiurgus to the mundane Gods unfolded. The difference between the primarily and secondarily immortal, and the primarily and secondarily indissoluble. And that the mundane Gods are neither primarily immortal, nor primarily indissoluble.

Chapter IX ... 492

That part of the speech of the Demiurgus unfolded, in which he says to the mundane Gods, "Learn now therefore what I say to you indicating my desire."

Chapter X ... 496

The development of the remaining part of the speech of the Demiurgus.

Chapter XI ... 498

Who the junior Gods are, and why they are thus called.

Chapter XII ... 501

Farther important particulars respecting the fabrication of the mundane Gods, collected from the *Timæus* and unfolded.

Chapter XIII ... 503

Continuation of the development of these particulars.

Chapter XIV ... 506

The peculiarities of the celestial Gods separately discussed. Why the one sphere of the fixed stars comprehends a multitude of stars, but each of the planetary spheres convolves only one star. And that in each of the planetary spheres, there is a number of satellites, analogous to the choir of the fixed stars, subsisting with proper circulations of their own.

Chapter XV ... 509

The nature of the Moon, Mercury, Venus, and the Sun unfolded.

Chapter XVI ... 513

Extract from the Oration of the Emperor Julian to the Sovereign Sun.

Chapter XVII ... 517

Extract from the MS. Scholia of Proclus on the *Cratylus* of Plato concerning Apollo, in which the principal powers of the God are unfolded.

Chapter XVIII 521

The nature of the Muses unfolded from the above MS. Scholia.

Chapter XIX 523

The nature of Mars, Jupiter, and Saturn, unfolded. The manner in which each of the seven planetary divinities becomes an animal, and is suspended from a more divine soul; and what kind of perfection it affords to the universe.

Chapter XX 525

That all the celestial Gods are beneficent, and after a similar manner the causes of good. And that the participation of them, and the mixture of material with immaterial influences, become the causes of the abundant difference in secondary natures.

Chapter XXI 527

The nature of Minerva unfolded from the Commentaries of Proclus on the *Timæus*. The spear and shield with which this Goddess, in the statues of her, is represented as armed, explained from Iamblichus. And observations respecting the mundane allotment of this Goddess.

Chapter XXII 531

The nature of the great mundane divinity, the earth, unfolded from Proclus on the *Timæus* of Plato.

Chapter XXIII 535

The manner in which the earth is said to be the most ancient, and first of the Gods within the heavens, explained.

Chapter XXIV 538

On the essence of the sublunary deities. What Plato says of them in the *Timæus* unfolded.

Chapter XXV 542

Where the sublunary Gods are to be arranged. And the meaning of the subsequent words of Plato developed.

Chapter XXVI 545

The nature of the sublunary Gods more fully unfolded. On the dæmoniacal order. And that about each of the fabricators of generation, there is a co-ordinate angelical, dæmoniacal, and heroical multitude, which retains the appellation of its producing monad.

Chapter XXVII 548

What Pythagoras says in the *Sacred Discourse*. What the Orphic traditions are concerning Phanes, Night, Heaven, Saturn, Jupiter, and Bacchus. That Plato begins the Theogony of the sublunary Gods from Heaven and Earth, and not from Phanes and Night. And why he does so.

Chapter XXVIII 550

Of the two principles of Heaven and Earth. What each of them is; and particularly concerning the power of Heaven.

Chapter XXIX 553

The whole theory of Earth unfolded. And also the theory of Ocean and Tethys. That the causes of these are in the intellectual Gods, and likewise in the sensible universe.

Chapter XXX 558

The theory of Phorcys, Saturn and Rhea, unfolded.

Chapter XXXI 562

The nature of the sublunary Jupiter and Juno unfolded. And why Plato comprehends in this ennead, viz. Heaven and Earth, Ocean and Tethys, Phorcys, Saturn, Rhea, Jupiter and Juno, the Gods who are the fabricators of generation.

Chapter XXXII 566

Why Plato denominates the sublunary deities, "such as become apparent when they please." General observations respecting the Gods that govern generation.

Chapter XXXIII 568

On the summit, or monad of all the mundane Gods, Bacchus. And on the mundane soul which is the immediate participant of the Bacchic intellect.

Chapter XXXIV 573

How the mundane Gods are characterized in the *Parmenides* of Plato.

Chapter XXXV 575

A development of what Plato says in the *Phædrus*, about Boreas and Orithys, the Centaurs, Chimæras, Gorgons, Pegasuses, Typhons, Achelous, and the Nymphs.

Chapter XXXVI 580

The meaning of Plato unfolded, in what he says about Pan, Tartarus, Prometheus, Cadmus, and the Syrens

Chapter XXXVII 582

A development of Plato's theological conceptions respecting Nature, Fate, and Fortune.

Chapter XXXVIII 587

What Time, Day and Night, Month and Year are, so far as they are deities, according to the theology of Plato.

Chapter XXXIX 592

A discussion of the order of divine souls, who are deified by always participating of the Gods.

Chapter XL 597

A development of the nature of Love, from the MS. Commentary of Proclus on the *First Alcibiades* of Plato.

Chapter XLI 600

A continuation of the same subject.

Chapter XLII 602

The nature of dæmons more fully disclosed. An extract from the MS. Commentary of Proclus on the *First Alcibiades*, on this subject.

Chapter XLIII 605

On the dæmons who are allotted the superintendence of mankind.

Chapter XLIV 609

On the dæmon of Socrates. The peculiarity of this dæmon; and that it belonged to the Apolloniacal series.

Chapter XLV 611

Important information concerning dæmons from the MS. Scholia of Proclus on the *Cratylus* of Plato. And also from the MS. Commentary of Olympiodorus on the *Phædo* of Plato.

Chapter XLVI 614

The nature of those human souls that are of an heroic characteristic unfolded. What Plato says of these souls in the *Cratylus*. His meaning elucidated from the MS. Scholia of Proclus on that dialogue.

Chapter XLVII 620

How the triple genera that are the perpetual attendants of the Gods, are indicated in the *Parmenides* of Plato.

Chapter XLVIII 623

An elucidation from Proclus of what Plato says in the *Timæus*, in celebration of the divinity of the World, so far as the whole of it is a God.

Chapter XLIX 626

A further elucidation from Proclus of the same subject.

Chapter L 631

The meaning of the words of Plato, "And causing circle to revolve in a circle, he established heaven (ie the world) one, only solitary nature," unfolded from Proclus.

Chapter LI 635

What Plato says in the *Timæus* about the name of the World, with elucidations of Proclus.

INTRODUCTION

I rejoice in the opportunity which is afforded me of presenting the *truly* philosophic reader, in the present work, with a treasure of Grecian theology; of a theology, which was first mystically and symbolically promulgated by Orpheus, afterwards disseminated enigmatically through images by Pythagoras, and in the last place scientifically unfolded by Plato and his genuine disciples. The peculiarity indeed, of this theology is, that it is no less scientific than sublime; and that by a geometrical series of reasoning originating from the most self-evident truths, it develops all the deified progressions from the ineffable principle of things, and accurately exhibits to our view all the links of that golden chain of which deity is the one extreme, and body the other.

That also which is most admirable and laudable in this theology is, that it produces in the mind properly prepared for its reception the most pure, holy, venerable, and exalted conceptions of the great cause of all. For it celebrates this immense principle as something superior even to being itself; as exempt from the whole of things, of which it is nevertheless ineffably the source, and does not therefore think fit to connumerate it with any triad, or order of beings. Indeed, it even apologises for attempting to give an appropriate name to this principle, which is in reality ineffable, and ascribes the attempt to the imbecility of human nature, which striving intently to behold it, gives the appellation of the most simple of its conceptions to that which is beyond all knowledge and all conception. Hence it denominates it *The One,* and *The Good;* by the former of these names indicating its transcendent simplicity, and by the latter its subsistence as the object of desire to all beings. For all things desire good. At the same time however, it asserts that these appellations are in reality nothing more than the parturitions of the soul which standing as it were in the vestibules of the adytum of deity, announce nothing pertaining to the ineffable, but only indicate her spontaneous tendencies towards it, and belong rather to the immediate offspring of the first God, than to the first itself.

Hence, as the result of this most venerable conception of the supreme, when it ventures not only to denominate the ineffable, but also to assert something of its relation to other things, it considers this as pre-eminently its peculiarity, that it is the principle of principles; it being necessary that the characteristic property of principle, after the same manner as other things, should not begin from multitude, but should be collected into one monad as a summit, and which is the principle of all principles. Conformably to this, Proclus, in the second book of this work[†] says, with matchless magnificence of diction: "Let us as it were celebrate the first God, not as establishing the earth and the heavens, nor as giving subsistence to souls, and the generation of all animals; for he produced these indeed, but among the last of things; but prior to these, let us celebrate him as unfolding into light the whole intelligible and intellectual genus of Gods, together with all the supermundane and mundane divinities - as the God of all Gods, the unity of all unities, and beyond the first adyta,[‡] - as more ineffable than all silence, and more unknown than all essence, - as holy among the holies, and concealed in the intelligible Gods."

The scientific reasoning from which this dogma is deduced is the following: As the principle of all things is *The One*, it is necessary that the progression of beings should be continued, and that no vacuum should intervene either in incorporeal or corporeal natures. It is also necessary that every thing which has a natural progression should proceed through similitude. In consequence of this, it is likewise necessary that every producing principle should generate a number of the same order with itself, *viz. nature*, a natural number; *soul*, one that is psychical (*i.e.* belonging to soul); and *intellect*, an intellectual number. For if whatever possesses a power of generating, generates similars prior to dissimilars, every cause must deliver its own form and characteristic peculiarity to its progeny; and before it generates that which gives subsistence to progressions far distant and separate from its nature, it must constitute things proximate to itself according to essence, and conjoined with it through similitude. It is therefore necessary from these premises, since there is one unity the principle of the universe, that this unity should produce from itself, prior to every thing else, a multitude of natures characterised by unity, and a number the most of all things allied to its cause; and these natures are no other than the Gods.

According to this theology therefore, from the immense principle of principles, in which all things causally subsist, absorbed in superessential light, and involved in unfathomable depths, a beauteous progeny of principles proceed, all largely partaking of the ineffable, all stamped with the occult characters of deity, all possessing an overflowing fullness of good. From these dazzling summits, these ineffable blossoms, these divine propagations, being, life, intellect, soul, nature and body depend;

[†] See page 166.

[‡] *i.e.* The highest order of intelligibles.

monads suspended from *unities*, deified natures proceeding from deities. Each of these monads too, is the leader of a series which extends from itself to the last of things, and which while it proceeds from, at the same time abides in, and returns to its leader. And all these principles and all their progeny are finally centred and rooted by their summits in the first great all-comprehending one. Thus all beings proceed from, and are comprehended in the first being; all intellects emanate from one first intellect; all souls from one first soul; all natures blossom from one first nature; and all bodies proceed from the vital and luminous body of the world. And lastly, all these great monads are comprehended in the first one, from which both they and all their depending series are unfolded into light. Hence this first one is truly the unity of unities, the monad of monads, the principle of principles, the God of Gods, one and all things, and yet one prior to all.

No objections of any weight, no arguments but such as are sophistical, can be urged against this most sublime theory which is so congenial to the unperverted conceptions of the human mind, that it can only be treated with ridicule and contempt in degraded, barren, and barbarous ages. Ignorance and priestcraft, however, have hitherto conspired to defame those inestimable works,[†] in which this and many other grand and important dogmas can alone be found; and the theology of the Greeks has been attacked with all the insane fury of ecclesiastical zeal, and all the imbecil flashes of mistaken wit, by men whose conceptions on the subject, like those of a man between sleeping and waking, have been *turbid and wild, phantastic and confused, preposterous and vain.*

Indeed, that after the great incomprehensible cause of all, a divine multitude subsists, co-operating with this cause in the production and government of the universe, has always been, and is still admitted by all nations, and all religions, however much they may differ in their opinions respecting the nature of the subordinate deities, and the veneration which is to be paid to them by man; and however barbarous the conceptions of some nations on this subject may be when compared with those of others. Hence, says the elegant Maximus Tyrius, "You will see one according law and assertion in all the earth, that there is one God, the king and father of all things, and many Gods, sons of God, ruling together with him. This the Greek says, and the Barbarian says, the inhabitant of the Continent, and he who dwells near the sea, the wise and the unwise. And if you proceed as far as to the utmost shores

---

[†] *Viz.* the present and other works of Proclus, together with those of Plotinus, Porphyry, Iamblichus, Syrianus, Ammonius, Damascius, Olympiodorus, and Simplicius.

of the ocean, there also there are Gods, rising very near to some, and setting very near to others."† This dogma, too, is so far from being opposed by either the Old or New Testament, that it is admitted by both, though it forbids the religious veneration of the inferior deities, and enjoins the worship of one God alone, whose portion is Jacob, and Israel the line of his inheritance. The following testimonies will, I doubt not, convince the liberal reader of the truth of this assertion.

In the first place it appears from the 32nd chapter of Deuteronomy, v. 8 in the Septuagint version, that "*the division of the nations was made according to the number of the angels of God,*" and not according to the number of the children of Israel, as the present Hebrew text asserts. This reading was adopted by the most celebrated fathers of the Christian church, such as, among the Greeks, Origen, Basil and Chrysostom, and among the Latins, Jerom and Gregory. That this too, is the genuine reading, is evident from the 4th chapter of the same book and the 19th verse, in which it is said, "And lest thou lift up thine eyes unto heaven, and when thou seest the sun and the moon, and the stars, *even* all the host of heaven, shouldst be driven to worship them, and serve them, *which the Lord thy God hath divided unto all nations under the whole heaven.*" Here it is said that the stars are divided to all the nations, which is equivalent to saying that the nations were divided according to the number of the stars; the Jewish legislator at the same time, considering his own nation as an exception, and as being under the government of the God of Israel alone. For in the following verse it is added, "But the Lord hath taken you (*i.e.* the Jews), and brought you forth out of the iron furnace, *even* out of Egypt, to be unto him a people of inheritance, as *ye* are to this day." By the angels of God therefore (in Deuteron. 32 v. 8) the stars are signified; and these in the same book (chapter 17 v. 3) are expressly called Gods; "And hath gone and served other Gods, and worshipped them, *either the sun or moon, or any of the host of heaven, which I have not commanded.*" In the 3rd chapter also, and the 24th verse, it is implied in the question which is there asked, that the God of the Jews is superior to all the celestial and terrestrial Gods "For what God is there *in heaven, or in earth*, that can do according to thy works, and according to thy might?" As the

---

† Ενα ιδιος αν εν πασα γη ομοφωνον και λογον, οτι θιος εις παντων βασιλευς και πατηρ, και θεου πολλοι, θεου παιδες, συναρχοντες θεῳ. Ταυτα και ο ελλην λεγει, και ο βαρβαρος λεγει, και ο ηπειρωτης και ο θαλαττιος, και ο σοφος και ο ασοφος. Κᾳν επι του ωκιανου ελθης τ ας ηϊονας, κᾳκει θεοι, τοις μεν ανισχοντες αγχου μαλα, τοις δε καταδυομενοι. Dissert. I. Edit. Princ. [See TTS vol. VI.]

attention of the Jews was solely confined to the worship of the God of Abraham, Isaac and Jacob, they but little regarded the powers whom they conceived to be subordinate to this God, and considering all of them as merely the messengers of their God, they gave them the general appellation of *angels;* though as we shall shortly prove from the testimony of the Apostle Paul, they were not consistent in confounding *angels* properly so called with *Gods.*

But that the stars are not called Gods by the Jewish legislator as things inanimate like statues fashioned of wood or stone, is evident from what is said in the book of Job, and the Psalms: "Behold even the moon and it shineth not, yea the stars are not pure in his sight. How much less man that is a worm, and the son of man which is a worm?" (Job xxv v. 5 and 6.) And, "When I consider thy heavens, the work of thy fingers, the moon and the stars which thou hast ordained; what is man that thou art mindful of him, and the son of man that thou visitest him." (Psalm viii v. 3 and 4.) It is evident therefore from these passages, that the heavens and the stars are more excellent than man; but nothing inanimate can be more excellent than that which is animated. To which may be added, that in the following verse David says, that God has made man a little lower than the angels. But the stars, as we have shown, were considered by Moses as angels and Gods; and consequently, they are animated beings, and superior to man.

Farther still, in the Septuagint version of verse the 4th of the 19th Psalm, God is said *to have placed his tabernacle in the sun,* (εν τω ηλιω εθετο το σκηνωμα αυτου which is doubtless the genuine reading, and not that of the vulgar translation, "In them (*i.e.* the heavens) hath he set a tabernacle for the sun." For this is saying nothing more of the sun than what may be said of any of the other stars, and produces in us no exalted conception of the artificer of the universe. But to say that God dwells in the sun, gives us a magnificent idea both of that glorious luminary, and the deity who dwells enshrined, as it were, in dazzling splendour. To which we may add in confirmation of this version of the Septuagint, that in Psalm xi v. 4. it is said, "The Lord's *throne* is in *heaven.* And again in Isaiah lxvi v. 1. "Thus saith the Lord, the heaven is my throne, and the earth is my footstool." If therefore the heavens are the throne, and the sun the tabernacle of deity, they must evidently be deified. For nothing can come into immediate contact with divinity without being divine. Hence, says Simplicius,[†] "That it is connascent with the human soul to think the celestial bodies are divine, is especially

---

[†] In his commentary on the second book of Aristotle's treatise *On the Heavens.*

evident from those, (the Jews) who look to these bodies through preconceptions about divine natures. For they also say that the heavens are the habitation of God, and the throne of God, and are alone sufficient to reveal the glory and excellence of God to those who are worthy; than which assertions what can be more venerable?"

Indeed, that the heavens are not the inanimate throne and residence of deity, is also evident from the assertion in the 19th Psalm, "That the heavens *declare* the glory of God." For R. Moses, a very learned Jew, says,[†] "that the word *saphar*, to *declare* or *set forth* is never attributed to things inanimate." Hence he concludes, "that the heavens are not without some soul, which, says he, is no other than that of those blessed intelligences, who govern the stars, and dispose them into such letters as God has ordained; declaring unto us men by means of this writing, what events we are to expect. And hence, this same writing is called by all the ancients, *chetab hamelachim*, that is to say, *the writing of the angels*."

The Gods, therefore, which were distributed to all the nations but the Jews, were the sun and moon, and the other celestial bodies, yet not so far as they are bodies, but so far as they are animated beings. Hence the Hebrew prophets never reprobate and prohibit the worship of the stars as things which neither see, nor hear, nor understand, as they do the worship of statues. Thus in Deuteron. iv. and 28. "And there ye shall serve Gods the work of men's hands, wood and stone, which neither see nor hear, nor eat, nor smell." And the Psalmist, "They have a mouth but speak not, etc." These, and many other things of the like kind are said by the prophets of the Jews against the worship of images and statues, but never of the sun and moon, and the other stars. But when they blame the worship of the heavenly bodies, they assign as the cause that the people of Israel are not attributed to them as other nations are, in consequence of being the inheritance of the God that brought them out of the land of Egypt, and out of the house of bondage. This is evident from the before cited passage in the 4th chapter of Deuteronomy, in which it is said that the stars are divided into all nations under the whole heaven but the Jews.

Indeed, as the emperor Julian[‡] justly observes, "unless a certain ethnarchic God presides over every nation, and under this God there is an angel, a dæmon, and a peculiar genus of souls, subservient and

---

[†] See Gaffarel's *Unheard-of Curiosities*, p.391.

[‡] Apud Cyril.

ministrant to more excellent natures, from which the difference in laws and manners arises, - unless this is admitted, let it be shown by any other how this difference is produced. For it is not sufficient to say, "God said, and it was done," but it is requisite that the natures of things which are produced should accord with the mandates of divinity. But I will explain more clearly what I mean. God, for instance, commanded that fire should tend upward, and earthly masses downward; is it not therefore requisite, in order that the mandate of God may be accomplished, that the former should be light, and the latter heavy? Thus also in a similar manner in other things. Thus too, in divine concerns. But the reason of this is, because the human race is frail and corruptible. Hence also, the works of man are corruptible and mutable, and subject to all-various revolutions. But God being eternal, it is also fit that his mandates should be eternal. And being such, they are either the natures of things, or conformable to the natures of things. For how can nature contend with the mandate of divinity? How can it fall off from this concord? If, therefore, as he ordered that there should be a confusion of tongues, and that they should not accord with each other, so likewise he ordered that the political concerns of nations should be discordant; he has not only effected this by his mandate, but has rendered us naturally adapted to this dissonance. For to effect this, it would be requisite, in the first place, that the natures of those should be different, whose political concerns among nations are to be different. This, indeed, is seen in bodies, if any one directs his attention to the Germans and Scythians, and considers how much the bodies of those differ from those of the Lybians and Ethiopians. Is this therefore, a mere mandate, and does the air contribute nothing, nor the relation and position of the region with respect to the celestial bodies?

Julian adds, "Moses, however, though he knew the truth of this, concealed it; nor does he ascribe the confusion of tongues to God alone. For he says, that not only God descended, nor one alone with him, but many, though he does not say who they were. But it is very evident, that he conceived those who descended with God to be similar to him. If, therefore, not the Lord only, but those who were with him contributed to this confusion of tongues, they may justly be considered as the causes of this dissonance."

In short, that the heavens and the celestial bodies are animated by certain divine souls, was not only the opinion of the ancient poets and philosophers, but also of the most celebrated fathers of the church, and the most learned and acute of the schoolmen. Thus for instance, this is asserted by Jerom in his exposition of the 6th verse of the first chapter of Ecclesiastes. And by Origen in his book *On Principles*, who says that the heavenly bodies must be animated, because they are said to receive the mandates of God, which is only consentaneous to a rational nature. This too is asserted by Eusebius in his Theological Solutions, and by Augustine in his Enchiridion. Among the schoolmen too, this was the opinion of Albertus Magnus in his book De quatuor qutuor Coæquævis; of Thomas Aquinas in his treatise De Spiritualibus Creaturis; and of Johannes Scotus Super Secundo Sententiarum. To these likewise may be added, the most learned Cardinal Nicolaus Cusanus. Aureolus indeed strenuously contends for the truth of this opinion, and does not even think it improper to venerate the celestial bodies with outward worship (duliæ cultu) and to implore their favour and assistance. And Thomas Aquinas says, that he has no other objection to this than that it might be the occasion of idolatry. Hence, though it may seem ridiculous to most of the present time, that divine souls should be placed in the stars, and preside over regions and cities, tribes and people, nations and tongues, yet it did not appear so to the more intelligent Christians of former times.

I had almost forgotten however the wisest of the ancient Christians, but as he was the best of them, I have done well in reserving him to the last; and this is no other than the Platonic bishop Synesius. This father of the church therefore, in his third hymn, sings as follows:

> Σε, πατερ κοσμων,
> πατερ αιωνων,
> αυτουργε θεων,
> ευαγες αινειν.
> σε μεν οι νοεροι
> μελπουσιν, αναξ,
> σε δε κοσμαγοι,
> ομματολαμπεις,
> νοες αστεριοι,
> ομνουσι μακαρ,
> ους περι κλεινον
> σωμα χορευει.
> πασα σε μελπει
> γενεα μακαρων.
> οι περι κοσμον,
> οι κατα κοσμον,
> οι ζωναιοι,
> οι τ' αζωνοι
> κοσμου κοιρας

9

εφεπουσι, σοφοι
αμφιβατηρες,
οι παρα κλεινους
οιηκοφορους
ους αγγελικα
προχεει σειρα
το, τε κυδηεν
γενος ηρωων,
εργα τα θνητων
κρυφιαισιν οδοις
διανισσομενον,
εργα βροτεια
ψυχα τ' ακλινης,
και κλινομενα
ες μελαναυγεις
χθονιους ογκους

viz. "Thee, father of the worlds, father of the æones,[†] artificer of the *Gods*, it is holy to praise. Thee, O king, the intellectual Gods sing, thee, O blessed God, the *Cosmagi*, those fulgic eyes, and starry intellects, celebrate, round which the illustrious body [of the world] dances. All the race of the blessed sing thy praise, those that are about, and those that are in the world, the zonic Gods, and also the azonic,[‡] who govern the parts of the world, wise itinerants, stationed about the illustrious pilots [of the universe,] and which the angelic series pours forth. Thee too, the renowned genus of heroes celebrates, which by occult paths pervades the works of mortals, and likewise the soul which does not incline to the regions of mortality, and the soul which descends into dark terrestrial masses."

[†] What these are will be shortly explained, when we come to speak of the Apostle Paul.

[‡] Synesius does not here speak conformably to the Chaldean theologists, from whom he has derived these appellations. For the ζωναιοι and the αζωνοι, are according to them Gods, the former being the divinities of the stars, and the latter forming that order of Gods which is called by Proclus in the sixth book of this work απολυτος, *liberated*. Both these orders therefore, are superior to the angelic series. This unscientific manner however of calling both the highest and lowest divine powers by the common name of angels, is not peculiar to Synesius and the Jews, but to all the fathers of the church, and all the Christian divines that succeeded them.

In another part also of the same hymn, he informs us that he adored the powers that preside over Thrace and Chalcedon.

Ικετευσα θεους,
δρηστηρας οσοι
γονιμον Θρηκης
κατεχουσι πεδον,
οι τ' αντιπεραν
χαλκηδονιας
εφεπουσι γυιας.

i.e. "I have supplicated the ministrant Gods that possess the Thracian soil, and also that, in an opposite direction, govern the Chalcedonian land."

And in the last place he says (in Hymn I.)

Νοος αφθιτος, τοκηων
Θεοκοιρανων απορρωξ,
ολιγα μεν, αλλ' εκεινων
ολος ουτος, εις τε παντη
ολος εις ολον δεδυκως,
κοτος ουρανων ελισσει·
το δ' ολον τουτο φυλασσων,
νενεμημεναισι μορφαι,
μεμερισμενος παρεστη·
ο μεν, αστερων διφρειαις,
ο δ' ες αννελων χορειας
ο δε και ρεποντι δεσμῳ,
χθονιαν ευρετο μορφαν.

The substance of which is, "that incorruptible intellect which is wholly an emanation of divinity, is totally diffused through the whole world, convolves the heavens, and preserves the universe with which it is present distributed in various forms. That one part of this intellect is distributed among the stars, and becomes, as it were, their charioteer; but another part among the angelic choirs; and another part is bound in a terrestrial form."

I confess I am wholly at a loss to conceive what could induce the moderns to controvert the dogma, that the stars and the whole world are animated, as it is an opinion of infinite antiquity, and is friendly to the most unperverted, spontaneous, and accurate conceptions of the human mind. Indeed, the rejection of it appears to me to be just as absurd as it would be in a maggot, if it were capable of syllogizing, to infer that man is a machine impelled by some external force when he walks, because it never saw any animated reptile so large.

The sagacious Kepler, for so he is called even by the most modern writers,[†] appears to have had a conception of this great truth; but as he was more an astronomer than a philosopher, he saw this truth only partially, and he rather embraced it as subservient to his own astronomical opinions, than as forming an essential part of the true theory of the universe. But from what I have seen of the writings of Kepler, I have no doubt, if he had lived in the time of the Greeks, or if he had made the study of the works of Plato and Aristotle the business of his life, he would have become an adept in, and an illustrious and zealous champion of their philosophy. Kepler then (in *Harmonices Mundi*, lib. 4 p. 158) says, "That he does not oppose the dogma, that there is a soul of the universe, though he shall say nothing about it in that book. He adds, that if there is such a soul, it must reside in the centre of the world, which, according to him, is the sun, and from thence by the communication of the rays of light, which are in the place of spirits in an animated body, is propagated into all the amplitude of the world."[‡] In the following passages also he confidently asserts that the earth has a soul. For he says "That the globe of the earth is a body such as is that of some animal; and that what its own soul is to an animal, that the sublunary nature which he investigates will be to the

---

[†] Dr Gregory, in the 70th proposition of the first book of his *Elements of Astronomy*, says of Kepler, "That his archetypal ratios, geometrical concinnities, and harmonic proportions, show such a force of genius as is not to be found in any of the writers of physical astronomy before him. So that Jeremiah Horrox, a very competent judge of these matters, though a little averse to Kepler, in the beginning of his astronomical studies, after having in vain tried others, entirely falling in with Kepler's doctrine and physical reasons, thus addresses his reader: *Kepler is a person whom I may justly admire above all mortals beside: I may call him great, divine, or even something more; since Kepler is to be valued above the whole tribe of philosophers. Him alone let the bards sing of. - Him alone let the philosophers read; being satisfied of this, that he who has Kepler has all things.*"

I quote this passage, not from the justness of the encomium it contains; for it is extravagant, and by no means true; but that the reader may see what an exalted opinion some of the greatest of the moderns have had of the genius of Kepler.

[‡] "Et primum quidem de anima totius universi etsi non repugno, mihi tamen hoc libro IV dicam. Videtur enim (si est talis aliqua) in centro mundi, quod nihi sol est, residere, indeque in omnem ejus amplitudinem commercio radioram lucis, qui sint loco spirituum in corpore animali propagari."

earth."† He adds, "That he sees for the most part every thing which proceeding from the body of an animal testifies that there is a soul in it, proceeds also from the body of the earth. For as the animated body produces in the superficies of the skin hairs, thus also the earth produces [on its surface] plants and trees; and as in the former lice are generated, so in the latter the worms called erucæ, grasshoppers, and various insects and marine monsters are produced. As the animated body likewise produces tears, mucus, and the recrement of the ears, and sometimes gum from the pustules of the face, thus also the earth produces amber and bitumen. As the bladder too produces urine, thus likewise mountains pour forth rivers. And as the body produces excrement of a sulphureous odour, and crepitus which may also be inflamed, so the earth produces sulphur, subterranean fires, thunder, and lightning. And as in the veins of an animal blood is generated, and together with it sweat which is ejected out of the body, so in the veins of the earth, metals, and fossils, and a rainy vapour are generated."‡ And in cap. 7 p. 102, after having shown that there is in the earth the sense of touching, that it respires, and is subject in certain parts to languors, and internal vicissitudes of the viscera, and that subterranean heat proceeds from the soul of the earth, he adds, "That a certain image of the zodiac is resplendent in this soul, and therefore of the whole firmament, and is the bond of the sympathy of things celestial and terrestrial.§

Bishop Berkeley also was by no means hostile to this opinion, that the world is one great animal, as is evident from the following extract from his Siris, (p. 131).

"Blind fate and blind chance are at bottom much the same thing, and one no more intelligible than the other. Such is the mutual relation,

---

† "Denique terræ globus tale corpus erit, quale est alicujus animalis: quodque animali est sua anima, hoc erit telluri hæc, quam quærimus, natura sublunaris."

‡ "Videbam pleraque omnia, quæ ex corpore animantis provenientia, testantur animam in illo inesse, provenire etiam ex telluris corpore. Ut enim corpus in cutis superficie pilos, sic terra plantas arboresque profert; inque iis ibi pediculi, hic erucæ, cicadæ, variaque insecta et monstra marina nascuntur; et ut corpus lachrymas, blennam, auriumque recrementa, est ubi et gummi et faciei pustulis, sic tellus electrum, bitumen: utque vesica urinam, sic montes flumina fundunt; et ut corpus excrementum sulphurei odoris, crepitusque, qui etiam inflammari possunt, sic terra sulphur, ignes subterraneos, tonitrua, fulgura: utque in venis animantis generatur sanguis, et eum eo sudor, extra corpus ejectus; sic in venis terræ, metalia et fossilia, vaporque pluvius."

§ "Relucet igitur in anima telluris imago quædam circuli zodiaci sensibilis, totinsque adce firmamenti, vinculum sympathiæ rerum cœlestium et terrestrium."

connection, motion, and sympathy. The parts of this world, that they seem, as it were, animated and held together by one soul: and such is their harmony, order, and regular course, as shows the soul to be governed and directed by a mind. It was an opinion of remote antiquity that the world was an animal. If we may trust the Hermaic writings, the Ægyptians thought all things did partake of life. This opinion was also so general and current among the Greeks, that Plutarch asserts all others held the world to be an animal, and governed by providence, except Leucippus, Democritus, and Epicurus. And although an animal containing all bodies within itself, could not be touched or sensibly affected from without; yet it is plain they attributed to it an inward sense and feeling, as well as appetites and aversions; and that from all the various tones, actions, and passions of the universe, they supposed one symphony, one animal act and life to result.

"Iamblichus declares the world to be one animal, in which the parts, however distant each from other, are nevertheless related and connected by one common nature. And he teaches, what is also a received notion of the Pythagoreans and Platonics, that there is no chasm in nature, but a chain or scale of beings rising by gentle uninterrupted gradations from the lowest to the highest, each nature being informed and perfected by the participation of a higher. As air becomes igneous, so the purest fire becomes animal, and the animal soul becomes intellectual, which is to be understood, not of the change of one nature into another, but of the connection of different natures, each lower nature being, according to those philosophers, as it were, a receptacle or subject for the next above it to reside and act in.

"It is also the doctrine of Platonic philosophers, that intellect is the very life of living things, the first principle and exemplar of all, from whence, by different degrees, are derived the inferior classes of life; first the rational, then the sensitive, after that the vegetable, but so as in the rational animal there is still somewhat intellectual, again in the sensitive there is somewhat rational, and in the vegetable somewhat sensitive, and lastly in mixed bodies, as metals and minerals, somewhat of vegetation. By which means the whole is thought to be more perfectly connected. Which doctrine implies that all the faculties, instincts, and motions of inferior beings, in their several respective subordinations, are derived from, and depend upon intellect.

"Both Stoics and Platonics held the world to be alive, though sometimes it be mentioned as a sentient animal, sometimes as a plant or vegetable. *But in this, notwithstanding what has been surmised by some learned men, there seems to be no atheism. For so long as the world is supposed to be quickened by elementary fire or spirit, which is itself animated by soul, and directed by understanding, it follows that all parts thereof originally depend upon, and may be reduced unto, the same indivisible stem or principle, to wit, a supreme mind; which is the concurrent doctrine of Pythagoreans, Platonics, and Stoics."*

Compare now the Newtonian with this theory, that the heavenly bodies are vitalized by their informing souls, that their orderly motion is the result of this vitality, and that the planets move harmonically round the sun, not as if urged by a centripetal force, but from an animated tendency to the principle and fountain of their light, and from a desire of partaking as largely as possible of his influence and power. In the former theory all the celestial motions are the effect of violence, in the latter they are all natural. The former is attended with insuperable difficulties, the latter, when the principle on which it is founded is admitted, with none. And the former is unscientific and merely hypothetical; but the latter is the progeny of the most accurate science, and is founded on the most genuine and unperverted conceptions of the human mind.

I have said that I should prove from the testimony of the Apostle Paul, that the Jews were not consistent in confounding *angels* properly so called with Gods. And this appears to me to be evident in the first place from the following passage in Hebrews ii v. 9 πιστει νοομεν κατηρτισθαι τους αιωνας ρηματι θεου, εις το μη εκ φαινομενων τα βλεπομενα γενονεναι. This in the English version is erroneously rendered; "Through faith we understand, that the worlds were framed by the word of God, so that things which are seen, were not made of things which do appear." I say this is erroneously translated, because in the first place *the worlds* is evidently a forced interpretation of αιωνας; and even admitting it is not, leaves the passage very ambiguous, from the uncertainty to what worlds Paul alludes. If we adopt *ages*, which is the general sense of the word in the New Testament, we shall indeed avoid a forced and ambiguous interpretation, but we shall render the meaning of the Apostle trifling in the extreme. For as he has elsewhere said, "that all things were framed by the word of God," what particular faith does it require to believe, that by the same word he framed the ages?

In the second place, from the definition of faith, given in the first verse of this chapter, that it is "the evidence of *things not seen,"* it is clear, that Paul is speaking in this passage of something *invisible*. Since then αιωνας; is neither *worlds* nor *ages*, what shall we say it is? I answer, the *æones* of the Valentinians. And agreeably to this, the whole passage should be translated as follows: "By faith we understand, that the *æones* were framed by the word of God, in order that things which are seen, might be generated from such as do not appear (*i.e.* from things *invisible*)." Every one who is much conversant with greek authors, must certainly be convinced that εις το means *in order that;* and Bishop Pearson translates as I have done the latter part of this verse.

Now we learn from the second book of Irenæus against the heretics, that according to the Valentinians, all created things are the images of the *æones*, resident in the *pleroma*, or *fullness* of deity. And does it not clearly follow from the above version, that according to Paul too, the æones are the exemplars of visible or created things? To which we may add, that this sense of the passage clearly accords with the assertion that "faith is the evidence of things not seen." For here the things which do not appear are the *æones*; these, according to the Valentinians, subsisting in deity. So that from our version, Paul might say with great propriety, that "we understand by faith, that the *æones* were framed by the word of God, in order that things which are seen, might be generated from such as do not appear," for this naturally follows from his definition of faith.

I farther add, that among these *æones* of the Valentinians were νους, βυθος, σιγη, αληθεια, σοφια *i.e. intellect, a profundity, silence, truth, and wisdom,* which as Gale well observes in his notes on Iamblichus de Mysteriis etc. prove their dogmas to be of Chaldaic origin. For these words perpetually occur in the fragments of the Chaldaic oracles. And the middle of the Chaldean intelligible triad is denominated αιων *æon*,[†] *i.e. eternity*, and is also perfectly conformable to the theology of Plato, as is very satisfactorily shown by Proclus in the third book of the following work. According to the Chaldeans therefore, the æones are Gods; and considered as the exemplars of the visible universe, they are analogous to the ideas of Plato, which also are Gods, as is evident from

---

[†] Proclus begins the sixth book of the following work with observing that he has celebrated in the preceding book the hebdomadic *æon* of the intellectual Gods. The *æones* therefore, though the cause of them exists in the intelligible, properly belong to the intellectual order; and the Demiurgus or artificer of the universe subsists at the extremity of that order. But the demiurgus according to Orpheus, prior to the fabrication of the world absorbed in himself Phanes the exemplar of the universe. Hence he became full of ideas of which the forms in the sensible universe are the images. And as all intellectual natures are in each, it is evident that *things which are seen were generated from the invisible æones*, conformably to the assertion of Paul.

the *Parmenides* of that philosopher.[†] According to Paul too, as the *æones* are the fabricators of the visible world, they must be beings of a much higher order than angels, and consequently must be Gods; productive power being one of the great characteristics of a divine nature.

Again, in the Epistle to the Ephesians, chap. iv. 21. Paul says that God has exalted Christ "far above every principality, and power, and might, and dominion," υπερανω πασης αρχης και εξουσιας, και δυναμεως και κυριοτητος. And in the 6th chapter and 12th verse he conjoins with principalities and powers, *the rulers of the world*, i.e. the seven planets, προς τας αρχας, προς τας εξουσιας, προς τασ κοσμοκρατορας. Augustin[‡] confesses that he is ignorant what the difference is between those four words, (principality, power, might and dominion,) in which the Apostle Paul seems to comprehend all the celestial society. "Quid inter se distent quatuor illa vocabula quibus universam ipsam cœlestem societatem videtur Apostolus esse complexus, dicant qui possunt, si tamen possunt probare quod dicunt; ego me ista ignorare fateos." Ignatius also (in Epist. ad Trallianos) speaks of the angelic orders, the diversities of archangels and armies, the differences of the orders characterised by might and dominion, of thrones and powers, *the magnificence of the æones*,[§] and the transcendency of Cherubim and Seraphim," και γαρ εγω ου καθ᾽ ο, τι δεδεμαι, και δυναμαι νοειν τα επουρανια, και τας αγγελικας ταξεις, και τας των αρχαγγελων και στρατιων εξαλλαγας, δυναμεων τε και κυριοτητων διαφορας, θρονων τε και εξουσιων παραλλαγας, αιωνων δε μεγαλοτητας, των τε χερουβιμ και σεραφιμ τας υπεροχας.

The opinion of Grotius[*] therefore, is highly probable, that the Jews obtained the names of Powers, Dominations, and Principalities, from their Babylonic captivity; and Gale in his notes on Iamblichus[°] says, that certain passages of Zoroaster and Ostanes cited by the author of

---

[†] I refer the reader who is desirous of being fully convinced of this to the notes accompanying my translation of that dialogue, in vol. 3 of my Plato [TTS vol. XI.]

[‡] Ad Laurentium, c. 58.

[§] Here we see the *æones* are acknowledged by Irenæus to be beings of an order superior to angels.

[*] Ad Cap. 18. Mattheæi.

[°] De Myst. p. 204.

Arithm. Theolog. confirm this opinion of Grotius. Indeed, the appellation of αρχαι *principles*, which are the first of the four powers mentioned by Paul, was given by the Chaldeans to that order of Gods called by the Grecian theologists *supermundane* and *assimilative*, the nature of which is unfolded by Proclus in the sixth book of the following work; and Proclus in the fourth book of his MS. Commentary on the *Parmenides* of Plato shows that the order of Gods denominated νοητος και νοερος, *intelligible and at the same time intellectual*, is according to the Chaldean oracles[†] principally characterised by *domination*. In proof of this, the two following oracles are cited by him, the first, concerning the empyrean, and the second concerning the material Synoches.[‡]

Τοις δε πυρος νοερου νοεροις πρηστηρσιν απαντα
Εικαθε δουλευοντα, πατρος πειθηνιδι βουλη.

i.e. "All things yield ministrant to the intellectual presters of intellectual fire, through the persuasive will of the father." And

αλλα και υλαιοις οσα δουλευει Συνοχευσι.

i.e. "But likewise such as are in subjection to the material Synoches."

Farther still, Paul in the Epistle to the Romans, chap. viii v. 38, says "For I am persuaded that neither death nor life, nor *angels*, nor *principalities*, nor *powers*, nor things present, nor things to come, nor *height*, nor *depth*, nor any other creature, shall be able to separate us from the love of God, etc." From this arrangement therefore, it is evident that principalities and powers are not the same with angels; and as according to Paul they are beings so exalted, that in his Epistle to the Ephesians, he could not find any thing more magnificent to say of Christ, than that he is raised even above them, it follows that they must be Gods, since they are superior to the angelic order. It is remarkable too, that he co-arranges *height* and *depth* (υψωμα και βαθος) with principalities and powers; and βυθος is one of the *æones* according to the Valentinians.

In the first Epistle to the Corinthians likewise, chap. viii. v. 5. Paul expressly asserts that there is a divine multitude. For he says, "Though there be that are called Gods, whether in heaven or in earth, (as there

---

[†] See my Collection of these Oracles [TTS vol. VII.]

[‡] The Synoches form the second triad of the intelligible, and at the same time intellectual order of Gods.

be Gods many and Lords many;)" in the parenthesis of which verse, it is incontrovertibly evident that he admits the existence of a plurality of Gods, though as well as the heathens he believed that one God only was supreme and the father of *all* things. Nor am I singular in asserting that this was admitted by Paul. For the Pseudo-Dionysius the Areopagite in the second chapter of his treatise On the Divine Names observes concerning what is here said by Paul as follows: "Again, from the deific energy of God, by which every thing according to its ability becomes deiform, many Gods are generated; in consequence of which there appears and is said to be a separation and multiplication of the one [supreme] God. Nevertheless, God himself, who is the chief deity, and is superessentially the supreme, is still one God, remaining impartible in the Gods distributed from him, united to himself, unmingled with the many, and void of multitude." And he afterwards adds, "that this was in a transcendent manner understood by Paul, who was the leader both of him, and his preceptor, to divine illumination," in the above cited verse. And, "that in divine natures, unions vanquish and precede separations, and yet nevertheless they are united, after the separation which does not in proceeding depart from *The One*, and is unical."† Paul therefore, according to this Dionysius, considered the Gods, conformably to Plato and the best of his disciples, as deiform processions from *The One*, and which at the same time that they have a distinct subsistence from, are profoundly united to their great producing cause. Dionysius also employs the very same expression which Proclus continually uses when speaking of the separation of the Gods from their source; for he says that the divine multitude ανεκφοιτητος του ενος, *i.e.* does not depart from, but abides in *The One*. Hence Proclus in the fifth book of his MS Commentary On the *Parmenides* of Plato, speaking of the divine unities says, "Whichever among these you assume, it is the same with the others, because all of them are in each other, and are rooted in *The One*. For as trees by their summits (*i.e.* their roots) are fixed in the earth, and through these are

---

† Παλιν τη εξ αυτου θεωσει, τῳ κατα δυναμιν εκαστου θεοειδει θεων πολλων γιγνομενων, δοκει μεν ειναι και λεγεται του ενος θεου διακρισις και πολλαπλασιασμος· εστι δε ουδεν ηττον ο αρχιθεος και υπερθεος υπερουσιως, εις θεος, αμεριστος εν τοις μεριστοις, ηνωμενος, εαυτῳ, και τοις πολλοις αμιγης και απληθυντος. Και ταυτο υπερφυως εννοησας ο κοινος ημων και του καθηγεμονος επι την θειαν φωτοδοσιαν χειραγωγος, ο πολυς τα θεια, το φως του κοσμου, τα δε φησιν ενθεαστικως εν τοις ιεροις αυτου γραμμασι. Και γαρ ειπερ εισι λεγομενοι θεοι, ειτε εν ουρανῳ, ειτε επι γης, κ.λ. - Και γαρ επι των θεων αι ενωσεις των διακρισιων επικρατουσι και προκαταρχουσι, και ουδεν ηττον εστιν ηνωμενα, και μετα την του ενος ανικφοιτητον και ενιαιαν διακρισιν.

earthly, after the same manner also divine natures are rooted by their summits in *The One*, and each of them is a unity and one, through unconfused union with *The One Itself.*" Ην γαρ αν τουτων λαβης, την αυτην ταις αλλαις λαμβανεις, διοτι δη πασαι και εν αλληλαις εισι, και ενερριζονται τω ενι. Καθαπερ γαρ τα δενδρα ταις εαυτων κορυθαις ενιδρυνται τη γη, και εστι γηινα κατ' εκεινας, τον αυτον τροπον και τα θεια ταις εαυτων ακροτησιν ενερριζωται τω ενι, και εκαστον αυτων ενας εστι, και εν, δια την προς το εν ασυγχυτον ενωσιν.

This Dionysius, who certainly lived posterior to Proclus, because he continually borrows from his works, barbarously confounding that scientific arrangement of these deiform processions from *The One*, which is so admirably unfolded by Proclus in the following work, classes them as follows. The first order, according to him, consists of Seraphim, Cherubim and Thrones. The second of the divine essences characterized by dominion, might, and power. And the third of Principalities, Archangels, and Angels. Hence he has transferred the characteristics of the intelligible triad of Gods to Seraphim, Cherubim and Thrones. For symmetry, truth, and beauty, which characterize this triad, are said by Plato in the *Philebus* to subsist *in the vestibule of The Good;* (επι μεν τοις του αγαθου νυν ηδη προθυροις εφεσταναι) and Dionysius says[†] of his first order that *"it is as it were arranged in the vestibules of deity."* Goodness, wisdom, and beauty also, are shown by Proclus in the third book of the following work to belong to the intelligible triad; *goodness* to its summit, *wisdom* to the middle of it, and *beauty* to its extremity. And Dionysius says, that according to the Hebrews, the word Cherubim signifies *a multitude of knowledge, or an effusion of wisdom,* την δε χερουβιμ εμφαυνειν, πληθος γνωσεως, η χυσιν σοφιας. The characteristics of the Gods called νοητοι και νοεροι *intelligible and at the same time intellectual,* and of the Gods that are νοερος *intellectual* alone, he appears to have transferred to his middle triad which is characterized by *dominion, might, and power.* And he has adapted his third triad consisting of *Principalities, Archangels,* and *Angels* to the *supermundane, liberated,* and *mundane* orders of Gods. For the supermundane Gods are called by Proclus in the sixth book of the following work αρχαι *Principalities,* or *rulers,* which is the word employed by Dionysius and Paul. And the mundane Gods are said by Proclus (in Parmenid.) to be

---

[†] Ταις πρωταις ουσιαις, αι μετα την ουσιοποιον αυτων θεαρχιων ιδρυμεναι, και οιον εν προθυροις αυτης τιταγμεναι, πασης εισιν αορατου και ορατης υπερβεβηκυιαι γεγονυιας δυναμεως, ως οικειον οιητεον ειναι, και κατα παν ομοειδη την ιεραρχιαν. De Cœlest. Hierarch. cap. 7.

the sources of a *winged* life, and angels are celebrated by Dionysius as having *wings*. Hence it is evident that Dionysius has accommodated the peculiarities of the different orders of Gods to the nine orders which he denominates *celestial powers;* and his arrangement has been adopted by all succeeding Christian theologists.

Vestiges therefore of the theology of Plato may be seen both in the Jewish and Christian religion; and in a similar manner, a resemblance in the religions of all other nations to it might be easily pointed out, and its universality be clearly demonstrated. Omitting however, a discussion of this kind for the present, I shall farther observe respecting this theology, that the deification of dead men, and the worshipping men as Gods form no part of it when it is considered according to its genuine purity. Numerous instances of the truth of this might be adduced, but I shall mention for this purpose, as unexceptionable witnesses, the writings of Plato, the Golden Pythagoric verses,[†] and the treatise of

---

[†] "Diogenes Laertius says of Pythagoras, *That he charged his disciples not to give equal degrees of honour to the Gods and heroes.* Herodotus (in Euterpe) says of the Greeks, *That they worshipped Hercules two ways, one as an immortal deity and so they sacrificed to him: and another as a Hero, and so they celebrated his memory.* Isocrates (Encom. Helen.) distinguishes between the honours of heroes and Gods, when he speaks of Menelaus and Helena. But the distinction is no where more fully expressed than in the Greek inscription upon the statue of Regilla, wife to Herodes Atticus, as Salmasius thinks, which was set up in his temple at Triopium, and taken from the statue itself by Sirmondus; where it is said, *That she had neither the honour of a mortal, nor yet that which was proper to the Gods:* ουδε ιερα θνηητοις, αταρ ουδε θεοισιν ομοια. It seems by the inscription of Herodes, and by the testament of Epicteta extant in Greek in the *Collection of Inscriptions,* that it was in the power of particular families to keep festival days in honour of some of their own family, and to give *heroical honours* to them. In that noble inscription at Venice, we find three days appointed every year to be kept, and a *confraternity* established for that purpose with the laws of it. The first day to be observed in honour of the Muses and sacrifices to be offered to them as *deities.* The second and third days in honour of the *heroes* of the family; between which honour and that of deities, they shewed the difference by the distance of time between them, and the preference given to the other. But wherein soever the *difference* lay, that there was a *distinction* acknowledged among them appears by this passage of Valerius in his excellent oration extant in Dionysius Halicarnass. Antiq. Rom. lib. 11 p. 696. *I call*, says he, *the Gods to witness, whose temples and altars our family has worshipped with common sacrifices; and next after them, I call the Genii of our ancestors, to whom we give* δευτερας τιμας, *the second honours next to the Gods,* as Celsus calls those τας προσηκουσας τιμας *the due honours that belong to the lower dæmons.* From which we take notice, that the Heathens did not confound all *degrees of divine worship*, giving to the lowest object the same which they supposed to be due to the *celestial deities*, or the *supreme God.* So that if the distinction of divine worship will excuse from idolatry, the Heathens were not to blame for it." See Stillingfleet's answer to a book entitled *Catholics no Idolaters*, p. 510, 513, etc.

Plutarch On Isis and Osiris. All the works of Plato indeed, evince the truth of this position, but this is particularly manifest from his Laws. The Golden verses order, that the immortal Gods be honoured first as they are disposed by law; afterwards the illustrious Heroes, under which appellation, the author of the verses comprehends also angels and dæmons properly so called; and in the last place the terrestrial dæmons, *i.e.* such good men as transcend in virtue the rest of mankind. But to honour the Gods as they are disposed by law, is, as Hierocles observes, to reverence them as they are arranged by their fabricator and father; and this is to honour them as beings superior to man. Hence, to honour men, however excellent they may be, as Gods, is not to honour the Gods according to the rank in which they are placed by their Creator, for it is confounding the divine with the human nature, and is thus acting directly contrary to the Pythagoric precept. Plutarch too in his above-mentioned treatise most forcibly and clearly shows the impiety of worshipping men as Gods, as is evident from the following extract:

"Those therefore, who think that things of this kind [*i.e.* fabulous stories of the Gods as if they were men] are but so many commemorations of the actions and disasters of kings and tyrants, who through transcendency in virtue or power, inscribed the title of divinity on their renown, and afterwards fell into great calamities and misfortunes, these employ the most easy method indeed of eluding the story, and not badly transfer things of evil report, from the Gods to men; and they are assisted in so doing by the narrations themselves. For the Egyptians relate, that Hermes was as to his body, with one arm longer than the other; that Typhon was in his complexion red; but Orus white, and Osiris black, as if they had been by nature men. Farther still, they also call Osiris a commander, and Canopus a pilot, from whom they say the star of that name was denominated. The ship likewise, which the Greeks call Argo, being the image of the ark of Osiris, and which therefore in honour of it is become a constellation, they make to ride not far from Orion and the Dog; of which they consider the one as sacred to Orus, but the other to Isis.

"I fear, however, that this [according to the proverb] would be to move things immoveable, and to declare war, not only as Simonides says, against a great length of time, but also against many nations and families of mankind who are under the influence of divine inspiration through piety to these Gods; and would not in any respect fall short of transferring from heaven to earth, such great and venerable names, and of thereby shaking and dissolving that worship and belief, which has been implanted in almost all men from their very birth, would be opening great doors to the tribe of atheists, who convert divine into human concerns; and would likewise afford a large license to the impostures of Euemerus of Messina, who devised certain memoirs of an incredible and fictitious mythology,[†] and *thereby spread every kind of atheism through the globe, by inscribing all the received Gods, without any discrimination, by the names of generals, naval-captains, and kings, who lived in remote periods of time.* He further adds, that they are recorded in golden characters, in a certain country called Panchoa, at which neither any Barbarian or Grecian ever arrived, except Euemerus alone, who, as it seems, sailed to the Panchoans and Triphyllians, that neither have, nor ever had a being. And though the great actions of Semiramis are celebrated by the Assyrians, and those of Sesostris in Egypt; and though the Phrygians even to the present time, call all splendid and admirable actions Manic, because a certain person named Mania who was one of their ancient kings, whom some call Musdes, was a brave and powerful man; and farther still, though Cyrus among the Persians, and Alexander among the Macedonians, proceeded in their victories, almost as far as to the boundaries of the earth, yet they only retain the names of good kings, and are remembered as such, [and not as Gods.]

"But if certain persons, inflated by ostentation, as Plato says, having their soul at one and the same time inflamed with youth and ignorance, have insolently assumed the appellation of Gods, and had temples erected in their honour, yet this opinion of them flourished but for a short time, and afterwards they were charged with vanity and arrogance, in conjunction with impiety and lawless conduct; and thus,

  Like smoke they flew away with swift-pac'd fate.

And being dragged from temples and altars like fugitive slaves, they have now nothing left them, but their monuments and tombs. Hence Antigonus the elder said to one Hermodotus, who had celebrated him in his poems as the offspring of the sun and a God, 'he who empties my close-stool-pan knows no such thing of me.' Very properly also, did Lysippus the sculptor blame Apelles the painter, for drawing the picture of Alexander with a thunder-bolt in his hand, whereas he had

---

[†] Both Arnobius therefore and Minoclus Felix were very unfortunate in quoting this impostor to prove that the Gods of the ancients had formerly been men. Vid. Arnob. lib. 4. Adversus Gentes, et Minueii Felicia Octavo, p. 350, Parisiis, 1605.

represented him with a spear, the glory of which, as being true and proper, no time would take away."

In another part of the same work also, he admirably reprobates the impiety of making the Gods to be things inanimate, which was very common with Latin writers of the Augustan age, and of the ages that accompanied the decline and fall of the Roman empire. But what he says on this subject is as follows:

"In the second place, which is of still greater consequence, men should be careful, and very much afraid, lest before they are aware, they tear in pieces and dissolve divine natures, into blasts of wind, streams of water, seminations, earings of land, accidents of the earth, and mutations of the seasons, as those do who make Bacchus to be wine, and Vulcan flame. Cleanthes also somewhere says, that Persephone or Proserpine is the spirit or air that *passes through* (φερομενον) the fruits of the earth, and is then *slain*, (φονευομενον). And a certain poet says of reapers,

> Then when the youth the limbs of Ceres cut.

For these men do not in any respect differ from those who conceive the sails, the cables, and the anchor of a ship, to be the pilot, the yarn and the web to be the weaver, and the bowl, or the mead, or the ptisan, to be the physician. But they also produce dire and atheistical opinions, by giving the names of Gods to natures and things deprived of sense and soul, and that are necessarily destroyed by men, who are in want of and use them. For it is not possible to conceive that these things are Gods; since, neither can any thing be a God to men, which is deprived of soul, or is subject to human power. From these things however, we are led to conceive those beings to be Gods, who both use them and impart them to us, and supply them perpetually and without ceasing. Nor do we conceive that the Gods who bestow these, are different in different countries, nor that some of them are peculiar to the Barbarians, but others to the Grecians, nor that some are southern, and others northern; but as the sun and moon, the heavens, the land, and the sea, are common to all men, yet are differently denominated by different nations; so the one reason that adorns these things, and the one providence that administers them, and the ministrant powers that preside over all nations, have different appellations and honours assigned them according to law by different countries. Of those also that have been consecrated to their service, some employ obscure, but others clearer symbols, not without danger thus conducting our intellectual conceptions to the apprehension of divine natures. For some, deviating from the true meaning of these symbols, have entirely slipt into superstition; and others again flying from superstition as a quagmire, have unaware fallen upon atheism as on a precipice. Hence, in order to avoid these dangers, it is especially necessary that resuming the reasoning of Philosophy as our guide to mystic knowledge, we should conceive piously of every thing that is said or done in religion; lest that, as Theodorus said, while he extended his arguments with his right hand, some of his auditors received them with their left, so we should fall into dangerous errors, by receiving what the laws have well instituted about sacrifices and festivals in a manner different from their original intention."

The Emperor Julian, as well as Plutarch appears to have been perfectly aware of this confusion in the religion of the Heathens arising from the deification of men, and in the fragments of his treatise against the Christians, preserved by Cyril, he speaks of it as follows: "If any one wishes to consider the truth respecting you [Christians,] he will find that your impiety is composed of the Judaic audacity, and *the indolence and confusion of the Heathens.* For deriving from both, not that which is most beautiful, but the worst, you have fabricated a web of evils. With the Hebrews indeed, there are accurate and venerable laws pertaining to religion, and innumerable precepts which require a most holy life and deliberate choice. But when the Jewish legislator forbids the serving all the Gods, and enjoins the worship of one alone, whose portion is Jacob, and Israel the line of his inheritance, and not only says this, but also omits to add, I think, you shall not revile the Gods, the detestable wickedness and audacity of those in after times, wishing to take away all religious reverence from the multitude, thought that not to worship should be followed by blaspheming the Gods. This you have alone thence derived; but there is no similitude in any thing else between you and them. Hence, from the innovation of the Hebrews, you have seized blasphemy towards the venerable Gods; *but from our religion you have cast aside reverence to every nature more excellent than man, and the love of paternal institutes."*

"So great an apprehension indeed, says Dr. Stillingfleet,[†] had the Heathens of the necessity of *appropriate acts of divine worship,* that some of them have chosen to die, rather than to give them to what they did not believe to be God. We have a remarkable story to this purpose in Arrian and Curtius[‡] concerning Callisthenes. Alexander arriving at that degree of vanity, as to desire to have divine worship given him, and the matter being started out of design among the courtiers, either by

---

[†] Answer to *Catholics no Idolators,* Lond. 1676 p. 211.

[‡] Arrian. de Exped. Alex. 1. 4. et Curt. lib. 8.

Anaxarchus, as Arrian, or Cleo the Sicilian, as Curtius says; and the way of doing it proposed, *viz.* by incense and prostration; Callisthenes vehemently opposed it, *as that which would confound the difference of human and divine worship, which had been preserved inviolable among them.* The worship of the Gods had been kept up in temples, with altars, and images, and sacrifices, and hymns, and prostrations, and such like; *but it is by no means fitting,* says he, *for us to confound these things, either by lifting up men to the honours of the Gods, or depressing the Gods to the honours of men.* For neither would Alexander suffer any man to usurp his royal dignity by the votes of men; how much more justly may the Gods disdain for any man to take their honours to himself. And it appears by Plutarch,[†] that the Greeks thought it a mean and base thing for any of them, when sent on an embassy to the kings of Persia, to prostrate themselves before them, because this was only allowed among them in divine adoration. Therefore, says he, when Pelopidas and Ismenias were sent to Artaxerxes, Pelopidas did nothing unworthy, but Ismenias let fall his ring to the ground, and stooping for that was thought to make his adoration; which was altogether as good a shift as the Jesuits advising the crucifix to be held in the Mandarins' hands while they made their adorations in the Heathen temples in China.

"Conon[‡] also *refused to make his adoration, as a disgrace to his city;* and Isocrates[§] accuses the Persians for doing it, *because herein they shewed, that they despised the Gods rather than men, by prostituting their honours to their princes.* Herodotus mentions Sperchius and Bulis, who could not with the greatest violence be brought to give adoration to Xerxes, *because it was against the law of their country to give divine honour to men.*[*] And Valerius Maximus[°] says, *the Athenians put Timagoras to death for doing it;* so strong an apprehension had possessed them, that the manner of worship which they used to their Gods, should be preserved sacred and inviolable." The philosopher Sallust also in his treatise On the Gods and the World says, "It is not unreasonable to suppose that impiety is a species of punishment, and that those who

---

[†] Vit. Artaxers. Ælian. Var. hist. lib. 1. c. 21.

[‡] Justin. lib. 6.

[§] Panegyr.

[*] Lib. 7.

[°] Lib. 6. Cap. 3.

have had a knowledge of the Gods, and yet despised them, will in another life be deprived of this knowledge. And it is requisite to make the punishment of those who have honoured their kings as Gods to consist in being expelled from the Gods."†

When the ineffable transcendency of the first God, which was considered as the grand principle in the Heathen theology, by its most ancient promulgators Orpheus, Pythagoras, and Plato, was forgotten, this oblivion was doubtless the principal cause of dead men being deified by the Pagans. Had they properly directed their attention to this transcendency they would have perceived it to be so immense as to surpass eternity, infinity, self-subsistence, and even essence itself, and that these in reality belong to those venerable natures which are as it were first unfolded into light from the unfathomable depths of that truly mystic unknown, about which all knowledge is refunded into ignorance. For as Simplicius justly observes, "It is requisite that he who ascends to the principle of things should investigate whether it is possible there can be any thing better than the supposed principle; and if something more excellent is found, the same enquiry should again be made respecting that, till we arrive at the highest conceptions, than which we have no longer any more venerable. Nor should we stop in our ascent till we find this to be the case. For there is no occasion to fear that our progression will be through an unsubstantial void, by conceiving something about the first principles which is greater and more transcendent than their nature. For it is not possible for our conceptions to take such a mighty leap as to equal, and much less to pass beyond the dignity of the first principles of things." He adds, "This therefore is one and the best extension [of the soul] to [the highest] God, and is as much as possible irreprehensible; *viz.* to know firmly, that by ascribing to him the most venerable excellencies we can conceive, and the most holy and primary names and things, we ascribe nothing to him which is suitable to his dignity. It is sufficient however, to procure our pardon [for the attempt,] that we can attribute to him nothing superior."‡ If it is not possible therefore to form any ideas equal to the

---

† Και κολασεως δε ειδος ειναι αθειαν ουκ απεικος. Τους γαρ γνοντας θεους, και καταφρονησαντας, ευλογον εν ετερω βιω και της γνεωσεως στερεσθαι, και τους εαυτων βασιλεας ως θεους τιμησαντας, εδει την δικην αυτων ποιησαι των θεων εκπισειν. Cap. 18 [TTS vol. IV.]

‡ Και χρη τον επι τας αρχας αναβαινοντα ζητειν, ει δυνατον ειναι τι κρειστον της υποτεθεισης αρχης καν ευρεθη, παλιν επ' εκεινου ζητειν, εως αν εις τας ακροτατας εννοιας ελθωμεν, ων ουκετι σεμνοτερας εχομεν· και μη στησαι την αναβασιν. Ουδε γαρ ευλαβητεον μη κενεμβατωμεν, μειζονα τινα και υπερβαινοντα τας πρωτας αρχας περι

dignity of the immediate progeny of the ineffable, *i.e.* of the first principles of things, how much less can our conceptions reach that thrice unknown darkness, in the reverential language of the Egyptians,† which is even beyond these? Had the Heathens therefore considered as they ought this transcendency of the supreme God, they would never have presumed to equalize the human with the divine nature, and consequently would never have worshipped men as Gods. Their theology, however, is not to be accused as the cause of this impiety, but their forgetfulness of the sublimest of its dogmas, and the confusion with which this oblivion was necessarily attended.

In the last place, I wish to adduce a few respectable testimonies to prove that statues were not considered nor worshipped by any of the intelligent Heathens as Gods, but as the resemblances of the Gods, as auxiliaries to the recollection of a divine nature, and the means of procuring its assistance and favour. For this purpose, I shall first present the reader with what the philosopher Sallust says concerning sacrifices and the honours which were paid to the divinities, in his golden treatise On the Gods and the World. "The honours, says he, which we pay to the Gods are performed for the sake of our advantage; and since the providence of the Gods is every where extended, a certain habitude or fitness is all that is requisite in order to receive their beneficent communications. But all habitude is produced through imitation and similitude. Hence temples imitate the heavens, but altars the earth; statues resemble life, and on this account they are similar to animals; prayers imitate that which is intellectual; but characters superior ineffable powers; herbs and stones resemble matter; and animals which are sacrificed the irrational life of our souls. But from all these nothing happens to the Gods beyond what they already possess; for what accession can be made to a divine nature? But a conjunction with our souls and the Gods is by these means produced.

αυτων εννοουντες. Ου γαρ δυνατον τηλικουτον πηδημα πηδησαι τας ημετερας εννοιας, ως παρισωθηναι τη αξια των πρωτων αρχων, ου λεγω και υπερπτηναι· μια γαρ αυτη προς θεον ανατασις αριστη, και ως δυνατον απταιστος. Και ων εννοουμεν αγαθων τα σεμνοτατα, και αγιωτατα, και πρωτουργα, και ονοματα, και πραγματα αυτω ανατιθεντας ειδεναι βεβαιως, οτι μηδεν ανατεθεικαμεν αξιον· αρκει δε ημιν εις συγγνωμην, το μηδεν εχειν εκεινων υπερτερον. Simplic. in Epict. Enchir. p. 207 Lond. 1670. 8vo.

† Of the first principle, says Damascius (in M.S. περι αρχον) the Egyptians said nothing, but celebrated it as a darkness beyond all intellectual conception, a thrice unknown darkness, πρωτην αρχην ανυμνηκασαν, σκοτος υπερ πασαν νοησιν, σκοτος αγνωστον, τρις τουτο επιφημιζοντες.

"I think however, it will be proper to add a few things concerning sacrifices. And in the first place, since we possess every thing from the Gods, and it is but just to offer the first fruits of gifts to the givers; hence, of our possessions we offer the first fruits through consecrated gifts; of our bodies through ornaments; and of our life through sacrifices. Besides, without sacrifices, prayers are words only; but accompanied with sacrifices they become animated words; the words indeed corroborating life, but life animating the words. Add too, that the felicity of every thing is its proper perfection; but the proper perfection of every thing consists in a conjunction with its cause. And on this account we pray that we may be conjoined with the Gods. Since therefore life primarily subsists in the Gods, and there is also a certain human life, but the latter desires to be united to the former, a medium is required; for natures much distant from each other cannot be conjoined without a medium. And it is necessary that the medium should be similar to the connected natures. Life therefore must necessarily be the medium of life; and hence men of the present day that are happy, and all the ancients, have sacrificed animals. And this indeed not rashly, but in a manner accommodated to every god, with many other ceremonies respecting the cultivation of divinity."[†]

In the next place, the elegant Maximus Tyrius admirably observes concerning the worship of statues[‡] as follows: "It appears to me that as external discourse has no need, in order to its composition, of certain Phœnician, or Ionian, or Attic, or Assyrian, or Egyptian characters, but human imbecility devised these marks, in which inserting its dulness, it recovers from them its memory; in like manner a divine nature has no need of statues or altars; but human nature being very imbecile, and as much distant from divinity as earth from heaven, devised these symbols, in which it inserted the names and the renown of the Gods. Those, therefore, whose memory is robust, and who are able, by directly extending their soul to heaven, to meet with divinity, have, *perhaps*,[§] no

---

[†] See ch 15 & 16, of my translation of this excellent work. [TTS vol. IV, p. 19 ff.]

[‡] See my translation of his Dissertations, Dissertat. 38 [TTS vol. VI, p. 309 *et seq.*], the title of which is, *Whether statues should be dedicated to the Gods*.

[§] The philosopher Isidorus was a man of this description, as we are informed by Damascius in the extracts from his life preserved by Photius. For he says of him: ουτε τα αγαλματα προσκυνειν εθελων, αλλ' ηδη επ' αυτους τους θεους ιεμενος, εισω κρυπτομενους ουκ εν αδυτοις, αλλ' εν αυτω τω απορρητω, ο, τι ποτε εστι της παντελους αγνωσιας πως ουν επ' αυτους ιετο τοιουτους οντας; ερωτι δεινω απορρητω και τουτω και τις δε αλλος η αγνωστος και ο ερως; κια τινα τουτο φαμεν, ισασιν οι πειραθεντες·

need of statues. This race is, however, rare among men, and in a whole nation you will not find one who recollects divinity, and who is not in want of this kind of assistance, which resembles that devised by writing masters for boys, who give them obscure marks as copies; by writing over which, their hand being guided by that of the master, they become, through memory, accustomed to the art. It appears to me therefore, that legislators devised these statues for men, as if for a certain kind of boys, as tokens of the honour which should be paid to divinity, and a certain manuduction as it were and path to reminiscence.

"Of statues however, there is neither one law, nor one mode, nor one art, nor one matter. For the Greeks think it fit to honour the Gods from things the most beautiful in the earth, from a pure matter, the human form, and accurate art: and their opinion is not irrational who fashion statues in the human resemblance. For if the human soul is most near and most similar to divinity, it is not reasonable to suppose that divinity would invest that which is most similar to himself with a most deformed body, but rather with one which would be an easy vehicle to immortal souls, light, and adapted to motion. For this alone, of all the bodies on the earth, raises its summit on high, is magnificent, superb, and full of symmetry, neither astonishing through its magnitude, nor terrible through its strength, nor moved with difficulty through its weight, nor slippery through its smoothness, nor repercussive through its hardness, nor groveling through its coldness, nor precipitate through its heat, nor inclined to swim through its laxity, nor feeding on raw flesh through its ferocity, nor on grass through its imbecility; but is harmonically composed for its proper works, and is dreadful to timid animals, but mild to such as are brave. It is also adapted to walk by nature, but winged by reason, capable of swimming by art, feeds on corn and fruits, and cultivates the earth, is of a good colour, stands firm, has a pleasing countenance, and a graceful beard. In the resemblance of such a body, the Greeks think fit to honour the Gods."

He then observes, "that with respect to the Barbarians, all of them in like manner admit the subsistence of divinity, but different nations among these adopt different symbols." After which he adds, "O many and all-various statues! of which some are fashioned by art, and others

---

ειπειν δε αδυνατον, και νοησαι γε ουδεν μαλλον ραδιον. "He was not willing to adore statues, but approached to the Gods themselves, who are inwardly concealed not in adyta, but in the occult itself, whatever it may be of all-perfect ignorance. How therefore to them being such did he approach? Through vehement love, this also being occult. And what else indeed, could conduct him to them than a love which is also unknown? What my meaning is those who have experienced this love know; but it is impossible to reveal it by words, and it is no less difficult to understand what it is."

are embraced through indigence: some are honoured through utility, and others are venerated through the astonishment which they excite; some are considered as divine through their magnitude, and others are celebrated for their beauty! There is not indeed any race of men, neither Barbarian nor Grecian, neither maritime nor continental, neither living a pastoral life, nor dwelling in cities, which can endure to be without some symbols of the honour of the Gods. How, therefore, shall any one discuss the question whether it is proper that statues of the Gods should be fabricated or not. For if we were to give laws to other men recently sprung from the earth, and dwelling beyond our boundaries and our air, or who were fashioned by a certain Prometheus, ignorant of life, and law, and reason, it might perhaps demand consideration, whether this race should be permitted to adore these spontaneous statues alone, which are not fashioned from ivory or gold, and which are neither oaks nor cedars, nor rivers, nor birds, but the rising sun, the splendid moon, the variegated heaven, the earth itself and the air, all fire and all water; or shall we constrain these men also to the necessity of honouring wood, or stones or images? If, however, this is the common law of all men, let us make no innovations, let us admit the conceptions concerning the Gods, and preserve their symbols as well as their names.

"For divinity indeed, the father and fabricator of all things, is more ancient than the sun and the heavens, more excellent than time and eternity, and every flowing nature, and is a legislator without law, ineffable by voice, and invisible by the eyes. Not being able, however, to comprehend his essence, we apply for assistance to words and names, to animals, and figures of gold and ivory and silver, to plants and rivers, to the summits of mountains, and to streams of water; desiring indeed to understand his nature, but through imbecility calling him by the names of such things as appear to us to be beautiful. And in thus acting, we are affected in the same manner as lovers, who are delighted with surveying the images of the objects of their love, and with recollecting the lyre, the dart, and the seat of these, the circus in which they ran, and every thing in short, which excites the memory of the beloved object. What then remains for me to investigate and determine respecting statues? only to admit the subsistence of deity. But if the art of Phidias excites the Greeks to the recollection of divinity, honour to animals the Egyptians, a river others, and fire others, I do not condemn the dissonance: let them only know, let them only love, let them only be mindful of the object they adore."

With respect to the worship of animals, Plutarch apologizes for it in the following excellent manner in his treatise On Isis and Osiris.

"It now remains that we should speak of the utility of these animals to man, and of their symbolical meaning; some of them partaking of one of these only, but many of them of both. It is evident therefore that the Egyptians worshipped the ox, the sheep, and the ichneumon, on account of their use and benefit, as the Lemnians did larks, for discovering the eggs of caterpillars and breaking them; and the Thessalians storks, because, as their land produced abundance of serpents, the storks destroyed all of them as soon as they appeared. Hence also they enacted a law, that whoever killed a stork should be banished. But the Egyptians honoured the asp, the weezle, and the beetle, in consequence of observing in them certain dark resemblances of the power of the Gods, like that of the sun in drops of water. For at present, many believe and assert that the weezle engenders by the ear, and brings forth by the mouth, being thus an image of the generation of reason, [or the productive principle of things.] But the genus of beetles has no female; and all the males emit their sperm into a spherical piece of earth, which they roll about thrusting it backwards with their hind feet, while they themselves move forward; just as the sun appears to revolve in a direction contrary to that of the heavens, in consequence of moving from west to east. They also assimilated the asp to a star, as being exempt from old age, and performing its motions unassisted by organs with agility and ease. Nor was the crocodile honoured by them without a probable cause; but is said to have been considered by them as a resemblance of divinity, as being the only animal that is without a tongue. For the divine reason is unindigent of voice, and proceeding through a silent path, and accompanied with† justice, conducts mortal affairs according to it. They also say it is the only animal living in water that has the sight of its eyes covered with a thin and transparent film, which descends from his forehead, so that he sees without being seen, which is likewise the case with the first God. But in whatever place the female crocodile may lay her eggs, this may with certainty be concluded to be the boundary of the increase of the Nile. For not being able to lay their eggs in the water, and fearing to lay them far from it, they have such an accurate pre-sensation of futurity, that though they enjoy the benefit of the river in its access, during the time of their laying and hatching, yet they preserve their eggs dry and untouched by the water. They also lay sixty eggs, are the same number of days in hatching them, and those that are the longest lived among them, live just so many years; which number is the first of the measures employed by those who are conversant with the heavenly bodies.

"Moreover, of those animals that were honoured for both reasons, we have before spoken of the dog. But the ibis, killing indeed all deadly

---

† Instead of και δικης, I read και μετα δικης.

reptiles, was the first that taught men the use of medical evacuation, in consequence of observing that she is after this manner washed and purified by herself. Those priests also, that are most attentive to the laws of sacred rites, when they consecrate water for lustration, fetch it from that place where the ibis had been drinking; for she will neither drink nor come near unwholesome or infected water; but with the distance of her feet from each other, and her bill she makes an equilateral triangle. Farther still, the variety and mixture of her black wings about the white represents the moon when she is gibbous.

"We ought not, however, to wonder if the Egyptians love such slender similitudes, since the Greeks also, both in their pictures and statues, employ many such like resemblances of the Gods. Thus in Crete, there was a statue of Jupiter without ears. For it is fit that he who is the ruler and lord of all things, should hear no one.[†] Phidias also placed a dragon by the statue of Minerva, and a snail by that of Venus at Elis, to show that virgins require a guard, and that keeping at home and silence become married women. But the trident of Neptune is a symbol of the third region of the world, which the sea possesses, having an arrangement after the heavens and the air. Hence also, they thus denominated Amphitrite and the Tritons. The Pythagoreans likewise adorned numbers and figures with the appellations of the Gods. For they called the equilateral triangle Minerva Coryphagenes, or begotten from the summit, and Tritogeneia, because it is divided by three perpendiculars drawn from the three angles. But they called the *one* Apollo, being persuaded to this by the obvious meaning of the word Apollo [which signifies a privation of multitude] and by the simplicity of the monad.[‡] The duad they denominated strife and audacity; and the triad justice. For since injuring and being injured are two extremes subsisting according to excess and defect, justice through equality has a situation in the middle. But what is called the tetractys, being the number 36, was, as is reported, their greatest oath, and was denominated the world. For this number is formed from the composition of the four first even, and the four first odd numbers, collected into one sum.[§] If therefore the most approved of the philosophers did not think it proper to neglect or despise any occult signification of a divine nature

---

[†] *i.e.* Should be perfectly impartial.

[‡] Instead of διπλοτατοις μοναδος as in the original, which is nonsense, it is necessary to read, as in the above translation απλοτητι της μοναδος.

[§] For $2+4+6+8=20$; and $1+3+5+7=16$; and $20+16=36$.

when they perceived it even in things which are inanimate and incorporeal, it appears to me, that they in a still greater degree venerated those peculiarities depending on manners which they saw in such natures as had sense, and were endued with soul, with passion, and ethical habits. We must embrace therefore, not those who honour these kings, but those who reverence divinity through these, as through most clear mirrors, and which are produced by nature, in a becoming manner, conceiving them to be the instruments or the art of the God by whom all things are perpetually adorned. But we ought to think that no inanimate being can be more excellent than one that is animated, nor an insensible than a sensitive being, not even though some one should collect together all the gold and emeralds in the universe. For the divinity is not ingenerated either in colours, or figures, or smoothness; but such things as neither ever did, nor are naturally adapted to participate of life, have an allotment more ignoble than that of dead bodies. But the nature which lives and sees, and has the principle of motion from itself, and a knowledge of things appropriate and foreign to its being, has certainly derived an efflux and portion of that wisdom, which, as Heraclitus says, considers how both itself, and the universe is governed. Hence the divinity is not worse represented in these animals, than in the workmanships of copper and stone, which in a similar manner suffer corruption and decay, but are naturally deprived of all sense and consciousness. This then I consider as the best defence that can be given of the adoration of animals by the Egyptians.

With respect however to the sacred vestments, those of Isis are of various hues; for her power is about matter, which becomes and receives all things, as light and darkness, day and night, fire and water, life and death, beginning and end; but those of Osiris are without a shade and have no variety of colours, but have one only which is simple and luciform. Hence when the latter have been once used, they are laid aside and preserved; for the intelligible is invisible and intangible. But the vestments of Isis are used frequently. For sensible things being in daily use and at hand, present us with many developments and views of their different mutations: but the intellectual perception of that which is intelligible, genuine, and holy, luminously darting through the soul like a coruscation, is attended with a simultaneous contact and vision of its object. Hence Plato and Aristotle call this part of philosophy epoptic or intuitive, indicating that those who have through the exercise of the reasoning power soared beyond these doxastic, mingled and all-various natures, raise themselves to that first, simple, and immaterial principle, and passing into contact with the pure truth which subsists about it, they consider themselves as having at length obtained the end of philosophy.† And that which the present devoted and veiled priests obscurely manifest with great reverence and caution is that this God is the ruler and prince of the dead, and is not different from that divinity who is called by the Greeks Hades and Pluto, the truth of which assertion not being understood, disturbs the multitude, who suspect that the truly sacred and holy Osiris dwells in and under the earth, where the bodies of those are concealed who appear to have obtained an end of their being. But he indeed himself is at the remotest distance from the earth, unstained, unpolluted, and pure from every essence that receives corruption and death. The souls of men however, being here encompassed with bodies and passions, cannot participate of divinity except as of an obscure dream by intellectual contact through philosophy. But when they are liberated from the body, and pass into the invisible, impassive, and pure region, this God is then their leader and king, from whom they depend, insatiably beholding him, and desiring to survey that beauty which cannot be expressed or uttered by men; and which Isis, as the ancient discourse evinces, always loving, pursuing, and enjoying fills such things in these lower regions as participate of generation with every thing beautiful and good."

And lastly, the Emperor Julian, in a fragment of an Oration or Epistle on the duties of a priest, has the following remarks on religiously venerating statues: "Statues and altars, and the preservation of unextinguished fire, and in short, all such particulars, have been established by our fathers as symbols of the presence of the gods; *not that we should believe that these symbols are Gods, but that through these we should worship the Gods.* For since we are connected with body, it is also necessary that our worship of the Gods should be performed in a corporeal manner; but they are incorporeal. And they indeed have exhibited to us as the first of statues, that which ranks as the second genus of Gods from the first, and which circularly revolves round the whole of heaven.‡ Since, however, a corporeal worship cannot even be paid to these, because they are naturally unindigent, a third kind of statues was devised on the earth, by the worship of which we render the Gods propitious to us. For as those who reverence the images of kings,

---

† For τελοσ εχειν φιλοσοφιαν, it is necessary to read as in the translation, τελος εχειν φιλοσοφιας.

‡ Meaning those divine bodies the celestial orbs, which in consequence of participating a divine life from the incorporeal powers from which they are suspended, may be very properly called *secondary Gods*.

who are not in want of any such reverence, at the same time attract to themselves their benevolence; thus also those who venerate the statues of the Gods, who are not in want of any thing, persuade the Gods by this veneration to assist and be favourable to them. For alacrity in the performance of things in our power is a document of true sanctity; and it is very evident that he who accomplishes the former, will in a greater degree possess the latter. But he who despises things in his power, and afterwards pretends to desire impossibilities, evidently does not pursue the latter, and overlooks the former. For though divinity is not in want of any thing, it does not follow that on this account nothing is to be offered to him. For neither is he in want of celebration through the ministry of *words*. What then? Is it therefore reasonable that he should be deprived of this? By no means. Neither therefore is he to be deprived of the honour which is paid him through *works;* which honour has been legally established, not for three, or for three thousand years, but in all preceding ages, among all nations of the earth.

"But [the Galilæans will say,] O! you who have admitted into your soul every multitude of dæmons, whom, though according to you they are formless and unfigured, you have fashioned in a corporeal resemblance, it is not fit that honour should be paid to divinity through such works. *How, then, do not we [heathens] consider as wood and stones those statues which are fashioned by the hands of men? O more stupid than even stones themselves! Do you fancy that all men are to be drawn by the nose as you are drawn by execrable dæmons, so as to think that the artificial resemblances of the Gods are the Gods themselves?* Looking therefore to the resemblances of the Gods, we do not think them to be either stones or wood; for neither do we think that the Gods are these resemblances; since neither do we say that royal images are wood, or stone, or brass, nor that they are the kings themselves, but the images of kings. Whoever, therefore, loves his king, beholds with pleasure the image of his king; whoever loves his child is delighted with his image and whoever loves his father surveys his image with delight.[†] Hence also, he who is a lover of divinity gladly surveys the statues and images of the

---

[†] Dr. Stillingfleet quotes this part of the extract, in his answer to a book entitled *Catholics no Idolaters*, and calls Julian the devout emperor.

Gods; at the same time venerating and fearing with a holy dread the Gods who invisibly behold him.†

---

† "Dio Chrysostome (says Dr Stillingfleet in the before-cited work, p. 414) at large debates the case about images, in his Olympic Oration; wherein he first shows, that all men have a natural apprehension of one supreme God the father of all things; and that this God was represented by the statue made by Phidias of Jupiter Olympius, for so he said παρ' ᾧ νῦν ἐσμεν, *before whom we now are*; and then describes him to be the king, ruler, and father of all, both Gods and men. This image he calls the most blessed, the most excellent, the most beautiful, the most beloved image of God. He says there are four ways of coming to the knowledge of God, by nature, by the instructions of the poets, by the laws, and by images; but neither poets, nor lawgivers, nor artificers were the best interpreters of the deity, but only the philosophers who both understood and explained the divine nature most truly and perfectly. After this, he supposes Phidias to be called to account for making such an image of God, as unworthy of him; when Iphitus, Lycurgus, and the old Eleans, made none at all of him, as being out of the power of man to express his nature. To this Phidias replies, that no man can express mind and understanding by figures, or colours, and therefore they are forced to fly to that in which the soul inhabits, and from thence they attribute the seat of wisdom and reason to God, having nothing better to represent him by. And by that means joining power and art together, they endeavour by something which may be seen and painted, to represent that which is invisible and inexpressible. But it may be said, we had better then have no image or representation of him at all. No, says he; for mankind doth not love to worship God at a distance, but to come near and feel him, and with assurance to sacrifice to him and crown him. Like children newly weaned from their parents, who put out their hands towards them in their dreams as if they were still present; so do men out of the sense of God's goodness and their relation to him, love to have him represented as present with them, and so to converse with him. Thence have come all the representations of God among the barbarous nations, in mountains, and trees, and stones."

The same conceptions also about statues are entertained by the Brachmans in Benares on the Ganges. For Monsieur Bernier when he was at their university, and was discoursing with one of the most learned men among them, proposed to him the question about the adoration of their idols, and reproaching him with it as a thing very unreasonable, received from him this remarkable answer: "We have indeed in our temples many different statues, as those of Brahma, Mahaden, Genick, and Gavani, who are some of the chief and most perfect Deutas (or Deities); and we have also many others of less perfection, to whom we pay great honour, prostrating ourselves before them, and presenting them flowers, rice, oyles, saffron, and the like, with much ceremony. But we do not believe these statues to be Brahma or Bechen, etc. themselves, but only their images and representations, and we only give them that honour on account of the beings they represent. They are in our temples, because it is necessary in order to pray well, to have something before our eyes that may fix the mind. And when we pray, it is not the statue we pray to, but he that is represented by it." The Brahmans have also another way of defending their worship of statues, of which the same author gives the following account: "That God, or that sovereign being whom they call Achar (immutable) has produced or drawn out of his own substance, not only souls,

The Catholics have employed arguments similar to these, in defence of the reverence which they pay to the images of their saints. Indeed, it is the doctrine of the Church of England,[†] that the Catholics form the same opinions of the saints whose images they worship as the Heathens did of their Gods; and employ the same outward rites in honouring their images, as the Heathens did in the religious veneration of their statues. Thus as the Heathens had their *tutelar Gods,* such as were Belus to the Babylonians and Assyrians, Osiris and Isis to the Egyptians, and Vulcan to the Lemnians, thus also the Catholics attribute the defence of certain countries to certain saints. Have not the saints also to whom the safeguard of particular cities is committed, the same office as the *Dii Præsides* of the Heathens? Such as were at Delphi, Apollo; at Athens, Minerva; at Carthage, Juno; and at Rome, Quirinus. And do not the saints to whom churches are built and altars erected correspond to the Dii Patroni of the Heathens? Such as were in the Capitol, Jupiter, in the temple at Paphos, Venus, in the temple of Ephesus, Diana. Are not likewise, our Lady of Walsingham, our Lady of Ipswich, our Lady of Wilsdon, and the like, imitations of Diana Agrotera, Diana Coriphea, Diana Ephesia, Venus Cypria, Venus Paphia, Venus Gnidia, and the like? The Catholics too, have substituted for the marine deities Neptune, Triton, Nereus, Castor and Pollux, Venus, etc. Saint Christopher, Saint Clement, and others, and especially our Lady, as she is called by them, to whom seamen sing *Ave Maris Stella.* Neither has the fire escaped their imitation of the Pagans. For instead of Vulcan and Vesta, the inspective guardians of fire according to the Heathens, the Catholics have substituted Saint Agatha, on the day of whose nativity they make letters for the purpose of extinguishing fire. Every artificer likewise and profession has a special saint in the place of a presiding God. Thus scholars have Saint Nicholas and Saint Gregory; painters Saint Luke; nor are soldiers in want of a saint corresponding to Mars, nor lovers of one who is a substitute for Venus.

All diseases too have their special saints instead of Gods, who are invoked as possessing a healing power. Thus the venereal disease has

---

but also whatever is material and corporeal in the universe, so that all things in the world are but one and the same thing with God himself, as all numbers are but one and the same unity repeated." Bernier Memoires, tome 3, p. 171. 178.

From this latter extract it appears that the Brachmans as well as the ancient Egyptians, believe that the supreme principle is all things. According to the best of the Platonists likewise, this principle is *all things prior to all.* For by being *The One,* it is *all things* after the most *simple* manner, *i.e.* so as to transcend all multitude.

[†] See its *Homilies,* tome 2, p. 46.

Saint Roche; the falling sickness Saint Cornelius, the toothach Saint Apollin, etc. Beasts and cattle also have their presiding saints: for Saint Loy (says the Homily) is the horse-leach, and Saint Antony the swineherd, etc. The Homily adds,[†] "that in many points the Papists exceed the Gentiles in idolatry, and particularly in honouring and worshipping the relics and bones of saints, which prove that they be mortal men and dead, and therefore no Gods to be worshipped, which the Gentiles would never confess of their Gods for very shame." And after enumerating many ridiculous practices of the Catholics in reference to these relics, the Homily concludes with observing, "that they are not only more wicked than the Gentile idolaters, but also no wiser than asses, horses, and mules, which have no understanding."

In the second place the Homilies show[‡] that the rites and ceremonies of the Papists in honouring and worshipping their images or saints, are the same with the rites of the Pagans. "This, say they, is evident in their pilgrimages to visit images which had more holiness and virtue in them than others. In their candle-religion, burning incense, offering up gold to images, hanging up crutches, chairs, and ships, legs, arms and whole men and women of war, before images, as though by them, or saints (as they say) they were delivered from lameness, sickness, captivity, or shipwreck." In spreading abroad after the manner of the Heathens, the miracles that have accompanied images. "Such an image was sent from heaven, like the Palladium, or Diana of the Ephesians. Such an image was brought by angels. Such a one came itself far from the east to the west, as Dame Fortune fled to Rome. Some images though they were hard and stony, yet for tender-heart and pity wept. Some spake more monstrously than ever did Balaam's ass, who had life and breath in him. Such a cripple came and saluted this saint of oak, and by and by he was made whole, and here hangeth his crutch. Such a one in a tempest vowed to Saint Christopher, and scaped, and behold here is his ship of war. Such a one, by Saint Leonard's help, brake out of prison, and see where his fetters hang. And infinite thousands more miracles by like, or more shameless lies were reported."

After all this, I appeal to every intelligent reader, whether the religion of the Heathens, according to its genuine purity as delineated in this Introduction, and as professed and promulgated by the best and wisest men of antiquity, is not infinitely preferable to that of the Catholics? And whether it is not more holy to reverence beings the immediate

---

[†] Tome 2, p. 54.

[‡] p. 49

progeny of the ineffable principle of all things, and which are eternally centred and rooted in him; and to believe that in reverencing these, we at the same time reverence *the ineffable,* because they partake of his nature, and that through these as media we become united with him,† than to reverence men, and the images of men, many of whom when living, were the disgrace of human nature? The Church of England as we see prefers the Pagans to the Papists; and I trust that every other sect of Protestant Christians will unanimously subscribe to her decision. And thus much in defence of the theology of Plato, and the religious worship of the Heathens.

It now remains that I should speak of the following work, of its author, and the translation. The work itself then is a scientific development of the deiform processions from the ineffable principle of things, and this, as it appears to me in the greatest perfection possible to man. For the reasoning is every where consummately accurate, and deduced from self-evident principles; and the conclusions are the result of what Plato powerfully calls geometrical necessities. To the reader of this work indeed, who has not been properly disciplined in Eleatic and Academic studies, and who has not a genius naturally adapted to such abstruse speculations, it will doubtless appear to be perfectly unintelligible, and in the language of critical cant, nothing but jargon and revery. This, however, is what Plato the great hierophant of this theology predicted would be the case, if ever it was unfolded to the multitude at large. *"For as it appears to me, says he, there are scarcely any particulars which will be considered by the multitude more ridiculous than these; nor again, any which will appear more wonderful and enthusiastic to those who are naturally adapted to perceive them."*‡

In his seventh epistle also he observes as follows: "Thus much, however, I shall say respecting all those who either have written or shall write, affirming that they know those things which are the objects of my study (whether they have heard them from me or from others, or whether they have discovered them themselves) that they have not heard

---

† The ineffable principle of things, as is demonstrated in the *Elements of Theology* [TTS vol I], is beyond self-subsistence. Hence the first ineffable evolution from him consists of self-subsistent natures. As we therefore are only the dregs of the rational nature, many media are necessary to conjoin us with a principle so immensely exalted above us. And these media are the golden chain of powers that have deified summits, or that have the ineffable united with the effable.

‡ Σχεδον γαρ ως εμοι δοχει, ουκ εστι τουτων προς τους πολλους καταγελαστοτερα ακουσματα, ου δ' αυ προς τους ευφυεις θανμαστοτερα τε και ενθουσιαστικωτερα. Epist. 2.

any thing about these things conformable to my opinion: for I never have written nor ever shall write about them.† For a thing of this kind cannot be expressed by words like other disciplines, but by long familiarity, and living in conjunction with the thing itself, a light‡ as it were leaping from a fire will on a sudden be enkindled in the soul, and there itself nourish itself." And shortly after he adds; "But if it appeared to me that the particulars of which I am speaking could be sufficiently communicated to the *multitude* by writing or speech, what could we accomplish more beautiful in life than to impart a mighty benefit to mankind, and lead an intelligible nature into light, so as to be obvious to all men? I think, however, that an attempt of this kind would only be beneficial to a few, who from some small vestiges previously demonstrated are themselves able to discover these abstruse particulars. But with respect to the rest of mankind, some it will fill with a contempt by no means elegant, and others with a lofty and arrogant hope that they shall now learn certain venerable things.§

The prediction of Plato therefore, has been but too truly fulfilled in the fate which has attended the writings of the best of his disciples, among whom Proclus certainly maintains the most distinguished rank. This indeed, these disciples well knew would be the case; but perceiving that the hand of Barbaric and despotic power was about to destroy the schools of the philosophers, and foreseeing that dreadful night of ignorance and folly which succeeded so nefarious an undertaking, they

---

† Plato means by this, that he has never written perspicuously about *intelligibles* or *true beings*, the proper objects of intellect.

‡ This light is a thing of a very different kind from that which is produced by the evidence arising from truths perceptible by the multitude, as those who have experienced it well know.

§ Τασονδε γε μην περι ταντων εχω φραζειν των γεγραφοτων και γραψαντων, οσοι φασιν ειδεναι περι ων εγω σπουδαζω, ειτ' εμον ακηκοοτες, ειτ' αλλων, ειθ' ως ευροντες αυτοι, τουτους ουκ εστι κατα γε την εμην δοξαν περι του πραγματος επαϊειν ουδεν, ουκ ουν εμον γε περι αυτων εστι συγγραμμα, ουδε μη ποτε γενηται· ρητον γαρ ουδαμως εστιν, ως αλλα μαθηματα, αλλ' εκ πολλης συνουσιας γιγνομενης περι το πραγμα αυτο, και του συζην, εξαιφνης οιον απο πυρος πηδησαντος (lege πηδησαν) εξαφθεν φως, εν τη ψυχη γενομενον αυτο εαυτο ηδη τρεφει. - Ει δε μοι εφαινετο γραπτεα θ' ικανως ειναι προς τους πολλους και ρητα, τι τουτου καλλιον επεπρακτ' αν ημιν εν τω βιω, η τοις τι ανθρωποισι μεγα οφελος γραψαι, και την φυσιν εις φως τοις πασι προσαγαγειν; αλλ' ουτε ανθρωποις ηγουμαι την επιχειρησιν περι αυτων λεγομενην αγαθον, ει μη τισιν ολιγοις, οποσοι δυνατοι ανευρειν αυτοι δια μικρας ενδειξεως· των τε δη αλλων, τοις μεν καταφρονησεως ουκ ορθως εμπλησειεν αν ουδαμη εμμελους, τους δε υψηλης και χαυνης ελπιδος, ως σεμν' αττα μεμαθηκοτας.

benevolently disclosed in as luminous a manner as the subject would permit, the arcana of their master's doctrines, thereby, as Plato expresses it, giving assistance to Philosophy, and also preserving it as a paternal and immortal inheritance, to the latest posterity. Proclus in the first book of this work has enumerated the requisites which a student of it ought to possess; and it is most certain that he who does not possess them, will never fathom the depths of this theology, or perceive his mind irradiated with that admirable light, mentioned by Plato in the foregoing extract, and which is only to be seen by that eye of the soul which is better worth saving than ten thousand corporeal eyes.

With respect to the diction of Proclus in this work, its general character is that of purity, clearness, copiousness, and magnificence; so that even the fastidious critic, who considers every Greek writer as partially barbarous who lived after the fall of the Macedonian empire, must, however unwillingly, be forced to acknowledge that Proclus is a splendid exception. The sagacious Kepler, whose decision on this subject, outweighs in my opinion, that of a *swarm* of modern critics, after having made a long extract from the commentaries of Proclus on Euclid, gives the following animated encomium of his diction. "Oratio fluit ipsi torrentis instar, ripas inundans, et cœca dubitationum vada gurgitesque occultans, dum mens plena majestatis tantarum rerum, luctatur in angustiis linguæ, et conclusio nunquam sibi ipsi verborum copia satisfaciens, propositionum simplicitatem excedit." *i.e.* "His language flows like a torrent, inundating its banks, and hiding the dark fords and whirlpools of doubts, while his mind full of the majesty of things of such a magnitude, struggles in the straits of language, and the conclusion never satisfying him, exceeds by the copia of words, the simplicity of the propositions." If we omit what Kepler here says about the struggle of the mind of Proclus, and his never being satisfied with the conclusion, the rest of his eulogy is equally applicable to the style of the present work, so far as it is possible for the beauties of diction to be combined with the rigid accuracy of geometrical reasoning.

With respect to the life of Proclus, it has been written with great elegance by his disciple Marinus; and a translation of it by me prefixed to my version of the commentaries of Proclus was published in 1788. From the edition of that life therefore, by Fabricius, the following particulars relative to this very extraordinary man are extracted, for the information of the reader who may not have the translation of it in his possession. According to the accurate chronology then of Fabricius, Proclus was born at Byzantium in the year of Christ 412, on the 6th of the Ides of February, and died in the one hundred and twenty-fourth year after the reign of the emperor Julian, on the seventeenth day of the

Attic Munichion, or the April of the Romans, Nicoragoras the junior, being at that time the Athenian archon. His father Patricius, and his mother Marcella, were both of them of the Lycian nation, and were no less illustrious for their virtue than their birth. As soon as he was born, his parents brought him to their native country Xanthus, which was sacred to Apollo. And this, says Marinus, happened to him by a certain divine allotment. "For, he adds, I think it was necessary that he who was to be the leader of all sciences, should be nourished and educated under the presiding deity of the Muses." The person of Proclus was uncommonly beautiful; and he not only possessed all the moral and intellectual virtues in the highest perfection, but the vestigies of them also, which are denominated the physical virtues, were clearly seen, says Marinus, in his last and shelly vestment the body. Hence he possessed a remarkable acuteness of sensation, and particularly in the most honourable of the senses, sight and hearing, which, as Plato says, were imparted by the Gods to men for the purpose of philosophizing, and for the well being of the animal life. In the second place, he possessed so great a strength of body, that it was neither injured by cold, nor any endurance of labours, though these were extreme, both by night and day. In the third place, he was, as we have before observed, very beautiful. "For not only," says Marinus, "did his body possess great symmetry, but a living light as it were beaming from his soul was efflorescent in his body, and shone forth with an admirable splendour, which it is impossible to describe." Marinus adds, "Indeed he was so beautiful, that no painter could accurately exhibit his resemblance; and all the pictures of him which were circulated, though very beautiful, were very inferior to the beauty of the original." And in the fourth place, he possessed health in such perfection, that he was not ill above twice or thrice in the course of so long a life as seventy-five years.

Such then were the corporeal prerogatives which Proclus possessed, and which may be called the forerunners of the forms of perfect virtue. But he possessed in a wonderful manner what Plato calls the elements of a philosophic genius.[†] For he had an excellent memory, learned with facility, was magnificent and graceful, and the friend and ally of truth, justice, fortitude, and temperance. Having for a short space of time applied himself in Lycia to grammar, he went to Alexandria in Egypt, and was there instructed in rhetoric by Leonas who derived his lineage from Isaurus, and in grammar by Orion, whose ancestors discharged the sacerdotal office among the Egyptians, and who composed elaborate treatises on that art. A certain good fortune however, says Marinus,

---

† See the sixth book of the *Republic* of Plato.

brought him back to the place of his nativity. For on his return his tutelar Goddess exhorted him to philosophy, and to visit the Athenian schools. Having therefore, first returned to Alexandria and bade farewell to rhetoric, and the other arts which he had formerly studied, he gave himself up to the discourses of the philosophers then resident at Alexandria. Here, he became an auditor of Olympiodorus,† the most illustrious of philosophers, for the sake of imbibing the doctrine of Aristotle; and was instructed in the mathematical disciplines by Hero, a religious man, and eminently skilful in teaching those sciences. Proclus however, not being satisfied with the Alexandrian schools, went to Athens, "with a certain splendid procession," says Marinus, "of all eloquence and elegance, and attended by the Gods that preside over philosophy, and by beneficent dæmons. For that the succession of philosophy, might be preserved legitimate and genuine, the Gods led him to the city over which its inspective guardian presides." Hence Proclus was called κατ' εξοχην *by way of eminence,* the *Platonic Successor.* At Athens therefore, Proclus fortunately met with the first of philosophers, Syrianus,‡ the son of Philoxenus, who not only much assisted him in his studies, but made him his domestic as to other concerns, and the companion of his philosophic life, having found him such an auditor and successor as he had a long time sought for, and one who was capable of receiving a multitude of disciplines and divine dogmas.

In less than two whole years therefore, Proclus read with Syrianus all the works of Aristotle, *viz.* his logic, ethics, politics, physics, and theological science. And being sufficiently instructed in these as in certain *proteleia,* or things preparatory to initiation, and lesser mysteries, Syrianus led him to the mystic discipline of Plato, in an orderly progression, and not according to the Chaldean oracle with a transcendent foot. He likewise enabled Proclus to survey in conjunction with him, says Marinus, truly divine mysteries, with the eyes of his soul free from material darkness, and with undefiled intellectual vision. But Proclus employing sleepless exercise and attention, both by night and by

---

† This Olympiodorus is not the same with the philosopher of that name whose learned commentaries on certain dialogues of Plato are extant in manuscript; as in these, not only Proclus, but Damascius who flourished after Proclus is celebrated.

‡ This truly great man appears to have been the first who thoroughly penetrated the profundity contained in the writings of the more ancient philosophers, contemporary with and prior to Plato, and to have demonstrated the admirable agreement of their doctrines with each other. Unfortunately but few of his works are extant.

day, and synoptically and judiciously committing to writing what he heard from Syrianus, made so great a progress in a little time, that by then he was twenty-eight years of age, he had composed a multitude of works and among the rest his commentaries on the *Timæus* which are truly elegant and full of science. But from such a discipline as this, his manners became more adorned; and as he advanced in science he increased in virtue.

Marinus after this, shows how Proclus possessed all the virtues in the greatest possible perfection; and how he proceeded from the exercise of the political virtues, which are produced by reason adorning the irrational part as its instrument, to the cathartic virtues which pertain to reason alone, withdrawing from other things to itself, throwing aside the instruments of sense as vain, repressing also the energies through these instruments, and liberating the soul from the bonds of generation. He then adds, "Proclus having made a proficiency, through these virtues, as it were by certain mystic steps, recurred from these to such as are greater and more telestic, being conducted to them by a prosperous nature and scientific discipline. For being now purified, rising above generation, and despising its thyrsus-bearers,† he was agitated with a divinely inspired fury, about the first essences, and became an inspector of the truly blessed spectacles which they contain. No longer collecting discursively and demonstratively the science of them, but surveying them as it were by simple intuition, and beholding through intellectual energies the paradigms in a divine intellect, assuming a virtue which can no longer be denominated prudence, but which ought rather to be called wisdom, or something still more venerable than this. The philosopher therefore energizing according to this virtue, easily comprehended all the theology of the Greeks and Barbarians, and that which is adumbrated in mythological fictions, and brought it into light, to those who are willing and able to understand it. He explained likewise every thing in a more enthusiastic manner, and brought the different theologies to an harmonious agreement. At the same time also, investigating the writings of the ancients, whatever he found in them genuine, he judiciously

---

† Socrates in the *Phædo* of Plato, Orphically calls the multitude thyrsus-bearers as living Titanically. For the thyrsus, says Olympiodorus, (in MS. comment in Phæd.) is a symbol of material and partible fabrication, on account of its divulsed continuity, whence also it is a Titanic plant. "For it is extended, says he, before Bacchus, instead of his paternal sceptre, and through this they call him into a partial nature." He adds, "Besides the Titans are thyrsus-bearers; and Prometheus concealed fire in a reed, whether by this we are to understand that he draws down celestial light into generation, or impels soul into body, or calls forth divine illumination, the whole of which is ungenerated, into generation."

adopted; but if he found any thing of a spurious nature, this, he entirely rejected as erroneous. He also strenuously subverted by a diligent examination such doctrines as were contrary to truth. In his associations too with others, he employed no less force and perspicuity. For he was a man laborious beyond measure; as, in one day, he gave five, and sometimes more lectures, and wrote as many as seven hundred verses. Besides this, he went to other philosophers, and spent the evening in conversation with them. And all these employments he executed in such a manner as not to neglect his nocturnal and vigilant piety to the Gods, and assiduously supplicating the sun when rising, when at his meridian altitude, and when he sets."

Marinus farther observes of this most extraordinary man, "that he did not seem to be without divine inspiration. For words similar to the most white and thick-falling snow[†] proceeded from his wise mouth, his eyes appeared to be filled with a fulgid splendour, and the rest of his face to participate of divine illumination. Hence Rufinus, a man illustrious in the *Republic*, and who was also a man of veracity, and in other respects venerable, happening to be present with him when he was lecturing, perceived that his head was surrounded with a light. And when Proclus had finished his lecture, Rufinus rising, adored him, and testified by an oath the truth of the divine vision which he had seen."

Marinus also informs us, "that Proclus being purified in an orderly manner by the Chaldean purifications, was an inspector of the lucid Hecatic visions, as he himself somewhere mentions in one of his writings. By opportunely moving likewise a certain Hecatic sphærula,[‡] he procured showers of rain, and freed Athens from an unseasonable heat. Besides this, by certain phylacteria or charms, he stopt an

---

[†] Alluding to the beautiful description given of Ulysses in the third book of the Iliad, v 22 which is thus elegantly paraphrased by Pope.
> But when he speaks what elocution flows!
> Soft as the fleeces of descending snows
> The copious accents fall with easy art;
> Melting they fall and sink into the heart.

[‡] Nicephorus in his commentary on Synesius de Insomniis, p. 362, informs us that the Hecatic orb is a golden sphere, which has a sapphire stone inclosed in its middle part, and through its whole extremity characters, and various figures. He adds, that turning this sphere round, the Chaldeans perform invocations which they call Iyngæ. Thus too, according to Suidas, the magician Julian of Chaldæa, and Arnuphis the Egyptian brought down showers of rain, by a magical power. And by an artifice of this kind, Empedocles was accustomed to restrain the fury of the winds; on which account he was called αλεξανεμος, *an expeller of wind.*

earthquake, and had made trial of the divining energy of the tripod, having been instructed by certain verses respecting its failure. For when he was in his fortieth year, he appeared in a dream to utter the following verses:

> High above æther there with radiance bright,
> A pure immortal splendour wings its flight;[†]
> Whose beams divine with vivid force aspire,
> And leap resounding from a fount of fire.

And in the beginning of his forty-second year he appeared to himself to pronounce with a loud voice these verses:

> Lo! on my soul a sacred fire descends,
> Whose vivid power the intellect extends;
> From whence far beaming thro' dull body's night,
> It soars to æther deck'd with starry light;
> And with soft murmurs thro' the azure round,
> The lucid regions of the Gods resound.

Besides, he clearly perceived that he belonged to the Mercurial series; and was persuaded from a dream, that he possessed the soul of Nichomachus the Pythagorean."[‡]

[†] This signifies that the divine splendour which is the cause of the prophetic energy, would leave the earth, in consequence of the then existing inaptitude of persons, places, and instruments, to receive it.

[‡] No opinion is more celebrated, than that of the metempsychoses of Pythagoras; but perhaps no doctrine is more generally mistaken. By most of the present day it is exploded as ridiculous; and the few who retain some veneration for its founder, endeavour to destroy the literal, and to confine it to an allegorical meaning. By some of the ancients this mutation was limited to similar bodies; so that they conceived the human soul might transmigrate into various human bodies, but not into those of brutes. And this was the opinion of Hierocles, as may be seen in his Commentary on the Golden Verses. But why may not the human soul become connected with subordinate, as well as with superior lives, by a tendency of inclination? Do not similars love to be united; and is there not in all kinds of life something similar and common? Hence when the affections of the soul verge to a baser nature, while connected with a human body, these affections, on the dissolution of such a body, become enveloped as it were, in a brutal nature, and the rational eye, in this case, clouded by perturbations, is oppressed by the irrational energies of the brute, and surveys nothing but the dark phantasms of a degraded imagination. But this doctrine is vindicated by Proclus with his usual acuteness, in his admirable Commentaries on the *Timæus*, lib. V, 329D, as follows: "It is usual, says he, to enquire how human souls can descend into brute animals. And some indeed, think that there are certain similitudes of men to brutes, which they call savage lives: for they by no means think it possible that the rational essence can become

In the last place, Marinus adds, "that the lovers of more elegant studies may be able to conjecture from the position of the stars under which he was born, that the condition of his life, was by no means among the last or middle, but among the first orders, we have thought fit to expose in this place the following scheme of his nativity."

Ascendant	8° 19′ ♈	Midheaven	4° 42′ ♑
	☉ 16° 26′ ♒		☽ 17° 29′ ♊
	☿ 4° 42′ ♒		♀ 0° 23′ ♓
	♂ 29° 50′ ♐		♃ 24° 41′ ♉
	♄ 24° 23′ ♉		☊ 24° 33′ ♏
The new moon preceeding his birth			8° 51′ ♒

And thus much for the life of Proclus.

With respect to the translation of the following work, *On the Theology of Plato*, I can only say that I have endeavoured to render it as faithful as possible, and to preserve the manner as well as the matter of the author; this being indispensably necessary, both from the importance of the subject, and the scientific accuracy of the reasoning with which it is discussed. I have added a seventh book in order to render the work complete; for without the development of the mundane Gods, and the more excellent genera their perpetual attendants, it would obviously be incomplete. From the catalogue of the manuscripts in the late French

the soul of a savage animal. On the contrary, others allow it may be sent into brutes, because all souls are of one and the same kind; so that they may become wolves and panthers, and ichneumons. But true reason indeed, asserts that the human soul may be lodged in brutes, yet in such a manner, as that it may obtain its own proper life, and that the degraded soul may, as it were, be carried above it, and be bound to the baser nature by a propensity and similitude of affection. And that this is the only mode of insinuation, we have proved by a multitude of arguments, in our Commentaries on the *Phædrus*. If however, it be requisite to take notice, that this is the opinion of Plato, we add that in his *Republic* he says, that the soul of Thersites assumed an ape, but not the body of an ape: and in the *Phædrus*, that the soul descends into a savage life, but not into a savage body. For life is conjoined with its proper soul. And in this place he says it is changed into a brutal nature. For a brutal nature is not a brutal body, but a brutal life."

King's library, it is evident that Proclus had written a seventh book[†] as some chapters of it are there said to be extant in that library. These I have endeavoured, but without success, to obtain. The want of this seventh book by Proclus, will doubtless be considered by all the friends of Greek literature, and particularly by all who are lovers of the doctrines of Plato, as a loss of no common magnitude. It is, however, a fortunate circumstance, that in the composition of the seventh book I have been able to supply the deficiency arising from the want of that which was written by Proclus, in a great measure from other works of Proclus himself, and particularly from his very elegant and scientific commentaries on the *Timæus* of Plato. So that I trust the loss is in some measure supplied; though I am sensible, very inadequately, could it be compared with the book which was written by a man of such gigantic powers of mind as Proclus, and who had also sources of information on the subject, which at the present period, it is impossible to obtain.

The Greek text of Proclus abounds with errors, so that the emendations which I have made, and the deficiencies which I have supplied in this volume, amount to more than four hundred. And the Latin translation of Portus is so very faulty, as to be almost beyond example bad. Having discovered this to be the case, and having in so many places corrected the original, I scarcely think that any of my critical enemies will be hardy enough to say, that any part of this volume was translated from the Latin, where the Greek could be obtained. As I am conscious however, that in what is now offered to the public, I had no other view than to benefit those who are capable of being benefited by such sublime speculations; that wishing well to all mankind, and particularly to my country, I have laboured to disseminate the philosophy and theology of Plato, as highly favourable to the interests of piety and good government, and most hostile to lawless conduct and revolutionary principles; and that I have done my best to deserve the esteem of the wise and worthy part of mankind, I am wholly unconcerned as to the reception it may meet with from the malevolent, though I wish for the approbation of the candid critics of the day. For in all my labours I have invariably observed the following Pygthagoric precept: "Do those things which you judge to be beautiful, though in doing them you should be without renown; for the rabble is a bad judge of a good thing."[‡]

[†] Proclus at the end of the first book of this work says, "that divine names will be accurately discussed by him, when he comes to speak of partial powers." This, however, is not done by him in any one of the six books that are extant; which shows that another book is wanting.

[‡] Ποιει α κρινεις ειναι καλα, κqν ποιων μελλης αδοξησειν· φαυλος γαρ κριτης καλου πραγματος οχλος. Demophilus.

An explanation of certain terms which are unusual, or have a meaning different from their common acceptation, and which there was a necessity of introducing in the translation of this work.

COMPOSITE, συνθετος. I have used the word composite instead of *compounded*, because the latter rather denotes the mingling than the contiguous union of one thing with another, which the former, through its derivation from the Latin word *compositus*, solely denotes.

DEMIURGUS OF WHOLES, δημιουργος των ολων. The artificer of the universe is thus denominated, because he produces the universe so far as it is a *whole,* and likewise all the wholes it contains, by his own immediate energy; other subordinate powers co-operating with him in the production of parts. Hence he produces the universe *totally* and *at once.*

DESIRE, επιθυμια. Is an irrational appetite solely directed to external objects, and to the gratification arising from the possession of them.

DIANOIA, διανοια, from whence *dianoetic*, is the discursive energy of reason; (διεξοδικη του λογου ενεργεια) or according to its most accurate signification, it is that power of the soul which reasons scientifically, deriving the principles of its reasoning from intellect, or the power which sees truth intuitively.

DOXASTIC, formed from δοξα *opinion*, is the last of the gnostic powers of the rational soul; and knows *that* a thing is, but is ignorant of the cause of it, or *why* it is. The knowledge of the διοτι or *why* a thing is, being the province of dianoia.

GUEST, ξενος. This word, in its more ample signification in the Greek, denotes a *stranger,* but properly implies one who receives another, or is himself received at an entertainment. In the dialogues of Plato therefore, (and consequently in this work of Proclus when he cites the dialogues in which this word occurs) wherever one of the speakers is introduced as a ξενος, I have translated this word *guest*, as being more conformable to the genius of Plato's dialogues, which may be justly called rich mental banquets, and consequently the speakers in them may be considered as so many guests. Hence in the *Timæus*, the persons of that dialogue are expressly spoken of as guests from having been feasted with discourse.

HYPARXIS, υπαρξις. The first principle, or foundation as it were, of the essence of a thing. Hence, also, it is the summit of essence.

IMPARTICIPABLE, αμεθεκτος. One thing is said to be imparticipable with respect to another, to which it is superior, when it is not consubsistent with it.

INTELLECTUAL PROJECTION. The immediate energy of intellect is thus denominated, because it is an intuitive perception, or an immediate darting forth, as it were, to its proper object, the intelligible.

MONAD, μονας, in divine natures is that which contains *distinct*, but at the same time *profoundly-united* multitude, and which produces a multitude exquisitely allied to itself. But in the sensible universe, the first monad is the world itself, which comprehends in itself all the multitude of which it is the cause in conjunction with the cause of all. The second monad is the inerratic sphere. In the third place, the spheres of the planets succeed, each of which is also a monad, comprehending an appropriate multitude. And in the fourth and last place are the spheres of the elements, which are in a similar manner monads. All these monads likewise are denominated ολοτητες, *wholenesses*, and have a perpetual subsistence.

PERMANENCY, στασισ. The proper word for rest, in Greek, is ηρεμια. And Simplicius justly observes, that not every στασις is ερεμια, but that only which is after motion. This word is employed by Plato in the *Sophista*, to express one of the five genera of being, *viz. essence, permanency,* (στασις), *motion, sameness,* and *difference*; in which place it evidently does not signify rest.

PHANTASY or *Imagination,* φαντασια, is, μορφωτικη νοησις, *i.e. a figured intelligence,* because all the perceptions of this power are *inward* and not external, like those of sense, and are accompanied with *figure*.

PSYCHICAL, ψυχικος, *i.e. pertaining to soul,* in the same manner as *physical* is *something pertaining to nature.*

REASON, λογος. This word in Platonic writers signifies either that inward discursive energy called reasoning; or a certain productive and seminal principle; or that which is indicative and definitive of a thing. Hence λογοι or *reasons* in the soul, are, gnostically producing principles.

UNICAL, ενιαιος, that which is characterized by unity.

UNIFORM, ενοειδης. This word when it occurs in Proclus, and other Platonic writers, signifies that which has the form of *The One,* and not as in Johnson, that which keeps its tenour, or is similar to itself.

BOOK I

CHAPTER I

O Pericles, to me the dearest of friends, I am of opinion that the whole philosophy of Plato was at first unfolded into light through the beneficent will of superior natures, exhibiting the intellect concealed in them, and the truth subsisting together with beings, to souls conversant with generation (so far as it is lawful for them to participate of such supernatural and mighty good); and again, that afterwards having received its perfection, returning as it were into itself, and becoming unapparent to many† who professed to philosophize, and who earnestly desired to engage in the investigation of true being, it again advanced into light. But I particularly think that the mystic doctrine respecting divine concerns, which is purely established on a sacred foundation, and which perpetually subsists with the gods themselves, became thence apparent to such as are capable of enjoying it for a time, through one man,‡ whom I should not err in calling the primary leader and hierophant of those true mysteries, into which souls separated from terrestrial places are initiated, and of those entire and stable visions, which those participate who genuinely embrace a happy and blessed life. But this philosophy shone forth at first from him so venerably and arcanely, as if established in sacred temples, and within their adyta, and being unknown to many who have entered into these holy places, in certain orderly periods of time, proceeded as much as was possible for it into light, through certain true priests, and who embraced a life corresponding to the tradition of such mystic concerns. It appears likewise to me, that the whole place became splendid, and that illuminations of divine spectacles every where presented themselves to the view.

These interpreters of the *epopteia* (or mystic speculations) of Plato, who have unfolded to us all-sacred narrations of divine concerns, and who were allotted a nature similar to their leader, I should determine to

---

† It is a remarkable historical fact, as I have observed in my *History of the Restoration of the Platonic Theology* [TTS vol. VII], that the philosophy of Plato was in a manner lost for many centuries after the death of its great master. For its depths were not penetrated prior to Plotinus, who lived about two hundred and fifty years after the birth of Christ.

‡ Meaning Plato.

be the Egyptian Plotinus, and those who received the theory from him, I mean Amelius and Porphyry, together with those in the third place who were produced like virile statues from these, *viz*.: Iamblichus and Theodorus,[†] and any others, who after these, following this divine choir, have energized about the doctrines of Plato with a divinely-inspired mind. From these, he[‡] who, after the gods, has been our leader to everything beautiful and good, receiving in an undefiled manner the most genuine and pure light of truth in the bosom of his soul, made us a partaker of all the rest of Plato's philosophy, communicated to us that arcane information which he had received from those more ancient than himself, and caused us, in conjunction with him, to be divinely agitated about the mystic truth of divine concerns.

To this man, therefore, should we undertake to return thanks adequate to the benefits which we have received from him; the whole of time would not be sufficient. But if it is necessary, not only[§] that we should have received from others the transcendant good of the Platonic philosophy, but that we should leave to posterity monuments of those blessed spectacles of which we have been spectators, and emulators to the utmost of our ability, under a leader the most perfect of the present time, and who arrived at the summit of philosophy; perhaps we shall act properly in invoking the gods, that they will enkindle the light of truth in our soul, and in supplicating the attendants and ministers of better natures to direct our intellect and lead it to the all-perfect, divine, and elevated, end of the Platonic theory. For I think that every where he who participates in the least degree of intelligence, will begin his undertakings from the Gods, and especially in explications respecting the Gods: for we can no otherwise be able to understand a divine nature than by being perfected through the light of the Gods; nor divulge it to others unless governed by them, and exempt from multiform opinions, and the variety which subsists in words, preserving at the same time the interpretation of divine names. Knowing therefore this, and complying with the exhortation of the Platonic *Timæus*, we in the first place establish the Gods as leaders of the doctrine respecting themselves. But

---

[†] Both these philosophers were the disciples of Porphyry. For an account of the former, of whom the Emperor Julian says, that he was posterior indeed in time to Plato, but not in genius, see my *History of the Restoration of the Platonic Theology* [TTS vol. VII].

[‡] Meaning his preceptor Syrianus.

[§] The word $\mu o \nu o \nu$ is omitted in the original.

may they in consequence of hearing our prayers be propitious to us, and benignantly approaching, guide the intellect of our soul, and lead it about the Vesta of Plato, and to the arduous sublimities of this speculation; where, when arrived, we shall receive all the truth concerning them, and shall obtain the best end of our parturient conceptions of divine concerns, desiring to know something respecting them, inquiring about them of others, and, at the same time, as far as we are able, exploring them ourselves.

CHAPTER II

And thus much by way of preface. But it is necessary that I should unfold the mode of the proposed doctrine, what it is requisite to expect it will be, and define the preparatives which a hearer of it ought to possess; that being properly adapted, he may approach, not to our discourses, but to the intellectually-elevated and deific philosophy of Plato. For it is proper that convenient aptitudes of auditors should be proposed according to the forms of discourses, just as in the mysteries, those who are skilful in concerns of this kind, previously prepare receptacles for the Gods, and neither always use the same inanimate particulars, nor other animals, nor men, in order to procure the presence of the divinities; but that alone out of each of these which is naturally capable of participating divine illumination, is by them introduced to the proposed mystic rites.

The present discourse, therefore, will first of all be divided by me into three parts. In the beginning, considering all those common conceptions concerning the Gods, which Plato summarily delivers, together with the power and dignity every where of theological axioms; but in the middle of this work, speculating the total orders of the Gods, enumerating their peculiarities, defining their progressions after the manner of Plato, and referring every thing to the hypotheses of theologists; and, in the end, speaking concerning the Gods which are in different places celebrated in the Platonic writings, whether they are supermundane or mundane, and referring the theory respecting them to the total genera of the divine orders.

In every part of this work, likewise, we shall prefer the clear, distinct, and simple, to the contraries of these. And such things as are delivered through symbols, we shall transfer to a clear doctrine concerning them; but such as are delivered through images, we shall transmit to their exemplars. Such things too as are written in a more affirmative way, we shall examine by causal reasonings; but such as are composed through demonstrations, we shall investigate; and besides this, explain the mode of truth which they contain, and render it known to the hearers. And of things enigmatically proposed, we shall elsewhere discover perspicuity, not from foreign hypotheses, but from the most genuine writings of Plato. But with respect to the things which immediately occur to the hearers, of these we shall contemplate the consent with things themselves. And from all these particulars, one perfect form of the Platonic theology will present itself to our view, together with its truth which pervades through the whole of divine intellections, and the one intellect which generated all the beauty of this theology, and the mystic evolution of this theory. Such, therefore, as I have said, will be my present treatise.

But the auditor of the proposed dogmas is supposed to be adorned with the moral virtues, and to be one who has bound by the reason of virtue all the illiberal and inharmonious motions of the soul, and harmonized them to the one form of intellectual prudence: for, as Socrates says, it is not lawful for the pure to be touched by the impure. But every vicious man is perfectly impure; and the contrary character is pure. He must likewise have been exercised in all the logical methods, and have contemplated many irreprehensible conceptions about analyses, and many about divisions, the contraries to these, agreeably, as it appears to me, to the exhortation of Parmenides to Socrates. For prior to such a contest in arguments, the knowledge of the divine genera, and of the truth established in them, is difficult and impervious. But in the third place, he must not be unskilled in physics. For he who has been conversant with the multiform opinions of physiologists, and has after a manner explored in images the causes of beings, will more easily advance to the nature of separate and primary essences. An auditor therefore of the present work, as I have said, must not be ignorant of the truth contained in the phenomena, nor unacquainted with the paths of erudition, and the disciplines which they contain; for through these we obtain a more immaterial knowledge of a divine essence. But all these must be bound together in the leader intellect. Being likewise a partaker of the dialectic of Plato,[1] meditating those immaterial energies which are separate from corporeal powers, and desiring to contemplate by intelligence[†] in conjunction with reason [true] beings, our auditor must genuinely apply himself to the interpretation of divine and blessed dogmas, and fill his soul, according to the Oracle, with profound love;

[†] Instead of νοησις μετα λογου, it is necessary to read, νοησει μετα λογου.

since, as Plato somewhere observes, for the apprehension of this theory, a better assistant than love cannot be obtained.

He must likewise be exercised in the truth which pervades through all things, and must excite his intelligible eye to real and perfect truth. He must establish himself in a firm, immovable, and safe kind of divine knowledge, and must be persuaded not to admire any thing else, nor even to direct his attention to other things, but must hasten to divine light with an intrepid reasoning energy, and with the power of an unwearied life; and in short, must propose to himself such a kind of energy and rest as it becomes him to possess who intends to be such a coryphæus as Socrates describes in the *Theætetus*. Such then is the magnitude of our hypothesis, and such the mode of the discourses about it. Before, however, I enter on the narration of the things proposed, I wish to speak about theology itself, its different modes, and what theological forms Plato approves, and what he rejects; that these being previously known, we may more easily learn in what follows, the auxiliaries of the demonstrations themselves.

CHAPTER III

All, therefore, that have ever touched upon theology, have called things first, according to nature, Gods; and have said that the theological science is conversant about these. And some, indeed, have considered a corporeal essence, as that alone which has any existence, and have placed in a secondary rank with respect to essence, all the genera of incorporeal natures, considering the principles of things as having a corporeal form, and evincing that the habit in us by which we know these, is corporeal. But others, suspending indeed all bodies from incorporeal natures, and defining the first hyparxis† to be in soul, and the powers of soul, call (as it appears to me) the best of souls, Gods; and denominate the science which proceeds as far as to these, and which knows these, theology. But such as produce the multitude of souls from another more ancient principle, and establish intellect as the leader of wholes, these assert that the best end is a union of the soul with intellect, and consider the intellectual form of life as the most honourable of all things. They doubtless too consider theology, and the discussion of intellectual essence, as one and the same. All these, therefore, as I have said, call the first and most self-sufficient principles of things, Gods, and the science respecting these, theology.

---

† Hyparxis, is the summit of any nature, or blossom, as it were, of its essence.

The divine narration however, of Plato alone, despises all corporeal natures with reference to principles. Because, indeed, every thing divisible and endued with interval, is naturally unable either to produce or preserve itself, but possesses its being, energy and passivity through soul, and the motions which soul contains. But Plato demonstrates that the psychical essence [*ie.* the essence pertaining to soul] is more ancient than bodies, but is suspended from an intellectual hypostasis. For every thing which is moved according to time, though it may be self-moved, is indeed of a more ruling nature than things moved by others, but is posterior to an eternal motion. He shows, therefore, as we have said, that intellect is the father and cause of bodies and souls, and that all things both subsist and energize about it, which are allotted a life conversant with transitions and evolutions.

Plato, however, proceeds to another principle entirely exempt from intellect, more incorporeal and ineffable, and from which all things, even though you should speak of such as are last, have necessarily a subsistence. For all things are not naturally disposed to participate of soul, but such things only as are allotted in themselves a more clear or obscure life. Nor are all things able to enjoy intellect and being, but such only as subsist according to form. But it is necessary that the principle of all things should be participated by all things, if it does not desert any thing, since it is the cause of all things which in any respect are said to have a subsistence. Plato having divinely discovered this first principle of wholes, which is more excellent than intellect, and is concealed in inaccessible recesses; and having exhibited these three causes and monads, and evinced them to be above bodies, I mean soul, the first intellect, and a union above intellect, produces from these as monads, their proper numbers; one multitude indeed being uniform,† but the second intellectual, and the third psychical. For every monad is the leader of a multitude co-ordinate to itself. But as Plato connects bodies with souls, so likewise he connects souls with intellectual forms, and these again with the unities of beings. But he converts all things to one imparticipable unity. And having run back as far as to this unity, he considers himself as having obtained the highest end of the theory of wholes; and that this is the truth respecting the Gods, which is conversant with the unities of beings, and which delivers their

---

† Wherever this word occurs in this translation, it signifies that which is characterised by unity.

progressions and peculiarities, the contact of beings with them, and the orders of forms which are suspended from these unical[†] hypostases.

But he teaches us that the theory respecting intellect, and the forms and the genera revolving about intellect, is posterior to the science which is conversant with the Gods themselves. Likewise that the intellectual theory apprehends intelligibles, and the forms which are capable of being known by the soul through the projecting energy of intellect; but that the theological science transcending this, is conversant with arcane and ineffable hyparxes, and pursues their separation from each other, and their unfolding into light from one cause of all: whence, I am of opinion, that the intellectual peculiarity of the soul is capable of apprehending intellectual forms, and the difference which subsists in them, but that the summit, and, as they say, flower of intellect and hyparxis, is conjoined with the unities of beings, and through these, with the occult union of all the divine unities. For as we contain many gnostic powers, through this alone we are naturally capable of being conjoined with and participating this occult union. For the genus of the Gods cannot be apprehended by sense, because it is exempt from all bodies; nor by opinion and dianoia,[‡] for these are divisible and come into contact with multiform concerns; nor by intelligence in conjunction with reason, for knowledge of this kind belongs to true beings; but the hyparxis of the Gods rides on beings, and is defined according to the union itself of wholes. It remains, therefore, if it be admitted that a divine nature can be in any respect known, that it must be apprehended by the hyparxis of the soul, and through this, as far as it is possible, be known. For we say that every where things similar can be known by the similar; *viz.* the sensible by sense, the doxastic[§] by opinion, the dianoetic by dianoia, and the intelligible by intellect. So that the most unical nature must be known by *The One*, and the ineffable by that which is ineffable.

Indeed, Socrates in the *[First] Alcibiades* rightly observes, that the soul entering into herself will behold all other things, and deity itself. For verging to her own union, and to the centre of all life, laying aside multitude, and the variety of the all manifold powers which she

---

[†] *ie.* Of the nature of *The One*.

[‡] *i.e.* The discursive energy of reason, or the power of the soul that reasons scientifically.

[§] *i.e.* The object of opinion.

contains, she ascends to the highest watch-tower of beings. And as in the most holy of the mysteries, they say, that the mystics at first meet with the multiform, and many-shaped[†] genera; which are hurled forth before the Gods, but on entering the interior parts of the temple, unmoved, and guarded by the mystic rites, they genuinely receive in their bosom divine illumination, and divested of their garments, as they would say, participate of a divine nature; - the same mode, as it appears to me, takes place in the speculation of wholes. For the soul when looking at things posterior to herself, beholds the shadows and images of beings, but when she converts herself to herself she evolves her own essence, and the reasons which she contains. And at first indeed, she only as it were beholds herself; but, when she penetrates more profoundly into the knowledge of herself, she finds in herself both intellect, and the orders of beings. When however, she proceeds into her interior recesses, and into the adytum as it were of the soul, she perceives with her eye closed, the genus of the Gods, and the unities of beings. For all things are in us psychically, and through this we are naturally capable of knowing all things, by exciting the powers and the images of wholes which we contain.

And this is the best employment of our energy, to be extended to a divine nature itself, having our powers at rest, to revolve harmoniously round it, to excite all the multitude of the soul to this union, and laying aside all such things as are posterior to *The One*, to become seated and conjoined with that which is ineffable, and beyond all things. For it is lawful for the soul to ascend, till she terminates her flight in the principle of things; but arriving thither, beholding the place which is there, descending thence, and directing her course through beings; likewise, evolving the multitude of forms, exploring their monads and their numbers, and apprehending intellectually how each is suspended from its proper unity, then we may consider her as possessing the most perfect science of divine natures, perceiving in a uniform manner the progressions of the Gods into beings, and the distinctions of beings about the Gods. Such then according to Plato's decision is our theologist; and theology is a habit of this kind, which unfolds the hyparxis itself of the Gods, separates and speculates their unknown and unical light from the peculiarity of their participants, and, announces it to such as are worthy of this energy, which is both blessed and comprehends all things at once.

[†] *i.e.* Evil dæmons.

CHAPTER IV

After this all-perfect comprehension of the first theory, we must deliver the modes according to which Plato teaches us mystic conceptions of divine natures. For he appears not to have pursued every where the same mode of doctrine about these; but sometimes according to a deific energy, and at other times dialectically, he evolves the truth concerning them. And sometimes he symbolically announces their ineffable peculiarities, but at other times he recurs to them from images, and discovers in them the primary causes of wholes. For in the *Phædrus* being inspired by the Nymphs, and having exchanged human intelligence for a better possession, fury, he unfolds with a divine mouth many arcane dogmas concerning the intellectual Gods, and many concerning the liberated rulers of the universe, who lead upwards the multitude of mundane Gods to the monads which are intelligible and separate from [mundane] wholes. But relating still more about those Gods who are allotted the world, he celebrates their intellections, and mundane fabrications, their unpolluted providence and government of souls, and whatever else Socrates delivers entheastically [or according to a divinely-inspired energy] in that dialogue, as he clearly asserts, ascribing at the same time this fury to the deities of the place.

But in the *Sophista*, dialectically contending about being, and the separate hypostasis of *The One* from beings, and doubting against those more ancient than himself, he shows how all beings are suspended from their cause, and the first being, but that being itself participates of the unity which is exempt from the whole of things, that it is a passive one, but not *The One* itself, being subject to and united to *The One*, but not being that which is primarily one. In a similar manner too, in the *Parmenides*, he unfolds dialectically the progressions of being from *The One*, and the transcendency of *The One*, through the first hypotheses, and this as he asserts in that dialogue, according to the most perfect division of this method. And again, in the *Gorgias*, he relates the fable concerning the three demiurgi [or fabricators] and their demiurgic allotment, which indeed is not only a fable, but a true narration. But in the *Banquet*, he speaks concerning the union of Love. And in the *Protagoras*, about the distribution of mortal animals from the Gods; in a symbolical manner concealing the truth respecting divine natures, and as far as to mere indication unfolding his mind to the most genuine of his hearers.

If likewise, you are willing that I should mention the doctrine delivered through the mathematical disciplines, and the discussion of divine concerns from ethical or physical discourses, of which many may be contemplated in the *Timæus*, many in the dialogue called the *Politicus*, and many may be seen scattered in other dialogues; here likewise to you who are desirous of knowing divine concerns through images, the method will be apparent. For all these shadow forth the powers of things divine. The *Politicus*, for instance, the fabrication in the heavens. But the figures of the five elements delivered in geometrical proportions in the *Timæus*,[†] represent in images the peculiarities of the Gods who ride on the parts of the universe. And the divisions of the psychical essence in that dialogue shadow forth the total orders of the Gods.

I omit to mention that Plato composes polities, assimilating them to divine natures, and to the whole world, and adorns them from the powers which it contains. All these therefore, through the similitude of mortal to divine concerns, exhibit to us in images, the progressions, orders, and fabrications of divine natures. And such are the modes of theologic doctrine employed by Plato.

It is evident however, from what has been already said, that they are necessarily so many in number. For those who treat of divine concerns in an indicative manner, either speak symbolically and fabulously, or through images. But of those who openly announce their conceptions, some frame their discourses according to science, but others according to inspiration from the Gods. And he who desires to signify divine concerns through symbols is Orphic, and in short, accords with those who write fables concerning the Gods. But he who does this through images is Pythagoric. For the mathematical disciplines were invented by the Pythagoreans, in order to a reminiscence of divine concerns, at which, through these as images they endeavour to arrive. For they refer both numbers and figures to the Gods, according to the testimony of their historians. But the entheastic character, or he who is under the influence of divine inspiration, unfolding the truth itself by itself concerning the Gods, most perspicuously ranks among the highest initiators. For these do not think proper to unfold the divine orders, or their peculiarities to their familiars, through certain veils, but announce their powers and their numbers, in consequence of being moved by the Gods themselves. But the tradition of divine concerns according to science, is the illustrious prerogative of the philosophy of Plato. For Plato alone, as it appears to me, of all those who are known to us, has attempted methodically to divide and reduce into order, the regular

---

[†] $\varepsilon\nu\ \tau\iota\mu\alpha\iota\omega$ is omitted in the Greek.

progression of the divine genera, their mutual difference, the common peculiarities of the total orders, and the distributed peculiarities in each. But the truth of this will be evident when we frame precedaneous demonstrations about the *Parmenides*, and all the divisions which it contains.

At present we shall observe that Plato does not admit all the fabulous figments of dramatic composition, but those only which have reference to the beautiful and the good, and which are not discordant with a divine essence. For that mythological mode which indicates divine concerns through conjecture is ancient, concealing truth under a multitude of veils, and proceeding in a manner similar to nature, which extends sensible figments of intelligibles, material, of immaterial, partible, of impartible natures and images, and things which have a false being, of things perfectly true. But Plato rejects the more tragical mode of mythologizing of the ancient poets, who thought proper to establish an arcane theology respecting the Gods, and on this account devised wanderings, sections, battles, lacerations, rapes and adulteries of the Gods,[†] and many other such symbols of the truth about divine natures, which this theology conceals; this mode he rejects, and asserts that it is in every respect most foreign from erudition. But he considers those mythological discourses about the Gods, as more persuasive, and more adapted to truth and the philosophic habit, which assert that a divine nature is the cause of all good, but of no evil, and that it is void of all mutation, ever preserving its own order immutable, and comprehending in itself the fountain of truth, but never becoming the cause of any deception to others. For such types of theology, Socrates delivers in the *Republic*.

All the fables therefore of Plato, guarding the truth in concealment, have not even their externally apparent apparatus discordant with our undisciplined and unperverted anticipation respecting the Gods. But they bring with them an image of the mundane composition, in which both the apparent beauty is worthy of divinity, and a beauty more divine than this, is established in the unapparent lives and powers of the Gods. This therefore, is one of the mythological modes respecting divine concerns, which from the apparently unlawful, irrational, and inordinate, passes into order and bound, and regards as its scope the composition of the beautiful and good.

---

† See the fables in which these things are asserted of the Gods admirably unfolded by Proclus in the Introduction to the second and third books of the *Republic* of Plato, in Vol. I of my Plato. [TTS vol. IX.]

But there is another mode which he delivers in the *Phædrus*. And this consists in every where preserving theological fables, unmixed with physical narrations, and being careful in no respect to confound or exchange theology, and the physical theory with each other. For, as a divine essence is separate from the whole of nature, in like manner, it is perfectly proper that discourses respecting the Gods should be pure from physical disquisitions. For a mixture of this kind is, says he, laborious: and to make physical passions the end of mythological conjecture, is the employment of no very good man; such for instance, as considering through his [pretended] wisdom, Chimæra, Gorgon, and things of a similar kind, as the same with physical figments. Socrates, in the *Phædrus*, reprobating this mode of mythologizing, represents its patrons as saying under the figure of a fable, that Orithya sporting with the wind Boreas and being thrown down the rocks, means nothing more, than that Orithya who was a mortal, was ravished by Boreas through love. For it appears to me, that fabulous narrations about the gods, should always have their concealed meaning more venerable than the apparent. So that if certain persons introduce to us physical hypotheses of Platonic fables, and such as are conversant with sublunary affairs, we must say that they entirely wander from the intention of the philosopher, and that those hypotheses alone, are interpreters of the truth contained in these fables, which have for their scope, a divine, immaterial, and separate hypostasis, and which looking to this, make the compositions and analyses of the fables, adapted† to our inherent anticipations of divine concerns.

CHAPTER V

As we have therefore enumerated all these modes of the Platonic theology, and have shown what compositions and analyses of fable are adapted to the truth respecting the Gods, let us consider, in the next place, whence, and from what dialogues principally, we think the dogmas of Plato concerning the Gods may be collected, and by a speculation of what types or forms we may be able to distinguish his genuine writings, from those spurious compositions which are ascribed to him.

The truth then concerning the Gods pervades, as I may say, through all the Platonic dialogues, and in all of them conceptions of the first philosophy, venerable, clear, and supernatural, are disseminated, in some

---

† For οικειαις, it is necessary to read οικειας.

indeed, more obscurely, but in others more conspicuously; conceptions which excite those that are in any respect able to participate of them, to the immaterial and separate essence of the Gods. And, as in each part of the universe, and in nature herself, the demiurgus of all that the world contains, established resemblances of the unknown hyparxis of the Gods, that all things might be converted to a divine nature, through their alliance with it, in like manner I am of opinion, that the divine intellect of Plato weaves conceptions about the Gods in all his writings, and leaves nothing deprived of the mention of divinity, that from the whole of them, a reminiscence of wholes may be obtained, and imparted to the genuine lovers of divine concerns.

If however, it be requisite to lay before the reader those dialogues out of many, which principally unfold to us the mystic discipline about the gods, I should not err in ranking among this number, the *Phædo* and the *Phædrus*, the *Banquet*, and the *Philebus*, and together with these, the *Sophista* and *Politicus*, the *Cratylus* and the *Timæus*. For all these are full through the whole of themselves, as I may say, of the divine science of Plato. But I should place in the second rank after these, the fable in the *Gorgias*, and that in the *Protagoras*; likewise the assertions about the providence of the Gods in the *Laws* and, such things as are delivered about the Fates, or the mother of the Fates, or the circulations of the universe in the tenth book of the *Republic*. Again, you may, if you please, place in the third rank those Epistles, through which we may be able to arrive at the science about divine natures. For in these, mention is made of the three kings; and very many other divine dogmas worthy of the Platonic theory are delivered. It is necessary therefore, looking to these, to explore in these each order of the Gods.

Thus from the *Philebus*, we may receive the science respecting the one good, and the two first principles of things, together with the triad† which is unfolded into light from these. For you will find all these distinctly delivered to us by Plato in that dialogue. But from the *Timæus*, you may obtain the theory about intelligibles, a divine narration about the demiurgic monad: and the most full truth about the mundane Gods. But from the *Phædrus*, [you may acquire a scientific knowledge of] all the intelligible and intellectual genera, and of the liberated orders of Gods, which are proximately established above the celestial circulations. From the *Politicus*, you may obtain the theory of the fabrication in the heavens, of the uneven periods of the universe, and the intellectual causes of those periods. But from the *Sophista*, the whole

---

† τριαδος is omitted in the original.

sublunary generation, and the peculiarity of the Gods who are allotted the sublunary region, and preside over its generations and corruptions. But with respect to each of the Gods, we may obtain many conceptions adapted to sacred concerns from the *Banquet*, many from the *Cratylus*, and many from the *Phædo*. For in each of these dialogues, more or less mention is made of divine names, from which it is easy for those who are exercised in divine concerns to discover by a reasoning process the peculiarities of each.

It is necessary however, to evince that each of the dogmas accords with Platonic principles, and the mystic traditions of theologists. For all the Grecian theology is the progeny of the mystic tradition of Orpheus; Pythagoras first of all learning from Aglaophemus the orgies of the Gods, but Plato in the second place receiving an all-perfect science of the divinities from the Pythagoric and Orphic writings. For in the *Philebus* referring the theory about the two species of principles [bound and infinity] to the Pythagoreans, he calls them men dwelling with the Gods, and truly blessed. Philolaus therefore, the Pythagorean, has left us in writing many admirable conceptions about these principles, celebrating their common progression into beings, and their separate fabrication of things. But in the *Timæus*, Plato endeavouring to teach us about the sublunary Gods, and their order, flies to theologists, calls them the sons of the Gods, and makes them the fathers of the truth about those divinities. And lastly, he delivers the orders of the sublunary Gods proceeding from wholes, according to the progression delivered by them of the intellectual kings. Again, in the *Cratylus* he follows the traditions of theologists, respecting the order of the divine processions. But in the *Gorgias*, he adopts the Homeric dogma, respecting the triadic hypostasis of the demiurgi. And in short, he every where discourses concerning the Gods agreeably to the principles of theologists; rejecting indeed, the tragical part of mythological fiction, but establishing first hypotheses in common with the authors of fables.

CHAPTER VI

Perhaps, however, some one may here object to us, that we do not in a proper manner exhibit the every where dispersed theology of Plato, and that we endeavour to heap together different particulars from different dialogues, as if we were studious of collecting together many things into one mixture, instead of deriving them all from one and the same fountain. For if this were the case, we might refer different dogmas to different treatises of Plato, but we shall by no means have a precedaneous doctrine concerning the Gods, nor will there be any dialogue which presents us with an all-perfect and entire procession of the divine genera, and their co-ordination with each other. But we shall be similar to those who endeavour to obtain a whole from parts, through the want of a whole prior to parts, and to weave together the perfect from things imperfect; when, on the contrary, the imperfect ought to have the first cause of its generation in the perfect. For the *Timæus*, for instance, will teach us the theory of the intelligible genera; and the *Phædrus* appears to present us with a methodical account of the first intellectual orders. But where will be the co-ordination of intellectuals to intelligibles? And what will be the generation of second from first natures? In short, after what manner the progression of the divine orders takes place from the one principle of all things, and how in the generations of the Gods, the orders between *The One*, and all-perfect number, are filled up, we shall be unable to evince.

Farther still, it may be said, where will be the venerableness of your boasted science about divine natures? For it is absurd to call these dogmas which are collected from many places, Platonic; and which, as you acknowledge, are introduced from foreign names to the philosophy of Plato; nor are you able to evince one whole entire truth about divine natures. Perhaps, indeed, they will say, certain persons, junior to Plato, have delivered in their writings, and left to their disciples, one perfect form of theology. You, therefore, are able to produce one entire theory about nature from the *Timæus*; but from the *Republic*, or *Laws*, the most beautiful dogmas about manners, and which tend to one form of philosophy. Alone, therefore, neglecting the treatise of Plato, which contains all the good of the first philosophy, and which may be called the summit of the whole theory, you will be deprived of the most perfect knowledge of beings, unless you are so much infatuated, as to boast on account of fabulous fictions, though an analysis of things of this kind abounds with much of the probable, but not of the demonstrative. Besides, things of this kind are only delivered adventitiously in the Platonic dialogues; as the fable in the *Protagoras*, which is inserted for the sake of the politic science, and the demonstrations respecting it. In like manner, the fable in the *Republic* is inserted for the sake of justice; but in the *Gorgias*, for the sake of temperance. For Plato combines fabulous narrations with investigations of ethical dogmas, not for the sake of the fables, but for the sake of the leading design, that we may not only exercise the intellectual part of the soul, through contending reasons, but that the divine part of the soul may more perfectly receive the knowledge of beings, through its sympathy with more mystic concerns. For, from other discourses, we appear similar to those who are compelled to the reception of truth; but from fables we suffer in an ineffable manner, and call forth our unperverted conceptions, venerating the mystic information which they contain.

Hence, as it appears to me, Timæus with great propriety thinks it fit that we should produce the divine genera, following the inventors of fables as the sons of the Gods,[†] and subscribe to their always generating secondary natures from such as are first, though they should speak without demonstration. For this kind of discourse is not demonstrative, but entheastic, and was invented by the ancients, not through necessity, but for the sake of persuasion, not regarding mere discipline, but sympathy with things themselves. But if you are willing to speculate not only the causes of fables, but of other theological dogmas, you will find that some of them are scattered in the Platonic dialogues for the sake of ethical,[‡] and others or the sake of physical considerations. For in the *Philebus*, Plato discourses concerning bound and the infinite, for the sake of pleasure and a life according to intellect. For I think the latter are species of the former. In the *Timæus*, the discourse about the intelligible Gods, is assumed for the sake of the proposed physiology. On which account it is every where necessary that images should be known from paradigms; but that the paradigms of material things should be immaterial, of sensibles, intelligible, and that the paradigms of physical forms should be separate.

But again in the *Phædrus*, Plato celebrates the supercelestial place, the subcelestial profundity, and every genus under this, for the sake of amatory mania: the manner in which the reminiscence of souls takes place, and the passage to these from hence. But every where, as I may say, the leading end is either physical or political, while the conceptions about divine natures take place, either for the sake of invention or perfection. How, therefore, can such a theory as yours be any longer venerable and supernatural, and worthy to be studied beyond every thing, when it is neither able to evince the whole in itself, nor the perfect, nor that which is precedaneous in the writings of Plato, but is destitute of all these, is violent and not spontaneous, and does not possess a genuine, but an adventitious order, as in a drama? And such are the objections which may be urged against our design.

[†] $των θεων$ is omitted in the original.

[‡] For $μυθικων$, it is necessary to read, $τα μεν ηθικων$.

CHAPTER VII

I, however, to an objection of this kind, shall make a just and perspicuous reply. I say then, that Plato every where discourses about the Gods agreeably to ancient rumour, and to the nature of things. And sometimes indeed, for the sake of the cause of the things proposed, he reduces them to the principles of the dogmas; and thence, as from a watch tower, contemplates the nature of the thing proposed. But sometimes he establishes the theological science as the leading end. For in the *Phædrus* his subject respects intelligible beauty, and the participation of beauty pervading from thence through all things; and in the *Banquet* it respects the amatory order.

But if it be necessary to survey in one Platonic dialogue, the all-perfect, whole, and connected, extending as far as to the compleat number of theology, I shall perhaps assert a paradox, and which will alone be apparent to our familiars. We ought however to dare, since we have entered on such like arguments, and affirm against our opponents, that the *Parmenides*, and the mystic conceptions it contains, will accomplish all you desire. For in this dialogue all the divine genera proceed in order from the first cause, and evince their mutual connexion and dependence on each other. And those which are highest indeed, connate with *The One*, and of a primary nature, are allotted a unical, occult, and simple form of hyparxis; but such as are last, are multiplied, are distributed into many parts, and are exuberant in number, but inferior in power to such as are of a higher order; and such as are middle, according to a convenient proportion, are more composite than their causes, but more simple than their proper progeny. And in short, all the axioms of the theologic science, appear in perfection in this dialogue, and all the divine orders are exhibited subsisting in connexion. So that this is nothing else than the celebrated generation of the Gods, and the procession of every kind of being from the ineffable and unknown cause of wholes. The *Parmenides*, therefore, enkindles in the lovers of Plato, the whole and perfect light of the theological science. But after this, the before mentioned dialogues distribute parts of the mystic discipline about the Gods, and all of them, as I may say, participate of divine wisdom, and excite our spontaneous conceptions respecting a divine nature. And it is necessary to refer all the parts of this mystic discipline to these dialogues, and these again to the one and all-perfect theory of the *Parmenides*. For thus, as it appears to me, we shall suspend the more imperfect from the perfect, and parts from wholes, and shall exhibit reasons assimilated to things, of which, according to the Platonic

Timæus, they are interpreters. Such then is our answer to the objection which may be urged against us; and thus we refer the Platonic theory to the *Parmenides*; just as the *Timæus* is acknowledged by all who are in the least degree intelligent, to contain the whole science about nature.

CHAPTER VIII

I appear, however, by these means, to have excited for myself a twofold contest against those who attempt to investigate the writings of Plato; and I see two sorts of persons, who will oppose what has been said. One of these does not think proper to explore any other design in the *Parmenides*, than exercise through opposite arguments, or to introduce in this dialogue a crowd of arcane and intellectual dogmas, which are foreign from its intention. But the other sort, who are more venerable than these, and lovers of forms assert, that one of the hypotheses is about the first God, another about the second God, and the whole of an intellectual nature, and a third, about the natures posterior to this, whether they are the more excellent genera, or souls, or any other kind of beings. For the investigation of these particulars does not pertain to the present discourse.

These, therefore, distribute three of the hypotheses after this manner. But they do not think proper to busy themselves about the multitude of Gods, the intelligible, and the intellectual genera, the supermundane and mundane natures, or to unfold all these by division, or busily explore them. For according to them, though Plato in the second hypothesis, treats about intellectual beings, yet the nature of intellect is one, simple, and indivisible. Against both these therefore, must he contend, who entertains that opinion of the *Parmenides*, which we have before mentioned. The contest however against these is not equal. But those who make the *Parmenides* a logical exercise, are again attacked by those who embrace the divine mode of interpretation. And those who do not unfold the multitude of beings, and the orders of divine natures, are indeed, as Homer says, in every respect venerable and skilful men, but yet for the sake of the Platonic philosophy, we must doubt against them, following in this our leader to the most holy and mystic truth. It is proper likewise to relate as far as contributes to our purpose, what appears to us to be the truth respecting the hypotheses of the *Parmenides*; for thus perhaps by a reasoning process, we may embrace the whole theology of Plato.

CHAPTER IX

In the first place then, let us consider those, who draw down the design of this dialogue from the truth of things to a logical exercise, and see whether they can possibly accord with the writings of Plato. It is therefore evident to every one, that Parmenides proposes to himself to deliver in reality the dialectic method, and that with this view he cursorily assumes it in a similar manner in each of the things which have a real being, as, in sameness, difference, similitude, dissimilitude, motion, and permanency, etc.; exhorting at the same time, those who desire to discover the nature of each of these in an orderly method, to this exercise, as to a great contest. He likewise asserts that it was by no means an easy undertaking to him who was so much advanced in years, assimilates himself to the Ibycean horse, and presents us with every argument to prove that this method is a serious undertaking, and not a contest consisting in mere words. How therefore, is it possible, that we can refer to empty arguments those conceptions[†] about which the great Parmenides, evincing that they require much serious discussion, composed this discourse? How likewise is it reasonable to suppose that an aged man would busy himself with mere verbal contests, and that he who loved to speculate the truth of things, would bestow so much study on this method, - he who considered every thing else, as having no real existence, and who ascended to the high watch-tower of being itself? Indeed, he who admits this must suppose that Parmenides is satirized by Plato in this dialogue, by thus representing him drawn down to juvenile contests, from the most intellectual visions of the soul.

But if you are willing, let us consider in addition to the above, what Parmenides promises, and on what subject engaging to speak, he entered on this discussion. Was it not then about being according to his doctrine, and the unity of all beings, to which extending himself, his design was concealed from the vulgar, while he exhorts us to collect the multitude of beings into one undivided union? If, therefore, this is the one being, or that which is the highest, and which is perfectly established above the reasons conversant with opinion, is it not absurd to confound dogmas about intelligibles with doxastic arguments? For indeed, such a form of discourse is not adapted to the hypothesis about true beings, nor does the intellection of unapparent and separate causes harmonize with dialectic exercises; but these differ from each other, so far as intellect is established above opinion, as Timæus informs us, and

---

† For ἐπιστολας, it is necessary to read ἐπιβολας.

not Timæus only, but likewise the dæmoniacal Aristotle, who, discoursing on a power of this kind, exhorts us to make our investigations, neither about things perfectly unapparent to us, nor about such as are more known.

It is far therefore from being the case, that Parmenides, who places the science of beings above that which appears to be truth to those who rank sense before intellect, should introduce doxastic knowledge to an intellective nature, since a knowledge of this kind is dubious, various, and unstable; or that he should speculate true being with this doxastic wisdom, and inane discussion. For a various form of knowledge does not harmonise[†] with that which is simple, nor the multiform with the uniform, nor the doxastic with the intelligible.

But still further, nor must this be omitted, that such a mode of discourse is perfectly foreign from the discussion of Parmenides. For he discourses about all beings, and delivers the order of wholes, their progression beginning from *The One*, and their conversion ending in the one. But the argumentative method is very remote from scientific theory. Does it not therefore appear, that Plato must have attributed a discordant hypothesis to Parmenides, if it be said that he merely regards an exercise through opposite arguments, and that for the sake of the power employed in this exercise, he excites the whole of this evolution of reasons? Indeed, it will be found that in all the other dialogues, Plato attributes hypotheses to each of the philosophers adapted to their peculiar tenets. Thus to Timæus, he assigns the doctrine about nature; to Socrates that of a republic; to the Elean guest, that about being; and to the priestess Diotima, that respecting love. Afterwards, each of the other dialogues confines itself to those arguments which are adapted to the writings of the principal person of the dialogue. But Parmenides alone will appear to us wise in his poems, and in his diligent investigation of true being, but in the Platonic scene, he will be the leader of a juvenile muse. This opinion, therefore, accuses Plato of dissimilitude of imitation, though he himself condemns the poets, for ascribing to the sons of the Gods a love of money, and a life subject to the dominion of the passions. How, therefore, can we refer a discussion of doxastic and empty arguments to the leader of the truth of beings?

But if it be necessary that omitting a multitude of arguments, we should make Plato himself a witness of the proposed discussion, we will cite if you please what is written in the *Theætetus* and *Sophista*; for from these dialogues what we assert will be apparent. In the *Theætetus* then

---

[†] For μονον αρμοστεον, it is necessary to read ειδος αναρμοστεον.

Socrates being excited by a young man to a confutation of those who assert that being is immoveable, attacks among these an opinion of this kind entertained by Parmenides, and at the same time assigns the cause. "I blush," says he, "for Parmenides, who is one of these, more than for all the rest; for I, when very young, was conversant with him when he was very elderly, and he appeared to me to possess a certain profundity perfectly generous. I am afraid therefore, lest we do not understand what has been asserted, and much more am I fearful that we fall short of the meaning of Parmenides." With great propriety therefore do we assert, that the proposed discussion does not regard a logical exercise, and make this the end of the whole, but that it pertains to the science of the first principles of things. For how could Socrates using a power of this kind, and neglecting the knowledge of things, testify that the discourse of Parmenides possessed a depth perfectly generous? And what venerableness can there be in adopting a method which proceeds doxastically, through opposite reasons, and in undertaking such an invention of arguments?

Again, in the *Sophista*, exciting the Elean guest to a perspicuous evolution of the things proposed by him, and evincing that he was now accustomed to more profound discourses: "Inform me," says he, "whether it is your custom to give a prolix discussion of a subject which you are able to demonstrate to any one by interrogations; I mean such discussions as Parmenides himself formerly used, accompanied with all-beautiful reasons, and of which I was an auditor when I was very young, and he was very elderly?" What reason then can be assigned, why we should not believe Socrates, when he asserts that the arguments of Parmenides were all-beautiful, and possessed a generous profundity, and why we should degrade the discussion of Parmenides, hurl it from essence and being, and transfer it to a vulgar, trifling, and empty contest, neither considering that discourses of this kind are alone adapted to youth, nor regarding the hypothesis of *being* characterized by *The One*, nor any thing else which opposes such an opinion?

But I likewise think it is proper that the authors of this hypothesis, should consider the power of dialectic, such as it is exhibited by Socrates in the *Republic*; - how, as he says, it surrounds all disciplines like a defensive enclosure, and elevates those that use it, to *The Good Itself*, and the first unities, purifies the eye of the soul, establishes it in true beings, and the one principle of all things, and ends at last in that which is no longer hypothetical. For if the power of this dialectic is so great, and the end of this path so mighty, it is not proper to confound doxastic arguments, with a method of this kind. For the former regards the opinions of men, but the latter is called garrulity by the vulgar. And the one is perfectly destitute of disciplinative science, but the other is the defensive enclosure of such sciences, and the passage to it is through these. Again, the doxastic method of reasoning has for its end[†] the apparent, but the dialectic method endeavours to arrive at *The One* itself, always employing for this purpose steps of ascent, and at last, beautifully ends in the nature of *The Good*.

By no means therefore, is it fit that we should draw down to doxastic arguments, a method which is established among the most accurate sciences. For the merely logical method which presides over the demonstrative phantasy, is of a secondary nature, and is alone pleased with contentious discussions; but our dialectic, for the most part, employs divisions and analyses as primary sciences, and as imitating the progression of beings from *The One*, and their conversion to it again. But it likewise sometimes uses definitions and demonstrations, and prior to these the definitive method, and the dividing method prior to this. On the contrary, the doxastic method is deprived of the incontrovertible reasonings of demonstration. Is it not, therefore, necessary that these powers must be separated from each other, and that the discussion of Parmenides, which employs our dialectic, must be free from the empty variety of mere argument, and must fabricate its reasonings with a view to being itself, and not to that which is apparent? And thus much may suffice in answer to those who reprobate our hypotheses. For if all this cannot convince them, we shall in vain endeavour to persuade them, and urge them to the speculation of things.

CHAPTER X

But a greater and more difficult contest remains for me, against those lovers of the speculation of beings, who look to the science of first causes, as the end proposed in the hypothesis of the Platonic *Parmenides*; and this contest we will accomplish, if you please, by numerous and more known arguments.

And in the first place, we shall define what that is, about which our discourse against them will be employed; for this, I think, will render the mystic doctrine of Plato concerning divine natures, apparent in the highest degree. There are, therefore, nine hypotheses which are discussed by Parmenides in this dialogue, as we have evinced in our commentaries upon it. And the five precedaneous hypotheses suppose

---

[†] τελος is omitted in the original.

that *The One* has a subsistence, and through this hypothesis, that all beings, the mediums of wholes, and the terminations of the progressions of things, may be supposed to subsist. But the four hypotheses which follow these, introduce *The One*, not having a subsistence, according to the exhortation of the dialectic method, show that by taking away *The One*, all beings, and such things as have an apparent existence, must be entirely subverted, and propose to themselves the confutation of this hypothesis. And some of the hypotheses evidently conclude every thing according to reason, but others (if I may be allowed the expression) perfectly evince things more impossible than impossibilities; which circumstance some prior to us perceiving, as it appears to me, necessarily to happen in these hypotheses, have considered it as deserving discussion,[†] in their treatises on this dialogue.

With respect to the first of the hypotheses therefore, almost all agree in asserting, that Plato through this celebrates the superessential principle of wholes, as ineffable, unknown, and above all being. But all do not explain the hypothesis posterior to this after the same manner. For the ancient Platonists, and those who participated the philosophy of Plotinus assert that an intellectual nature presents itself to the view in this hypothesis, subsisting from the superessential principle of things, and endeavour to harmonize to the one and all-perfect power of intellect, such conclusions as are the result of this hypothesis. But that leader of ours to truth about the Gods, and confabulator of Plato (that I may use the language of Homer) who transferred what was indefinite in the theory of the more ancient philosophers, to bound, and reduced the confusion of the different orders to an intellectual distinction, in the writings which he communicated to his associates; - this our leader, in his treatise on the present subject, calls upon us to adopt a distinct division of the conclusions, to transfer this division to the divine orders, and to harmonize the first and most simple of the things exhibited to the first of beings; but to adapt those in the middle rank to middle natures, according to the order which they are allotted among beings; and such as are last and multiform, to ultimate progressions. For the nature of being is not one, simple, and indivisible; but as in sensibles, the mighty heaven is one, yet it comprehends in itself a multitude of bodies; and the monad connectedly contains multitude, but in the multitude there is an order of progression; and of sensibles, some are first, some middle, and some last; and prior to these, in souls, from one soul a multitude of souls subsists, and of these, some are placed in an

---

[†] For διαιτης, I read διατριβης.

order nearer, but others more remote from their wholeness, and others again fill up the medium of the extremes; - in like manner, it is doubtless necessary that among perfectly true beings, such genera as are uniform and occult, should be established in the one and first cause of wholes, but that others should proceed into all multitude, and a whole number, and that others should contain the bond of these, in a middle situation. It is likewise by no means proper to harmonize the peculiarities of first natures with such as are second, nor of those that possess a subject order, with such as are more unical, but it is requisite that among these, some should have powers different from others, and that there should be an order in this progression of true beings, and an unfolding of second from first natures.

In short, being which subsists according to, or is characterized by *The One*, proceeds indeed from the unity prior to beings, but generates the whole divine genus, *viz.* the intelligible, intellectual, supermundane, and that which proceeds as far as to the mundane order. But our preceptor likewise asserts, that each of the conclusions is indicative of a divine peculiarity. And though all the conclusions harmonize to all the progressions of *the one being*, or of being characterized by *The One*, yet I am of opinion, it is by no means wonderful, that some conclusions should more accord with some hypotheses than with others. For such things as express the peculiarity of certain orders, do not necessarily belong to all the Gods; but such as belong to all, are doubtless by a much greater reason present with each. If, therefore, we ascribe to Plato, an adventitious division of the divine orders,[†] and do not clearly evince that, in other dialogues, he celebrates the progressions of the Gods from on high to the extremity of things, sometimes in fables respecting the soul, and at other times, in other theological modes, we shall absurdly attribute to him, such a division of being, and together with this, of the progression of *The One*. But if we can evince from other dialogues, that he (as will be manifest in the course of this work) has celebrated all the kingdoms of the Gods, in a certain respect, is it not impossible, that in the most mystic of all his works, he should deliver through the first hypothesis, the exempt transcendency of *The One* with respect to all the genera of beings, to being itself, to a psychical essence, to form, and to matter, but that he should make no mention of the divine progressions, and their orderly separation? For if it is proper to contemplate last things only, why do we touch on the first principle before other things? Or if we think fit to unfold the

---

[†] For πραξεων, it is necessary to read ταξεων.

multitude of the proper hypotheses, why do we pass by the genus of the Gods, and the divisions which it contains? Or if we unfold the natures subsisting between the first and last of things, why do we leave unknown the whole orders of those divine beings, which subsist between *The One*, and natures that are in any respect deified? For all these particulars evince, that the whole discourse is defective, with respect to the science of things divine.

But still farther, Socrates, in the *Philebus*, calls upon those that love the contemplation of beings, to use the dividing method, and always to explore the monads of total orders, and the duads, triads, or any other numbers proceeding from these. If this then is rightly determined, it is doubtless necessary that the *Parmenides*, which employs the whole dialectic method, and discourses about being which is characterized by *The One*, should neither speculate multitude about *The One*, nor remain in the one monad of beings, nor in short, introduce to *The One* which is above all beings, the whole multitude of first beings immediately, but should unfold, as in the first order, such beings as have an occult subsistence, and are allied to *The One*; but as in the middle rank, those genera of the Gods which subsist according to progression, and which are more divided than the extremely united, but are allotted a union more perfect, than such as have proceeded to the utmost; and should unfold as in the last rank, such as subsist according to the last division of powers, and together with these, such as have a deified essence. If, therefore, the first of the hypotheses is about *The One* which is above all multitude, it is doubtless necessary that the hypothesis which follows this, should not unfold being itself in an indefinite and indistinct manner, but should deliver all the orders of beings. For the dividing method does not admit, that we should introduce the whole of multitude at once to *The One*, as Socrates teaches us in the *Philebus*.

Besides, we may evince the truth of what we assert from the very method of the demonstrations. For the first of the conclusions become immediately manifest from the least, most simple, most known, and as it were common conceptions. But those which are next in order to these, become apparent through a greater multitude of conceptions, and such as are more various. And the last conclusions are entirely the most composite. For he always uses the first conclusions, as subservient to the demonstration of those that follow,† and presents us with an intellectual paradigm of the order observed in geometry, or other disciplines, in the connexion of these conclusions with each other. If,

---

† For εχοντων, it is necessary to read εχομενων.

therefore, discourses bring with them an image of the things of which they are interpreters, and if, as are the evolutions from demonstrations, such must the order necessarily be of the things exhibited, it appears to me to be necessary, that such things as derive their beginning from the most simple principles, must be in every respect of a more primary nature, and must be arranged as conjoined with *The One*; but that such as are always multiplied, and suspended from various demonstrations, must have proceeded farther from the subsistence[†] of *The One*.

For the demonstrations which have two conclusions, must necessarily contain the conclusions prior to themselves; but those which contain primary, spontaneous, and simple conceptions, are not necessary united with such as are more composite, which are exhibited through more abundant media, and which are farther distant from the principle of beings. It appears therefore, that some of the conclusions are indicative of more divine orders, but others, of such as are more subordinate; some, of more united, and others, of more multiplied orders; and again, some, of more uniform, and others, of more multiform progressions. For demonstrations are universally from causes, and things first. If, therefore, first are the causes of second conclusions, there is an order of causes, and things caused, in the multitude of the conclusions. For, indeed, to confound all things, and speculate them indefinitely in one, neither accords with the nature of things, nor the science of Plato.

CHAPTER XI

Again, therefore, let us discuss this affair in another way, and view with the dianoetic power, where any thing futile is delivered. For let it be said, if you please, and we will first of all allow it, that the conclusions of this second hypothesis are about true being. But as this is multitude, and not only one itself, like *The One* prior to beings; for being is that which is passive to *The One*, as the Elean guest in the *Sophista* informs us; and as it is universally acknowledged by our opponents, who establish that which is first as *The One*, but intellect, as *one many*, soul, as *one and many*, and body as *many and one*:- as therefore, this has been asserted a thousand times, I mean that in true being there is multitude together with union, whether will they say that these things harmonize with the whole of being, but not with its parts, or both with the whole and its parts? And again, we ask them, whether

---

[†] For αποστασεως, it is necessary to read υποστασεως.

they attribute all things to each part of being, or whether they ascribe different things to different parts?

If, therefore, they are of opinion, that each particular should alone harmonize with the whole of being, being will consist of non-beings, that which is moved, of things immoveable, that which abides, of things deprived of permanency, and universally, all things will consist of their opposites, and we shall no longer agree with the discourse of Parmenides, who says that the parts of *being characterized by The One*, are in a certain respect wholes, and that each of them is one and being, in a manner similar to the whole. But if we attribute all things to each part, and there is nothing which we do not make all things, how can the summit of being, and that which is most eminently one, contain a wholeness, and an incomprehensible multitude of parts? How can it at one and the same time contain the whole of number, figure, motion and permanency, and in short all forms and genera? For these differ from each other, and the hypothesis will assert things impossible. For things near to, will be similarly multiplied with things remote from *The One*, and that which is first, will not be a less multitude than that which is last; nor again, will the last of things be a less one than the first, and things in the middle will have no difference with respect to division from the extremes.

As therefore, it is not proper to ascribe all this multitude of conclusions to the whole alone, nor to consider all things in a similar manner in all the parts of being, it remains that different conclusions must harmonize with different things. It is necessary, therefore, that either the enumeration of the conclusions, should be inordinate, or ordinate. But if they say they are inordinate, they neither speak agreeably to the dialectic method, nor to the mode of demonstrations, which always generate things secondary from such as are first, nor to the science of Plato, which always accompanies the order of things. But if they say the conclusions are regular, I think it is entirely necessary, that they should either begin from things first according to nature, or from things last. But if from things last *being characterised by The One* will be the last, and that which is moved according to time, the first. This, however, is impossible. For that which participates of time, must by a much greater priority participate of first being. But that which participates of first being does not necessarily participate of time. First being, therefore is above time. If then Plato begins from first being, but ends in that which participates of time, he proceeds supernally from the first to the last parts of true being. Hence, the first conclusions are to be referred to the first orders, the middle for the same reason, to the middle orders, and the last, as is evident, to such as are last. For it is necessary, as our discourse has evinced, that different conclusions should be assigned to different things, and that a distribution of this kind should commence from such things as are highest.

But likewise, the order of the hypotheses, as it appears to me, is a sufficient argument of the truth of our assertion. For with us *The One* which is exempt from all multitude, is allotted the first order, and from this the evolution of all arguments commences. But the second order after this, is about true beings, and the unity which these participate. And the third order in regular succession, is about soul. Whether, therefore, is it about every soul or not? In answer to this, we shall observe, that our leader Syrianus has beautifully shown, that the discourse about whole souls is comprehended in the second hypothesis. If, therefore, the order of these three hypotheses proceeds according to the nature of things, it is evident that the second is produced from the first, and the last from the second. For I would ask those who are not entirely unskilled in discourses of this kind, what can be more allied to *The One*, than being characterized by *The One*, which the first of the conclusions of the second hypothesis unfolds? Or what can be more allied to soul, than that which participates of time, which subsists divisibly, and which is the last thing exhibited in this hypothesis? For the life of partial as well as of total souls is according to time. And first being is that which first participates of *The One*, and through its connexion with being, has a redundant hyparxis with respect to the imparticipable unity. But if this hypothesis is the middle, and if we aptly harmonize the highest conclusions with things highest, we should doubtless harmonize middles with middles. For this hypothesis commencing from first being, proceeds through all the genera posterior to it, till it ends in a nature participating of time.

But, farther, from the common confession of those interpreters of Plato, who were skilled in divine concerns, we can demonstrate the same things as we have above asserted. For Plotinus, in his book *On Numbers*, enquiring whether beings subsist prior to numbers, or numbers prior to beings, clearly asserts that the first being subsists prior to numbers, and that it generates the divine number. But if this is rightly determined by him, and being is generative of the first number, but number is produced by being, it is not proper to confound the order of these genera, nor to collect them into one hypostasis, nor, since Plato separately produces first being, and separately number, to refer each of the conclusions to the same order. For it is by no means lawful, that cause and the thing caused, should have either the same power, or the same order: but these are distinct from each other; and the science concerning them is likewise distinct, and neither the nature, nor the definition of them is one and the same.

But, after Plotinus, Porphyry in his treatise *On Principles*, evinces by many and beautiful arguments, that intellect is eternal, but that at the same time, it contains in itself something prior to the eternal, and through which it is conjoined with *The One*. For *The One* is above all eternity, but the eternal has a second, or rather third order in intellect. For it appears to me to be necessary that eternity should be established in the middle of that which is prior to the eternal, and the eternal. But of this hereafter. At the same time, thus much may be collected from what has been said, that intellect contains something in itself better than the eternal. Admitting this, therefore, we ask the father of this assertion, whether this something better than the eternal is not only being characterized by *The One*, but is a whole and parts, and all multitude, number and figure, that which, is moved, and that which is permanent; or whether we are to ascribe some of the conclusions to it, but not others? For it is impossible that all these can accord with a nature prior to eternity, since every intellectual motion, and likewise permanency, are established in eternity. But if we are to ascribe some of the conclusions to it, and not others, it is evident that other orders in intellect are to be investigated, and that each of the conclusions is to be referred to that order, to which it appears particulary adapted. For intellect is not one in number, and an atom, as it appeared to be to some of the ancients, but it comprehends in itself the whole progression of first being.

But the third who makes for our purpose after these, is the divine Iamblichus, who, in his treatise *Concerning the Gods*, accuses those who place the genera of being in intelligibles, because the number and variety of these is more remote from the one. But afterwards he informs us where these ought to be placed. For they are produced in the end of the intellectual order, by the Gods which there subsist. How the genera of being, however, both are, and are not in intelligibles, will be hereafter apparent. But if, according to his arrangement of the divine orders, intelligibles are exempt from the genera of being, much more are they, exempt from similitude and dissimilitude, equality and inequality. Each of the conclusions, therefore, ought not in a similar manner to be accommodated to all things, so as to refer them to the whole breadth of the intelligible, or intellectual order. Hence from what the best of the interpreters have said, when philosophizing according to their own doctrines, both the multitude of the divine orders, and of the Platonic arguments, are to be considered as proceeding according to an orderly distinction.

In addition, likewise, to what has been said, this also may be asserted, that we cannot, on any other hypothesis, obtain a rational solution of the many doubts which present themselves on this subject, but shall ignorantly ascribe what is rash and vain to this treatise of Plato. For in the first place, why are there only so many conclusions, and neither more nor less? For there are fourteen conclusions. But as there are so many, we cannot assign the reason of this, unless we distribute them in conjunction with things themselves. In the second place, neither shall we be able to find the cause of the order of the conclusions with respect to each other, and how some have a prior, and others a posterior establishment, according to the reason of science, unless the order of the conclusions proceeds in conjunction with the progression of beings. In the third place, why do some of the conclusions become known from things proximately demonstrated, but others from proceeding demonstrations? For that *The One* is a whole and contains parts, is demonstrated from being, which is characterized by *The One*; but its subsistence in itself and in another, is placed in a proximate order, after the possession of figure, but is demonstrated from whole and parts. Or why are some things often demonstrated, from two of the particulars previously evinced, but others from one of them? For we shall be ignorant of each of these, and shall neither be able scientifically to speculate their number, nor their order, nor their alliance to each other, unless following things themselves, we evince that this whole hypothesis is a dialectic arrangement, proceeding from on high through all the middle genera, as far as to the termination of first being.

Again, if we should say, that all the conclusions demonstrate syllogistically only, in what respect shall we differ from those, who assert that the whole of this discussion consists of doxastic arguments, and only regards a mere verbal contest? But if it is not only syllogistic, but likewise demonstrative, it is doubtless necessary, that the middle should be the cause of, and by nature prior to the conclusion. As, therefore, we make the conclusions of the proceeding reasons, the media of those that follow, the things which the arguments respect, must doubtless have a similar order as to being, and their progeny must be the causes of things subject, and generative of such as are secondary. But if this be admitted, how can we allow that all of them have the same peculiarity and nature? For cause, and that which is produced from cause, are separated from each other.

But this likewise will happen to those who assert that one nature is to be explored in all the arguments, that they will by no means perceive how in the three first conclusions, *The One* remains unseparated from being, but is first separated in the fourth conclusion. But in all the following conclusions, *The One* is explored considered as subsisting itself by itself. Is it not therefore necessary, that these orders must differ from each other? For that which is without separation, in consequence of having an occult and undivided subsistence, is more allied to *The One*, but that which is separated, has proceeded farther from the first principle of things.

Again, if you are willing to consider the multitude of arguments, and the extent of the hypothesis, how much it differs from that which follows it, - neither from this will it appear to you to be entirely about one and an unseparated nature. For reasonings about divine concerns, are contracted in the more principal causes, because in these the occult is more abundant than the perspicuous, and the ineffable than the unknown. But they become multiplied and evolved, by proceeding to divine orders more proximate to our nature. For such things as are more allied to that which is ineffable, unknown, and exempt in inaccessible places, are allotted an hyparxis more foreign from verbal enunciation. But such things as have proceeded farther, are both more known to us, and more apparent to the phantasy, than such as have a prior subsistence.

This, therefore, being abundantly proved, it is necessary that the second hypothesis, should unfold all the divine orders, and should proceed on high, from the most simple and unical to the whole multitude, and all the number of divine natures, in which the order of true being ends, which indeed is spread under the unities of the Gods, and at the same time is divided in conjunction with their occult and ineffable peculiarities. If, therefore, we are not deceived in admitting this, it follows, that from this hypothesis, the continuity of the divine orders, and the progression of second from first natures, is to be assumed, together with the peculiarity of all the divine genera. And indeed, what their communion is with each other, and what their distinction proceeding according to measure, likewise, the auxiliaries which may be found in other dialogues respecting the truth of real beings, or the unities which they contain, are all to be referred to this hypothesis. For, here we may contemplate the total progressions of the Gods, and their all-perfect orders, according to theological science. For as we have before shown that the whole treatise of the *Parmenides* has reference to the truth of things, and that it was not devised as a vain evolution of words, it is doubtless necessary, that the nine hypotheses which it discusses, employing the dialectic method, but speculating with divine science, should be about things and certain natures, which are either middle or last. If, therefore, Parmenides acknowledges that his whole discourse will be about *The One*, and how it subsists with respect to itself, and all other things, it is evident that the speculation of *The One*, must commence from that which is highest, but end in that which is the last of all things. For the hyparxis of *The One* proceeds from on high, as far as to the most obscure hypostasis of things.

CHAPTER XII

As the first hypothesis, however, demonstrates by negations the ineffable supereminence of the first principle of things, and evinces that he is exempt from all essence and knowledge, - it is evident that the hypothesis after this, as being proximate to it, must unfold the whole order of the Gods. For Parmenides does not alone assume the intellectual and essential peculiarity of the Gods, but likewise the divine characteristic of their hyparxis through the whole of this hypothesis. For what other *one* can that be which is participated by being, than that which is in every being divine, and through which all things are conjoined with the imparticipable one? For as bodies through their *life* are conjoined with soul, and as souls through their *intellective* part, are extended to total intellect, and the first intelligence, in like manner true beings through *The One* which they contain are reduced to an exempt union, and subsist in unproceeding union with this first cause.

But because this hypothesis commences from that which is *one being*, or *being characterized by The One*, and establishes the summit of intelligibles as the first after *The One*, but ends in an essence which participates of time, and deduces divine souls to the extremities of the divine orders, it is necessary that the third hypothesis should demonstrate by various conclusions, the whole multitude of partial souls, and the diversities which they contain. And thus far the separate and incorporeal hypostasis proceeds.

After this follows that nature which is divisible about bodies, and inseparable from matter, which the fourth hypothesis delivers supernally suspended from the Gods. And the last hypothesis is the procession of matter, whether considered as one, or as various, which the fifth hypothesis demonstrates by negations, according to its dissimilar similitude† to the first. But sometimes, indeed, the negations are privations, and sometimes the exempt causes of all the productions. And what is the most wonderful of all, the highest negations are only enunciative, but some in a supereminent manner, and others according to deficiency. But each of the negations consequent to these is affirmative; the one paradigmatically, but the other iconically, or after the manner of an image. But the middle corresponds to the order of soul, for it is composed from affirmative and negative conclusions. But it possesses negations co-ordinate to affirmations. Nor is it alone multiplied, like material natures,‡ nor does it possess an adventitious one; but *The One* which it contains, though it is still one, yet subsists in motion and multiplication, and in its progressions is, as it were, absorbed by essence. And such are the hypotheses which unfold all beings, both separable and inseparable, together with the causes of wholes, as well exempt, as subsisting in things themselves, according to the hyparxis of *The One*.

But there are four other hypotheses besides these, which by taking away *The One*, evince that all things must be entirely subverted, both beings and things in generation, and that no being can any longer have any subsistence; and this, in order that he may demonstrate *The One* to be the cause of being and preservation, that through it all things participate of the nature of being, and that each has its hyparxis suspended from *The One*. And in short, we syllogistically collect this through all beings, that if *The One* is, all things subsist as far as to the last hypostasis, and if it is not, no being has any subsistence. The One, therefore, is both the hypostatic and preservative cause of all things; which Parmenides also himself collects at the end of the dialogue. With respect, however, to the hypothesis of the *Parmenides*, its division, and the speculation of its several parts, we have sufficiently treated in our commentaries on that dialogue; so that it would be superfluous to enter into a prolix discussion of these particulars at present. But as from what has been said, it appears whence we may assume the whole of theology, and from what dialogues we may collect into one the theology distributed according to parts, we shall in the next place treat about the common dogmas of Plato, which are adapted to sacred concerns, and which extend to all the divine orders, and shall evince that each of these is defined by him according to the most perfect science. For things

---

† For ανομοιοτητα, it is necessary to read ομοιοτητα.

‡ Instead of οτε ως ολα, read ουτε ως τα ενυλα.

common are prior to such as are peculiar, and are more known according to nature.

CHAPTER XIII

In the first place, therefore, we shall assume the things which are demonstrated in the *Laws*, and contemplate how they take the lead, with respect to the truth about the Gods, and are the most ancient of all the other mystic conceptions about a divine nature. Three things, therefore, are asserted by Plato in these writings; that there are Gods; that their providence extends to all things; and that they administer all things according to justice, and suffer no perversion from worse natures.

That these then obtain the first rank[†] among all theological dogmas, is perfectly evident. For what can be of a more leading nature, than the hyparxis of the Gods, or than boniform providence, or immutable and undeviating power? Through which they produce secondary natures uniformly, preserve themselves in an undefiled manner, and convert them to themselves. But the Gods indeed govern other things, but suffer nothing from subordinate natures, nor are changed with the variety of the things to which their providence extends. We shall learn, however, how these things are defined according to nature, if we endeavour to embrace by a reasoning process the scientific method of Plato about each of them; and prior to these, survey by what irrefragable arguments he proves that there are Gods; and thus afterwards consider such problems as are conjoined with this dogma.

Of all beings, therefore, it is necessary that some should move only, but that others should be moved only, and that the natures situated between these, should both move and be moved. And with respect to these last it is necessary, either that they should move others being themselves moved by others, or that they should be self-motive. These four hypostases likewise, are necessarily placed in an orderly series, one after another; that which is moved only and suffers, depending on other primary causes; that which moves others, and is at the same time moved, being prior to this; that which is self-motive, and which is beyond that which both moves and is moved, beginning from itself, and through its own motion imparting the representation of being moved, to other things; and that which is immoveable, preceding whatever participates either producing or passive motion. For every thing self-motive, in consequence of possessing its perfection in a transition

---

† For αρχη δευτερα, it is necessary to read αρχειοτερα.

and interval of life, depends on another more ancient cause, which always subsists according to sameness, and in a similar manner, and whose life is not in time, but in eternity. For time is an image of eternity.

If, therefore, all things which are moved by themselves, are moved according to time, but the eternal form of motion is above that which is carried in time, the self-motive nature will be second in order, and not the first of beings. But that which moves others, and is moved by others, must necessarily be suspended from a self-motive nature: and not this alone, but likewise every alter-motive fabrication, as the Athenian guest demonstrates. For if all things, says he, should stand still, unless self-motive natures had a subsistence among things, there would be no such thing as that which is first moved. For that which is immoveable, is by no means naturally adapted to be moved, nor will there then be that which is first moved; but the alter-motive nature is indigent of another moving power. The self-motive nature, therefore, alone, as beginning from its own energy, will move both itself and others in a secondary manner. For a thing of this kind imparts the power of being moved to alter-motive natures, in the same manner as an immoveable nature imparts a motive power to all beings. In the third place, that which is moved only, must first of all be suspended from things moved by another, but moving others. For it is necessary, both that other things, and the series of things moved, which extends in an orderly manner from on high to the last of things, should be filled with their proper media.

All bodies, therefore, belong to those things which are naturally moved only, and are passive. For they are productive of nothing, on account of possessing an hypostasis endued with interval, and participating of magnitude and bulk; since every thing productive and motive of others, naturally produces and moves, by employing an incorporeal power.

But of incorporeal natures, some are divisible about bodies, but others are exempt from such a division about the last of things. Those incorporeals, therefore, which are divisible about the bulks of bodies, whether they subsist in qualities, or in material forms, belong to the number of things moved by another, but at the same time moving others. For these, because they possess an incorporeal allotment, participate of a motive power; but because they are divided about bodies, are deprived of the power of verging to themselves, are divided together with their subjects, and are full of sluggishness from these, they are indigent of a motive nature which is not borne along in a foreign seat, but possesses an hypostasis in itself. Where, therefore, shall we obtain that which moves itself? For things extended into natures possessing bulk and interval, or which are divided in these, and subsist inseparably about them, must necessarily either be moved only, or be motive through others. But it is necessary, as we have before observed, that a self-motive nature should be prior to these, which is perfectly established in itself, and not in others, and which fixes its energies in itself, and not in things different from itself. There is, therefore, another certain nature exempt from bodies, both in the heavens and in these very mutable elements, from which bodies primarily derive the power of being moved. Hence, if it be requisite to discover what such an essence as this is, (rightly following Socrates, and considering what the end of things is,) which by being present to alter-motive natures, imparts to them a representation of self-motion, to which of the above mentioned natures shall we ascribe the power of things being moved from themselves? For all inanimate natures are alone alter-motive, and whatever they suffer, they are adapted to suffer, through a certain power externally moving and compelling. It remains, therefore, that animated natures must possess this representation, and that they are self-motive in a secondary degree, but that the soul which is in them, primarily moves itself, and is moved by itself, and that through a power derived from itself as it imparts life to bodies, so likewise it extends to them from itself a representation of being moved by themselves.

If, therefore, the self-motive essence is more ancient than alter-motive natures, but soul is primarily self-motive, from which the image of self-motion is imparted to bodies, soul will be beyond bodies, and the motion of every body, will be the progeny of soul, and of the motion it contains. Hence it is necessary that the whole heaven and all the bodies it contains possessing various motions, and being moved with these different motions, according to nature (for a circulation is natural to every body of this kind) should have ruling souls, which are essentially more ancient than bodies, and which are moved in themselves, and supernally illuminate these with the power of being moved. It is necessary, therefore, that these souls which dispose in an orderly manner the whole world and the parts it contains, and who impart to every thing corporeal which is of itself destitute of life, the power of being moved, inspiring it, for this purpose, with the cause of motion, should either move all things conformably to reason, or after a contrary manner, which it is not lawful to assert. But if indeed, this world and every thing in it which is disposed in an orderly manner, and is moved equally and perpetually according to nature, as is demonstrated, partly in the mathematical disciplines, and partly in physical discussions, is suspended from an irrational soul, which moving itself moves also other things, neither the order of the periods, nor the motion which is bounded by one reason, nor the position of bodies, nor any other or those things which are generated according to nature, will have a stable cause, and which is able to distribute every thing in an orderly manner, and according to an invariable sameness of subsistence. For every thing irrational is naturally adapted to be adorned by something different from itself, and is indefinite and unadorned in its own nature. But to commit all heaven to a thing of this kind, and a circulation revolving according to reason, and with an invariable sameness, is, by no means adapted, either to the nature of things, or to our undisciplined conceptions. If however, an intellectual soul, and which employs reason, governs all things, and if every thing which is moved with a perpetual lation, is governed by a soul of this kind, and there is no one of the wholes in the universe destitute of soul (for no body is honourable if deprived of such a power as this, as Theophrastus somewhere says) if this be the case, whether does it possess this intellectual, perfect, and beneficent power, according to participation, or according to essence? For if, according to essence, it is necessary that every soul should be of this kind, since each according to its own nature is self-motive. But if, according to participation, there will be another intellect subsisting in energy, more ancient than soul, which essentially possesses intellection, and by its very being pre-assumes in itself the uniform knowledge of wholes; since it is also necessary that the soul which is essentialized according to reason, should possess that which pertains to intellect through participation, and that the intellectual nature should be twofold; the one subsisting primarily in a divine intellect itself; but the other, which proceeds from this, subsisting secondarily in soul. To which, you may add, if you please, the presence of intellectual illumination in body. For whence is the whole of this heaven either spherical or moved in a circle, and whence does it revolve with a sameness of circulation according to one definite order? For how could it always be allotted the same idea and power immutably according to nature, if it did not participate of specific formation according to intellect? For, soul, indeed, is the supplier of motion; but the cause of a firm establishment, and that which reduces the unstable mutation of things that are moved, into sameness, and also a life which is bounded by one reason, and a circulation which subsists with invariable sameness, will evidently be superior to soul.

Body, therefore, and the whole of this sensible nature belong to things which are alter-motive. But soul is self-motive, binding in itself all corporeal motions; and prior to this is intellect which is immoveable. Let no one, however, suppose that I assert this immobility of intellect to resemble that which is sluggish, destitute of life,[†] and without respiration, but that it is the leading cause of all motion, and the fountain, if you are willing so to denominate it, of all life, both of that which is converted to itself, and of that which has its hypostasis in other things. Through these causes also, the world is denominated by Timæus, an animal endued with soul and intellect; being called by him an animal according to its own nature, and the life pervading to it from soul, and which is distributed about it, but animated or endued with soul, according to the presence of a divine soul in it, and endued with intellect, according to intellectual domination. For the supply of life, the government of soul, and the participation of intellect connect and contain the whole of heaven.

If, however, this intellect is essentially intellect, since Timæus indicating that the essence of intellect is the same with its intellection, denominates it divine; for he says, that soul receiving a divine intellect led an upright and wise life; if, therefore, this be the case, it is necessary that the whole world should be suspended from its divinity, and that motion indeed should be present to this universe from soul, but that its perpetual permanency and sameness of subsistence should be derived from intellect, and that its one union, the conspiration in it and sympathy, and its all-perfect measure should originate from that unity,[‡] from which intellect is uniform, soul is one,[§] every being is whole and perfect according to its own nature, and every thing secondary together with perfection in its own proper nature, participates of another more excellent peculiarity, from an order which is always established above it. For that which is corporeal being alter-motive, derives from soul the representation of self-motive power, and is through it an animal. But soul being self-motive participates of a life according to intellect, and energizing according to time, possesses a never-ceasing energy, and an ever-vigilant life from its proximity to intellect. And intellect possessing its life in eternity, always subsisting essentially in energy,[*] and fixing all

---

[†] For αξων read αζων.

[‡] For και της εναδος, read, και απο της εναδος.

[§] For και ο νου, ενοειδη μια και η ψυχη, read, και ο νους ενοειδης, και η ψυχη μια.

[*] For αιων ενεργεια, read, αει ων ενεργεια.

its stable intellection at once in intellect, is entirely deific through the cause prior to itself. For it has twofold energies as Plotinus says, some as intellect, but others as being inebriated with nectar. And elsewhere he observes, that this intellect, by that which is prior to itself and is not intellect, is a god; in the same manner as soul, by its summit which is above soul, is intellect; and as body, by the power which is prior to body, is soul.

All things therefore, as we have said, are suspended from *The One* through intellect and soul as media. And intellect indeed has the form of unity; but soul has the form of intellect; and the body of the world is vital. But every thing is conjoined with that which is prior to itself. And of natures posterior to these, one in a more proximate, but the other in a more remote degree, enjoys that which is divine. And divinity, indeed, is prior to intellect, being primarily carried in an intellectual nature; but intellect is most divine, as being deified prior to other things; and soul is divine, so far as it requires an intellectual medium. But the body which participates of a soul of this kind, so far as body indeed, is also itself divine; for the illumination of divine[†] light pervades supernally as far as to the last dependencies; yet it is not simply divine; but soul, by looking to intellect, and living from itself, is primarily divine.

My reasoning is also the same about each of the whole spheres, and about the bodies they contain. For all these imitate the whole heaven, since these likewise have a perpetual allotment; and with respect to the sublunary elements, they have not entirely an essential mutation, but they abide in the universe according to their wholenesses, and contain in themselves partial animals. For every wholeness has posterior to itself more partial essences. As, therefore, in the heavens, the number of the stars proceeds together with the whole spheres, and as in the earth the multitude of partial terrestrial animals subsists together with their wholeness, thus also it appears to me to be necessary that in the wholes which have an intermediate subsistence, each element should be filled up with appropriate numbers. For how in the extremes can wholes which subsist prior to parts, be arranged together with parts, unless there is the same analogy of them in the intermediate natures?

But if each of the spheres is an animal, and is always established after the same manner, and gives completion to the universe, as possessing life indeed, it will always primarily participate of soul, but as preserving its own order immutable in the world, it will be comprehended by

---

[†] The sense requires that θειον should be here supplied.

intellect, and as one and a whole, and the leader and ruler of its proper parts, it will be illuminated by divine union. Not only the universe, therefore, but each also of its perpetual parts is animated and endued with intellect, and as much as possible is similar to the universe.† For each of these parts is a universe with respect to its kindred multitude. In short, there is indeed one corporeal-formed wholeness of the universe, but there are many others under this, depending on this one; there is one soul of the universe, and after this, other souls, together with this disposing in an orderly manner the whole parts of the universe with undefiled purity; one intellect, and an intellectual number under this, participated by these souls; and one god who connectedly contains at once all mundane and supermundane‡ natures, and a multitude of other gods, who distribute intellectual essences, and the souls suspended from these, and all the parts of the world. For it is not to be supposed that each of the productions of nature is generative of things similar to itself, but that wholes and the first of mundane beings should not in a much greater degree extend in themselves the paradigm of a generation of this kind. For the similar is more allied, and more naturally adapted to the reason of cause than the dissimilar, in the same manner as the same than the different, and bound than the infinite. These things, however, we shall accurately survey in what follows. But we shall now direct our attention to the second of the things demonstrated in the *Laws*, *viz.* that the Gods providentially attend at once to wholes and parts, and shall summarily discuss the irreprehensible conception of Plato about the providence of the Gods.

CHAPTER XIV

From what has been said, therefore, it is evident to every one, that the Gods being the causes of all motion, some of them are essential and vivific, according to a self-motive, self-vital, and self-energetic power. But others of them are intellectual, and excite by their very being all secondary§ natures to the perfection of life, according to the fountain and principle of all second and third progressions of motion. And

---

† Instead of ομοιον μη κατα δυναμιν, it is necessary to read και κατα δυναμιν τω παντι ομοιον, as both the sense of the whole sentence and the version of Portus require.

‡ It seems requisite to supply here the word υπερκοσμιων as in the translation.

§ For δευτερον read δευτερα.

others are unical, or characterized by unity, deifying by participation all the whole genera of themselves, according to a primary, all-perfect, and unknown power of energy, and who are the leaders of one kind of motion, but are not the principle of another. But again others supply to secondary natures motion according to place or quality, but are essentially the causes of motion to themselves. For every thing which is the cause of essence to other things is much prior to this the cause to itself of its own proper energies and perfection. Farther still, that which is self-motive is again the principle of motion, and being and life are imparted by soul to every thing in the world, and not local motion only and the other kinds of motion, but the progression into being is from soul, and by a much greater priority from an intellectual essence, which binds to itself the life of self-motive natures and precedes according to cause all temporaral energy. And in a still greater degree do motion, being, and life proceed from a unical hyparxis, which connectedly contains intellect and soul, is the source of total good, and proceeds as far as to the last of things. For of life indeed, not all the parts of the world are capable of participating, nor of intellect and a gnostic power; but of *The One* all things participate, as far as to matter itself, both wholes and parts, things which subsist according to nature, and the contraries to these; and there is not any thing which is deprived of a cause of this kind, nor can any thing ever participate of being, if it is deprived of *The One*. If, therefore, the Gods produce all things, and contain all things, in the unknown comprehensions of themselves, how is it possible there should not be a providence of all things in these comprehensions, pervading supernally as far as to the most partial natures? For it is every where fit that offspring should enjoy the providential care of their causes. But all alter-motive are the progeny of self-motive natures. And things which subsist in time, either in the whole of time, or in a part of it, are the effects of eternal natures; because that which always is, is the cause of that which sometimes exists. And divine and unical genera, as they give subsistence to all multiplied natures, precede them in existence. In short, there is no essence, or multitude of powers, which is not allotted its generation from *The One*. It is necessary, therefore, that all these should be partakers of the providence of preceding causes, being vivified indeed from the psychical gods, and circulating according to temporal periods; and participating of sameness and at the same time a stable condition of forms from the intellectual gods;[†] but receiving into themselves the

---

[†] It is necessary here to supply the words, εκ των νοερων θεων.

presence of union, of measure, and of the distribution of good from the first Gods. It is necessary, therefore, either that the Gods should know that a providential care of their own offspring is natural to them, and should not only give subsistence to secondary beings, and supply them with life, essence and union, but also previously comprehend in themselves the primary cause of the goods they contain, or, which it is not lawful to assert, that being Gods, they are ignorant of what is proper and fit.

For what ignorance can there be of beautiful things, with those who are the causes of beauty, or of things good, with those who are allotted an hyparxis defined by the nature of *The Good*? But if they are ignorant, neither do souls govern the universe according to intellect, nor are intellects carried in souls as in a vehicle, nor prior to these do the unities of the Gods contractedly comprehend in themselves all knowledge, which we have acknowledged they do through the former demonstrations. If, therefore, they are not deprived of knowledge, being the fathers, leaders and governors of every thing in the world, and[†] to them as being such a providential care of the things governed by, and following them, and generated by them, pertains, whether shall we say that they knowing the law which is according to nature, accomplish this law, or that through imbecility they are deprived of a providential attention to their possessions or progeny, for it is of no consequence as to the present discussion which of these two appellations you are willing to adopt? For if through want of power they neglect the superintendence of wholes, what is the cause of this want of power? For they do not move things externally, nor are other things indeed the causes of essence, but they assume the government of the things they have produced, but they rule over all things as if from the stern of a ship, themselves supplying being, themselves containing the measures of life, and themselves distributing to things their respective energies.

Whether also, are they unable to provide at once for all things, or they do not leave each of the parts destitute of their providential care? And if they are not curators of every thing in the world, whether do they providentially superintend greater things, but neglect such as are less? Or do they pay attention to the less, but neglect to take care of the greater? For if we deprive them of a providential attention to all things similarly, through the want of power, how, while we attribute to them a greater thing, *viz.* the production of all things, can we refuse to grant that which is naturally consequent to this, a providential attention to

---

[†] καɩ is omitted in the original.

their productions? For it is the province of the power which produces a greater thing, to dispose in a becoming manner that which is less. But if they are curators of less things, and neglect such as are greater, how can this mode of providence be right? For that which is more allied, and more similar to any thing, is more appropriately and fitly disposed by nature to the participation of the good which that thing confers on it. If, however, the Gods think that the first of mundane natures deserve their providential care, and that perfection of which they are the sources, but are unable to extend their regard to the last of things, what is it which can restrain the presence of the Gods from pervading all things? What is it which can impede their unenvying and exuberant energy? How can those who are capable of effecting greater things, be unable to govern such as are less? Or how can those who produce the essence even of the smallest things, not be the lords of the perfection of them, through a privation of power? For all these things are hostile to our natural conceptions. It remains, therefore, that the Gods must know what is fit and appropriate, and that they must possess a power adapted to the perfection of their own nature, and to the government of the whole of things. But if they know that which is according to nature, and this to those who are the generating causes of all things is to take care of all things, and an exuberance of power, - if, this be the case, they are not deprived of a providential attention of this kind. Whether, also, together with what has been said, is there a will of providence in them? Or is this alone wanting both to their knowledge and power? And on this account are things deprived† of their providential care? For if indeed knowing what is fit for themselves, and being able to accomplish what they know, they are unwilling to provide for their own offspring, they will be indigent of goodness, their unenvying exuberance will perish, and we shall do nothing else than abolish the hyparxis according to which they are essentialized. For the very being of the Gods is defined by the good, and in this they have their subsistence. But to provide for things of a subject nature, is to confer on them a certain good. How, therefore, can we deprive the Gods of providence, without at the same time depriving them of goodness? And how if we subvert their goodness is it possible, that we should not also ignorantly subvert their hyparxis which we established by the former demonstrations? Hence it is necessary to admit as a thing consequent to the very being of the Gods that they are good according to every virtue. And again, it is consequent to this that they do not

---

† For απηωρηνται it is requisite to read, παρηρηται.

withdraw themselves from a providential attention to secondary natures, either through indolence, or imbecility, or ignorance. But to this I think it is also consequent that there is with them the most excellent knowledge, unpolluted power, and unenvying and exuberant will. From which it appears that they provide for the whole of things, and omit nothing which is requisite to the supply of good.

Let, however, no one think that the Gods extend such a providence about secondary things, as is either of a busy or laborious nature, or that this is the case with their exempt transcendency, which is established remote from mortal difficulty. For their blessedness is not willing to be defiled with the difficulty of administration, since even the life of good men is accompanied with facility, and is void of molestation and pain. But all labours and molestation arise from the impediments of matter. If, however, it be requisite to define the mode of the providence of the Gods, it must be admitted that it is spontaneous, unpolluted, immaterial, and ineffable. For the Gods do not govern all things either by investigating what is fit, or exploring the good of every thing by ambiguous reasonings, or by looking externally, and following their effects as men do in the providence which they exert on their own affairs; but pre-assuming in themselves the measures of the whole of things, and producing the essence of every thing from themselves, and also looking to themselves, they lead and perfect all things in a silent path, by their very being, and fill them with good. Neither, likewise, do they produce in a manner similar to nature, energizing only by their very being, unaccompanied with deliberate choice, nor energizing in a manner similar to partial souls in conjunction with will, are they deprived of production according to essence; but they contract both these into one union, and they will indeed such things as they are able to effect by their very being, but by their very essence being capable of and producing all things, they contain the cause of production in their unenvying and exuberant will. By what busy energy, therefore, with what difficulty, or with the punishment of what Ixion, is the providence either of whole souls, or of intellectual essences, or of the Gods themselves accomplished, unless it should be said, that to impart good in any respect is laborious to the Gods? But that which is according to nature is not laborious to any thing. For neither is it laborious to fire to impart heat, nor to snow to refrigerate, nor in short to bodies to energize according to their own proper powers. And prior to bodies, neither is it laborious to natures to nourish, or generate, or increase. For these are the works of natures. Nor again, prior to these, is it laborious to souls. For these indeed produce many energies from deliberate choice, many from their very being, and are the causes of many motions by alone being present. So that if indeed the communication of good is according to nature to the Gods, providence also is according to nature. And these things we must say are accomplished by the Gods with facility, and by their very being alone. But if these things are not according to nature, neither will the Gods be naturally good. For the good is the supplier of good; just as life is the source of another life, and intellect is the source of intellectual illumination. And every thing which has a primary subsistence in each nature is generative of that which has a secondary subsistence.

That however, which is especially the illustrious prerogative of the Platonic theology, I should say is this, that according to it, neither is the exempt essence of the Gods converted to secondary natures, through a providential care for things subordinate, nor is their providential presence with all things diminished through their transcending the whole of things with undefiled purity, but at the same time it assigns to them a separate subsistence, and the being unmingled with every subordinate nature, and also the being extended to all things, and the taking care of and adorning their own progeny. For the manner in which they pervade through all things is not corporeal, as that of light is through the air, nor is it divisible about bodies, in the same manner as in nature, nor converted to subordinate natures, in the same manner as that of a partial soul, but it is separate from body, and without conversion to it, is immaterial, unmingled, unrestrained, uniform, primary and exempt. In short, such a mode of the providence of the Gods as this, must at present be conceived. For it is evident that it will be appropriate according to each order of the Gods. For soul indeed, is said to provide for secondary natures in one way, and intellect in another. But the providence of divinity who is prior to intellect is exerted according to a transcendency both of intellect and soul. And of the Gods themselves, the providence of the sublunary is different from that of the celestial divinities. Of the Gods also who are beyond the world, there are many orders, and the mode of providence is different according to each.

CHAPTER XV

The third problem after these we shall connect with the former, and survey how we are to assume the unpervertible in the Gods, who perform all things according to justice, and who do not in the smallest degree subvert its boundary, or its undeviating rectitude, in their providential attention to all other things, and in the mutations of human affairs. I think therefore, that this is apparent to every one, that every where that which governs according to nature, and pays all possible attention to the felicity of the governed, after this manner becomes the leader of that which it governs, and directs it to that which is best. For neither has the pilot who rules over the sailors and the ship any other precedaneous end than the safety of those that sail in the ship, and of the ship itself, nor does the physician who is the curator of the diseased, endeavour to do all things for the sake of any thing else than the health of the subjects of his care, whether it be requisite to cut them, or administer to them a purgative medicine. Nor would the general of an army or a guardian say that they look to any other end, than the one to the liberty of those that are guarded, and the other to the liberty of the soldiers. Nor will any other to whom it belongs to be the leader or curator of certain persons, endeavour to subvert the good of those that follow him, which it is his business to procure, and with a view to which he disposes in a becoming manner every thing belonging to those whom he governs. If therefore we grant that the Gods are the leaders of the whole of things, and that their providence extends to all things, since they are good, and possess every virtue, how is it possible they should neglect the felicity of the objects of their providential care? Or how can they be inferior to other leaders in the providence of subordinate natures? Since the Gods indeed always look to that which is better, and establish this as the end of all their government, but other leaders overlook the good of men, and embrace vice rather than virtue, in consequence of being perverted by the gifts of the depraved.

And universally, whether you are willing to call the Gods leaders, or rulers, or guardians, or fathers, a divine nature will appear to be in want of no one of such names. For all things that are venerable and honourable subsist in them primarily. And on this account indeed, here also some things are naturally more venerable and honourable than others, because they exhibit an ultimate resemblance of the Gods. But what occasion is there to speak further on this subject? For I think that we hear from those who are wise in divine concerns paternal, guardian, ruling and pæonian powers celebrated. How is it possible therefore that the images of the Gods which subsist according to nature, regarding the end which is adapted to them, should providentially attend to the order of the things which they govern, but that the Gods themselves with whom there is the whole of good, true and real virtue, and a blameless life, should not direct their government to the virtue and vice of men? And how can it be admitted, on this supposition, that they exhibit virtue victorious in the universe, and vice vanquished? Will they not also thus corrupt the measures of justice by the worship paid to them by the depraved, subvert the boundary of undeviating science, and cause the gifts of vice to appear more honourable than the pursuits of virtue? For this mode of providence is neither advantageous to these leaders, nor to those that follow them. For to those who have become wicked, there will be no liberation from guilt, since they will always endeavour to anticipate justice, and pervert the measures of desert. But it will be necessary, which it is not lawful to assert, that the Gods should regard as their final end the vice of the subjects of their providence, neglect their true salvation, and consequently be alone the causes of adumbrant good. This universe also and the whole world will be filled with disorder and incurable perturbation, depravity remaining in it, and being replete with that discord which exists in badly governed cities. Though is it not perfectly impossible that parts should be governed according to nature in a greater degree than wholes, human than divine concerns, and images than primary causes?

Hence if men properly attend to the welfare of men in governing them, honouring some, but disgracing others, and every where giving a proper direction to the works of vice by the measure of virtue, it is much more necessary that the Gods should be the immutable governors of the whole of things. For men are allotted this virtue through similitude to the Gods. But if we acknowledge that men who corrupt the safety and well-being of those whom they govern, imitate in a greater degree the providence of the Gods, we shall ignorantly at one and the same time entirely subvert the truth concerning the Gods, and the transcendency of virtue. For this I think is evident to every one, that what is more similar to the Gods is more happy than those things that are deprived of them[†] through dissimilitude and diversity. So that if among men indeed, the uncorrupted and undeviating form of providence is honourable, it must undoubtedly be in a much greater degree honourable with the Gods. But if with them, mortal gifts are more venerable than the divine measures of justice, with men also earth-

---

[†] For αυτου it is necessary to read αυτων.

born gifts will be more honourable than Olympian goods, and the blandishments of vice than the works of virtue. With a view therefore to the most perfect felicity, Plato in the *Laws* delivers to us through these demonstrations, the hyparxis of the Gods, their providential care extending to all things, and their immutable energy; which things, indeed, are common to all the Gods, but are most principal and first according to nature in the doctrine pertaining to them. For this triad appears to pervade as far as to the most partial natures in the divine orders, originating supernally from the occult genera of Gods. For a uniform hyparxis, a power which providentially takes care of all secondary natures, and an undeviating and immutable intellect, are in all the Gods that are prior to and in the world.

CHAPTER XVI

Again, from another principle we may be able to apprehend the theological demonstrations in the *Republic*. For these are common to all the divine orders, similarly extend to all the discussion about the Gods, and unfold to us truth in uninterrupted connexion with what has been before said. In the second book of the *Republic* therefore, Socrates describes certain theological types for mythological poets, and exhorts his pupils to purify themselves from those tragic disciplines, which some do not refuse to introduce to a divine nature, concealing in these as in veils the arcane mysteries concerning the Gods. Socrates therefore, as I have said, narrating the types and laws of divine fables, which afford this apparent meaning, and the inward concealed scope, which regards as its end the beautiful and the natural in the fictions about the Gods, - in the first place indeed, thinks fit to evince, according to our unperverted conception about the Gods and their goodness, that they are the suppliers of all good, but the causes of no evil to any being at any time. In the second place, he says that they are essentially immutable, and that they neither have various forms, deceiving and fascinating, nor are the authors of the greatest evil lying, in deeds or in words, or of error and folly. These therefore being two laws, the former has two conclusions, *viz*. that the Gods are not the causes of evils, and that they are the causes of all good. The second law also in a similar manner has two other conclusions; and these are, that every divine nature is immutable, and is established pure from falsehood and artificial variety. All the things demonstrated therefore, depend on these three common conceptions about a divine nature, *viz*. on the conceptions about its goodness, immutability and truth. For the first and ineffable fountain of good is with the Gods; together with eternity, which is the cause of a power that has an invariable sameness of subsistence; and the first intellect which is beings themselves, and the truth which is in real beings.

CHAPTER XVII

That therefore, which has the hyparxis of itself, and the whole of its essence defined in the good, and which by its very being produces all things, must necessarily be productive of every good, but of no evil. For if there was any thing primarily good, which is not God, perhaps some one might say that divinity is indeed a cause of good, but that he does not impart to beings every good. If, however, not only every God is good, but that which is primarily boniform and beneficent is God, (for that which is primarily good will not be the second after the Gods, because every where, things which have a secondary subsistence, receive the peculiarity of their hyparxis from those that subsist primarily) - this being the case, it is perfectly necessary that divinity should be the cause of good, and of all such goods as proceed into secondary descents, as far as to the last of things. For as the power which is the cause of life, gives subsistence to all life, as the power which is the cause of knowledge, produces all knowledge, as the power which is the cause of beauty, produces every thing beautiful, as well the beauty which is in words, as that which is in the phænomena, and thus every primary cause produces all similars from itself and binds to itself the one hypostasis of things which subsist according to one form, - after the same manner I think the first and most principal good, and uniform hyparxis, establishes in and about itself, the causes and comprehensions of all goods at once. Nor is there any thing good which does not possess this power from it, nor beneficent which being converted to it, does not participate of this cause. For all goods are from thence produced, perfected and preserved; and the one series and order of universal good, depends on that fountain. Through the same cause of hyparxis therefore, the Gods are the suppliers of all good, and of no evil. For that which is primarily good, gives subsistence to every good from itself, and is not the cause of an allotment contrary to itself; since that which is productive of life, is not the cause of the privation of life, and that which is the source of beauty is exempt from the nature of that which is void of beauty and is deformed, and from the causes of this. Hence, of that which primarily constitutes good, it is not lawful to assert that it is the cause of contrary progeny; but the nature of goods proceeds from thence undefiled, unmingled and uniform.

And the divine cause indeed of goods is established eternally in itself, extending to all secondary natures, an unenvying and exuberant participation of good. Of its participants, however, some preserve the participation with incorruptible purity, receiving their proper good in undefiled bosoms, and thus through an abundance of power possess inevitably an allotment of goods adapted to them. But those natures which are arranged in the last of the whole of things, entirely indeed enjoy according to their nature the goodness of the Gods; for it is not possible that things perfectly destitute of good should either have a being, or subsist at first; but receiving an efflux of this kind, they neither preserve the gift which pervades to them, pure and unmingled, nor do they retain their proper good stably, and with invariable sameness, but becoming imbecil, partial and material, and filled with the privation of vitality of their subject, they exhibit to order indeed, the privation of order, to reason irrationality, and to virtue, the contrary to it, vice. And with respect indeed to the natures which rank as wholes,[†] each of these is exempt from a perversion of this kind, things more perfect in them always having dominion according to nature. But partial natures through a diminution of power always diverging[‡] into multitude, division and interval, obscure indeed the participation of good, but substitute the contrary in the mixture with good, and which is vanquished by the combination. For neither here is it lawful for evil to subsist unmingled, and perfectly destitute of good; but though some particular thing may be evil to a part, yet it is entirely good to the whole and to the universe. For the universe is always happy, and always consists of perfect parts, and which subsist according to nature. But that which is preternatural is always evil to partial natures, and deformity, privation of symmetry, perversion, and a resemblance of subsistence are in these. For its proper perfection, but to the universe it is incorruptible and indestructible.

And every thing which is deprived of good, so far indeed as pertains to itself, and its own subsistence, is deprived of it through imbecility of nature; but it is good to the whole, and so far as it is a part of the universe. For it is not possible that either a privation of life, or deformity and immoderation, or in short privation can be inserted in the

---

† For αλλων it is necessary to read, ολων.

‡ For εμβαινοντα read εκβαινοντα.

universe; but its whole number is always perfect, being held together by the goodness of wholes. And life is every where present, together with existence, and the being perfect, so far as each thing gives completion to the whole. Divinity therefore, as we have said, is the cause[†] of good; but the shadowy subsistence of evil does not subsist from power, but from the imbecility of the natures which receive the illuminations of the Gods. Nor is evil in wholes, but in partial natures, nor yet in all these. For the first of partial natures and partial intellectual genera are eternally boniform. But the media among these, and which energize according to time, connecting the participation of the good with temporal mutation and motion, are incapable of preserving the gift of the Gods immoveable, uniform and simple; by their variety obscuring[‡] the simplicity of this gift, by their multiform its uniform nature, and by their commixture its purity and incorruptibility. For they do not consist of incorruptible first genera, nor have they a simple essence, nor uniform powers, but such as are composed of the contraries to these, as Socrates somewhere says in the *Phædrus*. And the last of partial natures and which are also material, in a much greater degree pervert their proper good. For they are mingled with a privation of life, and have a subsistence resembling that of an image, since it is replete with much of non-entity, consists of things hostile to each other, and of circumstances which are mutable and dispersed through the whole of time, so that they never cease to evince in every thing that they are given up to corruption, privation of symmetry, deformity, and all-various mutations, being not only extended in their energies, like the natures prior to them, but being replete both in their powers and energies with that which is preternatural, and with material imbecility. For things which become situated in a foreign place, by co-introducing whole together with form, rule over the subject nature; but again receding to that which is partial, from their proper wholeness, and participating of partibility, imbecility, war and the division which is the source of generation, they are necessarily all-variously changed. Neither, therefore, is every being perfectly good; for there would not be the corruption and generation of bodies, nor the purification and punishment of souls. Nor is there any evil in wholes: for the world would not be a blessed god, if the most principal parts of which it consists were imperfect. Nor are the Gods the causes of evils, in the same manner as they are of goods; but evil

---

[†] It is necessary here to supply the word $αιτιον$.

[‡] For $παρασκευαζοντα$ it is requisite to read $περισκιαζοντα$.

originates from the imbecility of the recipients of good, and a subsistence in the last of things. Nor is the evil which has a shadowy subsistence in partial natures unmingled with good. But this participates of it in a certain respect, by its very existence being detained by good. Nor in short, is it possible for evil which is perfectly destitute of all good to have a subsistence. For evil itself is even beyond that which in no respect whatever has an existence, just as the good itself is beyond that which is perfectly being. Nor is the evil which is in partial natures left in a disordered state, but even this is made subservient to good purposes by the Gods, and on this account justice purifies souls from depravity. But another order of gods purifies from the depravity which is in bodies. All things however are converted as much as possible to the goodness of the Gods. And wholes indeed remain in their proper boundaries, and also the perfect and beneficent genera of beings. But more partial and imperfect natures are adorned and arranged in a becoming manner, become subservient to the completion of wholes, are called upward to the beautiful, are changed, and in every way enjoy the participation of the good, so far as this can be accomplished by them.

For there cannot be a greater good to each of these, than what the Gods impart according to measures to their progeny: But all things, each separately, and all in common, receive such a portion of good, as it is possible for them to participate. But if some things are filled with greater, and others with less goods, the power of the recipients, and the measures of the distribution must be assigned as the cause of this. For different things are adapted to different beings according to their nature. But the Gods always extend good, in the same manner as the sun always emits light. For a different thing receives this light differently according to its order, and receives the greatest portion of light it is capable of receiving. For all things are led according to justice, and good is not absent from any thing, but is present to every thing, according to an appropriate boundary of participation. And as the Athenian guest says, all things are in a good condition, and are arranged by the Gods. Let no one therefore say, that there are precedaneous productive principles of evil in nature, or intellectual paradigms of evils, in the same manner as there are of goods, or that there is a malefic soul, or an evil-producing cause in the Gods, nor let him introduce sedition and eternal war against the first good. For all these are foreign from the science of Plato, and being more remote from the truth wander into barbaric folly, and gigantic mythology. Nor if certain persons speaking obscurely in arcane narrations, devise things of this kind, shall we make any alteration in the apparent apparatus of what they indicate. But the truth indeed of those things is to be investigated, and in the mean time, the science of Plato must be genuinely received in the pure bosoms of the soul, and must be preserved undefiled and unmingled with contrary opinions.

CHAPTER XVIII

In the next place, let us survey the immutability and simplicity of the Gods, what the nature of each of them is, and how both these appear to be adapted to the hyparxis of the Gods, according to the narration of Plato. The Gods, therefore, are exempt from the whole of things. But filling these, as we have said, with good, they are themselves perfectly good; each of them according to his proper order possesses that which is most excellent; and the whole genus of the Gods is at once allotted predominance according to an exuberance of good. But here again, we must oppose those who interpret in a divisible manner that which is most excellent in the Gods, and who say, that if the first cause is most excellent, that which is posterior to the first is not so. For it is necessary, say they, that what is produced should be inferior to that by which it is produced. And this indeed is rightly asserted by them. For it is necessary in the Gods, to preserve the order of causes unconfused, and to define separately their second and third progressions. But together with a progression of this kind, and with[†] the unfolding into light of things secondary from those that are first, that which is most excellent must also be surveyed in each of the Gods. For each of the Gods in his own characteristic peculiarity is allotted a transcendency which is primary and perfectly good. One of them indeed, that we may speak of something known, is allotted this transcendency, and is most excellent as possessing a prophetic power, another as demiurgic, but another as a perfector of works. And Timæus indicating this to us, continually calls the first demiurgus the best of causes. For the world, says he, is the most beautiful of generated natures, and its artificer is the best of causes; though the intelligible paradigm, and which is the most beautiful of intelligibles is prior to the demiurgus. But this is most beautiful and at the same time most excellent, as the demiurgic paradigm; and the maker and at the same time father of the universe is most excellent, as a demiurgic God. In the *Republic* also, Socrates speaking of the Gods, very properly observes, that each of them being as much as possible most beautiful and most excellent, remains always with a simplicity of subsistence in his own form. For each of them

---

[†] For το it is necessary to read τη.

being allotted that which is first and the summit in his own series, does not depart from his own order, but contains the blessedness and felicity of his own proper power. And neither does he exchange his present for a worse order; for it is not lawful for that which possesses all virtue to be changed into a worse condition; not does he pass into a better order. For where can there be any thing better than that which is most excellent? But this is present with each of the divinities according to his own order, as we have said, and also with every genus of the Gods.

It is necessary therefore that every divine nature should be established immutably, abiding in its own accustomed manner. Hence from these things the self-sufficiency, undefiled purity, and invariable sameness of subsistence of the Gods is apparent. For if they are not changed to a more excellent condition of being, as possessing that which is best in their own nature, they are sufficient to themselves, and are not in want of any good. And if they are not at any time changed to a worse condition, they remain undefiled, established in their own transcendencies. If also they guard the perfection of themselves immutably, they subsist always with invariable sameness. What the self-sufficiency therefore of the Gods is, what their immutability, and what their sameness of subsistence, we shall in the next place consider.

The world then is said to be self-sufficient, because its subsistence is perfect from things perfect, and a whole from wholes; and because it is filled with all appropriate goods from its generating father. But a perfection and self-sufficiency of this kind is partible, and is said to consist of many things coalescing in one, and is filled from separate causes according to participation. The order of divine souls also, is said to be self-sufficient, as being full of appropriate virtues, and always preserving the measure of its own blessedness without indigence. But here likewise the self-sufficiency is in want of powers. For these souls have not their intellections directed to the same intelligibles; but they energize according to time, and obtain the complete perfection of their contemplation in whole periods of time. The self-sufficiency therefore of divine souls, and the whole perfection of their life is not at once present. Again, the intellectual world is said to be self-sufficient, as having its whole good established in eternity, comprehending at once its whole blessedness, and being indigent of nothing, because all life and all intelligence are present with it, and nothing is deficient, nor does it desire any thing as absent. But this, indeed, is sufficient to itself in its own order, yet it falls short of the self-sufficiency of the Gods. For every intellect is boniform, yet is not goodness itself, nor primarily good; but each of the Gods is a unity, hyparxis and goodness. The peculiarity however of hyparxis changes the progression of the goodness of each. For one divinity is a perfective goodness, another is a goodness connective of the whole of things, and another is a collective goodness. But each is simply a goodness sufficient to itself. Or it may be said, that each is a goodness possessing the self-sufficient and the all-perfect, neither according to participation, nor illumination, but by being that very thing which it is. For intellect is sufficient to itself by participation, and soul by illumination, but this universe, according to a similitude to a divine nature. The Gods themselves, however, are self-sufficient through and by themselves, filling themselves, or rather subsisting as the plenitudes of all good.

But with respect to the immutability of the Gods, of what kind shall we say it is? Is it such as that of a [naturally] circulating body? For neither is this adapted to receive any thing from inferior natures, nor is it filled with the mutation arising from generation, and the disorder which occurs in the sublunary regions. For the nature of the celestial bodies is immaterial and immutable. But this indeed is great and venerable, as in corporeal hypostases, yet it is inferior to the nature of the Gods. For every body possesses both its being, and its perpetual immutability from other precedaneous causes. But neither is the impassive and the immutable in the Gods such as the immutability of souls. For these communicate in a certain respect with bodies, and are the media of an impartible essence, and of an essence divided about bodies. Nor again is the immutability of intellectual essences equivalent to that of the Gods. For intellect is immutable, impassive, and unmingled with secondary natures, on account of its union with the Gods. And so far indeed as it is uniform, it is a thing of this kind; but so far as it is manifold, it has something which is more excellent, and something which is subordinate, in itself. But the Gods alone having established their unions according to this transcendency of beings, are immutable dominations, are primary and impassive. For there is nothing in them which is not one and hyparxis. But as fire abolishes every thing which is foreign to it and of a contrary power, as light expels all darkness, and as lightning proceeds through all things without defilement, thus also the unities of the Gods unite all multitude, and abolish every thing which tends to dispersion and all-perfect division. But they deify every thing which participates of them, receiving nothing from their participants, and do not[†] diminish their own proper union by the participation.

[†] *ουχ* is omitted in the original.

Hence also the Gods being present every where, are similarly exempt from all things, and containing all things are vanquished by no one of the things they contain; but they are unmingled with all things and undefiled. In the third place, this world indeed is said to subsist with invariable sameness, so far as it is allotted an order in itself which is always preserved indissoluble. At the same time however, since it possesses a corporeal form, it is not destitute of mutation, as the Elean guest observes. The psychical order likewise is said to obtain an essence always established in sameness; and this is rightly said. For it is entirely impassive according to essence; but it has energies extended into time, and as Socrates says in the *Phædrus*, at different times it understands different intelligibles, and in its progressions about intellect comes into contact with different forms. Besides these also, much-honoured intellect is said both to subsist and to understand with invariable and perpetual sameness, establishing at once in eternity its essence, powers, and energies. Through the multitude however of its intellections, and through the variety of intelligible species and genera, there is not only an invariable sameness, but also a difference of subsistence in intellect. For difference there is consubsistent with sameness. And there is not only a wandering of corporeal motions, and of the psychical periods, but likewise of intellect itself, so far as it produces the intelligence of itself into multitude; and evolves the intelligible. For soul indeed evolves intellect, but intellect the intelligible, as Plotinus somewhere rightly observes, when speaking of the intelligible subjections. For such are the wanderings of intellect and which it is lawful for it to make. If therefore we should say that a perpetual sameness of subsistence is primarily in the Gods alone, and is especially inherent in them, we shall not deviate from the truth, and we shall accord with Plato, who says in the *Politicus*, that an eternally invariable sameness of subsistence alone pertains to the most divine of all things. The Gods, therefore, bind to themselves the causes of a sameness of this kind, and guard with immutable sameness their proper hyparxis established according to the unknown union of themselves. And such is the immutability of the Gods, which is contained in self-sufficiency, impassivity and sameness.

CHAPTER XIX

In the next place, let us consider what power the simplicity of the Gods possesses; for this Socrates adds in his discourse concerning a divine nature, not admitting that which is various, and multiform, and which appears different at different times, but referring to divinity the uniform and the simple. Each of the divinities therefore, as he says, remains simply in his own form. What then shall we conclude respecting this simplicity? That it is not such as that which is defined to be one in number. For a thing of this kind is composed of many things, and abundantly mingled. But it appears to be simple so far as it has distinctly a common form. Nor is it such as the simplicity which is in many things according to an arranged species or genus. For these are indeed more simple than the individuals in which they are inherent, but are replete with variety, communicate with matter, and receive the diversities of material natures. Nor is it such as the form of nature. For nature is divided about bodies, verges to corporeal masses, emits many powers about the composition subject to it, and is indeed more simple than bodies, but has an essence mingled with their variety. Nor is it such as the psychical simplicity. For soul subsisting as a medium between an impartible essence, and an essence which is divided about bodies, communicates with both the extremes. And by that which is multiform indeed in its nature it is conjoined with things subordinate, but its head is established on high, and according to this it is especially divine, and allied to intellect.

Nor again is the simplicity of the Gods such as that of intellect. For every intellect is impartible and uniform, but at the same time it possesses multitude and progression; by which it is evident that it has a habitude to secondary natures, to itself, and about itself. It is also in itself, and is not only uniform, but also multiform, and as it is said, is one many. It is therefore allotted an essence subordinate to the first simplicity. But the Gods have their hyparxis defined in one simplicity alone, being exempt indeed from all multitude so far as they are gods, and transcending all division and interval, or habitude to secondary natures, and all composition. And they indeed are in inaccessible places, expanded above the whole of things, and eternally ride on beings. But the illuminations proceeding from them to secondary natures, being mingled in many places with their participants which are composite and various, are filled with a peculiarity similar to them. Let no one therefore wonder, if the Gods being essentialized in one simplicity according to transcendency, various phantasms are hurled forth before the presence of them; nor, if they being uniform the appearances are multiform, as we have learnt in the most perfect of the mysteries. For nature, and the demiurgic intellect extend corporeal-formed images of things incorporeal, sensible images of intelligible, and of things without interval, images endued with interval. For Socrates also in the *Phædrus* indicating things of this kind, and evincing that the mysteries into which souls without bodies are initiated are most blessed, and truly perfect, says, that they are initiated into entire, simple and immoveable visions, such souls becoming situated there, and united with the Gods themselves, but not meeting with the resemblances which are emitted from the Gods into these sublunary realms. For these are more partial and composite, and present themselves to the view attended with motion. But illuminated, uniform, simple, and, as Socrates says, immoveable spectacles exhibit themselves to the attendants of the Gods, and to souls that abandon the abundant tumult of generation, and who ascend to divinity pure and divested of the garments of mortality. And thus much is concluded by us respecting the simplicity of the Gods. For it is necessary that the nature which generates things multiform should be simple[†] and should precede what is generated, in the same manner as the uniform precedes the multiplied. If, therefore, the Gods are the causes of all composition, and produce from themselves the variety of beings, it is certainly necessary that *The One* of their nature which is generative of the whole of things, should have its subsistence in simplicity. For as incorporeal causes precede bodies, immoveable causes things that are moved, and impartible causes all partible natures, after the same manner uniform intellectual powers precede multiform natures, unmingled powers, things that are mingled together, and simple powers, things of a variegated nature.

CHAPTER XX

In the next place, let us speak concerning the truth which is in the Gods; for this in addition to what has been said is concluded by Socrates, because a divine nature is without falsehood, and is neither the cause of deception or ignorance to us, or to any other beings. We must understand therefore, that divine truth is exempt from the truth which consists in words, so far as this truth is composite, and in a certain respect is mingled with its contrary, and because its subsistence consists of things that are not true. For the first parts do not admit of a truth of this kind, unless some one being persuaded by what Socrates asserts in the *Cratylus*, should say that these also are after another manner true. Divine truth also is exempt from psychical truth, whether it is surveyed in opinions or in sciences, so far as it is in a certain respect divisible, and is not beings themselves, but is assimilated to and co-harmonized with beings, and as being perfected in motion and mutation falls short of the

---

[†] After απλουν in the original, it is requisite to insert ειναι και.

truth which is always firm, stable and of a principal nature. Divine truth is likewise again exempt from intellectual truth, because though this subsists according to essence, and is said to be and is, beings themselves, through the power of sameness, yet again, through difference, it is separated from the essence of them, and preserves its peculiar hypostasis unconfused with respect to them. The truth therefore of the Gods alone, is the undivided union and all-perfect communion of them. And through this the ineffable knowledge of the Gods, surpasses all knowledge, and all secondary forms of knowledge participate of an appropriate perfection. But this knowledge alone of the Gods contractedly comprehends these secondary forms of knowledge, and all beings according to an ineffable union. And through this the Gods know all things at once, wholes and parts, beings and non-beings, things eternal and things temporal, not in the same manner as intellect by the universal knows a part, and by being, non-being, but they know every thing immediately, such things as are common, and such as are particulars, though you should speak of the most absurd of all things, though you should speak of the infinity of contingencies, or even of matter itself.

If, however, you investigate the mode of the knowledge and truth of the Gods, concerning all things that have a subsistence in any respect whatever, it is ineffable and incomprehensible by the projecting energies of the human intellect; but is alone known to the Gods themselves. And I indeed admire those Platonists that attribute to intellect the knowledge of all things, of individuals, of things preternatural, and in short, of evils, and on this account establish intellectual paradigms of these. But I much more admire those who separate the intellectual peculiarity from divine union. For intellect is the first fabrication and progeny of the Gods. These therefore assign to intellect whole and first causes, and such as are according to nature, and to the Gods a power which is capable of adorning and generating all things. For *The One* is every where, but whole is not every where. And of *The One* indeed matter participates and every being; but of intellect and intellectual species and genera, all things do not participate. All things therefore are alone from the Gods, and real truth is with them who know all things unically. For on this account also, in oracles the Gods similarly teach all things, wholes and parts, things eternal, and such as are generated through the whole of time. For being exempt from eternal beings, and from those that exist in time, they contract in themselves the knowledge of each and of all things, according to one united truth. If therefore any falsehood occurs in the oracles of the Gods, we must not say that a thing of this kind originates from the Gods, but from the recipients, or the instruments, or the places, or the times. For all these contribute to the participation of divine knowledge, and when they are appropriately co-adapted to the Gods, they receive a pure illumination of the truth which is established in them. But when they are separated from the Gods through inaptitude, and become discordant with them, then they obscure the truth which proceeds from them. What kind of falsehood therefore can be said to be derived from the Gods, who produce all the species of knowledge? What deception can there be with those who establish in themselves the whole of truth? In the same manner, as it appears to me, the Gods extend good to all things, but always that which is willing and able receives the extended good, as Socrates says in the *Phædrus*. And a divine nature indeed is causeless of evil, but that which departs from it, and gravitates downwards, is elongated through itself; thus also, the Gods indeed are always the suppliers of truth, but those natures are illuminated by them, who are lawfully their participants. For the Elean wise man says, that the eye of the soul in the multitude, is not strong enough to look to the truth.

The Athenian guest also celebrates this truth which subsists primarily in the Gods; for he says that truth is the leader to the Gods of every good, and likewise of every good to men. For as the truth which is in souls conjoins them with intellect, and as intellectual truth conducts all the intellectual orders to *The One*, thus also the truth of the Gods unites the divine unities to the fountain of all good, with which being conjoined, they are filled with all boniform power. For every where the hyparxis of truth has a cause which is collective of multitude into one; since in the *Republic* also, the light proceeding from *The Good* and which conjoins intellect with the intelligible, is denominated by Plato truth. This characteristic property therefore, which unites and binds together the natures that fill and the natures that are filled, according to all the orders of the Gods, must be arranged as originating supernally and proceeding as far as to the last of things.

CHAPTER XXI

To us however discussing what pertains to every divine nature, what we assert will be known from those commonly received truths adduced in the *Phædrus*, and which we have before mentioned. Socrates therefore says that every thing divine is beautiful, wise, and good[†] and

---

[†] δυνατον is erroneously printed instead of αγαθον.

he indicates that this triad pervades to all the progressions of the Gods. What therefore is the goodness, what the wisdom, and what the beauty of the Gods? With respect to the goodness of the Gods therefore, we have before observed, that it preserves and gives subsistence to the whole of things, that it every where exists as the summit, as that which fills subordinate natures, and as pre-existing in every order analogous to the first principle of the divine orders. For according to this all the Gods are conjoined with the one cause of all things, and on account of this primarily derive their subsistence as Gods. For in all beings there is not any thing more perfect than the good, and the Gods. To the most excellent of beings therefore, and which are in every respect perfect, the best and most perfect of things is adapted.

CHAPTER XXII

But in the *Philebus*, Plato delivers to us the three most principal elements of *The Good, viz.* the desirable, the sufficient, and the perfect. For it is necessary that it should convert all things to itself, and fill all things, and that it should be in no respect deficient, and should not diminish its exuberance. Let no one therefore conceive the desirable to be such as that which is frequently extended in sensibles as the object of appetite. For such is apparent beauty. Nor let him suppose it to be such as is indeed able to energize upon and excite to itself the natures which are able to participate it, but which at the same time may be apprehended by intelligence, and is educed by us according to a projecting energy, and an adhesion of the dianoetic power. For it is ineffable, and prior to all knowledge extends to all beings. For all things desire *The Good*, and are converted to it. But if it be requisite summarily to unfold the characteristic peculiarity of the desirable, as the supplier of light proceeds by his rays into secondary natures, converts the eye to himself, causes it to be solar-form, and to resemble himself, and through a different similitude conjoins it with his own fulgid splendour, thus also I think the desirable of the Gods allures and draws upward all things to the Gods in an ineffable manner by its own proper illuminations, being every where present to all things, and not deserting any order whatever of beings. Since even matter itself is said to be extended to this desirable, and through this desire is filled with as many goods as it is able to participate. It is therefore the centre of all beings, and all beings, and all the Gods have their essences, powers and energies about this. And the extension and desire of things towards this is inextinguishable. For all beings aspire after this desirable which is unknown and incomprehensible. Not being able therefore either to know or receive that which they desire, they dance round it, and are parturient and as it were prophetic with respect to it. But they have an unceasing and never-ending desire of its unknown and ineffable nature, at the same time that they are unable to embrace and embosom it. For being at once exempt from all things, it is similarly present to and moves all things about itself, and is at the same time by all of them incomprehensible. By this motion also and this desire it preserves all things. But by its unknown transcendency through which it surpasses the whole of things, it preserves its proper union unmingled with secondary natures. Such therefore is the desirable.

But the sufficient is full of boniform power, proceeds to all things, and extends to all beings the gifts of the Gods. For we conceive such a sufficiency as this to be a power pervading and protending to the last of things, extending the unenvying and exuberant will of the Gods, and not abiding in itself, but unically comprehending the super-plenitude, the never-failing, the infinite, and that which is generative of good in the divine hyparxis. For the desirable being firmly established, and surpassing the whole of things, and arranging all beings about itself, the sufficient begins the progression and multiplication of all good, calls forth that which is primary in the uniform hyparxis of the desirable, by its own prolific[†] exuberance, and by the beneficent replenishings which pervade to all things, and copiously produces and imparts it to every being. It is owing to the sufficient therefore, that the stability of divine natures, and that which proceeds from its proper causes is full of goodness, and that, in short, all beings are benefited, abiding in, proceeding from, and being united to their principles, and essentially separated from them. Through this power therefore, the intellectual genera give subsistence to natures similar to themselves, souls desire to generate, and imitate the beings prior to souls, natures deliver their productive principles into another place, and all things possess, in short, the love of generation. For the sufficiency of the goodness of the Gods, proceeding from this goodness, is disseminated in all beings, and moves all things to the unenvying communication of good; intellect indeed to the communication of intellectual, but soul of physical, and nature of natural good.

All things therefore abide through the desirable of goodness, and generate and proceed into second and third generations through the sufficient. But the third thing, the perfect, is convertive of the whole of

---

[†] Instead of μονιμῳ it is necessary to read γονιμῳ.

things, and circularly collects them to their causes; and this is accomplished by divine, intellectual, psychical and physical perfection. For all things participate of conversion, since the infinity of progression is through this again recalled to its principles; and the perfect is mingled from the desirable and sufficient. For every thing of this kind is the object of desire, and is generative of things similar to itself. Or in the works of nature also, are not perfect things every where lovely and prolific through the acme of their beauty? The desirable therefore establishes all things, and comprehends them in itself. The sufficient excites them into progressions and generations. And the perfect consummately leads progressions to conversions and convolutions. But through these three causes, the goodness of the Gods fixing the unical power and authority of its proper hypostasis in this triad, is the primary and most principal fountain and vestal seat of things which have any kind of subsistence whatever.

CHAPTER XXIII

After this, wisdom is allotted the second order, being the intelligence of the Gods, or rather the hyparxis of their intelligence. For intelligence indeed, is intellectual knowledge; but the wisdom of the Gods is ineffable knowledge, which is united to the object of knowledge and the intelligible union of the Gods. But it appears to me that Plato especially surveyed this in the triad [of the beautiful, the wise and the good,] as may be inferred from the conceptions scattered about it in many places. I say then that Diotima in the *Banquet* is of opinion that wisdom is full of that which is known, and that it neither seeks, nor investigates, but possesses the intelligible. Hence, she says, that no one of the Gods philosophizes, nor desires to become wise; for a God is wise. Hence that which is philosophic is imperfect, and indigent of truth; but that which is wise is full and unindigent, and has every thing present which it wishes and desires nothing. But the desirable and the appetible are proposed to the philosopher. Socrates, however, in the *Republic* considers that which is generative of truth and intellect, as affording an indication of wisdom, to our souls indeed the ascent to divine plenitude being accomplished through knowledge,† but to the Gods intellect being present from the fullness of knowledge.‡ For the progression in them

---

† For γεννησεως it is requisite to read γνωσεως.

‡ The same emendation is necessary here as above.

is not from an imperfect habit to the perfect; but from a self-perfect hyparxis a power prolific of inferior natures proceeds. But in the *Theætetus* he indicates that the perfective of things imperfect, and that which calls forth concealed intelligence in souls, pertain to wisdom. For he says, it compels me to obstetrication, but prevents me from generating. It is evident therefore, from these things, that the genus of wisdom is triadic. Hence it is full of being and truth, is generative of intellectual truth, and is perfective of intellectual natures that are in energy, and itself possesses a stable power. We must admit therefore, that these things pertain to the wisdom of the Gods. For this wisdom is full indeed of divine goodness, generates divine truth, and perfects all things posterior to itself.

CHAPTER XXIV

In the next place let us consider the beautiful, what it is, and how it primarily subsists in the Gods. It is said therefore to be boniform beauty, and intelligible beauty, to be more ancient than intellectual beauty, and to be beauty itself, and the cause of beauty to all beings; and all such like epithets. And it is rightly said. But it is separate not only from the beauty which is apparent in corporeal masses, from the symmetry which is in these from psychical elegance, and intellectual splendour, but also from the second and third progressions in the Gods; and subsisting in the intelligible place of survey, it proceeds from this to all the genera of the Gods, and illuminates their superessential unities, and all the essences suspended from these unities, as far as to the apparent vehicles of the Gods. As therefore through the first goodness all the Gods are boniform, and through intelligible wisdom they have a knowledge ineffable, and established above intellect, thus also, I think, through the summit of beauty, every thing divine is lovely. For from thence all the Gods derive beauty, and being filled with it, fill the natures posterior to themselves, exciting all things, agitating them with Bacchic fury about the love of themselves, and pouring supernally on all things the divine effluxion of beauty.

Such therefore, in short, is divine beauty, the supplier of divine hilarity, familiarity and friendship. For through this the Gods are united to and rejoice in each other, admire, and are delighted in communicating with each other, and in their mutual replenishings, and do not desert the order which they are always allotted in the distributions of themselves. Plato also delivers three indications of this beauty, in the *Banquet* indeed, denominating it the delicate; for the perfect and that which is most blessed, accedes to the beautiful through the participation of goodness. But he thus speaks of it in that dialogue: That which is truly beautiful, is delicate, perfect and most blessed." One of the indications therefore of the beautiful, is a thing of this kind, *viz.* the delicate. But we may assume another indication of it from the *Phædrus*, *viz.* the splendid. For Plato attributing this to the beautiful says: "It was then that we were permitted to see splendid beauty shining upon us etc." And afterwards he adds: "And arriving hither we apprehended it shining most manifestly through the clearest of the senses." And at last he says: "But now beauty alone has this allotment to be most splendid and most lovely." These two things therefore are to be assumed as indications of beauty. Another indication of beauty is this, that it is the object of love, which now also Plato appears to me to have called most lovely.; And in many other places he shows that the amatory fury is conversant with the beautiful, defining, and in short, suspending love from the monad of beauty. "For love, says he, is conversant with the beautiful."

Because, therefore, beauty converts and moves all things to itself, causes them to energize enthusiastically, and recalls them through love, it is the object of love, being the leader of the whole amatory series walking on the extremities of its feet, and exciting all things to itself through desire and astonishment. But again because it extends to secondary natures plenitudes from itself, in conjunction with hilarity and divine facility, alluring, enflaming, and elevating all things, and pouring on them illuminations from on high, it is delicate, and is said to be so by Plato. And because it bounds this triad, and covers as with a veil the ineffable union of the Gods, swims as it were on the light of forms, causes intelligible light to shine forth, and announces the occult nature of goodness, it is denominated splendid, lucid and manifest. For the goodness of the Gods is supreme and most united; their wisdom is in a certain respect now parturient with intelligible light, and the first forms; but their beauty is established in the highest forms, is the luminous precursor of divine light, and is the first thing that is apparent to ascending souls, being more splendid and more lovely to the view and to embrace than every luciferous essence, and when it appears is received with astonishment. This triad therefore filling all things, and proceeding through all things, it is certainly necessary that the natures which are filled should be converted to and conjoined with each of the three through kindred, and not through the same media. For of different things that are filled by this triad there is a different medium; and different powers are converted to a different perfection of the Gods. I think therefore, it is manifest to every one, and it is frequently asserted by Plato, that the cause which congregates all secondary natures to divine beauty, which familiarizes them to it and is the source of their being filled with it, and of their derivation from thence, is nothing else than love, which always conjoins according to the beautiful, secondary to the first[†] Gods, and the more excellent genera, and the best of souls. But again, truth is certainly the leader to, and establishes beings in, divine wisdom, with which intellect being filled, possesses a knowledge of beings, and souls participating of this energize intellectually. For the full participation of true wisdom is effected through truth, since this every where illuminates intellective natures, and conjoins them with the objects of intellection, just as truth also is the first thing that congregates intellect and the intelligible. To those however who hasten to be conjoined with the good, knowledge and co-operation are no longer requisite, but collocation, a firm establishment and quiet are necessary.

CHAPTER XXV

What therefore is it which unites us to the good? What is it which causes in us a cessation of energy and motion. What is it which establishes all divine natures in the first and ineffable unity of goodness. And how does it come to pass that every thing being established in that which is prior to itself according to the good which is in itself again establishes things posterior to itself according to cause? It is, in short, the faith of the Gods, which ineffably unites all the genera of the Gods, of dæmons, and of happy souls to *The Good*. For it is necessary to investigate *The Good* neither gnostically, nor imperfectly, but giving ourselves up to the divine light, and closing the eyes of the soul, after this manner to become established in the unknown and occult unity of beings. For such a kind of faith as this is more ancient than the gnostic energy, not in us only, but with the Gods themselves, and according to this all the Gods are united, and about one centre uniformly collect the whole of their powers and progressions.

If however it be requisite to give a particular definition of this faith, let no one suppose that it is such a kind of faith as that which is conversant with the wandering about sensibles. For this falls short of science, and much more of the truth of beings. But the faith of the Gods surpasses all knowledge, and according to the highest union conjoins secondary with first natures. Nor again, let him conceive a

---

[†] Instead of προς αυτον it is requisite to read πρωτιστοις.

faith of a similar species with the celebrated belief in common conceptions; for we believe in common conceptions prior to all reasoning. But the knowledge of these is divisible, and is by no means equivalent to divine union; and the science of these is not only posterior to faith, but also to intellectual simplicity. For intellect is established beyond all science, both the first science, and that which is posterior to it. Neither, therefore, must we say that the energy according to intellect is similar to such a faith as this. For intellectual energy is multiform, and is separated from the objects of intellection through difference; and in short, it is intellectual motion about the intelligible. But it is necessary that divine faith should be uniform and quiet, being perfectly established in the port of goodness. For neither is the beautiful, nor wisdom, nor any thing else among beings, so credible and stable to all things, and so exempt from all ambiguity, divisible apprehension and motion, as *The Good*. For through this intellect also embraces another union more ancient than intellectual energy, and prior to energy. And soul considers the variety of intellect and the splendour of forms as nothing with respect to that transcendency of *The Good* by which it surpasses the whole of things. And it dismisses indeed intellectual perception, running back to its own hyparxis; but it always pursues, investigates, and aspires after *The Good*, hastens as it were to embosom it, and gives itself to this alone among all things without hesitation. But why is it necessary to speak of the soul? For these mortal animals, as Diotima somewhere says, despise all other things, and even life itself and being, through a desire of the nature of *The Good;* and all things have this one immoveable and ineffable tendency to *The Good;* but they overlook, consider as secondary, and despise the order of every thing else. This, therefore, is the one secure port of all beings.

This also is especially the object of belief to all beings. And through this the conjunction and union with it is denominated faith by theologists, and not by them only, but by Plato likewise, (if I may speak what appears to be to be the case) the alliance of this faith with truth and love is proclaimed in the *Laws*. The multitude therefore are ignorant, that he who has a conception of these things, when discoursing about their contraries, infers the same thing with respect to the deviations from this triad. Plato then clearly asserts in the *Laws* that the lover of falsehood is not to be believed, and that he who is not to be believed is void of friendship. Hence it is necessary that the lover of truth should be worthy of belief, and that he who is worthy of belief should be well adapted to friendship. From these things therefore, we may survey divine truth, faith and love, and comprehend by a reasoning process their stable communion with each other. If, however, you are willing, prior to these things we will recall to our memory that Plato denominates that virtue fidelity which conciliates those that disagree, and subverts the greatest of wards, I mean seditions in cities. For from these things faith appears to be the cause of union, communion and quiet. And if there is such a power as this in us, it is by a much greater priority in the Gods themselves. For as Plato speaks of a certain divine temperance, justice and science, how is it possible that faith which connectedly comprehends the whole order of the virtues should not subsist with the Gods? In short, there are these three things which replenish divine natures, and which are the sources of plenitude to all the superior genera of beings, *viz.* goodness, wisdom and beauty. And again, there are three things which collect together the natures that are filled, being secondary indeed to the former, but pervading to all the divine orders, and these are faith, truth and love. But all things are saved through these, and are conjoined to their primary causes; some things indeed, through the amatory mania, others through divine philosophy, and others through theurgic power, which is more excellent than all human wisdom, and which comprehends prophetic good, the purifying powers of perfective good, and in short, all such things as are the effects of divine possession. Concerning these things therefore, we may perhaps again speak more opportunely.

CHAPTER XXVI

Again, let us, if you are willing, from other dialogues investigate the common dogmas of Plato about divine natures. Whence therefore, and what dogmas shall we assume, while we proceed in our search according to nature? Are you willing that we should in the next place recall to our memory what is written in the *Phædo*? Socrates therefore says in the demonstrations of the immortality of the soul which are derived from its similitude to divinity, that the essence which is superior to the soul, (and to which the soul is naturally similar, and being similar participates of an immortal allotment) is divine and immortal, intelligible and uniform, indissoluble and possesses an invariable sameness of subsistence; but that the essence which is inferior to the soul, is entirely the contrary, to which also it pertains to be corrupted and to be passive. For a thing of this kind is sensible and multiform, and is dissoluble because it is a composite; and he predicates among these all such things as pertain to a corporeal subsistence. Let us therefore direct our attention to these common dogmas, and examine after what manner each of them pertains to the Gods.

In the first place then what is that which we look to when we speak of that which is said to be divine? From what has been said therefore, it is evident that every God subsists according to the highest union of beings. For to us ascending from bodies, the Gods have appeared to be superessential unities, the generators, perfectors and measurers of essences, and who bind all first essences to themselves. But that which is divine, is not only hyparxis and *The One* in each order of being, but at the same time is that which participates and that which is participated; of which the latter is a God, but the former is divine. Whether however, prior to the participated unities, there is something which is separate and participated will be evident in what follows. But at present we shall define that which is divine to be a thing of this kind, *viz.* being which participates of *The One*, or *The One* subsisting contractedly together with being. For we assume all things in the Gods except *The One*, as suspended from them and secondary, *viz.* essence, life and intellect. For the Gods do not subsist in, but prior to these, and they produce and contain these in themselves, but are not defined in them. But it is necessary not to be ignorant that these are in reality thus distinguished from each other. In many places, however, Plato magnificently celebrates the participants of the Gods by the same names, and denominates them Gods. For not only the Athenian guest in the *Laws* calls a divine soul a God, but also Socrates in the *Phædrus*. For he says "That all the horses and charioteers of the Gods are good and consist of things good;" and afterwards still more clearly, "and this is the life of the Gods." But this is not yet wonderful. For is it not admirable that he should denominate those beings Gods who are always conjoined with the Gods, and who together with them give completion to one series? For in many places he calls dæmons Gods, though they are essentially posterior to, and subsist about the Gods. For in the *Phædrus* and *Timæus*, and in other dialogues, you will find him extending the appellation of the Gods even as far as to dæmons. But what is still more paradoxical than these things, he does not refuse to call certain men Gods; for in the *Sophista* he thus denominates the Elean guest.

From all that has been said therefore, this must be assumed, that with respect to a God, one thing is simply a God, another according to union, another according to participation, another according to contact, and another according to similitude. For of super-essential natures indeed, each is primarily a God; of intellectual natures, each is a God according to union, and of divine souls, each is God according to participation. But divine dæmons are Gods according to contact with the Gods; and the souls of men are allotted this appellation through similitude. Each of these however is, as we have said, rather divine than a God. Since the Athenian guest calls intellect itself divine; but that which is divine is posterior to the first deity, in the same manner as that which is united is posterior to *The One* that which is intellectual, to intellect, and that which is animated, to soul. And always those natures that are more uniform and simple have the precedency; but the series of beings ends in *The One Itself.* Let this, therefore, be the definition and distinction of that which is divine.

In the next place, let us survey the immortal. For with Plato there are many orders of immortality, pervading from on high as far as to the last of things; and the last echo, as it were, of immortality, is in those visible natures that are perpetual; which the Elean guest, in his discourse about the circulation of the universe, says, are allotted from the father a renovated immortality. For every body is allotted a being and a life dependent on another cause; but is not itself naturally adapted to connect, or adorn, or preserve itself. The immortality of partial souls is, I think, more manifest and more perfect than this; which Plato evinces by many demonstrations in the *Phædo,* and in the 10th book of the *Republic.* But I mean by the immortality of partial souls, that which has a more principal subsistence, as containing in itself the cause of eternal permanency. We shall not, however, err if prior to both these we establish the immortality of dæmons. For the genera of these through which they subsist are incorruptible, and they neither verge to mortality, nor are filled with the nature of things which are generated and corrupted. But I infer that the immortality of divine souls is still more venerable and essentially more transcendent than that of dæmons; which divine souls we say are primarily self-motive, and are the fountains and principles of the life divided about bodies, and through which bodies obtain a renovated immortality. If, however, prior to these you conceive the Gods themselves, and the immortality in them, and how in the *Banquet* Diotima does not attribute an immortality of this kind even to dæmons, but defines it to subsist in the Gods alone, such an immortality as this will appear to you to be separate, and exempt from the whole of things. For there eternity subsists, which is the fountain of all immortality, and through it all things live and possess life, some things indeed a perpetual life, but others a life dispersed into non-being. In short, therefore, that which is divine is immortal so far as it generates and comprehends in itself a perpetual life. For it is immortal, not as participating of life, but as the supplier of a divine life, and as deifying life itself, whether you are willing to call such a life intelligible, or by any other name.

In the next place let us direct our attention to the intelligible. It is denominated, therefore, in opposition to that which is sensible and which is apprehended by opinion in conjunction with sense. For the intelligible is first unfolded into light in the most principal causes. For soul is indeed intelligible, is of this allotment, is exempt from sensibles, and obtains an essence separated from them. Prior to soul also intellect is intelligible; for we rather think it fit to arrange soul in the middle, than to connumerate it with the first essences. That likewise is denominated intelligible, which is more ancient than intellect, which replenishes intelligence, and is itself by itself perfective of it, and which Timæus arranges prior to the demiurgic intellect and intellectual energy, in the order of a paradigm. But beyond these is the divine intelligible, which is defined according to union itself, and a divine hyparxis. For this is intelligible as the object of desire to intellect, as perfecting and comprehending intellect, and as the plenitude of being. In one way, therefore, we must denominate the intelligible as the hyparxis of the Gods; in another way as true being and the first essence; in another way as intellect and all intellectual life; and in another way as soul and the psychical order. It is likewise necessary not to fashion the different natures of things conformably to names. Such, therefore, is the order of this triad; so that what is divine indeed is unmingled and ranks as the first; that which is immortal is the second; and that which is intelligible the third. For the first of these is deified being; the second is life subsisting according to the immortality of the Gods; and the third is intellect, which is denominated intelligible in consequence of being replete with union.

CHAPTER XXVII

After this, it follows in the next place, that we should consider the uniform, the indissoluble, and that which has an invariable sameness of subsistence, from the same causes, and these as the precursors of, and pervading through all the divine orders. For the uniform, indeed, has the highest subsistence, is present with the divine monad, and appears to be especially adapted to that which is primarily being[†] and in which also every participable genus of unities ends. For *The One* is prior to these, as will be evident as we proceed. But the indissoluble is the second. For it comprehends and binds the extremes according to divine union; since the dissoluble is such as it is through the want of connexion and of a power which collects multitude into one. And that which has an invariable sameness of subsistence is eternal, and is full of the

---

[†] For το ον it is necessary to read τῳ οντι.

perpetuity of the Gods; from which also the participation of immortality and eternal sameness is derived to other things. The uniform, therefore, pertains to the same thing as the divine; but the indissoluble to the same thing as the immortal; and that which has an invariable sameness of subsistence we must refer to the intelligible.

And do you not see how these are severally after a manner co-adapted to each other? For the first of these, through the first unity which is participated by being is, as it is fit it should be, uniform. For if a god subsists according to *The One*, that which is divine will doubtless be uniform. But that which through one cause of life is immortal, is also similarly indissoluble. For life is the bond of dissoluble natures; which also Timæus indicating to us, opposes the dissoluble to the immortal: "for you are not immortal, says the demiurgus, yet you shall never be dissolved, nor be subject† to the fatality of death." Every thing mortal, therefore, is dissoluble; but the immortal is indissoluble. That, however, which has a renovated immortality is for the same reason neither indissoluble, nor mortal. For being in the middle of both it is neither of the extremes, according to each opposition. But the third of these being established according to the plenitude of whole intelligibles subsists at once and is invariably the same. For the intelligible is the cause of sameness and of eternal permanency; and intellect through this is entirely eternal. These triads, therefore, proceed from the first and most principal causes, in the same manner as we demonstrated of the before-mentioned triads. But those things, indeed, we shall consider hereafter.

These things, therefore, being discussed, let us direct our attention to the unbegotten in divine natures, and unfold what we assert it to be. For we say that all [true] being is without generation, and Socrates demonstrates in the *Phædrus*, that souls are unbegotten. Prior to these, also, the Gods themselves are established above generations and a subsistence according to time. How, therefore, shall we define the unbegotten when applied to a divine nature, and according to what reason? Is it because divinity is exempt from all generation, not only from that which subsists in the parts of time, such as we assert the generation of material natures to be, nor from that only which is extended into the whole of time, such as Timæus demonstrates the generation of the celestial bodies to be, but also from the psychical generation? Since Timæus denominates this to be unbegotten according to time, but to be the best of generated natures. And in short, a divine nature is exempt from all division and essential separation. For the

---

† For γευσεσθε read τευξεσθε.

progression of the Gods is always according to a union of secondary natures, which are uniformly established in the natures prior to them, the things producing containing in themselves the things produced. The indivisible, therefore, the unseparated and the united are in reality unbegotten. So that if certain generations of the Gods are spoken of by Plato in fabulous figments, as in the fable of Diotima, the generation of Venus is celebrated, and of Love at the birth of Venus, it is necessary not to be ignorant after what manner things of this kind are asserted, and that they are composed for the sake of symbolical indication; and that fables for the sake of concealment call the ineffable unfolding into light through causes, *generation*. For in the Orphic writings, indeed, the first cause is on this account denominated Time; since again, for another reason, it is thus denominated, in order that a subsistence according to cause may be the same as a subsistence according to time. And the progression of the Gods from the best of causes is properly denominated generation according to time. To Plato, therefore, mythologizing, it is adapted to devise things of this kind conformably to theologists; but when he is discoursing dialectically, and investigating and unfolding divine natures intellectually and not mystically, it is then adapted to him to celebrate the unbegotten essence of the Gods. For the Gods primarily establish in themselves the paradigm of non-generation. But an intellectual nature is in a secondary degree unbegotten, and after this the psychical essence. And in bodies there is an ultimate resemblance of unbegotten power; which some posterior to Plato perceiving, have indefinitely shown that the whole heaven is unbegotten. The Gods, therefore, are unbegotten. But there is an order in them of first, middle, and last progressions, and a transcendency and subjection of powers. There are also in them uniform comprehensions of causes; but multiform progenies of things caused. And all things, indeed, are consubsistent in each other; but the mode of subsistence is various. For some things as replenishing subsist prior to secondary natures; but others, as being filled aspire after more perfect natures, and participating of their power become generative of things posterior to themselves, and perfective of their hyparxis.

CHAPTER XXVIII

Looking to these things, therefore, we may unfold what is said of paternal causes, and of the prolific powers of mothers in fables. For every where, we may suppose that the cause of a more excellent and more uniform nature is paternal;[†] but we may say that the cause of a more subordinate and partial nature pre-exists in the order of a mother. For with the Gods a father is analogous to the monad, and the cause of bound; but a mother, to the duad, and to the infinite power which is generative of beings. The paternal cause, however, is with Plato uniform, and is established in a more elevated order than the natures which proceed from it, and subsists prior to its progeny in the allotment of the desirable. Again, the maternal cause has the form of the duad; and at one time presents itself to the view in fables as more excellent than its progeny, but at another time as essentially subordinate to it; as in the *Banquet*, Plato calls Poverty the mother of Love. And this is not only the case in fabulous figments, but also in the philosophic theory of beings, as is evident in the *Timæus*. For there Plato calls being the father, but matter the mother and nurse of generation. The powers, therefore, which are prolific and perfective of secondary natures, and the suppliers of life and causes of separation are mothers, being established above the natures produced by them. But the powers which receive the natures that proceed into light, which multiply their energies, and extend even the subordinate allotment of the progeny, are also themselves called mothers. Again, however, the progeny of such like causes, at one time indeed, proceed according to union from their proper principles, and are filled from both the paternal and maternal cause; but at another time they contain the bond of them, being arranged in the middle, conveying the gifts of the fathers to the maternal bosoms, and converting the receptacles of them to the completions of primary causes. But of the natures which subsist from twofold pre-existing principles, some are assimilated to the paternal cause; and such like genera of Gods are productive, defensive, and comprehensive. For to produce, to contain, and to defend, pertain to the cause of bound. But others are assimilated to the maternal cause, and are prolific, and vivific, and the suppliers of motion, of the multiplication of powers, of variety and progressions. For all these are the progeny of infinity and the first multitude.

CHAPTER XXIX

Thus much therefore may suffice concerning the unbegotten hyparxis of the Gods. It now remains, I think, to speak of divine names. For Socrates in the *Cratylus* thinks fit to unfold in a remarkable degree the rectitude of names in divine natures. And Parmenides indeed, in the

---

[†] πατρικον is omitted in the original.

first hypothesis, as he denies of *The One* every thing else that is known, and all knowledge, so likewise he denies of it name and language. But in the second hypothesis, besides all other things he shows that this one may be spoken of and[†] that it has a name. In short therefore, it must be admitted that the first, most principal and truly divine names are established in the Gods themselves. But it must be said that the second names, which are the imitations of the first, and which subsist intellectually, are of a dæmoniacal allotment. And again, we may say that those names which are the third from the truth, which are logically devised, and which receive the ultimate resemblance of divine natures, are unfolded by scientific men, at one time energizing divinely, and at another intellectually, and generating moving images of their inward spectacles. For as the demiurgic intellect establishes resemblances about matter of the first forms contained in himself, and produces temporal images of things eternal, divisible images of things indivisible, and adumbrated images as it were of true beings, - after the same manner I think the science that is with us representing intellectual production, fabricates resemblances of other things, and also of the Gods themselves, representing that which is void of composition in them, through composition; that which is simple, through variety; and that which is united, through multitude; and thus fashioning names, ultimately exhibits images of divine natures. For it generates every name as if it were a statue of the Gods. And as the theurgic art through certain symbols calls forth the exuberant and unenvying goodness of the Gods into the illumination of artificial statues, thus also the intellectual science of divine concerns, by the compositions and divisions of sounds, unfolds the occult essence of the Gods. Very properly therefore, does Socrates in the *Philebus* say, that on account of his reverence of the Gods, he is agitated with the greatest fear respecting their names. For it is necessary to venerate even the ultimate echoes of the Gods, and venerating these to become established in the first paradigms of them. And thus much concerning divine names,[2] which at present may be sufficient for the purpose of understanding the theology of Plato. For we shall accurately discuss them when we speak of partial powers.

[†] και is omitted in the original.

BOOK II
CHAPTER I

The most proper beginning however of the theory proposed by us is that from which we may be able to discover the first cause[†] of all beings. For being impelled from this in a becoming manner, and having our conceptions purified respecting it, we shall with greater facility be able to distinguish other things. About these things therefore we must speak from the beginning as follows: It is necessary that all beings, and all the natures of beings should either be many only, there being no one in them, neither in each, nor in all of them; or that they should be one only, there being no multitude, but all things being compelled into one and the same power of existence; or it is necessary that they should be both one and many, and that being should be one in order that neither multitude itself by itself may vanquish beings, nor that we may be forced to bring together into the same thing all things and their contraries at once. These things therefore being three, which of them shall we choose? And to which of the above mentioned assertions shall we give our suffrage. It is necessary therefore severally to discuss the absurdities which attend these positions, and thus to survey after what manner the truth subsists.

If then beings are many, and in such a manner many, as we have mentioned from the beginning, so that *The One* is not any where to be found, many absurdities will happen to be the result, or rather all the nature of beings will at once from the first be destroyed, as there will immediately be nothing which is capable of participating *The One*. For it must be admitted that every being is either one certain thing, or nothing. And that indeed which is a certain being, is also one; but that which is not even one being, has not any existence whatever. Hence, if many things have a subsistence, each of the many is something or a certain one. But if each of them is nothing, or not even one thing, neither is it possible for the many to exist; for the many are many so far as each individual of the multitude exists. If, therefore, the many alone have a subsistence, and *The One* in no respect is, neither will the many exist. For things which are in no respect one have not any existence whatever. But if *The One* is not, by a much greater priority neither

---

[†] For ουσιαν it is necessary to read αιτιαν.

have the many an existence. For it necessarily follows that none of the things from which the many consist will have a subsistence.

Farther still, if the many alone have a subsistence (as has been said) all things will be infinitely infinite; and if you receive any one of the infinities whatever, this also will be immediately infinite. And with respect to the things from which this consists and which are infinite, each of these likewise will be infinite. For let something of the many be assumed, which we say is not one, this therefore will be multitude according to its own nature, since it belongs to beings, but is not nothing. If however it is multitude, this also will consist of many things, and will be many. And if you assume something of these manys, this will immediately appear to you not to be one, but many. There will likewise be immediately the same reasoning in these, and in a similar manner each, (because we falsely speak of each) will be multitude in energy. And each, as I may say, will be infinite, or rather will be infinitely infinite. For there is nothing which will not be something of this kind; since a part is many, and in a similar manner the part of a part; and this to infinity. For multitude proceeding will never stop, nor infinity, in consequence of being deprived of the nature of *The One*. To make beings however, to be infinitely infinite, is impossible both with respect to truth, and to the thing proposed by us. For if being is infinitely infinite, being can neither be known, nor discovered; since the infinite is entirely incomprehensible and unknown. If also being is infinitely infinite, there will be something more infinite than the infinite. But if that something is more infinite, this will be less infinite. That, however, which is less infinite, since it is not perfectly infinite, will evidently be finite, so far as it falls short of the nature of the infinite. If, therefore, there is something which is itself according to multitude more infinite than that which is infinite in multitude there will be something more than the infinite, and the infinite will be less, yet not according to multitude. This however is impossible. Hence there is not the infinitely infinite.

Again therefore, according to this hypothesis, the same things will be according to the same, similar and dissimilar. For if all the manys are not one, and each thing according to all things is not one, that which is not one will evidently suffer the same passion in consequence of the privation of *The One*. All things therefore being deprived of *The One*, after the same manner, they will on this account subsist similarly with respect to each other. But things which subsist similarly, so far as they thus subsist, are evidently similar to each other. Hence the many will be similar to each other, so far as they are deprived of *The One*. They will likewise according to this privation of *The One* be perfectly dissimilar. For it is necessary that things which are similar should suffer the same passion; so that things which do not suffer any thing that is the same, will not be similar. But things which suffer any thing that is the same, suffer also one thing. Hence things which are deprived of every one, will not suffer any thing that is the same. The many therefore will be similar and dissimilar according to the same. But this is impossible. Hence it is impossible for the many to exist which are in no respect one.

Moreover, the many will be the same with and different from each other according to the same. For if all things are similarly deprived of *The One*, so far indeed as all of them are similarly deprived they will be the same according to this privation; since things which subsist after the same manner according to habit are the same, and also things which are after the same manner deprived according to privation. But so far in short, as each of them is deprived of every one, so far the many will be different from each other. For if *The One* in the many is the same, that which is in no respect one, will in no respect be the same. The many therefore will be the same and not the same with each other. But if they are the same and not the same it is evident that they are different from each other. For that which is the same and not the same, so far as it is not the same, is not the same, by nothing else than the different. Farther still therefore, these many will be moveable and immoveable, if *The One* is not. For if each of them is not one, they will be immoveable according to the privation of *The One*. For if that which is not one should be changed, each of them would have *The One*; since privations being changed, entirely lead into habits the things that are changed. It is necessary however that what is not one should remain immoveable according to the privation of *The One*, though this very thing is itself impossible, viz. that the many should stand still. For every thing which stands still is in something which is the same, viz. it is either in the same form, or in the same place. But every thing which is in the same, is in one thing which is the same. For the same in which it is, is one thing. Every thing therefore which stands still is in one thing. The many, however, do not participate of *The One*. But it is perfectly impossible that things which do not participate of *The One*, should be in one certain thing. And things which are not in one thing cannot stand still, since things which stand still are entirely in one and the same thing. It is impossible therefore, that the many should stand still, and remain immoveable. It has been demonstrated however, that the many must necessarily stand immoveable. The same things therefore, and the same passion, (I mean the privation of the habit of *The One*,) are moveable and immoveable. For things immoveable, and things which stand still, so far as they are unstable, so far they must necessarily appear to be moveable.

Moreover, there is no number of beings if *The One* in no respect is; but all things and each thing will not be one. For the particle of number, the monad, is one, and every number itself is one. For if there are five monads, there is also the pentad; and if three monads, the triad. But the triad itself is a certain unity, and so is the pentad. So that if there is no one, there will neither be any part, nor the whole of numbers. For how can there be any number *The One* not existing? For *The One* is the principle of numbers. But the principle not existing, neither is it possible that the things which proceed from this principle should exist. Hence *The One* not existing, neither will there be any number.

Again, therefore, neither will there be any knowledge of beings if *The One* is not. For it will not be possible either to speak or think of any being. For each thing itself, and every thing of which we can speak, and in which we impress the nature of *The One*, will have no existence, because neither does *The One* exist. Hence neither will there be any discourse nor any knowledge. For discourse is one thing consisting of many things, if it is perfect. And knowledge then exists, when that which knows becomes one with that which is known. But union not existing, there will at the same time be no knowledge of things, and it will be impossible to speak about things which we know. To which we may add, that the inexplicable in the several infinites, will necessarily always fly from the bound of knowledge. For immediately each apparent infinite which he who possesses knowledge desires to understand, will escape the gnostic power hastening to come into contact with, and adhere to it, since it is incapable either of contact or adhesion. If, therefore, the many alone have an existence, *The One* having no subsistence whatever, so many absurdities, and a still greater number must necessarily happen to those who adopt such an hypothesis.

But if *The One* which is *The One Itself* alone has a subsistence, and there is nothing else (for if there were there would not only be one but many things; since one and another thing are more than one, and are not one thing only) if this be the case, there will neither be among all things either whole, or that which has parts. For every thing which has parts is many, and every whole has parts. But *The One* is in no respect many. Neither therefore will there be a whole, nor that which has parts. Farther still, neither is it possible that there should be a beginning, or end of any thing. For that which has a beginning, a middle, and an end, is divisible. But *The One* is not divisible, because neither has it any parts. Hence, neither has it a beginning, nor a middle, nor an end. Again, if *The One* alone has a subsistence, no being will have a figure. For every thing which has figure is either rectilinear or circular, or mixed from these. But if indeed it is rectilinear, it will have for its parts, the middle and the extremes. If it is circular, there will be one thing in it as a middle, but other things as extremes, to which the middle extends. And if it is mixed from the right and circular line, it will consist of many things, and will not be one.

Moreover, neither will any being be in itself, nor in another thing. For that which is in another thing is different from that in which it is. But *The One* alone existing and nothing else (for it will by no means be in another thing) there will be no being which is in another thing. But that which is in itself will at the same time comprehend and be comprehended; and in this, to comprehend will not be the same thing as to be comprehended; nor will there be the same[†] definition of both. There will therefore be two things, and no longer *The One* alone. Again, neither will any being be moved. For being moved indeed, it must necessarily be changed. But being changed it must be in another thing. If *The One* however alone has an existence, it is not possible for any thing to appear to be in something else. Hence it is not possible for any being to be changed. But every thing which stands still is necessarily in the same thing. And that which is in the same is in a certain same thing. The one however is in no same thing. For that which is in a certain thing, is either in itself, or in something else. But it has been demonstrated, that it is neither in itself, nor in another. Hence neither is it in a certain same thing. Neither therefore does any being stand still.

Moreover, it is impossible for any thing to be the same with, or different from any thing. For if there is nothing besides *The One Itself*, there is not any thing which will be either the same with, or different from another thing. For there will not be any other being. And *The One Itself* will not be different from itself; for it would be many and not one. Nor will it be the same with itself. For this thing which is same is in another, and same is not *The One Itself*. For *The One* is simply one, because is it not many. But that which is same is the same with another thing. Again, neither is it possible for any thing to be similar or dissimilar to anything. For every thing similar suffers a certain same

---

[†] For ουτος it is necessary to read αυτος.

passion; but every thing dissimilar a certain different passion. *The One*, however, cannot suffer any thing, nor can this be the case with any thing else besides *The One*; since nothing else has any existence whatever, if *The One* alone has a subsistence.

Farther still, in addition to these things we say that neither is it possible for any thing to be touched, nor to be separate, if there is nothing else besides *The One*. For how can things which have no existence be separate, or come into contact with any thing? But neither can *The One* either be separate from itself, or touch itself. For it would thus be passive to the being touched, and the being separate. But *The One* suffers no other thing besides itself. It is likewise requisite that no one thing should either be equal or unequal to any thing. For that which is equal to another thing, is said to be so with reference to another thing. And the like may be said of that which is unequal. Another thing, however, has no existence, if *The One* alone has a subsistence. But neither can *The One* be equal or unequal to itself. For if unequal, there will be one thing in it as greater, but another as less; so that it will be two things and not one. And if *The One* is equal to itself, *The One* will measure itself. This however is impossible. For *The One* will measure and be measured by itself, so that it will not be *The One Itself*. Neither therefore will there be any equality or inequality in beings. If however these things are impossible, neither can any being come into contact with another, and be separate, nor be similar or dissimilar, nor be same or different, nor again, stand still, or be moved, or in short be in any thing, or have figure, or be a whole, or have parts, if *The One* alone has a subsistence which is void of multitude, and is without all these things. Neither however, is it possible for the many alone to have a subsistence, as was before demonstrated. And hence it is necessary that every being should be both many and one.

If this however is the case, either *the many* must participate of *The One*, or *The One* of *the many*, or both must participate of each other, or neither of each other; but *the many* indeed must be separate, and *The One* must also be separate, in order that *the many* and *The One* may subsist, as reason evinces. If, therefore, neither *The One* participates of *the many*, nor *the many* of *The One*, the same absurdities will ensue as we brought together in the hypothesis of *the many* alone having a subsistence. For again, there will be *the many* separate from *The One*. For if *The One* subsists by itself, and *the many* do not in any respect participate of *The One*, *the many* will be infinitely infinite, they will be similar and dissimilar, same and different, moved and stable, and there will neither be any number nor any knowledge of *the many*. For the absence of *The One* compels all these consequences to be apparent in *the many*. It is impossible therefore, that neither *the many* should participate of *The One*, nor *The One* of *the many*.

If however, *The One* participates of *the many*, and *the many* of *The One*, and both these are in each other, it is necessary that there should be another nature besides these, which is neither one nor many. For both these being mingled in each other, it is necessary that there should be a cause of their mixture which conjoins *multitude* to *The One*, and *The One* to *multitude*. For it is necessary that every thing that is mingled, should have a cause of the mixture. For in short, if *The One* and *multitude* participate of each other, neither *The One* is the cause of essence to *multitude*, nor *multitude* to *The One*, but a certain third thing is the cause of essence to both, and which is prior to these. For what will that be which makes this to be multitude, and that to be one? And what is the cause of this communication and association with each other, *The One* so far as it is one never having communication with *the many*? For *the many* so far as many, and *The One* so far as one are different from each other. And so far as neither is from neither, they have no sympathy with each other. What therefore is it which collects these into one, since they fly from and are unmingled with each other? For being thus discordant with each other, they cannot desire each other, or if they did their congress must be fortuitous. For if this should happen to be the case, there was a time when these were separate from each other, since now also they subsist together casually. It is however impossible for *the many* to subsist separate from *The One*. The mixture therefore is not casual. But neither is the mixture from *the many*, if neither *The One* is the cause of *the many*, nor *the many* of *The One*. What therefore is this more excellent thing [which is the cause of the mixture?] For it is either one, or not one. But if indeed, it is *The One Itself*, we must again inquire concerning this, whether it participates of multitude or of nothing. For if this participates, it is evident that some other thing prior to this, will for the same reason present itself to the view, and this will be the case to infinity. But if a thing of this kind is entirely void of multitude, again that which was asserted at first will not be true, viz. that *the many* do not participate of *The One*, nor *The One* of *the many*. I mean however that which is the most principal and primarily one. But there is indeed a certain one in the many, and there is also the imparticipable one, and which is simply one, and nothing else. If however that which is prior to both, is *not*[†] one, it is necessary

---

[†] ουχ is omitted in the original.

that this *not one* should be more excellent than *The One*. All things however are, and are generated what they are, through *The One*. And together with *The One* indeed every being is preserved; but separate from *The One* proceeds to the corruption of itself. The mixture also of *The One* and *multitude*, which the non-one affords to beings, is communion and union. *The One*† therefore, and that which is *not one*‡, are the cause of nothing else to beings than of their being one. If however *The One* is the cause of a thing of this kind, that which is *not one* will not be the cause of that which is more excellent [than union.] But it is every where necessary that what is more excellent should be the cause to beings of another more excellent thing, according to its own power. For thus it will be more excellent as being more good, and as the cause from its own nature of a greater and more excellent good to those things to which a less good is the cause of less goodness. From these things therefore it is necessary, that *the many* should participate of *The One*, that *The One* should be unmingled with *multitude*, and that nothing should be better than *The One*, but that this should also be the cause of being to *the many*. For every thing which is deprived of *The One*, flies immediately into nothing, and to its own corruption. But that which is not many, is not at one and the same time not many and nothing. For to *The One* that which is nothing, or not one, is opposed, and to *the many* that which is not many is opposed. If, therefore, *The One* and *the many* are not the same, the not being many will not be the same with nothing. From thus considering the affair therefore, it appears that *The One* is beyond multitude, and is the cause of being to *the many*.

CHAPTER II

It is necessary however, that discussing the same subject after another manner, we should again see if we can in a certain respect follow what has been said, and refer it to the same end. It is necessary therefore, that there should either be one principle, or many principles; or rather, we should begin from hence. And if there are many principles, they must either possess sympathy with each other, or they must be divulsed from each other, and they must be either finite or infinite. But if there is one

---

† Instead of το ον it is necessary to read το εν.

‡ The εν in the original which immediately precedes ουχ εν seems to be superfluous, and is therefore omitted in the translation.

principle, this must either be not essence, or essence. And if it is essence, this must either be corporeal or incorporeal. And if incorporeal, it must either be separate from, or inseparable from bodies. And if separate, it must either be moveable or immoveable. But if it is not essence, it must either be inferior to all essence, or participated by essence, or imparticipable. If therefore there are many principles, and which have no sympathy with each other, no being will originate from them [conjointly,] nor will they be common to all things, but each will produce by itself. For what communication can there be between things which are naturally foreign, or what co-operation between things which are entirely of a different kind? In addition also to these things, there will be *the many* which do not participate of *The One*. For if there is a certain one common in all of them, they will not be perfectly separated essentially from each other. If therefore they are different, and there is nothing which is the same about them, they are alone many and by no means one. But if there are many principles, and which possess sympathy with each other, they will have something common, which leads all of them to sympathy, and similarly unfolds all of them to the view. For we call those things sympathetic, which happen to be passive to the same thing. But similars are entirely similar from participating one form and one nature. If however this be the case, it is necessary that that all [or universal] which is every where, and in all the principles, should be of a more principal nature than the many. This therefore gives them the power to generate sympathy with each other, and affords them communion according to nature.

Again, if there are indeed infinite principles, either the things which proceed from them are infinite, and there will thus be the infinite twice, or they are finite, and thus all the principles will not be principles. For things finite in number, will entirely proceed from finite principles. The principles therefore are in vain infinite. To which may be added, that infinity makes both the principles to be unknown, and the things which proceed from them. For the principles being unknown, it is necessary that the things which proceed from them should be unknown; since we then think that we know any thing when we know the causes and the first principles of it. But if the principles are finite, it is evident that there will be a certain number of them: for we say that number is a definite multitude. If however, there is a number of the principles, it is necessary that there should be a cause of the whole number of them. For every number is from one; and this, viz. *The One* is the principle of numbers. This therefore will be the principle of principles, and the cause of finite multitude, since number itself is one, and the end in the many is one, and it bounds the many by that which is one. But the principle being one, and this being essence, it is necessary if this is admitted to be either corporeal or incorporeal, that it must be acknowledged to be the principle of other things.

If therefore, body is the cause of the generation of beings, it is necessary indeed, that it should be divisible and have parts. For every body is in its own nature divisible; since every magnitude is a certain whole and that which is a whole consists of parts. These parts therefore, (but I mean each of them) must either severally participate a certain one, or not participate it. If therefore they do not participate it, they will be many alone, and by no means one. Hence, neither will that which consists from them be a whole. For there being no one, that which consists of all of them will not be one. But if each of the parts participates of something of this kind, and there is something which is the same in all of them, a thing of this kind must necessarily be incorporeal, and impartible according to its own nature. For if this also is itself corporeal, it is either wholly in each of the parts, or not wholly. If therefore, it is indeed wholly in each, it will itself be separated from itself. For the parts in which it is are separate from each other. But if it is not wholly in each of the parts, this also will be divisible, and will have parts after the same manner as the above mentioned parts; and there will again be the same inquiry concerning these, viz. whether in these also there is something common, or nothing; since if there is nothing common, we shall place *the many* separate from *The One*.

Let us however consider the whole; for every body is a whole, and has parts. What therefore will that be which is connective of the parts, since they are many? For it is necessary to say either that the whole is unific of the parts, or the parts of the whole, or that some third thing prior to both, which is neither a whole, nor has any part, connects and unites the whole with its parts, and the parts with the whole. But if the whole indeed is connective of the parts, the whole will be incorporeal and impartible. For if it is a body, this also will be partible, and will be indigent of a nature which is capable of connecting the parts; and this will be the case to infinity. But if the parts are connective of the whole, how can *the many* be connective of *The One;* and things divided, of that which consists from them? For on the contrary, it is necessary that *The One* should have the power of uniting *the many*, and not *the many* of uniting *The One*. And if that which connects both, is neither a whole nor has parts, it will be perfectly impartible. But being impartible, it is also necessarily without interval. For every thing which has interval has parts, and is divisible. But being without interval it is incorporeal; for every body possesses interval.

Farther still, it is necessary that the principle should be perpetual; for every being is perpetual or corruptible. Hence it must be admitted that the principle of beings is perpetual or corruptible. But if we should grant that this may be corrupted, there will be no being incorruptible. For the principle being destroyed, it will neither be itself generated from any thing, nor will another thing be generated from it. For it can neither be able to generate itself (since it is not, if it is not perpetual) nor can another thing be able to generate it, if it is the principle of all things. But if it is incorruptible, it will have the power of not being corrupted, and this power will be infinite, in order that it may exist to infinity through the whole of time. For every finite power of existence pertains naturally to that which is corruptible. But an infinite power pertains to perpetual natures, the existence of which continues to infinity. This infinite therefore, I mean the infinite according to power, is either impartible or partible. But if it is partible indeed, there will be the infinite in a finite body. For the principle is finite; since if it were infinite, there will be nothing else besides itself. But if it is impartible, the power of infinitely existing will be incorporeal. And the principle of beings is incorporeal,[†] so far as it is this power through which the subject of it always is. That it is impossible therefore, the principle of beings can be corporeal is from these things evident.

If however it is incorporeal, it must either be separate, or inseparable from bodies. But if inseparable indeed, it will have all its energies in bodies, and subsisting about them. For that is inseparable from body which is not any where naturally adapted to energize except in and with bodies. But if the principle is a thing of this kind, it is evidently necessary that none of the things which subsist according to it should be more powerful, or possess greater authority than the principle of all beings. If however, nothing is more excellent in bodies than the power which subsists in and energizes about bodies, and a corporeal essence there will not any where be intellect and the power which energizes according to intellect. For every such like motion [*i.e.* energy] proceeds from a power, which is entirely in its energies independent of body. But it neither was, nor is lawful for generated natures to surpass the power of their causes. For every thing which is in the things begotten is from primary natures, and the latter are the lords of the essence of the former. If therefore, the principle of beings is able to generate intellect

---

[†] The words $\alpha\sigma\omega\mu\alpha\tau\sigma\varsigma\ \epsilon\sigma\tau\iota$ are omitted in the original.

and wisdom, how is it possible it should not generate it, on account of and in itself? For one of two things is necessary, either that intellectual perception pertains in no respect to beings, or that it is inferior to them; and that if it exists it acts in bodies only. These things however, it is impossible to assert. But if that which is the first of beings, and which is the principle of all things is separate from bodies, it is perfectly necessary to admit that it is either immoveable or moved. And if indeed it is moved, there will be something else prior to it, about which it is moved. For every thing which is moved, is naturally adapted to be moved about something else which is permanent. And farther still, besides this, it is moved through desire of another thing. For it is necessary indeed that it should be moved in consequence of desiring a certain thing; because motion itself by itself is indefinite. But the end of it is that for the sake of which it subsists. It desires however, either something else, or itself. But every thing which desires itself is immoveable. For why should any thing that is present with itself want to be in another thing? For of things which are moved, the motion of that is less to which the good is nearer, but the motion is greater of that to which the good is more remote. But that which possesses good in itself, and for the sake of which it subsists, will be immoveable and stable; since being always in itself, it is in good. That however which is in itself is in same; for each thing is the same with itself. But of that which is in itself we say indeed that it stands still and is immoveable; while that which is not immoveable, is not in itself but in another, is moved towards another thing, and is perfectly indigent of good. If therefore the principle of being is moved, but every thing which is moved is moved through the want of good, and towards another thing which is the object of desire to it, there will be something else which is desirable to the principle of beings besides itself, and about which possessing a sameness of subsistence, we must say it is moved. This however is impossible. For the principle is that for the sake of which all things subsist, which all things desire, and which is indigent of nothing. For if it were in want of something, it would be entirely subordinate to that of which it is in want, and to which its energy is directed as the object of desire. But if the principle is immoveable (for this is what remains,) it is necessary that it should be one incorporeal essence, possessing an eternal sameness of subsistence. After what manner, however, does it possess *The One*? And how is it one essence? For if essence and *The One* are the same, it must be admitted that the principle of beings is essence. But if essence is different from *The One*, it must be granted that to be *The One* is not the same thing as to be essence. And if, indeed, essence is better than *The One,* according to this it must be said to be with the principle. But if *The One* is better than essence and beyond it, *The One* is also the principle of essence. And if they are co-ordinate to each other, the many will be prior to *The One*.[†] This, however, is impossible as we have before demonstrated. It is evident, indeed, that essence is not the same as *The One*. For it is not one and the same thing to say one, and that essence is one; but the former is not yet a sentence, and the latter is. To which may be added, that if essence and *The One* are the same, multitude will be the same as that which has no existence, and which is not essence. This, however, is impossible. For in essence the many are contained, and in that which is not essence is *The One*. But if essence and *The One* are not the same, they will not be co-ordinate to each other; for if they were co-ordinate there will be some other thing prior to them, if it is necessary that all things should subsist from one principle. And if one of these is better than the other, either *The One* is prior to essence, or essence is prior to *The One*. But if *The One* indeed is prior to essence, this and not essence is the principle of all things. For it is necessary that nothing should be better than the principle. And if essence is prior to *The One, The One* will be passive to essence, and not essence to *The One*. But if *The One* is passive to essence, it is necessary that *The One* and essence should be every thing, and that all such things as are one should be essence, but not that all such things as are essence should be one. There will, therefore, be a certain essence deprived of *The One*. If, however, this be the case, it will be nothing. For that which is deprived of *The One* is nothing. Hence *The One* is prior to essence.

But if that which is first is something which is not essence, it is absurd to assert that it is subordinate to essence. For the principle is that which has the greatest power and the most absolute authority, and is most sufficient to itself, and is not that which is most ignoble, and indigent of the many. And, in short, it is necessary that no secondary nature should be better than the principle; for it is requisite that beings should not be governed badly. But if, indeed, the principle has an order subordinate to the things which proceed from it, and the things proceeding from it are better than it, all things will be badly confounded, nor will the principle according to nature be any thing else than something which is not the most excellent of things, nor will things which proceed from the principle possess from it a power of

---

[†] For essence and *The One* being two things will participate of the many, *i.e.* of the first many, or two.

ruling over their principle. The principle of beings, therefore, will indeed be fortuitous, and also the beings which are its progeny. But this is impossible. For things which are fortuitous (if to have a fortuitous subsistence is this, not to exist according to intellect, nor with a view to a definite end) are disorderly, infinite, and indefinite, and are all of them things which have a less frequency of subsistence. But the principle is invariably principle, and other things proceed from it. If however, that which is not essence is better than all essence, it will either be participated by it, or it will be entirely imparticipable. If, however, essence participates of the principle, of what will it be the principle? And how will it be the principle of all beings? For it is necessary that the principle of beings should be no one of beings; since if it were any one of them, it is necessarily not the principle of all beings. But every thing which is participated by another thing is said to be that by which it is participated, and in which it primarily is. The principle, however, is separate, and belongs in a greater degree to itself than to other things. Besides, every thing which is participated proceeds from another more excellent cause; since that which is imparticipable is better than that which is participable. It is not, however, possible to conceive any thing better than that which is most excellent, and which we call the principle. For it is not lawful to assert that things secondary to the principle, and which proceed from it, are in any respect better than their principle. The cause therefore of all beings is above all essence, is separate from every essence, and is neither essence, nor has essence as an addition to its nature. For such an addition as this is a diminution of simplicity, and of that which is one.

CHAPTER III

See, therefore, the third argument after these, leading us to the same conclusion with the former arguments. For it is necessary that the cause of all beings should be that of which all beings participate, to which they refer the subsistence of themselves, and which separates itself from nothing that in any respect whatever is said to have an existence. For this alone is the object of desire to beings, which primarily, or in some other way, is itself the cause of their subsistence. And it is necessary that every thing which is produced with reference to, and on account of it, should have a certain habitude with relation to it, and through this also, a similitude to it. For every habitude of one thing towards another, is predicated in a twofold respect, either from both participating of one thing, which affords to the participants a communion with each other; or from one of them participating of the other; of which, indeed, the one as being more excellent, imparts something to that which is subordinate to itself; but the other, as being inferior, is assimilated to the more excellent nature, so far as it participates of it. Hence it is necessary, if all sensible natures possess a habitude to that which is first, aspire after, and subsist about it, either that there should be a certain third thing the cause of the habitude, or that the principle should impart to the natures posterior to itself, a tendency to itself, and that desire, through which every thing is preserved, and exists. Nothing else, however, is more excellent than that which is first. Hence, the habitude of beings, their existence, and their tendency to the first, are derived from thence. And all things participate of the principle of themselves, if it is necessary that this which is participated, should from thence become apparent in all beings, since it is the principle of all things, and deserts no being whatever. What, therefore, will this nature be, which is every where, and in all beings? Is it life and motion? But there are indeed many things which are deprived of these. Is, therefore, permanency every where, and in all things? But neither is this true. For motion, so far as it is motion, will not participate of permanency. Is much-honoured intellect, therefore, so far as it is intellect, participated by all beings? But this also is impossible. For all beings would have intellectual perception, and no being would be deprived of intellect.

Shall we say, therefore, that being itself and essence are participated by all things that in any respect whatever have a subsistence? But how is this possible? For that which is in generation, or passing into existence, is said to be, and is destitute of essence. Nor must we wonder, if it also, since it ranks among beings, should now participate of essence. For so far as it is in generation, it is not; but it ends in existence and essence when it is now actually generated, and is no longer rising into existence. All things, therefore, that have in any respect whatever a subsistence, do not participate of essence. What then will that be which is every where and by all things participated? Let us consider every being, and see what that is to which all beings are passive, and what it is which is common in all of them, as in essence, sameness, difference, permanency, and motion. Can we say, therefore, that each of these is any thing else than one thing, and not only separately, but this is also the case with the things which subsist from them; and in short, it is not possible in a certain respect to speak otherwise of all things, than this, that all things, and each thing is one. For if any thing should be deprived of *The One*, though you should speak of parts, or of beings, immediately, that which becomes destitute of *The One*, will be altogether nothing. Or with what intention do we say that a thing which is not is perfectly nothing, [or not even one thing] unless *The One* is the last thing which deserts beings. This it is, therefore, to become that which in no respect is, and to be perfectly deprived of *The One*. For it is possible for that which is not moved to be, and for that which has no being to have an hyparxis; but that which is not even one thing, and which is destitute of *The One Itself*, will be entirely nothing. Hence *The One* is present with all beings; and though you should speak of multitude itself, it is necessary that this also should participate of *The One;* for if it does not become one thing, it is not possible for it to subsist. And if even you divide the whole to infinity, immediately nothing else than one occurs. For either that which is divided does not subsist, or becoming to be, or subsisting something else, it will be immediately one.† *The One*, therefore, which is every where apparent, and is in all beings, and which deserts no being whatever, is either derived from *The One* which is simply one, or from that which is more excellent than *The One*. For it is not possible for *The One* to be otherwise passive, [*i.e.* to be consubsistent with something else] than from the first one, to which *The One* is no longer present, but which is *The One Itself,* or nothing else than one.

Again, therefore, from another principle we may arrive at the same conclusion, by speaking as follows: It is necessary either that the causes of beings and things caused should proceed to infinity, and that there should be nothing first or last in beings; or that there should be no first, but that there should be the last of things, infinity existing in one part only. Or on the contrary, it is necessary that beings should proceed to infinity from a definite principle, or that there should be a certain first and last, and a boundary of beings each way. And if there are boundaries of beings, things either proceed from each other, and the generation of beings is in a circle; or if they are not from each other, either one of them is from another, or the first indeed is one, but the last not one, or the contrary, or both are one, or each is not one. If, therefore, first things, and the causes of beings are infinite, each thing will consist of infinites. For that which proceeds from a certain principle, must necessarily participate of that principle from which it proceeds. But that which derives its subsistence from many causes, will be in its own nature multiform, as participating of many powers. And that which is produced from infinites prior to itself, will have infinite peculiarities derived from the principles, and adapted to itself. Every

---

† For ου it is necessary to read εν.

being, therefore, being infinite, and consisting of infinites, will render all things infinitely infinite, and there will neither be a knowledge of any being, nor any evolution of powers. For the power of the infinite is perfectly unknown, and incomprehensible, by those natures to whom it is infinite.

But if things are infinite in a descending progression, whether is each of them infinite always proceeding most downward, in the same manner as we say all things do, or is each whole indeed finite, but the beings which are produced from these are infinite? For if every being according to the beginning of itself is definite, but according to its end is infinite, there will neither be in parts nor in wholes a conversion of beings to their proper principle, nor will that which is second in order ever have a subsistence so as to be assimilated to the extremity of a pre-existent order; though as we frequently say, the summits of inferiors are conjoined with the boundaries of superiors. For where there is no last, by what contrivance can such a similitude of progression as this, and such a mutual coherence of beings be left, according to which secondary things are always conjoined to the natures prior to them? But if all things alone have an infinity of this kind, each being bounded by that which is posterior to itself, wholes will be subordinate to parts, and the parts of beings will be naturally more perfect [than wholes.] For wholes, indeed, will be without conversion to the principle prior to themselves; but parts will be converted to it after their progression. By how much the more, however, every being hastens to conjunction with that which is more perfect than itself, by so much the more must it necessarily excel, as it appears to me. And if this whole proceeding infinity is not convolved to the summit of itself, and circularly converted and perfected according to such a conversion [it will not desire its proper good.] If, however, we admit that there is an infinity both ways these things must necessarily happen.

In addition to these things, also, there will be no common object of desire to all beings, nor any union nor sympathy of them. For things which are perfectly infinite have not that which is first in them; but not having a first, we shall not be able to say what is the common end of beings, and why some things are more excellent, but others are allotted a subordinate nature. For we call one thing better and another less excellent, from proximity to that which is best, just as we define the more and the less hot from communion with that which is hot in the first degree. And in short, we form a judgement of the more and the less from a reference to that which is a maximum. It is necessary, therefore, that the boundary in beings should be that which is first and that which is last.

But if, indeed, these are from each other, the same thing will be older and younger, cause and at the same time the thing caused, and each thing will be first and last. For it makes no difference whether these are from each other, or the things which subsist between these. For the extremes being indifferent, how is it possible that a mutation according to essence should intervene? But if the one is from the other, whether is the first derived from the last, as some say, who generate things more excellent from things subordinate, and things more perfect from such as are more imperfect? In this case, however, must not that which is allotted the power of generating and producing the perfect, by a much greater priority perfect and adorn itself by its present power? And how is it possible that leaving itself to be of an inferior allotment it should definitely assign a more excellent order to another thing? For every thing aspires after its proper perfection, and simply desires good; though not every thing is able to participate of a thing of this kind. If, therefore, it has the power of producing this most perfect thing, that which is last will energize on account of itself prior to other things, and the whole of good, and all perfection, will be first established in itself.

But if that which is last is produced from that which is first, and the most imperfect from that which is most perfect, whether, is each of them one, or is this one, but that not one? If, however, that which is first, or that which is last, is not one, neither of them will be first or last. For, as there will be multitude in each, each of them will have the better and the worse; and neither will that which is best be unmingled with that which is inferior to it, nor that which is the most obscure of all things according to being, have so great a subjection entirely deprived of a more perfect nature; but there will be something more extreme than that which is last, and something more perfect than that which is first. For every where that which is best if it receives another addition through that which is inferior will be more perfect than that which does not abide in the best, [through not receiving this very addition.] If, therefore, we rightly assert these things, *The One* is the principle of all things, and the last of beings is one. For it is necessary, I think, that the end of the progression of beings should be assimilated to the principle, and that as far as to this, the power of the first should proceed.

Summarily, therefore, recapitulating what we have said, it is necessary either that the first principle should be one, or that there should be alone many† first principles, or one containing multitude in itself, or many participating of one. But if there are many first principles only, there will not be one thing from them. For what will make one and a whole, if there are many principles, and there is nothing which produces one? For it is certainly necessary that things posterior to the principles should be assimilated to them. Either, therefore, there will not be *The One* in any being, or it will not be from these principles; so that each of the things which in any respect whatever have a subsistence will be divided multitude alone. And again each of the parts of any being will be a thing of this kind, and we shall in no way whatever stop, dividing into minute parts essence and existence. For all things will be many, and *The One* will be no where in the universality of things, nor will either wholes or parts be apparent.

But if it is necessary, indeed, that there should be many principles, and that they should participate of *The One*, *The One* will be co-ordinated in the many. Again, however, it is necessary, that the unco-ordinated should every where be more ancient than the co-ordinated, and the exempt than the participated. For how is *The One* in each of the many except from one principle which co-arranges the multitude, and converts it to itself according to the communion of *The One*? Again, if the first one were multiplied, *The One* will be passive; for at the same time it will be one and not one, and will not be that which is one [only.] It is necessary, however, in each genus of things, that there should be that which is unmingled with an inferior nature, in order that there may be that which is mingled, in the same manner as we say respecting forms. For from the equal itself, things which are equal in these sublunary realms, appear indeed as equal, though they are filled with a contrary nature; and from that which is primarily being, that which is mingled with non-being is derived, and which presents itself to the view as being. And in short every where the simple unmingled subsistence of each thing precedes those things which through remission are mingled with the privations of themselves. *The One* therefore is by itself exempt from all multitude; and that which is one, and at the same time not one, is not the first one, but is suspended‡ from that which is primarily one; through the principle, indeed, participating of *The One*, but through the

---

† viz. which are multitude only without any participation of *The One*.

‡ For εξηρηται it is necessary to read εξηρτηται. The punctuation also of the text in this place, must be altered agreeably to the translation.

diminution arising from multitude, now manifestly exhibiting in itself the cause of separation.

CHAPTER IV

That *The One* therefore is the principle of all things, and the first cause, and that all other things are posterior to *The One*, is I think evident from what has been said. I am astonished however at all the other interpreters of Plato, who admit the existence of the intellectual kingdom, but do not venerate the ineffable transcendency of *The One*, and its hyparxis which surpasses the whole of things. I particularly, however, wonder that this should have been the case with Origen,† who was a partaker of the same erudition with Plotinus. For Origen ends in intellect and the first being, but omits *The One* which is beyond every intellect and every being. And if indeed he omits it, as something which is better than all knowledge, language and intellectual perception, we must say that he is neither discordant with Plato, nor with the nature of things. But if he omits it because *The One* is perfectly unhyparctic, and without any subsistence, and because intellect is the best of things, and that which is primarily being is the same as that which is primarily one, we cannot assent to him in asserting these things, nor will Plato admit him, and connumerate him with his familiars. For I think that a dogma of this kind is remote from the philosophy of Plato, and is full of Peripatetic innovation. If you are willing, however, we will adduce some arguments against this dogma, and against all others who are the patrons of this opinion, and we will strenuously contend for the doctrine of Plato, and show that according to him the first cause is beyond intellect, and is exempt from all beings, as Plotinus and Porphyry, and all those who have received the philosophy of these men, conceive him to assert.

We shall begin, therefore, from the *Republic*; for here Socrates clearly shows that *The Good* is established above being, and the whole intellectual order, following the analogy of the first goodness to the sun. For if, as the sovereign sun is to generation, to every thing visible, and to all visive natures according to the power generative of light, so it is necessary *The Good* should be with reference to intellect and intelligibles, according to a cause productive of truth, - if this be the case, we must say that the sun is exempt at one and the same time from visive and

---

† This Origen was not the Christian father of that name, but was somewhat junior to him.

visible natures, and must admit that *The Good* transcends the natures which are always intellective, and also those which are eternally intelligible. It is better, however, to hear the Platonic words themselves: "You may say that the sun not only imparts the power of being seen to visible natures, but also that he is the cause of their generation, increase, and nutriment, not being himself generation. Certainly. We may say, therefore, that things which are known, have not only this from *The Good* that they are known, but likewise that their being and essence are thence derived, whilst *The Good Itself* is not essence, but beyond essence, transcending it both in dignity and in power." Through all these things, therefore, it is evident how *The Good* and the first principle are defined by Plato to be expanded above not only the intellectual, but also the intelligible extent, and essence itself, according to union, in the same manner as it is inferred the sun surpasses all visible natures, and perfects and generates all things by his light. How, therefore, following Plato, can we admit that intellect is the best of things, and the cause of all things? How can we assert that being itself[†] and essence are the same with the principle which is the leader of all the divine progressions? For essence and intellect are said to subsist primarily from *The Good*, to have their hyparxis about *The Good*, to be filled with the light of truth proceeding from thence, and to obtain the participation which is adapted to them from the union of this light, which is more divine than intellect itself and essence, as being primarily suspended from *The Good*, and affording in beings a similitude to that which is first. For the light which is emitted from the sun causes every thing visible to be solar-form. And the participation of the light of truth renders that which is intelligible boniform and divine. Intellect, therefore, is a god through a light which is more ancient than intellectual light and intellect itself, and that which is intelligible and at the same time intellectual participates of a divine hyparxis through a plenitude of this light being appropriately imparted to it.[‡] And in short, every divine nature is that which it is said to be, on account of this light, and is through it united to the cause of all beings. By no means, therefore, is the first good to be considered as the same with intellect, nor must it be admitted that the intelligible is more ancient than all the hyparxis of the whole of things, since it is even subordinate to the light proceeding from *The*

[†] For $\alpha\upsilon\tau o\ \tau o\ \epsilon\nu$ it is necessary to read $\alpha\upsilon\tau o\ \tau o\ o\nu$.

[‡] This sentence is very erroneous in the original, as will be evident from comparing it with the above translation.

Good, and being perfected by this light, is conjoined according to its own order with *The Good Itself*. For we must not say that the intelligible is united to the first after the same manner as the light [of truth;] but the latter through continuity with *The Good* is established in it without a medium; while the former, through this light, participates of a vicinity to *The Good*; since in sensibles also, the solar light is primarily connascent with the circulation of the sun, ascends as far as to the centre of the whole sphere, and subsists of all sides about it. But all sensible natures through this obtain a similitude to the sun, each of them according to its own nature being filled with solar-form illumination. These things, therefore, will be sufficient to recall into the memory of those who love the contemplation of truth, the conceptions of Plato on this subject, and to evince that the order of intellect is secondary to the exempt transcendency of *The One*.

If, however, it is requisite to evince the same thing through many testimonies, let us survey what the Elean guest in the *Sophista* determines concerning these things. He says, therefore, it is necessary that the multitude of all beings, whether they are contraries or not, should be suspended from the one being, [*i.e.* from being characterized by the one;] but that the one being itself should be suspended from *The One*. For when we call the hot or the cold, or permanency or motion, being, we do not denominate each of these as the same with being itself. For if permanency were being itself, motion would not be being; or, if motion were such like being, permanency would not participate of the appellation of being. But it is evident that being accedes to permanency, to motion, and to every multitude of beings from one thing which is primarily being. This very thing, therefore, which is the cause of essence to all things, and which is participated by all other things, is a participant of this one, and on this account, as it is being alone, so also it is primarily being.[†] It is, however, being itself indeed, and is not allotted *to be*, from participation; but it is one according to participation, and on this account it is passive to *The One*. But it is being[‡] primarily. If, therefore, Plato gives to *The One* a subsistence beyond being, in the same manner as that which is first in wholes is supposed by him to transcend beings, how is it possible that being should not be posterior to *The One*, since it participates of it, and on this account is denominated one?

[†] For εν it is necessary to read ον.

[‡] Here also ον must be substituted for εν.

Moreover, Socrates in the *Philebus* clearly demonstrates the same thing to those who are able to know wholes from parts, viz. that intellect has not the same order as the first cause of all. Investigating, therefore, the good of the human soul and its end, of which participating in every respect sufficiently it will reap the fruits of a felicity adapted to its nature, he in the first place removes pleasure from an end of this kind, and after this intellect, because neither is this replete with all the elements of *The Good*. If, therefore, the intellect which is in us is an image of the first intellect, and the good of the whole of our life is not to be defined according to this alone, is it not necessary that in wholes also, the cause of good must be established above intellectual perfection? For if that which is primarily good subsisted according to total intellect, in us also and all other [intellectual natures,] self-sufficiency and appropriate good would be present through the participation of intellect. Our intellect, indeed, is disjoined from *The Good*, and is indigent, and on this account requires pleasure in order to the attainment of human perfection. But a divine intellect always participates of *The Good*, and on this account is divine. For it is boniform through the participation of good; but divine, as being suspended from the first deity. It is the same reasoning, therefore, which infers that *The Good* is exempt from the first intellect, and which defines felicity to consist not in intelligence only, but in the all-perfect presence of *The Good*. For the intellectual form of energy is itself by itself defective with respect to blessedness. And why is it requisite to be prolix? For Parmenides teaches us most clearly the difference of *The One* from essence and being, and shows that *The One* is exempt from all other things and from essence; for this he evinces of *The One* at the end of the first hypothesis. But how is it possible that the cause of essence, and which is exempt from it through supreme transcendency, should not also be beyond the intellectual order? For intellect is essence. But if in intellect there is permanency and motion, and Parmenides demonstrates that *The One* transcends both these, does he not immediately bring us to the ineffable cause of all things, which is prior to every intellect? And if every intellect is converted to itself, and is in itself, but *The One* is demonstrated to be neither in itself, nor in another, how can we any longer consider intellect as the same with the first cause of all? In what respect, also, will *The One* which is prior to being differ from the one being, which is the subject of the second hypothesis, if intellect is the best of things, and the first principle of all? For the one being participates of *The One;* but that which participates is secondary to that which is participated.

That *The One*, however, is according to Plato more ancient than intellect and essence, is through what has been said recalled to our memory.

CHAPTER V

In the next place, if *The One* is neither intelligible nor intellectual, nor in short participates of the power of being, let us survey what will be the modes of leading us to it, and through what intellectual conceptions Plato unfolds as far as he is able, to his familiars, the ineffable and unknown transcendency of the first. I say then, that at one time he unfolds it through analogy, and the similitude of secondary natures; but at another time he demonstrates its exempt transcendency, and its separation from the whole of things, through negations. For in the *Republic*, indeed, he indicates the ineffable peculiarity and hyparxis of *The Good*, through analogy to the sun; but in the *Parmenides*, he demonstrates the difference of *The One* with respect to all things posterior to it through negations. But he appears to me through one of these modes to unfold the progression from the first cause of all other things, and prior to other things, of the divine orders. For on this account the first cause is exempt from all the natures produced by it, because every where cause is established above its effects; and on this account the first is nothing of all things, because all things proceed from him. For he is the principle of all things, both of beings, and at the same time of non-beings. But again, according to the other of these modes, he adumbrates the conversion to the first of the things which have proceeded from it. For in each order of beings, through similitude to it there is a monad analogous to *The Good*, which has the same relation to the whole series conjoined with it, that *The Good* has to all the orders of the Gods. The cause, however, of this similitude is entirely the conversion of the whole of things to *The Good*. These, therefore, proceed from thence and are converted to it. And the progression indeed of all things demonstrates to us the ascent to the first through negations; but the conversion of all things demonstrates this to us through analogies. Let not, however, any one considering these negations to be such things as privations despise such a mode of discussion, nor defining the sameness in words analogously, and words in habitudes, endeavour to calumniate this anagogic progression to the first principle. For negations, as it appears to me, extend a triple peculiarity in things. And at one time, indeed, being more primogenial than affirmations, they are procreative and perfective of the generation of them. But at another time, they are allotted an order co-ordinate to affirmations, and negation is then in no respect more venerable than affirmation. And again, at another time, they are allotted an order subordinate to affirmations, and are nothing else than the privations of them. For with respect to non-being itself, with which there is also a negation of beings, at one time considering it as beyond being, we say that it is the cause and the supplier of beings; but at another time we evince that it is equivalent to being; just as I think, the Elean guest demonstrates [in the *Sophista*] that non-being is in no respect less, if it be lawful so to speak, than being; and at another time we leave it as a privation of, and indigent of being. For indeed, according to this mode, we call every generation, and matter itself, non-being.

Analogies, however, are assumed for the purpose alone of indicating the similitude of secondary natures to the first principle. And neither any reason, nor habitude, nor communion of this principle with things posterior to it, becomes apparent from these. For its exempt nature is not of such a kind as is beheld in the second and third orders of beings; but *The Good* transcends the whole of things in a much greater degree than intellect surpasses the natures posterior to itself, whether it be the demiurgic intellect, or the intellect of the whole world, or some other intellect from among the number of those that are called divine. Every intellect however, and every god, is allotted a transcendency with respect to subordinate natures, and those things of which it is the cause, inferior to that which the first principle has to every being; for this principle similarly transcends all things, and not some in a greater, but others in a less degree; since thus we should introduce a greater and less habitude of it to secondary natures. It is necessary, however, to preserve it without habitude to all things, and similarly exempt from the whole of things. But of other natures, some are indeed nearer, and others are more remote from it. For each thing proceeds from it, since it produces all things according to one cause. And different things are indeed converted to it in a different manner, this principle in the mean time, receiving no habitude or communion with things posterior to itself.

CHAPTER VI

The mode of demonstration, therefore, pertaining to *The One* is, as we have said, twofold. For again, Plato delivers to us twofold names of the ineffable cause. In the *Republic* indeed he calls it *The Good*, and demonstrates it to be the fountain of the truth which unites intellect and intelligibles. But in the *Parmenides*, he denominates such a principle as this *The One*, and shows that it gives subsistence to the divine unities.

Again therefore, of these names, the one is the image of the progression of the whole of things, but the other of their conversion. For because indeed all things derive their subsistence and proceed from the first principle, on this account referring *The One* to it, we demonstrate that it is the cause of all multitude and every progression. For whence is multitude unfolded into light except from *The One?* But because again the progressions from it are naturally converted to it, and desire its ineffable and incomprehensible hyparxis, we denominate it *The Good.* For what else is that which converts all things, and which is extended to all beings as the object of desire, but *The Good?* For all other things subsist distributedly, and are to some beings honourable, but to others not. And every thing which in any respect whatever is said to have a subsistence aspires after some things, and avoids others. But *The Good* is the common object of desire to all beings, and all things according to their nature verge and are extended to this. The tendency however of desiring natures is every where to the appropriate object of desire. *The Good* therefore converts, but *The One* gives subsistence to all secondary natures. Let not, however, any one suppose that the ineffable can on this account be named, or that the cause of all union is doubled. For here indeed we transfer to it names, looking to that which is posterior to it, and to the progressions from, or the circular conversions to it. Because, indeed, multitude subsists from it, we ascribe to it the appellation of *The One;* but because all things even as far as to things that have the most obscure existence, are converted to it, we denominate it *The Good.*

We endeavour therefore to know the unknown nature of the first principle, through the things which proceed from, and are converted to it; and we also attempt through the same things to give a name to that which is ineffable. This principle, however, is neither known by beings, nor is effable by any one of all things; but being exempt from all knowledge, and all language, and subsisting as incomprehensible, it produces from itself according to one cause all knowledge, every thing that is known, all words, and whatever can be comprehended by speech. But its unical nature, and which transcends all division, shines forth to the view dyadically in the natures posterior to it, or rather triadically. For all things abide in, proceed from, and are converted to *The One.* For at one and the same time, they are united to it, are in subjection to its union which is exempt from the whole of things, and desire the participation of it. And union indeed imparts a stable transcendency to all secondary natures, and which subsists in unproceeding conjunction with the cause of them. But subjection defines the progression of beings, and their separation from the imparticipable and first unity. And desire perfects the conversion of the subsisting natures, and their circular tendency to the ineffable. First natures therefore, being always entirely united, [to the ineffable] some more remotely, but others more proximately, and receiving through this union their hyparxis, and their portion of good, we endeavour to manifest through names the progression and conversion of the whole of things. But with respect to their stable comprehension, if it be lawful so to speak, in the first, and their union with the ineffable, this as being incomprehensible, and not to be apprehended by knowledge, those who were wise in divine concerns were unable to indicate it by words. But as the ineffable is primarily concealed in inaccessible places, and is exempt from all beings, thus also the union of all things with it is occult ineffable, and unknown to all beings. For every being is united to it, neither by intellectual injection, [or projection] nor the energy of essence; since things which are destitute of knowledge are united to the first, and things deprived of all energy, participate according to their order of a conjunction with it. That which is unknown therefore in beings according to their union with the first, we neither endeavour to know, nor to manifest by names, but being more able to look to their progression and conversion, we ascribe indeed to the first two names, which we derive as resemblances from secondary natures. We also define two modes of ascent to the first, conjoining that mode which is through analogy with the appellation of *The Good*, but that which is through negations with the appellation of *The One;* which Plato also indicating, in the *Republic* indeed calls the first *The Good,* and at the same time makes a regression to it through analogy; but in the *Parmenides* establishing it as *The One Itself*, he unfolds the transcendency of it which is exempt from beings, through negative conclusions. According to both these modes therefore, the first principle transcends both gnostic powers, and the parts of speech; but all other things afford us the cause of knowledge and of appellation. And the first principle indeed unically gives subsistence to all the unions and hyparxes of secondary natures; but the things posterior to this cause participate of it in a divided manner. These also, as we have before observed, become multiplied by abiding, proceeding and returning; but *The One* is at once perfectly exempt from all the prolific progressions, convertive powers, and uniform hypostases in beings. What the modes therefore are of the doctrine about the first, and through what names Plato endeavours to indicate it, and whence the names and the modes of this indication which is unknown to all things are derived, is, I think, through what has been said sufficiently manifest.

CHAPTER VII

If, however, it be requisite to survey each of the dogmas about it which are scattered in the writings of Plato, and to reduce them to one science of theology, let us consider, if you are willing, prior to other things, what Socrates demonstrates in the 6th book of the *Republic*, conformably to the before mentioned mode, and how through analogy he teaches us the wonderful transcendency of *The Good* with respect to all beings, and the summits of the whole of things. In the first place therefore, he distinguishes beings from each other, and establishing some of them to be intelligibles, but others sensibles, he defines science by the knowledge of beings. But he conjoins sense with sensibles, and giving a twofold division to all things, he places one exempt monad over intelligible multitude, and a second monad over sensible multitude, according to a similitude to the former monad. Of these monads also, he shows that the one is generative of intelligible light, but the other of sensible light. And he evinces that by the intelligible light indeed, all intelligibles are deiform, and boniform, according to participation from the first God; but that by the sensible light, according to the perfection derived from the sun, all sensible natures are solarform, and similar to their one monad. In addition also to what has been said, he suspends the second monad from that which reigns in the intelligible. And thus he extends all things, both the first and the last of beings, I mean intelligibles and sensibles, to *The Good*. Such a mode of reduction to the first as this, appears to me to be most excellent, and especially adapted to theology; viz. to congregate all the Gods in the world into one union, and suspend them from their proximate monad; but to refer the supermundane Gods to the intellectual kingdom; to suspend the intellectual Gods from intelligible union; and to refer the intelligible Gods themselves, and all beings through these, to that which is first. For as the monad of mundane natures is supermundane, as the monad of supermundane natures is intellectual, and of intellectual natures intelligible, thus also it is necessary that first intelligibles should be suspended from the monad which is above intelligibles and perfected by it, and being filled with deity, should illuminate secondary natures with intelligible light. But it is necessary that intellectual natures which derive the enjoyment of their being from intelligibles, but of good and a uniform hyparxis from the first cause, should connect supermundane natures by intellectual light. And that the genera of the Gods prior to the world, through receiving a pure intellect from the intellectual Gods, but intelligible light from the intelligible Gods, and a unical light from the father of the whole of things, should send into this apparent world the illumination of the light which they possess. On this account, the sun being the summit of mundane natures, and proceeding from the etherial profundities, imparts to visible natures supernatural perfection, and causes these as much as possible to be similar to the supercelestial worlds. These things therefore we shall afterwards more abundantly discuss.

The present discourse, however, suspends all things after the above mentioned manner from *The Good*, and the first unity. For if indeed the sun connects every thing sensible, but *The Good* produces and perfects every thing intelligible, and of these, the second monad [*i.e.* the sun] is denominated the offspring of *The Good* and on this account causes that which is sensible to be splendid, and adorns and fills it with good, because it imitates the primogenial cause of itself, - if this be the case, all things will thus participate of the good, and will be extended to this one principle, intelligibles indeed, and the most divine of beings without a medium, but sensibles through their monad [the sun].

Again therefore, and after another manner, Plato narrates to us in this extract from the *Republic* the analysis to the first principle. For he suspends all the multitudes in the world from the intelligible monads, as for instance, all beautiful things from the beautiful itself, all good things from *The Good*, and all equal things from the equal itself. And again, he considers some things as intelligibles, but others as sensibles; but the summits of them are uniformly established in intelligibles. Again, from these intelligible forms he thinks fit to ascend still higher, and venerating in a greater degree the goodness which is beyond intelligibles, he apprehends that all intelligibles, and the monads which they contain, subsist and are perfected through it. For as we refer the sensible multitude to a monad unco-ordinated with sensibles, and we think that through this monad the multitude of sensibles derives its subsistence, so it is necessary to refer the intelligible multitude to another cause which is not connumerated with intelligibles, and from which they are allotted their essence and their divine hyparxis.

Let not, however, any one fancy that Plato admits there is the same order of *The Good* in intelligible forms, as there is prior to intelligibles. But the good indeed, which is co-ordinated with the beautiful, must be considered as essential, and as one of the forms which are in intelligibles. For the first good, which by conjoining the article with the noun we are accustomed to call τα' γαθον or *The Good*, is admitted to be something superessential, and more excellent than all beings both in dignity and power; since Socrates also, when discussing the beautiful and the good, calls the one the beautiful itself and the other the good itself, and thus says he we must denominate all the things which we then very properly considered as many. Again, particularly considering each thing as being one, we denominate each thing that which it is, and thus Socrates leading us from sensible things that are beautiful and good, and in short from things that are participated, subsist in other things, and are multiplied, to the superessential unities of intelligibles and the first essences, from these again, he transfers us to the exempt cause of every thing beautiful and good. For in forms, the beautiful itself is the leader of many beautiful things, and the good itself of many goods, and each form alone gives subsistence to things similar to itself. But the first good is not only the cause of what is good, but similarly of things beautiful, as Plato elsewhere says; and "all things are for its sake, and it is the cause of every thing beautiful."

For again, in addition to what has been said, the good which is in forms is intelligible and known, as Socrates himself teaches; but *The Good* prior to forms is beyond beings, and is established above all knowledge. And the former is the source of essential perfection; but the latter is the supplier of good to the Gods so far as they are Gods, and is generative of goods which are prior to essences. We must not therefore apprehend that when Socrates calls the first principle *The Good*, from the name of idea, that he directly calls it the intelligible goodness; but though the first principle is superior to all language and appellation, we permit Socrates to call it the cause of every thing beautiful and good, transferring through the things which are proximately filled by it, appellations to it. For this I think Socrates indicating asserts in all that he says about *The Good*, that it is beyond knowledge and things that are known, and likewise beyond essence and being, according to its analogy to the sun. And after a certain admirable manner he presents us with an epitome of the negations of *The One* in the *Parmenides*. For the assertion that *The Good* is neither truth, nor essence, nor intellect, nor science, at one and the same time separates it from the superessential unities, and every genus of the Gods, and from the intellectual and intelligible orders, and from every psychical subsistence. But these are the first things, and through the first hypothesis of the *Parmenides*, these are taken away from the principle of the whole of things.

Moreover, neither when he celebrates *The Good* the leader of the divine orders, as the most splendid of being, does he denominate it *most splendid* as participating of light. For the first light proceeds from it to intelligibles and intellect, but he gives it this appellation as the cause of the light which is every where diffused, and as the fountain of every intelligible, or intellectual, or mundane deity. For this light is nothing else than the participation of a divine hyparxis. For as all things become boniform through participating of *The Good* and are filled with the illumination proceeding from thence, thus also the natures which are primarily beings are deiform; and as it is said, intelligible and intellectual essences become divine through the participation of deity. Looking therefore to all that has been said, we shall preserve the exempt transcendency of *The Good* with reference to all beings and the divine orders. But again, in each order of beings, we must grant that there is a monad analogous to it, not only in sensibles, as Plato says the sun is, but likewise in supermundane natures, and in the genera of Gods arranged from *The Good* prior to these. For it is evident that the natures which are nearer to the first cause and which participate of it in a greater degree, possess a greater similitude to it. And as that is the cause of all beings, so these establish monads which are the leaders of more partial orders. And Plato indeed arranges the multitudes under the monads; but extends all the monads to the exempt principle of the whole of things, and establishes them uniformly about it. It is necessary therefore that the theological science should be unfolded conformably to the divine orders, and that our conceptions about it should be transcendent, and unmingled and unconnected with other things. And we should survey indeed all secondary natures, subsisting according to and perfected about it; but we should establish it as transcending all the monads in beings, according to one excess of simplicity, and as unically arranged prior to the whole orders [of Gods.] For as the Gods themselves enact the order which is in them, thus also it is necessary that the truth concerning them, the precedaneous causes of beings, and the second and third progeny of these should be definitely distinguished.

This, therefore, is the one truth concerning the first principle, and which possesses one reason remarkably conformable to the Platonic hypothesis, viz. that this principle subsists prior to the whole orders in the Gods, that it gives subsistence to the boniform essence of the Gods, that it is the fountain of superessential goodness, and that all things posterior to it being extended towards it, are filled with good, after an ineffable manner are united to it, and subsist uniformly about it. For its unical nature is not unprolific, but it is by so much the more generative of other things, as it pre-establishes a union exempt from the things which have a subsistence. Nor does its fecundity tend to multitude and division; but it abides with undefiled purity concealed in inaccessible places. For in the natures also which are posterior to it, we every where see that what is perfect desires to generate, and that what is full hastens to impart to other things its plenitude. In a much greater degree therefore it is necessary that the nature which contains in one all perfections, and which is not a certain good, but good itself, and superfull, (if it be lawful so to speak) should be generative of the whole of things, and give subsistence to them; producing all things by being exempt from all things, and by being imparticipable, similarly generating the first and the last of beings.

You must not, however, suppose that this generation and progression is emitted in consequence of *The Good* either being moved, or multiplied, or possessing a generative power, or energizing; since all these are secondary to the singleness of the first. For whether *The Good* is moved, it will not be *The Good;* since *The Good Itself,* and which is nothing else, if it were moved would depart from goodness. How, therefore, can that which is the source of goodness to beings, produce other things when deprived of good? Or whether *The Good* is multiplied through imbecility, there will be a progression of the whole of things through a diminution, but not through an abundance of goodness. For that which in generating departs from its proper transcendency, hastens to adorn inferior natures, not through prolific perfection, but through a diminution and want of its own power. But if *The Good* produces all things by employing power, there will be a diminution of goodness about it. For it will be two things and not one, viz. it will be good and power. And if indeed it is in want of power, that which is primarily good will be indigent. But if to be *The Good Itself* is sufficient to the perfection of the things produced, and to the plenitude of all things, why do we assume power as an addition? For additions in the Gods are ablations of transcendent unions. Let *The Good* therefore alone be prior to power, and prior to energy. For all energy is the progeny of power. Neither, therefore, does *The Good* energizing give subsistence to all things through energy, nor being in want of power does it fill all things with powers, nor being multiplied do all things participate of good, nor being moved do all beings† enjoy the first principle. For *The Good* precedes all powers, and all energies, and every multitude and motion; since each of these is referred to *The Good* as to its end. *The Good* therefore is the most final of all ends, and the centre of all desirable natures. All desirable natures, indeed, impart an end to secondary beings; but that which pre-subsists uncircumscribed by all things is the first good.

---

† For παντα παροντα, I read παντα τα οντα.

CHAPTER VIII

After these things, however, let us direct our attention to the conceptions about the first principle in the epistle [of Plato] to Dionysius, and survey the manner in which he considers its ineffable and immense transcendency. But perhaps some one may be indignant with us for rashly drawing to our own hypotheses the assertions of Plato, and may say that the three kings of which he speaks are all of them intellectual Gods; but that Plato does not think fit to co-arrange or connumerate *The Good* with secondary natures. For such a connumeration ought not to be considered as adapted to the exempt transcendency of *The Good* with respect to other things, nor in short, must it be said that *The Good* contributes as the first with reference to another second or third cause to the completion of a triad in conjunction with other natures; but that it in a greater degree precedes every triad and every number, than the intelligible precede the intellectual Gods. How, therefore, can we connumerate with other kings *The Good* which is at once exempt from all the divine numbers, and co-arrange one as the first [king,] another as the second, and another as the third? Some one may also adduce many other things, indicating the transcendency of the first principle with respect to every thing divine. Such a one, however, in thus interpreting the words of Plato will remarkably accord with us who assert *The Good* to be imparticipable, to transcend all the intelligible and intellectual genera, and to be established above all the divine monads.

That Plato, indeed, admits the first God to be the king of all things, and says that all things are for his sake, and that he is the cause of all beautiful things, does not I think require much proof to those who consider his words by themselves apart from their own conjectures, by introducing which they violently endeavour to accord with Plato. But that we do not assert these things connumerating [the first God with secondary natures,] Plato himself manifests, neither calling the first king the first, but alone the king of all things, nor asserting that some things are about him, as he says that second things are about that which is second, and third things about that which is third, but[†] he says, in short, that all things are about him. And to the other kings, indeed, he introduces number and a divided kingdom; but to the king of all things he neither attributes a part of number, nor a distribution of dominion opposite to that of the others. Such a mode of words, therefore, neither

---

† For και here, it is necessary to read αλλα.

connumerates the king of all things with the other kings, nor co-arranges him as the leader of a triad with the second and third power. For of a triadic division the first monad, indeed, is the leader of first orders, and which are co-ordinate with itself; but the second of second; and the third of third orders. If, however, some one should apprehend that the first monad is the leader of all things, so as to comprehend at once both second and third allotments; yet the cause which subsists according to comprehension is different from that which similarly pervades to all things. And to the king of all things, indeed, all things are subject according to one reason and one order; but to the first of the triad, things first are subjected according to the same order; and it is necessary that things second and third should be subservient according to their communion with the remaining kings. Does not, therefore, what is here said by Plato remarkably celebrate the exempt nature of the first cause, and his unco-ordination with the other kingdoms of the Gods? Since he says that this cause similarly reigns over all things, that all things subsist about him, and that for his sake essence and energy are inherent in all things.

If also Socrates in the *Republic* clearly[†] teaches that the sun reigns over the world analogous to *The Good*, let no one dare to accuse this analogy as connumerating *The Good* with the king of mundane natures. For unless[‡] together with the similitude of secondary causes to the first principles, we think fit to preserve that exempt dominion [of the first cause] it will be impossible for us to evince that the super-mundane kings have their allotment analogous to the first cause, who subsists prior to the whole of things according to one transcendency. But what occasion is there to be prolix? For Plato indeed calls the first God king; but he does not think fit to give the others the same appellation, not only in the beginning of what he says about the first, but shortly after, he adds: "About the king himself and the natures of which I have spoken there is nothing of this kind." The first God, therefore, alone is called king. But he is called not only the king of things first, in the same manner as the second of things second, and the third of things third, but as the cause at once of all being and all beauty. Hence the first God precedes the other causes in an exempt and uniform manner, and according to a transcendency of the whole of things, and is neither

---

† For σοφως, it is necessary to read σαφως.

‡ In the original μη is wanting after ει.

celebrated by Plato as co-ordinated with them, nor as the leader of a triad.

That these things, however, are asserted by Plato about the first God we shall learn by recurring a little to the preceding words, which are as follows: "You say, that I have not sufficiently demonstrated to you the particulars respecting the first nature. I must speak to you, therefore, in enigmas, that in case the letter should be intercepted, either by land or sea, he who reads it may not understand this part of its contents. All things are situated about the king of all; and all things are for his sake; and he is the cause of every thing beautiful." In these words, therefore, Plato proposing to purify our conceptions about the first principle through enigmas, celebrates the king of all things, and refers to him the cause of the whole of things beautiful and good. Who, therefore, is the king of all things, except the unical God who is exempt from all things, who produces all things from himself, and is the leader of all orders according to one cause? Who is he that converts all ends to himself, and establishes them about himself? For if you call him, for whose sake all things subsist, the end of all ends, and the primogenial cause, you will not deviate from the truth concerning him. Who is he that is the cause of all beautiful things, shining upon them with divine light, and who encloses that which is deformed and without measure, and the most obscure of all things in the extremity of the universe?

If you are willing also from the words of Plato that follow the preceding, we will show that to be the recipient neither of language nor of knowledge is adapted to the first principle. For the words: "This your inquiry concerning the cause of all beautiful things is as of a nature endued with a certain quality." are to be referred to this principle. For it is not possible to apprehend it intellectually, because it is unknown, nor to unfold it, because it is uncircumscribed; but whatever you may say of it, you will speak as of a *certain thing;* and you will speak indeed *about* it, but you will not speak *it.* For speaking of the things of which it is the cause, we are unable to say, or to apprehend through intelligence what it is. Here therefore, the addition of quality, and the busy energy of the soul, remove it from the goodness which is exempt from all things, by the redundancy of its conceptions about it. This likewise draws the soul down to kindred, connate, and multiform intelligibles, and prevents her from receiving that which is characterized by unity, and is occult in the participation of *The Good.* And it is not only proper that the human soul should be purified from things co-ordinate with itself in the union and communion with that which is first, and that for this purpose it should leave all the multitude of itself behind, and exciting its own hyparxis, approach with closed eyes, as it is said, to the king of all things, and participate of his light, as much as this is lawful for it to accomplish; but intellect also, which is prior to us, and all divine natures, by their highest unions, superessential torches, and first hyparxes are united to that which is first, and always participate of its exuberant fullness; and this not so far as they are that which they are, but so far as they are exempt from things allied to themselves, and converge to the one principle of all. For the cause of all disseminated in all things impressions of his own all-perfect transcendency, and through these establishes all things about himself, and being exempt from the whole of things, is ineffably present to all things. Every thing therefore, entering into the ineffable of its own nature, finds there the symbol of the father of all. All things too naturally venerate him, and are united to him, through an appropriate mystic impression, divesting themselves of their own nature, and hastening to become his impression alone, and to participate him alone, through the desire of his unknown nature, and of the fountain of good. Hence, when they have run upwards as far as to this cause, they become tranquil, and are liberated from the parturitions and the desire which all things naturally possess of goodness unknown, ineffable, imparticipable, and transcendentally full. But that what is here said is concerning the first God, and that Plato in these conceptions leaves him unco-ordinated with and exempt from the other causes, has been, I think, sufficiently evinced.

CHAPTER IX

Let us in the next place consider each of the dogmas, and adapt them to our conceptions concerning cause, that from these we may comprehend by a reasoning process, the scope of the whole of Plato's theology. Let then one truth concerning the first principle be especially that which celebrates his ineffable, simple, and all-transcending nature; which establishes all things about him, but does not assert that he generates or produces any thing, or that he pre-subsists as the end of things posterior to himself. For such a form of words neither adds any thing to the unknown, who is exempt from all things, nor multiplies him who is established above all union, nor refers the habitude and communion of things secondary to him who is perfectly imparticipable. Nor in short, does it announce that it teaches any thing about him, or concerning his nature, but about the second and third natures which subsist after him.

Such then being this indication of the first God, and such the manner in which it venerates the ineffable, the second to this is that which converts all the desires of things to him, and celebrates him as the object of desire to and common end of all things, according to one cause which precedes all other causes. For the last of things subsists only for the sake of something else, but the first is that only for the sake of which all other things subsist: and all the intermediate natures participate of these two peculiarities. Hence they genuinely adhere to the natures which surpass them, as objects of desire, but impart the perfection of desires to subordinate beings.

The third speculation of the principle of things is far inferior to the preceding, considering him as giving subsistence to all beautiful things. For to celebrate him as the supplier of good, and as end preceding the two orders of things, is not very remote from the narration which says, that all causes are posterior to him, and derive their subsistence from him, as well those which are paternal, and the sources of good, as those that are the suppliers of prolific powers. But to ascribe to him a producing and generative cause, is still more remote from the all-perfect union of the first. For as it cannot be known or discussed by language, by secondary natures, it must not be said that it is the cause, or that it is generative of beings, but we should celebrate in silence this ineffable nature, and this perfectly causeless cause which is prior to all causes. If, however, as we endeavour to ascribe to him *The Good* and *The One*, we in like manner attribute to him *cause,* and that which is *final* or *paternal,* we must pardon the parturition of the soul about this ineffable principle, aspiring to perceive him with the eye of intellect, and to speak about him; but, at the same time, the exempt transcendency of *The One* which is immense, must be considered as surpassing an indication of this kind. From these things therefore, we may receive the sacred conceptions of Plato, and an order† adapted to things themselves. And we may say that the first part of this sentence sufficiently indicates the simplicity,‡ transcendency, and in short the unco-ordination with all things of the king of all. For the assertion that all things subsist about him, unfolds the hyparxis of things second, but leaves that which is beyond all things without any connexion with things posterior to it. But the second part

---

† For $\pi\rho\alpha\xi\iota\nu$, it is necessary to read $\tau\alpha\xi\iota\nu$.

‡ For $\tau\eta\varsigma\ \alpha\pi\lambda\sigma\tau\eta\tau\sigma\varsigma$ I read $\tau\eta\nu\ \alpha\pi\lambda\sigma\tau\eta\tau\alpha$.

celebrates the cause of all the Gods[†] as prearranged in the order of *end*. For that which is the highest of all causes, is immediately conjoined with that which is prior to cause; but of this kind is the final cause, and that for the sake of which all things subsist. This part therefore is posterior to the other, and is woven together with the order of things, and the progression of the Platonic doctrine.

Again, the third part asserts him to be productive of all beautiful things, and thus adds to him a species of cause[‡] inferior to the final. Whence also Plotinus, I think, does not hesitate to call the first God the fountain of the beautiful. It is necessary therefore to attribute that which is best to the best of all things, that he may be the cause of all, and in reality prior to cause. But this is *The Good*. This too, which is an admirable circumstance, may be seen in the words of Plato, that the first of these three divine dogmas, neither presumes to say any thing about *The Good,*, and this ineffable nature, nor does it permit us to refer any species of cause to it. But the second dogma leaves indeed *The Good* ineffable, as it is fit it should, but from the habitude of things posterior to it, enables us to collect the final cause; for it does not refuse to call it that for the sake of which all things subsist. But when it asserts that all things are for the sake of *The Good*, it excites in us the conception of the communion and co-ordination of that which is the object of desire with the desiring natures. And the third dogma evinces that *The Good* is the cause of all beautiful things. But this is to say something concerning it, and to add to the simplicity of the first cause, and not to abide in the conceptions of the end, but to conjoin with it the producing principle of things second. And it appears to me that Plato here indicates the natures which are proximately unfolded into light after the first. For it is not possible to say any thing concerning it except at one time being impelled to this from all things, and at another from the best of things: for it is the cause of hyparxis to all things, and unfolds its own separate union through the peculiarities of these. We ascribe to it therefore *The One* and *The Good,* from the donation which pervades to all things from it. For of those things of which all participate, we say there is no other cause than that which is established prior to all these.

[†] For του θεου it is necessary to read των θεων.

[‡] For αιτιον it is necessary to read αιτιου.

But *the about which* (το περι ο), *the on account of which* (το δι, ο[†]), and *the from which* (το αφ ου), particularly subsist in the intelligible Gods: and from these they are ascribed to the first God. For whence can we suppose the unical Gods derive their peculiarities, except from that which is prior to them? To this summit of intelligibles therefore the term *about* is adapted, because all the divine orders occultly proceed about this summit which is arranged prior to them. But the term *on account of which* pertains to the middle order of intelligibles: for all things subsist for the sake of eternity and an hyparxis perfectly entire. And the term *from which* is adapted to the extremity of intelligibles: for this first produces all things, and adorns them uniformly. These things, therefore, we shall indeed make more known in the doctrine which will shortly follow concerning the intelligible Gods.

CHAPTER X

In the next place, let us finish the discussion concerning the first God, with the theory of Parmenides, and unfold the mystic conceptions of the first hypothesis as far as pertains to the present purpose. For we shall refer the reader for the most perfect interpretation of them to our commentaries on that dialogue. In the first place therefore, it is requisite to determine this concerning the first hypothesis, that it comprehends as many conclusions negatively, as the hypothesis which follows it does affirmatively. For this latter demonstrates all the orders proceeding from *The One;* but the former evinces that *The One* is exempt from all the divine genera. From both these hypotheses however, it is obvious to every one how it is necessary that the cause of the whole of things should transcend his productions. For because *The One* is the cause of all the Gods, he transcends all things. And because he is exempt from them through transcendency, on this account he gives to all things their hypostases. For through being expanded above all things he causes all things to subsist. Since in the second and third orders also of beings, causes which are entirely exempt from their effects, more perfectly generate and connect their progeny than those causes do which are coordinate with their effects. And *The One* by ineffably producing all the divine orders, appears to be unically established above all. For in the productions posterior to it, cause is every where different from the things caused. And on this account nature indeed being incorporeal, is

---

[†] For δι' ου it is necessary to read δι' ο; since the former denotes the *instrumental*, but the latter the *final* cause.

a cause which transcends bodies; but soul being perfectly perpetual, is the cause of things generated; and intellect being immoveable is the cause of every thing that is moved. If, therefore, according to each progression of beings effects are denied of their causes, it is certainly necessary to take away all things similarly from the cause of all.

In the second place, I think it is necessary that the order of the negations should be defined by those who receive theology according to the intention of Parmenides; and that it should be admitted that they proceed indeed from the monads which subsist primarily in the divine genera, and that Parmenides takes away from *The One* all second and third natures, according to an order adapted to each. For that which transcends more principal causes must in a much greater degree subsist prior to those that are subordinate. Parmenides, however, does not begin his negations from the Gods that are united to the first; for this genus is with difficulty distinguished from *The One:* because being arranged naturally [immediately] after it, is most unical and occult, and transcendently similar to its producing cause. Parmenides therefore beginning where prior to all other things division and multitude are apparent, and proceeding regularly through all the second orders as far as to the last of things, again returns to the beginning, and shows how *The One* differs from the Gods that are most similar to it, and which primarily participate of it, according to one ineffable cause.

In the third place, in addition to what has been said, I determine concerning the mode of negations, that they are not privative of their subjects, but generative of things which are as it were their opposites. For because the first principle is not many, the many proceed from it, and because it is not a whole, wholeness proceeds from it, and in a similar manner in other things. And in thus determining I speak conformably to Plato, who thinks it proper to abide in negations, and to add nothing to *The One*. For whatever you add, you diminish *The One*, and afterwards evince that it is not *The One*, but that which is passive to [or participates] *The One*. For it is thus not one only, but in addition to this possesses something else also by participation. This mode therefore of negations is exempt, unical, primary, and is a departure from the whole of things, in an unknown and ineffable transcendency of simplicity. It is likewise necessary, having attributed such a mode as this to the first God, again to exempt him from the negations also. For neither does any discourse, nor any name belong to *The One*, says Parmenides. But if no discourse belongs to it, it is evident that neither does negation pertain to it. For all things are secondary to *The One*, things knowable and knowledge, and the instruments of knowledge, and after a manner that which is impossible presents itself at the end of the hypothesis. For if nothing whatever can be said of *The One*, neither is this discussion itself adapted to *The One*. Nor is it at all wonderful that the discourse of those who wish to know the ineffable by words should terminate in that which is impossible; since all knowledge when conjoined with an object of knowledge which does not at all pertain to it loses its power. For sense, if we should say that it pertained to that which is the object of science would subvert itself; and this would be the case with science and every kind of knowledge if we should say that they belonged to that which is intelligible; so that language when conversant with that which is ineffable, being subverted about itself, has no cessation, and opposes itself.[3]

CHAPTER XI

Let us now therefore, if ever, abandon multiform knowledge, exterminate from ourselves all the variety of life, and in perfect quiet approach near to the cause of all things. For this purpose, let not only opinion and phantasy be at rest, nor the passions alone which impede our anagogic impulse to the first, be at peace; but let the air be still, and the universe itself be still. And let all things extend us with a tranquil power to communion with the ineffable. Let us also, standing there, having transcended the intelligible (if we contain any thing of this kind,) and with nearly closed eyes adoring as it were the rising sun, since it is not lawful for any being whatever intently to behold him - let us survey the sun whence the light of the intelligible Gods proceeds, emerging, as the poets say, from the bosom of the ocean; and again from this divine tranquillity descending into intellect, and from intellect, employing the reasonings of the soul, let us relate to ourselves what the natures are from which, in this progression, we shall consider the first God as exempt. And let us as it were celebrate him, not as establishing the earth and the heavens, nor as giving subsistence to souls, and the generations of all animals; for he produced these indeed, but among the last of things; but, prior to these, let us celebrate him as unfolding into light the whole intelligible and intellectual genus of Gods, together with all the supermundane and mundane divinities - as the God of all Gods, the unity of all unities, and beyond the first adyta,[†] - as more ineffable

---

[†] For αδυνατων, it is necessary to read αδητων. For the occult and invisible order of Night and Phanes is called by Orpheus *the adytum*. So that by the *first adyta*, Proclus means the highest order of intelligibles.

than all silence, and more unknown than all essence, - as holy among the holies, and concealed in the intelligible Gods. And again after these things descending into a reasoning process from an intellectual hymn, and employing the irreprehensible science of dialectic, let us, following the contemplation of first causes, survey the manner in which the first God is exempt from the whole of things. And let our descent be as far as to this. But opinion and phantasy and sense, prevent us indeed from partaking of the presence of the Gods, and draw us down from Olympian goods to earth-born motions, Titannically divide the intellect that is in us, and divulse us from an establishment in wholes to the images of beings.

CHAPTER XII

What therefore will be the first conception of the science proceeding from intellect, and unfolding itself into light? What other can we assert it to be than that which is the most simple and the most known of all the conceptions contained in this science? What therefore is this? "*The One*, says Parmenides, if it is *The One* will not be many." For it is necessary that the many should participate of *The One;* but *The One* does not participate of *The One*, but is *The One* itself. Neither is that which is primarily one participable. For it would not be purely one if mingled with the many, nor that which is one, if it received the addition of that which is subordinate. *The One* therefore is exempt from the many. The many however subsist primarily in the summit of the first intellectual Gods, and in *the intelligible place of survey*, as we are taught in the second hypothesis. *The One*, therefore, entirely transcends an order of this kind, and is the cause of it. For the *not many*, is not privation, as we have said, but the cause of the many. This, therefore, Parmenides does not think it requisite to demonstrate, but as a thing most manifest to every one, he first evinces this, through the opposition as it were of the many to *The One*. But employing this he takes away that which follows; and he takes away that which is posterior to this by employing the conclusions prior to it, and this he always does, after the same manner. And at one time indeed, he assumes the elements of the demonstrations from proximate conclusions, but at another time from those that are more remote. For after this intelligible order of Gods, as we have said, he gives subsistence to that order which connectedly contains and bounds the extent of them, from their exempt cause. But this order is called by him in the second hypothesis parts and a whole.

These therefore he denies of *The One* employing the many for the purpose of distinguishing the subjects and *The One*. For, as he says, that which is a whole and has parts is many; but *The One* is beyond the many. If, therefore, *The One* transcends the intelligible simplicity, but whole and that which has parts proceed from it in order to become the bond of the whole of this distribution, is it not necessary that *The One* should neither be a whole, nor be indigent of parts? And I think it is through this transcendency that *The One* pre-subsists as the cause of this order of Gods, and that it produces this order, but in an exempt manner.

In the third place after these, we may survey the order which is allotted the boundary of the intellectual and at the same time intelligible Gods, proceeding from *The One*, and may behold *The One* perfectly expanded above it. For this order indeed subsists from the second genera, and from the intellectual wholeness of the genera. But *The One*, as has been demonstrated, is exempt according to cause from this wholeness. *The One* therefore has neither beginning, or middle, or end, nor has it extremes, nor does it participate of any figure. For through these Gods, the before mentioned order of Gods becomes apparent. Whether therefore, there be a perfective summit, or what is celebrated as the middle centre in these Gods, or a termination converting the end of these divinities to their beginning, *The One* is similarly beyond every triple distribution. For *The One* would have parts, and would be many, if it participated of things of this kind. But it has been demonstrated that *The One* unically subsists prior to the many, and to wholeness together with its parts, as the cause of them. And you see how Parmenides indeed exhibits to us one negation of the highest order, but two negations of the middle, and three of the last order. Besides this also, he shows that *The One* has no extremity. But the infinite is a thing of this kind. And separately from this he likewise shows that *The One* is unreceptive of all figures.

Again therefore, after these triple orders we must direct our attention to the intellectual Gods subsisting from these, and receiving a tripartite division, and must demonstrate that *The One* transcends these also. For such is *The One*, says Parmenides, since it is neither in itself, nor in another. For if it were in another, it would be on all sides comprehended by that in which it is, and would every where touch that which comprehends it. But in this case, it would have a figure, would consist of parts, and on this account would be many and not one. And if it were in itself it would entirely comprehend itself in itself. But comprehending and at the same time being comprehended, it will be two, and will be no longer primarily one. The discourse therefore proceeds to the same conclusion, and evinces that *The One* will not be one, by the summit of the intellectual order, if any one endeavours to mingle it with other things. Hence *The One* being perfectly exempt from this summit also, gives subsistence to it, this summit at one and the same time participating of the third of the Gods placed above it, but being produced from the second of these Gods, and being perfected from the first, and entirely established in it.

Moreover, *The One* likewise generates the second intellectual order, being unmingled with it. For *The One* neither stands still, nor is moved. It participates therefore of neither of these; but being similarly exempt from both, it at the same time transcends the middle orders of the intellectual progression of the Gods. For if it were moved, it would be moved in a twofold respect, viz. either according to a change in quality, or local motion. But it is not possible that *The One* can be changed in quality; for being thus changed it will be not one, and will fall off from a unical hyparxis. Nor can it be locally moved. For it is impossible that it should be moved in a circle, because it would have parts, viz. middle and extremes. And if it changed one place for another it would be partible. For it would be necessary that it should neither be wholly in that place to which it is moved, nor in that whence it begins to be moved. For if it were wholly in either of them, it would be immoveable, in consequence of partly not yet being moved, and partly having now ceased its motion. But if *The One* stands still, it is certainly necessary that it should abide in the same thing. But it has been demonstrated that *The One* is no where. Hence it is neither in itself, nor in another thing. In no respect therefore is *The One* moved, or does it stand still, which things [viz. motion and permanency] particularly belong to the middle order of intellectuals, as will be evident from the second hypothesis. For the first God produces this order also, being exempt from it.

In the third place, we may survey through what next follows, the last order of intellectuals, proceeding from *The One*, and subordinate to it. For in this order sameness and difference subsist unitedly. But at the same time *The One* subsists prior to both these. For different is said to be different both from itself and from other things. And in a similar manner same is the same with itself, and with other things. But *The One* is not indeed different from itself, because that which is different from *The One* will be not one. And it is not the same with other things, lest becoming the same with them, it should latently pass into their nature. Moreover, neither is *The One* different from other things. For it would be at the same time one, and would have as an addition the power of difference. For so far as it is different it will not be one; since difference is not *The One*. Hence being one and different, it will be many and not *The One*. Nor is *The One* the same with itself. For if *The One* and the same differ only in name, the many will not be in consequence of participating of sameness with each other. For it is impossible that the many should become one by participating of the many. But if *The One* and sameness are essentially different, that which is primarily one does not participate of sameness, lest by receiving sameness in addition to *The One*, it should become a passive one, and not that which is primarily one. If however the extremity of intellectuals is characterized by this tetrad, it is evident that *The One* existing beyond this also supernally unfolds it into light, and places over the wholes of the universe a tetradic monad, the source of ornament to all secondary natures. For from hence other things primarily receive a communication with *The One* which are also indeed produced and connectedly contained by *The One*.

But after the intellectual Gods, the ineffable transcendency of *The One* arranges the extent of the supermundane divinities, *The One* in the mean time, being occultly exempt from its supermundane progeny. And this extent indeed proximately subsists from the intellectual Gods, but uniformly receives its hyparxis from the first God. This, therefore, Parmenides produces through similitude and dissimilitude, from the deity which encloses the boundary of the intellectual monads. For the similar is that which is passive to sameness, in the same manner as dissimilitude is that which is passive to difference. Parmenides therefore demonstrates that *The One* transcends according to one simplicity such a peculiarity of the Gods also as this. For that which is established above the power of same and different, in a much greater degree transcends the genera which are allotted a subsistence according to similitude and dissimilitude.

What therefore remains after this? Is it not evident that it is the multitude of the mundane Gods? But this also is twofold, the one being celestial, but the other sublunary. Of these, therefore, the genus which revolves in the heavens, proceeds together with the equal, the greater and the less. But in the sublunary genus the equal is allotted a difference in multitude from the celestial equality, but the unequal is again divided by the power of the more and the less. According to another genus therefore of the divine orders, there will be a monad and a duad, but above indeed, they are allied to *The One* and to sameness, and beneath to multitude, and the intellectual cause of difference. Hence *The One* transcends all these. For the equal indeed every where consists of the same parts. By what contrivance therefore is it possible that the nature which at one and the same time is exempt from sameness, and the difference which is associated with it, should participate of equality and inequality?

Besides all these divine orders therefore we must intellectually survey the genera of deified souls, and which are distributed about the Gods. For in each of the divine progressions and in the progressions also of souls, the first genus presents itself to the view connascent with the Gods; since both in the heavens, and in the sublunary region divine souls receive the division of the Gods into the world, as the Athenian Guest in a certain place demonstrates. The psychical extent therefore, is characterized by time, and by a life according to time. But the peculiarity of divine souls is shown by Parmenides to consist in their being younger and at the same time older both than themselves and other things. For revolving always according to the same time, and conjoining the beginning with the end, as at one and the same time proceeding to the end of the whole period they become younger, but as at the same time circulating to the beginning of it, they become older. All their ages however, perpetually preserve the same measures of time. Again, there is sameness in them and difference, the former indeed preserving equality, but the latter inequality, according to time. *The One* therefore subsists prior to divine souls, and generates these also together with the Gods. We now therefore come to the end of the whole distribution of more excellent natures; and the cause of all intelligibles at once unfolds into light the genera that follow the Gods, and that are triply divided by the three parts of time. But this cause is demonstrated by the intellectual projections of Parmenides to be also exempt from these. For that which is beyond all time and the life which is according to time, can by no contrivance become subservient to the more partial periods of time.

That which is the first of all things therefore, unfolds into light all the Gods, divine souls, and the more excellent genera, and is neither complicated with its progeny, nor multiplied about them; but being perfectly exempt from them in an admirable simplicity, and transcendency of union, it imparts to all things indifferently progression and at the same time order in the progression. Parmenides therefore beginning from the intelligible place of survey of the first intellectual Gods, proceeds thus far, according to the measures of generation, giving subsistence to the genera of the Gods, and to the natures that are united to and follow the Gods,[†] and perpetually evinces that *The One* is ineffably exempt from all things. But again, from hence he returns to the beginning, and imitating the conversion of the whole of things, separates *The One* from the highest, viz. from the intelligible Gods. For thus especially we may survey the transcendency of *The One*, and the immense difference of its union from all other things, if we not only demonstrate that it is established above the second or third progressions in the divine orders, but also that it subsists prior to the intelligible unities themselves, and this in a manner conformable to the simplicity of their occult nature, and not through a variety of words, but through intellectual projection alone. For intelligibles are naturally adapted to be known by intellect. This therefore, Parmenides also evinces in reality, relinquishing logical methods, but energizing according to intellect, and asserting that *The One* is above essence, and *being* characterized by *The One*. For this assertion was not collected from the preceding conclusions. For the discourse about the first Gods themselves would be without demonstration, if it derived its credibility from things subordinate. At the same time therefore, Parmenides contends that all knowledge, and all the instruments of knowledge, fall short of the transcendency of *The One*, and beautifully end in the ineffable of that God who is beyond all things. For after scientific energies, and intellectual projections, a union with the unknown follows, to which also Parmenides referring the whole of his discussion, concludes the first hypothesis, suspending indeed all the divine genera from *The One*, but evincing that *The One* is unically exempt from all things, subsisting without the participation of intelligibles and sensibles, and in an ineffable manner giving subsistence to the participated monads. Hence also, *The One* is said to be beyond that one which is conjoined with essence, and at the same time to be beyond every participated multitude of unities.

[†] For των θεων it is necessary to read τοις θεοις.

BOOK III

CHAPTER I

Such therefore is the theology with Plato concerning the first God, as it appears to me, and so great is the transcendency which it is allotted with respect to all other discussions of divine concerns; at one and the same time venerably preserving the ineffable union of this God exempt from the whole of things, uncircumscribed by all gnostic comprehensions, and apart from all beings; and unfolding the anagogic paths to him, perfecting that parturient desire which souls always possess of the father, and progenitor of all things, and enkindling that torch in them, by which they are especially conjoined with the unknown transcendency of *The One*. But after this imparticipable, ineffable, and truly superessential cause, which is separated from all essence, power and energy, the discussion of the Gods immediately follows. For to what other thing prior to the unities is it lawful to be conjoined with *The One*, or what else can be more united to the unical God than the multitude of Gods? Concerning these therefore, we shall in the next place unfold the inartificial theory of Plato, invoking the Gods themselves to enkindle in us the light of truth. I wish however prior to entering on the particulars of this theory, to convince the reader, and to make it evident to him through demonstration, that there are necessarily as many orders of the Gods, as the Parmenides of Plato unfolds to us in the second hypothesis.

This therefore is I think prior to all other things apparent to those whose conceptions are not perverted, that every where, but especially in the divine orders, second progressions, are completed through the similitude of these to their proper principles. For nature and intellect, and every generative cause, are naturally adapted to produce and conjoin to themselves things similar, prior to such as are dissimilar to themselves. For if it is necessary that the progression of beings should be continued, and that no vacuum should intervene either in incorporeal natures, or in bodies, it is necessary that every thing which proceeds naturally should proceed through similitude. For it is by no means lawful that the thing caused should be the same with its cause; since a remission and deficiency of the union of the producing cause generates secondary natures. For again, if that which is second were the same as that which is first, each would be similarly the same, and one would not be cause, but the other the thing caused. If however, the one by its very being, or essentially, has an exuberance of productive power, but the other falls short of the power that produced it, these are naturally separated from each other, and the generative cause precedes in excellence the thing generated, and there is not a sameness of things which so greatly differ. But if that which is second is not the same with that which is first, if indeed it is different only, they will not be conjoined to each other, nor will the one participate of the other. For contact and participation, are indeed a communion of things conjoined, and a sympathy of participants with the natures they participate. But if it is at the same time the same with and different from that which is first, if indeed the sameness is indigent, and vanquished by the power which is contrary to it, *The One* will no longer be the leader of the progression of beings, nor will every generative cause subsist prior to things of a secondary nature, in the order of the good. For *The One* is not the cause of division, but of friendship. And *The Good* converts generated natures to their causes. But the conversion and friendship of things secondary to such as are primary is through similitude, but not through a dissimilar nature. If therefore *The One* is the cause of the whole of things, and if *The Good* is in an exempt manner desirable to all things, it will every where give subsistence to the progeny of precedaneous causes through similitude, in order that progression may be according to *The One*, and that the conversion of things which have proceeded may be to *The Good*. For without similitude there will neither be the conversion of things to their proper principles, nor the generation of effects. Let this therefore be considered as a thing admitted in this place.

But the second thing besides this, and which is demonstrated through this, is, that it is necessary every monad should produce a number co-ordinate to itself, nature indeed a natural, but soul a psychical, and intellect an intellectual number. For if every thing generative generates similars prior to dissimilars, as has been before demonstrated, every cause will certainly deliver its own form and peculiarity to its own progeny, and before it gives subsistence to far distant progressions, and things which are separated from its nature, it will produce things essentially near to it, and conjoined with it through similitude. Every monad therefore, gives subsistence to a multitude indeed, as generating that which is second to itself, and which divides the powers that pre-subsist occultly in itself. For those things which are uniformly and contractedly in the monad, present themselves to the view separately in the progeny of the monad. And this indeed the wholeness of nature manifests, since it contains in one the reasons, [*i.e.* productive principles] of all things both in the heavens and in the sublunary region; but distributes the powers of itself to the natures which are divided from it about bodies. For the nature of earth, of fire, and of the moon, possesses from the wholeness of nature its peculiarity and form, and energizes together with this wholeness, and contains its own allotment. This also the monad of the mathematical sciences and of numbers manifests. For this being all things primarily, and spermatically producing in itself the forms of numbers, distributes different powers to different externally proceeding numbers. For it is not possible that what is generated, should at once receive all the abundance of its generator. And it is necessary that the prolific power of everything that pre-exists in the cause[†] itself should become apparent. The monad therefore gives subsistence to a multitude about itself, and to number which distributes the peculiarities that abide collectively in itself. Since however, as was before observed, the similar is always more allied to cause than the dissimilar, there will be one multitude of similars to the monad, proceeding from the monad; and another of dissimilars. But again, the multitude which is similar to the monad is that in a divided manner which the monad is indivisibly. For if the monad possesses a peculiar power and hyparxis, there will be the same form of hyparxis in the multitude together with a remission with reference to the whole.

After this however, it is necessary to consider in the third place, that of progressions, such as are nearer to their cause are indicative of a greater multitude of things, and are at the same time in a certain respect equal to their containing causes; but that such as are more remote possess a less extended power of signification; and on account of the diminution of their power, change and diminish at the same time the amplitude of production. For if, of progressions, that which subsists the first in order is more similar to its principle, and that which gives subsistence to the greatest number is both with respect to essence and power more similar to the generating principle of all things, it is necessary that of secondary natures, such as are nearer to the monad, and which receive dominion after it, should give a greater extent to their productions; but that such things as are more separated from their primary monad should neither pervade in a similar manner through all things, nor extend their efficacious energies to far distant progressions. And again, as similar to this, it is necessary that the nature which gives subsistence to the greatest number of effects, should be arranged next to the monad its principle; and that the nature generative of a more numerous progeny, because it is more similar to the supplying cause of

---

[†] For αιτιαν it is necessary to read αιτια.

all things than that which is generative of a few, must be arranged nearer to the monad, according to hyparxis. For if it is more remote, it will be more dissimilar to the first principle; but if it is more dissimilar, it will neither possess a power comprehending the power of similar natures, nor an energy abundantly prolific. For an abundant cause is allied to the cause of all. And universally, that which is generative of a more abundant, is more naturally allied to its principle than that which is productive of a less numerous progeny. For the production of fewer effects is a defect of power; but a defect of power is a diminution of essence; and a diminution of essence becomes redundant on account of dissimilitude to its cause, and a departure from the first principle.

Again therefore, in addition to what has been said, we shall assert this which possesses the most indubitable truth, that prior to the causes which are participated, it is every where necessary that imparticipable causes should have a prior subsistence in the whole of things. For if it is necessary that a cause should have the same relation to its progeny as *The One* to all the nature of beings, and that it should naturally possess this order towards things secondary; but *The One* is imparticipable, being similarly exempt from all beings, as unically producing all things; - if this be the case, it is requisite that every other cause which imitates the transcendency of *The One* with respect to all things, should be exempt from the natures which are in secondary ranks, and which are participated by them. And again, as equivalent to this, it is requisite that every imparticipable and primary cause should establish monads of secondary natures similar to itself, prior to such as are dissimilar. I say, for instance, it is requisite that one soul should distribute many souls to different natures; and one intellect participated intellects to many souls. For thus the first exempt genus will every where have an order analogous to *The One*. And secondary natures which participate kindred causes will be analogous to these causes, and through the similitude of these will be conjoined with their imparticipable principle. Hence prior to the forms which are in other things, those are established which subsist in themselves; exempt causes prior to such as are co-ordinate; and imparticipable monads prior to such as are participable. And consequently (as that which is demonstrated at the same time with this) the exempt causes are generative of the co-ordinate, and imparticipable natures extend participable monads to their progeny. And natures which subsist from themselves produce the powers which are resident in other things. These things therefore being discussed, let us consider how each of the divine genera subsists through analogy,[†] and survey following Plato himself, what are the first and most total orders of the Gods. For having discovered and demonstrated this, we shall perhaps be able to perceive the truth concerning these several orders.

It is necessary therefore, from the before-mentioned axioms, since there is one unity the principle of the whole of things, and from which every hyparxis derives its subsistence, that this unity should produce from itself, prior to all other things, a multitude characterized by unity, and a number most allied to its cause. For if every other cause constitutes a progeny similar to itself prior to that which is dissimilar, much more must *The One* unfold into light after this manner things posterior to itself, since it is beyond similitude, and *The One Itself* must produce according to *union* things which primarily proceed from it. For how can *The One* give subsistence to its progeny except unically? For nature generates things secondary to itself physically, soul psychically, and intellect intellectually. *The One* therefore is the cause of the whole of things according to union, and the progression from *The One* is uniform. But if that which primarily produces all things is *The One*, and the progression from it is unical, it is certainly necessary that the multitude thence produced should be self-perfect unities, most allied to their producing cause. Farther still, if every monad constitutes a number adapted to itself, as was before demonstrated, by a much greater priority must *The One* generate a number of this kind. For in the progression of things, that which is produced is frequently dissimilar to its producing cause, through the dominion of difference: for such are the last of things, and which are far distant from their proper principles. But the first number, and which is connascent with *The One*, is uniform, ineffable, superessential, and perfectly similar to its cause. For in the first causes, neither does difference intervening separate from the generator the things begotten, and transfer them into another order, nor does the motion of the cause effecting a remission of power, produce into dissimilitude and indefiniteness the generation of the whole of things; but the cause of all things being unically raised above all motion and division, has established about itself a divine number, and has united it to its own simplicity. *The One* therefore prior to beings has given subsistence to the unities of beings.

For again, according to another mode [of considering the subject] it is necessary that primary beings should participate of the first cause through their proximate unities. For secondary things are severally

---

[†] For αναλυσεως it is necessary to read αναλογιας.

conjoined to the natures prior to them through similars; bodies indeed to the soul which ranks as a whole, through the several souls [which they participate]; but souls to universal intellect through intellectual monads; and first beings, through unical hyparxes to *The One*. For being is in its own nature dissimilar to *The One*. For essence and that which is in want of union externally derived, are unadapted to be conjoined with that which is superessential, and with the first union, and are far distant from it. But the unities of beings, since they derive their subsistence from the imparticipable unity, and which is exempt from the whole of things, are able to conjoin beings to *The One*, and to convert them to themselves.

It appears therefore to me, that Parmenides demonstrating these things through the second hypothesis, connects *The One* with being, surveys all things about *The One*, and evinces that this proceeding nature, and which extends its progressions as far as to the last of things is *The One*. For prior to true beings it was necessary to constitute the unities; since it neither was nor is lawful, says Timæus, for that which is the best of things to effect anything else than that which is most beautiful. But this is in a remarkable degree most similar to that which is best. To *The One* however, a unical multitude is most similar; since the demiurgus of the universe also being good, constituted all things similar to himself through goodness itself. Much more therefore, does the fountain of all good produce goodness naturally united to itself, and establish them in beings. Hence there is one God, and many Gods, one unity and many unities prior to beings, and one goodness, and many after the one goodness, through which the demiurgic intellect is good, and every intellect is divine, whether it be an intellectual or intelligible intellect. And that which is primarily superessential is *The One*; and there are many superessentials after *The One*. Whether therefore, is this multitude of unities imparticipable in the same manner as *The One Itself*, or is it participated by beings, and is each unity of beings the flower as it were of a certain being, and the summit and centre of it, about which each being[†] subsists? But if these unities also are imparticipable, in what do they differ from *The One*? For each of them is one, and primarily subsists from *The One*. Or in what being more redundant than the first cause were they constituted by it? For it is every where necessary that what is second being subordinate to that which is prior to itself, should

---

† For εν it is necessary to read ον.

fall short of the union of its producing[†] cause, and by the addition of a certain thing should have a diminution of the monadic simplicity of the first. What addition therefore, can we adduce, or what redundancy besides *The One*, if each of these also is by itself one? For if each of them is one and many, we shall appear to transfer to them the peculiarity of being. But if each is one only, in the same manner as *The One Itself*, why does this rank as the cause which is exempt from all things, but each of these is allotted a secondary dignity? Neither therefore shall we preserve the transcendency of the first with reference to the things posterior to it, nor can we admit that the unities proceeding from it are unconfused either with respect to themselves, or to the one principle of them.

But neither shall we be persuaded by Parmenides who produces *The One* together with being, and demonstrates that there are as many parts of *The One* as there are of being; that each being[‡] also participates of *The One*, but that *The One* is every where consubsistent with being; and in short, who asserts that *The One* of the second hypothesis participates of being, and is participated by being, the participation in each not being the same. For *The One* indeed participates of being, as not being primarily one, nor exempt from being, but as illuminating truly-existing essence. But being participates of *The One*, as that which is connected by it, and filled with divine union, and converted to *The One Itself* which is imparticipable. For the participated monads conjoin beings to *The One* which is exempt from the whole of things, in the same manner as participated intellects conjoin souls to the intellect which ranks as a whole, and as participated souls conjoin bodies to the soul which ranks as a whole. For it is not possible that the dissimilar genera of secondary natures should be united without media to the cause which is exempt from multitude; but it is necessary that the contact should be effected through similars. For a similar multitude, so far indeed as it is a multitude, communicates with the dissimilar; but so far as it is similar to the monad prior to itself, it is conjoined with it. Being established therefore, in the middle of both, it is united to the whole, and to *The One* which is prior to multitude. But it contains in itself remote progressions, and which are of themselves dissimilar to *The One*. Through itself also, it converts all things to that one, and thus all things are extended to the first cause of the whole of things, dissimilars indeed

---

[†] For παροντος it appears requisite to read παραγοντος.

[‡] Here also for εν it is necessary to read ον.

through similars,† but similars through themselves. For similitude itself by itself conducts and binds the many to *The One*, and converts secondary natures to the monads prior to them. For the very being of similars so far as they are similars is derived from *The One*. Hence, it conjoins multitude to that from which it is allotted its progression. And on this account similitude is that which it is, causing many things to be allied, to possess sympathy with themselves, and friendship with each other and *The One*.

CHAPTER II

If however it be requisite, not only by employing the intellectual projections of Parmenides to unfold the multitude of Gods participated by being, but also concisely to demonstrate the theory of Socrates about these particulars, we must recollect what is written in the *Republic*, where he says that the light proceeding from *The Good* is unific of intellect and of beings. For through these things *The Good* is demonstrated to be exempt from being and essence, in the same manner as the sun is exempt from visible natures. But this light being in intelligibles illuminates them, in the same manner as the solar-form light which is in visible natures. For visible natures no otherwise become apparent, and known to the sight, than through the light which is ingenerated in them. All intelligibles therefore become boniform through the participation of light, and through this light, every true being‡ is most similar to *The Good*. If, therefore, it makes no difference to speak of this light, or of *The One* (for this light conjoins intelligibles, and causes them to be one, as deriving its subsistence from *The One*) if this be the case, the deity proceeding from the first is participable, and all the multitude of unities is participable. And that indeed which is truly superessential is *The One*. But each of the other Gods, according to his proper hyparxis, by which he is a superessential God, is similar to the first; but they are participated by essence and being. According to this reasoning therefore, the Gods appear to us to be unities, and participable unities, binding indeed all beings to themselves, but conjoining through themselves to *The One* which similarly transcends all things, the natures posterior to themselves.

---

† For ανομοιων it is necessary to read ομοιων.

‡ οντως is omitted in the original.

Since therefore each of the Gods is indeed a unity, but is participated by some being, whether shall we say that the same being participates of each of the unities or that the participants of some of the unities are more, but of others less numerous? And if this be the case either the participants of the superior unities must be more, but of the inferior must be fewer in number, or vice versa. For it is necessary that there should be an order of the unities, in the same manner as we see that of numbers some are nearer to their principle, but others more remote from it. And that some are more simple, but others more composite, and exceed indeed in quantity, but suffer a diminution in power. But it is well that we have mentioned numbers. For if it is necessary to survey the order of the first monads with respect to each other, and their progression about beings, from these as images, in these also the monads which are nearer to *The One* will be participated by things which are more simple in essence, but those which are more remote from it, will be participated by more composite essences. For thus the participation will be according to the analogous; first monads being always participated by the first beings, but second monads by secondary beings. For again, if the first is exempt from all things, and is imparticipable, but that which is connascent with the most simple nature and *The One* is more similar to the imparticipable than that which is connascent with a more various and multiform nature, and which has more powers suspended from it, - if this be the case, it is perfectly obvious, that the unities which are nearer to *The One* are necessarily participated by the first and most simple essences; but that those which are more remote are participated by more composite essences, which are less in power, but are greater in number and multitude. For in short, additions in these unities are ablations of powers; and that which is nearer to *The One*, which surpasses the whole of things by an admirable simplicity, is more uniform, and is consubsistent with more total orders. And it happens according to the ratio of power, that the simplicity of the first unities is transcendent. For those things which are the causes of a greater number of effects, imitate as much as possible the cause of all things, but those which are the causes of fewer effects, have an essence more various than the natures that are prior to them.† For this variety distributes into minute

---

† Instead of τα μεν γαρ πλειονων αιτια, και των παντων αιτιων κατα την δυναμιν των προ αυτων ποικιλωτερων κατα την ουσιαν εστιν, it is necessary to read τα μεν γαρ πλειονων αιτια, και των παντων αιτιον κατα δυναμιν μιμουνται, τα δε των ελασσονων των προ αυτων ποικιλωτερα κατα την ουσιαν εστιν.

parts and diminishes the power which abides in one. Moreover, in participated souls also, such as are first and most divine subsist in simple and perpetual bodies. Others again are connected with bodies that are simple, but in conjunction with these with material bodies also. And others are connected at one and the same time with simple, material and composite bodies. For the celestial souls indeed rule over simple bodies, and such as have an immaterial and immutable subsistence. But the souls that govern the wholes of the elements, are at the same time invested with etherial garments, and at the same time through these are carried in the wholes of the elements, which as wholes indeed are perpetual and simple, but as material receive generation and corruption, and composition from dissimilar natures. And the souls that rank in the third order, are those which proximately inspire with life their luciform[†] vehicles, but also attract from the simple element material vestments, pour into these a secondary life, and through these communicate with composite and multiform bodies, and sustain through this participation another third life.

If, however, you are willing to survey the intellectual orders, some of these are arranged in the souls which rank as wholes, and in the most divine of mundane souls, which also they govern in a becoming manner. But others being arranged in the souls of the more excellent genera, are proximately participated by the rulers that are in them; and are participated secondarily by more partial essences. But again they arrange third intellectual orders in partial souls. And according as the power which they are allotted is diminished, in such proportion is participation in them more various, and far more composite than the participation of the natures that are prior to them. If, therefore, this is the mode of participation in all beings, it is certainly necessary that of the Gods also those that are nearer to *The One*, should be carried in the more simple parts of being, but that those which have proceeded to a greater distance should be carried in the more composite parts of being. For the participations of second genera are divided after this manner according to a similitude to them.

Again therefore, we may summarily say, that after the one principle of the whole of things, the Gods present themselves to our view as self-perfect monads, participated by beings.[‡] How many orders therefore

---

[†] For αυτοειδεσιν it is requisite to read αυγοειδεσιν.

[‡] In the original here, about a line and a half is so defective, that not being able to supply the deficiency, I have not attempted to translate it.

there are of beings we shall afterwards unfold, and show what beings are allotted a more simple, and what a more various hyparxis. Of all beings then, the last is that which is corporeal. For this derives its being, and all its perfection from another more ancient cause, and is neither allotted simplicity nor composition, nor perpetuity, nor incorruptibility from its own power. For no body is either self-subsistent, or self-begotten; but every thing which is so contracting in one, cause, and that which proceeds from cause, is incorporeal and impartible. And in short, that which is the cause of hyparxis to itself, imparts also to itself an infinite power of existence. For never deserting itself, it will never cease to be, or depart from its own subsistence. For every thing that is corrupted, is corrupted through being separated from the power that supplied it with being. But that which imparts being to itself, as it is not separated from itself, is allotted through itself a perpetual essence. No body however, since it is not the cause of perpetuity to itself, will be perpetual. For every thing which is perpetual possesses an infinite power. But body being finite is not the cause of infinite power. For infinite power is incorporeal, because all power is incorporeal. But this is evident, because greater powers are every where. But no body is capable of being wholly every where. If therefore, no body imparts to itself power, whether the power be infinite or finite, but that which is self-subsistent imparts to itself the power of being, and of existing perpetually, no body will be self-subsistent. Whence therefore is being imparted to bodies, and what is it which is adapted proximately to supply them with being? Must we not say that the cause of being to bodies primarily is that which by being present renders the nature of body more perfect than its kindred bodies [when they are deprived of it?] This indeed is obvious to every one. For it is the province of that which imparts perfection to connect also the essence of secondary natures, since perfection itself is the perfection of essence. What therefore is that of which bodies participating, are said to be better than the bodies which do not participate of it? Is it not evident that it is soul? For we say that animated bodies are more perfect than such as are inanimate. Soul therefore is primarily beyond bodies; and it must be admitted that all heaven and every thing corporeal is the vehicle of soul. Hence, these two orders of beings present themselves to our view; the one indeed being corporeal, but the other which is above this, psychical.

With respect to the soul itself however, whether is it the same with or different from intellect? For as the body which participates of soul is perfect, thus also the soul is perfect which participates of intellect. And of the soul indeed, which is able to live according to reason, all things do not participate; but of intellect and intellectual illumination rational souls participate, and also such things as partake of any kind of knowledge. And soul indeed energizes according to time; but intellect comprehends in eternity both its essence, and at the same time its stable energy. And not every soul indeed is adapted to preserve immutably and without diminution the perfection of itself; but every intellect is always perfect, and possesses a never-failing power of its own blessedness. The intellectual genus therefore is essentially beyond the psychical; since the former, neither in whole nor in partial intellects, admits the entrance of the nature of evil; but the latter being undefiled in whole souls, departs in partial souls from its own proper blessedness. What therefore is the first of beings? Shall we say intellect, or prior to this the extent of life? For soul indeed is self-vital, supplying itself with life; and intellect is the best and most perfect, and as we have said, an eternal life. But the life of intellect is indeed in a certain respect intellectual, and is mingled from the intellectual and vital peculiarity. It is necessary however, that there should be life itself. Whether therefore is life or intellect the more excellent thing? But if gnostic beings only participate of intellect, but such beings as are destitute of knowledge participate of life, (for we say that plants live) it is certainly necessary that life should be arranged above intellect, being the cause of a greater number of effects, and imparting by illumination more gifts from itself than intellect. What then? Is life the first of beings? And is *to live* the same thing as *to be*? But this is impossible. For if life is that which is primarily being, and to be vital is the same thing as to have being, and there is the same definition of both life and being, every thing which participates of life would also participate of being, and every thing which participates of existence would likewise participate of life. For if each is the same thing all things would similarly participate of being and life. All vital natures indeed have essence and being; but there are many beings that are destitute of life. Being therefore subsists prior to the first life. For that which is more universal, and the cause of a greater number of effects, is nearer to *The One*, as has been before demonstrated. Soul therefore is that which is primarily established above bodies; but intellect is beyond soul;† life is more ancient than intellect; and being which is primarily being is established above all these. Every thing also which participates of soul, by a much greater priority participates of intellect; but not every thing which enjoys

---

† Instead of ζωης here it is necessary to read ψυχης.

intellectual efficiency, is also adapted to participate of soul. For of soul rational animals only participate; since we say that the rational soul is truly soul. For Plato in the *Republic* says, that the work of soul is to reason and survey beings. And every soul [*i.e.* every rational soul] is immortal, as it is written in the *Phædrus*; the irrational soul being mortal, according to the demiurgus in the *Timæus*. And in short, it is in many places evident that Plato considers the rational soul to be truly soul, but others to be the images of souls, so far as these also are intellectual and vital, and together with whole souls produce the lives that are distributed about bodies. Of intellect however, we not only admit that rational animals participate, but also such other animals as possess a gnostic power; I mean such as possess the phantasy, memory and sense; Since Socrates also in the *Philebus* refers all such animals to the intellectual series. For taking away intellect from the life which is according to pleasure, he likewise takes away not only the rational life, but every gnostic power of the irrational life. For all knowledge is the progeny of intellect, in the same manner as all reason is an image of soul.

Moreover, all things which participate of intellect, by a much greater priority participate of life, some things indeed more obscurely, but others more manifestly. But all living beings do not participate of intellectual power, since plants indeed are animals, as Timæus says, but they neither participate of sense, or phantasy; unless some one should say that they have a co-sensation of what is pleasing and painful. And in short, the orectic powers every where are lives, and the images of the whole of life, and the last productions of life; but they are of themselves destitute of intellect and without any participation of the gnostic power. Hence also, they are of themselves indefinite, and deprived of all knowledge.

Again therefore, all animals indeed receive a portion of being, and different animals a different portion, according to their respective natures; but all beings are not similarly able to participate of life; since we say that qualities and all passions, and the last of bodies, receive the ultimate effective energy of being, but we do not also say that they participate of life. Being therefore is more ancient than life; life than intellect; and intellect than soul. For it is necessary that the causes of a greater number of effects being more ancient and according to order more principal, should preside over causes which are able to produce and adorn fewer effects. Very properly therefore, does Plato in the *Timæus* give subsistence to soul from intellect, as being secondary to it according to its own nature. But in the *Laws* he says that intellect is moved similarly to a sphere fashioned by a wheel.† For that which is moved, is moved by participating of life, and is nothing else than real life about motion. And in the *Sophista* he exempts being from all the total genera of things, and from motion. For being, says he, according to its own nature, neither stands still, nor is moved. But that which neither stands still nor is moved, is beyond eternal life.

These four causes therefore being prior to a corporeal subsistence, *viz.* essence, life, intellect and soul, soul indeed participates of all the causes prior to itself, being allotted reason from its own peculiarity, but intellect, life and being, from more ancient causes. Hence it gives subsistence to things posterior to itself in a fourfold manner. For according to its being indeed, it produces all things as far as to bodies; according to its life, all things which are said to live, even as far as to plants; according to its intellect, all things which possess a gnostic power, even as far as to the most irrational natures; and according to its reason, the first of the natures that are able to participate of it.‡ But intellect being established beyond soul, and existing as the plenitude of life and being, adorns all things in a threefold manner, imparting indeed by illumination the power of the intellectual peculiarity to all gnostic beings, but supplying the participation of life to a still greater number, and of being to all those to whom primary being imparts itself. But life being arranged above intellect, pre-subsists as the cause of the same things in a twofold respect, vivifying secondary natures indeed, together with intellect, and filling from itself with the rivers of life, such things as are naturally adapted to live, but together with being supernally producing essence in all things. But being itself which is primarily being generates all things by its very existence, all lives, and intellects and souls, and is uniformly present to all things, and is exempt from the whole of things according to one cause which gives subsistence to all things. Hence it is the most similar of all things to *The One*, and unites the comprehension of beings in itself to the first principle of the whole of things, through which all beings, and non-beings, wholes and parts, forms and the privations of forms subsist, which privations do not necessarily participate of being, but it is entirely necessary that they should participate of *The One*.

These things as it appears to me persuaded the Elean guest in the *Sophista*, when discussing that which is perfectly being, to admit that not

---

† For εντονοις it is necessary to read εν τορνοις.

‡ For αυτοις read αυτης.

only being is there, but also life, intellect and soul. For if true and real being is venerable and honourable, intellect is there in the first place, says he. For it is not lawful for that which is of itself venerable and immaterial to be without intellect. But if intellect is in that which is perfectly being, intellect will entirely be moved. For it is not possible for intellect ever to subsist, either without motion or permanency. But if intellect is moved and stands still, there are in being both life and motion. Hence, from what has been said, three things become apparent, *viz.* being, life and intellect. Moreover, soul also in the next place is discovered through these things. For it is necessary, says he, that life and intellect which before were by themselves, should also be in soul. For every soul is a plenitude of life and intellect, participating of both, which the Elean guest indicating adds, "Shall we say that both these are inherent in it, but yet it does not possess these in soul?" For to *possess*, as some one says in a certain place, is secondary to *existing*. And soul indeed participates of each of these according to the peculiarity of itself; but it mingles the rational form of its own hyparxis, with the intellectual vivific power. But both intellect and life subsist prior to soul, the former as being moved and standing still at one and the same time, and the latter as being motion and permanency. These four monads also, soul, intellect, life and being are not only mentioned by Plato here, but in many other places. And as in soul all things subsist according to participation, so in intellect the things which are prior to it subsist, and in life that which is prior to life. For we say that life exists, or has a being. Or how could it be said to be arranged in being unless it participated of being? We likewise say that intellect is and lives. For it is moved, and is a portion of being. Hence it is the third of the more comprehensive monads. Prior however to beings which are participated, it is every where necessary that imparticipable causes should subsist, as was before demonstrated, conformably to the similitude of beings to *The One*. Being therefore which is primarily being, is imparticipable; but life first participates of being, yet is imparticipable, being exempt from intellect. And intellect is filled indeed from being and life; but is imparticipable in souls, and in the natures posterior to itself. Intellect also presides over soul, imparting to it by illumination the participation of life and being; but being imparticipable subsists prior to bodies. The last order of beings therefore is that to which bodies are annexed; celestial bodies indeed primarily, but sub-lunary bodies with the addition of material [vestments.] This therefore is the progression of beings, through life, intellect and soul, ending in a corporeal nature.

If, however, it is necessary that the superessential unities of the Gods which derive their subsistence from the imparticipable cause[†] of all things should be participated, some of them indeed, by the first orders in beings, others by the middle, and others by the last orders, as was before demonstrated, it is evident that some of them deify the imparticipable portion of being, but that others illuminate life, others intellect, others soul, and others bodies. And of the last unities indeed, not only bodies participate, but likewise soul, intellect, life and essence. For intellect in itself is a plenitude of life and being. But from the unities which are above this world intellect is suspended, and the psychical power, which pre-exists in intellect. From the unities above these, imparticipable and intellectual intellect is suspended. From those that are beyond these, the first and imparticipable life is suspended. And from the highest unities, the first being itself, and which is the most divine of beings, is suspended. Hence Parmenides beginning from the one being, produces from thence the whole orders of the Gods. These things therefore being previously determined by us, let us speak concerning the divine dialogues, beginning from on high, and producing from *The One* the whole orders of the Gods. Let us also, following Plato, in the first place demonstrate the several orders from other dialogues, by arguments which cannot be confuted. Afterwards, let us thus conjoin and assimilate the conclusions of Parmenides to the divine progressions, adapting the first conclusions to the first, but the last to the last progressions.

CHAPTER III

Again therefore, the mystic doctrine concerning *The One* must be resumed by us, in order that proceeding from the first principle, we may celebrate the second and third principles of the whole of things. Of all beings therefore, and of the Gods that produce beings, one exempt and imparticipable cause pre-exists, - a cause ineffable indeed by all language, and unknown by all knowledge and incomprehensible, unfolding all things into light from itself, subsisting ineffably prior to, and converting all things to itself, but existing as the best end of all things. This cause therefore, which is truly exempt from all causes, and which gives subsistence unically to all the unities of divine natures, and to all the genera of beings, and their progressions, Socrates in the *Republic* calls *The Good*, and through its analogy to the sun reveals its admirable and

---

[†] For $αιτων$ it is necessary to read $αιτιας$.

unknown transcendency with respect to all intelligibles. But again, Parmenides denominates it *The One*. And through negations demonstrates the exempt and ineffable hyparxis of this one which is the cause of the whole of things. But the discourse in the epistle to Dionysius proceeding through enigmas, celebrates it as that about which all things subsist, and as the cause of all beautiful things. In the *Philebus* however, Socrates celebrates it as that which gives subsistence to the whole of things, because it is the cause of all deity. For all the Gods derive their existence as Gods from the first God. Whether therefore, it be lawful to denominate it the fountain of deity, or the kingdom of beings, or the unity of all unities, or the goodness which is generative of truth, or an hyparxis exempt from all these things, and beyond all causes, both the paternal and the generative, let it be honoured by us in silence, and prior to silence by union, and of the mystic end may it impart by illumination a portion adapted to our souls.

But let us survey with intellect the biformed principles proceeding from and posterior to it. For what else is it necessary to arrange after the union of the whole theory, than the duad of principles? What[†] the two principles therefore are of the divine orders after the first principle, we shall in the next place survey. For conformably to the theology of our ancestors, Plato also establishes two principles after *The One*. In the *Philebus* therefore, Socrates says, that God gives subsistence to bound and infinity, and through these mingling all beings, has produced them, the nature of beings, according to Philolaus subsisting from the connexion of things bounded, and things infinite. If, therefore, all beings subsist from these, it is evident that they themselves have a subsistence prior to beings. And if secondary natures participate of these mingled together, these will subsist unmingled prior to the whole of things. For the progression of the divine orders originates, not from things co-ordinated and which exist in others, but from things exempt, and which are established in themselves. As therefore *The One* is prior to things united, and as that which is passive to The One, has a second order after the imparticipable union, thus also the two principles of beings, prior to the participation of and commixture with beings, are themselves by themselves the causes of the whole of things. For it is necessary that bound should be prior to things bounded, and infinity prior to infinites, according to the similitude to *The One* of things which proceed from it. For again, if we should produce beings immediately after *The One*, we shall no where find the peculiarity of *The One*

---

† For τινος it is necessary to read τινες.

subsisting purely. For neither is being the same with *The One*, but it participates of *The One*, nor in reality is that which is the first *The One*; for, as has been frequently said, it is better than *The One*. Where therefore is that which is most properly and entirely one? Hence there is a certain one prior to being, which gives subsistence to being, and is primarily the cause of it; since that which is prior to it is beyond union, and is a cause without habitude with respect to all things, and imparticipable, being exempt from all things. If however this one is the cause of being, and constitutes it, there will be a power in it generative of being. For every thing which produces, produces according to its own power, which is allotted a subsistence between that which produces and the things produced, and is of the one the progression and as it were extension, but of the other is the pre-arranged generative cause. For being which is produced from these, and which is not *The One Itself*, but uniform, possesses its progression indeed from *The One*, through the power which produces and unfolds it into light from *The One*; but its occult union from the hyparxis of *The One*. This one therefore which subsists prior to power, and first pre-subsists from the imparticipable and unknown cause of the whole of things, Socrates in the *Philebus* calls *bound*, but he denominates the power of it which is generative of being, *infinity*. But he thus speaks in that dialogue, "God we said has exhibited the bound, and also the infinite of beings."

The first therefore and unical God, is without any addition denominated by him God; because each of the second Gods is participated by being, and has being suspended from its nature. But the first indeed, as being exempt[†] from the whole of beings, is God, defined according to the ineffable itself, the unical alone, and superessential. But the bound and the infinite of beings, unfold into light that unknown and imparticipable cause; bound indeed, being the cause of stable, uniform, and connective deity; but the infinite being the cause of power proceeding to all things and capable of being multiplied, and in short, being the leader of every generative distribution. For all union and wholeness, and communion of beings, and all the divine measures, are suspended[‡] from the first bound. But all division, prolific production, and progression into multitude, derive their subsistence from this most principal infinity. Hence, when we say that each of the divine orders

---

[†] For $\epsilon\xi\eta\rho\eta\tau\alpha\iota$ it is necessary to read $\epsilon\xi\eta\rho\tau\eta\tau\alpha\iota$.

[‡] Here also it is necessary for $\epsilon\xi\eta\rho\eta\tau\alpha\iota$ to read $\epsilon\xi\eta\rho\tau\eta\tau\alpha\iota$.

abides† and at the same time proceeds, we must confess that it stably abides indeed, according to bound, but proceeds according to infinity, and that at one and the same time it has unity and multitude, and we must suspend the former from the principle of bound, but the latter from that of infinity. And in short, of all the opposition in the divine genera, we must refer that which is the more excellent to bound, but that which is subordinate to infinity. For from these two principles all things have their progression into being, even as far as to the last of things. For eternity itself participates at once of bound and infinity; so far indeed, as it is the intelligible measure, it participates of bound; but so far as it is the cause of a never-failing power of existing, it participates of infinity. And intellect, so far indeed as it is uniform, and whole, and so far as it is connective of paradigmatical measures, so far it is the progeny of bound. But again, so far as it produces all things eternally, and subsists conformably to the whole of eternity, supplying all things with existence at once, and always possessing its own power undiminished, so far it is the progeny of infinity. And soul indeed, in consequence of measuring its own life, by restitutions and periods, and introducing a boundary to its own motions, is referred to the cause of bound; but in consequence of having no cessation of motions, but making the end of one period the beginning of the whole of a second vital circulation, it is referred to the order of infinity. The whole of this heaven also, according to the wholeness of itself, its connexion, the order of its periods, and the measures of its restitutions, is bounded. But according to its prolific powers, its various evolutions, and the never-failing revolutions of its orbs, it participates of infinity. Moreover, the whole of generation, in consequence of all its forms being bounded, and always permanent after the same manner, and in consequence of its own circle which imitates the celestial circulation, is similar to bound. But again, in consequence of the variety of the particulars of which it consists, their unceasing mutation, and the intervention of the more and the less in the participations of forms, it is the image of infinity. And in addition to these things, every natural production, according to its form indeed, is similar to bound, but according to its matter, resembles infinity. For these are suspended in the last place‡ from the two principles posterior to *The One*, and as far as to these the progression of their productive power extends. Each of these also is one, but form is

---

† μενειν is omitted in the original.

‡ For εσχατων it is necessary to read εσχατως.

the measure and boundary of matter, and is in a greater degree one. Matter however is all things in capacity, so far as it derives its subsistence from the first power. There, however, power is generative of all things. But the power of matter is imperfect, and is indigent of the hypostasis which is generative[†] of all things according to energy. Very properly therefore is it said by Socrates that all beings are from bound and infinity, and that these two intelligible principles primarily derive their subsistence from God. For that which congregates both of them, and perfects them, and unfolds itself into light through all beings is *The One* prior to the duad. And union indeed is derived to all things through that which is first; but the division of the two orders of things is generated from these primary causes, and through these is extended to the unknown and ineffable principle. Let it therefore be manifest through these things, what the two principles of beings are, which become proximately apparent from *The One*, according to the theology of Plato.

CHAPTER IV

In the next place let us show what the third[‡] thing is which presents itself to the view from these principles. It is every where therefore called that which is mixed, as deriving its subsistence from bound and infinity. But if bound is the bound of beings, and the infinite is the infinite of beings, and beings are the things which have a subsistence from both these, as Socrates himself clearly teaches us, it is evident that the first of things mingled, is the first of beings. This, however, is nothing else than that which is highest in beings, which is being itself, and nothing else than being. My meaning is, that this is evident through those things by which we demonstrate that what is primarily being, is comprehensive of all things intelligibly, and of life and intellect. For we say that life is triadic vitally, and intellect intellectually; and also that these three things being life and intellect are every where. But all things pre-subsist primarily and essentially in being. For there essence, life and intellect subsist, and the summit of beings. Life however is the middle centre of being, which is denominated and is intelligible life. But intellect is the boundary of being, and is intelligible intellect. For in the intelligible there is intellect, and in intellect the intelligible. There

---

[†] The word γεννητικης is omitted in the original.

[‡] τριτον is omitted in the original.

however intellect subsists intelligibly, but in intellect, the intelligible subsists intellectually.

And essence indeed is that which is stable in being, and which is woven together with the first principles, and does not depart from *The One*. But life is that which proceeds from the principles, and is connascent with infinite power. And intellect is that which converts itself to the principles, conjoins the end with the beginning, and produces one intelligible circle. The first of beings therefore is that which is mingled from the first principles, and is triple, one thing which it contains subsisting in it essentially, another vitally, and another intellectually, but all things pre-subsisting in it essentially. I mean however by the first of beings essence. For essence itself is the summit of all beings, and is as it were the monad of the whole of things. In all things therefore, essence is the first. And in each thing that which is essential is the most ancient, as deriving its subsistence from the Vesta of beings. For the intelligible is especially this. Since intellect indeed is that which is gnostic, life is intelligence, and being is intelligible. If however every being is mingled, but essence is being itself, prior to all other things essence is that which subsists as mingled from the two principles proceeding from *The One*. Hence Socrates indicating how the mode of generation in the two principles differs from that of the mixture says, "that God has exhibited bound and infinity." For they are unities deriving their subsistence from *The One*, and as it were luminous patefactions from the imparticipable and first union. But with respect to producing a mixture, and mingling through the first principles, by how much *to make* is subordinate to *the unfolding into light*, and *generation to patefaction*, by so much is that which is mixed allotted a progression from *The One*, inferior to that of the two principles.

That which is mixed therefore, is intelligible essence, and subsists primarily from [the first] God, from whom infinity also and bound are derived. But it subsists secondarily from the principles posterior to the unical God, I mean from bound and infinity. For the fourth cause which is effective of the mixture is again God himself; since if any other cause should be admitted besides this, there will no longer be a fourth cause, but a fifth will be introduced. For the first cause was God, who unfolds into light the two principles. But after him are the two principles bound and infinity. And the mixture is the fourth thing. If therefore the cause of the mixture is different from the first divine cause, this cause will be the fifth and not the fourth thing, as Socrates says it is. Farther still, in addition to these things, if we say that God is especially the supplier of union to beings, and the mixture itself of the principles is a union into the hypostasis of being, God is also certainly the cause of this primarily. Moreover, Socrates in the *Republic* clearly evinces that *The Good* is the cause of being and essence to intelligibles, in the same manner as the sun is to visible natures. Is it not therefore necessary, if that which is mixed is primarily being, to refer it to the first God, and to say that it receives its progression from him? If also the demiurgus in the *Timæus*, constitutes the essence of the soul itself by itself from an impartible and a partible essence, which is the same thing as to constitute it from bound and infinity; for the soul according to bound is similar to the impartible, but according to infinity, to the partible essence; - if therefore the demiurgus mingles the essence of the soul from these, and again separately, from same and different, and if from these being now pre-existent, he constitutes the whole soul, must we not much more say that the first God is the cause of the first essence? That which is mixed therefore, proceeds, as we have said, from the first God, and does not subsist from the principles alone posterior to *The One*, but proceeds also from these, and is triadic. And in the first place indeed, it participates from God of ineffable union, and the whole of its subsistence. But from bound, it receives hyparxis, and the uniform, and a stable peculiarity. And from infinity, it receives power, and the occult power which is in itself, of all things. For in short, since it is one and not one, the one is inherent in it according to bound, but the non-one according to infinity. The mixture however of both these, and its wholeness, are derived from the first God. That which is mixed therefore, is a monad, because its participates of *The One*; and it is biformed, so far as it proceeds from the two principles; but it is a triad, so far as in every mixture, these three things are necessary according to Socrates, *viz.* beauty, truth, and symmetry. Concerning these things however, we shall speak again.

In what manner, however, essence is that which is first mixed, we shall now explain. For this is of all things the most difficult to discover, *viz.* what that is which is primarily being, as the Elean guest also somewhere says; for it is most dubious how being is not less than non-being. In what manner therefore essence subsists from bound and infinity must be shown. For if bound and infinity are superessential, essence may appear to have its subsistence from non-essences. How therefore can non-essences produce essence? Or is not this the case in all other things which subsist through the mixture of each other? For that which is produced from things mingled together, is not the same with things that are not mingled. For neither is soul the same with the genera, from which, being mingled together, the father generated it, nor is a happy life the same with the life which is according to intellect, or with the life which is according to pleasure, nor is *The One* in bodies the same with its elements. Hence it is not wonderful, if that which is primarily being, though it is neither bound nor infinity, subsists from both these, and is mixed, superessential natures themselves not being assumed in the mixture of it, but secondary progressions from them coalescing into the subsistence of essence. Thus therefore being consists of these, as participating of both, possessing indeed the uniform from bound, but the generative, and in short, occult multitude from infinity. For it is all things occultly, and on this account, is the cause of all beings; which also the Elean guest, indicating to us, calls being the first power, as subsisting according to the participation of the first power, and participating of hyparxis from bound, and of power from infinity. Afterwards however, the Elean guest defines being to be power, as prolific and generative of all things, and as beings all things uniformly. For power is every where the cause of prolific progressions, and of all multitude; occult power indeed being the cause of occult multitude; but the power which exists in energy, and which unfolds itself into light, being the cause of all-perfect multitude. Through this cause therefore, I think, that every being, and every essence has connascent powers. For it participates of infinity, and derives its hyparxis indeed from bound, but its power from infinity. And being is nothing else than a monad of many powers, and a multiplied hyparxis, and on this account being is one many. The many however subsist occultly and without separation in the first natures; but with separation in secondary natures. For by how much being is nearer to *The One*, by so much the more does it conceal multitude, and is defined according to union alone. It appears to me also that Plotinus and his followers, frequently indicating these things, produce being from form and intelligible matter, arranging form[†] as analogous to *The One*, and to hyparxis, but power as analogous to matter. And if indeed they say this, they speak rightly. But if they ascribe a certain formless and indefinite nature to an intelligible essence, they appear to me to wander from the conceptions of Plato on this subject. For the infinite is not the matter of bound, but the power of it, nor is bound the form of the infinite, but the hyparxis of it. But being consists of both these, as not only standing in *The One*, but receiving a multitude of unities and powers which are mingled into essence.

---

† For $\pi\lambda\eta\theta o\varsigma$ in the original it is necessary to read $\epsilon\iota\delta o\varsigma$.

CHAPTER V

That therefore which is primarily being is through these things denominated by Plato that which is mixed. And through the similitude of it, generation also is mingled from bound and infinity. And the infinite indeed in this is imperfect power; but the bound in it is form and the *morphe* of this power. On this account we establish this power to be matter, not possessing existence in energy, and requiring to be bounded by something else. We no longer however say that it is lawful to call the power of being matter, since it is generative of energies, produces all beings from itself, and is prolific of the perfect powers in beings. For the power of matter being imperfect dissimilarly imitates the power of being; and becoming multitude in capacity, it expresses the parturition of multitude in the power of being.† Moreover, the form of matter imitates ultimately bound, since it gives limits to matter, and terminates its infinity. But it is multiplied and divided about it. It is also mingled with the privation of matter, and represents the supreme union of the hyparxis of being, by its essence always advancing to existence, and always tending to decay. For those things which subsist in the first natures according to transcendency, are in such as are last according to deficiency. For that also which is primarily being is mixed, is exempt from the bound of infinite life, and is the cause of it. But that which consists of the last‡ of forms and the first matter, is in its own nature void of life; since it possesses life in capacity. For there indeed generative causes subsist prior to their progeny, and things perfect prior to such as are imperfect. But here things in capacity are prior to such as are in energy, and concauses are subject to the things which are produced from them. This however, I think, happens naturally, because the gifts of the first principles pervade as far as to the last of things, and not only generate more perfect natures, but also such as have a more imperfect subsistence. And on this account that which is mixed is the cause of generation, and of the nature which is mingled here. The bound and infinity however, which are prior to being, are not only the

---

† The punctuation in the latter part of this sentence in the original is erroneous: for instead of και την εν εκεινη του πληθους ωδινα δυναμει γενομενη, το πληθος απεικασατο, it should be και την εν εκεινη του πληθους ωδινα δυναμει γενομενη το πληθος, απεικασατο.

‡ For πρωτου here, it is necessary to read εσχατου. For in this place Proclus is speaking of body.

causes of this nature, but also of the elements of it, of which that which is mixed is not the cause, so far as it is mixed. For bound and infinity are twofold. And one kind of these is exempt from the things mingled, but another kind is assumed to the completion of the mixture. For I think it is every where necessary that prior to things that are mingled, there should be such as are unmingled, prior to things imperfect, such as are perfect, prior to parts, wholes, and prior to things that are in others, such as are in themselves; and this Socrates persuades us to admit not in one thing only, but also in beauty and symmetry, and in all forms. If therefore the second and third genera of being and forms subsist prior to their participants, how can we assert that bound and infinity which pervade through all beings have their first subsistence as things mingled? It must be admitted therefore, that they are unmingled and separate from being, and that being is derived *from* them, and at the same time consists of *them*. It is derived *from* them indeed, because they have a prior subsistence; but it consists *of* them, because they subsist in being according to a second progression.

The genera of being also are twofold; some of them indeed being fabricative of beings, but others existing as the elements of the nature of each being. For some of them indeed pre-subsist themselves by themselves, as possessing a productive power; but others being generated from these constitute each particular being. Let no one therefore any longer wonder, how Socrates indeed in the *Philebus* establishes that which is mingled, prior to bound and infinity, but we on the contrary evince that bound and infinity are exempt from that which is mixed. For each is twofold, and the one indeed is prior to being, but the other is in being; and the one is generative, but the other is the element of the mixture. Of this kind also, are the bound and infinity of the mixed life, each being the element of the whole of felicity. Hence also each is indigent of each. And neither is intellect by itself desirable, nor perfect pleasure. It is necessary however, that the good should consist of all these, *viz.* of the desirable, the sufficient, and the perfect. Bound itself therefore and infinity, which are separate, subsist according to cause prior to that which is mixed. But the bound and infinity which are mixed are more imperfect than the mixture. Hence, from what has been said, it is evident what the things are of which the mixture consists.

CHAPTER VI

In the next place, we must speak of the triad, which is consubsistent with this mixture. For every mixture, if it is rightly made, as Socrates says, requires these three things, beauty, truth, and symmetry. For neither will any thing base, if it is introduced into the mixture, impart rectitude, since it will be the cause of error, and of inordinate prerogative, nor if truth is at any time separated, will it suffer the mixture to consist of things that are pure, and which are in reality subdued, but it will fill the whole with an image and with non-being. Nor without symmetry will there be a communion of the elements, and an elegant association. Symmetry, therefore, is necessary to the union of the things that are mingled, and to an appropriate communion. But truth is necessary to purity. And beauty to order; which also renders the whole lovely. For when each thing in the mixture has a place adapted to itself, it renders both the elements, and the arrangement resulting from them, beautiful. Here therefore, in the first mixture, these three things are apparent, symmetry, truth, and beauty. And symmetry indeed is the cause to the mixture, that being is one; truth is the cause of the reality of its existence; and beauty is the cause of its being intelligible. Hence it is intelligible and truly being. That also which is primarily being is more uniform, and intellect is conjoined to it, according to its familiarity with the beautiful. But each participates of existence, because it is being derived from being. That which is mixed however, is supreme among beings, because it is united to *The Good*. And it appears to me, that the divine Iamblichus perceiving these three causes of being, defines the intelligible in these three, *viz.* in symmetry, truth, and beauty, and unfolds the intelligible Gods through these in the Platonic theology. In what manner indeed, the intelligible breadth consists of these, will be most evident as we proceed. Now however, from what has been said, it is perfectly manifest why Socrates says that this triad is found to be in the vestibules of *The Good.* For what is primarily being participates of this triad through its union with *The Good.* For because indeed *The Good* is the measure of all beings, the first being becomes itself commensurate. Because the former is prior to being, the latter subsists truly and really. And because the former is good and desirable, the latter presents itself to the view as the beautiful itself. Here therefore, the first beauty also subsists; and on this account *The One* is not only the cause of good, but likewise of beauty, as Plato says in his *Epistles*. Beauty however subsists here occultly, since this order comprehends all things uniformly, in consequence of subsisting primarily from the principles [bound and infinity]. But where and how beauty is unfolded into light, we shall shortly explain.

CHAPTER VII

Such therefore, is the first triad of intelligibles, according to Socrates in the *Philebus*, viz. bound, infinite, and that which is mixed from these. And of these, bound indeed is a God proceeding to the intelligible summit, from the imparticipable and first God, measuring and defining all things, and giving subsistence to every paternal, connective, and undefiled genus of Gods. But infinite is the never-failing power of this God, unfolding into light all the generative orders, and all infinity, both that which is prior to essence, and that which is essential, and also that which proceeds as far as to the last matter. And that which is mixed, is the first and highest order of the Gods, comprehending all things occultly, deriving its completion indeed through the intelligible connective triad, but unically comprehending the cause of every being, and establishing its summit in the first intelligibles, exempt from the whole of things.

CHAPTER VIII

After this first triad subsisting from, and conjoined with *The One*, we shall celebrate the second, proceeding from this, and deriving its completion through things analogous[†] to the triad prior to it. For in this also it is necessary that being should participate, and that *The One* should be participated, and likewise that this one which is secondarily one, should be generative of that which is secondarily being. For every where participated deity constitutes about itself that which participates it. Thus whole souls render bodies consubsistent with their causes: and partial souls generate, in conjunction with the Gods, irrational souls. Much more therefore, do the Gods produce in conjunction with *The One* all things. Hence, as the first of the unities generates the summit of being, so likewise the middle unity constitutes the middle being. But every thing which generates, and every thing which makes or produces, possesses a power prolific of the things produced, according to which it produces, corroborates and connects its progeny. Again therefore, there will be a second triad unfolded into light analogously to the first. And one thing indeed, is the summit of it, which we call one, deity, and hyparxis. But another thing is the middle of it, which we call power. And another thing is the extremity of it, which we say is that which is

---

[†] For αλογων it is necessary to read αναλογων.

secondarily being. This however is intelligible life. For all things are in the intelligible, as was before demonstrated, *viz.* to be, to live, and to energize intellectually. And the summit indeed, of the intelligible order, is all things according to cause, and as we have frequently said, occultly. But the middle of it, causes multitude to shine forth, and proceeds from the union of being into manifest light. And the extremity of it, is now all intelligible multitude, and the order of intelligible forms. For forms have their subsistence at the extremity of the intelligible order. For it is necessary that forms should subsist first and become apparent in intellect. If therefore being abides exemptly in the first mixture, but now proceeds, and is generated dyadically from the monad, there will be motion about it; and if there is motion, it is also necessary that there should be intelligible life. For every where motion is a certain life, since some one calls even the motion of material bodies life. That which is first therefore, in this second triad, may be called bound; that which is second in it, infinity; and that which is the third, life. For the second triad also is a God, possessing prolific power, and unfolding into light from, and about itself, that which is secondarily being. Here however also, the triad is analogous to the first triad.

But again, it is necessary to comprehend by reasoning the peculiarity of this triad. For the first triad being all things, but intelligibly and unically, and as I may say, speaking Platonically, according to the form of bound, the second triad is indeed all things, but vitally, and as I may say, following the philosopher, according to the form of infinity, just as the third triad proceeds according to the peculiarity of that which is mixed. For as in the progression according to breadth, that which is mixed presents itself to the view as the third, so likewise in the progression according to depth of intelligibles, the third has the order of that which is mixed with reference to the superior triads. The middle triad therefore, is indeed all things, but is characterized by intelligible infinity. For the three principles after the first, orderly distribute for us the intelligible genus of the Gods. For bound indeed, unfolds into light the first triad; but infinity the second; and that which is mixed, the third. It is infinite power therefore, according to which the second triad is characterized. For being the middle, it subsists according to the middle of the first triad, being all things from all. For in each triad, there is bound, infinity, and that which is mixed. But the peculiarity of the monads being respectively different, evolves the intelligible order of the Gods. The middle triad however, thus subsisting, but I say thus, because it consists of all the things of which the triad prior to it consists, yet it contains and connects the middle of intelligibles according to infinite power, and is filled indeed from a more elevated union, but fills the union posterior to itself with the powers of being. And it is measured indeed, from thence uniformly, but measures the third triad by the power of itself. And it abides indeed, in the first triad stably, but it establishes in itself the triad which is next in order. And in short, it binds to itself the intelligible centre, and establishes one intelligible coherence; causing indeed that which is occult and possesses the form of *The One* in the first triad, to shine forth; but collecting the intelligible multitude of the third triad, and comprehending it on all sides. The being however, which gives completion to this triad is mixed, in the same manner as the being of the triad prior to it, and receives the peculiarity of life. For the infinity in this generates life.

It is likewise necessary that this triad should participate of the three things, symmetry, truth, and beauty. That which is primarily being however, principally subsists according to symmetry, which unites it, and conjoins it to *The Good*. But the second triad, principally subsists according to truth. For because it participates of that which is primarily being, it is being, and *truly* being. And the third triad principally subsists according to the beautiful. For there intelligible multitude, order and beauty, first shine forth to the view. Hence this being is the most beautiful of all intelligibles. This however will be discussed hereafter. As there is a triad therefore, in each of the mixtures, the first indeed, symmetry especially comprehends and connects; the second truth, and the third beauty. And this induced the divine Iamblichus to say, that Plato in these three defines the whole of the intelligible [order]. For all are in each, but one of these predominates more in one of the intelligible monads than in another. Moreover, the third triad presents itself to the view after this. For it is necessary that the extremity of being should also be deified, and should participate of an intelligible unity. For beings are not more in number than the unities, as Parmenides says, nor are the unities more numerous than beings; but each progression of being participates of *The One*; since this universe also, according to each part of itself, is governed by soul and intellect. By a much greater priority therefore, must the intelligible in its first, middle, and last hypostases, participate of the intelligible Gods.

CHAPTER IX

As the first unity therefore, after the exempt cause of all things, unfolds into light intelligible being, and the second unity, intelligible life, thus also the third constitutes about itself, intelligible intellect, and fills it with divine union, constituting power as the medium between itself and being, through which it gives completion to this being, and converts it to itself. In this therefore, every intelligible multitude shines forth to the view. For the whole of this being is intelligible intellect, life, and essence. And it is neither all things according to cause, in the same manner as that which is primarily being, nor does it cause all things to shine forth, as the second being does, but it is as it were all things according to energy, and openly. Hence also, it is the boundary of all intelligibles. For since the progression of beings is accomplished according to similitude, the first being is most similar to *The One*; the second, is parturient with multitude, and is the origin of separation; but the third, is now all-perfect, and unfolds into light in itself, intelligible multitude and form.

Farther still, as the first triad abides occultly in bound, and fixes in itself every thing that is stable in intelligibles; but the second abides and at the same time proceeds; so the third, after progression converts the intelligible end to the beginning, and convolves the order to itself. For it is every where the province of intellect to convert and converge to the intelligible. All these likewise are uniform [*i.e.* have the form of one] and intelligible, *viz.* the abiding, the proceeding, and the returning. For each of these is not asserted after the same manner in intelligibles. And the intelligible genus of Gods[†] is unical, simple, and occult, conjoining itself to *The One Itself* which is prior to beings; and unfolds[‡] into light nothing else than the transcendency of *The One*. For these three triads, mystically announce that unknown cause the first and perfectly imparticipable God. The first of them indeed, announcing his ineffable union; the second his transcendency, by which he surpasses all powers; and the third, his all-perfect generation of beings. For as they are able to comprehend the principle which surpasses both the union and the powers of all beings, so they exhibit to secondary natures, his[§] admirable transcendency; receiving indeed separately the unical power and dominion of the first God; but unfolding into light intelligibly the cause which is prior to intelligibles. For these Gods though they are allotted a simplicity which is equally exempt from all the divine orders,

---

[†] The words των μετα in the original immediately before το νοητον θεων γενος, are to be rejected as superfluous.

[‡] εκφαινει is omitted in the original.

[§] For εκεινοις, it is necessary to read εκεινης.

yet they fall short of the union of the father. Of this triad therefore, which converts all intelligibles to the first principle, and convolves the multitude apparent in itself to the stable union of the whole of things, one thing is bound, and unity and hyparxis; another, is infinity and power; and another is that which is mixed, essence, life, and intelligible intellect. But the whole triad subsists according to being, and is the intellect of the first triad. For the first triad is an intelligible God primarily. But the triad posterior to it is an intelligible and intellectual God. And the third triad is an intellectual God. These three deities also, and triadic monads, give completion to the intelligible genera. For they are monads according to their deities; since all other things are suspended from the Gods, and also powers and beings. But that are triads according to a separate division. For bound, infinity, and that which is mixed, have a threefold subsistence; but in one place indeed, all things are according to bound; in another, all things are according to infinity; and in another, all things are according to that which is mixed. And in one place, that which is mixed is essence, in another, it is intelligible life; and in another, intelligible intellect. In this last therefore, forms subsist primarily. For the separation of intelligibles, unfolds the order of forms; because form is being, but is not simply being. Hence that which is primarily being, is being itself, and is that which is being. But that which is the second being, is power, proceeding indeed from the first being, and existing as it were a duad generative of the multitude of beings, but not yet being multitude. And that which is the third being, is itself the multitude of beings; being there existing with separation. For being is the exempt cause of those things which forms constitute divisibly. And of the things of which being is productive collectively, of these, forms are the cause in a way attended with separation. Because forms indeed, are causes productive of separation in their effects, and also because forms are called the paradigms of beings. Being however, is the cause of all things posterior to itself, but is not the paradigm of them. For paradigms are the causes of things which are separated according to existence, and which have different characters of essence. After *The One* therefore which is prior to beings, that which is one-many occultly, and the united subsists. On this account, it is that which is divided into multitude, and which tends from the uniform to the splendid. But the last of intelligibles, is that from which a certain distribution into parts originates, and which is comprehensive of intelligible multitude.

CHAPTER X

Socrates therefore, in the *Philebus*, affords us such like auxiliaries to the theory of the intelligible triads. It is requisite however, not only to abide in these conceptions, but also to demonstrate the theology of Plato about these triads from other dialogues, and from them to point out one truth adapted to the things themselves. We shall assume therefore, what is written in the *Timæus*, and shall follow our leader [Syrianus] who has unfolded to us the arcane mysteries of these triads, and conjoin with the end of what has been said the beginning of the following discussion. In the *Timæus* therefore, Plato investigating what the paradigm of the whole world is, discovers that it is comprehensive of all intelligible animals, that it is all-perfect, that it is the most beautiful of intelligibles, that it is only-begotten, and that it is the intelligible of the demiurgus. He likewise denominates it animal itself, as being the intelligible paradigm of every animal, and of that which is the object of sense. Hence it is necessary that this animal itself, because it is all-perfect, and the most beautiful of intelligibles, should be established in the intelligible orders. For though there is intelligible animal in the demiurgus, yet it is rather intellectual than intelligible, and is not the most beautiful of all intelligibles, but is second to them in beauty and power. For primary beauty is in the intelligible Gods. In the demiurgus also, there are not only four forms of the things contained in the world, but there is all the multitude of forms. For in him the paradigms of individual forms pre-subsist. But animal itself is *totally* constitutive of all animals by the intelligible tetrad. The demiurgus likewise is not like animal itself only-begotten among beings, but subsists in conjunction with the vivific cause, together with which he constitutes the second genera of being, mingling them in the crater or bowl, in order to the generation of souls. For of the things of which intelligible animal is effective and at the same time generative, of these the demiurgus is allotted the cause in a divided manner, in conjunction with the crater. Hence, as I have said, animal itself is exempt from the demiurgus, and is, as Timæus every where denominates it, intelligible.

Nevertheless, because forms are first separated in it, and because it is all-perfect, it subsists in the third order of intelligibles. For neither that which is primarily, nor that which is secondarily being,[†] is all-perfect. For the former is beyond all separation; but the latter generates indeed, and is parturient with intelligibles, but is not yet the multitude of

---

[†] *viz.* Intelligible life, or life itself, or the first life.

beings. If therefore, neither of these is multitude, how can either of them be all-perfect multitude? If however all-perfect multitude shines forth in the third triad of intelligibles, as was a little before demonstrated, but animal itself is the first paradigm (for it is comprehensive of all intelligible animals, is an only-begotten paradigm, and is not conjoined with any other principle) it is necessary that animal itself should be established according to this order. For either there will not be an intelligible paradigm, (and in this case, how will sensibles be images of intelligibles? or how will the intelligible Gods be the fathers of the whole of things?) or if there is, it is the third in intelligibles. For the natures which are prior to the triad in intelligibles, are not all-perfect; since they are exempt from the division into multitude. But the natures posterior to it are not only-begotten. For they proceed together with others; the male indeed, with the female, and those that are of a demiurgic together with those that are of a generative characteristic. Nor are they the most beautiful of intelligibles; for beauty is in the intelligible. But animal itself is all-perfect, and at the same time only begotten. The first paradigm of beings therefore, is arranged in the third triad of intelligibles. Moreover, animal itself is eternal, as Timæus himself says. For says he, "the nature of animal is eternal." And again, in another place he asserts, "that the paradigm is through all eternity being." If therefore it is eternal, it participates of eternity. And if that which participates is every where secondary to that which is participated, animal itself is secondary to eternity. And if it is through all eternity being, it is filled with the whole power of eternity. If this however be the case, it subsists proximately after eternity. For that which enjoys the whole of causes, is arranged proximately after them.

CHAPTER XI

Moreover, if eternity has the same ratio to intelligible animal, which time has to that which is sensible, but the universe proximately participates of time (for time was generated together with the universe) it is certainly necessary that animal itself should primarily participate of eternity. Eternity therefore is beyond the first paradigm. For eternity indeed measures the existence of animal itself: but animal itself is measured and filled with perpetuity from it. To which may be added, that we assert eternity to be the cause of immortality to all things. Hence eternity is that which is primarily immortal. For as that which is primarily being is the cause of existence to all things, but that which is effective of form is itself prior to other forms, so that which is the cause of perpetuity and immortality, is itself primarily immortal. The dæmoniacal Aristotle also rightly calls eternity immortal and divine, and that from whence the existence and life of all things are suspended. If however it is that which is primarily immortal, and not according to participation, but is as it were immortality and perpetuity, it will be life, possessing from itself the ever, and exuberantly scattering the power of perpetuity, and extending it to other things, so far as each is naturally adapted to receive it. For the immortal is in life, and subsists together with life. Hence Socrates in the *Phædo*,[†] after many and beautiful demonstrations of the psychical immortality says, "God therefore, my dear Cebes, and the form itself of life, are much more immortal." Hence, intelligible life, and the God who is connective of this life, primarily possess the immortal, and are the fountain of the whole of perpetuity. But this is eternity. Eternity therefore has its subsistence in life, and will be established in the middle of the intelligible order.

Farther still, it is necessary to assert that intelligible eternity is one of these three things, *viz.* that it subsists either according to being, or according to life, or according to intelligible intellect. But being, as the Elean guest says, according to its own nature, neither stands still, nor is moved. For if being is being to all things, and essence is a thing of this kind, much more must this be the case with intelligible essence and that which is primarily being. For they are nothing else than essence only. But being unfolds motion and permanency, and the other genera of beings, in the second and third progressions of itself. The first being therefore, as we have said, is at one and the same time exempt from motion and permanency. But eternity according to Timæus *abides* in one. Hence also time imitates in its motion the intelligible permanency of eternity. Eternity therefore does not subsist according to that which is primarily being, nor yet according to intelligible intellect.[‡] For neither is soul time, which is moved through the whole of time. And in short, in divine beings, that which is participated is every where established above that which participates. But the eternal participates of eternity, just as that which is temporal participates of time. Eternity therefore is prior to intelligible intellect, and posterior to being; so that it is established in the middle of the intelligible breadth. And as animal itself is eternal, so likewise eternity is that which is always being. For as animal itself participates of eternity, so eternity participates of being,

---

[†] For Φαιδρῳ it is necessary to read Φαιδωνι.

[‡] It is necessary to supply αλλ' ουδε κατα τον νουν τον νοητον.

and is the cause of existence, of perpetual life, and intellection, and measures the essences, powers and energies of all things.

CHAPTER XII

Since, however, eternity subsists according to the middle centre of intelligibles, and animal itself according to the extremity of them, and the most splendid of that which is intelligible, what is that which is the first of intelligibles, and how is it denominated by Timæus? He says therefore of eternity, that while it abides in one, time proceeds according to number; and that by motion it adumbrates the permanency of eternity, but by number, its stable union. What therefore is that one, in which Timæus says eternity abides? For it is necessary either to say that it is the one of eternity, or *The One* which transcends all intelligibles, or the one of the first triad. But if indeed, we say that it is the imparticipable one, how is it possible that any thing can abide in that which is exempt from all things; and which neither admits the habitude nor communion of secondary natures with itself? For every thing which abides in any thing, is in a certain respect on all sides comprehended by that in which we say it abides. It is however perfectly impossible that the first one should either comprehend any being, or be co-arranged with beings. But if any one should suppose that it is the one of eternity, in which Timæus says eternity abides, in this case, eternity will be in itself. It is necessary however, that it should abide in itself, by having its subsistence in abiding in that which is prior to itself. For to abide in that which is prior to, is better than the establishment of things in themselves, in the same manner as it is more perfect than the collocation of better in less excellent natures. If therefore eternity abides in itself, to what shall we primarily assign permanency in that which is prior to itself? For it is necessary that this being more divine, should have its generation prior to that which is inferior to it. If therefore eternity can neither abide in itself, nor in *The One* which is prior to beings, it is evident that abiding in one according to Timæus, *it is established in the one of the first triad*, or rather in the whole of that triad. For, as we have before observed, the first triad is the cause of stability to all beings, in the same manner as the middle triad is the cause of their progression, and the third triad of their conversion to their principle.

CHAPTER XIII

Again therefore, three orders of intelligibles present themselves to our view, according to the doctrine of Timæus, *viz.* animal itself, eternity, and the one. And through this one, and the firm establishment in it, eternity has fixed the intelligible kingdom. But through eternity, animal itself defines the boundary of the intelligible Gods, according to a perpetual and invariable sameness. And animal itself indeed, having proceeded tetradically, is suspended from the duad in eternity. For eternity is *the ever in conjunction with being.* But the duad in eternity participates of the intelligible monad, which Timæus on this account denominates one, as being the monad and principle of all the intelligible breadth. Since otherwise indeed, he very properly calls the first triad one, in consequence of its being especially characterized according to bound, denominating it from bound. But he calls the middle triad dyadically, eternity, connecting the names; because this triad is defined according to intelligible power. And he denominates the third triad animal itself, transferring the appellation to the whole of it, from the extremity of the triad. The first triad therefore is the union of all the intelligibles, being in a certain respect co-ordinated with them. For the union is different from this which is exempt from intelligibles and imparticipable. It is also the supplier of stable power. For all things are established on account of it. But eternity is primary being, and is that which is primarily established. Hence, with respect to the permanency of the whole of things, we say that the first triad is that *on account of which* this permanency is effected; but that the second triad is that *by which* it is produced. For the firm establishment of beings is indeed *according* to this second triad, but is *on account* of the first. But the second triad is the proximate measure of all beings, and is co-ordinated with the things that are measured. There are also at one and the same time in it, bound and infinity; bound indeed, so far as it measures intelligibles; but infinity, so far as it is the cause of perpetuity, and the ever. For according to the oracle, eternity is the cause of never-failing life, of unwearied power, and unsluggish energy. Nevertheless, eternity is more characterized by infinity [than by bound.] For it comprehends in itself infinite time. And time indeed has bound and infinity in a divided manner. For according to its continuity, it is infinite; but according to the now it is bounded. For the now is a bound. But eternity establishes bound and infinity in the same. For it is a unity and power. And according to the one indeed, it is bound; but according to power infinite; which time† also demonstrates as from images; because the middle triad [of intelligibles] has bound, infinity, and that which is mixed. For whence is the bound of time derived except from eternal bound? For the temporal bound also is impartible, in the same manner as the bound of eternity is one. For the impartible is the image of *The One*. Whence likewise is the infinity of the continuity of time derived except from the power of the infinite? For the latter is a stable infinity, but the former an infinity which is moved. And as the latter stands still according to *The One*, so the former is moved according to number. Since whence is the alliance of time with lives, except from the first principle [of life, eternity?] But time proceeds through all temporal life.

Again, therefore, from these things it is evident, that eternity subsists according to the middle of the intelligible Gods. For here there is infinite life, and the cause of all life, intellectual, psychical, and that which subsists partibly in bodies. But eternity is the father and supplier of infinite life; since eternity is also the cause of all immortality and perpetuity. And Plotinus, exhibiting, in a most divinely inspired manner, the peculiarity‡ of eternity, according to the theology of Plato, defines it to be infinite life, at once unfolding into light the whole of itself, and its own being.⁴ For establishing its life in the intelligible centre, and through the one indeed measuring its being, and fixing it in that which is prior to itself, but through power causing it to be infinite, it unfolds indeed the uniform transcendency of the first triad, but defines the termination of the Gods, and extends from the middle on all sides, and to the all the intelligible breadth. Moreover the third triad is filled indeed with intelligible life,§ and on this account is an intelligible animal, and the first animal. For it primarily participates of the whole nature of this life; but unfolds into light in itself the first of forms, to which also the demiurgic intellect extending itself, constitutes the whole world, and is itself the intelligible universe, and the apparent world the sensible universe. Hence also, Plato denominates animal itself all-perfect. Or rather, if you are willing we will speak thus: that in this third triad, there are bound, infinity, and that which is mixed, which we have called intelligible intellect. Hence the whole triad is denominated only-begotten from the father which is in it. For the cause of bound imparts

---

† χρονος is omitted in the original.

‡ Instead of αϊδιοτητα, it is necessary to read ιδιοτητα.

§ ζωης is omitted in the original.

that which is unco-ordinated with other things, and an exempt transcendency. For that which comprehends, says Timæus, all such animals as are intelligible, will not be the second with any other; since again, it would be requisite that there should be another animal about it. Hence that which comprehends in one all intelligible animals is a whole. But every where whole is referred† to bound, and parts to infinity. So that if on this account animal itself is only-begotten, it will possess this peculiarity according to bound. But again, it is denominated eternal according to the power of it. For this power especially pertains to that which is eternal. For eternity is infinite power abiding in one, and proceeding stably. Animal itself, however, is all-perfect according to intellect. For that which unfolds in itself all the intelligible separation of being, is intelligible intellect. And that intellect, according to the decision of Plato, will be all-perfect, which comprehends all intelligibles, and defines the boundary of the intelligible order. The only-begotten, therefore, the eternal, the all-perfect, bound, infinity, and that which is mixed, manifest the nature of intelligible animal. On this account, Timæus also, in these three conclusions, reminds us of the paradigm, *viz.* in the conclusion which shows that the universe is only-begotten, and again, in the generation of time, and in the all-perfect comprehension of all animals.

If likewise Timæus says, that animal itself is the most beautiful of all intelligibles, and that this has the third order in intelligibles, it will not be wonderful. For it has been before asserted by us, that every where the cause of the best mixture is the triad symmetry, truth, and beauty. But beauty principally shines forth in the third progression of being, and exhibits its luminous nature together with intelligible forms, just as truth shines forth in the second, and symmetry in the first progression of being. If, however, truth is indeed the first, beauty the second, and symmetry the third, it is by no means wonderful, that according to order, truth and beauty should be prior to symmetry; but that symmetry being more apparent in the first triad than the other two, should shine forth as the third in the secondary progressions. For these three subsist occultly in the first triad. And truth indeed, so far as it is intelligible knowledge, is in the second triad; but beauty so far as it is the form of forms is in the third triad. For that this triad subsists there first, is evident from this, that truth is primarily in that which is especially being, prior to knowledge. But beauty, which pervades as far

---

† Instead of προ του περατος, and προ της απειριας, it is necessary to read προς του περατος, and προς της απειριας.

as to the last of beings, is necessarily in the first being, from which the last of beings are derived. And the first symmetry is in that which is primarily mixed. For every mixture requires symmetry, in order that what is produced from it may be one certain thing. Though these three things, therefore, pre-subsist there, for we assume, as acknowledged universally, that symmetry is there, and the most beautiful of intelligible animals, as Timæus says, yet at present we shall dismiss the further consideration of them, as we have elsewhere precedaneously discussed them, and have especially endeavoured to enforce what we conceive to be the opinion of Plato concerning their order. For we have spoken of these things in a treatise consisting of one book, in which we demonstrate that truth is co-ordinate to the philosopher, beauty to the lover, and symmetry to the musician; and that such is the order of these lives, such also is the relation of truth, beauty, and symmetry to each other.

Animal itself, therefore, may with the greatest justice, be called most beautiful, so far as it is eminently contained in intelligible beauty. For beauty is wont to be carried in forms, and is as it were the form of forms, unfolding that which is occult in *The Good*; causing its loveliness to shine forth, and attracting to its own splendour the desire which is concealed about it. And to *The Good* indeed, all things possess a silent and arcane tendency; but we are excited to the beautiful with astonishment and motion. For the illumination from it, and its efficacy, acutely pervade through every soul, and as being the most similar of all things to *The Good*, it converts every soul that surveys it. The soul also, beholding that which is arcane shining forth as it were to the view, rejoices in, and admires that which it sees, and is astonished about it. And as in the most holy of the mysteries, prior to the mystic spectacles, those that are initiated, are seized with astonishment, so in intelligibles prior to the participation of *The Good*, beauty shining forth, astonishes those that behold it, converts the soul to itself, and being established in the vestibules [of *The Good*] shows what that is which is in the adyta, and what the transcendency is of occult good. Through these things therefore, let it be apparent whence beauty originates, and how it first shines forth; and also that animal itself is the most beautiful of all intelligibles.

CHAPTER XIV

Since, however, Timæus says that the primary and intelligible paradigms have their subsistence in intelligible animal, and that all these are four, unfolding themselves first into light, according to the all-perfect tetrad, - this being the case, in the first place it deserves to be considered, that as species or *forms* present themselves to the view in the intelligible, it is necessary by a much greater priority, that the *genera* of beings should pre-subsist in intelligibles. For it is not possible to admit that forms are intelligible, but that genera are intellectual only. But as forms exist intelligibly indeed, according to their first subsistence, but the pleroma, or plenitude of them shines forth in the intellectual† gods, and divides that which is total into more partial decrements, produces the uniform into multitude, and expands that which is exempt into co-ordinate causes, thus also the genera of being are occultly and indivisibly in intelligibles, but are accompanied with separation in intellectuals. And on this account the first triad indeed has essence for that which is mixed; but the second has life, where there was motion and permanency, life both abiding and proceeding; and in the third there are sameness and difference. For the all-perfect multitude indeed, is through intelligible difference, but the united and that which is comprehensive in common of parts according to genera, and according to one, is through intelligible sameness. And all these subsist intelligibly, essentially, and uniformly in these triads.

In the first place therefore, this deserves to be inferred by those who love to survey the nature of things, and it is also fit that they should attribute co-ordinate genera to intelligible forms. For it neither was nor will be lawful for genera to shine forth secondarily‡ after forms. Hence much more must it be admitted that genera subsist in the intelligible after the above-mentioned manner, by those who admit that there are intelligible forms. In the next place, in addition to these things we must survey how this tetrad of forms subsists, and how it shines forth in intelligible intellect analogous to the principles. For it is divided into a monad and triad. For so far as the idea of the celestial gods is arranged prior to the others, it is defined according to a divine cause. It appears however to me that intelligible intellect returning to the principles of the whole of things, according to the conversion of itself, it becomes the plenitude of forms, and is all things intellectually and at the same time intelligibly, comprehending in itself the causes of beings, and being full of the ineffable and exempt cause of all things, constitutes the monad of the gods; whence also, Plato I think calls it the idea of the gods. But receiving the intellectual causes of the three principles posterior to *The*

---

† For νοετοις it is necessary to read νοεροις.

‡ For δευτερα it is necessary to read δευτερως.

One, it exhibits three ideas after this, one of them indeed, being the cause of air-wandering and volant animals, this cause proceeding analogous to bound. Hence also it constitutes gods that are uniform, elevating, undefiled, united to the celestial gods, and which receive measures second in dignity to theirs, and have the same relation to those gods that govern generation co-ordinately, as the celestial gods have to these, according to exempt transcendency. But it exhibits the cause of the aquatic gods, co-ordinate with generative and infinite power, and which produces gods that are the suppliers of motion and prolific abundance, and that are the inspective guardians of life; since also this water itself which is the object of sense is under the dominion of effusion, infinite lation and indefiniteness. Hence likewise it is attributed to vivific powers. And intelligible intellect exhibits the precedaneous cause of terrestrial and pedestrious gods, in a manner adapted to the nature of that which is mixed. It also generates gods who contain the end of the whole of things, who are stable, who subdue the formless nature of matter by the last forms, and fix the seat of mundane natures in the one centre of the universe. For deriving their subsistence from the first Vesta as it were, or seat of beings, they stably define this mundane seat. Thus therefore forms first unfold themselves into light in intelligible intellect, possessing their progression and order according to the first principles. It is necessary however, in addition to these things, to infer this in the third place, following Timæus, that according to this triad, the multitude of intelligible parts shines forth, and the whole is divided into an all-perfect order of parts. For that, says he, of which other intelligible animals both according to one, and according to genera are parts, is the first and most beautiful paradigm of the universe. But if other intelligible animals are parts of this, it is evident that it is a whole, comprehending in itself the multitude of intelligible parts, and that it is connective of all intelligible parts. It must be inferred therefore that this triad is the first cause of production and fabrication. For if it contains the primary paradigms of things, it is evident that the orderly distribution of secondary natures, originates from it. And if it is an animal constitutive of all animals, every psychical extent, and all the extent of bodies, have their progression from thence; and it will also comprehend the intelligible causes of all the vivific and demiurgic orders.

CHAPTER XV

Such conceptions therefore, as these, may be assumed from what is written in the *Timæus* concerning the three intelligible triads, conformably to what is said of them in the *Philebus*, surveying in each bound, infinity, and that which is mixed. If you are willing also, we will show from what is scattered in the *Sophista*, that Plato had the same conception as we have concerning the first principles. The Elean guest therefore, in that dialogue, doubting against the assertion of Parmenides that the universe is one, unfolding intelligible multitude, and showing how it is suspended from *The One*, at first indeed, he argues from the one being [or being characterized by the one] and reminds us that this is passive to *The One*, and participates of *The One*, but is not *The One Itself*, nor that which is primarily one. But afterwards, he produces the conception of the distinction between the imparticipable one and being, from whole. For if the one being is a whole, as Parmenides testifies, but that which is a whole has parts, and that which has parts, is not *The One Itself*, the one being will not be the same as *The One*. In the third place therefore, he argues from the all-perfect. For that which is perfectly divided, and is connective of many parts, can never have the same subsistence as that which is entirely one. And having proceeded thus far he shows that what is void of multitude, is in its own nature exempt from the one being, proceeding in the demonstration of this through three arguments. And at one time indeed, he begins from the one being, at another time from whole, and at another from all. It is better however to hear the words themselves of Plato. That *The One* therefore, is not the same with the one being, he proves through the following words. "But what with respect to those who assert that the universe is one? Must we not enquire to the utmost of our power what they say being is? Certainly. To this question therefore they may answer: Do you say there is one thing alone? We do say so. Or will they not speak in this manner? They will. What then, do you call being any thing? Yes. Do you call it *The One*, employing two names respecting the same thing? Or how do you say? What will be their answer after this O guest?" Through this therefore, Plato separating *The One* and being from each other, and showing that the conception of *The One* is different from that of being, and that these are not the same with each other, evinces that the most proper and primary one is exempt from the one being. For the one being does not abide purely in an hyparxis void of multitude and possessing the form of one. But *The One Itself* is exempt from every addition. For by whatever you may add to it, you will diminish its supreme and ineffable union. Hence it is necessary to arrange *The One* prior to the one being, and to suspend the one being from that which is one alone. For if *The One* and the one being were the same, and it made no difference to say one and being (since if they differed, *The One* would again be changed from the one being,) if therefore *The One* differs in no respect from the one being, all things will be one, and there will not be multitude in beings, nor will it be possible to denominate things, lest there should be two things, the thing and the name. For being exempt from all multitude, and all division, there will neither be a name of any thing, nor any discourse about it, but the name will appear to be the same with the thing. And neither will a name be the name of a thing, but a name will be the name of a name, if a thing is the same with a name, and a name is the same with a thing,† and a thing will be the thing of a thing. For all things will exist about a thing the same as about a name, through the union of the thing and the name. If therefore, these things are absurd, and *The One* is, and also being, and being participates of *The One*, *The One* and the one being are not the same.

But that whole also is not the same with *The One*, Plato afterwards demonstrates [in the same dialogue,] beginning as follows: "What then? Will they say that whole is different from the one being, or that it is the same with it? Undoubtedly they will and do say so. If therefore whole is, as Parmenides says, "that which is every where similar to the bulk of a perfect sphere, entirely possessing equal powers from the middle; for nothing is greater or more stable than this: " - if this be the case, it is necessary that being should have a middle and extremities. And having these, there is every necessity that it should have parts. Or how shall we say? Just so. Nothing however hinders but that when it is divided, it may have the passion of *The One* in all its parts, and that thus the all and whole may be one. Undoubtedly. But is it not impossible that that which suffers these things should be *The One*? Why? Because according to right reason, that which is truly one should be said to be entirely without parts. It must indeed necessarily be so. But such a thing as we have just now mentioned, in consequence of consisting of many parts would not accord with *The One*." Through these things therefore, the Elean guest arguing from wholeness after the one being, and also from the division of the parts of wholeness, demonstrates that the all is not one. For if whole is in beings, as Parmenides in his verses testifies it is, all things will not be *The One*. For *The One* is impartible; but whole possesses parts. Whole therefore is not *The One Itself*. For that transcends all things and wholeness; but whole is passive to *The One*. Hence also it is denominated whole; for it is not *The One Itself*. Hence all things are not one void of separation and multiplication.

---

† Instead of το πραγμα τῳ ονοματι, it is necessary to read το ονομα τῳ πραγματι.

Moreover, the all is comprehensive of many parts. For whole indeed, consists at first of two parts; but the all possesses a multitude of parts, and participating of wholeness at the same time is all, as being perfectly distributed into parts. This therefore is not *The One Itself*, but is passive to *The One*. For *The One Itself* is impartible. But it is impartible in such a manner as to be exempt from all parts. Hence the all is not the same with *The One*. We therefore, have divided whole and the all, but Plato conjoins them, when he says: "Nothing however hinders but that when it is divided, it may have the passion of the one in all its parts, and that thus the all and whole may be one." At the same time however, they are divided after the above mentioned manner. From these three arguments therefore, the Elean guest separates *The One* from the participants of *The One*, and doubts against those who assert all things to be one, *viz.* the one being, whole and the all; of which the all indeed participates of whole, and is a self-perfect multitude, consisting of many parts; but whole participates of being. For being is not whole, as Parmenides testifies. These therefore, having such an order as this, is it not necessary that the arguments of Plato should be made conformably to the three intelligible[†] triads? For it was requisite, since Parmenides defined the one being in intelligibles, that Plato should from thence derive his demonstrations of the distinction between *The One* prior to intelligibles, and the one which is in intelligibles. For the doubts against Parmenides, evince in many places that the one which is participated derives its subsistence from the imparticipable union. *The One*[‡] therefore is not in these triads, but the one being and whole. But with respect to the all, it is evident that it is in the extremity of the intelligible order. For that which is in every respect perfect, and all intelligible multitude, have their subsistence in that extremity. But whole is in the middle centre, and in the bond of the intelligible breadth. For whole is adapted to have a subsistence prior to the all; since the all is a whole, but whole is not necessarily all. For the all is divided multitude; but that which contains multitude in itself, and which is not yet separated is whole. And this especially pertains to eternity. For eternity is the measure of all intelligible multitude, just as whole is the coherence and union of the all. But the one being is in the first triad. For *The One* is especially the peculiarity of this triad, as Timæus also has demonstrated. And being which is occultly and intelligibly

---

[†] For νοερας here it is necessary to read νοητας.

[‡] It is requisite here to supply το εν.

being, and which is the cause of essence to all other things, primarily shines forth there. Again therefore, following the Elean guest, three triads present themselves to our view; the first indeed according to the one being; the second according to whole; and the third according to the all. To which also the demiurgus of the universe looking, adorns the sensible universe, defining the visible nature with reference to that intelligible all; but time with reference to the intelligible wholeness. On which account also time is continued. And as the intelligible whole comprehends two parts, but contains the parts in one boundary, after the same manner, time also is bounded by *the now*, but by its twofold parts is infinite. These things therefore, we shall shortly after more fully discuss when we speak concerning the Parmenides. For the conceptions of the Elean guest are the *proteleia* of the mysteries of the Parmenides. Before however we turn to the Parmenides, let us discuss, if it is agreeable to you, the three triads from the beginning, collecting the conception of Plato from his assertions that are scattered in many places.

CHAPTER XVI

There are three triads therefore, as we have frequently observed, and they are divided after this manner into bound, infinity, and that which is mixed. Hence there are triple intelligible bounds, triple infinities, and triple mixtures. But of every intelligible triad, the bound in each is denominated father; the infinite, power; and that which is mixed, intellect. And let not any one apprehend that these names are foreign from the philosophy of Plato. For it will appear that he uses these appellations in the before mentioned triads more than any one. For he denominates the first God father and lord in his Epistles. It is evident however, that as the first God surpasses even the paternal order, the first paternal is in the intelligible Gods. For these are they that are most eminently allied to *The One*, and that intelligibly unfold his ineffable and unknown union. If therefore the first God is denominated one and father from the natures that proximately proceed from him, - if this be the case, as the intelligible Gods are primarily unities, so likewise they are primarily fathers. For Plato gives names to the ineffable in a twofold respect, either from the summits of beings, or from all beings. For through these the transcendency of the one is known. Moreover, the Elean guest calls being that which is powerful and power. The first power therefore exists prior to being, and is united to the father; but it particularly accords with being, which also it fills. Hence being as participating of power is denominated powerful; but as united to it, and producing all beings according to it, it is called power. If however both

Plato himself, and his most genuine disciples, frequently call all [true] beings intellect (on which account, in many places they make three principles, *The Good*, intellect and soul, denominating every [true] being intellect) you will also have the third in these intellect. But it is necessary not to be ignorant of the difference. For with respect to intellect, one kind is intellect as with reference to hyparxis. For when we denominate the unity in each triad intelligible, as the object of desire to being, and as filling being, then we call that which ranks as the third in the triad intellect. For it is intelligible as essence and intellect, but not as the intellect of essence, but of father and deity. For every participated deity is intelligible, as being the plenitude of its participant. But another kind is intellect which is the intellect of essence; according to which we say that the being of the third triad, is the intellect of that which is primarily being. For this is essential intellect, being allotted its own essence by energizing.† For all things are essentially in it, and both the more simple genera, and the primary paradigms; for it is intelligible intellect. But the third kind is intellectual intellect, which subsists analogous to intelligible intellect, is conjoined with it, and is filled from it, possessing intellectually those things which are in the other intelligibly. And in short, it is necessary every where that such things as are first according to each series, should have the form of the things that are prior to them. Hence also they are called things first, and possess a certain transcendency of essence towards co-ordinate natures. Since therefore, that which is prior to intelligibles is God, the first intelligibles are Gods and unities. And since the intelligible is essential, the first intellects are essences. Since also intellect is every where according to its own nature intellectual, the first souls are intellectual. Because likewise, souls are the plenitudes of life, the first of bodies are most vital. And because the bodies that are perpetual are moved in a circle, the summits of material bodies are moved in conjunction with those bodies that are perpetual. This therefore is the cause why the unities are frequently called intelligibles, and beings intelligible intellects.

That Plato however knew this triad, I mean father, power and intellect, we shall learn by looking to the demiurgic order. For in this the triad is most remarkably apparent. Hence, on account of its union with the intelligible, it is filled with this triad, and possesses these things in a more divided manner than animal itself, or intelligible eternity. Immediately therefore, in the beginning of the fabrication in the *Timæus*, the demiurgus calls himself father, "Of which works I am the

---

† For αυτο το ενεργειν it is necessary to read αυτῳ τῳ ενεργειν.

demiurgus and *father*." But shortly after he unfolds his power, "Imitating my *power* in your generation." This therefore is also wonderful, that he has delivered to us the most theological conception concerning power. For in the first place indeed, he calls it the power of the father, when he says, "Of which works I am the demiurgus and father," and that the power is his, [is evident from the words,] "Imitating my power:" so that according to Plato power is of the father. And in the next place, he ascribes to this power a peculiarity generative of the whole of things; for this is evident from the words "In your generation." Power therefore is the cause of generation and of the progression of beings. And in the last place, he delivers the intellectual peculiarity of the demiurgus. "Having thus spoke, again into the former crater in which he had tempered the soul of the universe, he poured mingling the remainder of the former mixture." For to pour, to mingle, mixture, and to be productive of soul, pertain to intellect. Though what necessity is there for asserting these things, since prior to this he calls the demiurgus intellect. "Whatever ideas therefore *intellect* perceived by the dianoetic energy in animal itself, such and so many he conceived it necessary for this universe to contain." Hence the demiurgus is father, and power and intellect. And he possesses these things as much as possible on account of intelligibles. For he is a God as father, on account of them. He is also power, and the generator of wholes, and knows beings intellectually, on account of them. For in them intelligible knowledge first subsists. Much more therefore are father, power and intellect in intelligibles; from which also the demiurgus being filled, participates of this triad. For Plato assumes each of these analogously. For as the paternal triad in intelligibles gives subsistence to intelligible eternity, so the demiurgus makes those works to be indissoluble of which he is the father. And as in intelligibles, eternity proceeding according to all power generates intelligible animal itself, so the demiurgic power gives subsistence to mundane animals that are perpetual and divine, and imparts to the junior Gods another power which is generative of mortal animals. That any one therefore may assume these names from Plato is evident from what has been said.

Since however, being has an hypostasis triply in intelligibles, one is primarily being and prior to the eternal; but another is secondarily being, and the first eternity; and another is being ultimately, and is intelligible and eternal intellect. And here indeed there is being, but there eternity, and there intellect. And eternity is more comprehensive than intellect; but being than eternity. For every intellect is eternal, but not every thing eternal is intellect. For soul according to its essence is eternal, and every thing which participates of eternity, participates also by a much greater priority of being. For with perpetuity of existence, existence is entirely consubsistent. But that which participates of existence is not universally eternally being. For bodies also participate in a certain respect of the nature of existence, but they are not eternal. Intellect therefore constitutes an intellectual essence only, so far as it is intellect; since so far as it is also life and being it constitutes all things. But eternity constitutes both the intellectual and psychical essence. For the mixture [in the second triad] was intelligible life. But being constitutes the intellectual, the psychical, and the corporeal life. For matter also is being [most obscurely,] and is capacity indeed, but formless being, and non-being, falling off from the participation of being. If, however, some one should say that it is being in power or capacity, yet it has this power from being. For capacity is the forerunning participation of energy. And thus much concerning these things.

But what sufficient argument of division does Socrates afford us in the *Phædrus*, concerning these intelligible triads? And how from what is delivered by him may we recur to the conception of the hypostasis of the most principal Gods? Socrates therefore in that dialogue, being inspired by the Nymphs, celebrates every thing divine as beautiful, wise and good, and says that by these the soul is nourished. But is every thing divine is a thing of this kind, this is the case with the intelligible by a much greater priority. And all these indeed are every where, but in the first triad, the good principally subsists; in the second the wise; and in the third the beautiful. For in this there is the most beautiful of intelligibles. But in the second triad truth and the first intelligence subsist. And in the first there is the commensurate, which we say is the same as the good. But Socrates in the *Philebus* says that the element of the good is the desirable, the sufficient, and the perfect. The desirable therefore pertains indeed to bound; for it is the union and goodness of all the triad, and the triad converges about it. But the sufficient pertains to infinity. For sufficiency is a power capable of pervading to all things, and of being present to all things without impediment. And the perfect pertains to that which is mixed. For this is that which is primarily triadic; since every mixture has its coalition from the triad. The elements therefore of the good unfold to us the first triad; and the elements of intelligible wisdom, the second triad. But every thing wise is full of being, is generative of truth, and is convertive of imperfect natures to their perfection. The full therefore pertains to the second bound; for this is uniformly filled with the participation of the natures prior to itself. For the full is every where adapted to bound, just as that which cannot be filled is adapted to the infinite. But the prolific pertains to the second power, and to infinity. For that which does not abide in the fullness of itself, but is prolific and generative of other things, is especially indicative of divine infinity. And the convertive pertains to that which is mixed. For this as being allotted the end of the triad, converts every thing imperfect to the full, and unites itself prior to other things to the bound of the whole triad.

CHAPTER XVII

Moreover, the elements of beauty are the peculiarities of the third triad of intelligibles. But these are, as we have before observed, the lovely, the delicate, and the splendid. The lovely therefore, being arranged analogous to the desirable, pertains to bound. But the delicate being co-ordinate to the sufficient, pertains to the infinite power which is in the beautiful. And the splendid is of an intellectual peculiarity. For this is the beautiful of beauty; is that which illuminates all things, and astonishes those that are able to behold it. And as apparent beauty shining most manifestly, is seen through the clearest of the senses (for the objects of this sense have many differences according to Aristotle, and this sense pervades farther than the rest) so likewise intelligible beauty appears to the intellect of the soul shining intelligibly. For it is an intelligible form. And on this account the splendour of beauty is apparent to intellect. Splendid beauty therefore, as Socrates calls it, shines forth at the extremity of the intelligible order. For this is the most splendid of intelligibles, is intelligible intellect, and is that which emits the intelligible light, that when it appeared astonished the intellectual Gods, and made them admire their father, as Orpheus says. Such therefore is the preparation to the science of the intelligible Gods which may from these things be assumed. And now it will appear how beauty is indeed occultly in the end of the first intelligible triad, but subsists in the third triad so as to have manifestly proceeded into light. For in the former it subsists according to one form only; but in the latter it subsists triadically. It is also evident how each of the triads is at one and the same time a monad and a triad. For the first triad being characterized according to *The Good*, derives its completion from the three elements of *The Good*. But the second being characterized by the wise is contained in the triad of wisdom. And the third subsisting according to the beautiful, is all-perfect through the triad of beauty. If however the beautiful is occultly in the first triad, and shines forth triadically in the third, it is evident that intelligible intellect loves the first triad, and has love conjoined with its beauty. And this is the intelligible love of the first beauty. From these therefore, intellectual love proceeds, together with faith and truth, as we have before observed. For the three intelligible monads, the good, the wise and the beautiful, constitute three powers which lead upwards all other things, and prior to other things the intellectual Gods. Concerning these things however, we shall speak hereafter.

CHAPTER XVIII

Let us now then direct our attention to the theory of the *Parmenides*. But I wish again to remind the reader of what we have before demonstrated. It has been shown therefore, that it is necessary to divide the second hypothesis into the whole progressions of the one being; and that this hypothesis is nothing else than the generation and progression of the Gods, proceeding supernally from the supreme union of intelligibles as far as to a deified essence. For the discussion is not, as some say it is, in the first hypothesis, concerning God and the Gods. For it was not lawful to Parmenides to conjoin multitude with *The One*, and *The One* with multitude. For the first God is perfectly exempt from the whole of things. But in the first hypothesis essence, and even *The One Itself*, are taken away from the first God. That such an ablation, however, as this is not adapted to the other Gods is evident to every one. Moreover, neither does Parmenides in the first hypothesis speak about the intelligible Gods, as they say he does; for they assert that the negations are of these Gods, because they are conjoined with *The One*, and in simplicity and union precede[†] all the divine genera. For how can the similar or the dissimilar, or contact and the privation of contact, and all the other particulars which are denied of *The One*, be inherent in the intelligible Gods? They appear indeed to me to be right in asserting that the things which are taken away are similitudes of the Gods; but they do not speak rightly when they say that all of them are similitudes of the intelligible Gods. To which it may be added, in opposition to this assertion, that the discussion is again concerning the intelligible Gods in the second hypothesis. For the things which are denied in the first, are affirmed in the second hypothesis. This therefore, as I have said, is demonstrated that the conclusions with reference to each other have the order of prior and posterior, of causes and effects. It is necessary

---

† For προσχοντες it is necessary to read προεχοντες.

therefore, that proceeding from the beginning, we should adapt the first conclusions to the first orders, the middle conclusions to the middle orders, and the last conclusions to the last orders, and should demonstrate that as many questions are asked, as there are progressions of the divine orders. And in the first place, we must deliver the doctrine of Parmenides concerning the intelligible Gods, of whom we have proposed to speak; since Plato speaks about these in many places, partly indicating, and partly clearly unfolding his meaning.

It is necessary however, that we should collect into one the elaborate and syntopical theory about each order, since it would not be proper now to repeat the exposition which we have given in our commentaries on that dialogue. But assuming each of the conclusions itself by itself, I will endeavour to refer it to an appropriate order of the Gods, following in so doing the divine inspirations of our leader [Syrianus]. For we also through his assistance have with a divine head pursued these sacred paths about the theory of the *Parmenides*, being agitated with a divine fury, and wakened as from a profound sleep to this arcane mystic discipline. And thus much concerning the mode of the whole of the conclusions. But from hence I shall pass to the narration of the things proposed.

The first and imparticipable one therefore, which pre-exists beyond the whole of things, and not only beyond the unities that participate, but also those that are participated, is celebrated through the first hypothesis, being demonstrated to be the cause of all things ineffably, but not being defined itself in any one of all things, nor having any power or peculiarity of a kindred nature with the other Gods. But after this [imparticipable one,] that which is alone superessential and surpassing, and unmingled with all hyparxis, is a unity participated by being, and constituting about itself the first essence, and by the addition of this participation becoming more redundant than that which is primarily one. This however is a superessential hyparxis, and the hyparxis of the first intelligible triad. As there are therefore these two things in the first triad, *viz. The One* and being, and the former generates, but the latter is generated, and the former perfects, but the latter is perfected, it is necessary that the middle of both should be power, through which and together with which *The One* constitutes and is perfective of being. For the progression of being from *The One*, and its conversion to *The One*, is through power. For what else conjoins being to *The One*, or causes *The One* to be participated by being except power? For it is the progression of *The One*, and its extension to being. Hence, in all the divine genera powers precede progressions and generations. This triad therefore, *The One*, power and being, is the summit of intelligibles. The first of these indeed producing; the third being produced; and the second being suspended from *The One*, but coalescing with being.

CHAPTER XIX

This triad therefore, Parmenides delivers immediately in the beginning of the second hypothesis, adjoining to *The One* the most simple participation of essence. But he calls it the one being, and says that being participates of *The One*, and *The One* of being. The participation however of these is different. For *The One*[†] indeed so participates of being, as illuminating and filling, and deifying being; but being so participates of *The One*, as suspended from *The One*, and deified by it. But the habitude which is the middle of both, is not with them void of essence. For neither is the habitude which is among sensibles in no respect being, and much more is this the case with the habitude which is there. But this habitude is biformed. For it is of *The One*, and is connascent with being. For it is the motion of *The One*, and its progression into being. Parmenides delivers this triad, beginning what he says about it as follows: "See therefore from the beginning if *The One* is. Is it possible then for it to be, and yet not to participate of essence? It is not possible." But he ends speaking about it in the following words: "Will therefore that which is said be anything else than this, that *The One* participates of essence, when it is summarily asserted by any one that *The One* is? It will not." This therefore is the first intelligible triad, the one, being, and the habitude of both, through which being is of *The One* and *The One* of being, in a manner perfectly admirable; Plato indicating through these things, that the father is the father of intellect, and that intellect is the intellect of the father, and that power is concealed between the extremes. For deity is the father of the triad, and being is the intellect of this deity. Yet it is not intellect in the same way as we are accustomed to call the intellect of essence. For every such intellect stands still and is moved, as the Elean guest says. But that which is primarily being, neither stands still, nor is moved, as he also teaches. The first triad therefore is called one being; since power is here occultly. For the triad does not proceed from itself; but subsists without separation and uniformly, being primarily defined according to divine union. Hence, this is the first participation of essence, which participates of *The One* through power as the middle, which collects

---

[†] In the original εν ον, but the true reading is evidently εν alone.

together and separates both *The One* and being. And it is superessential indeed, but is conjoined with essence. We must never think therefore that all power is the progeny of essence. For the powers of the Gods are superessential, and are consubsistent with the unities themselves of the Gods. And through this power the Gods are generative of beings. Rightly therefore, does poetry every where assert that the Gods are able to do all things. For essential powers indeed are not capable of effecting all things; since they are not constitutive of superessential natures. The first triad therefore, is through these things unfolded to us by Parmenides.

CHAPTER XX

But immediately after this, the second triad is allotted a progression, which Parmenides characterizes by intelligible wholeness, as we have shown in the *Sophista*. For the first triad being uniform, and possessing all things intelligibly and occultly, *viz.* hyparxis, power and being, so that power which is the cause of division, subsisting between *The One* and being, is concealed, and becomes apparent through the communion of the extremes with each other, - the second triad proceeds, being characterized by the first intelligible power, and having the monads in itself distinguished from each other. For all things being united and without distinction in the first triad, distinction and separation shine forth in this triad. Being also and power are more divided from each other. And that which consists of these is no longer one being [or being characterized by *The One*,] but is a whole, so that it has *The One* and being in itself as parts. For above indeed [*i.e.* in the first triad] all things are prior to parts and wholeness. But in this triad there are both parts and a whole, power unfolding itself into light. For as there is separation here, there are parts and the whole consisting of these. The second triad therefore is called intelligible wholeness. But the parts of it, *The One* and being, I call the extremes. And power being here the middle, connects *The One* and being, and does not cause them to be one, in the same manner as in the first triad. Since also it is the middle of both, through its communion indeed with being, it renders *The One* one being; but through its communion with *The One*, it perfectly causes being to be one. And thus the one being consists of two parts, *viz.* of being which is characterized by *The One*, and of *The One* which is characterized by being, as Parmenides himself says. He begins therefore to speak about this triad as follows: "Again therefore, let us say if *The One* is what will happen. Consider then if it is not necessary that this hypothesis should signify *The One* to be a thing of such a kind as to have parts?" But he ends in the following words: "That which is one therefore is a whole, and has a part."

Through these things therefore Parmenides defines the second order of intelligibles to be a wholeness. For as existence is derived to all things from the first triad, so whole from the second, and an all-perfect division from the third. This however will be considered by us hereafter. Wholeness therefore is triple, being either prior to parts, or consisting of parts, or subsisting in a part, according to the doctrine of Plato. For in the *Politicus* indeed, he calls genus a whole, but species a part, not that genus derives its completion from species, but exists prior to it. And in the *Timæus* he says that the world is a whole of wholes. And all the world indeed derives its completion from parts that are wholes; but each of the parts is a whole, not as the universe is, but partially. Wholeness therefore, being triple as we have said, according to Plato, the unity, and the intelligible and occult cause of these is now delivered, unically comprehending and constituting three wholenesses; according to the hyparxis indeed of itself, the wholeness prior to parts; but according to its power, the wholeness which is from parts; and according to its being the wholeness which is in a part. For *The One* is prior to all multitude; but power communicates in a certain respect with both extremes, and comprehends in itself the peculiarities of them; and being in a certain respect participates of *The One*. Hence the first of the wholenesses, or that which is prior to parts is derived from a unical hyparxis. For it is a monad, and is itself constitutive of parts, and of the multitude which is in them. But the second wholeness is from power. For it derives its completion from parts, just as in the power which is collective of the one and being, and extremes in a certain respect shine forth to the view. And the third wholeness is from being. For being is a part, and is the progeny both of power and *The One*,† and possesses each of these partially. After the intelligible therefore, three wholenesses are divided according to the different order of beings. But the intelligible wholeness comprehends the three unically, and is the intelligibly connective monad of this triad, every way extending the powers of itself from the middle of the intelligible and occult order.

---

† Instead of οντος it is necessary to read ενος.

CHAPTER XXI

Immediately after this triad we may see another proceeding, in which all intelligible multitude shines forth, and which Parmenides indeed constitutes a wholeness, but a wholeness consisting of many parts. For after the occult union of the first triad, and the dyadic separation of the second, the progression of the third is generated, which has indeed its subsistence from parts, but the parts are many, with the multitude of which the triad prior to it is parturient. For in this triad there is a unity, and power, and being. But *The One* is multiplied, and also being and power. And thus all the triad indeed is a wholeness; but each of its extremes, *viz. The One* and being, as it is multitude conjoined through collective power, is again divided and multiplied. For this power conjoining unical multitude to the multitude of beings, of some of these it causes each through progression to be being characterized by *The One*, but of others each according to participation to be *The One* characterized by being. For here indeed there are two parts of the wholeness, *The One* and being; but *The One* participates of being, for it is conjoined with it; and being participates of *The One*. *The One* of being therefore, is again divided, so that *The One* and being generate a second unity conjoined with the part of being. But being participating of *The One*, is again separated into being and *The One*. For it generates a more partial being suspended from a more partial unity. And being consists of more partial deified beings, and is a more specific monad. The cause however of this progression is power. For power is effective of two things, and is the operator of multitude. For *The One* indeed calls forth into multitude, but being converts to the participation of the divine unities. Whence therefore does Parmenides begin to teach us concerning this triad? And where does he conclude his discourse about it? The beginning, therefore, of what he says on this subject is as follows: "What then? Can each of these parts of the one being, *viz. The One* and being, desert each other, so that *The One* shall not be a part of being, or being shall not be a part of *The One*? It cannot be.[†]" But he ends thus: "Will not, therefore, the one being after this manner be an infinite multitude? It seems so."

In the first place, therefore, it is proper to understand the manner of the progression of the divine genera; and that conformably to the intelligible monad, which we arrange according to *The One* being, the

---

[†] It is necessary to correct the text here, and to read as follows: τι ουν; των μοριων εκατερον τουτων του ενος οντος το, τε εν και το ον αρα απολειπεσθον, ἦ το εν. κ.τ.λ.

duad posterior to it which we call a wholeness [proceeds.] But we say that it consists of two parts which are separated by power, and that intelligible multitude presents itself to the view from the monad and the duad. For when all things are said to be parts of the one being, *viz.* secondary things, and such as become apparent through the separating cause of power, then Parmenides delivers the union which pervades from the monad to the third triad. But when power separating and conjoining the unities and beings, gives completion to multitude, then the participation of the duad becomes perfectly apparent, as I think Parmenides demonstrates when he says, "so that it is necessary two things should always be generated, and that there should never be one thing (only.)" This triad, therefore proceeds according to both the preexistent triads, flowing according to the Oracle, and proceeding to all intelligible multitude. For infinite multitude is indicative of this flux, and of the incomprehensible nature of power. Hence, in the first place, I have said that the hypostasis of this triad is through these things demonstrated to be suspended from the triads prior to it. And in the next place, I say, that this triad, according to Parmenides, is primogenial. For this first imparts the power of being generated; and Parmenides calls the multitude which is in it *in generation*, [*i.e. becoming to be*, or rising into *existence*.] For he says: "And the part will be *generated* from two parts at least." And again: "Whatever part is *generated*, will always have these parts." And in what follows: "So that it is necessary it should always be *generated* two things, and should never be one." Does he not, therefore, who frequently uses the word generation in teaching concerning the progression of the intelligible multitude, proclaim that the natures prior to this order are more united to each other? But this order proceeds to a greater extent, unfolds the occult nature of the triads prior to itself, and is primogenial, unfolding in itself prolific power.

In addition to these things also, it is necessary to consider the infinity of multitude, not as those think fit to speak, who assume the infinite in quantity, but since in the principles of the whole of things, there are bound and infinity, the former being the cause of the union, but the latter of the separation of multitude, Parmenides calls the first and intelligible multitude infinite, because all multitude indeed, according to its own nature, is infinite, as being the progeny of the first infinity. All intelligible multitude, however, is a thing of this kind. For it is the first multitude, and multitude itself. But multitude itself is the first progeny of intelligible infinity. Intelligible multitude, therefore, is on this account infinite, as unfolding into light the first infinity, and this infinity is the same with the all-perfect. For that which has proceeded to the all, and as far as it is requisite an intelligible nature should proceed, through the power which is generative of the whole of things, is infinite. For it cannot be comprehended by any other thing. But intelligible multitude is comprehensive of all intelligible multitude. For if indeed that which is primarily infinite, was infinite according to quantity, it would be requisite to admit that the intelligible is infinite multitude of this kind. Since, however, the intelligible is infinite power, it is necessary that the participant of the primarily infinite, should cause infinity to shine forth according to the power which is comprehensive of all prior natures. And if it be requisite to relate my own opinion, as that which is primarily one is primarily bound, so that which is primarily multitude is infinite multitude. For it receives the whole power of infinity, and producing all unities, and all beings, as far as to the most individual natures, it possesses never-failing power. It is, therefore, more total than all multitude, and is an incomprehensible infinite. Hence unfolding into light all multitude, it bounds and measures it by infinite power, and through wholeness introduces bound to all things. These things, therefore, may be assumed from Parmenides concerning the third intelligible triad.

CHAPTER XXII

Let us in the next place speak in common about all the intelligible triads.[5] With respect to the first triad, therefore, which is occult, and is allotted the intelligible summit in intelligibles, Plato at one time proceeding from the union which is in it, and its exempt transcendency with respect to the other triads, denominates it one, as in the *Timæus*. For eternity, says he, abides in one. But reason evinces that this one is the first triad of intelligibles. But at another time proceeding from the extremities which are in it, *viz.* that which is participated, and that which participates, he calls it the one being, considering the power which is comprehended in these as ineffable, in consequence of its subsisting uniformly and occultly. And at another time, he unfolds the whole of it, according to the monads which are in it, bound, infinity, and that which is mixed; bound indeed indicating its divine hyparxis, infinity its generative power, and that which is mixed, the essence proceeding from this power. Plato, therefore, as I have said, teaches us through these names the first intelligible triad; at one time indeed through one name, but at another through two names, and at another again through three names, unfolding it to our view. For there is a triad in it, according to which the whole is characterized; and a duad according to which the extremes communicate with each other; and a monad which exhibits the ineffable, occult, and unical nature of the first, through its own monads.

But the second triad after this, Plato denominates in the *Timæus* indeed, eternity; but in the *Parmenides* the first wholeness. How these, however, are allotted the same peculiarity we may learn by considering that every thing eternal is indeed a whole; *viz.* if it is perfectly eternal, and has the whole of its essence and energy at once present. For every intellect is a thing of this kind, perfectly establishing at once in itself, the whole of intellectual perception. It likewise does not possess one part of being, but is deprived of another part, nor does it partially participate of energy, but it summarily comprehends the whole of being, and the whole of intelligence. If, however, in its energies it proceeded according to time, but had an eternal essence, it would be allotted the whole of the latter, and this always stably the same, but would possess the former variably, so as to exert different energies at different times. Eternity, therefore, is every where the cause of wholeness to the natures to which it is primarily present. But whole also is every where comprehensive of perpetuity. For no whole abandons either its essence or its proper perfection; but that which is primarily corrupted and vitiated is a partial nature. For on this account also the whole world is perpetual, *viz.* because it is a whole, and this is likewise the case with all that the heavens contain, and with each of the elements. For every where wholeness is connective of subjects. Hence eternity is consubsistent with wholeness, and whole and eternity are the same. Each also is a measure, the one of things eternal, and of all perpetual natures, but the other of parts and of all multitude. Since, however, there are three wholenesses, one indeed being prior to parts, another subsisting from parts, and another in a part, - through the wholeness which is prior to parts, eternity measures those unities of divine natures which are exempt from beings; but through the wholeness which derives its subsistence from parts, it measures the unities that are co-ordinate with beings; and through the wholeness which is in a part, it measures all beings and whole essences. For these wholenesses being parts of the divine unities, they possess partibly what pre-exists unically in the unities. And, moreover, eternity is nothing else than the ever shining forth from the unity which is connected with being. But whole consists of two parts, *viz.* of *The One* and being, power existing as the collector of the parts. According to both these conceptions, therefore, the duad pertaining to the middle intelligible triad, unfolds the uniform and occult hypostasis of the first triad.

Moreover, in the *Timæus*, Plato calls the third triad of intelligibles, animal itself, intelligible, all-perfect, and only-begotten. But in the *Parmenides* he denominates it infinite multitude, and a wholeness comprehensive of many parts. And in the *Sophista* he perpetually calls it the intelligible distributed into many beings. All these assertions, therefore, are the progeny of one science, and tend to one intelligible truth. For when Timæus calls this triad intelligible animal, he also asserts it to be all-perfect, and comprehensive of intelligible animals as its parts, both according to one and according to parts. Hence animal itself is according to this a whole, comprehensive of intelligible animals as its parts. And Parmenides, when he shows that the one being is all-perfect multitude, demonstrates that it is consubsistent with this order. For the infinite will be all-powerful and all-perfect, as we have before observed, comprehending in itself an intelligible multitude of parts, which also it generates; some of these being more total, but others more partial, and as Timæus says, both according to one, and according to genera. Farther still, as he calls animal itself eternal and only-begotten, so Parmenides first attributes the ever and to be generated, to infinite multitude, when he says, "And thus, according to the same reasoning, whatever part is generated will always possess these two parts: for *The One* will always contain being, and being *The One*; so that two things will necessarily always be generated, and no part will ever be one."

Who, therefore, so clearly reminds us of eternal animal, and the primogenial triad, as Parmenides, first assuming in this order generation and the ever, and so continually using each of these? The same thing, therefore, is both an all-perfect animal, and all-powerful intelligible multitude. For the first infinity being power, and every intelligible subsisting according to it, and receiving from it a division into parts, I think it proper to call it all-powerful; thus avoiding the appellation of the infinite, which disturbs the multitude. That, however, which in these things is both difficult to understand, and for which Plato especially deserves to be admired, we must not omit, but demonstrate to the genuine lovers of truth. For intelligible animal comprehends four intelligible ideas, according to which it not only constitutes the genera of Gods, but also the more excellent kind of beings after the Gods, and also mortal animals themselves; for generating it extends the idea of air-wandering, the idea of aquatic, and the idea of terrestrial animals, from the Gods as far as to mortal animals. Since animal itself, therefore, comprehends four ideas, and through the same paradigms produces totally divine, dæmoniacal and mortal animals, this deservedly produces a doubt in those who love the contemplation of truth, how, the causes being the same, and the same primary paradigms pre-existing, some of the natures which are constituted are Gods, others dæmons, and others mortal animals. For all these being generated with reference to one form, how is it possible they should not have the same form and nature; since it is requisite that one idea should every where be generative of things that have a similar form? For on this account we admit the hypothesis of ideas, in order that the intelligible genus of Gods may possess and contain prior to multitude monads productive of similar natures. This doubt,[†] therefore, being so difficult, some one may solve it logically by saying, that all things which subsist according to one form are not synonymous, and that they do not similarly participate of their common cause, but some things primarily, and others ultimately. For each form is the leader of a certain series, beginning supernally, and subsiding as far as to the last of things. For according to the oracle, all things begin supernally to extend their admirable rays to the downward place. Hence it will not be wonderful that the same idea should pre-exist as the cause of Gods, dæmons, and mortal animals, producing all things totally, and delivering the more partial separation of things to the demiurgic order, in the same manner as this order delivers the production of individuals to the junior Gods. For intelligibles are the causes of whole series; but intellectuals of divisions according to common genera. Supermundane forms are the causes of specific differences; but mundane of things which are now individuals. For they are causes which are moved, and are the leaders of mutation to their progeny.

If however it be requisite to survey the thing itself by itself, and how one intelligible form is the cause[‡] of Gods, and dæmons, and mortals, Parmenides alone is able to satisfy us about the parts which are contained in the intelligible multitude. For he characterizes some things according to being, but others according *The One*. For the one being, indeed, is absorbed by *The One*, but being which is one is rather absorbed by being, and the one being, and being which is one, contain in themselves each of the intelligible animals. According to the one being, therefore, Parmenides constitutes the divine genera, together with an appropriate peculiarity. But according to being which is one, he constitutes the genera posterior to the Gods. And according to the one being indeed of being which is one, he constitutes the genera of dæmons, but according to being which is one, the mortal genera. And again, according to the one being of the one being he constitutes the first and highest genera of Gods; but according to the being which is one of it, the second genera, and which have an angelic order. And thus all things are full of Gods, angels, dæmons, animals, and mortal natures. And you

---

[†] Instead of $\alpha\pi\epsilon\iota\rho\iota\alpha\varsigma$, it is necessary to read $\alpha\pi\rho\rho\iota\alpha\varsigma$.

[‡] It seems requisite to supply the word $\alpha\iota\tau\iota\rho\nu$ after the words $\tau\rho$ $\epsilon\nu$ $\nu\rho\eta\tau\rho\nu$ $\epsilon\iota\delta\rho\varsigma$.

see how the medium is preserved of the more excellent genera. For being which is one is the angelic boundary of the one being which produces the Gods. But the one being is the dæmoniacal summit of being which is one, and which adorns secondary natures. As to the unions, however, of secondary natures, it is not immanifest that they approximate to multitude, and to the progression of the natures placed above them. Nor must you wonder if being which is one is the cause of angels, but the one being of dæmons. For in one place, being which is one is a part of the one being, but in another the one being is a part of being which is one. And here, indeed, the union is essential, but there essence has the form of *The One*. For the summit of being which is one is a thing of this kind. Deservedly, therefore, is intelligible multitude all-powerful, and intelligible animal all-perfect, as being at once the cause of all things, and this as far as to the last of things, Plato all but exclaiming, [In the words of the *Chaldean Oracle*,] "Thence a fiery whirlwind sweeping along, obscures the flower of fire, leaping at the same time into the cavities of the worlds." For the divine unities proceeding gradually, generate the multitude of all mundane natures. This triad, therefore, is the fountain and cause of all things; and from it all the life, and all the progression of the Gods, and the genera superior to us, and of mortal animals subsist. For it produces totally and uniformly all things, and binds to itself the whole principles of the divisible rivers of vivification, and the production of forms.

CHAPTER XXIII

Again, therefore, let us recur from the divided theory of intelligibles to the all-perfect and one science of them, and let us say to ourselves, that this intelligible genus of the Gods is unically exempt from all the other divine orders, and is neither called intelligible as known by a partial intellect, nor as comprehended by intelligence in conjunction with reason, nor yet as pre-existing in all-perfect intellect. For it transcends both total and partial intelligibles, and exists prior to all intellectual objects, being an imparticipable and divine intelligible. Hence, also, it is allotted the same transcendency with respect to all the intelligible orders, as *The One* with respect to every genus of the Gods. For this intelligible is imparticipable, and supernally fills the divine and intellectual orders. For if every intellect is intelligible to itself, it possesses this property through the intelligible Gods. For plenitude is derived to all things from thence. And thus the intelligible is at the same time exempt from intellect, existing itself by itself; and at the same time the intelligible is not external to intellect. For there is an intelligible which is conjoined with intellect; the co-ordinate being derived from that which is exempt, the participated from that which is imparticipable, that which is inherent from that which is pre-existent, and that which is multiplied from that which is uniform. Intelligible simplicity, therefore, must not be defined to be such as that which we are accustomed to assert of intelligibles. For in these *The One* becomes equal to multitude, and separation to the uniform sameness of essence. But intelligible simplicity is uniform, without separation and occult, excelling every divisible form of life, and intellectual multitude. Hence I do not place intelligible simplicity in the order of idea. For this form is partial, and is subordinate to intelligible union. But I consider it as the hyparxis of divine natures, and as generative of the whole of the good which is distributed to all divine natures, and in which the Gods themselves subsist. For the goodness of the Gods, is neither form nor habit, but the plenitude of divine self-sufficiency and divine power, according to which the Gods fill all things with good. In a much greater degree, therefore, are the intelligible Gods, because they are united to *The Good*, wholly full of superessential goodness, and being established in this, they contain in it the supreme hyparxis of themselves. Very properly, therefore, do we say that the intelligible Gods unfold the ineffable principle of all things, and his admirable transcendency and union; subsisting themselves indeed occultly, but comprehending multitude uniformly and unically; reigning over the whole of things exemptly, and being unco-ordinated with all the other Gods. For as *The Good* illuminates all things with superessential light, and exhibits the Gods who are the fathers of all things, so likewise the intelligible genus of Gods, according to a similitude to the good, imparts from itself to all the secondary Gods, intelligible plenitude. Hence, according to each distribution of the Gods, there is an appropriate intelligible multitude, just as a monad analogous to *The Good* exists prior to each of the divine orders. And this monad indeed is the pre-existent leader of union to secondary natures. But intelligible multitude is the pre-existent source of beauty, self-sufficiency, power, essence, and all intelligible goods. For the Gods antecedently and intelligibly comprehend all intellectual natures, and contain in themselves all† things according to supreme union.

---

† Instead of τα καθ' ενωσιν, it is requisite to read παντα καθ' ενωσιν, and then the end of this book will be complete, and not defective as the Latin translator Portus imagined it was.

BOOK IV

CHAPTER I

Let the discussion, therefore, of the intelligible Gods, unfolding the mystic doctrine of Plato concerning them be here terminated by us. But it entirely follows in the next place, that we should consider after the same manner the narration concerning the intellectual Gods. Since, however, of intellectuals some are both intelligible and intellectual, *viz.* such as according to the Oracle perceiving intellectually are at the same time intellectually perceived; but others are intellectual only; - this being the case, beginning from those that are intellectual and at the same time intelligible, we will in the first place determine what pertains to them in common, from which we shall render the doctrine concerning each order of them more perspicuous. Again, therefore, let us recall to our memory those things which we a little before demonstrated, *viz.* that there are three total monads which are entirely beyond the Gods that are divided according to parts, *viz.* essence, life and intellect. And these prior to the partial participate of the superessential unities. Essence, however, is exempt from the rest. Life is allotted the middle order. But intellect converts the end of this triad to the beginning. And all these are indeed intelligibly in essence; but intelligibly and intellectually in life; and intellectually in intellect. And as secondary natures always participate of the natures placed above them, but these prior to participation pre-subsist themselves by themselves; and as in each order there are these three things, the cause of abiding, the cause of proceeding, and the cause of conversion, though intellect is more formalized according to conversion, but life according to progression, and essence according to permanency; - this being the case, it is certainly necessary that the first intellectual Gods being essentialized according to life should conjoin imparticipable intellect, and the intelligible genus of Gods, and that they should uniformly connect the various progressions of secondary, but unfold and expand the stable hyparxis of precedaneous causes. For imparticipable life is a thing of this kind, circumscribing that which is primarily being and intellect, and participating indeed of being, but participated by intellect. But this is the same thing as to assert that intelligence is filled indeed from the intelligible, but fills intellect from itself. For being is the intelligible, but life is intelligence. And being indeed is characterized according to a divine hyparxis; but life according to power; and intellect according to intelligible intellect. For as being is to hyparxis, so is intellect to being. And as intelligible power is to each of the extremes, so is life to the intelligible and to intellect. And as power is generated from the one and hyparxis, but constitutes in conjunction with *The One* the nature of being, so life proceeds indeed from being, and gives subsistence to a power different from that which is in being. As also *The One Itself* which exists prior to being, imparts to being from itself a second unity, so likewise life being allotted an hypostasis prior to intellect, generates intellectual life. For true being and the intelligible which precede the rest, supply both life and intellect with union. Imparticipable life, therefore, but which participates of the intelligible monads is the second after being, is generative of imparticipable intellect, and giving completion to this medium, and containing the bond of intelligibles and intellectuals, is illuminated by Gods who are allotted a union secondary to the occult subsistence of intelligibles, but preceding according to cause the separation of intellectual natures. For the unical, indivisible, simple, and primary natures of intelligibles, subsides through the medium of these Gods into multitude and separation, and the inexplicable evolution of the divine orders. Whence also, I think, the Gods who connectedly contain life which is infinite, being the middle of the intelligible and intellectual Gods, and carried in the divisions of themselves as in a vehicle, are called intelligible and at the same time intellectual; being filled indeed, from the first intelligibles, but filling the intellectual Gods. For we call the intelligible Gods intelligible, not as co-ordinate with intellect. For the intelligible which is in intellect is one thing, and that which produces the intellectual Gods another: and we denominate the Gods that subsist according to life intelligible and at the same time intellectual, not as giving completion to intellect, nor as being established according to intellectual intelligence, and imparting to intellect the power of intellectual perception, but to the intelligible the power of being intellectually perceived, but we give them this appellation, as deriving their subsistence from the intelligible monads, but generating all the intellectual hebdomads. And because they are illuminated indeed with intelligible life, but subsist prior to intellectuals, according to a generative cause, we think fit to denominate them in common, connecting their names from the extremes, in the same manner as they also are allotted a peculiarity collective of wholes in the divine orders.

It is evident, therefore, that they subsist according to this medium, and that they are proximate to the intelligible Gods, who are both monadic and triadic. For the intelligible triads, with reference indeed to the highest union and which is exempt from all things, are triads; but with reference to the divided essence of triads, they are monads, unfolding into light from themselves total triads. Since intelligibles, therefore, in their triadic progression, do not depart from a unical hyparxis, the intelligible and at the same time intellectual Gods subsist triadically, exhibiting in themselves the separation of the monads, and through divine difference, proceeding into multitude, and a variety of powers and essences. For the natures which subsist more remote from the one principle [of all things,] are more multiplied than the natures which are prior to them;† and are diminished indeed in powers, and the comprehensions of secondary natures, but are divided into more numbers, and such as are more distant from the monad. They likewise relinquish the union which is the cause of primarily efficient natures, and variety is assumed by them in exchange for the occult hyparxis of those primary essences. According to this reasoning, therefore, the intelligible and intellectual separation is greater than the separation which is only intelligible. And of these again, the partial orders are allotted a much greater division, so as to unfold to us a multitude of Gods which cannot be comprehended in the numbers within the decad. Their peculiarities also are indescribable, and inexplicable by our conceptions, and are manifest only to the Gods themselves, and to the causes of them. Such, therefore, are the intelligible and intellectual Gods, and such is the peculiarity which they are allotted, a peculiarity connective of extremes, and which unfolds into light precedaneous, but converts secondary natures. For they intellectually perceive the Gods prior to them, but are objects of intellection to the Gods posterior to them. Hence also Timæus establishes all-perfect animal to be the most beautiful of intelligibles, because there are intelligibles posterior to it, which it surpasses in beauty, as being superior to them, and because it is the boundary of the first intelligibles, the natures posterior to it subsisting intellectually. According to this reasoning, therefore, the first intellectual Gods are also intelligible; and we do not, deriving these things from a foreign source, ascribe them to Plato, but they are asserted by us in consequence of receiving auxiliaries from him. This, however, will be more manifest through what follows.

CHAPTER II

In the next place, therefore, we shall discuss the manner in which the Gods who illuminate the breadth of imparticipable life proceed from the intelligible Gods. Since then the intelligible Gods establish in themselves uniformly things multiplied, occultly such as are divided, and according

---

† For $αυτης$ it is necessary to read $αυτων$.

to a certain admirable transcendency of simplicity, the various genera of beings, - hence the first intellectual Gods,[†] unfolding their indistinct union, and the unknown nature of their hypostasis, and being filled through intelligible power and essential life with the prolific abundance of wholes, are allotted a kingdom which ranks as the second after them. And they always indeed produce, perfect, and connect themselves, but receive from the intelligible Gods an occult generation; from intelligible power indeed, receiving a peculiarity generative of all things; but from intelligible life which pre-exists according to cause in the intelligible, receiving the nature which is spread under them. For life is primarily indeed in intelligibles; but secondarily in intelligibles and intellectuals; and in a third degree in intellectuals; existing indeed according to cause in the first, but according to essence in the second, and according to participation in the last of these. The first intellectual, therefore, proceed from the intelligible Gods, multiplying indeed their union, and their unical powers, unfolding their occult hyparxis, and through prolific, connective, and perfective causes assimilating themselves to the essential, entire, and all-perfect transcendencies of intelligibles. For in intelligibles there were three primarily effective powers; one indeed constituting the essence of wholes; another measuring things which are multiplied; and another being productive of the forms of all generated natures.

And conformably to these, the intelligible and intellectual powers subsist; one indeed, by its very essence producing the life of secondary natures, according to a certain intelligible comprehension; but another being connective of every thing which is divided, and imparting by illumination the intelligible measure to those natures that relinquish the one union [of all things;] and another supplying all things with figure, and form and perfection. The intelligible and intellectual orders of the Gods, therefore, are generated according to all the intelligible causes. From power indeed, being allotted the peculiarity of progression; but from life receiving the portion of being which is suspended from them. For life is conjoined with power; since life is of itself infinite, all motion having infinity consubsistent with its nature, and the power of infinity, is generative of the whole of things. But from the triadic hypostasis of intelligibles, they receive a distribution into first, middle and last. For it is necessary that all things should be detained by a triadic progression, and that this should be the case prior to all [other] things with the intelligible and at the same time intellectual genera of Gods. For

---

[†] It is necessary to supply in this place in the original, νοεροι θεοι.

because they subsist as the middle of wholes, and give completion to the bond of the first orders, according to their summit indeed, they are assimilated to intelligibles, but according to their extremity, to intellectuals. And they are partly indeed intelligible, and partly intellectual. For everywhere the progressions of the divine genera are effected through continued similitude. And the first of subordinate are united to the ends of pre-existent causes. As however, the first and the last in the middle of wholes are both intelligible and intellectual, it is necessary there should be a connective medium of these, according to which medium the peculiarity of these Gods is principally apparent. For that which is intelligible and at the same time intellectual, in one part indeed is more abundant than, but in another equally communicates with both these. From these things, therefore, the continuity of the progression of the divine orders appears to be admirable. For the extremity of intelligibles indeed was intellectual, yet as in intelligibles. But the summit of intelligibles and at the same time intellectuals, is intelligible indeed, yet it possesses this peculiarity vitally. And again, the end of intelligibles and at the same time intellectuals, is intellectual, but it is vitally so. But the beginning of intellectuals, is intelligible, and presides over the intellectual Gods, yet it has the intelligible intellectually. And thus all the divine genera are allotted an indissoluble connexion and communion, an admirable friendship, and well-ordered diminution, and a transcendency, partly co-ordinate and partly exempt. That which proceeds too, is always in continuity with its producing cause; and secondary natures together with a firm establishment in their causes, make a progression from them. There is likewise one series and alliance of all things; secondary natures always subsisting from those prior to them, through similitude. After what manner, therefore, the intelligible and at the same time intellectual Gods, unfold themselves into light from the intelligible Gods, may through these things be recollected.

CHAPTER III

In the next place, let us show how they are divided in their progressions, and what difference the triads of these Gods are allotted with respect to the intelligible triads. These Gods, therefore, are also divided triply, after the above mentioned manner; being conjoined indeed to the intelligible, through their summit; but to the intellectual through their end; and through the middle bond of the extremes, being allotted the peculiarity of each equally, and extending to both the intelligible and intellectual genera of Gods, as the centre of these twofold orders, uniformly containing the communion of wholes. They are likewise divided triply, because in these all things, *viz.* essence, life, and intellect, are vitally, in the same manner as they are intelligibly in the Gods prior to them, and intellectually in the Gods that derive their subsistence from these. And essence indeed is the intelligible of life; but life is the middle and at the same time the peculiarity of this order; and intellect is the extremity, and that which is proximately carried in intellectuals as in a vehicle. All things therefore subsisting in these Gods, there will be a division of them into first, middle, and last genera. And in the third place, they are divided triply, because it is necessary that life should abide, proceed, and be converted to its principles; since of beings, the first triad was said to establish all things, and prior to other things the second triad. Eternity, therefore, abides stably in the first triad. But the triad posterior to this, is the supplier to wholes [and therefore to all things,] of progression, motion, and life according to energy. And the third triad is the supplier of conversion to the one, and of perfection which convolves all secondary natures to their principles. Hence it is necessary that the intelligible and at the same time intellectual Gods, should primarily participate of these three powers, and should abide indeed in the summit of themselves; but proceeding from thence, and extending themselves to all things, should again be converted to the intelligible place of survey, and conjoin to the beginning of their generation the end of their whole progression.

The intelligible and at the same time intellectual Gods therefore are, as I have said, triply divided. And essence indeed is that which ranks as first in them, but life is the middle, and intellect the extremity of them. Since however, each of these three is perfect, and participates of the intelligible monads, I mean of the essence which is there, of intelligible life, and of intelligible intellect, they are tripled according to the participation of primarily efficient causes. And the intelligible of life indeed possesses essence, intellect, and life intelligibly; but the intelligible and intellectual of it, possesses essence, life and intellect, intelligibly and at the same time intellectually; and the intellectual of it possesses these intellectually and intelligibly.† And every where indeed, there is a triad in each of the sections, but in conjunction with an appropriate peculiarity. Hence three intelligible and at the same time intellectual

---

† In the original, after καὶ νουν in this sentence, it is necessary to supply νοητως και νοερος, το δε νοερον. And after νοερως, it is also requisite to supply και νοητως, as in the above translation.

triads present themselves to our view, which are indeed illuminated by the divine unities, but each of them contains an all-various multitude. For since in intelligibles, there was an all-powerful and all-perfect multitude, how is it possible that this multitude should not in a much greater degree, be evolved and multiplied, in the Gods secondary to the intelligible order, according to the prolific cause of them? Each triad therefore comprehends in itself a multitude of powers, and a variety of forms, producing intelligible multitude into energy, and unfolding into light the generative infinity of intelligibles. And we indeed, being impelled from the participants, discover the peculiarity of the participated superessential Gods. But according to the order of things, the intelligible and intellectual monads generate about themselves essences, and all lives, and the intellectual genera. And through these, they unfold the unknown transcendency of themselves preserving by itself the pre-existent cause of the whole of things. There are however, as we have said, three intelligible triads. And there are also three triads posterior to these, which appear to be tripled from them, according to their prolific perfection.

But it is necessary that the peculiarity of the intelligible, and also of the intelligible and at the same time intellectual triad, should be defined according to another mode. For in the intelligible order indeed, each triad had only the third part of being; for it consisted of bound, and infinity, and from both these. But this was essence indeed in the first triad, intelligible life in the second, and intelligible intellect in the third. The natures however prior to these were unities and superessential powers, which give completion to the whole triads. But in the intelligible and at the same time intellectual order, each triad has essence, life and intellect; one indeed intelligibly and at the same time intellectually, but more intelligibly, so far as it is in continuity with the first intelligibles; but another intellectually and intelligibly, but more intellectually, because it is proximately carried in intellectuals; and another according to an equal part, as it comprehends in itself both the peculiarities. Hence the first triad, that we may speak of each, was in intelligibles, bound, infinity, and essence; for essence was that which was primarily mixed. But here the first triad is essence, life and intellect, with appropriate unities. For essence is suspended from the first deity [of this triad,] life from the second, and intellect from the third. And these three superessential monads, unfold the monads of the first triad. But again, the second triad after this, was in the intelligible order, a superessential unity, power, and intelligible and occult life. Here however, essence, life and intellect are all vital, and are suspended from the Gods who contain the one bond of the whole of this order. For as the first unities were allotted a power unific of the middle genera, so the second unities after them, exhibit the connective peculiarity of primarily efficient causes. After these therefore, succeeds the third triad, which in the intelligible order indeed was unity, power, and intelligible intellect; but here it consists of three superessential Gods, who close the termination of the intelligible and at the same time intellectual Gods, and begird all things intellectually, I mean essence, life and intellect. They are likewise the suppliers of divine perfection,[†] imitating the all-perfect intelligible triad, just as the connectedly containing Gods imitate the intelligible measure, and the Gods prior to these, the generative cause of intelligibles. The three intelligible therefore, and at the same time intellectual triads, are thus generated, and are allotted such a difference as this, with respect to the intelligible triads.

CHAPTER IV

Again however, returning to Plato, let us accord with him, and exhibit the science which pre-exists with him concerning each of these triads. And in the first place, let us assume what is written in the *Phædrus*, and survey from the words themselves of Socrates, how he unfolds to us the whole of the orderly distinction of these triads, and the differences which it contains. In the *Phædrus* therefore, there are said to be twelve leaders who preside over the whole [of mundane concerns,] and who conduct all the mundane Gods, and all the herds of dæmons, and convert them to the intelligible nature. It is also said that Jupiter is the leader of all these twelve Gods, that he drives a winged chariot, adorns and takes care of all things, and brings all the army of Gods that follow him, first indeed to the place of survey within the heaven, and to the blessed spectacles, and discursive energies of the intelligibles which are there. But in the next place Jupiter brings them to the subcelestial arch which proximately begirds the heaven, and is contained in it, and after this to the heaven itself, and the back of heaven; where also divine souls stand, and being borne along together with the heaven, survey all the essence that is beyond it. Socrates further adds, that prior to the heaven there is what is called the supercelestial place, in which true and real essence, the plain of truth, the kingdom of Adrastia, and the divine choir of virtues subsist, and that souls being nourished through the intellection

---

[†] For τελειοτατοι it is necessary to read τελειοτητος.

of these monads, are happily affected, following [in their contemplation] the circulation of the heaven.

These things therefore, are asserted in the *Phædrus*, Socrates being clearly inspired by divinity, and discussing mystic concerns. It is necessary however, prior to other things, to consider what the heaven is of which Socrates speaks, and in what order of beings it is established. For having discovered this, we may also survey the subcelestial arch, and the supercelestial place.† For each of these is assumed according to habitude towards the heaven; the one indeed being primarily placed above it, but the other being primarily arranged under it.

CHAPTER V

What therefore is the heaven to which Jupiter leads the Gods? For if we should say that it is the sensible heaven, as certain other persons say it is, it will be necessary that the more excellent genera should be converted to things naturally subordinate to themselves. For if Jupiter the mighty leader in the heaven proceeds to this sensible heaven, and leads to it all the Gods that follow him, he will have a conversion to things subordinate, and posterior to himself. And together with Jupiter, this will also be the case with all the leaders, and the Gods and dæmons suspended from these; though the same Socrates in the *Phædrus* says, that even a partial soul when perfected is conversant with sublime concerns, and governs the whole world. How is it possible therefore, that the leaders of whole souls should be converted to the sensible heaven, and exchange the intelligible place of survey for an inferior allotment, when through these souls they preside over the universe, in order that they may illuminate mundane natures with a liberated and unrestrained power? In addition to these things also, what are the blessed intellections of the Gods within this sensible heaven, and what are the evolutions of all the knowledge of sensibles?‡ For in short the Gods know sensibles, not by a conversion to them, but by containing in themselves the causes of them. Hence intellectually perceiving themselves, they know sensibles causally, and rule over them, not by looking to them, and verging to the subjects of their government, but

---

† After την υπουρανιαν αψιδα, it is obviously necessary to add και τον υπερουρανιον τοπον.

‡ The sentence that immediately follows this in the original, is so defective, as to be perfectly unintelligible. I have not therefore, attempted to translate it.

by converting through love inferior natures to themselves. Neither therefore, is it lawful for the Gods who adorn the whole of heaven, and think it worthy their providential care, to be ever situated under the circulation of this heaven; nor is there any blessedness in the contemplation of the things which exist under it; nor are the souls that are converted to this contemplation among the number of those that are happy, and that follow the Gods, but they rank among those that exchange intelligible for doxastic nutriment, such as Socrates says, the souls are that are lame, that have broken their wings, and are in a merged condition. Since therefore passions of this kind belong to partial souls, and these not such as are happy, how can we refer a conversion to the sensible heaven to the ruling and leading Gods?

Further still, Socrates says that souls standing on the back of the heaven, are carried round by the circumvolution itself of the heaven; but Timæus, and the Athenian guest say, that souls lead every thing in the heavens by their own motions, externally cover bodies with their motions, and living their own life through the whole of time, impart to bodies secondarily efficient powers of motion. How therefore do these things accord with those who make this heaven to be sensible? For souls do not contemplate and dance round intelligibles, through the circulation of the heavens; but through the unapparent convolution of souls, bodies revolve in a circle, and about these perform their circulations. If therefore any one should say that the sensible heaven circumvolves souls, and that it is divided according to the back, the profundity, and the subcelestial arch, many absurdities must necessarily be admitted.

But if some one should say that the heaven is intelligible, to which Jupiter is the leader, but all the Gods, and together with these, dæmons follow him, he will unfold the divinely-inspired narrations of Plato consentaneously to the nature of things, and will follow the most celebrated of his interpreters. For Plotinus and Iamblichus are of opinion that this heaven is a certain intelligible. And prior to these, Plato himself in the *Cratylus* following the Orphic theogonies calls the father indeed of Jupiter, Saturn, but of Saturn, Heaven. And he evinces that Jupiter is the demiurgus of the whole of things through the names [by which he is called,] investigating for this purpose the truth concerning them. But he shows that Saturn is connective of a divine intellect; and that Heaven is the intelligence, or intellectual perception of the first intelligibles. For sight, says he, looking to the things above, is Heaven. Hence Heaven subsists prior to every divine intellect, with which the mighty Saturn is replete; but it intellectually perceives the things above, and such as are beyond the celestial order. The mighty Heaven therefore, is allotted a kingdom which is between the intelligible and intellectual orders. For the circulation mentioned in the *Phædrus* is intelligence, through which all the Gods and souls obtain the contemplation of intelligibles. But intelligence is a medium between intellect and the intelligible. It must be said therefore, that the whole of heaven is established according to this medium, and that it contains the one bond of the divine orders, being the father indeed of the intellectual genus, but being generated from the kings prior to it, which also it is said to see. But on one side of it the supercelestial place, and on the other the subcelestial arch must be arranged.

CHAPTER VI

Again therefore, if indeed the supercelestial place is the imparticipable and occult genus of the intelligible Gods, how can we establish so great a divine multitude there, and this accompanied with separation, *viz.* truth, science, justice, temperance, the meadow, and Adrastia? For neither do the fountains of the virtues, nor the separation and variety of forms, pertain to the intelligible Gods. For the first and most unical of forms extend the demiurgic intellect of wholes to the intelligible paradigm, and the comprehension of forms which is there. But Socrates in the *Phædrus* says that a partial intellect contemplates the supercelestial place. For this intellect is the governor of the soul, as it is well said by the philosophers prior to us. If therefore, it be necessary from this analogy to investigate the difference of intelligibles, as the demiurgic intellect indeed, is imparticipable, but a partial intellect is participable, so with respect to the intelligible, one indeed which is the first paradigm of the demiurgus, pertains to the first intelligibles, but another which is the first paradigm of a partial intellect pertains to the second intelligibles, which are indeed intelligibles, but are allotted an intelligible transcendency, as subsisting at the summit of intellectuals. But if the supercelestial place is beyond the celestial circulation, but is inferior to those intelligible triads, because it is more expanded; for it is the plain of truth, and is not unknown, is divided according to a multitude of forms, and possesses a variety of powers, and the meadow which is there nourishes souls, and is visible to them, the first intelligibles illuminating souls with ineffable union, but not being known by them through intelligence; - if this be the case, it is certainly necessary that the supercelestial place should subsist between the intelligible nature, and the celestial circulation. If Plato himself also admits that essence which truly is, exists in this place, how is it possible that he should not also admit it to be intelligible, and to participate of the first intelligibles? For because indeed it is essence it is intelligible; but because it truly is, it participates of being.

Moreover, possessing in itself a multitude of intelligibles, it will not be arranged according to the first triad; for the one being is there, and not the multitude of beings. But possessing a various life which the meadow indicates, it is subordinate to the second triad; for intelligible life is one, and without separation. And again, since it shines forth to the view with divided forms, all-various orders, and prolific powers, it falls short of the all-perfect triad [in intelligibles]. If therefore it is the second to these in dignity and power, but is established above the celestial order, it is intelligible indeed, but is the summit of the intellectual Gods. On this account also, nutriment is derived to souls from thence. For the intelligible is nutriment, since the first intelligibles also, *viz.* the beautiful, the wise and the good, are said to nourish souls. For by these, says Socrates, the wing of the soul is nourished; but by the contraries to these it is corrupted and destroyed. These things however, are indeed effected by the first intelligibles exemptly, and through union and silence. But the supercelestial place is said to nourish through intelligence and energy, and to fill the happy choir of souls with intelligible light, and the prolific rivers of life.

CHAPTER VII

After the supercelestial place however and the heaven itself, is the subcelestial arch, which it is obvious to every one ought to be arranged under the heaven, and not in the heaven. For it is not called by Plato the celestial, but the subcelestial arch. That it is also proximately situated under the celestial circulation, is evident from what is written concerning it. But if it be necessary to make the subcelestial arch being such, the same with the summit of intellectuals, and not with the end of the intelligible and intellectual Gods, it will be now necessary to contemplate what remains. For the summit of intellectuals separates itself from the kingdom of the heaven, but the subcelestial arch is on all sides comprehended by it. And the former indeed constitutes the whole of intellect, intellectual multitude, and as Socrates says, the blessed discursive energies of the Gods; but the latter only bounds the celestial series, and supplies the Gods with the means of ascending to the heaven. For when the Gods are elevated to the banquet, and the delicious food, and are filled with intelligible goods, then they proceed ascending, to the subcelestial arch, and through it are raised to the celestial circulation. Hence, if you say that the subcelestial arch is perfective of the Gods, and converts them to the whole of the heaven, and the supercelestial place, you will not wander from the meaning of Plato. For the Gods are indeed nourished by the intelligible, by the meadow, and by the divine forms, which the place above the heaven comprehends; but they are filled with this nutriment through the subcelestial arch. For through this they also participate of the celestial circulation. Hence they are converted indeed, through the subcelestial arch; but they receive a vigorous intellectual perception from the celestial order; and they are filled with intelligible goods from the supercelestial place. It is evident therefore, that the supercelestial place is allotted an intelligible summit; but the circulation of the heaven, the middle breadth; and the arch, the intelligible extremity. For all things are in it. And intellect indeed is convertive, but the intelligible is the object of desire. But divine intelligence gives completion to the middle, perfecting indeed the conversions of divine natures, and binding them to such as are first, but unfolding the tendencies to intelligibles, and filling secondary natures with precedaneous goods. I think however, that through these things we have sufficiently reminded the reader of the order of these three.

CHAPTER VIII

Perhaps, however, some one may ask us, why we here characterize the whole progression of the intelligible and at the same time intellectual gods, according to the middle, and why we call one of the extremes supercelestial, but the other subcelestial, from their habitude to the middle, indicating the exempt transcendency of the one, but the proximate and connected diminution of the other. Perhaps therefore, we may concisely answer such a one, that this whole genus of the intelligible and at the same time intellectual Gods, binds together both the extremes, being to the one the cause of conversion, but to the other of becoming unfolded into light, and being present with secondary natures. As therefore, we denominate all the intelligible Gods paternal and unical, characterizing them from the summit, and as we say that they are the boundaries of the whole of things, *viz.* those that are effective of essence, those that are the causes of perpetuity, and those that are the sources of the production of forms, after the same manner we unfold these middle Gods as the leaders of all bonds, from the middle which is in them. For the whole of this middle order is vivific, connective and perfective. But the summit of it indeed, unfolds the impressions of intelligibles, and their ineffable union. The termination of it converts intellectuals, and conjoins them to intelligibles. And the middle collects into, and fixes in itself as in a centre the whole genera of the Gods. For to the extremes also through reference to the middle we attribute the habitude of transcendency and diminution, calling the one above, but the other under the middle.

CHAPTER IX

Through these things therefore, we may concisely answer him, as I have said, who doubts concerning these names. Here however, it is fit that we should admire the divine science of Plato, because he has narrated the mode of the ascent of the whole of things to the intelligible conformably to the highest of initiators. For in the first place, he elevates souls and the Gods themselves to *the fountains*, through the liberated leaders. For the blessed and most abundant spectacles and discursive energies are particularly in these fountains, in which also theurgists place all their hope of salvation. They are therefore blessed through the unpolluted monads; but they are most abundant through the cause of divine difference; and they are spectacles and discursive energies, through the intellectual and paternal powers. But in the second place, Plato elevates souls and Gods from the fountains, and through the fountains to the leaders of perfection. For after many and divided intellections the good of the perfective Gods shines forth, being supernally expanded from the intellectual Gods themselves, and illuminating us, and prior to our souls, whole souls, and prior to these, the Gods themselves. But from the perfective Gods Plato elevates souls and Gods to the divinities, who are connective of all the intellectual orders. For the perfective Gods are suspended from these divinities, subsist together with them, and are comprehended by them. Such also is the communion and union of these Gods, that some of the most celebrated [interpreters of Plato] have supposed that there is an all-perfect and indivisible sameness among them, in consequence of not being able to apprehend by a reasoning process the separation which is in them. For here also, it may appear to some one that Plato calls the extremity of the celestial circulation, the arch. This however is not the case. For he does not denominate the arch celestial, but subcelestial. As therefore, the supercelestial is essential exempt from the heaven, thus also the subcelestial is inferior to the kingdom of the heaven. For the former indeed is indicative of transcendency, but the latter of a proximately-arranged diminution.

After this circulation however which is connective of the whole of things, Plato elevates souls and the Gods to the supercelestial place, and the intelligible union of intellectuals, where also the Gods abiding, are nourished, are in a happy condition, and are filled with ineffable and unical goods. For with theurgists also, the ascent to the ineffable and intelligible powers which are the summits of all intellectuals, is through the connective Gods. In what manner however, the Gods are here conjoined to the first intelligibles, Plato no longer unfolds through words; for the contact with them is ineffable, and through ineffables, as he also teaches in what he says about them in the *Phædrus*. And through this order, the mystic union with the intelligible and first-producing causes is effected. With us therefore, there is also the same mode of conjunction. And through this, the mode of theurgic ascent is more credible. For as wholes ascend to exempt principles, through the natures proximately placed above them, thus also parts imitating the ascent of wholes, are conjoined through middle steps of ascent, with the most simple and ineffable causes. For what Plato has delivered in this dialogue concerning whole souls, he afterwards unfolds concerning ours. And in the first place indeed, he conjoins them with the liberated Gods. Afterwards, through these he elevates them to the perfective Gods. Afterwards, through these, to the connective Gods, and in a similar manner, as far as to the intelligible Gods. Socrates therefore, narrating the mode of ascent to intelligible beauty, and how following the Gods, prior to bodies and generation, we were partakers of that blessed spectacle, says: "For it was then lawful to see splendid beauty, when we obtained together with that happy choir, this blessed vision and spectacle, we indeed following Jupiter, but others in conjunction with some other God, perceiving, and being initiated in those mysteries, which it is lawful to call the most blessed of mysteries." How then were we once conjoined with intelligible beauty? Through being initiated, says he, in the most blessed of mysteries. What else therefore, does this assert, than that we were conjoined with the perfective leaders, and were initiated by them, in order to our being replenished with beauty? Of what goods therefore, is the initiation the procurer? "Which orgies," says he, "were celebrated by us, when we were entire and impassive, and were initiated in, and became spectators of entire, simple, and quietly stable visions." The *entire* therefore, is derived to souls from the celestial circulation. For this contains, and is connective of all the divine genera, and also of our souls. Every thing however, which in the whole contains parts, comprehends also that which is divided, and collects that which is various into union and simplicity.

But the entire, quietly stable, and simple visions, are unfolded to souls supernally from the supercelestial place, through the connectedly-containing Gods. For the mystic impressions of intelligibles, shine forth in that place, and also the unknown and ineffable beauty of characters. For *muesis* and *epopteia*† are symbols of ineffable silence, and of union with mystic natures through intelligible visions. And that which is the most admirable of all is this, that as theurgists order the whole body to be buried, except the head, in the most mystic of initiations, Plato also has anticipated this, being moved by the Gods themselves. "For being pure," says he, "and liberated from this surrounding vestment, which we now denominate body, we obtained this most blessed *muesis* and *epopteia*, being full of intelligible light." For the pure splendour [which he mentions] symbolically unfolds to us intelligible light. Hence, when we are situated in the intelligible, we shall have a life perfectly liberated from the body. But elevating the head of the charioteer to the place beyond the heaven, we shall be filled with the mysteries which are there, and with intelligible silence. It also appears to me that Plato sufficiently unfolds the three elevating causes, love, truth, and faith, to those who do not negligently read what he has written. For what besides love conjoins with beauty? Where is the plain of truth, except in this place? And what else than faith is the cause of this ineffable *muesis*? For *muesis* in short, is neither through intelligence nor judgment, but through the unical silence imparted by faith, which is better than every gnostic energy, and which establishes both whole souls and ours, in the ineffable and unknown nature‡ of the Gods. These things however, have proceeded to this length from my sympathy about such like concerns.

---

† "The word τελετη or *initiation*," says Hermeas, in his MS. Commentary on the *Phædrus*, "was so denominated from rendering the soul perfect. The soul therefore was once perfect. But here it is divided, and is not able to energize wholly by itself." He adds: "But it is necessary to know that *telete, muesis* and *epopteia*, τελετη, μυησις, and εποπτεια, differ from each other. *Telete*, therefore, is analogous to that which is preparatory to purifications. But *muesis*, which is so called from closing the eyes, is more divine. For to close the eyes in initiation is no longer to receive by sense those divine mysteries, but with the pure soul itself. And εποπτεια *epopteia* is to be established in, and become a spectator of the mysteries."

‡ φυσει is omitted in the original

CHAPTER X

But again returning to the proposed theology, let us unfold the conceptions which Plato indicates to us concerning each order of the intelligible and at the same time intellectual Gods. The supercelestial place therefore is intelligible. Hence also Plato says that it is essence which truly is, and that it is visible to the intellect of the soul. It is likewise the one comprehension and union of the intellectual Gods. For it is not intelligible after such a manner as animal itself, nor as the first eternity, nor as that which is itself primarily the one being. For as these are primarily intelligibles, they are exempt from all other intelligibles, and pre-subsist by themselves. But the supercelestial place, is proximately established above the celestial circulation, and of this is the intelligible; yet it is not simply intelligible. And that we assert these things rightly, Socrates also testifies, imparting the intellection of this intelligible to souls likewise, through the heaven. For in this period, according to which they are carried round together with the circulation of the heaven, they behold indeed justice, they behold temperance, and they also behold science, and each of the beings which have a true and real existence; so that if the supercelestial place is intelligible, and real being, yet it is intelligible, as being above the heaven. The first intelligibles however, are intelligible according to their own essence and according to the exempt and first efficient cause of all intellectual natures. For the mighty Saturn likewise, though he is an intellectual God, and the fullness of intellect, is intelligible as with reference to the demiurgus; for he is the summit of the intellectual triad. Thus therefore, the place also which is above the heaven, is allotted an intelligible transcendency with respect to the celestial circulation, and is intelligible as in the first intellectuals.† Hence also it subsists analogous to the first triad of intelligibles. That triad however, was simply intelligible. For the intelligible which is in intelligibles, at once exists prior to all second and third intelligibles. But the supercelestial place is not simply intelligible; for it is the summit of intellectuals, and not of intelligibles. Hence Plato calls the first triad of intelligibles the one being; but he denominates the supercelestial place, truly-existing essence. For the former indeed, antecedes all beings in an admirable simplicity, and in the occult unity of being. For that being is the intelligible itself, and is not in one respect intelligible, but in another intellectual, nor is

---

† Instead of ως εν τοις πρωτιστοις νοητοις νοερος, it is necessary to read ως εν τοις πρωτιστοις νοεροις νοητος.

it that which is passive to [*viz.* participates of] being; but it is the seat, and the most ancient monad of being. This order however, [*viz.* the supercelestial place] falls short of the union of that triad, and participates of being, but is not simply being. Hence also Plato calls it essence, and essence which truly is, as receiving this intelligible and essential according to the essence of that which is primarily being. And the first triad indeed of intelligibles was paternal; for it subsists according to divine union and bound, and is the occult, and highest boundary of all intelligibles. But the supercelestial place is maternal, subsisting according to infinity, and the power of infinity. For this order is feminine and prolific, and produces all things by intelligible powers. Hence also, Plato calls it a place, as being the receptacle of the paternal causes, and bringing forth, and producing the generative powers of the Gods into the hypostasis of secondary natures. For having denominated matter also a place, he calls it the mother and nurse of the reasons [*i.e.* of the productive principles], which proceed into it from being, and the paternal cause.

According to this analogy, therefore, Plato thus denominates the supercelestial place, as feminine, and as being the cause of those things maternally, of which the intelligible father is the cause paternally. Matter however receives forms alone; but the mother and nurse of the Gods, not only receives, but also constitutes and generates secondary natures, together with the father. Nor does this generative deity produce from herself into an external place, her progeny, and separate them from her own comprehension, in the same manner as the natures which generate here, deliver their offspring into light external to themselves; but she generates, comprehends and establishes all things in herself. Hence also she is the place of them, as being a seat which on all sides contains them, and as by her prolific, and primarily efficient powers, preoccupying and containing in herself, all the progressions, multitude and variety of secondary natures. For all beings subsist in the Gods, and are comprehended and saved by them. For where can they recede from the Gods, and from the comprehension which is in them? And how, if they depart from them, can they remain even for the smallest portion of time? In a particular manner however the powers which are generative of divine natures, are said to comprehend their progeny, so far as they are the proximate causes of them, and constitute their essence with a more abundant division, and a more particular providence. For paternal causes produce secondary natures uniformly, exemptly, and without co-ordination, and comprehend, but unically their own progeny. And in simplicity indeed, they preoccupy the variety of them; but in union their multitude. It is evident therefore, from what has been said, that the supercelestial place is intelligible, and after what manner it is intelligible. In addition to these things also it is evident, how it is feminine; for place is adapted to the generative Gods through the above-mentioned causes. And the meadow is the fountain of a vivific nature, as will be shortly demonstrated. Socrates likewise assumes all the divine natures that are in this place, to be of this kind, [*viz.* to be of the feminine genus] I mean science herself, justice herself, temperance herself, truth herself, and Adrastia; which may especially be considered as a certain indication, that Plato particularly attributes the feminine to this order, and not only other theologians.

CHAPTER XI

What therefore is the cause through which Plato in the first place celebrates this deity negatively, analogous to *The One*? And what are the negations? For he denominates it, without colour, without figure, and without contact. And he takes away from it these three hyparxes, colour, figure, and contact. I say therefore, that this order being the summit of the intellectual Gods, is unknown and ineffable, according to its peculiarity, and is [only] to be known through intelligible impressions. For being the summit of intellectuals, it conjoins itself with intelligibles. For how could intellectuals be conjoined with intelligibles, unless they antecedently constituted an intelligible transcendency of themselves? But what connexion and communion could be surveyed of the whole orders of things, unless the extremities of such as are first possessed a certain similitude to the beginnings of such as are second? For on account of this similitude, these are connascent with each other, and all things subsist according to one series. As therefore, the end of intelligibles was intellectual, so likewise the beginning of intellectuals is allotted an intelligible hyparxis. And each of these indeed is intelligible; but the one is intelligible simply; and the other is not intelligible without the addition of the intellectual. These therefore, are consubsistent with each other. And the one indeed, is the paternal cause of the whole of things, so far as it is intelligible, and the intellectual which is in it is extended intelligibly. But the other is generatively constitutive of the same things, because it is intellectual, and intelligible good presides in the intellectual genus. All things therefore, are from both, exemptly indeed, from the intellectual of intelligibles, but co-ordinately, from the intelligible of intellectuals. And both indeed, rejoice in unknown hyparxes; and are alone, as Plato says, known by intelligible, mystic, and ineffable impressions. Hence also he calls the attempt boldness which endeavours to unfold the arcana concerning them, and to explain by words their unknown union.

From the end of the intelligible order however, the summit of intellectuals possesses its unknown peculiarity. For so far as it conjoins itself to the first intelligibles, and is filled with their unical, ineffable, and paternal hyparxis, so far also it exists in an unknown manner prior to intellectuals. Hence it is incomprehensible by the natures posterior to it; but it is known by those prior to it, being super-expanded into a continued union with them.[†] It likewise knows the natures prior to itself intelligibly; but this does not at all differ from uniform and ineffable knowledge. For intelligible knowledge is the union, cause, summit, and unknown and occult hyparxis of all knowledge. Since therefore, the one and united triad is, if it be lawful so to speak, the intellectual image of the unknown union of intelligibles, and presides over the same uniform and unknown power in intellectuals, as its own cause does, hence Plato mystically unfolds it through negations. For every where that which is highest, and that which is unknown, are analogous to the unical God. As therefore, we are taught to celebrate this God through negations, after the same manner we endeavour to unfold negatively the uniform and unknown summits of secondary orders. And in short, since Socrates in the *Phædrus* makes the ascent as far as to the supercelestial place, arranging it analogous to the first, as in this order, and in the ascent of souls, he celebrates it by negations. For in the *Timæus*, Plato contends that the one demiurgus through whom every demiurgic genus of Gods subsists, is ineffable and unknown; and every where that which is highest has this transcendency with respect to secondary natures. For it imitates the cause which is at once unically exempt from all beings. We celebrate this cause however, through negations alone, as existing prior to all things; but we unfold the summits which proceed analogous to it, affirmatively and at the same time negatively. As participating indeed, the natures prior to themselves, we celebrate them affirmatively. For Plato calls the supercelestial place essence which truly is, the plain of truth, the meadow, and the intelligible place of survey of the Gods, and he does not only call it without colour, without figure, and without contact, thus mingling affirmations with negations. For this order is a medium between the intelligible Gods and the first intellectual divine orders, containing the bond of both. And it guards indeed intellectually,

---

[†] For αυτην it is necessary to read αυτοις.

according to a uniform and unknown transcendency, but transmits the plenitudes of intelligibles as far as to the last of things. It likewise elevates all things at once, according to one common union, as far as to the intelligible father, and generates and produces them as far as to matter. Being therefore established between the unical and the multiplied Gods, it is unfolded, negatively indeed, through the unknown manner in which it transcends secondary natures, but affirmatively through its participation of the first natures. For the first demiurgus is called in the *Timæus* fabricator and father, and good, and all such names, so far as he participates of pre-existent causes; but so far as he is the monad of all fabrication, Plato leaves him unknown and ineffable, exempt from all the fabricators of things. For he says, "it is difficult to discover him, and when found, it is impossible to speak of him to all men." Thus therefore Plato unfolds the supercelestial place, affirmatively indeed, as being filled from the first causes, at one time indeed calling it essence, which truly is, at another the plain of truth, and at another, something else of this kind; but[†] so far as it transcends the intellectual Gods, and so far as it is supreme and unical, he celebrates it negatively, in the same manner as the principle which is exempt from all things.

CHAPTER XII

It follows therefore, in the next place, that we should consider what the negations are, and from what orders they are generated. In the *Parmenides* then, the negations of *The One* are produced from all the divine orders, because *The One* is the cause of all of them. And every thing divine according to the hyparxis of itself participates of the first principle; and *The One* in consequence of transcending these is in a much greater degree exempt from the natures posterior to these. For from these all things proceed; since they receive partibly the peculiarities of these. This however is evident from the other hypotheses, in which the same conclusions are again circulated, at one time being connected together negatively, and at another affirmatively. For what is there which could be able to subsist, unless it was antecedently comprehended according to cause in wholes? But in the *Phædrus*, the things which are denied of the intelligible summit of all intellectuals are the natures which are proximately established after this summit, *viz.* the sacred genera, the connective, the perfective, and the

---

† δε is omitted in the original, which the sense evidently requires to be inserted.

paternal of what are properly called intellectuals. For this summit being exempt from these, it also transcends all the intellectual Gods. For what every genus of the Gods is to *The One*, that the three orders posterior to this summit, are to it. Plato therefore denominates the celestial order which connectedly contains wholes, and illuminates them with intelligible light, colour; because likewise the apparent beauty of this sensible heaven is resplendent with all various colours, and with light. Hence he calls that heaven intellectual colour, and light. For the light proceeding from *The Good* is [in the orders] above [the heaven] unknown and occult, abiding in the adyta of the Gods; but it shines forth in this order, and from being unapparent becomes manifest. Hence it is assimilated to colour the offspring of light.

Farther still, if the heaven is sight beholding the things above, the intelligible of it may very properly be called colour which is conjoined with the sight. The cause therefore of the intelligibles in the heaven is without colour, but is exempt from them; for sensible colour is the offspring of the solar light. But Plato denominates the order which proximately subsists after the celestial order, and which we have called the subcelestial arch, figure. For the arch itself is the name of a figure. And in short, in this order, Parmenides also places intellectual figure. But Plato first attributes contact to the summit of intellectuals, as is evident from the conclusions of the *Parmenides*. For in the first hypothesis taking away figure from *The One*, he uses this as a medium, *viz.* that *The One* does not touch itself. "But *The One*," says he, "does not touch itself." And the conclusion is evident. Here therefore contact first subsists, and subsists according to cause. For of those things of which the demiurgus is proximately the cause, the father who is prior to him is paradigmatically the cause. In this order therefore, contact is the paradigm of the liberated Gods. Hence these three orders are successive, *viz.* colour, figure, and contact. And from these the supercelestial place is essentially exempt. Hence it is without colour, without figure, and without contact. Nor does it transcend these three privatively, but according to causal excellence. For it imparts to colour from intelligibles the participation of light; on figure it confers by illumination intellectual bound; and in contact it supernally inserts union and continuity, and perfects all things by its power, things which are touched indeed, through union, those that are figured, through the participation of bound, and those that are coloured, through the illumination of light. But it draws upward, and allures to itself every thing ineffably, and through intelligible impressions, and fills every thing with unical goods.

If therefore, we assert these things rightly, we must not admit the interpretation of those who are busily occupied in sensible colours, and contacts, and figures, and who assert that the supercelestial place is exempt from these. For these are trifling, and by no means adapted to that place. For even nature, not only that which exists as a whole, but that also which is partial, is exempt from sensible colours, from apparent figures, and from corporeal contact. What therefore is there venerable in this, if it is also present to natures themselves? But it is necessary to extend colours, and figures, and contacts, from on high as far as to the last of things, and to evince that the supercelestial place, is similarly exempt from all these. For soul also and intellect participate of figure; and contact is frequently in incorporeal natures, according to the communion of first with secondary beings, and it is usual to call these communications contacts, and to denominate the touchings of intellectual perceptions adhesions. We should not therefore be carried from things first to things last, nor compare the highest order of intellectuals with the last of beings, above which both soul and nature are established. For in so doing we shall err, and shall not attend to Plato, who exclaims that it is boldness to assert these things concerning it. For where is the boldness, and what the unknown power transcending our conceptions, in contemplating the truth of sensible colours, figures, and contacts. For an hypostasis of this kind is known by physiologists, and not by the sons of theologists. Such therefore is the power possessed by the negations through which Plato celebrates the supercelestial place.

CHAPTER XIII

Again then, let us in the next place survey the affirmations, how they exist according to the participation of the first intelligibles themselves. The supercelestial place therefore, is said to be essence which truly is, because it participates of that which is primarily being. For to be, and truly to be are present to all things, as the progeny of the intelligible essence. For as *the one* is from the first principle which is prior to intelligibles, so the nature of being is from intelligibles. For there the one being subsists, as Parmenides a little before taught us. But the supercelestial place is beheld by the governor of the soul, because it is allotted an intelligible transcendency with respect to the other intellectual Gods. Hence the intelligible good of it is rendered manifest from its being known by intellect. This intelligible therefore, in the same manner as that which is truly being, arrives to it from the unical

Gods. For they are primarily and imparticipably intelligibles, and the first efficient causes of all intelligibles. These things also concur with each other, *viz.* that which is truly being, and the intelligible. For every intelligible is truly being, and every thing which is truly being is intelligible. For intellect is intelligible according to the being which is in it; but according to its gnostic power it is intellect. Hence also every intellect is the supplier of knowledge; but every intelligible is the supplier of essence. For that which each is primarily, it imparts by illumination to the secondary orders.

CHAPTER XIV

In the third place therefore, the genus of true science is said to be established about the supercelestial place. For these two things ascend to the contemplation of that essence, *viz.* intellect the governor of the soul [but this is a partial intellect established indeed above souls, and elevating them to their paternal port] and true science which is the perfection of the soul. This therefore energizes about that place, as transitively revolving in harmonic measures about being. But intellect contemplates it, as employing simple intellection. Farther still, the science which is in us is one thing, but that which is in the supercelestial place another. And the former indeed is true, but the latter is truth itself. What therefore is it, and whence does it subsist? It is indeed a deity which is the fountain of all intellectual knowledge, and the first efficient cause of undefiled and stable intelligence.[†] But it shines forth in the first triad of intellectuals, because this is perfective of all other things and likewise of divine souls. For these ascending to this uniform power of all knowledge, perfect their own knowledge. For each of the undefiled souls, says Socrates, revolving together with Jupiter and the heaven, surveys justice, temperance and science. Hence, these three fountains are there, being intelligible deities, and the fountains of the intellectual virtues, and not being, as some think they are, intellectual forms. For Plato is accustomed to characterize these by the term itself, as for instance science itself and justice itself; and this Socrates says somewhere in the *Phædo*. But here when he says justice herself, temperance herself, and science herself, he appears to unfold to us certain self-perfect and intelligible deities, which have a triadic subsistence. And of these science indeed is the monad; but temperance has the second order; and justice the third. And science indeed is the

---

† For $\epsilon\nu\omega\sigma\epsilon\omega\varsigma$ it is necessary to read $\nu o\eta\sigma\epsilon\omega\varsigma$.

supplier of undefiled, firm and immutable intelligence; but temperance imparts to all the Gods the cause of conversion to themselves; and justice imparts to them the cause of the distribution of the whole of good according to desert. And through science indeed, each of the Gods intellectually perceives the natures prior to himself, and is filled with intelligible intelligence;† but through temperance he is converted to himself, and enjoys a second union, and a good co-ordinate to the conversion to himself; and through justice he rules over the natures posterior to himself, in a silent path, as they say, measures their desert, and supplies a distribution adapted to each. These three fountains therefore contain all the energies of the Gods. And science indeed proceeds analogous to the first triad of intelligibles. And as that triad imparts essence to all things, so this illuminates the Gods with knowledge. But temperance proceeds analogous to the second triad of intelligibles. For temperance imitates the connective and measuring power of that triad; since it measures the energies of the Gods, and converts each of them to itself. And justice proceeds analogous to the third triad of intelligibles. For it also separates secondary natures according to appropriate desert,‡ in the same manner as that triad separates them intelligibly by the first paradigms.

CHAPTER XV

After these things therefore, we may survey another triad pre-existing in this place, which also Socrates celebrates, *viz.* the plain of truth, the meadow, and the nutriment of the Gods. The plain of truth therefore, is intellectually expanded to intelligible light, and is splendid with the illuminations that proceed from thence. For as *The One* emits by illumination intelligible light, so the intelligible imparts to secondary natures a participation productive of essence. But the meadow is the prolific power of life, and of all-various reasons, is the comprehension of the first efficient causes of life, and is the cause of the variety, and generation of forms. For the meadows also which are here are productive of all-various forms and reasons, and bear water which is the symbol of vivification. And the nourishing cause of the Gods, is a certain intelligible union, comprehending in itself the whole perfection

---

† Here also it is requisite to adopt the same reading as before.

‡ Instead of κατα την προσηκουσαν εκεινη, it seems requisite to read κατα την προσηκουσαν αξιαν ωσπερ εκεινη, as in the translation.

of the Gods, and filling the Gods with acme and power, in order that they may bestow a providential attention to secondary natures, and may possess an immutable intellectual perception of such natures as are first. Above however, the Gods participate of these uniformly; but in a divided manner in their progressions.

With respect to the nutriment likewise, one kind is called by Plato ambrosia, but the other nectar. "For the charioteer," says he, "stopping the horses at the manger, places before them ambrosia, and afterwards gives them nectar to drink." The charioteer therefore, being nourished with intelligibles, unically participates of the perfection which is imparted through illumination by the Gods. But the horses participate of this divisibly; first indeed of ambrosia, and afterwards of nectar. For it is necessary that from ambrosia, they should stably and undeviatingly abide in more excellent natures; but that through nectar they should immutably provide for secondary natures. For they say that ambrosia is solid, but nectar liquid nutriment; which Plato also indicates when he says that the charioteer places before the horses ambrosia and afterwards gives them nectar to drink. Hence the nutriment of nectar manifests the unrestrained and indissoluble nature of providence, and its proceeding to all things in an unpolluted manner. But the nutriment of ambrosia manifests stability, and a firm settlement in more excellent natures. From both these however, it is evident that the Gods both abide and proceed to all things, and that neither their undeviating nature, and which is without conversion to subordinate beings, is unprolific, nor their prolific power and progression is unstable; but abiding they proceed, and being established in the divinities prior to themselves, they provide for secondary natures without being contaminated. Nectar and ambrosia therefore, are the perfections of the Gods, so far as they are Gods; but other things are the perfections of intellect, nature, and bodies. Hence Plato having assumed these in souls, calls the souls [which are nourished with these, Gods. For so far as they also participate of the Gods, so far they are filled with nectar and ambrosia. These however in their progressions have a bipartite division; the one indeed, being the supplier to the Gods of stable and firm perfection; but the other, of undeviating providence, of liberated administration, and of an unenvying and abundant communication of good, according to the two principles of the whole of things, which preside over a distribution of this kind. For it must be admitted that ambrosia is indeed analogous to bound, but nectar to infinity. Hence the one is as it were humid and not bounded from itself; but the other is as it were solid, and has a boundary from itself. Nectar therefore is prolific, and is perfective of the secondary presence of the Gods, and is the cause of power, of a vigour which provides for the whole of things, and of infinite and never-failing supply. But ambrosia is stable perfection, is similar to bound, is the cause to the Gods of an establishment in themselves, and is the supplier of firm and undeviating intellection. Prior to both these however, is the one fountain of perfection, and seat to all the Gods, which Plato calls nutriment, and the banquet, and delicious food, as unically perfecting indeed the divided multitude of the Gods, but converting all things to itself through divine intelligence. For δαις [the banquet] indeed manifests the divided distribution of divine nutriment; but θοινη [delicious food] the united conversion of the whole of things to it. For it is the intellectual perception of the Gods, so far as they are Gods. But nutriment connectedly contains both these powers, being the plenitude of intelligible goods, and the uniform perfection of divine self-sufficiency.

CHAPTER XVI

Concerning these things therefore, thus much may suffice as to the present theory. But it follows that we should discuss the division of the supercelestial place into three parts. For the intelligible summit of intellectuals is, as we have before observed, a triad. Immediately therefore, according to the first conception of this place, Plato unfolds its triadic nature, assuming indeed, three negatives, the uncoloured, the unfigured, and the untangible. Having likewise established three divinities in it, *viz.* science, temperance, and justice, our preceptor and leader [Syrianus] thinks fit to divide this triad into three monads, and also demonstrates this conformably to the Orphic theologies. If, however, it be requisite to discover the definite peculiarities of these three Goddesses, from what has been already laid down, we must understand, that the plain of truth, the meadow, and the nourishing cause of the Gods are posited there. To nourish therefore is the province of intelligible perfection. Hence the elevating impulse is given to the wing of the soul, and also intellectual perfection, according to the nourishment which flows from thence into the soul. But the peculiarity of the meadow, is to possess a power generative of reasons and forms; and of the causes† of the production of animals. Hence also souls are fed about the meadow; and the pabulum (νομη) is indeed nutriment, but in a divided manner.

---

† For εικων I read αιτιων.

The plain however of truth is the expansion and manifestation of intelligible light, the evolution of inward reasons, and perfection proceeding every where. This therefore† is the peculiarity of the third monad. But fecundity is the peculiarity of the second; and intelligible plenitude of the first. For all the supercelestial place is indeed illuminated with the light of truth. Hence all the natures that are contained in it are called true. And Socrates says, "that whatever soul attending on divinity has beheld any thing of reality shall be free from damage, till another period takes place." For every thing in that place is truly being and intelligible, and is full of divine union. In the first monads however [*i.e.* in the plain of truth and the meadow,] this intelligible light subsists contractedly, and is occultly established as it were in the adyta; but in the third monad [*viz.* in the nourishing cause of the Gods] it shines forth, and is co-expanded, and is co-divided with the multitude of powers. We may therefore from these things survey the differences of the three monads, in a manner conformable to the Platonic hypotheses. But if indeed science pertains to the first monad, temperance to the second, and justice to the third, from these things also the triad will be perfectly apparent. And does not science which is stable, and the uniform intelligence of wholes, and which at the same time is consubsistent with intelligibles, pertain to the power which is united to the intelligible father, and which does not proceed, nor separate its union from the deity of that father? but does not the genus of justice pertain to the power which is divided, which separates the intellectual genera, leads the intelligible multitude into order, and imparts by illumination distribution according to desert? And does not the genus of temperance pertain to the power which is the medium of both these, which is converted to itself, and possesses the common bond of this triad? For the harmonic, and a communication with the extremes according to reason, are the illustrious good of this middle power.

That we may not therefore be prolix, what has been said being sufficient to remind us of the meaning of Plato, those three deities are celebrated by us, which dividing the supercelestial place, are indeed all of them intelligible as in intellectuals, and are likewise summits, and collective of all things into one intelligible union. One of these however is so stably; another generatively; and another convertively, possessing a primary effective power in intellectuals. For one of them indeed, unites the monads of all the Gods and collects them about the

---

† *i.e.* Perfection proceeding every where.

intelligible; but another effects this about the progressions of the Gods; and another about their conversions. All of them however at the same time collect into one the whole of an hyparxis which always abides, proceeds, and returns. Hence also Plato elevates the Gods that are distributed in the world, to this one place, and converts them energizing about this as collective of the whole orders of the Gods to the participation of intelligibles. These monads, therefore, educe intelligible forms, fill them with the participation of divine union, and again recall the natures that have proceeded, and conjoin them to intelligibles. Concerning this whole triad however, what has been said may suffice.

CHAPTER XVII

It remains therefore, that we should pass to the discussion of Adrastia, Socrates indicating that she possesses her kingdom in this place. For that which defines the measures of a blameless life to souls from the vision of these intelligible goods, is certainly there allotted its first evolution into light. For the elevating cause, being secondary to the objects of desire, may be able to raise both itself and other things to the supercelestial place, through conversion. But that which defines and measures the fruits of the vision of the intelligible to souls, since it has its hyparxis in the intelligible, imparts by illumination beatitude to them from thence. It is established therefore, as I have said, in that place. But it rules over all the divine laws uniformly, from on high, as far as to the last of things. It likewise binds to the one sacred law of itself, all the sacred laws, *viz.* the intellectual, the supermundane, and the mundane. Whether therefore, there are certain Saturnian laws, as Socrates in the *Gorgias* indicates there are, when he says, "The law therefore which was in the time of Saturn is now also among the Gods;" or whether there are Jovian laws, as the Athenian guest asserts there are, when he says, "But justice follows Jupiter, which is the avenger of those that desert the divine law;" or whether there are fatal laws, as Timæus teaches there are, when he says, "That the demiurgus announced to souls the laws of fate;" - of all these the sacred law of Adrastia is connective according to one intelligible simplicity, and at the same time imparts existence of all of them, and the measures of power. And if it be requisite to relate my own opinion, the inevitable guardian power of this triad, and the immutable comprehension of order pervading every where, pre-subsist in this goddess. For these three deities not only unfold and collect all things, but they are also guardians according to the Oracle of the works of the father, and of one intelligible intellect.

This guardian power therefore, the sacred law of Adrastia indicates, which nothing is able to escape. For with respect to the laws of Fate, not only the Gods are superior to them, but also partial souls, when they live according to intellect, and give themselves up to the light of providence. And the Saturnian Gods are essentially exempt from the Jovian laws, and the connective and perfective Gods from the Saturnian laws; but all things are obedient to the sacred law of Adrastia, and all the distributions of the Gods, and all measures and guardianships subsist on account of this. By Orpheus also, she is said to guard the demiurgus of the universe, and receiving brazen drumsticks, and a drum made from the skin of a goat, to produce so loud a sound as to convert all the Gods to herself. And Socrates imitating this fabulous sound which extends a certain proclamation[†] to all things, in a similar manner produces the sacred law of Adrastia to all souls. For he says, "This is the sacred law of Adrastia, that whatever soul has perceived any thing of truth, shall be free from harm till another period," all but expressing the Orphic sound through this proclamation, and uttering this as a certain hymn of Adrastia. For in the first place indeed, he calls it θεσμος, *a sacred law*, and not νομος, *a law*, as he does the Saturnian and Jovian laws. For θεσμος is connected with deity, and pertains more to intelligibles [than to the intellectuals]; but νομος indicating intellectual distribution, is adapted to the intellectual fathers. And in the second place, he speaks of it in the singular and not in the plural number, as Timæus does of the fatal laws. In the third place therefore, he extends it to all the genera of souls, and evinces that it is the common measure of their happy and blessed life, and the true guard of those souls that are able to abide on high free from all passivity. For such is the meaning of the words, "And the soul that is able to do this always, shall always be free from harm." This sacred law therefore, comprehends all the undefiled life of divine souls, and the temporal blessedness of partial souls. And it guards the former indeed intelligibly, but measures the latter by the vision of intelligible goods. And thus much concerning Adrastia.

CHAPTER XVIII

With respect to what remains therefore, we shall summarily say, that the supercelestial place is the first triad of the intelligible and at the same time intellectual Gods, possessing three peculiarities, the unfolding into light, the collective, and the defensive.. It likewise comprehends all

---

[†] For κηρυγματι, it is requisite to read κηρυγμα τι.

these intelligibly, and in an unknown manner, conjoining indeed intellectuals to intelligibles, but calling forth the prolific powers of intelligibles, receiving in itself the plenitude of forms from the intelligible paradigms, and producing its own meadow from the fontal summit which is there. But from the one intellect it gives subsistence to the three virtues, perfects all itself by intelligible impressions, and in its ineffable bosoms receives the whole of intelligible light. At one and the same time also it abides in the occult nature of the intelligible Gods, and proceeds intelligibly from thence, shines forth to the view of intellectuals, and converts and draws upward by ineffable powers all the images of its proper union which it has disseminated in every thing. To this place likewise it is necessary that we should mystically approach, leaving in the earth all the generation-producing life, and the corporeal nature, with which on coming hither we were surrounded as with a wall, but exciting alone the summit of the soul to the participation of total truth, and the plenitude of intelligible nutriment.

CHAPTER XIX

After this intelligible and unknown triad however, which presides over all the intellectual[†] genera, let us survey the triad which connectedly contains the bond of them, intelligibly and at the same time intellectually. For it is necessary that prior to intellect and the intellectual Gods, the cause of connectedly containing should be in these Gods; and that this being established in the middle of the intelligible and intellectual order, should extend to all the divine multitudes, all the genera of beings, and all the divisions of the world. For what is it which primarily connects things? If, as some say, the nature of spirit and local motion, body itself which is connective of other things will require connexion. For every body according to its own composition is dissipable and divisible; which also the Elean guest indicating to those who make corporeal principles, says that the essence which is so much celebrated by them, is broken and dissipated. Body therefore, is not naturally adapted to be connective of other things, nor even if a power of this kind pertained to bodies, would spirit be able to afford us this power, because it is always defluous and dissipated, and diffusing itself beyond that which bounds it. But if we suppose that habits and connective forms which are divided about bodies illuminate their subjects with connexion, it is perfectly necessary that they should effect

---

[†] For νοητων, it is necessary to read νοερων.

this by being present with them; but how will these habits and forms connect themselves? For it is difficult to devise how this can be effected. For these being distributed about material bulks, and divided together with their subjects, require a boundary and connexion. But they are not naturally adapted to be bounded or connected from themselves; because they have not an essence self-begotten and self-subsistent. That however, which neither produces nor perfects itself, cannot connect itself. And moreover, every habit, and every material form is alter motive, and depends on another more ancient cause, and on this account is inseparable from subjects, not being able to verge to itself.

But if abandoning these, we should assert that souls which are incorporeal and self-begotten, are the first efficient causes of connexion, where shall we place the partible and at the same time impartible nature of souls, that which is mixed from the partible and impartible, that which participates of the genera of being, and that which is divided into harmonic reasons? For souls indeed, connect bodies and natures, because they participate of an impartible peculiarity; but they are in want of another connective nature which may impart the first principle of mixture to the genera, and of connexion to divided reasons. For the self-motive nature of souls being transitive, and extended to time, requires that which may connect its one life, and may render it total and indivisible. For the whole which is connective of parts, exists prior to parts; since the whole which consists of parts receives connexion introduced from something different from itself. But if proceeding with the reasoning power beyond souls, we survey intellect, whether the intellect which is participated, or if you are willing, that which is imparticipable and divine, and in short, if we survey at once the intellectual genus of the Gods, if this is primarily connective of beings, we shall find also in this all-various multitude, divisions of genera, and as Socrates says, many and blessed visions, and discussive energies. For the separation of divine natures, and the variety of forms, present themselves to the view in intellectuals, and also fabulous sections and generative powers. How therefore, can that which connects be primarily here, where the divisive genus shines forth? And how is it possible that intellectual multitude should not refer to another more ancient cause the participation of its proper connexion? For intellectual multitude is that which is primarily connected (since it is that which is primarily divided, and that which requires connexion is divisible, but the indivisible itself is beyond the connective hyparxis), but it is not that which primarily connects. For every thing which is connected, is connected by another thing which primarily possesses the power of connexion. It is evident therefore, from what has been said, that the connective order of beings is established prior to the intellectual Gods.

The intelligible indeed, and occult hyparxis, is the supplier of union to all things, as proximately subsisting after *The One*, and being indivisible and uniform. But connexion is the contraction of multitude into impartible communion; on which account it subsists as secondary to intelligibles. For the medium which was there was intelligible, and the united primarily-efficient cause of connexion. The connective however, of intelligibles and intellectuals, imitates the unific power of intelligibles. For there the three triadic monads were the unions of wholes; one of them indeed according to transcendency; another according to the middle centre; and another according to conversion. But in the intelligible and at the same time intellectual orders, these three triads are the second after those unions, and are connascent with multitude. Hence one of these triads is collective; another is connective of multitude; and another is of a perfective nature. For that which is collected, that which is connected† and that which is perfected, is multitude. Whether, therefore it is intellectual, or supermundane, or mundane, or any other multitude, it is collected, connected, and perfected through these three triads. And when collected indeed, it is elevated to the union of intelligibles, and is firmly established in them. When it is connected, it abides impartible and undissipated in its progeny. And when it is perfected, it receives completion from its proper parts or powers.

Since however, it is necessary that beings abiding, proceeding and returning should enjoy this triple providence, there are indeed three preexistent collective monads, three connective, and three perfective monads. And we do not say this, that on account of the good of secondary natures, first natures are thus divided, and preside over so many orders and powers; but they indeed are always the primary causes of good to things subordinate, while we from inferior natures recur to the causes of wholes. The intelligible therefore, and intellectual triads, perfect things triadically, and always connect and collect them into union. But the intelligible monads generate without separation and unically, their permanencies, progressions and conversions. With respect to other things however, we have partly spoken, and shall again partly speak concerning them.

---

† For $\sigma \upsilon \nu \epsilon \chi o \nu$, it is necessary to read $\sigma \upsilon \nu \epsilon \chi o \mu \epsilon \nu o \nu$.

CHAPTER XX

Let us therefore speak at present concerning the connective triad. This then, Socrates, in the *Phædrus*, calls the celestial circulation. Because indeed, it possesses the middle centre of imparticipable life, and is that which is most vital itself of life, he calls it circulation, as comprehending circularly, and on all sides all other lives, and divine intellections. For on account of this, souls also which are elevated to it, are perfected according to intellection, and are conjoined with intelligible spectacles. The circulation of the heaven, however, is always established after the same manner. For it is an eternal, whole, one, and united intelligence. But the circulation of souls is effected through time, subsists in a more partial manner, and is not an at-once-collected comprehension of intelligibles. Souls, therefore, are carried round in a circle, and are restored to their pristine state, the celestial circulation always remaining the same. Because, however, it gives completion to the bond of the intelligible and intellectual Gods, and connects all the orders in their abiding, proceeding, and returning, Socrates calls it celestial. For Timæus says, that this [sensible] heaven also, compresses on all sides the elements that are under it, and that on this account, no place is left for a vacuum. As, therefore, the apparent heaven is connective of all things that are under it, and is the cause of continuity, coherence and sympathy, (for the intervention of a vacuum would interrupt the continuity of things, and the subversion of this continuity would destroy the sympathy of bodies) thus also that intellectual heaven, binds all the multitudes of beings into an impartible communion, illuminating each with an appropriate portion of connexion. For intellect participates of the connective cause in one way, the nature of soul in another, and a corporeal state of being in another. For through the highest participation of connexion, intellect is impartible; but through second measures of participation, soul is partible and impartible, according to one mixture; and through an ultimate diminution, bodies possessing a partible hypostasis, at the same time remain connected, and do not in consequence of being dissipated perish, but enjoy their own division and imbecility. The whole of the connective triad therefore, is denominated heaven according to the hyparxes of itself; but the breadth of life which is spread under it is called circulation. For in things apparent to sense, the period of the heavens is motion, and is as it were the life of body.

CHAPTER XXI

If however it be requisite to discover the triadic nature of it from what has been laid down, we must employ the mode of analogy. Since therefore Plato himself calls the back of the heaven one thing, and its profundity another, it is evident that the celestial arch is the third thing; for the arch which is under this, he directly calls subcelestial. But as we say that the supercelestial place is established above the back of the heaven, so likewise we must grant that the subcelestial is different from the celestial arch. For the heaven is bounded, supernally indeed by the back, but beneath by the arch. And it is comprehended indeed by the supercelestial place, but it comprehends the subcelestial arch. It is evident therefore from these things, that the heaven presents itself to our view as triadic, according to its back indeed, connectedly containing all things in one simplicity; but according to its arch bounding the whole triad; and according to its profundity, itself proceeding into itself, and constituting the middle breadth of connexion and coherence. The back however, of the whole celestial order, is an intelligible deity, being perhaps allotted from hence this appellation. But it is intelligible as in the connective triad, externally compressing, and connectedly comprehending all the kingdom of the heaven. It likewise imparts to all the Gods by illumination a uniform and simple comprehension of secondary natures, and is supernally filled with intelligible union. Hence also, divine souls being led through all the celestial profundity, stand indeed on the back of the heaven, but the circulation carries them round as they stand; and thus they survey what is called the supercelestial place. The station therefore, is the establishment of souls in the intelligible watch tower of the heaven, extending to souls sameness, undefiled power, and undeviating intellection. But the circumduction is the participation of a life full of vigour, and the most acute energy. And the common presence of both these, comprehends the prolific energy, the quiet motion, and the stable intellection of intelligibles. But the celestial profundity, is the one continuity of the whole triad, and the middle deity which conjoins the whole[†] celestial order, proceeding indeed from the intelligible comprehension, but ending in the celestial arch, which defines the boundary of the whole of the heaven. There is therefore, one union and connexion of all this triad, and an indissoluble progression from the back as far as to the arch, through this middle deity which is connascent with both the extremes, and which unfolds

---

[†] For των ολων it is necessary to read την ολην.

indeed the connective multitude, but on each side is bounded by the extremes; one of which comprehends it supernally, but the other from beneath bounds its progression.

The celestial arch therefore remains, which is the boundary beneath of the triad, and this is also the case with the intellect which is in it, being filled indeed by life, but united by the intelligible, and converting all the triad to its principle. For the arch also is similar to the back of the heaven, though according to interval it is less. Through subjection therefore it is diminished; but through similitude it is converted to the celestial summit. And this is the celestial intellect which is the proximate *Synocheus*[†] of the subcelestial arch. Hence each[‡] arch is called the intellectual boundary of the intelligible and intellectual Gods. The whole connective triad therefore, is allotted such a division as this; the back (το νωτον) according to the intelligible (κατα το νοητον); the profundity according to life; and the arch according to intellect. But the whole of it is one and continued, because that which connects all other things, ought much more to be connective of itself. For each peculiarity of the Gods begins its energy from itself; the peculiarity indeed, which is collective, fixing itself collectively in the highest union; that which is convertive of wholes, converting itself to the principle; and that which is undefiled preserving itself prior to other things pure from matter. Hence the connective peculiarity also prior to its participants, connects itself intelligibly and intellectually, and through this connexion the nature of the heaven is asserted to be one and continued. For all the triad converges to itself, and preserves its proper wholeness united, and most similar to itself according to nature. And the arch indeed, proximately connects all intellectuals, and compresses them on all sides. But prior to this, the celestial profundity itself, which also comprehends the arch, binds together the whole orders. And prior to these, the celestial back uniformly comprehends according to one ambit of simplicity, all the celestial kingdom itself, and all things that are contained under it, and binds them to themselves, by connective power and hyparxis. For in the things also that are apparent to sense, the concave circumference of the heavens, proximately compresses the elements, and does not suffer them in their indefinite motions on all sides, to be dissipated and blown away. And still prior to these, the celestial bulk strongly compresses and impels all things to the middle,

---

[†] *i.e.* That which connectedly contains.

[‡] For εκατερον I read εκατερα, in order that it may agree with αψις.

and leaves no void place. But there is one comprehension of all these, *viz.* the back of the heavens, which is the cause to the heavens of similitude, and to the elements of contact with the heavens. For the smooth and equable nature of the back of the heavens as Timæus says, makes the whole of heaven similar to itself; and always the natures which comprehend are connective of the natures that are comprehended. It is necessary therefore from things that are apparent, to transfer the similitude to the father of the intellectual Gods, Heaven, and to survey how he is both one and triple, supernally indeed, and beneath, possessing the intelligible and intellect; but according to the middle possessing life, which being the cause of progressions and intervals, and generative powers, we have properly arranged according to interval under the celestial profundity;[†] since Plato himself also calls the summit the back. "For those," says he, "that are called immortals, when proceeding beyond the heaven they arrive at the summit, stand on the back of the heaven." He calls therefore, the summit of the celestial order, and beyond, the back of the heaven; which things are in a remarkable manner the prerogatives of the first of the Synoches. For connectedly containing all things in the one summit of his hyparxis, according to the Oracle, he wholly exists beyond, and is united to the supercelestial place, and to the ineffable power of it, being enclosed on all sides by it, and shutting himself in the uniform comprehension of intelligibles. For what difference is there between saying that the first of the Synoches is shut in the intelligible place of survey, and evincing that it is proximately comprehended by the supercelestial place, which was intelligible, but expanded in intellectuals? If however, that which is beyond is the first, the summit is evidently co-arranged with the rest, and is exempt from them. But if the first is a thing of this kind, being established according to the intelligible summit, and imparting by illumination to the other Gods, contact with the intelligible, and with the paternal port, it is indeed necessary that there should be a middle and an extremity, the one according to the celestial profundity, but the other according to the termination of the whole circulation. If however the circulation of the whole of the heaven is one and continued, the peculiarity of this order must be assigned as the cause of this. For being connective of the whole orders of the Gods, and prior to other things of itself, and being as it were the centre and bond of the divine genera, it in the first place binds and connects itself, and extends itself to one life. The heaven therefore is one and at the same time triple, and

---

[†] *Viz.* as forming the celestial profundity.

proceeds into three monads, being both unapparent and apparent and that which is between these, and imitating the intelligible Gods who subside into intelligible triads.

CHAPTER XXII

If you are willing however from what is written in the *Cratylus*, to see the peculiarity of this order, in the first place, let this be considered by you as an argument of the *Synoche* established in the middle, that a twofold habitude of it is delivered, one, towards intelligibles, but the other towards intellectuals. For it is said to see the things above, and to generate a pure intellect. Hence, of intelligibles it is the intelligence, but of intellectuals the intelligible. For the cause of intellect subsists prior to an intellectual cause, and that which is at once both these, especially gives completion to the middle order of intelligibles and intellectuals. For the collective deity, perceiving intelligibles, or rather being united to them, does not primarily give subsistence to a divine intellect. And the perfective deity, producing together with the middle divinity intellectuals, proximately perceives intellectually the celestial order, and not the intelligibles prior to the heaven. But the middle divinity alone, occupying the intelligible and intellectual centre, equally indeed extends to both, but perceiving intelligibles intellectually, it is the cause of intellectuals intelligibly. Since however, habitude to its causes precedes the power† in it which is generative of intellectuals, Socrates beginning from this habitude, delivers also a second power as suspended from it. But sight directed to things above is very properly assigned the appellation of *celestial,* as *seeing the things above.* This therefore, perfectly defines for us a habitude more ancient than the connectedly-containing order, jointly assuming it to be intellectual as with reference to intelligibles, and sight as with reference to the objects of sight, though it intellectually perceives itself, and is intelligible in itself. But the intelligible of it, as with reference to that which is primarily intelligible, is allotted an intellectual order. What follows however, unfolds the habitude of this middle to intellectuals. (For Socrates adds,) "Whence also, O Hermogenes, those who are conversant with things on high say that Heaven generates a pure intellect, and that this name is properly assigned to it." The order therefore, of the Heaven is expanded as a middle in the middle intellectual and intelligible Gods, comprehending at once the intelligible and intellectual in one impartible connexion,

---

† For δυναμεων it is necessary to read δυναμεως.

subsisting similarly with respect to each of these, and being equally distant from the first intellectuals, and the unical intelligibles. Hence it is said to perceive intellectually the things above, and thus to produce (a pure) intellect.

Assuming this therefore, in the first place from what has been laid down, in the next place we should attend to this, that the celestial order being triple, and the whole of it intellectually perceiving intelligibles, and producing intellectuals, the first monad indeed in an eminent manner intellectually perceives intelligibles. For it mingles itself with intelligibles, knows intelligible intellect, is united to the natures prior to itself, and is impartible as in impartibles, super-expanding itself towards intelligible simplicity. But the third monad is especially generative of intellectuals; since it is the intellect of the whole connective triad. And with the Orphic theologists also, heaven the father of Saturn is the third. But the middle monad produces together with the third the intellectual order of the Gods; but is conjoined together with the first to intelligibles, and is filled indeed with intelligible union from the first, but fills the third[†] with prolific powers. Do you not see therefore, how Plato through the peculiarity of the extremes, unfolds to us the whole celestial order? Conjoining indeed, the intelligible hyparxis of it to intelligibles; but its intellectual hyparxis to intellectuals; and affording us the means of collecting its hyparxis which is the middle of both these, and which proceeds according to a common peculiarity. For if you likewise wish to assume this from what has been said, the celestial light is conjoined to the light of intelligibles. For sight is nothing else than light. The middle order therefore, by its own light, and by the divine summit of itself is conjoined to the first natures; but by an intellectual nature, and the boundary of the whole triad, it generates intellect, and all the unpolluted deity of intellectuals. For it does not produce intellect by itself, but in conjunction with purity. For this Socrates himself asserts: "Whence also, they say, that a pure intellect is generated by it." Hence the celestial order is the first-efficient cause of the intellectual hyparxis, and of undefiled power. If however it is necessary that purity should not be inherent in intellect from accident, it is the deity of those beings that are exempt from secondary natures, and is the supplier of immutable power, which the mighty Heaven producing in conjunction with intellect, is at the same time the efficient cause of the Gods who are the sources of purity, and of the intellectual fathers. These

---

[†] For πρωτην it is necessary to read τριτην.

indications therefore of the truth concerning the connective Gods, may also be assumed from the *Cratylus*.

CHAPTER XXIII

It remains therefore that in conformity to what is written in the *Phædrus*, we should survey the subcelestial arch, and the peculiarity of the Gods that are there. Before however we begin the doctrine concerning it, I wish to premise thus much, that some of the most celebrated of the interpreters prior to us, conceiving that this subcelestial arch is a divine order arranged under the heaven, have thought fit to rank it immediately after the first God, calling the first God Heaven. But others have arranged both the heaven, and the subcelestial arch in the breadth of intelligibles. For the Asinæan philosopher indeed [Theodorus] being persuaded by Plotinus, calls that which proximately proceeds from the ineffable, the subcelestial arch, as in his treatise concerning names he philosophizes about these things. But the great Iamblichus conceiving the mighty heaven to be a certain order of the intelligible Gods, (and in one place he considers it to be the same with the demiurgus,) asserts that the order proximately established under the heaven, and as it were begirding it, is the subcelestial arch. And these things he has written in his Commentaries on the *Phædrus*. Let no one therefore think that we make any innovation concerning the theology of this order, and that we are the first who divide the subcelestial arch from the heaven; but that we are principally persuaded by Plato, who distinguishes these three orders, the supercelestial place, the celestial circulation, and the subcelestial arch; and that after Plato, we are persuaded by those who investigate his theory in a divinely-inspired manner, *viz*. by Iamblichus and Theodorus. For why is it necessary to speak of our leader [Syrianus,] who was truly a Bacchus, [*i.e.* one agitated with divine fury,] and who in a remarkable manner was full of deity about Plato, and caused as far as to us the admirable nature of the Platonic theory, and the astonishment with which it is attended, to shine forth?

He therefore in his treatise on the concord [of Orpheus, Pythagoras, and Plato, has most perfectly unfolded the peculiarity of this order, the subcelestial arch.] The two above-mentioned wise men, however, differ very much from each other in their theory. For Theodorus, in calling the first cause Heaven, does not any longer permit Heaven to be sight perceiving the things above, as Socrates in the *Cratylus* etymologizes it to be. For the first God neither sees, nor is sight, nor is inferior to any thing. Neither therefore does Theodorus admit this explanation of the name, nor does he celebrate the supercelestial place, as Socrates does under the influence of divine inspiration. For there is neither any place, not intelligible of *The One*, nor any multitude of forms, nor does the genus of souls ascend beyond the first God; since there is not any thing beyond him. But the divine Iamblichus, as he supposes that Heaven subsists indefinitely after the first cause, and as he has not delivered the peculiarity of its hyparxis, he is indeed pure from the above-mentioned doubts, but he should teach us what the celestial order is, how it subsists, and what genus of Gods prior to the demiurgus gives completion to it. He however who has perfected every thing [on this subject,] and has confirmed all that he has said by invincible arguments, is our preceptor [Syrianus,] who has surveyed all the orders between the first God, and the kingdom of the heaven, and who has intellectually beheld the peculiarity of this order, and has delivered to us his mystics the accurate truth concerning it. In this way therefore, our fathers and grandfathers differ from each other; but all of them in common distinguish the subcelestial arch from the celestial circulation.

CHAPTER XXIV

This therefore must also be supposed by us, and likewise in addition to this, that this order of Gods (the subcelestial arch,) is proximately arranged under the heaven. Hence, since the heaven being one and triple, is allotted the connective order, but the supercelestial place is allotted the highest order of the intelligible and at the same time intellectual Gods, it is undoubtedly necessary that the subcelestial arch should terminate the middle progression of the Gods, should close this whole order, and convert it to its principle, and that it should receive an order which is secondary indeed to the heaven, but which it convolves to the highest union, and should be connascently conjoined with the middle genera, but exist prior to intellectuals. For these indeed separate their kingdom from the celestial power; but the subcelestial arch is united to the heaven, and is comprehended by the celestial order. Whence also it is denominated subcelestial. As it is conjoined therefore, to the celestial circulation, and subsists proximately from it, it converts all secondary natures to intelligibles, and perfects them according to the intellectual place of survey. For since the intellectual Gods are generated according to conversion, and are convolved to themselves according to one spherical union, it is necessary that the perfective empire should be proximately established above them.

Hence, I am led to wonder at those who are ignorant of this divine order, and do not maintain the whole fountain of perfection; but some of them betake themselves to *entelechias*, of whom we admit thus much alone, that they also conjoin the perfect with the form of connexion. They are ignorant therefore, of the perfection which is separate from subjects, willingly embrace the resemblances of true perfections, and are conversant with these. Others again assign soul as the cause of perfection, who are ignorant that they do not vindicate to themselves a perfection pre-existing in eternity, and who begin from the life which energizes according to time, and possesses its perfection in periods. It is necessary, however, that a perfection the whole of which subsists at once, should be prior to that which is divided, and that stable perfection should be prior to that which is moved. For the motion itself which is according to time, is indigent of end, and of the desirable, and is evolved about it according to parts. In the third place, after these, others recur to intellect, and suppose the first perfection to be intellectual. For intellect indeed, is energy and intellectual perfection; but it aspires after divine perfection, subsists about it, and is converted to itself through it. It is necessary therefore, that the cause of conversion should exist prior to the intellectual genera which are converted to divine perfection, and that the leader of the perfection which is one, should be expanded above the natures which are perfected.

Deservedly therefore, does the subcelestial arch prior to all intellectual natures, pre-establish an order of Gods convertive and perfective of all the secondary divine genera. And on this account, Plato elevates the Gods and dæmons that follow Jupiter, to this arch, and through this to the heaven, and the supercelestial place. For when they proceed to the banquet, and delicious food, they ascend to the subcelestial arch. Hence through this they are perfected, participate of the circulation of the heaven, and are extended to the intelligible. For the intelligible is that which nourishes and fills all things. The perfective therefore is established under the connective order. And it perfects indeed all the natures that ascend to the intelligible, dilates souls to the reception of divine goods, and illuminates intellectual light. But comprehending in the bosoms of itself, the second genera of the Gods, it establishes all things in the connective circulation of wholes.

Through these things therefore, Socrates also shortly after says, that the souls that are elevated together with the twelve Gods, to intelligible beauty, are initiated [*viz.* rendered perfect] in the most blessed of the mysteries, and through this initiation, receive the mysteries with a pure soul, and become established in, and spectators of things ineffable.

Hence the initiation of the Gods is there; the first mysteries are there. Nor is it at all wonderful, if Plato also tolerates us in calling the Gods [of this order] *Teletarchs*, since, he says, that the souls that are there are *initiated*, the Gods themselves indeed initiating them. But how is it possible otherwise to denominate those who are the primary sources of *telete* or *initiation* than *Teletarchs*. For I indeed, perceiving so great an energy even as far as to the names themselves, do not see how they can be called differently. Initiation however, being one and triple, (for the perfective are co-divided with the connective Gods, Plato calls the one union of it the subcelestial arch, in the same manner as he calls the connective order Heaven. But the depth which is in it is indicated by his admitting that there is in it an extreme subjection, and a steep path to the summit of the arch. As therefore, in the order prior to this, we thought it proper to arrange the intelligible according to the summit, the vital according to the profundity, and the intellectual according to the extremity, which defines the whole celestial circulation, so likewise in this perfective order, we must consider the intelligible of the arch as its summit, denominating it after the same manner as the back of the heaven, because these are co-ordinate to each other; but we must consider the profundity as co-ordinate to life, through which souls proceed to the summit; and the extremity which closes the whole arch, as co-ordinate to intellect.

CHAPTER XXV

This whole order however, which is united to the order prior to it, we must analogously divide. For the perfective Gods are spread under all the connective triad. And one of these indeed, is the supplier to the Gods of stable[†] perfection, establishing all the Gods in, and uniting them to themselves. But another is the primary source of a perfection generative of wholes, exciting things which precede according to essence, to the providence of secondary natures. And a third is the leader of conversion to causes, convolving every thing which has proceeded, to its proper principle. For through this triad every thing which is perfect is self-sufficient, and subsists in itself; every thing which generates, is perfect, and generates full of vigour; and every thing which aspires after its proper principle, is conjoined to it, through its own perfection. Whether therefore, you assume the power of nature which is perfective of things that are generated, or the perfect number of the restitutions of

---

[†] For γονιμον it is necessary to read μονιμον.

the soul to its pristine state, or the perfection of intellect which is established according to energy in one, all these are suspended from the one perfection of the Gods, and being referred to it, some are allotted a greater, but others a less portion of a perfect hyparxis; and every perfection proceeds from thence. But in short, perfection is triple; one indeed being prior to parts, such as is the perfection of the Gods. For this has its subsistence in unity, pre-existing self-perfectly, prior to all multitude. For such indeed is *The One* of the Gods, not being such as *The One* of souls, or of bodies; since these indeed are in a kindred manner conjoined with multitude, and are co-mingled with essences. But the unities of the Gods are self-perfect, and subsist prior to essences, generating multitudes, and not being generated together with them. But another perfection is that which consists of parts, and which derives its completion through parts, such as is the perfection of the world; for it possesses the all-perfect from its plenitudes. And a third other perfection, is that which is in parts. But thus also each part of the world is perfect. For as this universe is a whole consisting of wholes, so likewise it is perfect from the perfect parts that are in it, according to Timæus. And in short, perfection is divided after the same manner as wholeness; for, as Timæus says, they are conjoined with each other.

Hence also the perfective genus is connascent with the connective, and the perfective monad is arranged under all the connective genera. And as the wholeness of the heaven which connectedly contains parts is triple, so likewise perfection is triple. And if it be requisite to deliver my own opinion, all the perfections are derived from all the leaders; but the perfection which is prior to parts, pertains in a greater degree to the first leader; that which consists of parts, to the middle; and that which is in a part, to the third leader. But prior to this triad, is the intelligible triad, which is uniform perfection, and an all-perfect hyparxis, and which Timæus also denominates perfect according to all things. There, however, the three perfections pre-existed unitedly, or rather, there was one fountain of every perfection. As therefore the connective† triad, is the evolution of the intelligible connexion, and the collective triad of the unific, and that which is the first in intelligibles, so likewise the perfective triad is the image of the all-perfect triad. For the intelligible and intellectual proceed analogous to the intelligible triads. Perfection therefore is triple, prior to parts, from parts, in a part. According to another mode also, perfection is stable, generative, convertive. And according to another conception, there is one perfection of intellectual

---

† For εκεινη it is necessary to read συνεκτικη.

and impartible essences, another of psychical essences, and another of the natures which are divisible about bodies. Very properly therefore, there are three leaders of perfection prior to the intellectual Gods, who constitute one order under the celestial circulation, who elevate through themselves all secondary natures to the intelligible, perfect them by intelligible light, convert and conjoin them to the kingdom of the heaven, impart an unsluggish energy to the natures that are perfected, and are the guardians of their undefiled perfection.

CHAPTER XXVI

Such are the conceptions which may be assumed from Plato concerning the third triad of the intelligible, and at the same time intellectual orders, which at one time he denominates the subcelestial arch, possessing a summit, middle, and extremity, but at another a blessed mystery, and of all mysteries the most ancient and august, through which he elevates souls and conjoins them to the mystic plenitude of intelligibles. For this triad opens the celestial paths, being established under the celestial circulation, and exhibits the self-splendid appearances of the Gods, which are both entire and firm, and expand to the mystic inspection of intelligible spectacles, as Socrates says in the *Phædrus*. For *telete* precedes *muesis*, and *muesis*, *epopteia*. Once we are initiated [*teleioumetha*] in ascending, by the perfective Gods. But we view with closed eyes [*i.e.* with the pure soul itself, *muoumetha*] entire and stable appearances, through the connective Gods, with whom there is the intellectual wholeness, and the firm establishment of souls. And we become fixed in, and spectators of [*epopteuomen*] the intelligible watch tower, through the Gods who are the collectors of wholes. We speak indeed of all these things as with reference to the intelligible, but we obtain a different thing according to a different order. For the perfective Gods initiate us in the intelligible through themselves. And the collective monads are through themselves the leaders of the inspection of intelligibles. And there are indeed many steps of ascent, but all of them extend to the paternal port, and the paternal initiation, in which may the teletarchs, who are the leaders of all good, likewise establish us, illuminating us not by words, but by deeds. May they also think us worthy of being filled with intelligible beauty under the mighty Jupiter, and perfectly free us from those evils about generation with which we are now surrounded as with a wall. May they likewise impart to us by illumination this most beautiful fruit of the present theory, which, following the divine Plato, we have sufficiently delivered to those who love the contemplation of truth.

CHAPTER XXVII

Let us now therefore again follow Parmenides in another way, who after the intelligible triads generates the intelligible, and at the same time, intellectual orders, and unfolds the continued progression of divine natures, through successive conclusions. For the connexion of the words, and their dependence on each other, imitates the indissoluble order of things, which always conjoins middles to extremes, and proceeds through middle genera to the last progressions of beings. This therefore we must survey prior to the several intellectual conceptions, how the intelligible, and at the same time, intellectual triads, proceed analogous to the intelligible triads, that we may comprehend by a reasoning process the well-arranged order of things. There were three intelligible triads therefore, *viz.* the one being, whole, and infinite multitude. And three intelligible, and at the same time, intellectual triads, have also presented themselves to our view, *viz.* number, whole, and the perfect. Hence from the one being, number is derived; from the intelligible whole, the whole that is in these; and from infinite multitude, the perfect. For the infinite which is there was all-powerful, and all-perfect, comprehending indeed all things, but being itself incomprehensible. To the all-powerful therefore and all-perfect, the perfect is analogous, possessing a perfection which is intellectual, and secondary to the first effective and intelligible perfection. The whole also which is both intelligible and intellectual is allied to the intelligible whole, but it differs from it, so far as the latter possesses wholeness according to the one union of the one being; but *The One* of the former appears to be itself by itself a whole, consisting of unical parts, and being appears to consist of many beings. These wholenesses therefore, being divided, differ from the wholeness which precedes according to union and is intelligible. For the wholenesses of this whole are parts of the intelligible wholeness.

In the third place therefore, we must consider number as analogous to the one being. For the one being is there indeed occultly, intelligibly, and paternally; but here in conjunction with difference it generates number, which constitutes the separation of forms and reasons.† For difference itself first shines forth in this order, being power indeed, and

---

† For λογον it is necessary to read λογων.

the duad in intelligibles; but here it is maternal, and a prolific fountain. For there power was collective of *The One*, and the one being; on which account also it was ineffable, as existing occultly in *The One* and in hyparxis. But here difference separates indeed being and *The One*. After this likewise, it multiplies *The One* proceeding generatively, and calls forth being into second and third progressions; breaking indeed being into many beings, and dividing *The One* into more partial unities. But according to each of these completing the decrements, the wholes remaining. Very properly therefore does Plato make the negations of *The One* from this. For here the many subsist, through difference which divides being and *The One*; since the whole also which is denied of *The One*, is intellectual and not intelligible. The negation therefore says that *The One* is not a whole, so that the affirmation is, *The One* is a whole. This whole however is intellectual and not intelligible. Parmenides also denies the many as follows: "*The One* is not many;" but the opposite to this is, *The One* is many. The multitude of intelligibles, however, does not make *The One* to be many, but causes the one being to be many. And in short, every intelligible is characterized by the one being. For in the intelligible being and *The One* are complicated, and are connascent with each other; and being is most unical. But when each of these proceeds into multitude, they are separated from each other, and evince a greater difference with respect to each other. Each of these also is divided into multitude through the prolific nature of difference. From these things therefore, it is evident that the intelligible and intellectual orders, being analogous to the intelligible orders, proceed in conjunction with diminution.

CHAPTER XXVIII

After this however, let us discuss each of them, beginning according to nature. First, therefore, the intelligible, and at the same time, intellectual number presents itself to our view; and which is connected with multitude. For every number is multitude. But with respect to multitude, one kind subsists unitedly, and another kind with separation. Number, however, is separate multitude; for there is difference in it. For in the intelligible there was power, and not difference, and this power generated multitude, and conjoined it to the monads. Number therefore is in continuity with intelligible multitude; and this is necessary. For the monad was there, and also the duad; since whole also was there, and was always monadic; and becoming to be two, has no cessation. Hence the monad and the duad were there, which are the first and exempt principles of numbers. And in these multitude was unitedly; since the monad which is the fountain of numbers, and the duad possess all multitude according to cause; the former paternally, but the latter maternally. And on this account intelligible multitude is not yet number, but is intelligibly established in the uniform principles, I mean the monad and the duad; generatively indeed, in the duad, but paternally in the monad. For the third God was father and mother; since if animal itself is in it, it is also necessary that the cause of the male and female should there primarily pre-exist. For these are in animals. Hence according to Timæus, and according to Parmenides, the maternal and the paternal cause are there. And in these, intelligible animals, and intelligible multitudes are comprehended. From these first principles also number together with difference proceed, and they generate the monads and the duads which are in number, and all numbers. For both the generative and the paternal subsist in these in a feminine manner.

All the monads likewise of this triad are paternal. Hence prior to other things they participate of the monadic cause, but according to the power of difference. For there indeed, I mean in the intelligible, the maternal was paternally; but here the paternal subsists maternally; just as there, the intellectual subsists intelligibly, but here the intelligible, intellectually. From that order therefore, the first number subsists proximately, but being generated analogous to the first triad of intelligibles, it also evidently proceeds from it. Hence also, Parmenides beginning his discourse about number, reminds us of the first hypothesis through which he generates the one being, asserting that *The One* participates of essence, and essence of *The One*, in consequence of *this* subsisting according to *that* triad. And this very properly. For being intelligible and intellectual, so far indeed, as it is allotted an intelligible order in intellectuals, it proceeds from the summit of intelligibles, but so far as it precedes the intellectual orders, it proceeds from the intellectual of intelligibles. In that intelligible triad, however, *The One* was of being, and being of *The One*, through the ineffable and occult union of these two, and their subsistence in each other. But in the intelligible and at the same time intellectual triad, difference presenting itself to the view, which is the image of the concealed and ineffable power in the first triad of intelligibles, and luminously exerting its own energy, separates *The One* from being, and being from *The One*, leads each into divided multitude, and thus generates total number. For number, as we have frequently said, is divided and not united multitude, and subsists from the principles according to a second progression, but is not occultly established in the principles. Hence also, it is simply different from multitude. And in intelligibles indeed, there is multitude; but in intellectuals number. For there indeed, number is according to cause; but here multitude is according to participation. For there indeed, division subsists intelligibly; but here union has an intellectual subsistence. If therefore number proceeds from these, and is allotted such an order, Parmenides very properly especially mentions these triads, asserting that *The One* participates of essence, and essence of *The One*,[†] and that through these the many become apparent. For one of these indeed, is the illustrious property of the first triad, but the other, of the third triad. And in the first triad indeed, participation[‡] was the pre-subsistence of the union of *The One* and being; but in the third triad many intelligibles present themselves to the view, Plato all but proclaiming that the most splendid of intelligibles subsists according to intelligible multitude, though multitude is there occult, and uniformly. For according to each order of divine natures, multitude is appropriately generated in the extremities.

CHAPTER XXIX

The intelligible number therefore of the intellectual genera, proceeds from these, and through these. And it possesses indeed properties incomprehensible by human reasonings, but which are divided into two first effective powers, *viz.* the power generative of wholes, and the power which collects into union all progressions. For according to the monad indeed, it collects intellectual multitude, and conjoins it to intelligibles; but according to the duad it produces multitude, and separates it according to difference. And according to the odd number indeed, it collects the many orders into indivisible union; but according to the even numbers, it prolifically produces into light all the genera of the Gods. For being established as the middle of the intelligible and intellectual Gods, and giving completion to the one bond of them, it is carried in its summit indeed, in intellectuals as in a vehicle, but being united to intelligibles, it evolves intelligible multitude, and calls forth its occult and unical nature into separation, and prolific generation. It also collects that which is intellectual into union and impartible communion. And not this only, but generating all things as far as to the last of things, according to the incomprehensible cause of the duad and the

---

[†] It is here necessary to supply καιι την ουσιαν του ενος.

[‡] Instead of ἠ μεθεξις, I read ἡ μεθεξις.

nature of the even number, it again unites the proceeding natures and convolves them according to the monad, and the sameness of the odd number. Through unity indeed, and the duad, it produces,[†] collects and binds all things intelligibly, occultly, and in an unknown manner to the intelligible, and effects this even in the last matter and the vestigies of forms which it contains. But through the even and odd number it constitutes the two co-ordinations, *viz.* the vivific and the immutable, the prolific and the effective, all the impartible genera of fabricating and animal-producing powers, those powers that preside over a partible life, or partible production, the more intellectual and singular mundane natures, and which belong to the better co-ordination, and those natures that are more irrational and multiplied, and which give completion to the subordinate series. And again, through this divided generation we may see that each of the proceeding natures, is united and at the same time multiplied, is indivisible and divided in its causes, and through diminution is separated from them. And we attribute indeed things that are more excellent and more simple to the nature of the odd number, but things that are less excellent and more various, to the nature of the even number. For every where indeed, the odd number is the leader of impartible, simple and unical goods; but the even number is the cause of divided, various, and generative progressions. And thus we may see all the orders of beings woven together according to divine number which is most ancient, intellectual, and exempt from all the dinumerated genera. For it is necessary that number should exist prior to the things that are numbered, and that prior to things which are separated there should be the cause of all separation, according to which the genera of the Gods are divided, and are distinguished in an orderly manner by appropriate numbers.

If therefore in intellectuals there are divisions, contacts, and separations of the proceeding natures, and likewise communications of co-ordinate natures, it is necessary that number should be prior to intellectuals, which divides and collects all things intelligibly by the powers of itself. And if all things subsist occultly, intelligibly, in an unknown manner and exemptly in this summit,[‡] there is a number of them, and a peculiarity unical and without separation. Number therefore subsists according to the middle bond of intelligibles and intellectuals, being

---

[†] It appears to me that the word προαγει is wanting in the original, and I have therefore supplied it in the translation.

[‡] It is requisite to supply in this place εν τη ακροτητι ταυτη.

indeed expanded above intellectuals through intelligible goods, but subordinate to intelligibles through intellectual separations. And it is assimilated indeed to intelligibles according to the power which is collective of many things into union, but to intellectuals according to the power which is generative of the many from *The One*. But from this highest place of survey of the intellectual Gods, it constitutes the first intellectual numbers themselves which have the nature of forms, are universal, and preside over the whole of generation and production. It likewise constitutes the second numbers, which are supermundane, and vivific, and measure the Gods that are in the world. But it constitutes as the third numbers, these celestial governors of the perpetual circulations, and who convolve all the orbs according to the intellectual causes of them. And it constitutes as the last numbers those powers that in the sublunary region connect and bound the infinity and unstable nature of matter by forms, and numbers and reasons, through which both the wholes and parts of all mortal natures are variegated with proper numbers. But it every where connects the precedaneous and more perfect genera of the Gods by the odd number, but the subordinate and secondary genera, by the even number. Thus for instance, in the intellectual orders, it produces the female and the prolific according to the even number, but the male and the paternal according to the odd number. But in the supermundane orders, it characterizes similitude and the immutable according to the odd number, but dissimilitude and a progression into secondary natures, according to the even number. For thus the Athenian guest also, orders that in sacred worship odd things should be distributed to the celestial, but even to the terrestrial powers. And according to each of these genera that which is of a more ruling nature must be referred to the odd number, but that which is subordinate, to the even number.

The nature of number, therefore, pervades from on high, as far as to the last of things, adorning all things, and connecting them by appropriate forms. For how could a perfect number comprehend the period of the whole world, as the Muses in Plato assert that it does? Or how could numbers, some of which are productive of fertility, and others of sterility, comprehend the descents of souls? Or how could some of them define the ascents of souls in less, but others in greater periods, as Socrates says in the *Phædrus*, where he delivers to us restitutions consisting of three thousand and ten thousand years? Or how could time itself which is unically comprehensive of the psychical measures, proceed according to number, as Timæus says it does, unless divine number exists prior to all these, which imparts to all things a principal cause of order according to numbers? Since all things therefore subsist through numbers and forms, numbers are allotted a progression from the intellectual summit. But forms have their generation from intelligible[†] forms. For forms subsist primarily in the third triad of intelligibles. But numbers are primarily in the first triad of intellectuals; since also in the effects of these, every number indeed is form, but not every form is number.

If, however, it be requisite clearly to unfold the truth, numbers are also prior to forms. For there are indeed superessential numbers, but there are not superessential forms. And according to this reasoning every form is number, as also the Pythagoreans said. For Timæus being a Pythagorean, not only asserts that there are intelligible forms, but also intelligible numbers; for he says that the intelligible forms are four. There however, number is intelligibly, and monadically according to cause. For intelligible animal is a monad, occultly containing the whole of number. But in the summit of intellectuals, number subsists separately, evolving the number which pre-exists in the monad according to cause and uniformly. For there is a difference, I think, between saying multitude in its cause, and multitude from its cause, and between saying united, and saying separated multitude. And the one indeed is prior to number, but the other is number. So that according to Timæus there are intelligible numbers together with forms, and prior to forms. And according to Parmenides, number is after multitude. For Timæus calls uniform and occult multitude the number of forms. But since number is primarily in the Gods, but forms participate of the divine unities, he denominates the first ideas four. For monad and triad, were primarily indeed in the Gods themselves, but secondarily in intellectuals; and superessentially indeed in the former, but formally in the latter. In intelligibles therefore, multitude was unically; but in intellectuals it subsists separately. But where there is separation there also there is number, as we have frequently observed. Hence likewise all the genera of the Gods are from hence generated. And they are divided, the paternal indeed and generative, among intelligibles and intellectuals; but the demiurgic and vivific, among intellectuals. And the genera indeed, that bind through similitude, are divided among supermundane natures; but those that are both exempt and distributed, are divided among the liberated Gods. And the celestial[‡] and sublunary genera, are divided

---

[†] For νοερων, it is necessary to read νοητων.

[‡] For υπουρανια, it seems to be necessary that we should read ουρανια.

among the mundane Gods. And in short, all the co-ordinations of beings receive their distinction and separation from this order. From these things therefore, it is evident what the peculiarities are which intelligible and at the same time intellectual number possesses, and of what it is the cause to the Gods.

CHAPTER XXX

In the next place, we must likewise assert that the first number[†] is of a feminine nature. For in this, difference first shines forth, separating *The One* from being, and dividing *The One* into many unities, and being into many beings. What therefore is the difference which is the cause of these things to the Gods? For if we should call it a genus of being, in the first place indeed, how is it prior to being? For separating being and *The One*, it is arranged between both of them. But existing as a middle, it calls forth indeed *The One* into generations, but it fills being with generative cause. If therefore, it is prior to being, how will it be one certain genus of being? And in the second place, after this, *the different* which is a genus of being, is every where essential, and is by no means inherent in superessential natures. But difference itself is primarily present with the unities themselves, and separates and produces many unities from one. How therefore, can superessential difference ever come to be the same with the difference which gives completion to essences?

In the third place, *that different* [which is a genus of being,] presents itself to the view in intellectuals, according to the demiurgic order. But difference itself is the intelligible summit of intellectuals. And the former indeed, subsists together with sameness; but the latter has by itself a subsistence in the intelligibles of intellectuals. To which also may be added, that in what follows, Plato as he proceeds makes mention of difference, and generates it in conjunction with sameness. How therefore, does he effect the same conclusion twice? For he does not employ such a repetition as this in any one of the other conclusions. For whole, which he seems to assume twice, is not the same whole, *viz.* the intellectual is not the same with the intelligible; but these, as we have said, differ from each other. For how could he unfold to us the different progressions of divine natures, if he collected the same conclusions? According to all these conceptions, therefore, we must

---

[†] In the original αριθμος is omitted.

separate the difference which is generative of numbers from the genus of beings.

But if difference itself is not the nature of the different, but a power generative of beings, it will be collective of being and *The One*. For every where power is allotted an hyparxis of this kind. For through power *The One* participates of being, and being of *The One*. Power therefore was the cause, not of division, but of communion, of contact without separation, and of the habitude of *The One* to being, and of being to *The One*. Hence it is necessary that it should neither be arranged according to intelligible power, not according to the intellectual difference of beings; but that being the middle of both, it should subsist analogous to intelligible power, but should generate in the extremities of intellectuals the portion of *the different*. What else therefore is it than the feminine nature of the Gods? Hence also it imitates intelligible power, and is prolific of many unities, and of many beings. And how could it otherwise separate number from itself, and the forms and powers of number, unless it was the cause of the divine progressions in a feminine manner. Multitude therefore is paternally in intelligibles, but maternally in intellectuals. Hence, in the former indeed, it subsists monadically, but in the latter according to number. Very properly therefore, in the second genera of the Gods also, union is derived from the male, but separation from the female divinities. And bound indeed proceeds from the males, but infinity from the females. For the male is analogous to bound, but the female to infinity. The female, however, differs from infinite power, so far as power indeed, is united to the father, and is in him; but the female is divided from the paternal cause. For power is not only in the female divinities, but is also prior to them, since the intelligible powers are in the male divinities, according to Timæus, who says that the power of the demiurgus is the cause of the generation of perpetual natures. For [the demiurgus says to the junior Gods] "imitating my power, produce and generate animals." Power therefore, is prior to the male and the female, and is in both, and posterior to both. For it pervades through all beings, and every being participates of power, as the Elean guest says. For power is every where. But the female participates in a greater degree of its peculiarity, and the male of union according to bound. That the first number therefore, which presents itself to the view from intelligibles, is of a feminine nature, is through these things evident.

CHAPTER XXXI

It remains then, that we should speak concerning the triadic division of it, following Parmenides. These three things therefore, have appeared to us from the beginning, according to the separation of *The One* from being, *viz.* *The One*, difference, and being; difference not being the same either with *The One* or being. For though *The One* and being were in intelligibles, yet difference first subsists here. Since however power above [*i.e.* in intelligibles] was collective, but here is the separator of the extremes, there are not only three monads, but also three duads, *viz.* *The One* in conjunction with difference, difference in conjunction with being, and *The One* in conjunction with being. For difference also is the cause of a separation of this kind, not preserving the union of the one being with genuine purity. There are therefore three monads, and three duads. But these likewise may become three triads, when we begin, at one time from *The One*, at another time from being, and at another from difference. Hence this triad subsists monadically, and triadically. But this is the same thing as to assert that difference and the first feminine nature generates in itself, monads, duads, and triads. For the divided assumption, generates for us different monads; but the conjoined assumption, duads, and triads, some indeed being vanquished by *The One*, others by difference, and others by being. And thus far the first deity presents itself to the view, being prolific of the first numbers; according to *The One* indeed, of unical numbers, but according to difference of generative, and according to being, of essential numbers.

Since however, from this deity which is intelligible, that which is posterior to it proceeds, it is evidently necessary that the monad, duad, and triad, should severally have prolific power. These powers therefore, Parmenides calls once, twice, thrice. For each of these is a power which is the cause of the above-mentioned essences that produce either separately, or connectedly. For there with respect to the generations of them, some of them are entirely peculiar, but others are common to secondary natures. The progeny therefore of these are, the oddly-odd, the evenly-even and the evenly-odd.[†] And of these, the oddly-odd indeed, as we have before observed, is collective into union of the divine progressions. But the evenly-even is generative of wholes, and proceeds as far as to the last of things. The evenly-odd however, is mixed, having its subsistence from both the even and the odd. Hence we must establish the first as analogous to bound, but the second as analogous to

---

[†] το αρτιοπερισσον is omitted in the original.

power, and the third as analogous to being. And you may see, how indeed in the first order all things had a primary subsistence, *viz.* monad, duad, triad; but how in this order, all things are secondarily and subordinately. And the mixture which is the triad, subsisted there indeed in one way, but here the evenly-odd subsists in another way. For there the extremes were odd, because they were intelligible; but here the even is more abundant, and the intelligible summit only is odd. For the middle of the triad is analogous to power. And there indeed, is the monad, which has all the forms of odd numbers according to cause, and the duad is there, which is occultly all the forms of even numbers, and also the triad, which is number primarily. But here both the odd and the even number now subsist in a twofold respect, in one place in an unmingled, and in another in a mingled manner. All things therefore, are here prolifically, but there, paternally and intelligibly. But *that* monad does not proceed from intelligibles, but subsists in them in unproceeding union. Hence, after these, and from these, we may survey the whole of number subsisting according to a third progression. "For these things," says Parmenides, "pre-existing, no number will be absent." Every number therefore, is generated through these in the third monad, and both *The One* and being become many, difference separating each of them. And every part indeed of being participates of *The One*; but every unity is carried as in a vehicle in a certain portion of being. Each of these however, is multiplied, intellectually separated, divided into minute parts, and proceeds to infinity. For as in intelligibles, we attribute infinite multitude to the third triad, so here, in this triad we assign infinite number to the third part of the triad. For in short every where, the infinite is the extremity, as proceeding in an all-perfect manner, and comprehending indeed all secondary natures, but being itself participated by none of them. In the first monad therefore, there were powers, but intelligibly. In the second, there were progressions and generations, but both intelligibly and intellectually. And in the third, there was all-powerful number, unfolding the whole of itself into light; and which also Parmenides denominates infinite. It is likewise especially manifest that it is not proper to transfer this infinity to quantity. For how can there be an infinite number, since infinity is hostile to the nature of number? And how are the parts of *The One* equal to the minute parts of being? For in infinites there is not the equal. But this indeed has been thought worthy of attention by those who were prior to us.

CHAPTER XXXII

The division therefore into three, having been demonstrated by us, we shall briefly observe, that *The One* appears to be many according to this order, *The One Itself* proceeding into a multitude of unities, and being in a similar manner becoming generated in conjunction with *The One*. For those three monads are the intelligible comprehensions of all orders, and they at once preside over all the progressions from intelligibles, produce all of them in an exempt manner, and collect them to the intelligible causes. Since however, Plotinus admits that number is prior to animal itself, and says that the first being produces from itself number, and that this is established as a medium between the one being, and animal itself, but is the basis and place of beings, it is worth while to speak likewise concisely about this. For if he says that animal itself has intelligible and occult number, as comprehended in the monad, he speaks rightly, and accords with Plato. But if he says that animal itself comprehends number, now separated, or which has a multiform subsistence, and is the progeny of difference, intelligible multitude is not a thing of this kind. For there indeed, *The One* is being, and being is *The One*. Hence animal itself is according to all things perfect. But in number, *The One* is separated from being, and being from *The One*, and each of the parts is no longer an intelligible whole, as an animal itself. For that is a whole of wholes; and every where *The One* was with being in the parts of it, and animal itself was only-begotten. But number proceeded after the twofold co-ordinations, I mean the monad and duad, the odd and the even number. How therefore can we place in animal itself the first number? If however, some one should say that number exists there, it is according to cause and intelligibly. But it is intellectually separated by difference. And farther still, in addition to these things, if animal itself is surveyed by some one in the demiurgic order, and he denominates it the plenitude of forms, and the intelligible of the demiurgic intellect, it will thus have intellectual number, as being arranged near the intellectual end. But if he should call intelligible animal number, in this case, there will be separation and difference in the Gods, whom we have asserted to be established above the whole of things, according to supreme union. For all section and division originate from the intellectual Gods; since here difference proceeds, adorning things in conjunction with *The One* and being. How therefore, does the division of the unities into minute parts, or the multiform nature of beings pertain to intelligibles? And how can the multitude of all forms accord with the first animal itself? For the tetrad was there, divided by the monad and triad, a division of this kind being adapted to the third order of intelligible forms. For as the one being is a monad, but eternity is a monad and duad, (for to be is conjoined with the ever) so animal itself is a monad and triad. Since however, it comprehends in itself the cause of all number, Timæus denominates it the tetrad which is comprehensive of the four first-effective causes. For the tetrad itself pre-exists as the fountain of all the production of forms. But in intelligibles the monad, duad and triad subsist unically; but in intellectuals in a divided manner.

Difference therefore necessarily generates all these for us with separation. For every where, the first of subordinate natures have the peculiar form of the natures that exist prior to them.[†] Hence, the first multitudes proceed indeed from *The One*, but they are unical, without separation, and without number, imitating the one principle of the whole of things. Very properly therefore, does Parmenides constitute multitude in intelligibles, according to the end [of the intelligible order]; but number in intellectuals according to the beginning [of the intelligible and at the same time intellectual order.] And these are conjoined with each other. Parmenides also pre-establishes unical and intelligible multitude, as the cause of intellectual numbers. And Timæus shows that animal itself is only-begotten, because it was monadically the cause of the whole of things, and not dyadically, nor according to divine difference. That number however, is the first thing in intellectuals, we have abundantly shown.

CHAPTER XXXIII

But Parmenides begins to speak about it as follows: "Proceed therefore, and still father consider this. What? We have said that *The One* participates of essence, so far as it is being. We have said so. And on this account the one being appears to be many." But he completes his discourse about the first monad thus: "Are not three things odd, and two even? How should they not?" And about the second monad, as follows: Hence there will be the evenly-even, and the oddly-odd, and the oddly-even, and the evenly-odd." But he completes his discourse about the third and all the succeeding triad, as follows:, "The one being therefore, is not only many, but it is likewise necessary that *The One*

[†] Instead of πανταχου γαρ τα πρωτιστα των υφισταμενων, την ιδιαν εχει μορφην, it is necessary to read πανταχου γαρ τα πρωτιστα των υφειμενων, των προϋφισταμενων, την ιδιαν εχει μορφην.

which is distributed by being should be many. Entirely so." The first triad, therefore, of the intelligible, and at the same time, intellectual Gods, is through these things unfolded to us by Plato, and which possesses indeed, according to the first monad the first powers of numbers, I mean the odd and the even, and is completed through these principles which were in intelligibles occultly, *viz.* monad, duad, triad. But according to the second monad it possesses the second powers of numbers which subsist from these [*i.e.* from the first powers]. For the section of the forms of the even number, is allotted a second order. And the oddly-odd is subordinate to the first odd numbers. But according to the third monad, it possesses the more partial causes of divine numbers. Hence also, a separation into minute parts, infinity, all-perfect division, and unical and essential number are here; receiving indeed, the unical and the essential from unity and being, but the separation of number from difference. For every where difference is in the three monads, but it particularly unfolds the multitudes of numbers, according to the third monad, generates more partial Gods, and divides being in conjunction with the Gods. For neither is deity in these imparticipable, because unity is not separate from being, nor is essence destitute of deity, because neither is being deprived of *The One*.

Since however, all things are in each of the monads, but unically and intelligibly in the first, generatively, and according to the peculiarity of difference in the second, and intellectually, and according to being in the third; - this being the case, Plato when unfolding to us the first monad, very properly begins from the monad, and proceeds as far as to the triad; but when teaching about the second, he begins from evenly-even numbers, and proceeds as far as to those that are evenly-odd, both which belong to the nature of the even number. And when he adds the third monad, he begins from being, and recurs through difference to *The One*. For having shown that being participates of number, he from hence leads us round to unical number, employing the mode of conversion in the conception of this monad.

CHAPTER XXXIV

If, however, it be requisite to survey the unknown peculiarity of divine numbers, and how the first order of intelligibles and intellectuals, and number which subsists according to this order, is the most ancient of all numbers, in the first place, we should consider the infinity mentioned by Parmenides, and see whether he does not say that intelligible multitude is infinite on account of this number, in consequence of its being unknown and incomprehensible by partial conceptions. For the all-perfect, and all-powerful peculiarity of divine numbers is exempt from the comprehension of partible natures, [such as ours]. They are therefore unknown, and on this account are said to be inexplicable, and not to be investigated. For number also in the last of things, and multitude, together with the known have likewise the unknown. And we are not able to comprehend the progression of every number in consequence of being vanquished by infinity. The incomprehensibility therefore, of this power which is unknown according to a discursive energy, is comprehended according to cause, in intelligible numbers and multitudes. For there would not be a thing of this kind in the last of numbers, unless the unknown pre-existed in intelligible numbers, and unless the former were ultimate imitations of the exempt incomprehensibility of the latter.

In the second place, after this, we may also add, that unical numbers are likewise of themselves unknown. For they are more ancient than beings, more single than forms, and being generative of, exist prior to the forms which we call intelligible. But the most venerable of divine operations manifest this, since they employ numbers, as possessing an ineffable efficacy, and through these effect the greatest, and most arcane of works. And prior to these nature ineffably, according to sympathy, imparts different powers to different† things, to some solar, but to others lunar powers, and renders the productions of these concordant with numbers. For in these monadic numbers also, the forms of numbers, such as the triad, the pentad, and the heptad, are one thing, but the unions of the forms another thing. For each of these forms is both one, and multitude. Hence form is unknown according to the highest union.

If therefore, monadic number participates of a certain unknown power, much more must the first number possess this peculiarity unically exempt from the whole of things. And besides this, we may also assume the anagogic power of numbers, not only because they define the periods of the physical restitutions, circumscribing our indefinite lation by appropriate measures, perfecting us according to these measures, and conjoining us to our first causes, but because likewise, number in a remarkable manner possesses a certain power of attracting to truth, as Socrates says in the *Republic*, leading us to intelligibles from a sensible

---

† Instead of αλληλοις, I read αλλοις.

nature.† As therefore, the last number is allotted this peculiarity, what ought we to say about the first number? Is it not this, that it unfolds intelligible light, especially persuades to an establishment in intelligibles, and through its own order announces to us the uniform power of principles? If therefore, we rightly assert these things, we shall in a greater degree admire Timæus, who having placed time over the perfections of souls, and the whole world, through which it would become more similar to animal itself says, that time proceeds according to number, and by number measures the existence of total souls. And as in intellectuals, number is established above the celestial circulation, collecting and causing it to be one, thus also in sensibles Timæus says, that time being number measures the celestial periods, and comprehends in itself the first causes of the perfection of the periods. If also, Socrates in the *Republic*, in the speech of the Muses, speaks about the one and entire period of the universe, which he says a perfect number comprehends, does it not through these things appear that divine number is perfective of wholes, and restores them to their pristine state, and that it measures all periods? The power likewise of collecting things imperfect to the perfect, accedes to all things from number, which elevates souls from things apparent to those that are unapparent, illuminates the whole world with the perfection of motion, and defines to all things measures, and the order of periods. But if not only a perfect number contains the period of a divine generated‡ nature, but another second number after this is the lord of better and worse generations, as the same Socrates says, number will not only restore things to their pristine state, but will also be of a generative nature. And it is evident that these things subsist in a divided manner, according to the second and third periods of numbers; but at once, and contractedly in the first of numbers. The first number therefore, is generative, mensurative, and perfective of generated natures.

CHAPTER XXXV

The first order therefore of intelligibles and intellectuals is thus surveyed by Parmenides. But after this the order which possesses the middle place of intelligibles and intellectuals, and which a little before

---

† Instead of $\alpha\pi\alpha\gamma\omega\nu\ \eta\mu\alpha\varsigma\ \alpha\pi\sigma\ \tau\omega\nu\ \nu\sigma\eta\tau\omega\nu\ \epsilon\pi\iota\ \tau\eta\nu\ \alpha\iota\sigma\theta\eta\tau\eta\nu\ \phi\upsilon\sigma\iota\nu$, it is necessary to read $\epsilon\pi\alpha\gamma\omega\nu\ \eta\mu\alpha\varsigma\ \epsilon\pi\iota\ \tau\omega\nu\ \nu\sigma\eta\tau\omega\nu\ \alpha\pi\sigma\ \tau\eta\varsigma\ \alpha\iota\sigma\theta\eta\tau\eta\varsigma\ \phi\upsilon\sigma\epsilon\omega\varsigma$.

‡ Every perpetually circulating body is called by Plato, a divine generated nature.

we called connective, presents itself to the view. It is however denominated in a three-fold respect, *viz.* one, many, whole, parts, finite, infinite. For since the separation of unities and beings from number, extends to it, *The One* and being, which we have said difference divides, become wholes. But the things proceeding from these, are the parts of these. And wholeness indeed connectedly contains parts, but these are contained by their wholeness, in one way indeed, by *The One*, but in another by being. For there indeed, I mean in the summit of the intellectual Gods, unity was the cause of multitude, at the same time being exempt from multitude, and generative of the many. But here unity is co-arranged with multitude. Hence also it is a whole which has reference to many unities as to parts. Since however, the connective order is triple, one division of it being intelligible, another intelligible and intellectual, and another intellectual, the first monad indeed subsists according to *The One* and the many; but the second, according to whole and parts; and the third, according to the finite and the infinite. For where the first triad ends, there the second has its beginning. Hence, in the triad prior to this, Parmenides infers that *The One* is many. And in this triad, he concludes the same thing together with what remains. There however, *The One* was generative of infinites; but here *The One* is comprehensive of many, the whole of parts, and the finite of infinites. Hence, there indeed, unity is exempt from the many; but here it is co-arranged with multitude. Hence also, the first co-arrangement generates whole together with parts; but the subsistence of whole and parts produces the finite and at the same time infinite. For these are successive to each other, *viz. The One*, the whole, the finite, and the things which are as it were in an opposite arrangement to these, the many, parts, infinites. And *The One* itself is indeed the principle of the rest. But whole has now a habitude with respect to parts, and a representation of the duad, and proceeds into a co-arrangement with reference to the parts. The finite however, is now multitude, participating of bound and *The One*, and is as it were a triad. For it is neither bound alone, as the monad, nor infinite alone, as the duad, but it participates of bound, which is primarily a triad. Every thing finite therefore is a whole, but not every whole is finite. For the infinite is a whole, whether it is multitude, or magnitude. And every whole indeed, is one, but not every one is a whole. For that which is without habitude to multitude is not a whole. *The One* therefore, is beyond whole; but whole is beyond the finite.

After the same manner also, infinite parts are said to be the parts of that which is finite. For the infinite of itself has no subsistence; by which also it is evident that the infinite is not in quantity in energy,[†] but in capacity. All parts however are not infinite. For according to bound they are characterized by one of the parts. And again, parts indeed are many, but the many are not entirely parts. The many therefore, are prior to parts; and parts are prior to infinites. Hence, as the many are to *The One*, so are parts to whole, and so are infinites to the finite. And these three connectedly-containing monads, give completion to the middle order of intelligibles and intellectuals. For unity indeed, is the supplier of stable and intelligible connection to all the secondary orders. But wholeness connects the progressions of divine natures, and produces one habitude of the orderly distribution of whole. And the finite monad imparts by illumination to the conversions of second natures, connection with the natures prior to them. And one of these indeed is analogous to the one being, on which account also it is intelligible. But another is analogous to the third order, in which there was *The One*, and the duad which generates infinite multitude. Such is the connective triad, which Parmenides exhibits to us through these things. *The One* therefore, is one and many, whole and parts, finite and infinite multitude. Let no one however be disturbed that Plato calls *The One* or being infinite multitude. For he calls *The One* and being when they have proceeded and are divided, infinite in multitude. For all multitude indeed, is referred to the intelligible infinity. But divided multitude, and which has proceeded perfectly, is most signally infinite.

Since therefore, all the primary causes of intellectuals are in this triad, and all things are disseminated in its bosoms, the first Synocheus indeed, comprehends these causes as multitude, being himself an intelligible unity, and the flower as it were of the triad. But the second comprehends indeed secondarily these causes, but co-arranged and co-multiplied with them. And the third, together with all-perfect division, connects the multitude comprehended in himself. Each of them also is connective, but one as bounding, another as giving completion to a whole, and another as uniting. Plato therefore made, and makes as he proceeds his demonstrations of *The One*. For the whole theory is concerning *The One*. But it is evident that being is co-divided with *The One*. For universally, it has been before observed that every deity proceeding thence is participable, and that every portion of being participates of deity. It is necessary however, not to stop in *The One*

[†] εν τη ενεργεια is omitted in the original.

alone, but to consider the same peculiarity† as imparted to being in a secondary degree, since Plato also produces *The One Itself* by itself according to the differences of the divine orders; which occasions me to wonder at those who think that all the conclusions of the second hypothesis are concerning intellect, and do not perceive that Plato omitting being surveys *The One Itself* by itself, as proceeding and generated, and receiving different peculiarities. For how in discoursing concerning intellect could he omit being, according to which intellect has its subsistence, power, and energy. For *The One* is beyond the nature of intellect; but being gives hyparxis to intellect, and intellect is nothing else than being. This opinion however of these men may be confuted by many other arguments. But if the three connective Gods are divided after the above-mentioned manner, and the intelligible connective deity is one many, but the intelligible and at the same time intellectual deity is whole and parts, and the intellectual is finite and infinite, each of them is very properly called *much*. For each of the Synoches according to his own peculiarity is a multitude. For the first about the many, receives many Synoches of a more partial nature. The second receives these according to parts. And the third, according to infinites. If therefore, there are certain partial Gods who are allotted this peculiarity, they are comprehended in this first triad.

CHAPTER XXXVI

Moreover, it is easy for every one to see how these things accord with what is written in the *Phædrus*. For the connective one accords with the back of the heaven that comprehends these. For *The One* and the back are the same, comprehending according to one simplicity the whole circulation. But whole is the same with the profundity of the heaven, and with as it were the bulk of it. For the celestial profundity is a whole extended from the back as far as to the arch. And end is the same with the arch. This therefore, is evident beyond every thing, and each of the other conclusions, is to be referred to the same conceptions. Hence from what has been said, it may be collected, that these three things pertain in a remarkable degree to the Synoches, *viz. The One*, whole, and the end [or the finite]. For what is so able to connect multitude as *The One* which is co-arranged with it? What is so connectedly-comprehensive of parts as whole? And how is it possible that the end [or bound,] should not be the cause of binding together

---

† For αϊδιοτητος, it is necessary to read ιδιοτητος.

things which are borne along to infinity. It terminates therefore, their progression, and brings back their dispersed section to the one essence of connection. And thus much concerning the connective triad.

CHAPTER XXXVII

But the third, as they say, to the saviour, and let us also following Plato in what remains celebrate the perfective order of the Gods. Because, therefore, the end of the connective order was the finite, [or the bounded] the perfective order has extremes. For the end [or bound] is the extremity. There however indeed *The One* was said to be the finite, but here it is said to have an extremity, as receiving according to participation that which has the power of terminating many things. And there indeed, *The One* was end or bound, which also connectedly contains the infinite; but here having an extremity, it will also have a middle and beginning, and will be perfect. For that which receives its completion from all these, is perfect. Here, therefore, the perfection which consists of parts is apparent. For the consummation of the parts, produces the perfect. Moreover, because such a one as this has a middle and extremes, it will have the figure of a circumference, or it will be rectilinear, or it will be mixed [from the right and circular line]. For all these require a middle and extremes; some indeed with simplicity, but others with connexion. Three peculiarities, therefore, again present themselves to our view; the first, indeed, being that which we said was to have extremes; the second, being according to the perfect; and the third, according to figure. And there are also three perfective leaders of wholes; one indeed being intelligible; another, intelligible and intellectual; and the third, intellectual. The intelligible leader, therefore, is said to have extremes, as being directly arranged under the end of the connective Gods, and in the boundaries of himself intelligibly comprehending all the intellectual orders. But the intelligible and intellectual leader, is defined according to the perfect, comprehending in himself the beginnings, middles, and ends of beings, and giving completion to the middle bond of the whole perfective triad. And the intellectual leader proceeds according to triadic figure, being the cause of bound and divine perfection; and imparting termination to things indefinite, but intellectual perfection to things imperfect. And this triad indeed is produced according to the connective triad. For the *end* in them is the cause of the possession of the *extremity*. But it is also produced from itself. For that which has extremes, having become a whole, constitutes the perfect through end [or bound]. But the perfect comprehending beginnings, middles and ends, unfolds figure. And thus the perfective triad proceeds supernally, as far as to the last of things, pervading to all things, and perfecting both whole and partial causes.

CHAPTER XXXVIII

And do you not see how each of the triads conjoins the summit of itself with the ends placed above it? For the one many was the end of the collective and unknown triad; and the same is the beginning of the connective triad. The end of the connective triad was the finite; and this again is the beginning of the perfective triad. For to have extremes manifests that which consists of ends or bounds. And thus the whole middle order is connected with and united to itself, and is truly the bond of total orders, itself establishing an admirable communion with itself, but conjoining intellectuals to intelligibles, and convolving them to one impartible union; above indeed, having the intelligible and unknown triad, but in the middle producing the triad which is connective of progressions, and at the end, the convertive empire, through which it proximately converts the intellectual to the intelligible Gods.

For on what account does intellect look to itself, and is in itself? Is it not because it is on all sides finite or bounded, converges to itself, and convolves its appropriate energies about itself? But why is it perfect, and full of intellectual goods? Is it not because it first participates of the perfection [of the above mentioned] leaders, and subsists according to them, possessing a self-perfect essence and intellectual perception? After what manner likewise, is it said to be a sphere, both by Plato, and other theologists? Is it not because it is the first participant of figure, and is intellectually figured according to it? All conversion, therefore, all perfection, and every intellectual figure, accede to the intellectual Gods, from the perfective triad. For the intelligible leader of perfection, gives perfection to the ends and summits and hyparxes of wholes. But the intelligible and intellectual leader terminates their progressions which extend from on high as far as to the last of things. And the intellectual leader comprehends in his own perfection, the conversions of all the Gods, and bounds and perfects through figures their progressions to infinity.

CHAPTER XXXIX

Looking therefore to this division, we may be able to survey causally many things which are to be found among other theologists. For why is one of the deities of the unknown triad carried in the first of the worlds, but another in the middle breadth, and another in the extremity? It is because the first of these was uniform, but the second proceeded according to difference, and the third, according to the infinite number of beings. But why of the three connective Gods, is the first empyrean, the second etherial, and the third material? It is because the first indeed subsists according to *The One*, and connectedly contains the one world. But the second subsists according to whole, and divides the etherial world. And the third according to the finite, and rules over material infinity. But why again, are the Teletarchs co-divided with the Synoches? Because the first having extremes governs like a charioteer the wing of fire. But the middle comprehending beginnings, ends and middles, perfects ether, which is also itself triple. And the third, which comprehends according to one union, the orbicular, the rectilinear, and the mixed[†] figure, perfects unfigured and formless matter; giving form indeed (μορφωσας) to the inerratic sphere, and the first matter, by the orbicular; but to the planetary sphere, and the second matter, by the mixed figure. For the spiral is there. And it gives form to the sublunary region, and the last matter by the rectilinear. For the motions according to a right line are in this region. Hence, the first triad is uniformly the cause of the division of the worlds. But the second has a more abundant representation of section, and of progression into parts; yet does not exhibit to us the multitude of the worlds. And the third unfolds the seven worlds, and the monad together with two triads. So great is the divine conception of Plato, that from these things we may survey the causes of what after his time became apparent.

For this, indeed, from what has been said appears to be very admirable, that according to each of the triads, the middle is characteristic of the whole triad. Thus for instance, in the unknown triad, difference is established as the middle between *The One* and being. But in the connective triad whole is the characteristic, which is the middle of *The One* and the finite. And in the perfective triad, the perfect is the characteristic, which is itself established as the middle of that which has extremes, and of figure. For difference is the feminine

---

† το μικτον is omitted in the original.

itself, and the prolific nature of the Gods. And whole is itself the form of connected comprehension, binding together many parts. And the perfect is itself the good of perfection, possessing a beginning, middle and end, and conjoining the end to the beginning, according to the peculiarity of conversion. Being also nothing else than a perfect governor it is the cause of the peculiarity of these Gods subsisting every where according to the middle centres. Hence the whole order of the intelligible, and at the same time, intellectual Gods, may be surveyed as having its subsistence in the middle. For the intelligible Gods, indeed, are especially defined according to hyparxes and summits; on which account also, they are called fathers, and unical Gods. For *The One* and father are in them the same. But the intellectual Gods are defined according to ends or extremities; and on this account, all of them are denominated intellects and intellectual. The intelligible, and at the same time, intellectual Gods, however, being middles, especially present themselves to the view according to the middles of the triads.

Farther still, this also may be considered in common about all these triads, that each according to the end proceeds to infinity. For the end of the first triad is number; of the second, the infinite in multitude; and of the third, the rectilinear, which itself participates of the nature of the infinite. And of this the cause is, that each of the triads according to its extremity is carried as in a vehicle in the material worlds, and comprehends according to one cause the infinity of the natures that are generated in them. In addition, likewise, to what has been said, we may survey the order of the triads, from the ends that are in them. For the end of the first triad is number; but of the second, the finite and the infinite; and of the third, the orbicular, the mixed figure, and the rectilinear. It is evident, therefore, that the first triad is monadic; but the second dyadic; and the third triadic. And the first of these indeed is analogous to the one being; but the second to the intelligible whole; and the third, to the all-perfect whole. But that these have this order with respect to each other, has been before observed. In short, therefore, every intelligible, and at the same time intellectual triad, is according to its summit indeed conjoined to the intelligible; but according to its middle, unfolds its proper power; and according to its termination, comprehends the infinity of secondary natures. And here we shall end the doctrine concerning the intelligible and intellectual Gods.

BOOK V

CHAPTER I

In the next place, let us survey another order of Gods, which is called intellectual, being indeed conjoined to the orders prior to it, but terminating the total progressions of the Gods, converting them to their principle, and producing one circle of the primarily-efficient and all-perfect orders. Let us also extend the intellect that is in us to the imparticipable and divine intellect, and distinguish the orders and diminutions of essence that are in it, according to the narration of Plato.

This intellectual hypostasis therefore of the Gods, is suspended indeed from more ancient causes, and is filled from them with total goodness and self-sufficiency. But after these causes, it establishes an illustrious empire over all secondary natures, binding to its dominion all the partial progressions of the Gods. And it is denominated indeed intellectual, because it generates an impartible and divine intellect. But it is filled from intelligibles, not as from those intelligibles which are co-arranged with intellect, nor as with those which are alone divided from intellect by the conception of the mind, but as establishing in itself unically all multitudes, and occultly containing the evolutions of the Gods into light, and the hyparxes of intelligibles. It is likewise allotted the total intellect of intellectuals, the variety of beings, and the multiform orders of divine natures; and it convolves the end of the whole progression† [of the Gods] to the one intelligible principle. For intellectuals are converted to intelligibles. And some intellectuals indeed are united and‡ firmly established prior to the divided Gods; but others are multiplied and through conversion are conjoined to primarily-efficient causes. The intellectual Gods however proceed from all the Gods prior to them, receiving indeed unions from *The One* that is prior to intelligibles; but essences from intelligibles; and being allotted lives all-perfect, connective and generative of divine natures, from the intelligible and at the same time intellectual Gods; but the intellectual peculiarity from themselves. They likewise convert to themselves all the divided orders, but establish themselves in intelligibles, existing wholly through the whole, pure and unknown knowledges, and fervid lives. Besides these things also, they

---

† For περιοδου it is necessary to read προοδου.

‡ After και it is necessary to supply τα μεν ενουται και.

are all-perfect essences, producing all secondary natures through subsisting from themselves, and being neither diminished by their progression, nor receiving an addition by their progeny; but through their own never-failing and infinite powers, being the fathers, causes, and leaders of all things. Nor are they co-divided with their progeny, nor do they depart from themselves in their progressions; but at once, and according to union they govern total multitudes, and all orders, and convolve them to the intelligible, and to occult good.

Whether therefore I may speak of life, it is not proper to think that it is such a life as we surveyed a little before. For that was imparticipable, but this is participated. And that indeed, was generative, but this is vivific. But it is not immanifest that these differ from each other. For the vivific cause indeed, is also evidently generative; but the generative cause is not entirely vivific. For it imparts figure to things unfigured, bound to things indefinite, and perfection to things imperfect. Or whether I may denominate the cause in intellectuals intelligible, it must not immediately be conceived to be such an intelligible, as that of which we have before spoken. For that was imparticipable, and prior to intellectuals, itself pre-existing by itself, and exempt from wholes; not being denominated intelligible, as the plenitude of intellect, but as the prior-cause of it, and the object of desire and love to it, subsisting uniformly unco-ordinated with it. The intelligible however which is now the subject of consideration, is participated, and co-arranged with intellect, is multiform, and contains in itself the divided causes of all things. Or whether we may call the Gods in this order fathers and fabricators, it must be admitted that this paternal and fabricative characteristic, is different from the hyparxis of the intelligible[†] fathers. For they indeed were generative of whole essences; but these pre-exist as the causes of divisible emanations, and of definite productions of form. And they indeed contained in themselves powers fabricative of the divine progressions; but these separate from themselves prolific causes, and are not conjoined to them according to union, but according to a communion subordinate to union. For the marriages which are celebrated by fables, and the concordant conjunction of divine natures, are in the intellectual Gods. But the demiurgic being mingled with the vivific effluxions, every genus of the Gods is unfolded into light, both the supermundane, and the mundane. This, however, will be hereafter discussed.

[†] For νοερων it is necessary to read νοητων.

CHAPTER II

Since however, we have, in short, surveyed the peculiarity of the intellectual Gods, it remains that we should deliver an appropriate theory concerning the division of them. For the intellectual order is not one and indivisible, but is allotted progressions more various than those of the more elevated genera. There will therefore be here also three fathers, who divide the whole intellectual essence; one indeed, being arranged according to the intelligible, but another according to life, and another according to intellect. They also imitate the intelligible fathers who divide the intelligible breadth in a threefold manner, and who are allotted a difference of this kind with respect to each other. For one of these intellectual fathers proceeds analogous to the first [intelligible] father, and is intelligible. But another proceeds analogous to the second [intelligible] father, and binds to himself the whole of intellectual life. And other proceeds analogous to the third father, and closes the whole intellectual, in the same manner as he closes the intelligible order.

But these fathers being three, and the first indeed, abiding in himself, but the second proceeding and vivifying all things, and the third glittering with fabricative productions, it is evidently necessary, that other triple Gods should be conjoined with them; of which, one indeed will be the source to the first intellectual God, of stable purity; but another, of undefiled progression, to the second God; and another of exempt fabrication, to the third. For in the Gods prior to these, the undefiled deities were according to cause, through union without separation, and a sameness collective of powers which are not in want of the communion of these. But in the intellectual Gods, where there is an all-perfect separation, as in total orders, and a greater habitude to secondary natures, unpolluted deity or power is necessary, which has the ratio of sameness, and undeviating subsistence, to the paternal cause, and which is co-divided with the fathers, so that each of the undefiled Gods is conjoined with a peculiar father.

These two triads therefore have presented themselves to our view, one indeed, of the intellectual fathers, but the other of the undefiled Gods. There is however, besides these two, a third other triadic monad, which is the cause of separation to intellectuals, and which subsists together with the above mentioned triads. For the fathers indeed are the suppliers of all essence; but the inflexible Gods, of sameness. But it is evidently fit that there should be also the cause of separation, and that this should be one and at the same time triple, separating the intellectual Gods from the above mentioned orders, from themselves, and from inferior natures. For why are they the leaders of another order, if they are not divided from the first orders? Why are they multiplied, and why do they differ from each other in their kingdoms, unless they are separated? Why also do they transcend the partial [Gods] unless they are also separated from these? The cause of separation therefore, will be for us one and a triple monad. But the paternal and undefiled causes will be each of them a uniform triad. And what is most paradoxical of all, the separative cause is more monadic; but the paternal and also the undefiled cause, are each of them more triadic. For the separative monad indeed, is the cause of separation to the other monads; but the others are the sources of communion and union to it. Hence each of these, being separated, becomes triadic; but the separative monad is monadic, in consequence of being united by these. For all intellectuals pervade through each other, and are in each other, according to a certain admirable communion, imitating the union of intelligibles, through being present and mingled with each other. The sphere also which is there, is the intellectual order, energising in and about itself, and proceeding into itself hebdomadically, being a monad and a hebdomad, the image, if it be lawful so to speak, of the all-perfect intelligible monad, and unfolding its occult union, through progression and separation. This first progression therefore of the intellectual Gods, which is separated by us into a heptad, we have perfectly celebrated.

Other secondary seven hebdomads, however, are to be considered under this, which produce as far as to the last of things, the monads of this heptad. For each monad is the leader of an intellectual hebdomad conjoined with it, and extends this hebdomad from on high, from the summit of Olympus, as far as to the last, and terrestrial orders. I say, for instance, the first paternal monad, indeed, constitutes seven such monads. But the second again constitutes seven vivific monads. And the third, seven demiurgic monads. Each likewise of the undefiled monads constitutes a number equal to that produced by the fathers. And the monad of separation constitutes seven [separative monads]. For all these causes proceed in conjunction with each other. And as the first triad of the fathers subsists together with the undefiled triad, and the divisive monad, after the same manner also, the second triads are allotted seven co-ordinate undefiled triads, and separative monads. Whence, therefore, does so great a number of intellectual Gods present itself to our view? It is evident, indeed, from what has been said. For the first hebdomad, indeed, the cause of the second hebdomads, and which has the relation of a monad to them, and which a little before we denominated an intellectual sphere, subsists according to the intelligible breadth, imitating the paternal nature of it through the paternal triad; but the eternity of its power, through undefiled sameness; and the multitude shining forth in its extremities, through the monad which is divisive of wholes. The remaining hebdomads, however, which are derived from this, proceed according to the intelligible and intellectual genera. For each monad, conformably to the summits of those genera, constitutes a monad co-arranged with the multitude proceeding from it; since every summit is uniform [*i.e.* has the form of the one,] as we have before demonstrated. But according to the middle and third progressions of those genera, each monad generates two triads. For the separation of them was apparent in the middle and ultimate progressions, as we have before observed. As, therefore, the intelligible, and at the same time, intellectual genera, produced the intelligible breadth, which is of a unical nature, into a triadic multitude, after the same manner also the intellectual monads call forth the intelligible, and at the same time intellectual triads, into intellectual hebdomads. And they constitute indeed the monads which are co-arranged with the hebdomads, according to the summits of the triads; but the two triads, according to the second and third decrements of those triads. Hence every hebdomad has the first monad indeed intelligible; but the second after this, and which is triadic, intelligible and intellectual; and the third triad, which is next in order, intellectual. All these likewise subsist as in intellectuals. For they are characterised according to the peculiarity of the constitutive monad.

In short, the intellectual powers proceed according to the intelligible orders; but they constitute these seven hebdomads according to the first intellectual orders. For it is indeed necessary that exempt causes should be assimilated to the intelligible Gods; but that co-arranged causes, and which proceed everywhere, should be assimilated to the intelligible, and at the same time, intellectual Gods; since these also are the first that divide the worlds triadically, and pervade as far as to the last of things, connectedly containing and perfecting all things. But the intelligible Gods contain the causes of wholes uniformly, and occultly. You may also say, that the intelligible Gods produce all things uniformly; for numbers subsist in them monadically. But the intelligible and intellectual Gods produce all things triadically. For the monads in these are divided according to number. And what the monad was in the former, the number is in the latter. And the intellectual Gods produce all things hebdomadically. For they evolve the intelligible, and at the same time, intellectual triads, into intellectual hebdomads, and expand their contracted powers into intellectual variety; since they define multitude itself and variety by numbers which are nearest to the monad. For the numbers of the partial are different from the numbers of the total orders in the Gods. And the whole of this intellectual number is indeed more expanded than the natures prior to it, and is divided into more various progressions, yet it does not desert its alliance with the monad. For hebdomadic multitude has an abundant affinity with the nature of the monad; since it is measured according to it, and primarily subsists from it. And the Pythagoreans, when they denominate the heptad *light according to intellect,* evidently admits its hyparxis to be intellectual, and on this account suspended from the monad. For *the unical,* which light manifests, is inherent from this in all the divine numbers. And thus much concerning the division of these intellectuals Gods.

CHAPTER III

It follows in the next place, that we should adapt the theory of Plato to this order, and show that he does not dissent from any of the theological dogmas concerning it. Since, therefore, we have demonstrated, that the celestial order, which we find in the *Cratylus* perfectly celebrated, possesses the middle bond of the intellectual, and at the same time, intelligible Gods, but that under this another order of Gods is immediately arranged, as Socrates shows in the *Phædrus,* called the subcelestial arch, and which we have considered as not divided from the heaven, - this being the case, what order is it which divides itself from the kingdom of heaven, but is the leader of the intellectual order of the Gods, and is primarily the supplier of intellect, according to the doctrine of Plato, as Socrates says in the *Cratylus,* except that which the mighty Saturn comprehends? For he calls this God the first and most pure intellect. This God, therefore, is the summit of a divine intellect, and, as he says, the purest part of it; separating himself indeed from the celestial order, but reigning over all the intellectual Gods; because he is full of intellect, but of a pure intellect, and is a God extended to the summit of the intellectual hypostasis. Hence also, he is the father of the mighty Jupiter, and is simply father. For he who is the father of the father of all things, is evidently allotted in a much greater degree the paternal dignity. Saturn, therefore, is the first intellect; but the mighty Jupiter is also an intellect, containing, as Socrates says in the *Philebus,* a royal soul, and a royal intellect.

And these Gods are two intellects, and intellectual fathers; the one, indeed, being intellectual; but the other intelligible, in intellectuals. For the Saturnian bonds which Socrates mentions in the *Cratylus,* are unific of the intelligence of Jupiter about the intelligible of his father, and fill the Jovian intellect with the all-perfect intelligence of the Saturnian intellect. And this I think is likewise evident from the analogy of souls to Plato. For as he binds souls about himself, filling them with wisdom and intelligence, thus also Saturn being the object of desire and love to Jupiter, contains him in himself by indissoluble bonds. And these things Socrates indicates in the *Cratylus*, jesting, and at the same time being serious in what he says. The object of desire therefore, and the intelligible to Jupiter, is Saturn. But the mighty Jupiter himself is a divine and demiurgic intellect. Hence, it is necessary that there should be a third other intellectual cause, generative of life. For Jupiter indeed is the cause of life, as Socrates says, but intellectually and secondarily. But we say that life is every where arranged prior to intellect. Hence, we must say that the queen Rhea, being the mother of Jupiter, but subordinate to the father Saturn, gives completion to this middle, existing as a vivific world, and establishing in herself the causes of the whole of life. These three paternal orders, therefore, have appeared to us in intellectuals: one of them indeed subsisting according to the intelligible power of intellectuals;[†] but another according to divine and intellectual life; and another according to intellectual intellect. For we celebrate the middle deity, herself by herself, as the mother of the demiurgus, and of wholes. When, however, we survey her together with the extremes, we denominate her a paternal cause, as being comprehended in the fathers; and as generating some things together with Saturn, but others in conjunction with Jupiter.

Moreover, Plato following Orpheus, calls the inflexible and undefiled triad of the intellectual Gods Curetic, as is evident from what the Athenian guest says in the *Laws*, celebrating the armed sports of the Curetes, and their rhythmical dance. For Orpheus represents the Curetes who are three, as the guards of Jupiter. And the sacred laws of the Cretans, and all the Grecian theology, refer a pure and undefiled life and energy to this order. For *το κορον to koron*, indicates nothing else than the pure and incorruptible. Hence, we have before said, that the mighty Saturn, as being essentially united to the cause of undefiled purity, is a pure intellect. The paternal Gods therefore are three, and the undefiled Gods also are three. Hence it remains that we should survey the seventh monad.

If, therefore, we consider the fabulous exections, both the Saturnian and the Celestial, of which Plato makes mention, and thinks that such like narrations should always be concealed in silence, that the arcane

---

[†] It appears from the version of Portus, that the words ο μεν κατα την νοητην δυναμιν νοερων are omitted in the original. Indeed, the sense requires that they should be inserted.

truth of them should be surveyed, and that they are indicative of mystic conceptions, because these things are not fit for young men to hear, - [if we consider these] we may obtain from them what the separative deity is, who accomplishes the divisions, and segregates the Saturnian genera indeed from the Celestial, and the Jovian from the Saturnian, and who separates the whole intellectual order from the natures prior and posterior to it, disjoins the different causes in it from each other, and always imparts to secondary natures, secondary measures of dominion. And let not any one be disturbed, or oppose me on hearing these things. How therefore does Plato reject exections, bonds, and the tragical apparatus of fables? For he thinks that all such particulars will be condemned by the multitude and the stupid, through ignorance of the arcana they contain; but that they will exhibit to the wise certain admirable opinions. Hence, he indeed does not admit such a mode of fiction, but thinks it proper to be persuaded by the ancients who were the offspring of the Gods, and to investigate their arcane conceptions. As therefore he rejects the Saturnian fables, when they are narrated to Euthyprhon, and the auditors of the *Republic*, yet at the same time admits them in the *Cratylus*, placing about the mighty Saturn and Pluto, other secondary bonds, - thus also, I think he forbids exections to be introduced to those who know only the apparent meaning of what is said, and does not admit that there is illegal conduct in the Gods, and nefarious aggressions of children against their parents, but he opposes, and confutes as much as possible such like opinions. He assents however to their being narrated to those who are able to penetrate into the mystic truth, and investigate the concealed meaning of fables, and admits the separation of wholes, whether [mythologists] are willing to denominate them exections for the purpose of concealment, or in whatever other way they may think fit to call them. For bonds and exections are symbols of communion and separation, and each is the progeny of the same divine mythology. Nor is there any occasion to wonder, if from these things we endeavour to confirm the opinion of Plato; but it is requisite to know how the philosophy of Plato admits all such particulars, and how it rejects them, and in what manner he apprehends they may be the causes of the greatest evils, and of an impious life to those that hear them. The seven intellectual Gods therefore, will through these conceptions appear to have been thought worthy of being mentioned by Plato.

CHAPTER IV

It is, however, I think, necessary syllogistically to collect the progression of them according to hebdomads, from images. The demiurgus therefore, [in the *Timæus*] fabricates the soul of the universe an image of all the divine orders, in the same manner as he fabricates this sensible world an image of intelligibles. And in the first[†] place indeed, he constitutes the whole essence of the soul, and afterwards divides it into numbers, binds it by harmonies, and adorns it with figures, I mean the rectilinear and the circular. After this also, he divides it into one circle and seven circles. Whence therefore, are this monad and hebdomad derived, except from the intellectual Gods? For figure, number and true being, are prior to them. As in the fabrication of the soul, after the subsistence of the psychical figure, the division of the circles according to the monad and hebdomad follows, thus also in the Gods, after intellectual and intelligible figure, the intellectual breadth, and that sphere of the Gods succeed. The multitude therefore of the seven hebdomads subsist from the divine intellectual hebdomad entering into itself. And on this account, the demiurgus thus divides the circles in the soul, because he and every intellectual order, produce an intellectual hebdomad from each monad. I do not however assert, and now contend, that the seven circles are allotted an hyparxis similar to the seven Gods that proceed from the demiurgus, but that the demiurgus dividing the soul according to circles, introduces number to the sections from the intellectual Gods, I mean the monadic and the hebdomadic number. For the monad indeed subsists according to the circle of sameness, but the division, according to the circle of difference. Shortly after however, it will appear that same and different belong to the demiurgic order.

Farther still, after the division of the circles, the demiurgus assumes some things which are symbols of the assimilative, and others which are symbols of the liberated Gods, and through these, he refers the soul to these orders of the Gods. If therefore figure is prior to the intellectual Gods, but the similar and dissimilar are posterior to them, it is evidently necessary that the monadic and at the same time hebdomadic, should be referred to this order, and that the progression from the monad to the hebdomad should pertain to this order. Each therefore of the seven intellectual Gods, is the leader of an intellectual hebdomad, as we may

---

[†] For πρωτην it is necessary to read πρωτως. It was also requisite to alter the punctuation in the preceding sentence.

learn from images. There however indeed, the hebdomad is one, and allied to itself. But in souls, the circles differ from each other, according to the divine peculiarities. For they receive number in such a manner as to preserve the proper nature which they are allotted, connectedly containing mundane natures, and convolving the apparent by their own circles. And thus much concerning these particulars, which afford arguments that are not obscure of the arrangement of them by Plato.

CHAPTER V

Again however, making another beginning, let us speak about each [of the intellectual Gods,] as much as is sufficient to the present theology. Let Saturn therefore, the first king of the intellectual Gods, be now celebrated by us, who according to Socrates in the *Cratylus* illuminates the pure and incorruptible nature of intellect, and establishing his own all-perfect power in his own summit of intellectuals, abides in, and at the same time proceeds from his father [Heaven]. He likewise divides intellectual government from the connective, and establishes the transcendency of the other intellectual Gods in connection with his own; but comprehends in himself the intelligible of the demiurgic intellect, and the plenitude of beings. Hence the Saturnian bonds, mystically, and obscurely signify the comprehension of this intelligible, and a union with it. For the intelligible is comprehended in intellect.

As therefore, the intelligible is indeed exempt from intellect, but intellect is said to comprehend it, thus also Jupiter is said to bind his father. And in placing bonds about his father, he at the same time binds himself [to him]. For a bond is the comprehension of the things that are bound. But the truth is as follows: Saturn is indeed an all-perfect intellect; and the mighty Jupiter is likewise an intellect. Each therefore being an intellect, each is also evidently an intelligible. For every intellect is converted to itself; but being converted to it energizes towards itself. Energizing however towards itself, and not towards externals, it is intelligible and at the same time intellectual; being indeed intellectual, so far as it intellectually perceives, but intelligible, so far as it is intellectually perceived. Hence also the Jovian intellect is to itself intellect, and to itself intelligible. And in a similar manner the Saturnian intellect is to itself intelligible, and to itself intellect. But Jupiter indeed is more intellect, and Saturn more intelligible. For the latter is established according to the intellectual summit, but the former according to the intellectual end. And the one indeed is the object of desire, but the other desires. And the one fills, but the other is filled.

Saturn therefore being intellect and intelligible, Jupiter also is in the second place intellect and intelligible. The intellectual however of Saturn is intelligible; but the intelligible of Jupiter is intellectual. Jupiter therefore, being at the same time intellectual and intelligible, intellectually perceives and comprehends himself, and binds the intelligible in himself. But binding this in himself, he is said to bind the intelligible prior to himself, and to comprehend it on all sides. For entering into himself, he proceeds into the intelligible prior to himself, and by the intelligible which is in himself, intellectually perceives that which is prior to himself. And thus the intelligible is not external to intellect. For every intellect possesses that which is in itself without any difference with respect to itself. But again, it intellectually perceives in itself that which is prior to itself. For every thing which is external to intellect, is foreign and adventitious, and pertains to an inferior nature. But that which is pre-established in the order of cause, and which pre-exists as the object of desire, is in the desiring natures themselves. For being converted to, and verging to themselves, they discover the causes of themselves, and all more ancient natures. And by how much more perfect and uniform the conversion of the desiring natures is about the objects of desire, by so much the more are they present with their own desirables. Hence every intellect, by intellectually perceiving itself, intellectually perceives likewise, all the natures prior to itself. And by how much the more it is united to itself, in a so much greater degree it is established in the intelligibles prior to itself. For the cause of any being, and which is the source of essence or of perfection to it, is not external to that being; but that which is subordinate to any being, is external to it, and is not the intelligible. On this account also, each of the divine natures is unconverted to that which is inferior to itself, but is converted to itself, and through itself reverts to that which is more excellent. And the intelligible indeed is not inferior to any intellect; but every intellect energising towards itself, and comprehending the intelligibles prior to itself, intellectually perceives them.

Some intelligibles likewise are such as are conjoined with intellect. But others are such as are proximately participated by it. And others are such as it sees more remotely, and which are more exempt from its nature. On this account, the demiurgic intellect is indeed at the same time intelligible and intellect, but has the intelligible of his father, which he binds as the fable says. He sees however animal itself, which is, according to Timæus, the most beautiful of all intelligibles. And if the illustrious Amelius, forming such conceptions as these, said that intellect is threefold, one being that which *is*, another that which *has*, and another that which *sees*, he rightly apprehends the conception of Plato, according to my opinion. For it is necessary that the second intellect should not only *have* the intelligible, but that it should *be* and *have* the intelligible; that it should *be* indeed the intelligible co-ordinate with itself, but *have* the intelligible prior to itself, so far as it participates of it. And it is necessary that the third intellect should *see* the intelligible, and should also *be* and *have* it; that it should *see* indeed the first intelligible; but *have* that which is proximately beyond itself; and that it should *be* the intelligible which is in itself, and which is conjoined with its own intelligence, and should be inseparable from it.

If therefore, as we said from the beginning, Jupiter intellectually perceives his father Saturn, Saturn is indeed intelligible, but Jupiter is intellect; being one intelligible himself, but participating of another. Hence also Plato does not simply call Saturn intellect, but a pure and incorruptible intellect. For he† in the intellectual is intelligible. Since however, he is not simply intelligible, but as in intellectuals, he is intellect, and is himself paternally so, being both father and intellect, and having the paternal intellectually. In intelligibles therefore, intellect is also father; but in intellectuals father is intellect. Hence Saturn is a pure, immaterial and perfect intellect, established above fabrication in the order of the desirable. But possessing such a peculiarity as this, he is full of all intelligibles intellectually, is at it were exuberant with intellections, and establishes twofold genera of Gods, some indeed in himself, but other posterior to himself. And he leads forth, indeed, the prolific powers of his father Heaven as far as to the last of things; but fills the demiurgic order with generative goods.

CHAPTER VI

Saturn however is the only one of the Gods who is said both to receive and give the royal dignity with a certain necessity, and as it were violence, cutting off the genitals of his father, and being himself castrated by the mighty Jupiter. For he bounds the kingdom of his father, and is bounded by the God posterior to himself. He is also filled from the natures placed above him, but fills the whole fabrication [of the universe] with prolific perfection. But separating himself from his father, he is exempt from his progeny. Being however one all-perfect intellect, he contains in himself the multitude of total intelligibles. And as he deifies the intellectual summit, he illuminates all things with intelligible light.

---

† For το γαρ it is necessary to read εκεινος γαρ.

CHAPTER VII

Very properly therefore, has this universe twofold lives, periods, and convolutions; the one being Saturnian, but the other Jovian, as the fable in the *Politicus* says. And according to one of the periods indeed, it produces all goods spontaneously, and possesses an innoxious and unwearied life. But according to the other it participates of material error, and a very mutable nature. For the life in the world being twofold, the one unapparent, and more intellectual, but the other more physical and apparent, and the one being defined according to providence, but the other proceeding in a disorderly manner according to fate; - this being the case, the second life indeed, which is multiform, and perfected through nature, is suspended from the Jovian order; but the more simple, intellectual, and unapparent life, is suspended from the Saturnian order. And these things the Elean guest clearly teaches, calling one of the circulations Jovian, but the other, Saturnian; though Jupiter also is the cause of the unapparent life of the universe, is the supplier of intellect, and the leader of intellectual perfection; but he elevates all things to the kingdom of Saturn, and being a leader in conjunction with his father, constitutes the whole mundane intellect. And if it be requisite to speak the truth clearly, each of the periods indeed, I mean the apparent, and the unapparent, participates of both these Gods; but the one indeed is more Saturnian, and the other is perfected under the kingdom of Jupiter.

That the mighty Saturn therefore is allotted a kingdom different from that of the Gods prior to him, the Elean guest clearly manifests in what he asserts prior to the fable. For he says, "We have heard from many respecting the kingdom of which Saturn was the founder." According to this wise man therefore, Saturn is one of the royal Gods. Hence also he presides over a kingdom different from that of his father. And while his father connectedly contains the middle centres of the intelligible and intellectual Gods, he is the leader of the intellectual orders and supplies all intellectual life, first indeed, to the Gods, but secondarily to the natures more excellent than ours, and in the last place to partial souls, when they are able to be extended to the Saturnian place of survey. For this universe, and all the mundane Gods, always possess this twofold life, and imitate the Saturnian intelligence indeed through unapparent and intellectual energy, but the demiurgic intellect of Jupiter, through a providential attention to secondary natures, and in short, through the visible fabrication. But partial souls at one time energise intellectually, and consecrate themselves to Saturn, but at another time after a Jovian manner, and pay a providential attention to secondary natures, without restraint. When however they revolve analogous to those[†] deities [Saturn and Jupiter] they intellectually perceive intelligibles, and dispose sensibles in an orderly manner, and live both these lives, in the same manner as the Gods and the more excellent genera. For their periods are twofold; one being intellectual, but the other providential. Their paradigms also are twofold; the Saturnian intellect being the paradigm of the one, and the Jovian intellect of the other. For the mighty Jupiter himself has a twofold energy, containing indeed intelligibles in intellect, but adorning sensibles by demiurgic production.

Since however the circulations are twofold, not only in wholes, but also in partial souls, the Elean guest says that in the Saturnian period, the generation of these souls is not from each other, as in men which are the objects of sensible inspection, nor as the first man with us is alone earth-begotten, so in partial souls one first soul is the offspring of man, but all of them are earth-begotten. For they are elevated from ultimate and terrestrial bodies, and embrace an unapparent,[‡] relinquishing a sensible life. He also says that neither do they verge to old age, and change from being younger to becoming older; but on the contrary, they are rendered more vigorous, proceed intellectually in a way contrary to generation, and as it were, divest themselves of the variety of life with which in descending they became invested. Hence likewise all the symbols which are adapted to youth are present with these souls, when they pass into this condition, such as a privation of hair, and a smoothness of the cheek instead of hoariness and beards. For they lay aside every thing which adheres to them from generation. But being situated there with Saturn, and living the life which is there, he says that there are abundance of fruits from trees, and many other [vegetable] substances, which the earth spontaneously produces. Being likewise naked, and without coverlets, they are for the most part fed in the open air; for they have a temperament of the seasons which is always the same. But they make use of soft beds, grass in abundance being produced for them from the earth. Souls therefore derive these and such like goods from the mighty God, in the Saturnian period. For they are thence filled indeed with vivific goods, and gather intellectual fruits from wholes; but do not procure for themselves perfection and blessedness, from partial energies. For doxastic nutriment indeed has divisible and

---

[†] For εκειναις, it is necessary to read εκεινοις.

[‡] For εμθανους it is necessary to read αφανους.

material conceptions; but intellectual nutriment has pure, impartible, and native conceptions, which the spontaneous obscurely signifies.

The production from the earth also signifies the prolific intellect of the Gods, which imparts to souls by illumination perfection and self-sufficiency. For on account of the exuberant abundance of good, they are able to impart an influx of it, according to the measure of felicity adapted to them. Hence, they are neither covered with garments, as when the proceeded into generation, nor have they superabundant additions of life, but they are purified themselves by themselves from all composition and variety, and extending their intellect to total good, they participate of it from the intellectual father, being guarded by the intellectual Gods, and receiving from them the measures of a happy life. They likewise pass through the whole of their existence with facility, lead a sleepless and pure life, being established in the generative powers of intelligibles; and being filled with intellectual goods, and nourished with immaterial and divine forms, they are said to live a life under Saturn.

CHAPTER VIII

Because, therefore, this God is the leader of all intellectual life, and every intellect as well that which is imparticipable, as that which is participable proceeds from this cause, hence it belongs to this mighty God to feed in a distributed manner, and to nourish souls. For because indeed he is intelligible in intellectuals, he nourishes souls, and souls are called the nurselings of Saturn. But because he does not fill them with first, and unical intelligibles, but with those that are multiplied by his own cause of separation, he is said to feed them distributedly, and as it were in a divided manner. And do you not see how through these things, this God appears to be co-ordinate to the first triad of the intelligible and intellectual Gods? For as Socrates, in the *Phædrus*, says, the souls are nourished in the supercelestial place, and in the intelligible meadow, so the Elean guest asserts that the souls that are fed under Saturn, are filled with intelligible goods. And it is not at all wonderful if souls are perfected by both these; intellectually indeed, under the kingdom of Saturn; but intelligibly under the order of the first intellectual Gods. For this God himself is nourished by that order. And on this account he is allotted a leading and primary transcendency in intellectuals, because they are filled from that order [through him] with occult and unapparent powers. And he is that among the intellectual fathers, which the order of the first intellectual Gods is in the intelligible and at the same time intellectual orders. Hence the intelligible everywhere becomes nutriment to ascending souls, but the connection with it is effected through the second and third Gods.

As therefore, the demiurgic order elevates souls to the Saturnian place of survey, thus also the Saturnian order elevates them to the subcelestial† arch. For having made many and blessed discursive energies in the kingdom of Saturn, they are again extended from hence to the perfective, and from thence to the celestial triad, from which contemplating the supercelestial place, they are now ineffably conjoined with the supreme goods of intelligibles. And after this manner the second orders always connect souls with the orders prior to them. Hence also, the theurgic art imitating the unapparent periods of souls, arranges initiations in the mysteries of the second Gods, prior to the more sublime mysteries. And through these, it causes us to pass to the intelligible place of survey. These things, therefore, Plato indicates concerning the Saturnian life, and the polity of souls under Saturn, not in the *Politicus* only, but also in the discourses of the Athenian guest. For in the fourth book of the *Laws* he celebrates the life under Saturn, obscurely signifying the undefiled nature, the facility, plentitude, and self-sufficiency of that energy, through fabulous fictions.

CHAPTER IX

If, however, it be requisite from these things, and from all the mystic discipline concerning this God, to consider and discuss the orders which he constitutes in wholes, in the first place, we must direct our attention to the three kings mentioned in the *Gorgias*, who distributing the kingdom of Saturn were produced by him, as being allotted in a divided manner a uniform and impartible dominion, and over whom he places the divine law, which is the cause of distribution according to intellect, both to the Gods themselves, and to all the natures posterior to the Gods. In the second place, we must consider the rulers and kings mentioned in the *Laws*, who are said to preside over the different allotments of souls, and who are not men, but dæmons of a more divine and excellent genus, who distribute to souls the measures of good, cut off their generation-producing lives, restrain their disorderly lation, retain them in the intelligible, and comprehend them in the kingdom of Saturn. In the third place, therefore, we must direct our attention to the dæmon Gods, who preside over the parts of the world, and the herds [of

---

† For υπερουρανιαν in this place, it is necessary to read υπουρανιαν.

souls] that are in it, as the Elean guest says in the *Politicus*, and who at one time come into contact with the objects of their government, and distribute to them intellectual, and all unapparent goods, but at another time withdraw themselves from the physical life of the world, recur to their own place of survey, and imitate the exempt transcendency of the demiurgus and father of the universe.

But after these things, we must survey the twofold circulations of the mundane Gods, *viz.* the Saturnian and the Jovian; for these Gods always have each of these, as the fable says in the *Politicus*. For it is evident that the mutation of the stars and the sun takes place in each of the revolutions. This period, therefore, being twofold, it is obvious to every one that the periods are full of Saturnian goods, and participate of the Saturnian series. And not only the mundane Gods, but likewise all the more excellent genera that follow the Gods, energize according to both these energies, and revolve according to the twofold circulations, through which souls also sometimes participate of an intellectual life, and proceed in this path, exchanging for sense intellect as the leader of their motion and circulation. Saturn, therefore, extends his kingdom supernally from the first Gods, as far as to partial souls, perfects all things, and fills them with intellectual goods, distributing to different natures different measures of good. For on account of this, law also subsists with him, as Socrates says in the *Gorgias*: "This law therefore was in the time of Saturn, and always was, and now is, among the Gods." For law is the distribution of intellect; but this God is the first, most pure, and incorruptible intellect.

If, however, this God is the primary leader of all division, and is the origin of intellectual separation, it is necessary on this account, that law should be with him, which distinguishes the orders of beings, divides the intellectual genera, and separates all forms according to a well-ordered progression; but imparts to all things by illumination the measure of hyparxis, connecting the order which is in them, preserving the boundaries of divine distribution immutable, and possessing the same dignity in the kingdom of Saturn, and in intellectuals, as Adrastia in the supercelestial place, and in the intelligible, and at the same time, intellectual orders. For from each of them an immutable guard, and the progression of order to all things are generated. But they differ from each other, because law indeed divides the one into multitude, defines the measures of intellectual subsistence, and distributes to every thing an appropriate good, producing the different measures of beings from the one [Saturnian] intellect. But Adrastia abiding in the intelligible, guards all things uniformly, and preserves total order in a firm undeviating manner, exempt from all division. Law, therefore, is a certain God which divides divine forms, and definitely imparts to every thing that which is adapted to it according to the plentitude proceeding from one uniform cause; and it is also co-existent with the Saturnian order, in which the separations of beings, and the all-perfect progression of forms first subsist. Hence the demiurgus likewise looking to this conducts all things according to law, and constitutes mundane providence an image of the union of the father; but fate and the fatal laws, an image of the division according to law. Souls, therefore, live according to law; in the Jovian period indeed being governed conformably to the laws of Fate; but in the Saturnian period living according to divine law they are subservient to the multitude [of divine forms] and are extended to the one cause of all; and ascending to the intelligible place of survey, they are subjected to the sacred law of Adrastia. For this law extends from on high as far as to the last of things, and defines to souls the measures of whole period, as Socrates says in the *Phædrus*. Who therefore this greatest God is, and what the goods are of which he is the cause to souls, and prior to these, to Gods and dæmons, the leaders of souls, let it, from these things be manifest.

CHAPTER X

Since however, theologists assert that an exemption from old age pertains to this order, as the Barbarians say, and Orpheus the theologist of the Greeks, (for he mystically says that the hairs of the face of Saturn are always black, and never become hoary) I admire the divinely-inspired intellect of Plato which unfolds the same things concerning this God to those who proceed in his steps. For he says that souls in the Saturnian period abandon old age, but return to youth, and remove from themselves hoariness, but have black hair. For he says that the white hairs of the more elderly become black; but the cheeks of those that have beards being rendered smooth, they are restored to the past season [of youth.] These things indeed are asserted by the Elean guest; similar to which are the assertions of Orpheus concerning this God.

> . . . . under Saturnian Jove
> Men liv'd immortal; moist and fragrant hair
> From the pure chin then sprouted, nor was mix'd
> With the white flower that marks infirm old age;
> But in its stead, a florid down appear'd.

In these verses he delivers the similitude of Saturnian souls to this God. For he says that they remove from the view the old age which they had acquired from generation and abandon material imbecility; and that they exert the juvenile and vigorous life of intellect. For it is no otherwise lawful for them to be assimilated to the God who is exempt from old age, than through intellectual puberty, and undefiled power. But the cause of this is, that king Saturn himself is the source of the unallured Gods, and the inflexible triad. Hence he is, as Socrates says, a pure intellect. For he is at the same time the intellect of the undefiled order, ranking as a summit, and riding as in a vehicle in the flourishing and vigorous[†] Gods that govern wholes. The souls also which are sent to him, wonderfully advance, in conjunction with intellectual energy, in vigour, and in a power undeviating, and free from any tendency to matter. Partial souls therefore, when they change their periods, at one time proceed to a more juvenile, and at another, to a more aged condition. But whole souls always live according to both these periods, and are conversant with Saturn according to the unapparent period, but govern the universe in conjunction with Jupiter, according to visible providence, at once receiving an increase according to both these periods, and becoming at one and the same time both older and younger. And this is what Parmenides indicates when he says, that *The One* proceeding according to time becomes at once younger and older. These things however, will hereafter be more manifest.

CHAPTER XI

Having therefore brought to an end the information concerning the king of the intellectual Gods, it evidently follows that we should in the next place celebrate the queen Rhea. For both Plato and Orpheus assert that she is the mother of the demiurgus of wholes, but a divinity posterior to Saturn. Thus therefore, we must speak concerning her. The stable and united cause of all intellectuals, and the principal and original monad, abiding in herself, unfolding into light all intellectual multitude, and again convolving it into herself, and embosoming her progeny, and the causes of wholes that emerge from her, analysing as it were after division the natures that are divided, and being paternally allotted the highest kingdom in intellectuals, this being the case, the vivific Rhea proceeds as the second from her proper principle, being allotted a maternal order in the whole paternal orders, and producing

---

[†] For ακμαιος, it is necessary to read ακμαιοις.

the demiurgus of wholes, prior to other Gods, and the immutable guard of the Gods. For this Goddess is the middle centre of the paternal intellectual triad, and the receiving bosom of the generative power which is in Saturn, calling forth indeed, to the generation of wholes, the causes which abide in him, but unfolding definitely all the genera of the Gods. And being filled indeed from the father prior to her with intelligible prolific power, but filling the demiurgus and father subsisting from her, with vivific abundance. Whence also the demiurgus is the cause of life to all things, as containing in himself the plenitude of intellectual life, and extending to all things the prolific cause of his mother. For as the middle Goddess multiplies the uniform powers of Saturn, and produces and causes them to preside over secondary natures, so the third father, at one and the same time unfolds, divides, and produces as far as to the last of things, the all-perfect abundance of the Saturnian monad, and the dyadic generation of the mother Rhea, so as not to leave the most material and disorderly part of the universe destitute of the power of Saturn.

This Goddess therefore, being the middle of the two fathers, one of which collects, but the other divides intellectual multitude, and the one through transcendency desiring to abide and to be established in himself, but the other hastening to produce, generate and fabricate all things, she educes indeed into herself, the demiurgic causes of wholes, but imparts her own proper power to secondary natures, in unenvying abundance. Hence also Plato assimilates her prolific exuberance to streams, as Socrates says in the *Cratylus*, evinces that this Goddess is a certain flux, and in what he asserts of her obscurely shows nothing else than her fontal nature, and a power unically comprehensive of the divisible rivers of life. For the first-effective flux is fontal; which also Socrates indicating in this Goddess, shortly after clearly says that the name of Tethys is the name of a fountain. Why therefore, is it any longer necessary to doubt about these things and to say where does Plato make mention of fontal Gods? For he himself denominates the causes of the subsistence of all the Gods, fontal fluxions. And besides this, if he admits that the mundane soul is the fountain and principle of life, because it proceeds both from an impartible and partible vivification, how is it possible that he should not in a much greater degree and more truly call the Goddess who comprehends in herself all life, fontal?

Concerning names however, it is not, I think, at all proper to contend, but we should survey the orders themselves of the first effective Gods, and see how Plato following theologists copiously unfolds them to us, celebrating after the Saturnian monad the kingdom of Rhea, constituting from these the demiurgus of wholes, and all the multitude of Gods which is woven together with him. For this Goddess binding together the breadth of intellectuals, and embosoming total life, emits all the intellectual powers in herself of the rivers of life; and by the summit of herself indeed is conjoined to the first father, and together with him generates wholes, and the genera of Gods that abide in him; but by her extremity is connascent with fabrication, and according to a kindred conjunction with fabrication, constitutes all the orders of Gods that are prior to the world, and that are in the world. Hence there also the causes of the demiurgi of wholes primarily subsist, and the more partial genera of life: and the union and total deity of all these, is at once exempt from the plenitudes of herself, and is at once co-arranged with them.

Thus therefore, she is both uniform and multiform, one and simple, though being self-perfect, she is a vivific world, proceeding from on high as far as to the last of things, and as far as to the extremities of the universe, giving subsistence to the vivific powers of the breadth of life. Hence also Plato refers the vivific causes of wholes to this Goddess, and through the last gifts of this divinity, indicates her total energy; which primarily indeed fills the whole demiurgus with intellectual and prolific power, but secondarily perfects all the genera of the Gods with the intellectual fruits of herself. According to a third order also, her total energy nourishes the souls that are the attendants of the Gods, with the rivers of divine perfection. And in the last orders, it imparts to mortal animals the gift of nature. This therefore is, I think, more known than every thing to those who admit that things divine are beyond the works of nature.

That however, which it is more fit the lovers of the contemplation of truth should consider, I say, is this, that Plato divides Ceres from[†] the whole vivific deity, and co-arranges her, at one time with Prosperpine, at another with Juno, and at another with the progeny of Jupiter, as we may learn in the *Cratylus*. In which dialogue indeed, he co-arranges Rhea with Saturn, but connects a certain common investigation and theory about Ceres, Jupiter, and Juno. In the *Laws* likewise celebrating the legislative Goddesses, he refers the whole of a legitimate life to the union of Ceres and Proserpine; since according to Orpheus this middle Goddess being conjoined with Saturn by her summit, is called Rhea; but producing Jupiter, and together with Jupiter unfolding the whole and partial orders of the Gods, she is called Ceres. And all the order of

---

[†] ἀπο is omitted in the original.

middle life is comprehensive of the other Titanidæ, and likewise of Ceres. For it pre-established this monad as a middle collective of all the orders in it, both those that are occult, and those that are divided about the generative powers of the Goddess. Each of these powers, however are triple. And this monad indeed conjoins the superior triad to Saturn, but weaves the inferior, together with the demiurgic order. It also evinces that the Cerealian monad being the middle, is co-arranged with, and is at the same time exempt from the demiurgus of wholes. For in conjunction with the whole order it constitutes, and together with Jupiter generates Proserpine. And thus we have celebrated the primogenial Goddess who is the middle of the fathers.

CHAPTER XII

Now however, after this Goddess, the demiurgus of wholes is in the third place to be celebrated, according to the order which he is allotted in the intellectual Gods, peculiarly unfolding for this purpose all the truth concerning him. And in the first place, we must remember that it is necessary the peculiarity of this third father should be demiurgic; and thus in the next place, following Plato, we must direct our attention to other particulars [respecting this God]. The first of the intellectual Gods therefore, who is parturient with multitude, who is the leader and source of all separation, and who separates himself from the uniform and first Gods, but generates the divided principles of wholes, - this God again converts his progeny to himself, and weaves together these parts with his own sameness, and exhibits himself as one intelligible world in intellectuals, bringing forth in himself, and retaining with himself his own offspring. But the second of the intellectual deities, is the vivific Goddess, who brings forth indeed in conjunction with the first intellectual God, occult multitude, (for she is conjoined to him according to supreme transcendency) but cannot endure to remain in this mode of generating, and in collecting the separation of wholes into unseparated union. Hence she separates the third intellect from the [first] father; but produces the multitude of the Gods, and of intellectual reasons, and fills the demiurgus with generative power. If, therefore, the first intellectual God is parturient with the generation of wholes; but the prolific vivification of the intellectual orders causes this generation to shine forth; - it is evident that the intellect of the intellectual fathers, according to his own order, produces and adorns all things, and calls forth indeed, the occult nature of his father, into separation and progression, but prepares total vivification to send forth the rivers of itself, as far as to the last of things. For it is every where the peculiarity of intellect to divide and unfold multitude, the plenitudes of life, and the unions of intelligibles. Intelligible intellect however contains multitude uniformly, or according to the form of one; for multitude pre-exists in the intelligible according to cause. But the intelligible, and at the same time, intellectual intellect, has indeed secondary measures of union, but is exempt from all perfect separation, abiding in the first principles of wholes. And intellectual intellect is the source of all division, and of the subsistence of partial natures; since it pre-establishes in itself all the multitude of forms, and this not tetradically only, as intelligible intellect, but it possesses one all-perfect intellectual cause of all forms. It is necessary therefore that the whole demiurgic principles should pertain to this intellect, that all the demiurgic Gods should proceed from this one third father, and that this should be the demiurgus of wholes. For as the first paradigms co-subsist in intelligible intellect, and in the third triad and the first father, so likewise we must place the first demiurgic monad in intellectual intellect, and the third father of the intellectual Gods. For on this account also the demiurgic is conjoined with the paradigmatic cause, according to the analogy which each is allotted among the fathers; one indeed in intelligibles, but the other in intellectuals. For one is the boundary of the intelligible, but the other of the intellectual order. But this is evident from what has been before said.

Farther still, fabrication being fourfold, and one indeed adorning wholes totally, another adorning wholes but partially, another adorning parts, but totally, and another weaving parts together with wholes, partially, - this being the case, it is evident that the cause of wholes which is the cause of them uniformly and indivisibly, is the most ancient of all the causes. It is necessary however, that this cause should either be prior to, or in, or posterior to the intellectual Gods. Where therefore shall we place it? For all the parts which are constituted by intellectuals are more partial than the one and total fabrication. For the division of wholes into three, and the leaders of divisible production, present themselves to the view in these orders. The natures therefore, that are prior to intellectuals, are defined according to other peculiarities of the Gods, as was before shown, and in short, they subsist according to union, and are expanded above the separation of intellectual forms.

CHAPTER XIII

It remains therefore that the one demiurgus of wholes must be arranged in intellectuals. But if indeed, he is the first father, he will be intelligible, will contain his progeny in himself, and will be the collector of separation. How therefore, does he divide the worlds? How does he generate the multitude of mundane natures? How does he speak to all the junior demiurgi at once? For the first father is unco-ordinated with the whole number of mundane natures, and also converts his first progeny to himself, flying as it were from multitude to union, and hastily withdrawing himself from all-various separation into intelligible transcendency. But if the one demiurgus of wholes is the vivific order, all things indeed, will be full of life, on account of the whole demiurgus. And the cause of souls, according to a probable reason will here become apparent subsisting prior to multitude. But how will he convert all things to himself? How is he called demiurgus and father? For the vivific deity, herself by herself, has a maternal dignity among the Gods, and is the supplier of progression to all things. But to produce forms, and to convert, are the illustrious and peculiar good of intellect. Neither therefore, is the demiurgus of wholes in the supermundane order. For all the natures there are partial, and either partially preside over wholes, or comprehend the productions of parts totally. Nor is he in intelligibles. For all the Gods there are fathers; and no one there is called[†] demiurgus and father. But the divine orders antecedently comprehend all things in a manner perfectly occult and unical. Nor is he in the intelligible and at the same time intellectual order. For to collect, connect, and perfect multitudes, is not the province of the demiurgic peculiarity. For this is the source of separation, and the production of forms, glittering with intellectual sections. But the intelligible and at the same time intellectual Gods, extend intellectual multitudes to the union of intelligibles. Nor again, is it possible to admit that the demiurgic cause is in the first or second order of intellectuals. For the summit of intellectuals is imparticipable by mundane natures, and is rather proposed to them in the order of the desirable; but is not productive of them. Hence, all the Gods in the world are elevated to the Saturnian place of survey; but proceed from another secondary principle, and through it are converted and conjoined to the exempt kingdom. And the middle centre being vivific, is not defined according to the paternal characteristic. For the generative very

---

[†] For εξηρηται, it appears to me that we should read εκει ειρηται.

much differs from the paternal, and the vivific from the demiurgic genus; so far, I think, as the principles of the whole orders, I mean bound and infinity, differ from each other. For the demiurgic and paternal order is referred to bound; but all vivific and generative power, to infinity.

CHAPTER XIV

I wonder therefore, at those interpreters of Plato, who do not make one fabrication but many, who assess that there are three demiurgi of wholes, and pass at one time to the second, and at another to the third demiurgus; and who divide what is said in the *Timæus*, and think fit to refer some of the assertions to one, but others to another cause. For that there is a demiurgic triad, and another multitude of Gods characterised according to the producing cause, I also admit, and think it will be granted by Plato. It is necessary however in each order prior to the triad, and prior to every multitude, that there should be a pre-existent monad. For all the orders of the Gods originate from a monad; because each of the whole orders is assimilated to the whole progression of the Gods. As therefore the subsistence of the Gods has the cause of its generation from the imparticipable one, thus also it is necessary that the perfect orders in the Gods, should have a pre-existent monad, and a first-effective principle. According to the same reasoning, all the vivific progressions are suspended from one vivification, and the demiurgic orders are extended to one fabrication. And it is not proper that there should be multitude without the monad. For there will neither be co-arrangement, nor a division of multitude according to intellect, unless the one and whole pre-exist. For on this account prior to all the divine progressions, the order of wholeness subsists, in order that it may comprehend parts, and may define them in, and about itself.

How therefore neglecting whole in fabrication, can we survey demiurgi divided according to parts? Though Plato himself thinks with respect to the paradigm of the universe, that the world should not be assimilated to any thing which naturally subsists in the form of a part, but to all perfect animal; and on this account he demonstrates that the world is only-begotten, because its paradigm is one. For if it were not one, but many paradigms, again it would be necessary that there should be another animal about it, of which it would be a part, and it would be more right to assert that the world is no longer similar to the many paradigms, but to that which comprehends them. For it is necessary that the one paradigm should precede the many, in the same manner as the one good subsists prior to participated goods, and that the whole world should be the image of one paradigm prior to many. For whether it is alone the image of many paradigms, whence will the world be one and a whole? And how is it possible it should not be more dishonourable than its parts? For these indeed, are assimilated to intelligibles, but the whole world is similar to no one of real beings. Or whether all the world subsists from a certain intelligible paradigm, if indeed there are many paradigms of one world, these also will be similar to each other, if they are the causes of the same image. It is necessary therefore, that sameness should be communicated to these from one form; or again, the world will be more venerable than its paradigms according to union. But if the paradigm is one, after the same manner also the demiurgic cause is one. For as there is one image from one paradigm, thus also the progeny being one, derives its subsistence from one demiurgus and father. For it is necessary that the paradigmatic cause should either be the same with the demiurgus, and should be established in him, or that it should be prior to the demiurgus, as we say it is, or that it should be posterior to the demiurgus, as some think proper to assert.

If however, the paradigm and the demiurgus are the same, the demiurgus will be one according to Plato. For the paradigm is only-begotten, as he demonstrates. But if the demiurgus exists prior to the paradigm, which it is not lawful to assert, but the paradigm is one, much more will the demiurgus be one. For the causes which are more elevated are allotted a more uniform hypostasis; since also the first cause of wholes is one. And if the paradigmatic cause has indeed the first order in beings, but the demiurgic cause the second order, and this universe the last order, being the resemblance of the former, and the progeny of the latter, how is it possible since the extremes are monadic, the middle multitude should be without the monad? For it is necessary that the paradigm being intelligible, should impart by illumination a greater degree of union to the universe than the demiurgic cause. And as the paradigm being only-begotten, comprehends in itself the first paradigms, after the same manner it is necessary that the demiurgic monad should be comprehensive of many demiurgi. For if the world derives its only-begotten subsistence from the paradigm, but through the demiurgus, the demiurgus also is indeed entirely one.

Farther still, I think that those who are the patrons of this opinion should direct their attention to that assertion of Socrates, that it is every where fit the many should be comprehended in the one. For on account of this we admit the hypothesis of forms [or ideas], and prior to other things we pre-establish intellectual monads. How therefore are intellectual forms extended to one principle, and how do each of them proceed from one demiurgic cause, but the whole demiurgic form is multiplied, and divided prior to the indivisible monad? For it is necessary that as all equals, whether they are intellectual, or psychical, or sensible, should be suspended from one first equality, all beautiful things, from beauty itself, and the many every where, from primary beings, thus also it is necessary that the multitude of demiurgi should be suspended from one fabrication, and should subsist about one demiurgic monad. For how can it be lawful to leave the one in forms rather than in the Gods? For forms indeed, have their hypostasis mingled with multitude; but the Gods are defined according to union itself. If therefore all the multitudes of forms are the progeny of monads, much more are the orders of the Gods allotted peculiarities which originate from monads, and which through monads are inherent in multitudes. But if this be the case, it is necessary that the whole demiurgus should subsist prior to the multitude of demiurgi, and that the three demiurgi should distribute the one cause of the generation of the universe.

Again therefore we assert from the beginning that it is necessary the demiurgic principle should either be one, or many, or one, and many. But if indeed, it is one alone, and the multitude in the world, and the different order which it contains subsist similarly from one demiurgic principle, how are mortal and immortal natures the progeny of the same cause without a medium? For all the natures that proceed from the one fabrication are immortal. But if the demiurgic principle is many only, whence is the common form of hyparxis communicated to the multitude, if it does not originate from one? For as the final cause is one, *viz. The Good*, as the paradigmatic cause is one, *viz.* animal itself, and as the world is a generated one, thus also after the same manner, the demiurgic cause is one. But if there are one and many demiurgic principles, whether does the one principle belong to partial or to total genera? If however, it belongs indeed to partial genera, how is it extended to the first and intelligible paradigm? For the supermundane genera subsist about the intellectual Gods, and according to intellectual paradigms. For being partial, they entirely assimilate the natures posterior to themselves to intellectuals, co-ordinately to themselves. Or how will it any longer preserve the union of total fabrication which produces wholes totally? For a thing of this kind pertains to no partial nature; but it belongs to a partial principle, to produce parts either totally[†] or partially, as we before observed. But if the demiurgic principle belongs to the total orders, it is necessary that it should either be intelligible or intellectual, or intelligible and intellectual. If however, it is of an intelligible nature, how is it divisive of wholes? How is it co-arranged with mundane natures? How is it said to fashion the universe? How from the genera of being does it produce soul, and the natures posterior to soul? For [on this hypothesis] we must admit that all these are in intelligibles, *viz.* figure, the genera of being, and these divided, the similar and the dissimilar, and other things through which the demiurgic principle constitutes the whole world. But if the demiurgic principle is of an intelligible and at the same time intellectual nature, how does he produce participated intellect? How does he separate the multiform orders of souls? How does he divide the parts, or the circles that are in them? For that which is generative of participated intellect, is imparticipable intellect. And that which has the power of dividing multitude will not [on this hypothesis] differ from that which connects the total genera of the Gods. And in short, the demiurgus of wholes, is called by Timæus intellect, and is frequently said to see, to discover, and to reason, but he is no where denominated by him intelligible and at the same time intellectual. For the intelligible and at the same time intellectual Gods, divide all things triadically. But the demiurgus, at one time indeed, divides the world into five parts, and at another divides the circles of the soul into hebdomads, that he may generate either the celestial spheres, or the seven parts of the soul. We must say therefore, that he is entirely secondary to the intelligible and at the same time intellectual Gods, and he is the cause of secondary goods to the world. But we must refer to those Gods the cause of united forms and reasons. That the demiurgic intellect however, is an intellectual God, is I think through these things sufficiently apparent at present.

CHAPTER XV

But Plato appears to me to have indicated the peculiarity of this God in a remarkable manner, by calling him intellect, and asserting that he sees intelligibles, but admitting that they are visible to him according to nature. For that which is truly intellect, and which establishes itself according to this hyparxis, is intellectual intellect. For intelligible intellect also, is indeed simply intelligible, and is of that allotment; but is said to be intellect, as being the cause of every intellectual nature.

[†] ολικως is omitted in the original.

And the intellect of the intelligible and at the same time intellectual Gods, has not its own nature unmingled with the intelligible. But intellectual intellect alone, is peculiarly intellect, being allotted the intellectual itself in intellectuals; just as the most principal of intelligibles, is primarily, the first, and the highest intelligible, which we denominate the one being, and that which is occultly being. This therefore is that which is simply intelligible. But that which is simply intellect is intellectual intellect. For the intelligible indeed possesses the summit, but intellect the end of wholes. And the intermediate natures partly pertain to the intelligible, and partly to intellect, and the intellectual nature. And the intelligibles indeed, that are primarily so, possess intellect according to cause; but the first of intellectuals have the intelligible according to participation; and the natures that are collective of these, conjoin the intelligible and intellectual peculiarity together. Since, therefore, Timæus also calls the demiurgus intellect indefinitely, and neither denominates him life, nor intelligible, in consequence of his peculiarity being alone intellectual, it is certainly necessary that he should be established at the end of the intellectual Gods.

For there intellect is intellect itself, and is not such an intellect as the Saturnian is. For Saturn also is intellect, but he is a pure and incorruptible intellect, which manifests his supreme empire in intellectuals, transcending the whole intellectual Gods. But the demiurgus is simply intellect. As therefore, the simply intelligible is the first of intelligibles, so that which is simply intellect, is the last of intellectuals. For all things are in each of the orders. For in intelligibles life and intellect pre-exist; and in the breadth of life, there are similarly life and intellect. And in intellectuals there is each of the rest. But in intelligibles indeed, being is according to essence, but life and intellect are according to cause. In intellectuals, intellect indeed is according to essence, but being and life are according to participation. And in the intermediate natures intellect is according to cause, but being is according to participation, and life according to essence. As therefore, that which is most vital in life is the middle, and as that which is especially intelligible is the summit in being, so in intellectuals, the extremity is that which is most intellectual. Hence if there is a certain intellect which is simply intellect, and a perceiving intellect, this is intellectual intellect, which Plato denominating the demiurgus unfolds to us the most manifest order, which it is allotted in intellectuals. On this account also, prior to all other things, the demiurgus constitutes participated intellect, as Timæus says. For placing intellect in soul, and soul in body, he fashioned the universe. Energizing therefore, according to his own essence, and producing by his very being, he constituted the intellect of the universe prior to all other things. For every participated proceeds from imparticipable intellect. Hence, as if Plato had said, that the generative cause which gives subsistence to participated intelligible, is that which is primarily being, so since the demiurgus first produces intellect from himself, he will be imparticipable and intellectual intellect. From these things therefore, it is evident what the hyparxis of the demiurgus and father is, and what order it is allotted in intellectuals according to Timæus.

CHAPTER XVI

Let us however after another manner syllogistically collect the peculiarity of the demiurgus, receiving from the *Timæus* the principles of the arguments on this subject. This therefore is known to every one, that Timæus calls the whole demiurgus fabricator and father, in the beginning of what he says concerning him. For he says, "It is difficult to discover the fabricator and father of the universe, and when found, it is impossible to speak of him to all men."[6] Hence, he does not think fit to call him either father alone, or fabricator alone, nor again connecting the two, father and fabricator, but on the contrary, he places the fabricative prior to the paternal. Now therefore, we must show in the first place, in what respect fabricator and father differ from each other; and in the next place, in addition to this, who the fabricator alone is, and who father and fabricator is, and how the fabricative and at the same time paternal peculiarity, is considered by Plato as adapted to the demiurgus.

If therefore, we divide all things into the Gods, and the progeny of the Gods, and this is the same thing as to divide them into superessential monads, and the progressions of beings, father indeed will be generative of the Gods and superessential unities; but fabricator will give subsistence to essences and beings. For again, according to this reason Timæus says, that the natures which are generated by the demiurgus are equal to the Gods; for the demiurgus is not only fabricator, but also father; but that those which are produced by the junior Gods, are allotted a mortal nature. For these Gods are alone producers and fabricators of things which participate of existence alone, and not of the superessential peculiarity. Hence through that by which they suffer a diminution with respect to the demiurgic monad, through this they are not allotted a power generative of things equal to the Gods. And through that by which the intellectual demiurgus is expanded above the junior Gods, through this he binds to himself the generations of all mundane natures.

But if again, we divide beings into the total and partial, father indeed, will appear to us to be the hypostatic cause of wholes, but fabricator of partial natures. For the former is the cause exemptly of things that are generated; but the latter proximately. And the former, produces indeed by his very being, energy giving perfection to his hyparxis; but the latter produces by energizing, his hypostasis being fixed according to energy. If also we again separately divide the generations of perpetual and mortal natures, we must refer the generation of perpetual natures to the paternal cause, but the generation of mortal natures to the fabricative cause. For the fabricator indeed produces that which is generated from non-being to being. For the Elean guest defines the effective art to be this. But the father constitutes things posterior to himself consubsistent with himself. For he is father by his very being, and has the power of generating united with himself. Each therefore, I mean the paternal and the effective or fabricative, is assimilated to the principle of bound. And the former indeed is the cause of union, but the latter of the production of forms. And the former is the cause of wholes, but the latter of an extension as far as to parts. And the one indeed, is the primary leader of simple, but the other of composite natures. Again however, in these the generative cause, and the cause which is productive of life, are opposed to each other; because the paternal cause indeed is connascent with generative powers, but the effective with vivific powers. And as the paternal and the effective causes pertain to the co-ordination of bound, so every thing prolific and vivific, pertains to vivification, and the first infinity.

These things, however, being thus divided by us, it is evident that the paternal indeed, is itself by itself primarily in the intelligible Gods. For they are the fathers of wholes, being fixed according to supreme intelligible union. And on this account, Plato also calls the first God father, from the natures which are proximately established after him, transferring to him the appellation of father. For every where indeed, it is usual with Plato to introduce names to the ineffable from secondary causes, and the causes which are posterior to it. But at one time indeed, he introduces the names from all beings, and at another from the first beings. For it neither was nor is lawful to refer names to him who is exempt from all beings, from subordinate natures, and which are placed in an order very remote from him. If therefore, all beings participate of the paternal peculiarity, we must say that Plato gives this name to *The One* from all beings; for there is not among all beings such a cause as this. Hence it is evident that Plato introduces to *The One* an appellation of this kind, from that which is the first and highest in the Gods. The intelligible Gods, however, are more ancient than all the divine orders, and subsist immediately after *The One*. The paternal cause therefore of beings is in the intelligible Gods, and the intelligible Gods are the fathers of all the divine genera, being established in the highest essences, and occultly producing wholes. And the first God indeed, is beyond the appellation of father, as he is likewise beyond all other names; and he is neither properly called *The Good*, or *The One*, through his ineffable and unknown transcendency. But the intelligible Gods are primarily superessential unities and goodnesses, and are the exempt fathers of beings.

The paternal peculiarity, therefore, originates supernally from the first intelligible triad; but the fabricative first presents itself to the view in the third triad. For that which generates all forms, and adorns all things with forms is the third triad of intelligibles. For there, as we have said, all-perfect animal subsists, which is comprehensive of the first and intelligible paradigms. Here therefore, the effective also or fabricative at the same time subsists. For animal itself constitutes the Gods, and produces the forms of all beings. Hence it is allotted the paternal peculiarity, according to the divine cause, but according to the formal cause, it unfolds into light the effective principle of wholes. But again, on the contrary, the effective and at the same time paternal peculiarity, is allotted its hypostasis in the demiurgic monad. Hence also the Demiurgus of wholes is the hypostatic cause of Gods. In a particular manner however, he fabricates the world, energising with forms and demiurgic reasons. For he constitutes intellect, souls and bodies, adorning all things with forms, some indeed with first, others with middle, and others with last forms.

Do you not see, therefore, how the end of intelligibles indeed, was paternal and at the same time effective; but the end of intellectuals is effective and at the same time paternal. There however, the paternal peculiarity is more predominant; but here the effective. For in both indeed, both causes pre-exist; nevertheless in the paradigm [*i.e.* in animal itself] the paternal is more prevalent, but in the demiurgus the effective. For the former produces by his very being; but the latter by energizing. And in the former indeed, fabrication [or effective energy] is essential; but in the latter essence is effective. Forms also are with both; but in the former intelligibly, and in the latter intellectually. From these things therefore, it is evident, that the demiurgic cause subsists analogous to the paradigmatic cause; and that it has the same order with respect to intellectuals, as that has with respect to intelligibles. And on this account Timæus also says that the demiurgus of wholes was extended to that paradigm. For he says, "Whatever ideas intellect perceived by the dianoëtic energy in animal itself, such and so many he conceived it necessary for the universe to contain." And together with this analogy, there is a diminution of the intellectual with reference to the intelligible. For the latter is more united; but the former is more separated. And the one indeed is pre-established in the order of the desirable; but the other is moved about the desirable. And the one fills with paternal power; but the other absorbs as it were and embosoms the whole prolific abundance of the desirable. And after this manner, the demiurgus of the universe is all-perfect, receiving whole intelligible powers, from all-perfect animal. For the universe is threefold; one indeed being intelligibly [all]; another intellectually; and another sensibly. For the world is perfect, from perfect natures, as Timæus says. And animal itself is perfect according to all things, as the same Timæus asserts. The demiurgus likewise, being the best of causes, is all-perfect.

Again therefore, resuming what we have said, we repeat, that the paternal cause commences from the supreme union of intelligibles; but the paternal and at the same time effective cause is consubsistent in the intelligible paradigm; and the effective and at the same time paternal cause is defined according to the whole demiurgus. But the cause which is alone effective and fabricative, pertains to the junior Gods who give subsistence to partial and mortal things. The peculiarity therefore of the demiurgic cause is effective and paternal. And this Timæus asserts, not only in the beginning of the discourse about it, in which he says, "[To discover] therefore, the artificer and father of this universe, etc.;" but also in the speech to the junior Gods, he does the same thing; for the demiurgus in a similar manner says to them: "Gods of Gods of whom I am the demiurgus and father, [Whatever is generated by me is indissoluble, I being willing that it should be so.]" For he does not call himself father and demiurgus, but demiurgus and father, just as there [Timæus calls him] fabricator and father. And not in the *Timæus* only is this mode of the arrangement of the names defined, but in the *Politicus* also, the Elean guest speaking about the world says that it imitates the instructions of its demiurgus and father; and in the beginning indeed, he uses these names more accurately, but in the end more negligently. Since Plato therefore, every where preserves this order of names unchanged, it is evident to those who are not entirely unskilled in things of this kind, that he defines the demiurgic monad according to this peculiarity, and that he considers it to be effective and at the same time paternal. For because indeed, it is the end of the intellectual triad, it is allotted a paternal transcendency with respect to all the second genera of Gods; but because it produces from itself all the partial genera and species of beings, it possesses an effective cause of the natures to which it gives subsistence. And because indeed, it is father, power is in it, and at the same time intellect. For the demiurgus himself says, "Imitating the power which I employed in your generation." And again, Timæus says concerning the demiurgus; "Whatever ideas, therefore, intellect perceived by the dianoëtic energy in animal itself, such and so many he conceived it necessary for the universe to contain."† Hence he is father, and the power of the father is in him, and intellect. All these however, are in him intellectually, and not intelligibly. Hence, I think he is called father indeed, not simply, but together with effector and demiurgus; and power, not by itself, but the power of the demiurgus and father. For he who calls himself demiurgus and father, says that it is the power of himself. But he is immediately called intellect, without the addition of power, and the other appellations. "Whatever ideas therefore intellect perceived," etc. For all things are in him intellectually, and both power and father, by which he imitates the intelligible paradigm. For in him all things were intelligibly,‡ *viz.* bound, infinity, and that which is mixed from both these. These, however, are father, power, and intellect. But the intellectual of the paradigm indeed was intelligible in the intelligible Gods, subsisting prior to an intellectual cause. The intellectual however of the demiurgus, is of itself intellectual, being intellectual in intellectuals, as was before observed. Because indeed, as we have said, he is father, power is in him, and also intellect. But because these are defined according to the effective and demiurgic, he is co-arranged with the vivific order, and together with it constitutes the genera of life, and vivifies the whole world. What this order is however, and where it is arranged, we shall shortly survey. But thus much is evident from what has been said, that so far as he is the demiurgus, he requires contact with the vivific order, together with it generates total lives, and conjoins it to himself. Disseminating, however, all the measures of life in it, and

---

† In the original this reads "Whatever ideas intellect perceived in animal itself, such and so many he conceived by the dianoëtic energy it necessary for this universe to contain." But this is better phrased in Taylor's translation of Plato's *Timæus* which is given here. PT.

‡ For νοερως, it is necessary to read νοητως.

together with it adorning and producing them, he again converts them to himself. For it belongs to him to generate all things, and to recall all things to himself, no less than to generate them, because he is established at the end of the intellectual order, and is the demiurgic intellect. As he is therefore demiurgic, he gives subsistence to all things; but as intellect, he convolves multitude to union, and converts it to himself. He also accomplishes both these, by the words which he delivers to the junior Gods. For he fills them with demiurgic and prolific power, collects them to himself, constitutes himself the object of desire as it were to the multitude of Gods, and extends about himself all the demiurgi in the world.

CHAPTER XVII

In the third place therefore, let us purify our conceptions about the demiurgic cause according to other projecting energies of intellect, following for this purpose Timæus. In the first place then, Timæus in the beginning of the theory concerning the demiurgus, sufficiently exhibits his goodness, and his unenvying and abundant communication of demiurgic reasons, being impelled to this from the seat of goodness which is inherent in him, and from his exuberant deity. For his goodness and his unenvying abundance, are not as it were a certain habit of good, and a power, or a form itself by itself existing prior to many goods, but it is one ineffable participation of good, and *The One* of the demiurgic order; according to which the demiurgus also is a God, and fills all things with their proper good. For because there is deity in him which desires to adorn and arrange all things, and an hyparxis which is extended to the providence of the whole of things, on this account he establishes the principle of fabrication. His goodness therefore is nothing else than demiurgic deity. But his will is the progeny of the energy of his goodness, bounding the end of his power. For since in the demiurgus of wholes are, as we have said, father, power, and intellect, and these subsist in him intellectually, according to each of these he is filled with the participation of *The One*. And through goodness indeed, that which is paternal in him, and which is as it were the intelligible of intellect, is illuminated. But through will, his power is governed, and is extended to one intelligible good. And through providence, his intellect is perfect, and gives subsistence to all things. All these likewise are the progeny of the one deity in the demiurgus.

In the first place, therefore, as I have said, Timæus unfolds through these things the divine peculiarity of the demiurgus. But in the second place, he presents to our view the intelligible cause which is in him, and also the united paradigmatic cause of wholes which he contains. For to make all things similar to himself, evinces that he is the intelligible paradigm of every thing beautiful and good in the world. For because he gives subsistence to all things by his very being, that to which he gives subsistence is the image of himself. And according to this reasoning the demiurgus is not only a God, but he contains in himself the intelligible, and true being, and antecedently comprehends not only the final cause of mundane natures, but also the paradigmatic cause. But again, in the third place, Timæus celebrates the demiurgic power, and the principle which abolishes every thing disorderly and indefinite, and prepares the beautiful alone and the good to have dominion in wholes. For the assertion that the demiurgus to the utmost of his power suffered nothing evil and vile to exist, indicates his unconquerable power, which adorns things material in an unpolluted manner, and imparts by illumination bound to indefinite, and order to disorderly natures.

In which part of the *Timæus*, likewise, this dogma of Plato will appear to you to be admirable, that matter is generated from some one of the Gods situated above the demiurgus. For the demiurgus receiving matter occupied by the vestiges of forms, thus himself introduces into it all the perfection of ornament and arrangement. Matter, therefore, and the whole of that which is the subject of bodies, proceed supernally from the first principles, which on account of their exuberance of power, are able to generate even the last of beings. But the demiurgus of the universe, imparts by illumination, order, bound and ornament, and the whole world is fabricated an image of intelligibles, through the communication of forms.

In the fourth place, therefore, let us survey how Timæus unfolds to us the demiurgic intellect. "By a reasoning process", says he, "the demiurgus discovered from the things which are visible according to nature, that no work which is destitute of intelligence can ever become more beautiful than that which possesses intellect." What therefore is this reasoning? What is the discovery, and whence does it originate? Reasoning, therefore, is indeed distributed intellection, looking to itself, and in itself investigating good. For every one who reasons, passes from one thing to another, and being converted to himself, searches after good. The demiurgic intellect, therefore, in adorning and arranging the universe subsists analogously to him who reasons; for he emits the divided causes of mundane natures, which pre-exist unitedly in intelligibles. For those things which intelligible intellect constitutes uniformly and exemptly, these intellectual intellect separating, distributing into parts, and as it were fabricating by itself, generates. Reasoning therefore is the being filled with the intelligible, and an all-perfect union with it. By which also it is evident that it is not fit to think this reasoning [of the demiurgus] is either investigation or doubt, or a wandering of divine intellect, but that it is stable intelligence intellectually perceiving the multiform causes of beings. For intellect is always united to the intelligible, and is filled with its own intelligibles. And in a similar manner it is intellect in energy, and intelligible. For at one and the same time, it intellectually perceives and is perceived, discovers itself, entering into itself, and the reasoning also finds what this intelligence is, but not according to transition. For the intelligence of the Gods is eternal. And invention with them is not the discovery of that which is absent; for all things are always present to the intellect of the Gods. The intelligible likewise there is not separated from intellect. The conversion, therefore, of intellect to itself may be called reasoning; but the being filled from intelligibles invention. And intelligibles themselves may be denominated things visible according to nature. For because Timæus had denominated the unadorned subject of bodies when it was vanquished by the obscure vestiges of forms, visible, hence, I think, he calls intelligibles visible according to nature. For it is according to nature, to intellect to look to these and not to things subordinate to these. As, therefore, he says, that intellect itself sees intelligibles, after the same manner also he calls intelligibles things naturally visible, and converts intellect to the intelligible, as that which sees to that which is seen. If, therefore, intellect sees animal itself, and assimilates to it the whole world, it may be said that animal itself is visible to the demiurgus of the universe. For there the most splendid of intelligibles subsists; and this is that which we before demonstrated, when we said that there the fountain of beauty shines forth, which Socrates, in the *Phædrus*, denominates splendid and fulgid.

CHAPTER XVIII

Such therefore are the concepts which are to be assumed of the demiurgic cause, and from these things they are to be derived. We shall however obtain one perfection of the summit of the dogmas concerning it, if we are able to survey the words which this cause extends to the junior demiurgi, and to unfold the concealed meaning of them. This, therefore, we shall also do, establishing the following principle of the explanation of them: The energies and powers of the Gods are twofold. And some indeed abide in, and energize about them, and have for their end one hypostasis, and which is united to essence. But others proceed from them, exhibit an efficacious power about secondary natures, and coexist with the multitude of their recipients, and with the peculiarity of essence. These, however, being twofold, the secondary are suspended from those that are prior to them, are defined about them, and receive their proper hyparxis according to them. For it is every where necessary that eternally proceeding should be the images of internal energies, evolving the at-once-collected nature of their indivisibility; multiplying that in them which is united, and dividing their impartibility.

According to this reasoning, therefore, the energy of nature is also twofold, one being that which abides in it, according to which it connects itself, and the reasons it contains, but the other proceeding from it, through which also bodies are filled with these physical powers, which being moved by nature, act on each other, and physically suffer by each other. Again, the motion of the soul likewise is twofold. And the one indeed is self-motive, is converted to itself, is of itself, concurs with the life of the soul, and is without any difference with respect to it. But the other is incumbent on alter-motive natures, moves these, and about these extends the power of itself. The energy of intellect, therefore, is likewise twofold. And one indeed is intellectual, is united to true beings, and is impartible, being co-existent with the intelligible itself of intellect, or rather being the intelligible itself, and intellect. For intellect is not of itself in capacity, and afterwards receiving energy, intellectually perceives the intelligible; but is one simple energy. For the multitude of it is unical, and its energy is directed to itself. But the other energy of intellect is directed to externals, and to things which are able to participate of intellect. For these intellect causes to be intellectual through itself, splendidly as it were emitting the light of its own intelligence, and imparting it to others. It is necessary, therefore, that the divine and demiurgic intellect itself, should always indeed be united to the intelligible, and that it should have the plenitude and self-sufficiency of demiurgic intelligence eternally established according to a union exempt from wholes; to which, as it appears to me, Timæus also looking says, that the father of the universe abides in his accustomed manner, and withdraws himself to his own place of survey, delivering the fabrication of mortal natures to the mundane Gods. For so far as he is exempt from the beings posterior to himself and is unco-ordinated with the more partial multitude of Gods, so far he is converted to himself, and surveys and intellectually perceives the natures prior to himself, according to one uniform union. But in consequence of the more ruling and leading Gods being extended towards him, he emits from himself secondary energies, to all the partial orders.

Timæus, therefore, fashions through words, these powers and efficacious energies which proceed from the whole and one fabrication to the demiurgic multitude of Gods. For words are the images of intellections; because indeed they evolve that which is contracted in intelligibles, but lead forth that which is impartible into a partible hypostasis. They likewise transfer that which abides in itself into habitude to another thing. And it is evident that the reasons which are impelled from nature, are certain natural [powers], and render that which receives them physical. But the reasons which are generated from soul, are indeed vivific, but render the inanimate nature which participates of them [animated] and moved from itself, through the power of the soul, as Socrates says in the *Phædrus*, and communicate to it the resemblance of self-motion. And the reasons which are generated from intellect, illuminating the natures posterior to it, distribute all intellectual goods to their recipients, being the suppliers of true knowledge, of purity and a more simple life. After the same manner also the demiurgic words produce in the junior Gods, whole, impartible, and united measures of exempt fabrication, and fill their essences with demiurgic providence. They likewise render them second demiurgi, and emulous of their father. For he indeed gives subsistence to the whole plenitudes of the world. But they, imitating him, fabricate all partial natures in conjunction with wholes. And he produces the essence of perpetual natures. But they fashioning mortal natures according to one generation-producing circle, likewise transmute these. And as the one demiurgus governs the whole periods of the universe, thus also the many demiurgi convolve the divisible circles of the natures that are borne along† in generation. If, therefore, we assert these things rightly concerning the words proceeding from the demiurgus to the multitude of mundane Gods, and they are efficacious, fabricative, and convertive of their recipients to a union with him, and are also perfective of the beneficent reasons which they contain, we shall no longer seem to speak paradoxically, if we say that these words extend to the Gods in the world the participation of all the powers that are firmly established in the father, and of the causes prior to, and subsisting after him. And as he convolving the end of the intellectual Gods, is the plenitude of all things, so likewise the demiurgic words proceeding from him, produce in the junior Gods the peculiarities, as I may say, of all the divine genera

---

† For φυρομενων read φερομενων.

that are above the world, through which they are suspended from all the orders prior to them; just I think as the whole of this world [is suspended from the mundane Gods who]† fabricate all mortal natures, and impart to different things a different power, and an efflux of divine powers.

What, therefore, in short, is it which Plato indicates the Gods derive through these words from the first demiurgus, and the all-perfect fabrication? In the first place, indeed, they derive this, that they are Gods of Gods. For the vocal address proceeding to them from the father, is the supplier of divine power, and is allotted an efficacious presence in its participant, as we before observed. But in the next place, these words impart to them an indissoluble power. The demiurgus of wholes, however, comprehends in himself the cause of dissolution, in order that they may indeed be essentially indissoluble, but according to the cause of binding, not indissoluble. In the third place, therefore, the demiurgus produces in them from on high, through these words, a renovated immortality. For the assertion that they are neither immortal, nor shall be subject to the fatality of death, establishes them in this form of immortality, which the fable in the *Politicus* denominates renovated. In addition to this also, the words testify that they derive from the father a power perfective of wholes. For if the world is imperfect without the subsistence of mortal animals, it is doubtless necessary that those who preside over the generation of them should be the causes of perfection to the universe. And in the last place, these words impart to the junior Gods a paternal and generative empire derived from the exempt and intellectual cause of wholes; and insert in them the proximate powers of regeneration. For through these words, the junior Gods again receive in themselves the natures that are corrupted, fabricate parts from wholes, and again effect the dissolution of parts into their wholes. And universally the words of the demiurgus subject the perpetually-generated course of nature, to the fabrication of the junior Gods. In short therefore, the demiurgus fills the junior Gods with divine union, fills them with a firm establishment, and fills them with a perpetuity adapted to their nature. But he pours into them the all-various causes of perfective powers, of vivific rivers, and demiurgic measures. Hence also, the many demiurgi refer the fabrication of particulars to the one and whole providence of the father, and the

---

† There is evidently something wanting in the original in this part; and as it appears to me after καθαπερ (οιμαι) και ο συμπας ουτοσι κοσμος, it is requisite to supply the words εις τους εγκοσμιους θεους ανηρτηται, οι.

principles of demiurgic works which they receive from him, to his efficacious production. And all of them indeed are filled with all powers, because all of them participate of the demiurgic words which proceed into them from the father. But some of them are more characterised by one peculiarity than another.

And some of them indeed are the suppliers of union to their progeny; others, of indissoluble permanency; others, of perfection; and others, of life. But others preside over regeneration, and being allotted in a distributed manner in the universe, the powers which subsist unitedly in the one demiurgus, they are subservient to the providence of the father. And every thing which is generated by the many demiurgi, is in a much greater degree produced by the one fabrication; which governs mortal natures indeed, eternally, things that are moved, immovably, and partible natures impartibly. It is not however necessary that the progeny of that one demiurgus should be suspended from the motion of the junior Gods. For every where the one fabrication is more comprehensive than that which is multiplied. And the more causal of divine natures energize prior to their own offspring, and together with them constitute the progeny that proceed from them. The first [demiurgic] God, therefore, produces from and through himself the divine genera† of the universe, according to his beneficent will. But he governs mortal natures through the junior Gods, generating indeed these also from himself, but other Gods producing them as it were with their own hands. For he says, "these being generated *through* me will become equal to the Gods." The cause, therefore, *through which*, is to be attributed to the junior Gods; but the cause *from which*, even in the production of mortal natures is to be referred to the whole demiurgus. For always the first of those things that are constituted, produce in conjunction with their monad the generation of secondary natures. And all things indeed proceed *from* that monad, but some things immediately; and *through* it, but some things through other media receive the providence that emanates from it. For these middle genera of causes are allotted the providential inspection of secondary natures from the first effective monad.

---

† It appears from the version of Portus that the words θεια γενη are omitted in the original.

CHAPTER XIX

Concerning the words, therefore, in the *Timæus*, which the demiurgus delivers to the Gods in the world, thus much may suffice at present. But after these, it is fit to survey the secondary measures of total demiurgic providence, which the demiurgus extends from himself to the many and divisible souls. For having constituted these, divided them equal in number to divine animals, and disseminated them about the world, he inserts in them fabricative boundaries, defines the whole periods of them, inscribes in them the laws of Fate, proposes the apparent measures of their generation-producing life, legally institutes, and adorns in a becoming manner all the rewards of virtue, and the works of vice, intellectually comprehends in one the end of every period, and co-arranges with a view to this the whole polity of partial souls. All[†] souls, therefore, of an immortal condition, being allotted a progression from the demiurgus, are filled from him with an united and intellectual providence. Because, however, progeny which are suspended from their causes participate of the perfective efficacy which proceeds from them, divine souls, indeed, primarily subsisting from thence, become auditors of the words of their father immediately; but partial souls participate of the uniform providence of the demiurgus secondarily, and with greater partibility. Hence also the demiurgus, as a legislator, defining to these all the measures of their life, he thus extends demiurgic words, unitedly comprehending the divided nature of the whole of their life, convolving in sameness without time their temporal mutability, and collecting uniformly, according to one simplicity, the multiform and diversified nature of the energy which exists about them. But to divine souls he immediately unfolds the providence of himself, and exhorts them to join with him in a providential inspection of the whole world, to fabricate, adorn and dispose in conjunction with him, mortal natures, to govern generated beings according to the measures of justice, and to lead and convolve all things, following demiurgic providence. Very far therefore, are those interpreters of Plato from according with the fabrication of the universe, who admit that partial are the same with whole souls, and who attribute the same essence to all souls; because all of them are allotted their generation from one demiurgus.

For in the first place, the father in the course of his fabrication adorning, and disposing in an orderly manner partial souls, poured

---

[†] For πασι, it is necessary to read πασαι.

mingling, the remainder of the former mixture, says Timæus, and produced the second and third genera. But in a progression of this kind, the words effective of conversion which he extends to divine souls, are intellectual, and demiurgic, and impart to them generative powers, and perfective goods; but those which he extends to partial souls, are the definite sources of generation, of the laws of Fate, of justice, and all-various periods. If, therefore, every thing which proceeds from the demiurgus is essentially imparted to souls, it is indeed necessary that different measures of words should be the causes of different powers; and that to some among the number of divisible souls, the demiurgus should distribute a polity exempt from mundane affairs, but to others a polity arranged under these souls, and supernally governed by them. These things, however, may elsewhere be more copiously demonstrated.

CHAPTER XX

After the demiurgic words therefore, again returning to the demiurgic intellect, let us survey following Plato, who the demiurgus is, who convolves the end itself of the intellectual triad to the beginning, and after what manner it is fit to denominate him according to the Grecian theology. Or rather, prior to this let us summarily show what we may assume concerning him according to the narration of Timæus. For we shall more easily learn those particulars, if we assent to these. For directly, in the beginning of the theology concerning him, he is celebrated as the fabricator and father of the world. And he is neither called fabricator alone, nor father and fabricator, but at one and the same time manifestly possessing both peculiarities, he is rather characterised by the fabricative, than by the paternal cause. But he is denominated the demiurgus of wholes, according to his goodness, unenvying and exuberant will, and his power which is able to adorn and arrange all things, and even such as are of a disorderly nature. He is however particularly unfolded to us as the supplier of beauty, symmetry and order, and as the best of causes; and this because he is allotted the uniform, and first effective power of the whole demiurgic series. But he gives subsistence to intellect and soul, and at the same time to all the life in the world; since he fabricated the whole world an animal animated, and endued with intellect. Being likewise full of every intelligible, and extending himself to intelligible and all-perfect animal and conjoining this to himself through similitude, he fabricates the sensible universe only-begotten, in the same manner as the separate paradigm [animal itself] transcending wholes, unitedly constitutes the intelligible universe.

Moreover, he is likewise the fabricator of bodies, and the perfector of works, binding all things by the most excellent analogies, and co-adapting their powers, bulks, and numbers by the most beautiful bonds. Farther still, he constituted the universe a whole from wholes, and perfect from perfect parts, that it might be free from old age and disease, and might contain in itself all the genera of the elements. He likewise adorned it with the first figure, and with the most simple and most comprehensive of all figures. Besides these things, he is also the cause of self-sufficiency to the universe, and of a circulation into itself, in order that suffering all things from, and effecting all things in itself, it might not be in want of any thing externally situated. And he is indeed the supplier of intellectual motion, and of a life which is evolved according to time, and which effects[†] a mutation always according to the same, and similarly, and about the same things. Farther still, he is the father of soul, and of all the genera in soul, of the division in it, and all the harmonic reasons it contains, constituting it in the world, as a self-moved and immortal lyre; and he is also the divider of the one, and the seven circles in it, and in short, is the maker and fabricator of figure and morphe.[‡]

In addition to these things likewise, he generates from himself the whole of time, according to the imitation of eternity, together with all the measures of time, and the Gods that unfold these measures into light. But he especially constitutes the whole sun, enkindling its light from his own intellectual essence, in order that possessing a transcendency exempt from the other Gods it might be the king of the universe. Moreover, he fabricates[§] all the multitudes of mundane Gods and dæmons, and all celestial and sublunary natures, in order that he may evince this only begotten and self-sufficient God [the world] to be the image of the intelligible and all-perfect God; fixing the earth indeed, as a first seat or Vesta, in it, but distributing by lot the other elements to divine souls and dæmons. Besides all this likewise, he converts to himself the genera of Gods that have proceeded from him, and fills all things with undefiled generation, with perpetual life, demiurgic perfection, and generative abundance. He also constitutes divisible souls together with their vehicles, divides them about their leading Gods,

---

[†] For ποιουμενον, it is necessary to read ποιουμενης.

[‡] Morphe pertains to the colour, figure, and magnitude of superficies.

[§] For δημιουργου, it is necessary to read δημιουργει.

arranges different souls under different Gods, unfolds to them the laws of Fate, measures their descents into generation, establishes rewards to their contests in their periodic revolutions, and institutes, as I may say, the whole of their polity in the world.

But after all these things, he introduces a boundary to the providence of wholes, and returning to his own place of survey, delivering to the junior Gods the superintendence of mortal natures, and abiding in his own accustomed manner, is the paradigm to the demiurgi in the world of providential attention to beings of a second order. And as in the fabrication of wholes the paradigm is intelligible animal, so in the arrangement of partial natures, the paradigm is intellectual animal, in which all forms shine forth in a divided manner, according to their own nature. For Timæus says, "the children understanding the order of their father, were obedient to it", and he abiding, and paternally, and eternally producing all things, they adorn and arrange the mortal genera demiurgically, and according to time. Hence the providence of the demiurgus presents itself to the view, extending from on high as far as to the production of these, and what is here said by Plato, is as it were a hymn to the demiurgus and father of this universe, celebrating his productions, and the benefits which he confers on the world.

And it is requisite that being persuaded by what is here clearly written, we should investigate all the other enquiries about the demiurgus. My meaning is, that we should investigate what we mentioned a little before, who the demiurgus is, and how we ought to denominate him according to the sentiments of the Greeks; and on what account, Timæus neither delivers the name of him, nor unfolds to us who he is, but says, "that it is difficult to discover him, and that when discovered, it impossible to speak of him to all men." Now therefore, I think, from what has been already said, it is evident even to those who are but in a small degree intelligent, that according to the decision of Plato, it is the great Jupiter, who is now celebrated by us as the demiurgus. For if, as we have observed, the kingdom of Saturn is the summit of the whole intellectual triad, and the intelligible transcendency of intellectuals, but the maternal and vivific fountain of Rhea, is the middle centre, and the receiving bosom of the generative power of Saturn, it is manifest to every one, that the mighty Jupiter is allotted the end of this triad. For from the before mentioned causes, one of which indeed is paternal, but the other generative, he is the God having a paternal subsistence, who is said to reign, receiving the intellectual dominion of his father. If, therefore, it is necessary that the demiurgus should convolve the end of this intellectual triad, as was before demonstrated, and to effect this, is the province of the royal power of Jupiter, we must evidently acknowledge that the Jovian empire is the same as that of the demiurgus, and that Jupiter is the demiurgus celebrated in the *Timæus*.

CHAPTER XXI

If, however, it be necessary to consider this as worthy of further discussion, and to demonstrate that the theology in the *Timæus* about the demiurgus, accords with what is elsewhere written by Plato concerning this God, let us in the first place assume what is delivered in the *Critias*, because this dialogue proximately follows the *Timæus*, and is composed according to an analogy to it, delivering the hypostasis of the same things in images, the primary paradigms of which Timæus celebrates through the fabrication of the world. Here, therefore, Plato, (that I may derive what I say from the beginning) relating the warlike preparations of the Athenians, in former times, and the insolence and usurpation of the Atlantics, who were the progeny of Neptune, but destroyed the divine seed, through the mixture of human and mortal pursuits, and conducted themselves insolently to all men, collects indeed the Gods to a consultation concerning them, in the same manner as poets inspired by Phœbus, and forms a common assembly of the Gods. But Jupiter is the author of the whole polity of them, and converts the multitude of them to himself. And as in the *Timæus* the demiurgus convolves all the mundane Gods to himself, so Jupiter in the *Critias* providentially attending to the whole of things, collects the Gods to himself.

In the next place, therefore, let us consider what Plato says concerning this God, and how it accords with what was before said by Timæus. "But Jupiter the God of Gods who reigns legitimately, and who is able to perceive every thing of this kind, when he saw that an equitable race was in a miserable condition, and was desirous of punishing them, in order that by being chastised they might possess more elegant manner, collected all the Gods into their most honourable habitation, whence being seated as in the middle of the whole world, he beholds all such things as participate of generation." Here, directly in the beginning, king Jupiter being celebrated as the God of Gods, does it not accord with what is written in the *Timæus*, where he is said to be the father and cause of all the mundane Gods? For what other God is it who reigns over all the Gods, except the cause of their subsistence and essence? Who is it also that calls the mundane deities, Gods of Gods? Is it not him who binds to himself the principle of fabrication? If, therefore, he imparts to his progeny to be Gods of Gods, in a much greater degree it pertains to him to be celebrated as the God of all [the mundane] Gods. To which, therefore of the Gods prior to the world, does it particularly belong to punish offenders except to him who defines to souls all their measures, unfolds to them the laws of the universe, and legally institutes such things as are fit concerning justice and injustice, in order that afterwards he may not be accused of the vices of each of them? Moreover, to congregate all the Gods into their most honourable habitation, from which the whole of generation may be seen, and which possesses the middle of the universe, is to attribute to him a providence exempt from multitude, but extending equally to the whole world; which things indeed are the illustrious goods of the demiurgic monad. For to convert all the Gods to himself, and to survey the whole world pertains exemptly to the demiurgus of the universe. For what else is multitude able to participate proximately, except the monad from which it derives its subsistence? And who can convert all the Gods in the world to himself, but the fabricator of their essence, and of their allotment in the universe?

CHAPTER XXII

We must establish this, therefore, as one and the first argument in proof of the thing investigated. But if you are willing, we will derive a second argument from what is said by Socrates in the *Cratylus*, in which he discusses the meaning of the names, from which he may represent to us the essence of Jupiter. For he is not led to the nature of this God from one name, as he is in the names of other Gods, such as Saturn, Rhea, Neptune, and Pluto, but from two names which tend to one thing, and which divisibly indicate the one and united essence of Jupiter, he unfolds the power of this God, and the peculiarity of his hyparxis. For the common rumour concerning him, denominates him in a twofold respect. And at one time calling him (δια) *dia*, we worship him in our prayers and hymns; but at another time we celebrate him as (ζηνα) *zena*, a word derived from *life*. Being therefore at the same time called (ζευς) *Zeus*, and delighting in the appellation of *dia*, he is similarly denominated from both names by the Greeks. And these names manifest the essence and order which he is allotted among divine natures. And neither of these names indeed, is by itself sufficiently able to make known the peculiarity of the God; but when conjoined with each other and forming a sentence, they have the power of unfolding the truth concerning him.† How, therefore, from both the names the power of this king is signified, and the precedaneous order of his hypostasis in the Gods, we may hear Socrates himself saying, "That the name of his father‡ who is called Jupiter is beautifully posited; but that it is not easy to apprehend the meaning of it, because in reality the name of Jupiter is as it were a sentence. Dividing it however into two parts, some of us use one part, and some another. For some indeed call him *zena*, but others *dia*. And these parts collected into one evince the nature of the God, which we say a name ought to effect. For there is not any other who is more the author of life to us, and to all other things than he who is the ruler and king of all things. It happens, therefore, that this God is rightly denominated, *on account of* whom *life* is present to all living beings. But it is divided into two parts, as if I should say that there is one name from *dia* and *zena*." The mode, therefore, of collecting the names into one, and of rendering the hyparxis of this God apparent through both, is manifest to every one.

If, however, he is the supplier of life to all things, as he is said to be, and is the ruler and king of all such things as are said to live, to whom can we assert this peculiarity pertains, if we omit the demiurgus? And is it not necessary, that according with what is said in the *Timæus*, we should refer to him the principle of vivification. For the demiurgus renders the whole world animated, endued with intellect, and an animal, and constitutes the triple life which is in it, one indeed being impartible and intellectual, another partible and corporeal, and another between these, impartible and at the same time partible. It is he likewise who conjoins each of the celestial spheres to the circulations of the soul, inserts in each of the stars a psychical and intellectual life, and produces in the sublunary elements leading Gods and souls, and in addition to all these things, constitutes the divisible genera of life, and imparts to the junior Gods the principle of mortal animals. All things therefore in the world are full of life, through the power of the demiurgus and father. And this world is one animal, deriving its completion from containing all animals, through the never-failing cause of the power by which it was generated. And there is no other who is the supplier of life to all things, and through whom all things live, some indeed more clearly, but others more obscurely, than the demiurgus of wholes. For he also is intellectual animal, in the same manner as the all-perfect paradigm is

---

† For αυτων it seems necessary to read αυτου.

‡ *i.e.* Of the father of Tantalus.

intelligible animal. Hence likewise, these are conjoined to each other. And the one indeed is paternally the cause of wholes; but the other demiurgically. And as animal itself constitutes intelligibly, all intelligible and sensible animals, according to one cause, thus also the demiurgus fabricates intellectually according to a second order, the animals in the world.

As animal itself likewise proximately subsists from intelligible life, so the demiurgus is generated from intellectual life, and is the first that is filled with the rivers of vivification. Hence he illuminates all things with life, unfolding the depths of the animal-producing deity, and calling forth the prolific power of the intellectual Gods. If therefore, all things live through the demiurgic cause, they also participate of soul and intellect, and, as I may say, of all vivification, through the providence of this God. But he who pours the rivers of life on all things in the world from himself, and is the ruler and king of wholes, is the mighty Jupiter, as Socrates says in the *Cratylus*, and evidently appears to be the same with the demiurgus. And the divinely-inspired intellectual conception of Timæus concerning the demiurgus, accords with the theology of Socrates about Jupiter. If likewise each of them denominates the knowledge of this God difficult to be apprehended, and one of them says that it is difficult to discover him, and when discovered, that it is impossible to speak of him to all men, but the other asserts that it is not easy to understand the name of Jupiter, do they not in this respect accord with each other in what they say concerning this God? Besides this also, the composition of the names, and the coalition of the two names into one hyparxis, appear in a remarkable degree to be adapted to the demiurgus. For a biformed† essence, and generative power, are attributed to him according to other theologists. For the duad sits with him, according to which he generates all things; concerning which Timæus also introduces him speaking to the demiurgi in the world, and saying, "Imitating my power." And through this he produces and vivifies all things. Hence it is necessary through names also to consecrate the duad to him according to ancient rumour. For he glitters with intellectual sections, divides and collects wholes, and constitutes one indissoluble order from many things. And this the power of the names indicates, extending us from divided intellection, to one self-perfect and uniform theory.

All these particulars therefore, clearly demonstrate to us that Plato considers the demiurgus of wholes to be the same with Jupiter. For he

---

† For δυσειδες, it is necessary to read δυοειδες.

who alone is the cause of life to all things, and who is the king of all things, is the demiurgus of the universe. And he who in a remarkable manner rejoices in a duad of names, is he who arranges and adorns the whole world. And it appears to me, as I have frequently said, that in consequence of being allotted the end of the intellectual triad, converting this to the beginning, and being full of the middle fountains of life, but uniting himself to the watch-tower of his father, and producing into himself the simplicity of an intelligible subsistence, according to the peculiarity of first-effective causes, he is also allotted a duad of names. And as he received his essence from both [ie from Saturn and Rhea] and possesses indeed bound from his father, but infinite power from the generative deity of his mother, thus also he possesses one of the names from his father, and from the uniform perfection which is in him; but the other from total vivification. And through both, as he is allotted an essence, so likewise an appellation. For it is obvious to every one, that the term (διά) *dia*,[†] *on account of which*, is a sign of a total essence. "Let us declare, says Timæus, on account of what cause [the composing artificer constituted generation and the universe]. He was good." But the name of life pertains of itself to the middle order of beings. The demiurgus therefore obtains one of these names, *viz. dia*, from the intellectual summit, and the paternal union. For according to the participation of it, he is one,[‡] bound, and intelligible. But he obtains the other name from the middle order of intellectuals. For there life, and the vivific bosoms are allotted their hypostasis. The demiurgic intellect however, shining forth from both, participates also of the names through composition. For we call him *dia* and *zena*, because life proceeds to all things on account of him, and to live is inherent in all [vital natures] on account of him. And thus after a manner the position of the names indicates the progression of the demiurgus from both the precedaneous causes.

CHAPTER XXIII

Again therefore, let us direct our attention to what is written in the *Philebus*, and survey how, in what is there said, Socrates refers the fabrication of the universe to Jupiter. For admitting that intellect adorns and arranges all things, in the same manner as the wise men prior to

---

[†] In the original διο, but it is evidently necessary to read διά.

[‡] For ενεστι, it is necessary to read εν εστι.

him, and that it governs the sun and moon, and all the circulation [of the heavens] he demonstrates that the whole world participates of soul, and intellectual inspection, and that we also derive the participation of these from wholes; but that the universe is not and was not from chance, and likewise the most divine of visible natures, as many physiologists assert, while the natures which the universe contains participate of soul and intellect. Having therefore, as we have said, demonstrated these things, and shown that what the whole world contains is greater and more perfect than what we contain, and that wholes have a greater authority, and a more ruling essence than partial natures, and having placed intellect over wholes, as that which adorns and arranges the universe, and likewise assigned this province to soul, through the inspection of intellect, (for intellect is not present to the world without soul) he afterwards recurs to imparticipable intellect, to the author of participated intellect and soul, and the fabricator of the whole world, and he denominates and celebrates this fabricator, who contains the causes of the plenitudes in the world, as no other than Jupiter the great king and ruler of wholes, conformably to the rumour of the Greeks. He likewise extends about him all the providence of the world, and places in him the whole cause of the arrangement and ornament of the universe.

It is better however, in the next place, to hear the words themselves of Plato. He gives therefore to the world an intellectual superintendence, and adds this to the before mentioned demonstrations, that there is, as we have frequently observed, an abundance of infinity in the world, and a sufficiency of bound, and that there is a certain cause in them by no means vile and contemptible, which adorns and co-arranges the years, the seasons, and the months, and which may most justly be called wisdom and intellect. But again, because it is necessary that participated intellect should govern the world through soul as a medium, (for it is impossible that intellect should be present to any thing without soul, as Timæus also asserts) hence it is requisite that soul also should preside over the universe, and that proximately having dominion over the natures it contains, it should govern the world according to intellect. This therefore Socrates having in the next place added, he subjoins as follows: "Moreover, wisdom and intellect could never be without soul." For how could the impartible and eternal essence of intellect be immediately conjoined with a corporeal nature? It is necessary therefore that intellect should preside over wholes, that it may connect the order in the world, well-being, and all things. For order and well-being are the progeny of an intellectual essence. But it is necessary that soul primarily participating of intellect, should illuminate body with the light proceeding from thence, and fill all things with intellectual arrangement. It must be admitted therefore, that the world is animated and endued with intellect. Hence from this Socrates ascends to the cause itself of the whole world, which produced intellect and soul, and generated the total order [of the universe.]

"Hence, (Socrates adds) you may say that in the nature of Jupiter there are a royal soul and a royal intellect through the power of cause; and that in the other Gods there are other beautiful things, whatever they are, by which their deities love to be distinguished, and from which they delight in taking their respective denominations." One of these two things therefore is necessary, either that which is here said is said concerning the world, or concerning the demiurgus of wholes. For if the world is Jupiter, the participated intellect in the world is royal, and the soul also is royal which governs the universe, and arranges and adorns it according to intellect. And these things are evidently present to the world through the power of the cause by which it was constituted, and which rendered it a partaker of intellect and animated. And thus Jupiter will be that which is adorned and fabricated, and not the adorner and fabricator of all things. If, however, it is necessary that the power of cause should be comprehensive in an exempt manner of a royal intellect and a royal soul, we must admit that the nature of Jupiter is in the demiurgic order and power; and intellect and soul will be in him according to cause, since he imparts both these to his progeny. Of these two opinions therefore, every one may adopt that which he pleases, but to me, when I consider what is here said, and every other assertion of Plato concerning this God, it by no means appears to be necessary to refer the nature of Jupiter to the whole world. For neither does the only-begotten subsistence of the world accord with the kingdom of Jupiter, since the Saturnian triad, and which distributes the dominion of the father, is manifestly celebrated by Plato himself; nor can that which is cause to all things, as it is said in the *Cratylus*, refer† to the world. For the world is among the number of things which participate of life from another. As I have said therefore, we must leave this opinion, as by no means adapted to Plato, though it is adopted by some of his interpreters. But considering cause to be the same as Jupiter, we must say that soul and intellect are established in him exemptly; and that Jupiter participates of both these, from the Gods that are prior to him; of intellect indeed, from his father, but of soul from

---

† For διαφερει, it is necessary to read αναφερει.

the queen [Rhea] who is the deity of vivification. For there the fountain of soul subsists, just as in Saturn, there is intellect according to essence. For every where the intelligible unically comprehends the intellect which is co-ordinate with it. And thus much concerning these particulars.

CHAPTER XXIV

In the next place, we may conjoin with this the mythological conceptions in the *Protagoras*, and arrive at the same conclusion, considering in common with the *Timæus*, how the opinions delivered to us concerning the mighty Jupiter, through the Protagorean fable, accord with the assertions about the demiurgus. The fable says, therefore, that Prometheus adorning the human race, and providentially attending to our rational life, that it may not perish by being merged in the furies of earth, and the necessities of nature, as some one of the Gods says, bound nature to the arts, extended these which are imitations of intellect, as it were to sportive souls, and through these excited our gnostic and dianoetic power to the contemplation of forms. For every artificial production is effective of form, and adorns the matter which is the subject of it. The fable also adds, that Prometheus providentially attending to the arts gave them to souls, and that he received them from Vulcan and Minerva. For in these Gods the cause of all arts is primarily comprehended; Vulcan primarily imparting the fabricative power of them; but Minerva supernally illuminating their gnostic and intellectual power. Not only however, is the invention of arts necessary to souls in generation, but also a certain other science, the political, which is more perfect than the arts, and which is able to arrange and adorn them, and to lead souls through virtue to a life according to intellect. But as Prometheus was unable to impart this life to us, because the political science is primarily with the mighty Jupiter, but it was not possible (says the fable) for Prometheus to enter latently into the tower of Jupiter, (for the guards of Jupiter are terrible, defending him exempt from all partial causes,) - hence Jupiter sent the messenger Hermes to men, who brought with him prudence and shame, and in short the political science. Jupiter also ordered Hermes to impart similarly to all men these virtues, and to distribute to all souls the knowledge of things just, beautiful, and good, but not in a divided manner, as different arts are distributed to different persons. And some men indeed are judges of these things, but others are ignorant either of all, or of some of the arts.

In what is here said, therefore, Plato primarily refers to Jupiter the paradigm of the political science, as is evident from the words themselves. But he produces the progression of this science, and the communication and participation of the Hermaical series, and extends its essential presence, which we participate in common, to all souls. For to distribute to all of them, is to insert in souls essentially a science of this kind. These things, therefore, being laid down, let us consider to whom we must say the political science especially pertains, and who it is that primarily established a polity in the universe, that formed divine to govern mortal natures, divided wholes from parts, and produced self-motive and intellectual natures more ancient than those that are deprived of the presence of intellect. Is it not the demiurgus, who is the cause to us of all these goods, who governs the whole world according to rectitude, binds it by the best analogies, establishes every polity in it, possesses and comprehends the laws of Fate, and extends the sacred laws of Adrastia, as far as to the last of things, and arranges and adorns by justice all celestial and sublunary natures? For he who introduces partial souls into the universe as into their habitation, and imparts to them a total polity which is the best of all polities, and is governed by the most excellent laws, is he who denominates these laws the laws of Fate, who defines the measures of Justice, and legally institutes all things, as Timæus says. Is it not therefore superfluous to endeavour to prove that he who possesses the first paradigm of the political science, is according to Plato the demiurgus?

If, however, these things are true, and according to the fable in the *Protagoras* it must be admitted that the political science first subsists in Jupiter, it is evident from what has been said, that the demiurgus of the universe is Jupiter. For to what other cause can we grant the primary form of political science to belong, than to that which arranges and adorns the universe? If the polity in the heavens is the first and most perfect of all polities, as Socrates in the *Republic* says it is. Who likewise is he that produces all things, and co-arranges them when produced to each other, in order to the elegant disposition of the universe? If, therefore, the first and most perfect demiurgus of the universe is political, but the political science first subsists with Jupiter, being established with him on a sacred foundation, proceeds from thence to all secondary natures, and adorns and arranges both wholes and parts according to intellect, it is evidently necessary that the demiurgus of wholes should be the same with Jupiter, and that there should be one hyparxis of both, which administers every thing in the world according to rectitude, and circularly leads every thing confused and disorderly into order. For, says Timæus, it is not lawful for that which is best to effect any thing else than that which is most beautiful. How therefore is it possible that he who adorns and arranges wholes through Themis, and together with her produces all things, should not essentially possess in himself the whole of the political science?

How is it possible likewise that he should not be the first Jupiter, who definitely imparts to all things that which is divine, and weaves one polity from all things, but is exempt from all partial causes and the Titannic genera, and is guarded by his own undefiled powers, beyond the whole world? For the guards which surround him, obscurely signify his immutable order, and the undeviating defence of fabrication, through which being firmly established in himself, he pervades through all things without impediment, and being present to all his progeny, is according to supreme transcendency expanded above wholes. Moreover, the citadel of Jupiter, according to the rumours of theologists, is a symbol of intellectual circulation, and of the highest summit of Olympus, which all the wise suspend from the intellectual watch tower of Jupiter, to which he extends all the mundane Gods, imparting to them from thence intellectual powers, divine light, and vivific illuminations, and compressing all the profundities of the worlds by one most simple circulation, through which the summit also of the apparent worlds is denominated the period of sameness, and the most prudent and uniform circulation, as Timæus says, expressing the unical intellectual power of demiurgic conversion, and being allotted the same transcendency with respect to all the sensible world that the supreme summit of Jupiter possesses with respect to all the arrangement of the firmaments. These things may also be assumed by us as subservient to the proposed investigation, from the fabulous fictions in the *Protagoras*.

CHAPTER XXV

We may, however, approach still nearer to the truth, and assume in the present discussion, the fable in the *Politicus*. For in this it will appear that Plato in a remarkable manner considers the demiurgus of the universe to be the same with Jupiter, and even as far as to the very names asserts the same things as Timæus. The Elean guest, therefore, as we have before observed, assigns [in this dialogue] twofold circulations to the whole of this world, the one intellectual, and which elevates souls but the other proceeding into nature, and imparting things contrary to the former. And the one indeed, being unapparent, and governed by divine providence, but the other apparent, and convolved according to the order of Fate. He also places twofold motive causes over these circulations. For every mutation and period require a certain moving cause. And prior to the causes that move the circulations, he asserts that there are as it were twofold ends of the periods, and assigns first-effective causes of the motions, co-ordinate to the moving causes, and to the circulations themselves which differ from each other. Jupiter therefore moves, and circularly leads one of the periods, whether you are willing to call it intellectual, or providential, or in whatever other way you may denominate it, and he also supplies the world with life, and imparts to it a renovated immortality. But he pre-establishes his father Saturn as the object of desire to, and the end of the whole of this circulation. For he leads back wholes, and converts them to himself.

Moreover, he extends happy souls to the watch-tower of his father, *viz.* those souls whose corporeal nature is obliterated, and whose circulation is to the incorporeal and the impartible. All the generation-producing† symbols likewise of these souls are amputated, and the form of their life is transferred to the intellectual summit. For these souls are also said to be the nurselings of Saturn, but to commit the government of themselves to Jupiter, and through him to be extended to the intelligible, and the Saturnian dominion. For the intelligible is nutriment, as it is said by the Gods themselves. And as Socrates in the *Phædrus* elevates souls through the circulation of the heaven to the supercelestial place, where souls are nourished, survey true beings, and the unknown order of the Gods, with the highest powers of themselves, and as he there says, intellectually perceive with the heads of the charioteers, - thus also the Elean guest circularly leads souls under Jupiter, to the Saturnian watch-tower, and asserts that such as have ascended are nourished by Saturn, and calls them the nurselings of the God. For every where indeed, the intelligible is perfective of, and has the power of filling an intellectual life, and the summit of intellectuals extends perfection. These souls likewise participate of the natures that are beyond, establish themselves in more elevated intellectuals, and ascend as far as to the unknown order, but remote from *The Good*, and the one principle of all things. But the souls [that ascend through the circulation of the heaven] are extended to the first intellect, which is imparticipable, and the intelligible itself, and when they are there, and have established their life in the occult order as in a port, they ineffably participate of the union proceeding from *The Good*, and of the light of truth.

---

† For τελεσιουργα, it is necessary to read γενεσιουργα.

With respect however to what remains respecting the twofold periods, as we have said, the world itself indeed moves itself, being moved according to its own nature, and giving completion to the order of Fate. But the first-effective cause of this motion of the world, and of its life, is the God who illuminates it with the power of being moved and of living, and is the mighty Jupiter. Hence also this period is said to be Jovian, so far as Jupiter is the cause of this apparent arrangement, just as Saturn is the cause of the intellectual and unapparent arrangement. It is better, however, to hear Plato himself discussing these things. That there are, therefore, twofold circulations of the universe, and that the God who moves it is the leader of the one, but of the other the world itself convolving itself, Plato here teaches us. But as was just now said, and which is the only thing that remains, the universe is at one time co-governed by another divine cause, again acquiring life, and receiving a renovated immortality from the demiurgus; but at another time, when he lays aside as it were the handle of his rudder, the world being left by itself, moves for a time by itself, so as frequently to proceed in an inverted order.

Again, however, that one of the periods, *viz.* the apparent, is Jovian, but that the other is referred to the kingdom of Saturn, Plato himself determines in what follows, subjoining these words, after the celebration of that life, and of the undefiled polity of the souls that are there, which is liberated from all corporeal pains, and the servitude about matter: "You have heard, Socrates, what was the life of men under Saturn; but you yourself have seen what the condition of the present life is, which is said to be under Jupiter." And moreover, that of these two circulations, (since the apparent is under Jupiter) Jupiter is the cause and maker of it, is obvious to every one, and that again Jupiter is the power that moves the unapparent circulation, which is Saturnian, may be demonstrated from what is written. For it is necessary that these two Gods should either rule over each of these circulations, or that one of them should rule over the unapparent, but the other over the present circulation. If, however, Jupiter moves the universe according to this period, the world can no longer be said to convolve itself, and to govern every thing it contains. Nor will it be true neither that the whole is convolved by divinity with twofold and contrary circulations, nor again, that two certain Gods convolve it whose decisions are contrary to each other. For if Saturn indeed moves it according to one circulation, but Jupiter moves it according to a period contrary to that of Saturn, two Gods will move it according to contrary circumvolutions. If, however, these things are impossible, it is indeed manifest to every one that both the divine causes preside over the circulation according to the Saturnian convolution; Saturn indeed as the supplier of an intellectual life; but Jupiter, as elevating all things to the Saturnian empire, and establishing them in his own intelligible. And thus that period may be called Saturnian, in consequence of Saturn imparting the first effective cause of the whole [of an intellectual] life. But according to this more physical circulation, and which is known to every one, Fate and connate desire move the universe.

Jupiter, however, is the cause of this motion exemptly, who gives Fate and an adscititious life to the world. These things, therefore, being demonstrated by us, let us consider what the particulars are which are asserted of the God who moves the world according to the other period. And they are these; "that the world indeed at another time is conjointly governed by another divine cause, again acquiring life, and receiving a renovated immortality from the demiurgus." It is obvious, therefore, to every one, that the Elean guest says, that the God who moves the universe according to the Saturnian period, supplies it with life, and imparts to it a renovated immortality, and that he clearly calls him the demiurgus. Hence, if it is Jupiter who conjointly governs that period, as has been demonstrated, he will be the demiurgus of the world, and the supplier of immortality. And what occasion is there to say much on the subject? For if the same God is the cause of life, and is denominated the demiurgus, again the *Cratylus* will present itself to us, and Jupiter according to this will be the same with the demiurgus. For life accedes to all things from Jupiter, as it is asserted in that dialogue. Moreover, in what follows, as Timæus calls the cause of the circulation of Fate, demiurgus and father, after the same manner the Elean guest denominates this cause, and also calls it the maker. "For the world", says he, "revolves, remembering the doctrine of the demiurgus and father." Properly, therefore, do we denominate the whole of this period Jovian, because the world moves and convolves itself, according to the doctrine of Jupiter, and the order imparted to it from him. Again, therefore, Jupiter is demiurgus and father. And here also the Elean guest preserves the same order of the divine names as Timæus. For he does not† call him father and demiurgus, but on the contrary, in the same manner as Timæus, demiurgus and father; because the demiurgic peculiarity in him is more manifest than the paternal deity. These things, however, have been copiously investigated before; and it has been shown in what respect the demiurgic is different from the paternal

---

† For καιγαρ it is necessary to read ου γαρ.

genus, how they are complicated with each other,† where the paternal subsists essentially, but the demiurgic according to cause, and where again, the demiurgic subsists essentially, but the paternal, according to participation.

CHAPTER XXVI

It will remain, therefore, that we should make mention of what is written in the *Laws* concerning Jupiter. For perhaps in them also it will appear that Plato assigns the same order to the demiurgus and to Jupiter. As the equalities, therefore, according to which polities are adorned, are twofold, and the one polity indeed proposes the equal according to number, and proceeds through things which differ from each other according to an equal law; but the other embraces in all things, the equality which is according to desert; and also, since equality subsists according to ratio, - this being the case, each of these equalities exists in the providence of the world. For the essence of the soul, indeed, is primarily divided by its fabricator by the equality according to ratio; but it is also consummately filled with the remaining middles, and bound with them through the whole of itself. The several bodies [of the world] likewise, participate of a certain common essence, in the fabrication of things; and on this account they are allotted the equality which is according to number. But all things are arranged and adorned through the best of analogies, and the demiurgus according to this inserts both in wholes and parts, an indissoluble order in the universe, and an adaptation of them to each other.

This equality, therefore, the Athenian guest exhorts his citizens particularly to honour, in consequence of assimilating his city to the universe. He also says that it is a thing of this kind, but that it is not likewise easy for every one to perceive the most true and excellent equality; for it is the judgment of Jupiter. What therefore is the cause on account of which the Athenian guest asserts this analogy to be the judgment of Jupiter? What other cause can we assign than its contributing to the perfection of the world, and its power and dominion in the fabrication of wholes? For that which gives an orderly distinction to the genera of causes, contrives the most beautiful bond of them, and weaves together one order from wholes, is according to Timæus the power of this analogy. For it established soul in the middle (of the universe) analogous to intellect and a corporeal nature. For soul is the

---

† For εν αλλοις, it is requisite to read εν αλληλοις.

middle of an impartible and partible essence. And by how much it surpasses a partible, by so much it falls short of an impartible hypostasis. The power of this analogy, however, binds the soul from double and triple ratios, and connects the whole of it proceeding from and at the same time returning to (its principles,) by the primary and self-motive boundaries of equality. It likewise constitutes the corporeal series from the four first genera. And it adapts indeed the extremes to each other through the middles, but mingles the middles according to the peculiarity of the extremes. It reduces, however, all things to one world, and one indissoluble order connectedly comprehended in the universe. If, therefore, we acknowledge that this equality has dominion in the whole fabrication of things, the best of analogies is the judgment of the demiurgus, and according to the decision of him who generated wholes it is allotted that great dominion in the fabrication of the universe, which we have before shown it to possess. Hence if the same analogy is the judgment of Jupiter, as the Athenian guest says it is, it is obvious to every one that the nature of Jupiter is demiurgic. For it is not any thing else which judges of the dignity of this analogy than that which employs it in the arrangement of wholes. And to this the legislator establishing himself analogous, binds and in a particular manner adorns the city which is assimilated to the universe, by this analogy.

CHAPTER XXVII

From these things, therefore, and from all that has been previously said, we confidently assert, following Plato and paternal rumours, that Jupiter is the demiurgus of the universe; and we may collect into one, the scattered opinions of the ancients on this subject; of whom, some, indeed, refer the paradigm of the world, and the demiurgic cause to the same order; but others divide these from each other. And some place all-perfect animal prior to the demiurgus; but others afford an hypostasis to it after the demiurgus. For if the demiurgus is, as has been said, the great Jupiter, and the paradigm proposed to the demiurgus in order to the generation of the world, is all-perfect animal, these are at the same time united to each other, and are allotted an essential separation. And animal itself, indeed, intelligibly comprehends in itself the whole Jovian series; but Jupiter the demiurgus of the universe intellectually pre-establishes in himself the nature of animal itself. For animal itself is the supplier of life to all things, and all things primarily live on account of it, and Jupiter being the cause of life, possesses the paradigm and the generative principle of the essence of all animals. Justly, therefore, does

Timæus, in Plato, having called the intelligible paradigm animal, conjoin the demiurgic intellect to the first intelligible animal; and through the all-perfect union of the demiurgus and father with it, he also arranges and adorns this universe. For Jupiter binding to himself the fabrication of the universe, and being an intellectual animal, is united to intelligible animal, and being allotted a progression analogous to it, constitutes all things intellectually, which proceed from animal itself intelligibly.

For, as we have said, the intelligible hypostases being triple, and one indeed, being allotted its hyparxis according to existence and the one being; but another according to intelligible life, and the middle centre of the intelligible breadth, where eternity, all life, and intelligible life subsist, as Plotinus somewhere says; and another according to intelligible multitude, the first plenitude of life, and the all-perfect paradigm of wholes, - this being the case, the three kingdoms of the intellectual Gods are divided analogous to the three intelligible hypostases. And one indeed, the mighty Saturn, being allotted an hyparxis according to the summit of intellectuals, and having a paternal transcendency, possesses a dominion analogous to the summit of the intelligible Gods, and the occult order. And as in that order, all things are uniformly, and are ineffably, and without separation united, thus also this God again converts to himself, and conceals in himself the natures that have proceeded from him, imitating the occult of the first summit. But again the order which comprehends the middle genera of wholes, and is filled indeed, from the generative power of Saturn, but fills from itself the whole fabrication with vivific rivers, has the same order in intellectuals which eternity has in intelligibles, and the uniform cause of the life which is there. And as eternity proximately generates intelligible animal, which is also denominated eternal, through the participation of eternity, thus also the middle bosom of the intellectual Gods, unfolds the demiurgus of the universe, and the vivific fountain of wholes. But the third king, *viz.* the fabricator and at the same time father, is indeed co-ordinate to the remainder of the intelligible triad, *viz.* to all-perfect animal. And as that is an animal, so likewise is Jupiter. And Jupiter indeed is intelligibly in all-perfect animal; but all-perfect animal is intellectually in Jupiter. The extremities likewise of the intelligible and intellectual Gods are united to each other; and in them, separation is co-existent with union. And one of them, indeed, is exempt from fabrication; but the other is converted to the intelligible, is filled from thence with total goods, and is allotted a paternal transcendency through the participation of it. The maker, therefore, and father of the universe, who has firmly established in himself the uniform strength and power of all fabrication, who possesses and comprehends the primary cause of the generation of wholes, and who stably fixes in himself all things, and again produces them from himself in an undefiled manner, being allotted such an order as this among the intellectual fathers, is celebrated, as I may say, through the whole of the *Timæus*, in which dialogue, his prolific and paternal power is unfolded, and his providence which pervades from on high as far as to the extremities of the universe. He is also frequently celebrated by Plato in other dialogues, so far as it is possible to celebrate his uniform and united power,† and which through transcendency is exempt from wholes.

CHAPTER XXVIII

If however some one recollecting what is said in the beginning of the *Timæus* about him, *viz.* that it is difficult to discover him, and when found, impossible to speak of him to all men, should enquire in the first place, why since the Grecian theology ascribes such a name to the demiurgus, as we have before mentioned, Timæus says that he is ineffable, and established above all the indication which subsists in words. In the next place, if he should inquire why intelligible animal which is arranged above the demiurgus is both denominated, and is made known by many signs, but the demiurgus who has established his kingdom in an order secondary to that of all-perfect animal, and is an intellectual God, (all-perfect animal receiving an intelligible transcendency) is left by Timæus ineffable, as we have said, and unknown, perhaps we also, following Plato, may be able to dissolve all such doubts. For every order of the Gods originates from a monad, and presides over its proper series according to the first-effective cause. And such things indeed as are nearer to this principle are more total than those that are more remote from it. But more total natures are manifestly seen to be less‡ distant from the monad, and conjoin things which are diminished according to essence to the natures that are prior to them. Every order of the Gods likewise is a whole united to itself through the whole, is allotted one indissoluble connection, both in wholes and parts, and through the monad which collects every order into one, it is converted about itself, is suspended from this, and is wholly convolved according to it.

---

† δυναμιν is omitted in the original.

‡ For πλεον it is evidently necessary to read ηττον.

If, therefore, we assert these things truly, in each order a monad is allotted a transcendency with respect to multitude, analogous to *The Good*. And as the unical cause of whole goods, and which is incomprehensible by all things, is exempt from all things, constitutes all things about itself, generates them from itself, and hastily withdraws the unions of all things to its own ineffable superunion, thus also the uniform and generative principle of every co-ordinate multitude, connects, guards and perfects the whole series of itself, imparts good to it from itself, and fills it with order and harmony. It is likewise that to its own progeny, which *The Good* is to all beings, and is the object of desire to all the natures that originate from itself. Thus, therefore, the union of the intelligible father subsists prior to the whole paternal order; the one wholeness of the Synoches is prior to the connective order; and the first effective cause of life, to the vivific order.

Hence also, of every demiurgic series, which is suspended from the triad of the sons of Saturn, the monad which proximately fabricates wholes, and is established above this triad, comprehends in itself all the demiurgic Gods, converts them to itself, and is of a boniform nature. The one fountain likewise of all the demiurgic numbers, subsists, as I may say, with respect to all this order analogous to *The One*, and to the one principle of all things. Timæus therefore, indicating these things to us, asserts directly in the beginning of the generation of the world, that this monad which proximately fabricates wholes, is difficult to be known, and is indescribable, as having the same ratio as the ineffable and unknown cause of all beings. Whence likewise, I think, he calls the demiurgus the best of causes, and the father of this universe, as being allotted the highest order among the demiurgi, and convolving to himself, and producing from himself all the effective principles. *That* one however, Parmenides demonstrates to be perfectly unknown and ineffable; but Timæus says that it is difficult to discover the maker and father of the world, and impossible to speak of him to all men; which assertion falls short of the cause that flies from all knowledge, and all language, and appears to verge to the nature of things known and effable. For when he says that it is impossible to speak of him to all men, he does not leave him entirely ineffable and unknown. And the assertion that it is difficult to discover him, is not the sign of a peculiarity perfectly unknown. For because the demiurgus has established a kingdom analogous to *The Good*, but in secondary and manifold orders of it, he participates indeed of the signs of *The Good*, but is allotted the participation in conjunction with an appropriate peculiarity, and a communion with beings adapted to him. And as he is good, but not *The Good Itself*, so likewise he is difficult to be known by the natures posterior to him, but is not unknown. He is also celebrated in mystic language, but is not perfectly ineffable. You may see however, the order of things, and the remission in them proceeding in a downward progression. For *The Good* indeed, is exempt from all silence, and all language. But the genus of the intelligible Gods rejoices in silence, and is delighted with ineffable[†] symbols. Hence also, Socrates in the *Phædrus*, calls the vision of the intelligible monads the most holy initiations, as being involved in silence, and perceived intellectually in an arcane manner. But the vision of intellectuals is indeed effable, yet is not effable and known to all men, but is known with difficulty. For through diminution with respect to the intelligible, it proceeds from silence and a transcendency which is to be apprehended by intelligence alone, into the order of things which are now effable.

If however, this be the case, all-perfect animal is much more ineffable and unknown than the demiurgic monad. For it is at once the monad of every paradigmatic order, and is intelligible, but not intellectual. How therefore, do we endeavour to denominate, and as it were unfold it, but thus magnificently celebrate the demiurgic cause? And how do we class this cause in the same rank with things ineffable? For this will not be acting conformably to Plato, who arranges animal itself beyond the demiurgus; but this will be giving an hypostasis to it in a secondary order of Gods, where it will be ranked, and will be effable and known more than the demiurgic monad. To which may be added, that to denominate that all-perfect animal most beautiful, but the demiurgus the best of causes, gives indeed the same analogy to these causes with respect to each other, as there is of *The Good* with respect to the beautiful. And as *The Good* is prior to the beautiful, (for the first beauty, as Socrates says in the *Philebus*, is in the vestibules of *The Good*) so likewise the best[‡] indeed, remarkably participates of *The Good*, but the most beautiful, of beauty.

CHAPTER XXIX

In addition to these things therefore, it must also be asserted by us, that the most beautiful and the best, are simply indeed related to each other according to order, as *The Good* is to the beautiful. For the series

---

[†] For $αριστοις$, it is necessary to read $αρρητοις$.

[‡] For $αρρητον$, it is necessary to read $αριστον$.

of the whole of goodness is expanded above all the progression and arrangement of the beautiful. Every where, therefore the best is prior to the most beautiful. And the one, indeed, with reference to an inferior order, will be the best, but the other with reference to a more excellent order, will be the most beautiful. I say for instance, that the most beautiful, as in intelligibles, will have this peculiarity; but the best as in intellectuals. And if the most beautiful, in supermundane natures, is a thing of this kind, the best will be said to be best as with reference to the Gods in the world. Hence, if the best of causes is the leader of the demiurgic series, and according to it is allotted a transcendency of this kind, but the most beautiful of intelligible animals pre-establishes the illustrious power of beauty in a higher order, by what contrivance can it on this account be shown that intelligible and all-perfect animal is subordinate to the intellectual cause? And that the demiurgus is converted to that which is posterior to himself? Or how can it be said that animal itself is visible to him, and all-perfect animal, and that which is comprehensive of all intelligibles, if it is made to be comprehended by another? For thus the demiurgus will be more comprehensive than animal itself, if the former indeed being characterized according to the best, is expanded above the paradigm, but the latter being denominated as most beautiful is secondary to the demiurgic cause.

Moreover, as that all-perfect and intelligible animal is particularly considered by Timæus according to a formal nature, and not according to the union which is in it, and an hypostasis which is above all forms,[†] he very properly grants that animal itself may be known and manifested by words, but considers the demiurgus as in a certain respect ineffable, and superior to knowledge. For both indeed, I mean the demiurgus and animal itself, participate of union, and prior to a formal essence, are contained in *The One*. And if you assume the unities which are in them, you must admit the unity of the paradigm to be intelligible, but the demiurgic unity to be intellectual, and that an intelligible hyparxis is nearer to the first one, which is unknown and incomprehensible by all things, than an intellectual hyparxis. But if you are willing to survey the forms of the paradigm by themselves, according to which it is said to be the paradigm of every thing in the world, and the goodness and union of the demiurgus, the former will appear to you to be known and effable: but the demiurgic cause will be seen to participate of the unknown and ineffable peculiarity of the gods. For again, Timæus was

---

[†] Instead of του παντος, it is doubtless necessary to read τα παντα. For the demiurgus also has an hypostasis which is above the forms of the universe.

in a remarkable degree in want of the demiurgus and father, as the producing cause of wholes, and the generator of the world. But to generate, to produce and provide are the peculiarities of Gods, so far as they are Gods. Hence also Timæus denominates the peculiarity of the demiurgus according to which he is a God, the cause of the generation of the universe, and the most proper principle of the arrangement of wholes. But he denominates the peculiarity of the paradigm to be that which comprehends the first forms, according to which the world also is invested with forms. For it is the image of the paradigm, but the effect of the demiurgus. It belongs, therefore, to the paradigm to be the first of forms, but to the demiurgus to be the best of causes, according to his goodness, and the hyparxis of essence. For, as we have said, to generate, to give subsistence to, and to provide for other things, especially pertain to the Gods, and not to the natures which are primarily suspended† from them; but the latter are allotted through the former an abundance prolific of secondary natures. It appears to me that Socrates in the *Republic* indicating these things, does not say that the sun is the cause of generation, till he had declared him to be the progeny of the superessential principle of all things: just as Timæus does not begin the fabrication of the universe, till he had celebrated the goodness of the demiurgus of wholes. For each [*i.e.* the demiurgus and the sun] is a producing cause according to *The Good*, the former indeed of the universe, but the latter of a generated nature; but not according to the intellect which is in them, or life, or any other form of essence. For these through the participation of *The Good* constitute the natures posterior to themselves. And thus through these things we have answered the before-mentioned doubts.

CHAPTER XXX

Of the problems pertaining to total fabrication, it now remains for me to relate what my opinion is respecting the Crater, and the genera that are mingled in it. For these also Timæus co-arranges with the demiurgic monad, in the generation of the soul. The demiurgus, therefore, mingles the elements of the hypostasis of souls; but the middle genera of being are mingled. The much-celebrated Crater, however, receives this mixture, and generates souls in conjunction with the demiurgus. Hence, in the first place, the genera of being must be admitted to be twofold. And it must be granted indeed, that some of them give completion to

---

† For εξηρημενοις, it is necessary to read εξηρτημενοις.

total hypostases, but others, to such as are partial; and that the hyparxes of first effective and united causes, are established in the intelligible Gods. For there essence subsists primarily in the summit of intelligibles, and motion and permanency are in the middle centre. For intelligible eternity abides in one, and at once both abides and is the occult cause of all life. Hence, Plotinus also calls eternity life which is one and total: and again, in another part of his works he calls it intelligible life. But the third from him, Theodorus, denominates it permanency. And both these opinions harmonize with each other; because permanency also is in eternity, (for according to Timæus, eternity abides in one) and motion. For eternity is intelligible life, and that which participates of it is intelligible animal. Moreover, sameness and difference, are in the extremity of intelligibles. For whence does multitude originate, but from difference? And whence is the communion of parts with wholes, and the hyparxis of things which are divided in each other derived but from sameness? For that one participates of being, and being of *The One*. All the parts likewise of the one being pervade through each other in an unconfused manner; for at one and the same time sameness and difference are there occultly. And the whole intelligible breadth is allotted its hypostasis according to the first and most uniform genera. As essence likewise presents itself to the view in conjunction with *The One*, according to the first triad, so motion and permanency shine forth in the second, and sameness and difference in the third triad. And all things are essentially in the intelligible; just as life and intellect are there intelligibly. For since all beings proceed from intelligibles, all things pre-exist there according to cause. And motion and permanency are there essentially, and sameness and difference uniformly.

Again, in the middle genera of the intelligible and intellectual hypostases, the same things subsist secondarily and vitally. In the summit of them indeed, essence subsists. For Socrates in the *Phædrus* speaking about this order, characterizes the whole of it from essence. For the truly-existing essence which is without colour, without figure, and without contact, subsists after this manner. But in the middle centre there are motion and permanency. For there the circulation of the heaven subsists, as the same Socrates says; being established indeed undeviatingly, in one form of intelligence; but being moved in, and about itself; or rather being motion and eternal life. But in the extremity of this order, sameness and difference are vitally established. Hence it is converted to the beginning according to the nature of sameness, is divided uniformly, proceeds into more numbers, and generates from itself more partial monads.

Again, in the third orders, the highest of the intellectual Gods possesses all things according to essence, and is the intelligible itself and true being in intellectuals, again recalling the separation which is in himself into undivided union. But the middle order subsists according to motion and at the same time permanency. For it is a vivific deity, abiding and at the same time proceeding, being established with purity, and vivifying all things by prolific powers. And the third progression subsists according to sameness, together with difference. For this separates itself from the fathers, and is conjoined to them through intellectual conversion. And it binds, indeed, at once the natures posterior to itself, to each other, according to the common powers of forms, and at the same time separates them by intellectual sections. But in this order, all genera and species first shine forth to the view; because it is especially characterized according to difference, being allotted the end of all the total hypostases. From this likewise it proceeds to all things, *viz.* to participated intellect, the multiform orders of souls, and the whole of a corporeal nature. For, in short, it constitutes triple genera of the natures posterior to itself; some indeed, being impartible and the first; others being media between partible and impartible natures; and others being divided about bodies. And through these things it generates all the more partial genera of beings. That we may therefore again return to what has been before said, the genera must be admitted to subsist every where, yet not every where after the same manner; but in the highest orders of divine natures indeed, they subsist uniformly, without separation, and unitedly, where also permanency participates of motion, and motion of permanency, and there is one united progression of both. In the more partial orders, however, it must be admitted that the same things subsist in a divided manner, and together with an appropriate remission. For since the first and most total of forms are in the extremity of intelligibles, it is indeed necessary that genera should have the beginning of their hypostasis in intelligibles. And if the demiurgic cause is generative of all the partial orders, it comprehends the first genera of the hypostasis of them. As likewise the fountain of all forms subsists in this cause, though there are intelligible forms, so the genera of being pre-exist in it, though there are other whole genera prior to it. And the divine Iamblichus somewhere rightly observes that the genera of being present themselves to the view in the extremity of the intelligible Gods. The present theology likewise, following things themselves, gives a progression to these as well as forms supernally, from the intelligible Gods. For such things as subsist according to cause, occultly, and without separation in the first essences [*i.e.* in intelligibles] these subsist in a divided and partible manner, and according to the nature of each, in intellectuals. For from hence, all the divisible orders of beings are filled both with these genera, and with formal hyparxes. And on this account, the demiurgus also is said to comprehend all genera, and to have the fountain of forms, because he generates all the partial rivers [of life] and imparts to them from himself by illumination all the measures of subsistence. Hence triple genera of all beings proceed from the demiurgus, some indeed being impartible, others partible† and others subsisting between these, being more united indeed than the partible, but more separated than the impartible genera; but subsisting according to the middle of both, and connectedly containing the one bond of beings. And the demiurgus indeed produces the intellectual essence, through the first and impartible genera; but the corporeal essence through the third and partible genera; and the psychical hypostasis which is in the middle of these, through the middle genera in beings. Moreover, he generates every intellectual and impartible nature from himself, and fills them with total generative power. But he constitutes the psychical essence, in conjunction with the Crater; and the corporeal essence, in conjunction with total Nature.

CHAPTER XXXI

That in this arrangement likewise we follow Timæus, any one may learn from the following considerations: The demiurgus producing the intellect of the universe, himself produces it from his own essence alone, unfolding it at once according to one union, in consequence of constituting it eternally, and no mention whatever is here made of the Crater. But the demiurgus in arranging and adorning soul prior to body, mingles the genera, and energizes in conjunction with the Crater. And in fashioning the body of the universe, and describing the heaven, he fabricates it in conjunction with Necessity. For the nature of the universe, says Timæus, was generated mingled from intellect and necessity. And neither does he here assume the Crater in order to the arrangement of bodies. But it has been abundantly shown by us elsewhere, that Plato calls physical production, a production through necessity, and does not, as some suppose, consider necessity to be the same with matter. It is evident, therefore, that the demiurgus produces the generation of bodies together with total Nature, mingles the partible

---

† The words τα δε μεριστα are omitted in the original, but evidently ought to be inserted.

genera in the first Nature, and thus produces bodies from intellect and necessity. For bodies receive[†] from intellect indeed, good and union; but from necessity a progression which terminates in interval and division. He arranges and adorns, however, the self-motive essence of souls, in conjunction with the Crater. And neither intellect, nor bodies, require a cause of this kind. The demiurgus indeed is the common source of the triple genera. But the Crater is the peculiar cause of souls, and is co-arranged with the demiurgus and filled from him, but fills souls. And receiving from thence indeed the powers of prolific abundance, it pours them on souls according to the measures of their respective essences. To some of them likewise it orderly distributes the summits of the genera [of being], to others the middle progressions of the genera, and to others, the terminations of them. Hence the Crater is indeed essentially vivific, since souls also are certain lives, but it is the first-effective cause of souls, according to the peculiarity of hyparxis, and is the uniform and all-perfect monad, not of every life, but of that which is psychical. For from this Crater the soul of the universe subsists, and likewise the second and third genera of partible souls, and of those souls that are allotted a progression between these.

The whole number, therefore, of the psychical order proceeds from the Crater, and is divided according to the prolific powers which it contains. Hence the Crater is said to be the cause of souls, the receptacle of their fabrication, and the generative monad of them, and the like. For it is said to be so rightly, and conformably to the mind of Plato. If, however, the Crater is co-arranged with the demiurgus, and equally constitutes with him the genera of souls, it is indeed necessary that this Crater should be fontal, in the same manner as the whole demiurgus. Hence the Crater is the fountain of souls, but is united to the demiurgic monad. And on this account, Socrates also in the *Philebus* says, that in Jupiter there is a royal soul, and a royal intellect. For that which we at present denominate fontal, he calls royal; though the name of fountain when applied to souls is well known to Plato. For Socrates, in the *Phædrus*, says, that the self-motive nature is the fountain and principle of motion to such other things as are moved.

And you see that as a twofold divine monad prior to souls is delivered by theologists, the one being indeed fontal, but the other of a primary ruling nature, Plato likewise gives to the progeny of these twofold appellations, assuming one name from the more total, but the other from the more partial monad. For the self-motive nature, is a fountain

---

[†] For δεχομεθα, it is necessary to read δεχομενα.

indeed, as being the offspring of the fontal soul, but it is a principle, as participating of the primary ruling soul. If therefore, the name of fountain, and also of principle is assigned by Plato to souls, what occasion is there to wonder if we denominate the exempt monads of them, fountains and principles? Or rather from these things that is demonstrated. For whence is a ruling power imparted to all souls except from the ruling monad? For that which similarly extends to all souls, is necessarily imparted to them from one and the same cause. If therefore, some one should say it is imparted by the demiurgus, so far as he is the demiurgus, it is necessary that in a similar manner it should be inherent in all other things which proceed from the demiurgic monad. But if it proceeds from the definite and separate cause of souls, that cause must be denominated the first fountain and principle of them.

Moreover, that of these two names, the ruling is more allied to souls than the fontal, as being nearer to them according to order, Plato manifests in the same dialogue. For calling the self-motive nature the fountain and at the same time principle of the motion of the whole of things, he nevertheless frames his demonstration of its unbegotten subsistence from principle alone. For, says he, principle is unbegotten. For it is necessary that every thing which is generated should be generated from a principle. If therefore, demonstrations are from things proximate to the things demonstrated, it is necessary that principle should be more proximate to souls than fountain. Farther still, if every thing which is generated is generated from a principle, as Plato says, but souls are in a certain respect generated, as Timæus says, there is also a precedaneous principle of souls. And as they are the principles of things which are generated according to time, so after another manner principle subsists prior to souls, which are generated. And as they are unbegotten according to the generation of bodies, thus also the principle of souls is exempt from all generation. Through these things therefore, it is demonstrated by us, that the Crater is the fountain of souls, that after the fountain there is a primary ruling monad of them, and that this monad is more proximate to souls than the fountain, but is established above them, as being their prolific cause. And all these particulars we have demonstrated from the words of Plato.

CHAPTER XXXII

Again therefore, let us return to the things proposed, and teach in a greater degree the lovers of the contemplation of truth, concerning this Crater. For the whole vivific deity having established in the middle of the intellectual kings the prolific cause of divine natures, and according to her highest, most intellectual and all-perfect powers, being occultly united to the first father, but according to more partial and secondary causes from them, being conjoined to the demiurgus, and establishing one conspiration together with him of the generation of the partial orders, Timæus mystically mentions those more ancient powers of the Goddess, and which abide in the first father. But with respect to those powers that are co-arranged with the demiurgus, and adorn together with him the natures in the universe, some of these he delivers more clearly but the whole of others through indication. For the secondary monads themselves of the Goddess are triple, as the wise assert, one of them being the fountain of souls, the second, being the fountain of the virtues, but the third being the fountain of Nature which is suspended from the back of the Goddess. The demiurgus therefore, also assumes these three hypostases to his own prolific production. And the Crater indeed, as we have said, is the fountain of souls, unically containing the whole and perfect number of them.† And as the demiurgus is allotted a paternal cause with respect to the psychical generation, so the Crater is prolific, and is allotted the ratio and order of a mother. For such things as Jupiter produces paternally in souls, the fountain of souls produces maternally and generatively.

Virtue however, energizes by itself, and adorns and perfect wholes. And on this account, the universe having participated of soul, immediately also participates of virtue. "For the demiurgus, says Timæus, having placed soul in the middle, extended it through the universe, and besides this surrounded the body of it externally with soul as with a veil, and causing circle to revolve in circle, constituted heaven one, alone and solitary, but through *virtue* able to converse with itself, and being in want of no other thing, but sufficiently known and friendly itself to itself." At one and the same time therefore the world is animated, lives through the whole of its life according to virtue, and possesses from the virtues as its highest end, friendship with itself, and an all-perfect knowledge of itself. For it is itself sufficiently known and friendly to itself through virtue.

Moreover, nature also is consubsistent with the generation of body. For the demiurgus generates body through necessity, and fashions it together with its proper life. And on this account, shortly after, having constituted partial souls, he shows to them the nature of the universe, and the laws of Fate. For in consequence of possessing the cause of total

---

† For $\alpha \upsilon \tau o \upsilon$, it is necessary to read $\alpha \upsilon \tau \omega \nu$.

Nature and Fate, he also exhibits these to souls. For the demiurgus is not converted to things posterior to himself, but primarily contains in himself the things which are exhibited, and unfolds to souls the powers of himself. Hence, the paradigm of all Nature, and the one cause of the laws of Fate pre-subsist in him. For the fountain of Nature, is called the first Fate by the Gods themselves. "You should not look upon Nature, for the name of it is fatal." Hence also, Timæus says, that souls at one and the same time see the laws of Fate, and the nature of the universe, *viz.* they see as it were mundane Fate, and the powers of it. And the Elean guest in the *Politicus*, denominates the motive cause of the more physical circulation of the universe, Fate. For he says that "Fate and connate desire convolve the world." And the same person likewise clearly acknowledges that the world possesses this power from the demiurgus and father. For he says that all the apparent arrangement and circulation are derived from Jupiter. It is demonstrated therefore, that according to these three causes of the vivific Goddess which are co-arranged with the demiurgus, the world is perfected by him, *viz.* according to the fontal Crater, the fountain of the virtues, and the first-effective cause of nature.

It is likewise manifest that again in these things Plato does not refuse to employ the name of fountain. For in the *Laws* he calls the power of prudence which is essentially inherent in souls, and which is productive of the virtues in us, the fountain of intelligence. And he also says, that two other fountains are imparted to us by nature, *viz.* pleasure and pain. As, therefore, we before demonstrated that souls are called the fountains of motions, on account of the one fountain of them, of which they participate, thus also when Plato calls the first progeny of Nature fountains, it is obvious to every one, that he will permit the exempt cause itself of them to be denominated a fountain. After the same manner, likewise, since he magnificently celebrates the essential power of virtue in us, as the fountain of intelligence, he will not be compelled to hear a name which does not at all pertain to his philosophy, if some one should be willing to denominate, the first monad of the virtues, a fountain. But where shall we have the name of fountain posited by him in the intellectual Gods? In the *Cratylus*, therefore, he says that Tethys is the occult name of a fountain, and he calls Saturn himself and the queen Rhea fluxions. For these divinities are rivers of the intelligible fountains, and proceeding from fountains placed above them, they fill all the natures posterior to themselves with the prolific rivers of life. And the Crater itself likewise is fontal. The Gods, therefore, also denominate the first-effective causes of partial natures, fontal craters.

376

These things, however, we shall more fully investigate elsewhere. Let it be considered also, that we have here sufficiently examined the particulars concerning the demiurgic monad, according to the narration of Plato.

CHAPTER XXXIII

In the next place, let us survey those causes and leaders of uncontaminated purity, and see if Plato any where appears to remind us of this order of Gods, and of the inflexible power proceeding from them to all the divine genera. For the first-effective triad of the immutable order, is united to the triad of the intellectual kings and the progressions of the former are co-divided with the monads of the latter. And the summit of the triad, and as it were, the flower of the inflexible guard of wholes is united to the first intellectual king. But the middle centre of the triad, is in a kindred manner conjoined to the second intellectual king, proceeds together with him, and subsists about him. And the extremity[†] of the whole triad is connected with the third intellectual king, is converted with him to the principle [of the intellectual order,] and together with him is convolved to the one union of the father of all the intellectual Gods. And after this manner, indeed, the three unpolluted guardians of the intellectual fathers, are monadically divided. But together with this division they have also an hypostasis united to each other. All of them, likewise, are in a certain respect in each of the fathers, and all of them energize about all. And after a certain manner indeed according to their proper hypostasis, they are divided from the fathers; but after another manner they are impartibly assumed with them, and at one and the same time they are allotted an equally-dignified order with the fathers, and appear to possess an essence subordinate to them.

Such, therefore, being their nature, they preserve, indeed, the whole progressions of the fathers undefiled, but supply them with inflexibility in their powers, and immutability in their energies. They are suspended, however, from total purity. And if some of the ancients have in any of their writings surveyed in intellect that which always subsists with invariable sameness, which receives nothing into itself from subordinate natures, and is not mingled with things inferior, they celebrate all such goods as these, as pervading to intellect, and other natures, from these Gods. For the oration in the *Banquet* of Plato, celebrates in a

---

[†] το εσχατον is omitted in the original.

remarkable manner the immiscibility of the divine essence with secondary natures; and that which transcends the whole of things in purity and immutable power, arrives to the Gods through the guardian cause. And as the intellectual fathers, are the suppliers of prolific production, both to all other things, and to the inflexible Gods, thus also, the undefiled Gods, impart the power of purity, both to the fathers, and to the other divine orders. At one and the same time, therefore, the three unpolluted Gods subsist with the three intellectual kings, are the guardians of the father themselves, establish about them an immutable guard, and firmly fix themselves in them. Hence also, the Athenian guest, as he arranges and adorns his polity through the best analogy, through which the demiurgus binds and constitutes the whole number [of the elements,] so likewise he appoints a guard to all the inhabitants of the region, that nothing, as much as possible, may be without defence; imitating in this the intellectual Gods themselves who guard all things by the undefiled leaders. And it appears to me that on this account he calls the rulers [of his polity] guardians of the laws, or [simply] guardians, because the inflexible guardians are consubsistent with the intellectual leaders of the whole worlds.

CHAPTER XXXIV

These arguments, however, will be more remote from that divine triad, and are referred to it from ultimate images. But perhaps omitting these, we may abound with greater conceptions, and more conducive to the investigation of the thing proposed, and speculating together with Plato the divine genera, we may discover how he also celebrates this order of Gods, and constitutes them together with the three kings that are now discussed, just as by other theologists also, we are mystically instructed in the truth concerning them. In the fable therefore of Protagoras, Plato indicating to us the exempt watch-tower of Jupiter, and the transcendency of his essence which is unmingled with all secondary natures, through which he is inaccessible and unrevealed to the partible genera of Gods, refers the cause of this to his[†] immutable guard, and the defensive order by which he[‡] is surrounded. For on account of this, all the demiurgic powers indeed are firmly established in themselves. But all the forms [that are in him] are according to supreme transcendency

---

[†] For αυτων, it is necessary to read αυτου.

[‡] The same emendation is here also necessary, as above.

exempt from secondary natures. And in short, the demiurgic intellect [through this order] abides after its accustomed manner. For the fable says that the guards of Jupiter are terrible to all things. And on this account such [partible] genera of Gods (one of which also Prometheus is) cannot be immediately conjoined with the undefiled and Olympian powers of the demiurgus. If, therefore, Socrates himself in the form of a fable clearly delivers to us the guard about the demiurgus, is it not through these things evident that the guardian genus is consubsistent with the intellectual Gods? For as the Oracles say, that the demiurgic order is surrounded with a burning guard, thus also Plato says that guards stand round it, and defend inflexibly the summit of it exempt from all secondary natures.

But in the *Cratylus*, Socrates unfolding through the truth which is expressed in names, who Saturn is, demonstrates indeed his[†] peculiar hyparxis, according to which he subsists as the leader of the total intellectual orders. He likewise unfolds to us the monad of the unpolluted order, which is united with Saturn. For Saturn, as he says in that dialogue, is a pure intellect. For, he adds, the *koron* (το κορον) of him, does not signify his being a boy, but the purity, and incorruptible nature of intellect. After an admirable manner therefore, the fabricator of these divine names, has at one and the same time conjoined the Saturnian peculiarity, and the first monad of the unpolluted triad. For the union of the first father with the first of the unpolluted Gods, is transcendent, and hence this inflexible God is called *silent* by the Gods, is said to accord with intellect, and to be known by souls according to intellect alone: because he subsists in the first intellect according to one union with it. Saturn therefore, as being the first intellect, is defined according to its proper order, but as a pure and incorruptible intellect, he has the undefiled conjoined in himself. And on this account, he is the king of all the intellectual Gods. For as intellect he gives subsistence to all the intellectual Gods, and as a pure intellect, he guards the total orders of them. The two fathers therefore, [Saturn and Jupiter] are shown by the words of Plato to be co-arranged with the immutable Gods, according to union indeed, the first, but according to separation the third.

If you are willing however, to survey the one inflexible guard of them with respect to each other, according to which the third father is stably in the first, as being the intellect of him, and energizing about him again direct your attention to the bonds in the *Cratylus*, of which indeed,

---

[†] For αυτης, it is requisite to read αυτου.

partible lives, and the lives deprived of intellect, and which are stupidly astonished about matter, are unable to participate. But a divine intellect itself, and the souls which are conjoined to it, participate of these bonds according to an order adapted to them. For the Saturnian bonds, appear indeed to bind the mighty Saturn himself, but in reality, they connect about him in an undefiled manner the natures that throw the bonds around him. For a bond is the symbol of the connective order of the gods, since every thing which is bound is connected by a bond. Again therefore from these things, the guardian good which extends from the connective Gods to the intellectual kings is apparent, since it unites, and collects them into one. For a bond guards that which is connected by it. But the immutable Gods inflexibly preserve their own appropriate orders. For the guardship of these Gods is twofold; the one indeed, being primary and uniform, and suspended from the triad of the connective Gods; but the other being co-existent with the intellectual kings, and defending them from a tendency to all secondary natures. For all the intellectual fathers ride on the unpolluted Gods, and are established above wholes, through their inflexible, undeviating, and immutable power.

If however, it be not only necessary that these two fathers should participate of this guardian order, but that the middle vivific deity of them should be allotted a monad of the immutable Gods co-ordinate to herself, it is indeed necessary that the first [guardianship] of the unpolluted leaders in the intellectual fathers, should be triadic, and should have the same perfect number with the three intellectual Gods. It is likewise necessary that the first of these leaders should be stably united to the first [of the intellectual kings]; but that the second should in a certain respect be separated from the second of these kings, together with a union with him. And that the third should now be entirely separated from the third king. And thus the unpolluted proceeds conformably to the paternal order, and is after the same manner with it triadically divided. The first of the unpolluted Gods likewise guards the occult nature of Saturn, and the first-effective monad which transcends wholes, and establishes perfectly in him the causes that proceed from, and again return to him. But the second, preserves the generative power of the queen Rhea, pure from matter, and undefiled, and sustains from the incursions of secondary natures her progression to all things, on which she pours the rivers of life. And the third preserves the whole fabrication of things established above the fabrications, and firmly abiding in itself. It likewise guards it so as to be inflexible, one, and all-perfect with respect to the subjects of its providential case, and expanded above all partial production.

CHAPTER XXXV

Let us now then from this indefinite and common doctrine about these Gods, adduce the Grecian rumour concerning it, as delivered to us by Plato, and demonstrate that he as far as to the very names follows the theologists of the Greeks, just as in the mystic theory of the three kings, and the narration of the unpolluted Gods, he does not depart from their interpretation. For who that is in the smallest degree acquainted with the divine wisdom of the Greeks, does not know that in their arcane mysteries, and other concerns respecting the Gods, the order of the Curetes, is in a remarkable manner celebrated by them, as presiding over the undefiled peculiarity, as the leader of the goddess [Rhea,] and as binding in itself the guardianship of wholes? These Gods therefore, are said to guard the queen Rhea, and the demiurgus of wholes, and proceeding as far as to the causes of partible vivification and fabrication, to preserve the Proserpine and Bacchus which are among these causes, exempt from secondary natures, just as here [i.e. in the intellectual order], they defend the vivifications of total life, and the first-effective monads of all-perfect fabrication. Not only Orpheus therefore, and the theologists prior to Plato knew this Curetic order, and knowing, venerated it, but the Athenian guest also in the *Laws* celebrates it. For he says, that the armed sports of the Curetes in Crete, are the principal paradigms of all elegant motion. And now, neither is he satisfied with having mentioned this Curetic order, but also adds the one unity of the Curetes, *viz.* our mistress Minerva, from which the mystic doctrine also of theologists prior to him, suspends the whole progression of the Curetes. He likewise, surrounds them above with the symbols of Minerva, as presiding over an ever-flourishing life, and vigorous intellection; but beneath, he manifestly arranges them under the providence of Minerva. For the first Curetes indeed, as being the attendants of the intelligible and occult Goddess, are satisfied with the signs that proceed from thence; but those in the second and third orders, are suspended from the intellectual Minerval monad.

What then is it, that the Athenian guest says concerning this monad, which converts to itself in an undefiled manner the Curetic progressions? "The *Core* (κορη) *i.e.* virgin, and mistress that is with us, being delighted with the discipline of dancing, did not think it proper to play with empty hands; but being adorned with an all-perfect panoply, she thus gave perfection to dancing." Through these things therefore, the Athenian guest clearly shows the alliance of the Curetic triad to the Minerval monad. For as that triad is said to sport in armour, so he says that the Goddess who is the leader of them [*i.e.* of their progression] being adorned with an all-perfect panoply, is the source to them of elegant motion. And as he denominates that triad Curetic, from purity, so likewise he calls this goddess *Core*, as being the cause of undefiled power itself. For *koron* (το κορον) as Socrates[†] says in the *Cratylus*, signifies the pure and incorruptible. Whence also the Curetes are allotted their appellation, as presiding over the undefiled purity of the Gods. And the monad of them is particularly celebrated as a mistress and as Core [a virgin] she being the supplier of an inflexible and flourishing dominion to the Gods. The word *koron* therefore, as we have said, is a symbol of purity, of which these Gods are the primary leaders, and according to which[‡] they are participated by others. But their being armed, is a symbol of the guardian power according to which they connect wholes, guard them exempt from secondary natures, and preserve them established in themselves. For what other benefit do men derive from arms except that of defence? For these are in a particular manner the safeguard of cities. Hence fables also ascribing to the unpolluted Gods an unconquerable strength, give to them an armed apparatus. Hence adorning the one unity of them with an all-perfect panoply, they establish it at the summit of the progression of these Gods. For the all-perfect precedes things which are divided according to parts, and the panoply exists prior to the partible distribution of guardian powers. And it appears to me that through these particulars Plato again asserts the same things as were afterwards revealed by the Gods. For what they denominate *every kind of armour*, this Plato celebrates as adorned with an *all-perfect panoply*. [For the Gods say,] "Armed with every kind of armour, he resembles the Goddess." For the all-perfect in the habit of Pyrrhich arms, and the undefiled in power, pertain, according to Plato, to the Minerval monad; but according to the narration of the Oracles they pertain to that which is furnished with every kind of arms.

Farther still, rhythm and dancing are a mystic sign of this deity, because the Curetes contain the undefiled power of a divine life; because they preserve the whole progressions of it always arranged according to

---

[†] Κρατης is erroneously printed in the original for Σωκρατης.

[‡] For καθ' εν it is necessary to read καθ' ην.

one divine boundary; and because they sustain these progressions from the incursions of matter. For the formless, the indefinite, and the privation of rhythm, are the peculiarities of matter. Hence, the immaterial, the definite, and the undefiled, are endued with rhythm, are orderly, and intellectual. For on this account, the heavens also are said to form a perpetual dance, and all the celestial orbs participate of rhythmical and harmonious motion, being filled with this power supernally from the unpolluted Gods. For because they are moved in a circle they express intellect, and the intellectual circulation. But because they are moved harmonically, and according to the first and best rhythms, they participate of the peculiarity of the guardian Gods. Moreover, the triad of the unpolluted leaders is suspended from the summit of the intellectual Gods. And that it proceeds from this summit, Plato himself teaches us, by placing the first cause of purity in Saturn the king of all the intellectual hebdomad. For *purity* (το κορον) is there primarily, as he informs us in the *Cratylus*, and the first-effective cause of purity, pre-exists unically in Saturn. For on this account also, the Minerval monad, is called *Core* (a virgin) and the Curetic triad is after this manner celebrated, being suspended from the purity in the intellectual father.

CHAPTER XXXVI

Concerning the undefiled leaders, thus much we have had to say, according to the narration of Plato. The monad therefore, now remains, which closes the number of all the intellectual hebdomad, and is the first and uniform cause of all division, which must in the next place be discussed by us. The sections therefore, of the intellectual Gods which are celebrated by all the wise in divine concerns among the Greeks, and which obscurely signify the separations in those Gods, are effected in them through the seventh monad, which is the cause of division, and according to which they separate themselves from the Gods that are placed above them, proceeding into another order, are allotted a union exempt from subordinate natures, and by themselves have a definite order, and a progression bounded according to number. Plato however, allows indeed poets that are inspired by Phœbus, to signify things of this kind obscurely and mystically; but he excludes the multitude from hearing these things, because they believe without examination in the fabulous veils of truth. And this is what Socrates reprobates in Euthyphron, who was thus affected in consequence of being ignorant of divine concerns. According to the divinely-inspired intellect of Plato therefore, transferring all such particulars to the truth concerning wholes, and unfolding the concealed theory which they contain, we shall procure for ourselves the genuine worship of a divine nature. For Socrates himself in the *Cratylus*, unfolds to us the Saturnian bonds, and their mystic meaning, and in a remarkable manner demonstrates that the visions of those ancient and illustrious men do not fall off from the truth.

After the same manner therefore, he will permit his friends to assume intellectual sections, and the power which is productive of these, according to divinely-inspired conceptions, and will suffer them to survey these together with bonds in the intellectual Gods. Farther still, the fable in the *Gorgias*, in a clearer manner separates the empire of Jupiter from the Saturnian kingdom, and calls the former the second from, and more recent than the latter. What is the cause, therefore, which separates these paternal monads? What intellectual power produced the intellectual empire from that which is exempt from it? For it is necessary that there should be with the Gods themselves the first-effective fountain of division, through which Jupiter also separates himself from the monad his father, Saturn from the kingdom of the Heaven, and the natures posterior to Jupiter, proceeding into an inferior order, are separated from his all-perfect monad.

Moreover, the demiurgus himself in the production of the genera posterior to himself, at one and the same time is the cause to them of union, and the source of their all-various divisions. For fabricating the soul one whole, he separates it into parts, and all-various powers. And in the *Timæus* where the demiurgus is said to do this, Plato himself does not refuse to call these separations, and essential divisions, *sections*. He likewise cuts off parts from thence, places them in that which is between these, and again separates parts from the whole, and thus the mixture from which he had cut off these parts, was now wholly consumed. Is it therefore any longer wonderful that the framers of fables should denominate the divisions of the intellectual leaders, sections, since even Timæus himself who does not devise fables, but indicates the essential progression of souls into multitude, uses as a sign the word section? And does not also Plato in the greatest degree accord with the highest of theologists, when he delivers to us the demiurgus glittering with intellectual sections? As therefore the demiurgus, when producing the essence of souls, constitutes it according to true being, when generating life, he generates it according to the life which is in real beings, and produces the intellect which is in souls according to the intellect which is in himself, - thus also when cutting the essence of the soul from itself,

384

and separating it, he energizes according to the sections and separations which are in the intellectual order, and according to the one and intellectual cause of them. According to Plato, therefore, there is a first monad of the total divisions in intellectuals, and together with the twofold triads, I mean the paternal and the undefiled, it gives completion to the whole intellectual hebdomad. And we, following Plato, and other theologists, concede the same things.

CHAPTER XXXVII

Let us now, however, return to the beginning, and demonstrate that Parmenides delivers the same things concerning this intellectual hebdomad, and that he produces this hebdomadic *aiōn (eternity)* and the peculiarity of the Gods which is intellectual alone, in continuity with the triple orders of the intelligible, and at the same time intellectual Gods. And, in the first place, let us survey what he says concerning the father of the intellectual Gods, and the undefiled power which is co-arranged with him. For after the threefold figure, and the order of the Gods which perfects all things, that which is in itself[†] and in another, becomes apparent. These things, however, are demonstrated to be signs of the intellectual summit of the intellectual monads. For the first father of the Gods in this order, at one and the same time is allotted a paternal transcendency with respect to those posterior to him, and is the intellect of the first intelligibles. For every imparticipable intellect is said to be the intellect of the natures prior to itself, and towards them, from whom it is produced, it has an intellectual conversion, and in them as first-effective causes it establishes itself. Whence also the demiurgic intellect is the intellect of the natures above itself, and proximately indeed of its own father, from which likewise it proceeds, but eminently of the intelligible unities beyond [Saturn].

The first king, therefore, in intellectuals, is both an intellectual father, and a paternal intellect. He is, however, the intellectual father indeed of the Gods that proceed from himself; but he is the paternal intellect of the intelligibles prior to himself. For he is indeed intellectual essentially; but he has an intelligible transcendency in intellectuals; because he is also established analogous to the unknown order of the intelligible, and at the same time, intellectual Gods, and to the occult order of the intelligible triads. And as they are expanded above the triadic hypostases of the Gods posterior to themselves, thus also the

---

[†] For εν αυτῳ it is necessary to read εν εαυτῳ.

father of intellectuals, is a father expanded above the whole intellectual hebdomad, in consequence of being a paternal intellect. And analogously to the above-mentioned orders of Gods, he establishes himself in them, and is filled from them with paternal and intelligible union. On this account also, he is occult, shuts in himself the prolific powers of himself, and producing from himself total causes, he again establishes them in, and converts them to himself.

These things, therefore, Parmenides also indicating, magnificently celebrates this order by these twofold signs, and characterizes the first king and father of the intellectual[†] Gods through these peculiarities. For he is in himself, and in another. For so far indeed as he is a total intellect, his energy is directed to himself, but so far as he is in the intelligibles prior to himself, he establishes in another the all-perfect intelligence of himself. For, indeed, this subsistence in another, is more excellent than the subsistence of a thing in itself; since, as Parmenides himself concludes, the subsistence of Saturn in another, pertains to him according to whole, but the subsistence of him in himself, according to parts. Where, therefore, does *the another* pre-exist? And to what order of the Gods prior to Saturn does it belong? Or is not this also divinely unfolded by our preceptor? For he says that this *another*, remarkably pertains to that order, according to which the power of difference first shines forth, being the progeny of intelligible and paternal power. Hence in the first triad *the another* was occultly, so far as power also had there an occult subsistence; but it particularly shines forth in the first order of the intelligible, and at the same time, intellectual Gods. For there the first difference, the feminine nature of the Gods, and the paternal and unvocal power subsist.

[Saturn therefore] who is the first of the intellectual fathers being intelligible, so far as he is a whole, establishes himself in the intelligible triads prior to himself, from which also he is filled with united and occult goods. And on this account he is said to be in another. With respect to those triads indeed, *the another* is occultly and according to cause in the intelligible [*i.e.* in the first triad] of intelligibles; but according to essence in the intelligible of the intelligible, and at the same time, intellectual Gods. All intelligibles therefore are united; the intelligible indeed of the intelligible and intellectual Gods being united to the intelligible of the intelligibles prior[‡] to intellectuals; but the

---

[†] For νοητων, it is obviously necessary to read νοερων.

[‡] For πρωτων, it is necessary to read προ των.

intelligible of intellectuals, to both. And the subsistence indeed in another, adheres to the difference which is according to unical number. But unical number is suspended from the occult union of the one being; on which account also it is unical.

Farther still, we also say, that there is a twofold conversion in those orders, the one indeed being towards themselves, but the other towards the causes of them, (for it neither was nor will be lawful for divine natures, to convert themselves in any respect to natures posterior to themselves). And the intelligible Gods generate all things stably; but the intelligible and intellectual Gods who illuminate imparticipable life, impart the original cause of progression to all things; and the intellectual Gods arrange and adorn wholes according to conversion. Hence, it is indeed necessary that the summit of intellectuals which pours forth from itself the whole and all-perfect form of conversion, should be characterized by both the convertive symbols, and should be at one and the same time converted to itself, and to the natures prior to itself. Hence, because indeed, it is converted to itself, it is *in itself;* but because it is converted to the intelligible orders beyond itself, it is *in another.* For the *another* is more excellent than the whole intellectual order. As, therefore, the summit of intelligibles primarily subsists according to the intelligible peculiarity itself, and is firmly established above wholes; and as the summit of intelligibles and intellectuals primarily unfolds the peculiarity of this order, subsisting according to divine diversity, and being to all things the cause of all-various progressions; - thus also the intelligible deity of intellectuals, exhibits from himself according to union the twofold forms of conversion, being indeed *in another* according to the more excellent form of conversion, but *in himself* according to the less excellent form. For to be converted to himself is inferior to the conversion to more excellent natures.

Again, therefore, the subsistence *in another* is the illustrious prerogative of the intelligible and paternal peculiarity. For *the another* is intelligible, and difference was the power proceeding from the intelligible fathers, and from the natures firmly established in them. Hence, that which is comprehended in this power, and is filled from it, is paternal and intelligible. But the subsistence of a thing *in itself* is the proper sign of the unpolluted monad. For as we have before observed, the summits of the two intellectual triads are conjoined. And the monad of the guardian triad has eternally established itself in the paternal monad, and again establishes in, and converts to itself the natures which have proceeded from itself. And the first intellectual father is indeed father on account of himself, but on account of the unpolluted [monad,] he comprehends in himself the genera of himself, stably recalls them [when they have proceeded from him] to himself, and in his own allness[†] contains the intelligible multitudes of intellectuals in unproceeding[‡] union with their monad.

The first leader, therefore, of the guardian order subsists in conjunction with the father. And the father indeed comprehends the unpolluted cause, but is comprehended by the first intelligibles. And as he is intelligibly established in them, so likewise he has established in himself, and constituted about himself, the one summit of the inflexible Gods. In the *Parmenides*, therefore, also the same God appears to us to be a pure intellect. Because, indeed, he is intellect, being extended to the intelligible place of survey, and on this account being *in another*, so far as he is wholly established in it. But again, because he is pure and immaterial, being converted to himself, and shutting *in himself* all his own powers. For the parts of this wholeness, are more partial powers, which hasten indeed to a progression from the father, but are on all sides established and comprehended by the wholeness. And the wholeness itself is a deity, connectedly containing in itself intelligible parts, being parturient indeed with intellectual multitude, generating all things stably, and again embosoming and collecting to itself its progeny, and as the more tragical fables say, absorbing and depositing them in itself. For the progeny of it are twofold; some indeed, being, as it were, analyzed into it; but others being divided from it. And some abiding in it through the first unpolluted monad; but others proceeding according to the prolific cause of the intellectual Gods, surmounting the union of the father, and being the primary leaders of another order, and of the arrangement and ornament of secondary natures. The first order therefore of the intellectual Gods, is thus delivered to us by Parmenides.

CHAPTER XXXVIII

The second order however, after this, is that which comprehends the middle genera of wholes, is the cause to all things of progression and prolific power, and is in continuity with the first order of the intellectual Gods. What else therefore than life is every where in continuity with the intelligible and true being? For it is the medium between intellect and the intelligible, conjoining intellect to the

---

† For εαυτοτητι read παντοτητι.

‡ For εκφοιτητα read ανεκφοιτητα.

intelligible, and expressing the intelligible power which collects together *The One* and being. As the intelligible therefore is to *The One* and hyparxis, so is life to power, and intellect to being. And as in intelligibles, *The One* is the object of desire, but being aspires after the participation of *The One,* and power collects being to the participation of *The One,* and *The One* to a communion with being, (for *The One* here is not imparticipable, and exempt from all power) so likewise the intelligible is the object of desire to intellect, but intellect is filled with it. And life binds indeed intellect to the intelligible, but unfolds the intelligible to intellect. Whence also, I think, those who are wise in all divine concerns, call *The One* and hyparxis intelligible. But that which is primarily being, they call† the first intellect, conformably to this analogy. Life therefore, is the medium between being and intellect, in the same manner as power subsists between *The One* and being. And all these, *viz.* the intelligible, life, and intellect are primarily in intelligibles; but secondarily in intelligibles and intellectuals; and according to a third diminution, in intellectuals. In intelligibles however, being is according to essence; for there intellect is primarily according to cause. But in intellectuals, intellect indeed is according to essence, but the natures prior to intellect, are according to participation. Since therefore, life is surveyed in a threefold respect, in intelligibles indeed according to cause; but in intelligibles and intellectuals, according to hyparxis; and in intellectuals,‡ according to participation, it is indeed necessary that the life which is in the intellectual order, should both be life, and participate of the causes generative of life prior of itself. *The One* therefore of the intellectual Gods which is arranged in the middle, is not motion, but that which is moved. For prior to this, it has been demonstrated by Plato, that all life is motion. For soul is self-motive because it is self-vital. And intellect is on this account moved, because it has the most excellent life. The first vivific cause, therefore, of the intellectual Gods, is primarily allotted motion. If, however, it was the first-effective and highest life, it would be requisite to denominate it motion, and not that which is moved. But since it is life as in intellectuals, but is filled from exempt life, it is at the same time motion, and that which is moved. Very properly, therefore, does Parmenides demonstrate that *The One* in this order is moved, because it proceeds from the causes of all life that

---

† For αναλυοντες, it is necessary to read ανακαλουντες.

‡ In the original, after εν δε τοις νοητοις και νοεροις, it is necessary to supply καθ' υπαρξιν, εν δε τοις νοεροις, κ.τ.λ.

are placed above it, and is analogous to the middle centre of intelligibles, and to the middle triad of intelligibles and intellectuals. Hence also, Socrates in the *Phædrus* calls this middle triad Heaven; for the whole of it is life and motion. But that which is moved, is the middle in intellectuals, as being filled from it, [*i.e.* from the life in the middle triad of intelligibles and intellectuals;] since eternity also, which is arranged according to the intelligible wholeness, is all-perfect life, and all life according to Plotinus. There, however, the middle is life according to cause; but in intellectuals, it is life according to participation; and in the order between these, it is life according to essence, proceeding indeed from intelligible life, (as Parmenides also manifests, characterizing both according to wholeness, though the wholeness in intelligibles is different from that which is in intelligibles and intellectuals, as we have before observed,) but producing after this, intellectual life. For that which is moved, is indeed entirely allied to the circulation of the Heaven, and to intellectual and intelligible life.

Moreover, the permanency which is co-ordinate with this motion, is not one certain genus of being, as neither is motion. For beings indeed are naturally adapted to participate of the genera of being; but the superessential goods of the Gods, are expanded above the order of beings. If, therefore, Parmenides here, assuming *The One Itself* by itself, surveys in this motion and permanency, he evidently does not attribute the elements of being to the Gods, but assigns to them peculiarities appropriate, all-perfect, and transcending wholes. And thus asserting that *The One* is moved and stands still, according to motion, indeed, he delivers the vivific hyparxis of the Gods, the generative fountain of wholes, and the leading cause of all things. But according to permanency, he delivers the unpolluted monad co-ordinated with motion, and which connectedly-contains the middle centres of the guardian triad. For as the summit of the guardian triad, is united to the first father, according to the first hypostasis, thus also the deity who contains the middle bond of the unpolluted leaders, is by a congeniality of nature consubsistent with the motive cause of all the Gods, which moves wholes, and is primarily moved from itself. And through this deity, the prolific power of this Goddess [Rhea] is firmly established in herself. Producing likewise, and multiplying all things, she is [through this deity] exempt from wholes, and inflexibly exists prior to her progeny. With respect, therefore, to motion here and permanency, the former indeed is the fountain of the life and generative power that proceeds to all things; but the latter,[†] establishes the whole vivific fountain in itself, but is from thence filled with the prolific rivers of life. Parmenides, therefore, delivering to us these things, and the progression of them, demonstrates that that which is moved is generated from that which is in another, but that which stands still, from that which is in itself. For the first monad of the paternal triad constitutes the natures posterior to it. And after the same manner, the highest of the unpolluted triad, and which is intelligible as in this triad, imparts at one and the same time the middle and last monad of the triad. On this account, also, motion here is better than permanency. For as a subsistence in another is according to cause more ancient than the subsistence of a thing in itself, so likewise that which is moved, is causally more ancient than that which is permanent. For the unpolluted Gods, are in power subordinate to the fathers, and are comprehended in them.

CHAPTER XXXIX

The third, therefore, to the Saviour, as they say, and let us direct our attention to the demiurgic monad, unfolding itself into light together with the co-ordinate Gods it contains. In the first place, then, here also the communion of *The One* with other things is apparent, and we must no longer consider *The One* alone by itself, but according to its habitude towards other things., Because, therefore, the demiurgic order produces wholes from itself, and arranges and adorns a corporeal nature, it also generates all the second and ministrant causes of the Gods. For what occasion is there to say that the term *other things*, is a sign of a corporeal condition of being, since formerly the Pythagoreans thought fit to characterize an incorporeal nature by *The One*, but indicated to us the nature which is divisible about body, through the term *others?* In the second place, the number of the conclusions [in this part of the *Parmenides*] is doubled. For *The One* is no longer demonstrated to be alone same, or different, as it is to be in itself, and in another, or to be moved, and stand still, but it is demonstrated to be the same with itself,[‡] and different from itself, and to be different from other things, and the same with other things. But this twice appeared to us before to

---

[†] In the original ἡ δε is omitted.

[‡] After αλλα in the original it is necessary to supply the words και ταυτον εαυτῳ, και ετερον εαυτου.

be entirely adapted to the demiurgic monad, both according to other theologists, and to Socrates in the *Cratylus*, who says that the demiurgic name is composed from two words. In the third place, therefore, the multitude of causes is here separated, and all the monads of the Gods present themselves to the view, according to the demiurgic progression. For the demiurgic order is apparent, the prolific power co-ordinate with it, the undefiled monad the cause of exempt providence, and the distributive fountain of wholes; and together with these, as I may say, all the orders about the demiurgus are apparent, according to which he produces and preserves all things and being exempt from the things produced, is firmly established in himself, and separates his own kingdom, from the united empire of his father.

How, therefore, and through what particulars do these things become apparent? We reply, that *the same with itself* (for this Parmenides first demonstrates) represents to us about the nature of *The One*, the monadic and paternal peculiarity, according to which the demiurgus also subsists. Hence, likewise, *The One* is said to be the same with itself. For *the another* is in the demiurgus according to the transcendency of different causes; but *the same,* appears to be a sign of his proper, *viz.* of his paternal, hyparxis. For being one, and the exempt father and demiurgus of wholes, he establishes his proper union in himself. And in this one, Parmenides in a remarkable manner shows the uniform, and that which is allied to bound. But *the same with other things,* is the singular good of prolific power, and of a cause proceeding to, and pervading through all things without impediment. For the demiurgus is present to all things which he produces, and is in all things the same, which he arranges and adorns, pre-establishing in himself the generative essence of wholes. If, therefore, we rightly assert these things, bound and infinity subsist in him demiurgically. And the one indeed is in the sameness which is separate from other things, but the other is in the power which generates other things. For every where power is prolific of secondary natures. But the principle which subsists according to bound, is the supplier of an united and stable hypostasis.

Moreover, *the different from other things,* manifests his undefiled purity, and his transcendency which is exempt from all secondary natures. For the first intellect was on this account pure and incorruptible, as Socrates says in the *Cratylus*, because it is established above co-ordination of communion† with all sensible natures. For as some one of the Gods says, he does not incline his power to matter, but is at once exempt

---

† For κοινωνιαν, it is necessary to read κοινωνιας.

from all fabrication. But the demiurgic intellect receiving from thence total power, and a royal dominion, adorns indeed sensibles, and constitutes the whole of a corporeal nature. Together however, with prolific abundance, and the providential attention to secondary natures, he transcends his progeny, and abides in his own accustomed manner, as Timæus says, through the inflexible guard which subsists with him, and the power imparted to him from it, which is uncontaminated with other participants. Hence, through the never-failing supply of good, and providential energies, and the generation of subordinate natures, he is *the same with them*. For he is participated by them, and fills his progeny with his own providential care. But through his purity, undefiled power, and inflexible energies, he is separate from wholes, is disjoined from them, and is imparticipable by other things. And as the first king of intellectuals is allotted his non-inclination to matter, through the guard which is united to him, and through the undefiled monad; and as the vivific goddess possesses her stable and inflexible power from the second cause of the guardian Gods; thus also the demiurgic intellect preserves a transcendency exempt from other things, and a union separated from multitude, through the third monad of the leaders of purity. For the cause of separate providence is a guard co-ordinate with the demiurgus, who hastens to produce† all things, and to pervade through all things. But the guard which is the supplier of stable power, is co-ordinate with the vivific deity, who is moved to the generation of wholes. And with the intellect that is multiplied according to intellectual conceptions [*i.e.* with Saturn,] the guard is co-ordinate, that imparts an undefiled union of the conversion of all his energies to himself. The monad, therefore, remains, which is arranged as the seventh of these intellectual monads, which is present with, and energizes with all of them, but particularly unfolds itself into light in the demiurgic order, and which Parmenides also producing for us together with the whole demiurgus, defines it in *difference*, in the same manner as he does the undefiled cause in the demiurgus. He says however, that this difference separates the demiurgic monad itself from itself. For we have before observed that this order is the supplier of separation to all the Gods. As therefore, the demiurgus is the same with himself, through the paternal union, after the same manner he is separated from himself and his father through this difference. Whence therefore, does he derive this power? From being in himself, says Parmenides, and in another. For these were indeed unitedly in the first father, but

---

† The word παραγειν is omitted in the original, but ought doubtless to be inserted.

separately in the third. Separation therefore, pre-existed there according to cause; but in the demiurgus it shines forth, and unfolds the power of itself.

That the cause however of division, is in a certain respect in the first father, Parmenides manifests in the first hypothesis, when he says, "that every thing which is in itself is in a certain respect a duad, and is separated from itself." There however, the duad is occultly; but here it subsists more clearly, where also all intellectual multitude shines forth to the view. For difference is the progeny of the firmly-abiding duad which is there. This therefore separates the demiurgic intellect from the Gods prior to it, and divides the monads in it from each other. For if so far as it is in another, it is united to the intelligible of itself, but so far as it is in itself if it separated from it, because it proceeds according to each order of its own intelligible, - if this be the case, it is necessary that this difference should be the cause to it of separation from its father. All the intellectual monads therefore, have appeared to us to subsist co-ordinately with each other. And the subsistence indeed, *in another* is the sign of the father. But the subsistence *in itself,* is the sign of the first unpolluted monad. Again, *motion* is the sign of vivific goodness; but *permanency* of the inflexible power conjoined with motion. And *sameness with itself, and with another,* is the sign of the demiurgic peculiarity; but the being *different from other things,* is the sign of the guard about the demiurgus. And in the last place, *the being different from itself,* is the sign of the seventh intellectual monad, which is according to cause indeed, and occultly in the first father, but is allotted its hypostasis more clearly in the demiurgus. Parmenides likewise appears to me, when dividing the signs of fabrication, to have unfolded in the middles themselves, the peculiarities of the undefiled monad, and of the dividing monad, so far as they also are in a certain respect comprehended in the fabrication. For he shows in the first of the conclusions that *The One* is *the same with itself;* in the second, that it is *different from itself;* in the third, that it is *different from other things;* and in the fourth that it is *the same with other things.* For he co-arranges indeed, the dividing power with the paternal union; but connects with a transcendency separate from secondary natures, the providential cause of them. For in the Gods, it is necessary that union should exist prior to separation, and a purity unmingled with secondary natures, prior to a providential inspection of them; through which likewise, being every where, they are no where, being present with all things, they are exempt from all things, and being all things, they are not any of their progeny.

BOOK VI

CHAPTER I

The hebdomadic *aion* (eternity) therefore, of the intellectual Gods has been through these things celebrated by us, following the mystic conceptions of Plato. But after this, let us in the next place contemplate the multiform progressions of the ruling orders, and refer the one union of them to the intellectual theory of Parmenides. For this order is woven together in continuity with the demiurgus and father of wholes, proceeds from, is perfected by, and converted to him, according to his perfective power. Hence also, it is necessary to connect the narration about the governors of the universe, with the discussion concerning the demiurgus, and to assimilate words to the things of which they are the interpreters. For all the series of the ruling Gods, are collected into the intellectual fabrication as into a summit, and subsist about it. And as all the fountains are the progeny of the intelligible father, and are filled from him with intelligible union, thus likewise, all the orders of the principles or rulers, are suspended according to nature from the demiurgus, and participate from thence of an intellectual life. And let no one be offended with me on hearing in this place the names of fountain and principle, nor accuse these names, as not at all pertaining to Plato. For, as we have before observed, Plato does not leave unnoticed any one of these mystic names. But in his discussions about souls, when he denominates them the fountains and principles of motion, he at the same time indicates the difference between the peculiarity of fountain, and the peculiarity of principle, and the inferiority of principle with respect to the exempt transcendency of fountain.

He likewise manifests that the self-vital extends to all things as far as to soul, from fountain; but the unbegotten from principle. And this is because the *fontal genus* indeed of the Gods is self-begotten, and first-effective, and produces other things from itself; but the ruling genus of the Gods, and which has the relation of a principle, though it proceeds from the fountains, and is allotted a more partial order among beings, yet it is expanded above every thing which is generated, and neither is in a certain respect connected with generated natures, nor communicates with a sensible nature. For the mundane Gods, indeed, are in a certain respect generated; whence also, they are denominated generated by Timæus, and this whole world is likewise called by him a generated god. But the ruling Gods, and who have the relation of principles, are perfectly exempt from generated natures, and are not co-arranged with them. Hence also, the unbegotten is most particularly adapted to them. Those Gods, however, who preside over the liberated dominion being the media between the unbegotten and generated Gods, come into contact indeed with the latter, but do not give completion to the choir of mundane Gods. Hence, they are in a certain respect both generated and unbegotten. The Gods, therefore, who are the summits of supermundane natures, and the rulers of wholes, are alone allotted an unbegotten subsistence in the orders that proceed from the demiurgus. Hence, likewise, this peculiarity is from thence derived to souls. For, as Plato says, principle is unbegotten. For it is necessary that every thing which is generated should be generated from a principle, but that the principle should not be generated from any thing.

At the same time, therefore, it is manifest through these things, how the [ruling] principles proceed from the Gods prior to them. For they are not allotted a progression from them according to motion, nor in short, according to mutation; but the orders of the ruling Gods subsist by their very being, according to their prolific power, and unenvying and exuberant will; and the self-begotten power of the intellectual Gods, gives to the principles also the first generation from itself. Whether, therefore, some one is willing to adopt these, or other names of the divine orders, we shall consider it as a thing of no consequence. But receiving the peculiarity of them, whatever it may be, according to the rumours of theologists, we shall transfer their mystic tradition to the Platonic narration. For thus we shall make the investigation of what follows conformable to what has been before said, and what we assert will be adapted to the things themselves.

CHAPTER II

Again therefore, let us assume the principles of the science concerning these Gods, and demonstrate that the theory pertaining to them is consequent to the first causes. The intelligible Gods therefore, surpass wholes according to supreme transcendency, and primarily participate the union and divine light, in which all the Gods perfectly establish their hypostases. They likewise unically produce all things from themselves, according to the paternal and exuberant will of the communication of good, and pre-establish in themselves occultly the first effective causes of secondary natures. For the whole and common measures of forms pre-subsist in them, and they comprehend according to one cause the uniform genera of being, and prior to these, bound and infinity, from which the superessential orders of the Gods generate all beings.

But in the second rank after these, the intelligible and at the same time intellectual Gods subsist, being divided indeed according to the same number, and preserving the measure of the all-perfect triad in a second order, but producing into multitude the unities of intelligibles, and transferring the unical boundaries of those triads into essential hypostases, and which participate of *The One*. Instead of powers however, which are whole, without separation, and occult, they are transferred into divided causes, and which proceed far from *The One*.

Again, in the third rank after the intelligible Gods, those that are called intellectual are arranged at one and the same time indeed, proceeding into an order diminished with respect to that which is prior to it, and changing the number according to which they subsist. For instead of the perfective triads, they are intellectually divided according to hebdomads. And with respect to the hebdomads, the division of them into two triads, is supernally derived from the first triads; but the terminations of them into monads, express the ends of those orders. For every thing which is the peculiarity of difference and multitude, proceeds from thence to all the genera.

Again therefore, from these, the multiform orders of the ruling principles are generated, being divided indeed, analogous to all the intelligible Gods, and to those that are prior to these intellectual Gods, *viz.* to those that are called intelligible and at the same time intellectual. They have however, their proximate and peculiar hypostasis from the one fabrication; but their united generation together with intellectuals, from the third triad of intelligibles. For that all-perfect cause produces also from itself, the whole orders of the Gods. Hence likewise Parmenides denominates it infinite multitude, as unfolding into light all the genera of being, and all the orders of divine natures, and as being sufficient through one all-perfect power to the generation of wholes.

Farther still, we may also assert this of these leading and ruling Gods, that the intellectual monads make their progression according to imparticipable intellect, in the same manner as the Gods prior to them illuminate imparticipable life, and prior to all things, the intelligible Gods constitute about themselves truly existing and intelligible essence. For every God is participated indeed by beings, and on this account falls short of the unity which is imparticipable and exempt from all things. But a different deity proceeds according to a different peculiarity. And some of the Gods indeed, being defined according to the ineffable good itself, comprehend the intelligible causes of wholes. But others produce the vivific powers, and connectedly contain the first genera of the Gods. Others again, unfold into light all the intellectual involutions, and preside over the participants of the unities that produce divided hypostases. Since therefore, the intellectual Gods primarily subsist according to imparticipable intellect, and on this account are denominated intellectual, the orders that first proceed immediately after them, illuminate the summit of participated intellect, and are intellectual indeed, as with reference to the inferior orders, and which are now divided according to providential energies about the world. But they are secondary to the first intellectuals, and are allotted a more partial government; just as the first of intellectuals, are indeed intelligible with respect to the Gods produced from them, but fall short of the union of first intelligibles. As therefore, they unfold into light the first and imparticipable life, which the intelligible monads pre-established in themselves according to cause only, and occultly; (for all the causes of wholes are pre-assumed there according to one ineffable union) after the same manner also, these Gods, shining forth the first of the intellectuals, express the Gods from whom they derive their subsistence, and are intellectual indeed, but produce the pure, uniform, and total hyparxis of the fathers, into a secondary, and multiplied progression, which is divided about themselves, and into a diminution of essence. By first emissions also from the first-effective, and self-subsistent fountains, they shine forth similarly to the intellectual Gods.

Hence also, they bind to themselves the ruling and generative causes of all the partial orders, and which exist prior to these orders both in dignity and power. And in short, they have the same transcendency with respect to the other Gods [subordinate to them], which the intelligible Gods have to those that are produced from them. For the intelligible Gods being expanded above all the intellectual genera,[†] have pre-established the intelligible hyparxis, by itself, unmingled and pure; and these ruling Gods have also established in themselves the supermundane union, and this peculiarity perfectly exempt from mundane natures. And as in the imparticipable and total hypostases, there is indeed, the intelligible genus, itself by itself; there is also the intellectual which is foreign from this; and there is that which is collective of both, which is celebrated as subsisting in the middle, and is denominated intelligible and at the same time intellectual, - thus also, in these partial orders, the peculiarity of the supermundane Gods, pre-

---

[†] For γονων, it is necessary to read γενων.

exists by itself exempt from the parts of the universe, unco-ordinated with this world, and on all sides comprehending it according to cause.

But the essence of all the mundane Gods is allotted the third order, being proximately carried as in a vehicle in the parts of the world, giving completion to this one and only begotten God, and connectedly-containing the different progressions in it. The government however of the liberated Gods is allotted the middle bond of the extremes, possessing sovereign authority over all [mundane] natures, and in a certain respect communicating with the divisions about the world, but unitedly ascending at the same time into many of its parts, and collecting the divided numbers of the mundane Gods into unical bounds, and more simple causes. Every genus likewise, of the mundane Gods is spread under this liberated order, being on all sides connected, contained, and perfected by it, and filled with the first of goods. If therefore, there is any thing supermundane in the Gods, and if it imparts a certain definite hyparxis of essence to them, and defines a certain peculiarity of powers and a transcendency of order by itself, we must admit that it primarily subsists in the ruling Gods, being derived to them from the intellectual fathers, unmingled with a mundane nature. And this supermundane order indeed is universal, as with reference to all the partible rivers of the Gods, but it is partial, as with reference to the all-perfect, one and whole kingdom of the intellectual Gods. For it is every where necessary that the leading causes of secondary orders, should be in a certain respect assimilated to the terminations of the orders established above them.

And thus the progression of the Gods is one and continued, originating supernally from the intelligible and occult unities, and ending in the last division of a divine cause. For, as in sensibles the most gross and solid bodies, are not immediately connascent with the etherial expanse, but those which are simple and more immaterial than others, are proximately spread under the celestial periods, and of containing bodies, those which are primarily[†] contained, are allotted a greater communion than those which are situated remotely, and are conjoined to them through other media; thus also, in the divine essences prior to the world, the second orders are in continuity with those prior to them. The progressions of beings however, are completed through similitude. But the terminations of the higher orders are united to the beginnings of second orders. And one series and indissoluble order, extends from on high, through the surpassing goodness of the first cause, and his

---

† It appears to me that πρωτως is in this place omitted in the original.

unical power. For because indeed, he is *one*, he is the supplier of union; but because he is *The Good*, he constitutes things similar to him, prior to such as are dissimilar. And thus all things are in continuity with each other. For if this continuity were broken, there would not be union. And things dissimilar to each other being placed in a consequent order, that which is more similar to the principle, would not have a more ancient and honourable progression into being. If therefore, we assert these things rightly, it is necessary that the first hypostases of the partial orders should be total, according to an intellectual transcendency which they are allotted in the divided genera of the Gods, and thus that they should causally comprehend all secondary natures, and conjoin them to the Gods prior to themselves. The order of the ruling Gods therefore, is in continuity with the kingdom of the intellectual Gods. Hence also, Parmenides proximately constitutes it from the demiurgic monad. These things however, will afterwards be apparent.

CHAPTER III

For the present, however, let us survey the common peculiarity of the whole of this order, that we may to the utmost of our power admire the divinely-inspired intellection of Plato, which unfolds to us the most mystic of dogmas. The progression, therefore, of these Gods is said to be supermundane, as we have observed, and to have the second dominion in wholes, after the intellectual Gods. But being defined according to the hyparxis itself of this essence, it unfolds indeed the united nature of the intellectual Gods; but produces into multitude the causes comprehended in them. It also arranges and adorns the more partial genera of beings, from total and first-effective monads, divides them according to the best† order, and co-arranges them to each other. But it collects and binds all secondary natures, and inserts in them an admirable communion of essences and powers. Besides this, likewise, it conjoins all the natures posterior to itself, to those prior to itself, and calls forth the beneficent will of exempt causes, into the providential care of secondary natures, but establishes the hyparxes of subordinate in first essences, and imparts to all beings continuity, and one series of hypostasis. Conferring also all these benefits, it comprehends in itself the supply of them according to one peculiarity. For it assimilates all things, subordinate natures, to those prior to them, and co-ordinate natures, to each other. And through this similitude, at one, and the

† For $\alpha\rho\iota\sigma\tau\alpha$, I read $\alpha\rho\iota\sigma\tau\eta\nu$.

same time, indeed, it unfolds the essences and multiform powers of them, and is the collector of many things into union, and of divided natures, into the divine communion of goods.

From hence, therefore, the orders of different images primarily subsist. For every image is produced according to a similitude to its paradigm. But that which assimilates secondary to first natures, and binds all things through similitude, especially pertains to these Gods. For what else is able to assimilate the world itself, and every thing in the world to their paradigms, but this supermundane genus of Gods? For all intellectuals constitute the natures in the world according to one union, and an allperfect providence, and impartibly preside over the essence of them. But the liberated genus of Gods, in a certain respect now comes into contact with the world, and co-operates with the mundane Gods. It is necessary, therefore, that the assimilating nature should every where according to essence indeed be exempt from the things assimilated, and which are impressed through similitude; but that it should adorn secondary natures with separation, and a division according to species. For how would it be possible for it to assimilate some things to others, and appropriately conjoin all things to their paradigms, unless it proceeded as far as to the last forms and separated all those things from each other, of which there are immoveable pre-existing causes? For the demiurgus, indeed, appears to assimilate all things to himself, as Timæus says, being good, he produced all things similar to himself on account of his beneficent will. He likewise imparts to the world the order of time, by this mean rendering the world more similar to intelligible animal. And in short, on account of the similitude of the universe to its paradigm, he produces all things, and perfects his own fabrication.

In the demiurgus, however, all things, and likewise the second genera of Gods, are according to cause. And as he is the plenitude of all the natures prior to himself, thus also, he comprehends the united causes of the natures posterior to himself. Hence, he perfects the universe, energizes assimilatively, vivifies wholes, is the father of souls, the plastic framer of bodies, the supplier of harmony, the author of bonds, the cause of the impartible and partible genera, and the maker of all figures. And these things, indeed, he constitutes unically; but the Gods posterior to him in a divided manner. Let not, however, any one assert, that the assimilative nature is primarily in the demiurgus, but [let him rather say] that existence is present to the demiurgus according to sameness.† But if from him similitude subsists in all things, and his

---

† For κατα τουτο, it is necessary to read κατα ταυτον.

very being is in sameness, as Parmenides teaches us, we must indeed admit, that such a genus of Gods [as the assimilative] is proximate to him, which also first unfolds his whole fabrication, and inserts it in secondary natures, but is essentially different from and posterior to him, and falls short of the first-effective principle of all things which he contains. In short, the demiurgic monad, and all the multitude co-arranged with it, presides over the similitude of wholes, uniformly, originally, and impartibly; but the order of the ruling Gods, divides indeed that which is united in the demiurgic fabrication, expands that which is total in the energy of the intellectual Gods, and produces into variety the simplicity of their providence. Hence similitude extends from these to all the natures in the world, and to the first, middle, and last forms of life. For that which is assimilated presides over a second form of communion with appropriate principles, on account of progression from causes.

If, however, you are willing by investigating each particular to survey the providence pervading to all things through similitude, you will find that the whole world is the image of the perpetual Gods on account of this, and also that all the wholenesses in it are in a similar manner suspended from their paradigms, that whole souls always dance about the intelligible, and that the more excellent genera that follow the Gods, and such of our souls as are happy, are on account of similitude extended from the wandering produced by generation, to their proper fountain. In short, you will find, that all progressions and conversions are effected and perfected on account of the cause of similitude. For every thing which proceeds subsists through similitude to its generator, and every thing which is converted, in consequence of being assimilated to its proper principles, makes a conversion to them. Moreover, similitude eternally guards the never-failing nature of all the forms in the world, extending supernally from the Gods themselves. And the stable similitude of forms, brings back again to the circle of generation, the unstable mutation of particulars, not only in immaterial, but also in material forms which are conversant with mutability. And it closes in a finite period, the infinite variety of generated natures. But it refers the all-various division of reasons [i. e. of productive principles] to their united and first-effective cause. And on this account, the world being perpetually all-perfect, is completely filled by total genera and species. Hence also, it is similar to intelligible animal, possessing and comprehending all such things after the manner of an image, as all-perfect animal possesses paradigmatically.

We must not, therefore, suppose that the genus of similitude is something small, and extended only to a few things, since it is the cause of perfection to the whole world, gives completion through similitude to its first generation and self-sufficiency, and supplies from itself, its entire comprehension of all things. But neither must we admit that a production of this kind, is to be referred to one certain intellectual form. For that which extends[†] to all the superessential, essential, psychical, incorporeal, and corporeal genera, exists prior to all forms and genera, and to incorporeal and corporeal causes. For the Gods in the world, do not proceed assimilated to their causes, on account of the intellectual form of similitude. Nor on account of the paradigmatic idea of the dissimilar, are the superessential unities of the Gods divided, the intellectual nature separated from itself, and the psychical essences allotted a progression in order; but, I think, that both similitude and dissimilitude have their hypostasis analogous to intellectual sameness and difference. And as they are primarily in the Gods themselves, but secondarily in intellectual forms, being unfolded into light together with the hyparxes of the Gods, thus also, this similitude and dissimilitude, are allotted indeed a precedaneous hyparxis in the superessential unities, but a successive hyparxis in the descending progressions of beings. And on this account Parmenides, as he evinced that *The One* is moved and stands still, is same and different, separate from being, thus also he demonstrates to us the similar and the dissimilar in the uniform hyparxes themselves of the Gods. And Socrates indeed presents to our view in the beginning of the dialogue, the similar and the dissimilar, and defines each paradigm of these to be separate, and exempt from the many similars and dissimilars. But Parmenides recurring to the superessential hypostases of wholes, produces beings from thence, according to the peculiarities of the first causes.

For as every thing in generation is adorned with forms from essences, thus also the peculiarities of hyparxes extend to all essences from superessential natures. For generation is the image of essence; but essence has its progression according to superessential union. The genus of similitude, therefore, is primarily in the Gods; but is divided secondarily in intellectual forms. And on this account the progressions of the whole of things are according to similitude; but the conversions of all things to their principles are through similitude, it being said that all things proceed, and receive the power of conversion from divinity. The intelligible paradigm indeed pre-assumes in itself the occult cause of the

---

[†] For διακρινον, it is necessary to read διατεινον.

assimilative Gods. For it is not sluggish from itself, and established unprolific. But it produces all things essentially assimilated to itself, constitutes them paternally, and is by its very being alone. It likewise imparts by illumination hyparxis to secondary natures, and the power of assimilation to itself. But again, that which is demiurgic of the divine genera, being suspended from the precedaneous cause of the intelligible paradigm, and adhering to, and energizing about it, assimilates indeed all things both to itself and the paradigm, but does not define its proper hyparxis in the genus of similitude. For it comprehends intellectually and unitedly the causes of the similitude of wholes, and employs such like genera of Gods as ministrant to the generation of secondary natures. But the tribe of ruling Gods, being wholly arranged in the partible orders, but first unfolding the intellectual fabrication of the father, is suspended indeed from him† through the similitude of the causes pre-existing in him, but extends and expands all things to the demiurgic union. It converts, however, the partible genera of the Gods to impartible intellectual sameness. But it assimilates the proceeding orders to the intelligible paradigms, and gives completion to the one series of all beings. Very properly, therefore, do those who are wise in divine concerns assert, that the last triad of intelligibles is the cause of the fontal and ruling Gods, and that the whole series of rulers subsists about the intellectual father. For the genus of assimilating natures pertains to the perfect paradigm, just as the genus of things assimilated pertains to the extremity of the intellectual order. For all things are assimilated to the first paradigm, and the conversion of all secondary natures to it is through similitude. And with the demiurgus of wholes, the cause of intellectual sameness and difference is united, being partibly unfolded into light through the power of similitude and dissimilitude, and producing the one and whole form of that fabrication in all beings through divided energies, and the separations of essence. Through these things, therefore, we have reminded the reader, that the first and most total of the partible divine genera, and which is united to the intellectual orders, is allotted the assimilative peculiarity, and being defined according to this, conjoins all things to the demiurgic monad; and [we have also shown] how it proceeds from the intelligible paradigm to all mundane natures, and is the primary origin of their generation.

---

† For αυτο, I read αυτῳ.

CHAPTER IV

Again, it follows in addition to what has been said, that we should separate all the assimilative powers, properly arrange them, and survey them proceeding about the one essence of the Gods. Plato, therefore, asserts that the first and most ruling of these powers, are those that unfold the intellectual production of the father, and expand it to all the divided orders of beings. But that the second, are those which are connective of wholes, and which preserve one series and indissoluble connexion of the divine progressions. And that the third, are those which are the primary leaders of perfection to all secondary natures, and produce through similitude self-perfect conversions to principles. But next to these he arranges those powers that extend all the proceeding genera of the Gods to impartible monads, and which pre-exist as the collectors of partible natures. Farther still, he likewise asserts that other assimilative powers give subsistence to the divided genera, and are definitely the suppliers of existence and essence to first and last natures. And besides all these, that other powers are the causes of undefiled distribution, and of perpetually stable perfection.

Moreover, together with these, I should arrange the authors of prolific production, and those that pour upon and distribute to all secondary natures the partible rivers of life. And further still, after these, I should arrange the powers that elevate secondary beings, cut off every thing material, confused, and inordinate, and are the suppliers of all goods. For there is no one of all the beautiful things in the world that does not proceed from this[†] order of Gods, which fills its participants with divine goods. Or whence indeed is the world always established in its proper principles, whence does its circulation remain immutable, and whence is the universe connected by indissoluble bonds? For the ends of its periods become the principles of the subsequent revolutions. But the circle of generation imitates the invariable supply of the celestial orbs, and all things are converted to more divine natures. Matter, indeed, is assimilated to beings, through the last representations of the production of form. But that which is moved in a confused and disordered manner, is circularly led to order and bound by demiurgic reasons, being assimilated to natures which always subsist with invariable sameness and permanency. Things, however, which are borne along in a diversified generation, and multiform mutations, are assimilated to the celestial orbs, and being moved in an all-various manner, follow the revolutions

---

[†] Instead of εκ της διακοσμησεως, it is necessary to read εκ ταυτης διακοσμησεως.

of the heavenly bodies. But the convolutions of the heavens, represent as in images the psychical periods; and the circulations of the spheres inscribe as it were the intellections of the celestial souls. Time itself, likewise, which proceeds according to number, and forms a circular dance, is in a certain respect† assimilated to stable intellections, and to [eternity] the measure of all intelligibles. For the whole of this time was generated an image of eternity abiding in one, since it is evolved after the same manner according to number. All things, therefore, are allotted a progression into existence, and the distribution of perfection according to measure, from the assimilative leaders, and connect the essence of themselves through similitude.

Moreover, this order of Gods in a particular manner, presides over the sympathy of things in the world, and their communion with each other. For all things concur with each other through similitude, and communicate the powers which they possess. And first natures, indeed, impart by illumination the gift of themselves to secondary natures, in unenvying abundance. But effects are established in their causes. An indissoluble connexion, likewise, and communion of wholes, and a colligation of agents and patients, are surveyed in the world. For in effects their generative causes subsist through similitude. And in causes, the progeny that proceed from them are contained according to comprehension. All things, likewise, are in each other, and similitude is the collector of all things. On this account, also, celestial, impart to sublunary natures, an exuberant and unenvying communication of their own effluxions; but sublunary, being in a certain respect assimilated to celestial natures, participate of an appropriate perfection. A chain likewise extends from on high, as far as to the last of things, secondary, always expressing the powers of the natures prior to them, progression indeed diminishing the similitude, but all things at the same time, and even such as most obscurely participate of existence, bearing a similitude to the first causes, and being co-passive with each other, and with their original causes. For there is naturally a twofold similitude in things which have proceeded from their causes. For they are assimilated to each other, according to their progression from *The One*, and their conversion again to it, and they are also assimilated to their ruling and first-effective causes. And through the former similitude, indeed, the elements conspire, are connascent, and are mingled with each other. But through the latter, they hasten to their proper principles, and are

---

† For οπως, it is necessary to read πως, and in consequence of this, the sentence should not be, as it is in the original, interrogatory.

conjoined with their paradigms. On this account, all things which participate of the solar effluxion, are suspended from the circulation of the sun; I mean, not only the genera that are more excellent than us, but likewise the number of souls, animals, plants, and stones. But all things adhere to the Mercurial circulation, which receive the peculiarity of this God. And the like takes place in the other [mundane] Gods. For all of them are leaders and rulers in the universe. And many orders indeed of angels dance round them; many numbers of demons; many herds of heroes; the copious multitude of partial souls; the multiform genera of mortal animals; and the various powers of plants. And all things indeed aspire after their leaders, and in all things there is an impression of their proper monad; but in some this impression is more clear, and in others more obscure; since similitude also subsists in a greater degree, in the first progeny, but is obscured in the middle, and last progeny, according to the ratio of progression. Images, therefore, and paradigms, are allotted their hypostasis on account of collective similitude. And every thing on account of similitude is familiar to itself, and to co-ordinate natures. But there is an unshaken friendship between the co-ordinate natures in the world through the presence of similitude; since contraries, also, and things which are most distant from each other, are irreprehensibly bound through it, and connected so as to produce the perfection of the universe.

In short, therefore, we may say, that the assimilative leaders of wholes, produce and generate all things from themselves. For progressions are through similitude; and every thing which is constituted, is wont to be assimilated to its generative cause. The assimilative rulers also convert all things to their principles; for every conversion is through similitude. They likewise bind co-ordinate natures to each other. For the communion of the one cause [of all] produces similitude indeed in its participants, but from this, it inserts in them an indissoluble connexion. They also cause all things to sympathize, be friendly, and familiar with each other; exhibiting indeed, through participation, more elevated in more abject natures; but subordinate in more perfect essences, through causal comprehension. They likewise extend series and periods from on high, as far as to the last of things. And they produce monads indeed, into diminution, through appropriate numbers; but collect multitudes into union, through communion according to essence. They also adapt wholes to parts; but comprehend parts in wholes. And things imperfect, indeed, they perfect, through contact with ends; but they guard immutably perfect natures, through a similar cause. They likewise lead into definite order, by similar forms and reasons, the sea of dissimilitude; but they terminate the very-mutable generation of sublunary natures, by stable paradigms. Thus much, therefore, we have to say in common concerning the order of divine natures, which we assert to be proximate indeed to the intellectual Gods, but to be the leader, and cause of the assimilation of all secondary natures to their proper principles.

CHAPTER V

In the next place, I wish prior to the theory of Parmenides to teach, what the Gods are, possessing this peculiarity, of whom Plato makes mention in other dialogues. For perhaps thus the doctrine of Parmenides will become more credible, and more manifest to reason. The ruling Gods, therefore, are divided in a threefold manner; and some of them indeed are united to the intellectual kings, and extend the whole series under themselves to a union with those kings; but others give completion to the middle genera, and distribute the all-perfect progression of these Gods; and others close the end of this order, and unfold the powers of these divinities to secondary natures. This being the case, those Gods that are arranged in the summits, do not immediately participate of the similitude of the assimilative Gods; but some of them are in a certain respect established above it, and are essentially connected with the intellectual Gods; but others proceed from it, and are mingled with the secondary genera. Hence, those only who give completion to the middle breadth, genuinely define in themselves the hyparxis of this order. We, therefore, likewise beginning from these, shall embrace by a reasoning process the whole theory of Plato. For we shall find in these, the perfect measures of the ruling order, perfectly delivered to us by him.

Again, therefore, let us refer the whole progression of these middle orders to a triad, it being allotted a division of this kind supernally, from the three intellectual fathers. Hence, indeed, this whole order of Gods, is suspended from the demiurgic monad. But the demiurgic intellect produces indeed some of them from itself and the intellectual father; but others from itself,[†] and the whole vivification; and others from appropriate rivers. Hence, also, of the Gods that thus derive their subsistence, some are allotted a paternal dignity, and are ruling fathers; but others are allotted a generative; and others an elevating and

---

[†] From the version of Portus, it appears necessary after the words τους μεν, αφ' εαυτου τε, to supply the words του νοερου πατρος, τους δε αφ' εαυτου τε κ.τ.λ.

convertive dignity. But since a certain order of the unpolluted Gods is conjoined with each of the intellectual kings, it is indeed necessary that in the ruling Gods also, a second progression from them should shine forth to the view, and that on this account the guardian order should be connascent with the above-mentioned triple orders, being appropriately consubsistent with each of them; *viz.* paternally indeed in the first; but vivifically in the middle; and intellectually and convertively in the third order. And thus it is necessary that this whole order of Gods should be divided by paternal powers, and prolific progressions, by powers that lead upward all secondary natures, and by those that are of an undefiled guardian characteristic. For being allotted their hypostasis from the intellectual Gods, some indeed ascend totally into parts, but others partibly pour on wholes, the exuberant powers of themselves. They likewise distribute the providence of the demiurgus and father, some indeed arranging and adorning the universe with the first, middle, and last forms of production; others educing the rivers of life, and pouring them on all things; others elevating the natures that have proceeded, and recalling them to the father; and others presiding over purity, and being the guardians of secondary natures.

CHAPTER VI

Again, therefore, receiving the beginning of the theory of Plato from the paternal cause, we assert as follows: The demiurgus and father of this universe, being allotted this order in the intellectual kings, as was before demonstrated, as he produced wholes totally, and referred all things to the one form of the world, and the one perfection of the universe, thus also he arranged and adorned the parts of the world, and gave completion to the whole, contriving that all immortal and mortal natures should be generated for the sake of the universe. And this is what Plato introduces him saying in the *Timæus* to the junior Gods; 'That mortal natures therefore may exist, and that this universe may be truly all, convert yourselves according to nature to the fabrication of animals.' Since, however, after the monad, it is every where necessary that a multitude should be generated proximate to the monad, and that prior to an all-perfect division, united number should subsist (for that which has proceeded to all things is not allied to that which abides, nor is it possible that what is all-variously divided, should be connascent with that which is impartible) - this being the case, the demiurgus of wholes, produces indeed from himself, and his father a number proximate to the monad of the fathers. But the three [fathers] deriving their subsistence from one father, and first receiving the power and dominion of fabrication, produce other second and third fabricators from themselves, till through a diminution proceeding according to [appropriate] measures, they evolve the whole demiurgic number, the cause of which indeed, the demiurgic monad comprehends in itself.

The orderly progression, however, of multitude becomes at length apparent. And thus the three ruling fathers of wholes, separate their productions, by first, middle, and last boundaries of fabrication, and are all of them total, but they are fabricators and fathers of parts totally; through being in continuity indeed with the monad, not changing the form of production; but on account of diminished progression, not possessing an energy impartibly extended to all things. And the one demiurgus indeed, being arranged prior to the triad, comprehends in himself uniformly the productions of all [the demiurgi]. But these three fathers multiply the unical dominion and power of the first demiurgus, divide his impartible production, and lead forth into secondary natures the stable energy of the father. And the exempt monad indeed comprehends in itself the all-perfect measure of the triad, according to supreme union; but the triad unfolds into light from itself the undivided power of the monad.

Plato, therefore, celebrates indeed, in other dialogues, these three fabricators and fathers, but particularly in the *Gorgias*, adducing as a witness of the theory concerning them, divinely-inspired poetry, he refers the whole progression of them to Saturn the father of the intellectual Gods, and from thence gives to them their first production into light. He exempts, however, the demiurgic intellect from the triadic division of them, co-arranges it with the father, and says, that they have an intellectual dominion secondary to him. He likewise calls them the sons of Saturn, but indicates that they are allotted their progression from Jupiter. For there is a twofold Jupiter both according to Plato, and all the theology, as I may say, of the Greeks; the one indeed convolving the end of the intellectual triad to the beginning; but the other being allotted the summit of the ruling triad. And the one being the demiurgus of wholes totally; but the other being allotted the first parts of divided fabrication. And the one indeed being arranged prior to the three fathers; but the other being the first of the three, and proximate to the remaining fathers. Whence, also, I think that many who discuss these particulars are ignorant that Jupiter the demiurgus of the universe, is not the first of the three fathers, and that Saturn the leader and ruler of the intellectual kings, is not the same with the demiurgic intellect. For of those who immediately suspend the triad of the ruling fathers from the paternal kingdom of Saturn, some indeed refer the whole fabrication of things to Saturn himself; but others ascribe to the summit of the triad the generation of wholes. Is not, however, each of these impossible? For the one abiding in himself, and converting to himself every thing which has proceeded, is exempt from demiurgic production; but the other being divided oppositely to the total† fathers, will not be the impartible fabricator of wholes. For it is necessary that the whole and all-perfect demiurgus of the world, should neither be connumerated with the many‡ demiurgi, nor be the same with the cause which is stable, and perfectly established in itself. For he has a subsistence contrary to the cause which recalls that which has proceeded, and again exhibits it unemanent from itself. To be present likewise to all things by no means accords with that nature which energizes separately, and takes away its generative power. How, therefore, can he who converts his own children to himself, and shuts his own progeny in himself, possess the same power with the demiurgus who unfolds all things into light, and produces them into multitude? And how can he who is allotted the universe in conjunction with the remaining demiurgi, be uniformly the cause of the universe?

For, if you are willing, consider each of these three demiurgi, and survey what will happen from this assertion. For we say that the first of them is the cause of essence, and of existence to the fabrications in the world; but that the second is the source of the motion, life, and generation of sensibles; and that the third is the cause of the divided production of form, of partible circumscription, and of the circular conversion of wholes to their one principle. We likewise definitely assert these things, admitting that the fabrication of each of the three extends to the whole world. But surveying the peculiar mode of fabrication in each, we say that the first is the effector of essence, the second of life, and the third of intellect. And that the first is the cause of hyparxis, the second of motion, and the third of conversion. Hence, the whole world, so far as it participates of being, is produced from the first father; but so far as it subsists through motion, and is generation, it receives its progression from the second father; and so far as it is perfectly divided, and after all-various division, is converted to its proper principle, it is produced from the third father.

---

† For της ολης, it is necessary to read τοις ολοις.

‡ For τοις ολοις, it is necessary to read τοις πολλοις.

CHAPTER VII

These things, therefore, being thus determined, we may see how in the *Timæus*, the demiurgus and father of this universe, at one and the same time impartibly constitutes the world, gives to it essence, and supplies it with existence, fashioning bodies, generating souls in the middle of an impartible and partible essence, and constituting intellects ingenerably [*i.e.* without generation] and indivisibly, from the first genera. And farther still, besides these things, he distributes different motions to souls and bodies, divides each of them all-variously, according to harmonic reasons, binds them by analogies, and converts them to himself, and his own will. How, therefore, can we any longer rank such a demiurgus as this in the same order with one of these three fathers. For those things which they are said to give to the universe divisibly, he constitutes impartibly from himself. Nor does he produce some things precedaneously, and others according to accident, but by his very being he generates essence, supplies motions, and extends the divisions of mundane forms, and after the progression of other things, converts all things to himself, abiding in his own accustomed manner.

In the second place, therefore, we say that the three demiurgi differ from each other, because the first paternally comprehends the rest, and is the father of this whole triad. But the second is the power of the triad, and participates of the extremes according to the peculiarity of powers. And the third is the intellect of the triad, and contains the paternal, and intellectual power [by participation]. And in short, the first is the father of both; but the second is the power of both; and the third is the intellect of both. How, therefore, can the demiurgus of wholes be the same with one of the above mentioned fathers? For he, as Timæus says, is the father of all the world, and is allotted in himself a paternal power and divine intellect, converting all things to the watchtower of himself. Again, therefore, we find that the partible peculiarities of the three demiurgi, pre-exist in him impartibly and uniformly. And as the demiurgic triad participates of union with him, on account of the uncircumscribed transcendency of the monad, thus also the monad antecedently and occultly comprehends in itself the triad, according to the power of cause. Nor is it proper to confound these with each other, but it is requisite to exempt the monad from the triad, and to suspend the triad from the monad. And neither ought we to make the three fathers, the rulers of total fabrication, nor to rank the first of them in the same order with the one demiurgus. For a co-ordinated entirely differs from an exempt cause. And that which produces all things according to comprehension perfectly differs from that which is similarly present to all things, and is equally distant from all things. Besides this also, multitude is every where suspended from its proper monad. And as *The One* precedes the total orders of things, so likewise each order of the Gods has its progression from a monad; since also each God is allotted a union which antecedes the multitude he contains. But if the whole genus of the Gods, and each God proceed after the same manner, it is also necessary that each of the divided orders should have the same mode of subsistence.

In the third place we say that both Plato and the ancient theology of the Greeks assert, that these three demiurgi divide the uniform kingdom of their father Saturn. And that one of these three every where arranges and adorns the first of wholes, another the middles, and another the extremities of wholes; and that each is allotted this order, not in fabrication only, but also in the providence of partial souls. For of these, some indeed are arranged and perfected under the first, prior to generation; but others, that give completion to generation, are arranged under the second; and others, that require purification after generation, are perfected under the third. Moreover, the first demiurgus, as it is written in the *Timæus*, produces the whole world. For he constitutes the circulation of the *same*, and arranges and adorns the circulation of the *different*, and all sublunary natures as far as to the earth, which he fabricated to be the guardian of night and day, being immovably fixed about the axis which is extended through the poles of the universe. He also fills the whole parts of the world with their proper numbers, and gives generation to all of them, both to those that revolve manifestly, and to those that become manifest when they please. Again, he defines the whole period to partial souls, the measures of their descent into generation, the vicissitudes of the present life, and their restitutions to their kindred star,[†] and he is also said to unfold to them all the laws of Fate, and to point out to them the nature of the universe. Hence, he is not one[‡] of these three fathers, nor is he co-arranged with them, but is perfectly exempt from the triad. According likewise to the proper prerogative of his empire, he is expanded separately above each, and in common above all of them. And the operations indeed, of these fathers, are divided about him, and are distinguished by more partial boundaries. But his fabrication is uncircumscribed, is one whole, and is impartible.

[†] The word αστρον is omitted in the original.

[‡] εν is omitted in the original.

CHAPTER VIII

Let it therefore, from these things be manifest, that the demiurgic monad, is exempt from the ruling fathers, and that according to one undivided cause he generates beings eternally. But if Jupiter is according to Plato, the one and whole fabricator of the only-begotten world, as we have before demonstrated, and we grant these things without being deceived, and if, as it is now said, and Socrates in the *Gorgias* teaches us, the first of the demiurgi that divide the kingdom of Saturn, is in a similar manner called Jupiter, there will be according to this theory a twofold Jupiter, the one being an intellectual God prior to the three fathers; but the other being of a ruling, assimilative, and principal nature, and arranged at the summit of the three. For Jupiter, Neptune, and Pluto, divide, says Plato, the kingdom of their father, three leaders of wholes subsisting from one great king as it were, and producing the one fountain of the demiurgic series, into one all-perfect principal triad, which Plato also indicating, denominates the providence divided in the three a kingdom, attributing the first-effective, and the uniform to the Gods prior to these. If these however, are not the only orders of Jupiter, but there is also another Jovian multitude, how this proceeds will be evident in what follows. For all these three fathers participate of the same appellation, and are after the same manner celebrated by poets inspired by Phoebus; but one is called simply Jupiter, another marine Jupiter, and another subterranean Jupiter. The leader however of the three, possesses primarily the paternal dignity in the triad, and the appellation of the great Jupiter. For on account of the supreme union which he is allotted with the fontal demiurgus, who is beyond the three, he also participates of the same name as the total Jupiter, without any distinction. And on this account, I think, Socrates in the *Cratylus*, unfolding to us the arcane and mystic discipline concerning the Gods, from names, and at one time co-arranging Jupiter with Saturn, and at another with the remaining demiurgi, does not think it worth while to speak twice about the same things, but in the intellectual conceptions about the all-perfect demiurgus, he also thinks fit to deliver the arcane discipline concerning the first of the three demiurgi, through the truth of names. For in a certain respect, it was not possible for him to do otherwise who shows that the theory in things accords with names; since also, the father of this triad, is inseparably united to the whole demiurgus. But of these things enough.

If you are willing however, we will add the following observations to what has been said. For perhaps some one may apprehend that the fable in the *Gorgias*, gives to the three sons of Saturn, a progression from Saturn proximately, but not, as we have said, through the demiurgic monad as a medium. For again, the three are said to divide the kingdom of Saturn, but not of the whole demiurgus and father. That we may not however, ignorantly wander beyond measure from the conception of Plato, and the truth of things, in consequence of following fabulous fictions, we must affirm from the beginning, that both the whole demiurgus, and this triad of the ruling fathers, proceed from the father of the intellectual Gods. But the whole demiurgus proceeding from a whole, impartibly participates of his father. For he abides in the allness of his power, and imitates, if it be lawful so to speak, his uniform and unmultiplied nature, by being monadic and whole, and the father of things first, middle and last. But the three demiurgi, in a divided manner participate of, and proceed from their generating cause, being divided indeed from each other, but dividing his unical providence. And Saturn indeed, is a God one and numerous, establishing multitude in himself, and occultly comprehending it in appropriate boundaries. But Jupiter expresses the paternal monad, and produces the unical nature of it into the providence of wholes. And the three sons of Saturn unfold into light the multitude which is there, in the all-perfect boundary of the triad. Hence also they are said to divide the kingdom of their father,[†] which Jupiter possessed indivisibly. Hence, if it be requisite to speak boldly, he indeed is a proceeding father, hastening to arrange and adorn, and being parturient in order to the generation of wholes. But they distribute his providence. This however, is the same thing as to say they distribute the providence of Jupiter. For the progression to them was from each of these divinities, from Saturn indeed, according to the *from which* ($\alpha\phi$' ov), but from Jupiter according to the *by which* ($v\phi$' ov.)[‡] For Jupiter indeed, unfolds them into light; but they proceed from the Saturnian adyta.

If again, you are willing [to consider the affair] according to the *Parmenides* of Plato, since in the Saturnian order there are both wholeness and parts, if you assume the subsistence there of *that which is in another*, according to whole, but of *that which is in itself*, according to parts, Jupiter indeed, who is prior to the three, proceeds from his father according to whole; but the three demiurgi, according to parts. Hence, Jupiter reigns, possessing in himself, as Socrates says in the

---

[†] For $\pi\alpha\nu\tau o\varsigma$ it is necessary to read $\pi\alpha\tau\rho o\varsigma$.

[‡] $\alpha\phi$' ov signifies an occult, but $v\phi$' ov, a manifest progression.

Philebus, a royal intellect. But they reign in a divided manner, and are allotted the universe according to parts. Hence therefore, the Elean guest in the *Politicus*, celebrates these two intellectual kings, one indeed, being the cause of the unapparent life to wholes, and of the other circulation, but the other being the source of the manifest order of things, and of the present period; and he attributes to Jupiter the cause of both these periods. But at one time indeed, he ascribes this cause to Jupiter, as leading all things in the universe to the kingdom of Saturn; but at another, as binding to himself the providence of secondary natures. For he is united to his father by intellectual bonds, of which Socrates makes mention in the *Cratylus*. He is likewise a whole extended to a whole, and as it were adapts himself by his own light to the light of his father, and possesses a second dominion. Hence also, he is said to define the providence of his father. The Athenian guest however [in the *Laws*,] extending us to the one demiurgic kingdom, to the law, and the total justice which are there asserts, "that God, as it is said, possesses the beginning, middle, and end of all beings, and bounds all things by a circular progression according to nature, in a direct path." For because we do not think it right to consider Plato here as speaking of the first God, or of any other of the intellectual or intelligible fathers, but of the whole demiurgus, it is sufficient for those who are moderately able to understand things of this kind, that he is said to bound all things in a direct path, and to proceed circularly according to nature. It is also sufficient, that Justice is said to be the attendant of this God, being the avenger of those who transgress the divine law. For the first God, and all the Gods who are established above the perfective order, are exempt from this rectilinear, and also from the circular progression, as Parmenides teaches us. They likewise transcend all motion. But the first that proceeds after motion, is the whole and all-perfect demiurgus. To this divinity therefore, it pertains to bound wholes in a direct path, to proceed circularly, and to be followed by Justice. For we say indeed, that the thing which follows, follows that which is moved.

Moreover, the Gods who are secondary to the demiurgus, have not a unical dominion over wholes as he has, nor do they antecedently assume the beginnings, middles and ends of all beings. But some of them indeed, preside over partial natures totally, as these three fathers; but others preside over wholes partibly, as those who pour upon all things the rivers of life, in a divided manner; and others preside over parts partibly, as the last of the demiurgi, and who are conversant with the world. The one and impartible demiurgus of wholes therefore, alone comprehends in himself, the beginning, middle, and end of all beings, and equally rules over all secondary natures according to one cause. But Justice follows him, bounding the desert of the whole of things, and circumscribing each thing in its proper limits. And these things the Athenian guest manifests in the above-mentioned words; but Orpheus clearly refers them to the whole demiurgus. For he says that total Justice follows him, now reigning over, and beginning to arrange and adorn the universe.

> Justice th' abundant punisher of crimes,
> Aid and defence of all things, follows Jove.

Moreover, that Jupiter comprehends the beginnings, middles and ends of wholes, the theologist says, in addition to these things,

> Jove's the beginning, and the middle's Jove,
> And all things flow from Jove's prolific mind.

And it appears to me that Plato looking to all the Grecian theology, and particularly to the Orphic-mystic discipline says, that God, according to the ancient assertion, possesses the beginning, middle, and end of all things, bounding the whole of things in a direct path, and proceeding circularly according to nature, and that he has Justice for his attendant, through which every thing that departs from the providential empire of Jupiter is converted to it, and obtains an appropriate end. Through these things therefore, we have reminded the reader, that the Athenian guest also looking to the whole demiurgus, proclaims things of this kind to his pupils. If however, these things are rightly determined, it is indeed entirely necessary to exempt the one demiurgus, according to essence, from these three [demiurgi]. For if one of them indeed, comprehends the beginnings of every thing in the world, but another the middles, and another, every where convolves the ends, is it not necessary that he who uniformly rules over the universe, should be established above divided causes? But, the Athenian guest gives to him a power generative of this triad [of demiurgi]. For if he comprehends the beginnings, middles, and ends of the whole of things, according to the primary cause indeed, he generates the demiurgus, who arranges and adorns first natures; but according to middle causes, the demiurgus who gives completion to the middle boundaries of fabrication; and according to the end, the demiurgus who adapts an appropriate production to the last of things.

CHAPTER IX

The Athenian guest therefore, does all but clearly say, that the distribution to the three sons of Saturn, the measures of providence, and in short, progression, are suspended† from the great Jupiter, and that it is he who supernally defines their allotments, and uniformly comprehends all of them in himself. Moreover, with respect to the assertions, that he bounds all things in a direct path, and that he proceeds circularly according to nature, the former of these, manifests the progression of wholes from him; for the direct is a symbol of progression; but the latter manifests the conversion of wholes to him. For he being intellectually converted in, and to himself, convolves all things to the watch-tower of himself. But if the straight and the circular first subsist in the perfective Gods, the demiurgus of wholes is filled indeed from thence, but fills the natures posterior to himself with the powers that proceed from him. And as according to the triple cause of wholes, he constitutes the triad of demiurgi in conjunction with his father, thus also according to these twofold powers, he generates twofold [orders of] Gods; one indeed, which adorns a sensible nature, according to the straight which is in him; but the other which elevates all things to him, according to the circular. Moreover, because he proceeds indeed from the whole fabrication, (i.e. from Rhea) but participates of the perfective triad, he connects this straight and circular with motion. For to bound according to the straight, and to proceed circularly, designate motion; the former indeed, being significant of motion proceeding to all things, and adorning all things with boundaries, forms and reasons; but the latter, of motion convolving to itself, and calling upward all things to itself.

Again, therefore, Plato placing in the one demiurgus the cause of the triad, exempts him, who abides as it were in himself, from production according to parts; but attributes to the triad a division according to the demiurgus. For Timæus also, by placing in him a paternal cause, a generative power, and a royal intellect, theologizes the same things about him as the Athenian guest. The paternal, indeed, is every where principal; but power belongs to the middle; and intellect closes the end of the triad. For power, according to the Oracle, is with them; [i.e. with father and intellect], but intellect is from him, [i.e. from the father]. Hence, of the natures which have proceeded, one is the father of the whole triad, but another the intellect of it. And one indeed is allotted

---

† For εξηρηται, it is necessary to read εξηρτηται.

the beginning of total fabrication; but another, gives completion to the middle of the generation of wholes; and another, bounds the end of it. Nor must we here omit to observe the accuracy of Plato, but survey[†] how the Athenian guest magnificently celebrates the extremities of the three demiurgi, by more singular names, calling one the *beginning*, and the other the *end*, but that which is between the extremes even in causes, he manifests through multitude. For he denominates it *middles*; since power also, as being co-ordinate with the infinite, or rather being a certain infinity, is the cause of multitude and division to wholes. Hence also, of the three demiurgi, one indeed, is the cause to mundane natures of a stable[‡] collocation; but another, of generation proceeding to all things; and another, of the circulation of things to the principle of their progression.

Let us, however, return whence we digressed, to the discussion concerning the first demiurgus, in which it was said, that Jupiter, Neptune, and Pluto divide the kingdom of their father. For prior to these, the demiurgus received the kingdom of his father in an undivided and uniform manner. For both the demiurgic monad and the triad, were thence allotted their progression from the beginning, and their dominion over secondary natures; but the former impartibly, and the latter partibly; and the former monadically, but the latter triadically. That you may not, therefore, think that these three proceed after the same manner from the father, as the one king who is prior to the three, Socrates, [in the *Gorgias*] in the form of a fable, says that they divide the kingdom of the father, and on this account require secondary laws, and a subordinate order, and which is adapted to parts. For the law under Saturn, and the law of Jupiter who recently possesses the kingdom [of his father] appear to be by no means adapted to the providence of those powers who produce a partial and various form of life. And do you not see how Socrates gives to total Jupiter and to Saturn an exempt transcendency, and connects one law with both kingdoms; but to the three demiurgi that divide the kingdom, he definitely assigns as it were another polity, and more various laws commensurate to the subjects of their providential care? For he says that Pluto, and the curators were present enquiring of Jupiter respecting the second legislation; but that he placed over partible lives, other judges, and laws adapted to these lives. Again, therefore, Jupiter, who definitely assigns things of this kind, and

---

[†] For επιστησωμεν, I read επισκεψωμεν.

[‡] For γονιμου, it is necessary to read μονιμου.

who generates the three judges, is not the same with the Jupiter who is prior to the three [demiurgi]. For the latter was together with his father according to a prior law, and the simplicity of a divine life; but the former together with Pluto, leads into order and bound the variety of partial natures, and is the leader of secondary laws.

The divine law, therefore, is with the intellectual kings, Saturn and Jupiter; and also Justice the avenger of those who transgress the divine law, as the Athenian guest says. But other more various laws are with the three sons of Saturn, and also judges co-ordinate to such like laws, as it is written in the *Gorgias*. And there indeed, [*i.e.* with the intellectual kings], all things are impartibly, and unitedly; but here,[*i.e.* with the three sons of Saturn], all things subsist in a divided and partible manner. And the things which are there being primary, the law indeed is more Saturnian. But Justice follows the great Jupiter. And the laws indeed pertaining to secondary natures, confer perfection under the first of the sons of Saturn. But the judges give completion to the empire of the third of these sons. And Pluto participates from the second Jupiter of the separation of the laws; in the same manner as the total Jupiter receives from Saturn the one law which is to be the co-administrator with him in the total fabrication of things. In short, the Jupiter who is co-arranged with Neptune and Pluto, is the summit of the ruling triad; but the Jupiter who is co-arranged with Saturn and the mistress Rhea, is the third of the intellectual triad.† Hence also, Socrates, in the Cratylus, at one time ascends from Jupiter to Saturn, and conjoins the two kingdoms; but at another time he proceeds from Jupiter to Neptune and Pluto, and unfolds this one ruling triad; just as in the *Gorgias*, he weaves together the Saturnian and Jovian order, when he says that there is one and the same law in both. He co-arranges therefore, the second and more partial Jupiter with Pluto, according to the apparent correction of the prior law, and the distribution of the second laws. And thus much may suffice concerning these particulars.

---

† For νεαρας, it is necessary to read νοερας.

CHAPTER X[†]

It now remains that we should begin to speak about these three fathers, following the mystic narrations of Plato, since all of them are suspended from the demiurgic monad, and present themselves to our view as the second [in rank] after it. These three leaders, therefore, of wholes, and rulers, are emitted indeed from the intellectual fathers, and are divided according to them; but they are unfolded into light in all the partible orders of the Gods. For among the rulers they are allotted the first order, and are analogous to the intelligible and intellectual fathers, in the whole assimilative series, and having made a second progression in the liberated Gods, they rule over the universe. Together also with the mundane Gods, they give completion to the apparent order of things, being allotted in one way an essence in the heavens, but in another way distributing the total parts in the sublunary region, but every where energizing paternally and demiurgically, expanding the one fabrication, and adapting it to parts.

With respect, however, to the allotment and distribution of them, in the first place, if you please, it is according to the whole universe, the first of them producing essences, the second lives and generations, and the third administering formal divisions. And the first indeed establishing in the one demiurgus all things that thence proceed; but the second calling all things into progression; and the third converting all things to itself. In the second place, the allotment and division of them are according to the parts of the universe. For the first of them adorns the inerratic sphere, and the circulation of it; but the second governs the planetary region, and perfects the multiform, efficacious, and prolific motions in it; and the last administers the sublunary region, and

---

[†] The following observations were written in the margin of the manuscript copy of this work of Proclus, by some scholiast or commentator: "For end and that which is perfected, and the possession of beginning, middle and end, first subsist in the intelligible and at the same time intellectual Gods. And on this account figure, also, there presents itself to the view. This triad, therefore, in the whole assimilative series is analogous to intelligibles and intellectuals, as having from them [for $απ'$ $αυτης$, it is necessary to read $απ'$ $αυτων$] the beginning, middles, and end. For the demiurgus produced this triad according to the similitude of this perfective triad, and connected the straight and the circular motion. For to bound in a direct path, and to proceed circularly, are definitive of motion, as was said by Proclus in the Chapter prior to this. And as this triad has these properties from intelligibles and intellectuals, thus also the whole series of assimilative Gods possess them from this triad. Hence this triad of partial demiurgi, is analogous to the intelligible and intellectual fathers, *i.e.* to the perfective power."

intellectually perfects the terrestrial world. Again, in the third place, we may survey in that which is generated, these three demiurgic progressions; since Timæus also here makes mention of the offspring of Saturn. Jupiter, therefore, administers the summit of generated natures, and governs the spheres of fire and air. But Neptune all-variously moves the middle and very-mutable elements, and is the inspective guardian of every moist essence, which is beheld in air and water. And Pluto providentially attends to the earth, and to every thing in the earth. Hence also he is called terrestrial Jupiter.

In the fourth place, therefore, in the whole of generation, Jupiter indeed is allotted the summits, and the parts which are raised above others, in which also are the allotments of happy souls, as Socrates says in the *Phædrus*, because they then live under Jupiter, beyond generation. But Neptune is allotted cavities, and cavernous places, with which generation, motion, and the incursion of concussions are conversant. Hence, they call this God, the earth-shaker. And Pluto is allotted the places under the earth, various streams, Tartarus itself, and in short, the places in which souls are judged and punished. Whence also, of souls themselves, they say that such of them as have not yet proceeded into generation, but abide in the intelligible, are Jovian; but that such as are conversant with generation, are arranged under Neptune; and that such as are purified and punished after generation, and wander under the earth, according to a journey of a thousand years, or which are again converted and led back to their principle, are perfected under Pluto.

In the fifth place, therefore, we must say that the allotments of these divinities, are divided according to the centres of the universe. And Jupiter, indeed, has the eastern centre, as being allotted an order analogous to fire; but Neptune, the middle centre, which pertains to vivification, and according to which especially generation enjoys celestial natures; and Pluto the western centre, since we say that the west is coordinate to earth, as being nocturnal, and the cause of the unapparent. For shadow is from earth, and earth is the privation of light from west to east. In short, according to every division of the world, we admit that the first and most leading parts are Jovian; but we say that the middle parts pertain to the kingdom of Neptune; and we consider the last parts as belonging to the empire of Pluto.

CHAPTER XI

Through these things, therefore, the triad of the ruling fathers has been celebrated by us. Let us, however, survey another order in this progression, prolific, and vivific, and which is delivered by Plato in a divinely-inspired manner. For the proximate decrements and generations from all the intellectual fathers, are unfolded into light in the assimilative Gods. For here the partible progressions exist of things which there subsist uniformly, since it is lawful for progeny which every where are allotted an order inferior to their causes, to give multitude to the monads, and to multiply the stable hypostases of them, and to render the energies of the simplicity, which is in first natures, more composite. As, therefore, from the paternal monad [Saturn] a triad subsists of ruling demiurgi, thus also from the vivific fountain [Rhea] which is allotted the middle centre in the intellectual Gods, the vivific order of the assimilative Gods is emitted. And here also there is a triad connectedly contained by one monad; since the paternal triad also subsists according to one perfect intellect, and was, as we have said, monadic. After the same manner, therefore, the triad which is the supplier of life is monadic, being indeed full of prolific power, and full of undefiled perfection. It likewise participates of the whole vivification, and through the rivers of life, fills all secondary natures with generative goods, and produces the vivific light, into the unenvying and exuberant participation of subordinate essences. And it converts indeed all things to itself, but is present to all things, and imparts to them its own appropriate powers. It likewise pervades from on high, as far as to the last parts of the world, but every where preserves the union of itself unmingled with its participants. And it embosoms indeed the generative, perfect, and beneficent light of the demiurgic monad; but weaves together with the third father [Pluto] the order of life; and co-arranges the boundaries of wholes in a becoming manner.† In short, it extends itself from the middle to all the genera of rulers, both the first and the last. And together with them indeed, it perfects all secondary natures, and co-arranges that which is generative, with the demiurgus. In addition to these things also, it illuminates all things with an analogous power, and connects the undefiled with the convertive peculiarity. For stable power pertains indeed to the demiurgic genera, but undefiled purity to the elevating genera.

Plato, therefore, in the same manner as Orpheus, calls this triad by one name; but in a certain respect he also indicates the multitude of the powers it contains. For all the theology of the Greeks denominates the second vivification *Coric*, (*i.e. Virginal*) and conjoins it with the whole vivific fountain. Plato also says, that it has its hypostasis from this fountain, and energizes together with it. For effects are never divulsed

---

† For δε ὄντως, it is necessary to read δεόντως.

from the providence of their causes. But wanderings indeed, and investigations, [belong to the powers that energize providentially, just as†] participations according to periods pertain to the subjects of providential energy. The divine cause, however, of a partible life [*i.e.* Proserpine] conjoins herself from eternity, with the whole vivific fountain [*i.e.* with Ceres] which theologists call the mother of the ruling Goddess. And Plato every where conjoins Proserpine with Ceres. And he pre-establishes indeed, the latter as a generative cause; but he celebrates the former as being filled from the latter, and filling secondary natures. Since, however, the Coric order is twofold, one indeed shining forth above the world, where it is also co-arranged with Jupiter, and constitutes with him the one demiurgus of partible natures [*i.e.* Bacchus], but the other, and which is secondary, shining forth in the world, where also it is said to be ravished by Pluto, and to animate the extremities of the universe, which are under the administration of Pluto, - this being the case, Plato perfectly unfolds to us both these, at one time indeed conjoining Proserpine with Ceres, but at another with Pluto, and evincing that she is the wife of this God. For the rumour of theologists who delivered to us the most holy mysteries in Eleusis, says, that above indeed, Proserpine abides in the dwellings of her mother, which her mother had fabricated in inaccessible places, exempt from the universe, but that beneath she governs terrestrial concerns in conjunction with Pluto, rules over the recesses of the earth, extends life to the extremities of the universe, and imparts soul to things which are of themselves inanimate, and dead. Where also you may wonder that Proserpine associates with Jupiter indeed and Pluto, the former, as fables say violating, but the latter ravishing the Goddess, but is not connected with Neptune. For he alone of the sons of Saturn, is not conjoined with Proserpine. [The reason, however, of this is,] that Neptune possessing the middle centre in the triad, is allotted a vivific dignity and power, and is characterized according to this. From himself, therefore, he has the vivific cause, animates the whole of his proper allotment, and fills it with middle life from his own peculiarity. For Pluto indeed is the supplier of wisdom and intellect to souls according to Socrates in the Cratylus. But Jupiter is the cause of existence to beings, as the father of the triad. Proserpine, therefore, being co-arranged with the extremes, and prior to the world, with Jupiter indeed paternally, but in the world with Pluto, according to the beneficent will of the father, in the former

---

† It appears to me that after και αι ζητησεις in the original, there are wanting the words των προνοουντων, ωσπερ.

case she is said to be violated by Jupiter, but in the latter, to be ravished by Pluto, in order that the first and last of fabrications may participate of vivification. For as the whole fountain of life [Rhea] being conjoined with the whole, according to one impartible cause, illuminates all things with life, thus also Proserpine, weaving in conjunction with the leaders of the universe, things first, middle, and last, illuminates them with the vivification of herself.

Moreover, we may know from Plato, through these signs, the union of the whole triad, since denominating it *Core* (*i.e.* a virgin or Proserpine) he celebrates it with Ceres. But again, we must survey where it is that he indicates the division of the triad. For there are three monads in it, and one of them is arranged, as being the highest, according to hyparxis, but another is arranged according to the power which is definitive of life, and another according to vivific intellect. And theologists indeed are accustomed to call the first of these coric, (*i.e.* virginal) Diana, but the second Proserpine, and the third, Coric Minerva. I speak, however, of the authors of the Grecian theology, since among the Barbarians [*i.e.* the Chaldeans], the same things are manifested through other names. For they indeed call the first monad, Hecate, but the middle monad, Soul, and the third, Virtue. Since, therefore, these things are made known to us after this manner by the names of the Greeks, Plato indeed indicates the order of Coric Minerva, by denominating Minerva Mistress, celebrating her as Core, asserting that she is the cause of the whole of virtue, and calling her the lover of wisdom, and the lover of war, and also Ethonoe, as being intelligence in manners. For all these names sufficiently represent to us her intellectual and ruling nature, and that power of her which promptly supplies the whole of virtue. But in the same dialogue, he indicates the order of Proserpine, celebrating her as Pherephatta, and employing this name, which is likewise used by all other theologists. These things he manifests in the Cratylus, where he unfolds the truth concealed in the name of Pherephatta. And in the same dialogue he indicates the order of Diana, by calling her skilful in virtue. For it is evident that the whole triad being united to itself, the first [monad] of the triad,† unically comprehends the third, the third is converted to the first, and the middle has a power extending to both. There are, therefore, these three vivific monads, *viz.* Diana, Proserpine, and our mistress Minerva. And the first of these indeed is the summit of the whole triad, and which also converts to herself the third. But the second is a power

---

† For τριας here, it is necessary to read τριαδος.

vivific of wholes. And the third is a divine and undefiled intellect, comprehending in one, in a ruling manner, total virtues. Timæus, therefore, manifests this, calling the third monad (Minerva) philosophic, as being full of intellectual knowledge, and true wisdom; but philopolemic, as the cause of undefiled power, and the inspective guardian of the whole of fortitude. And again, the Athenian guest, calls her Core, as being a virgin, and as purifying from all conversion to externals.

If, however, you are willing, we will survey the triad of Core, from what is said in the Cratylus concerning Pherephatta. She is called, therefore, wisdom, and is said to come into contact with that which is generated and borne along: she also produces fear in those that hear her name, and excites astonishment in the multitude. With respect to the appellation of wisdom, therefore, it is evident that it is a sign [of the characteristic property] of Minerva, and the summit of virtue. For if in us, all the sciences are the first of the virtues, how is it possible that wisdom should not be rightly denominated, the first-effective cause of all the virtues? And if philosophy pertains to her, so far as she is wisdom, and immaterial intelligence, but not because she is indigent of wisdom, (for no one of the Gods, says Diotima, philosophizes), on this account, therefore, she is not indigent of wisdom; and the intellectual good of the ruling order entirely pertains to her. But to come into contact with that which is borne along, and with generation, will in a particular manner be adapted to soul. For it is soul that knows every thing which is generated, and continually communicates with it. She, likewise, in a certain respect comes entirely into contact with that which is borne along. Moreover, the incommensurability of Pherephatta with multitude, and the terror and astonishment which she excites, are indicative of the power in her which is exempt from all things, which is unapparent to the many and unknown. For the Barbarians also [*i.e.* the Chaldeans] call the Goddess who is the leader of this triad, dire and terrible. Hence Plato does not more clearly indicate these things to us about this mighty Goddess [than the Barbarians;] but he announces names adapted to the theology concerning her.

To the Core, therefore, that is beneath, and that associates with Pluto, all the above-mentioned particulars are inherent according to participation, and, as some one might say, according to similitude to the total Core; but they are inherent in the ruling Core, according to the first hypostasis. And in reality these three Goddesses are consubsistent. As, likewise, the whole vivific deity comprehends in herself the fountains of virtue and soul, which the demiurgus also imparts to the world, causing it to subsist perfectly, thus too, this deity [Core] possessing the primary cause of all the partible forms of life, possesses likewise the principle of souls, and of the virtues, and on this account, the ascent to partial souls [such as ours], is through similitude, and virtue is a similitude to the Gods. Hence also, the form of each of these, I mean of virtue and soul, pre-subsist in the assimilative Gods; since, likewise, the immortality of souls is inferred by Socrates, from their similitude to divinity. If, therefore, they are allotted immortality essentially, it is indeed necessary that the cause which assimilates them [to divinity] should primarily be in the Gods. For they are assimilated to their fountain. But they participate of similitude from the assimilative causes. Hence in these, the cause of such an immortality of souls as this, shines forth. On this account also, Socrates arguing from similitude says, it is fit that souls should govern and despotically rule over bodies, since they are allotted the power of governing and despotically ruling, from the same cause from which they derive their similitude [to divinity.] The one cause itself, therefore, of all the partible forms of life, pre-exists in the assimilative rulers. But one, whole, and impartible virtue exists prior to all the virtues which afford a similitude [to a divine nature.] And neither is the essential similitude of souls, nor the similitude of virtue, derived from any other source than that of these rulers and principles.

Since, however, there are, as we have said, triple monads in Core; and one, indeed, establishes all things in itself; but another leads all things into generation; (for it belongs to soul to generate) and another converts all things to itself; (for this is the illustrious work of virtue) and since all things are perfectly pre-arranged in Core, - this being the case, the monad which associates with Pluto, participates, indeed, in a certain respect of the extremes, but is particularly allotted its progression according to the middle. Hence also, it is called Proserpine, because it comes into contact, as we have observed, with generation and things which are borne along. For the unmingled and the virginal were adapted to the extremes. But mixture, and a contact with generated natures, are adapted to the middle, which rejoices in progressions and multiplications. This ravishment therefore, of Core, is indeed perfectly established in Proserpine. But she also imparts herself, and the vivification proceeding from herself to the last of things. Hence likewise, Socrates in the *Cratylus* co-arranges Proserpine with Pluto, but every where ranks total Core with Ceres, and comprehends her in the name of Core. The power however, which proceeds from her to the realms beneath, he comprehends in the name of Proserpine. For the psychical nature is in this power essentially; but the remaining things are in it, as we have said, according to representation, and not primarily. And thus much concerning the vivific triad, since Plato has delivered to us but few auxiliaries about it, from which as from firestones rubbed against each other, it is possible to enkindle the light of truth.

CHAPTER XII

In the third place, let us discuss the elevating, among the ruling Gods, and the triad which converts all things to their principle. For since there are three intellectual monads, as we have said, which are prearranged in the Gods prior to these, three triads of the ruling Gods proceed conformably to those monads; the paternal triad indeed, conformably to the first intellectual monad; (whence also they are called the sons of Saturn, and are said to have divided the kingdom of their father) but the vivific triad conformably to the middle monad; (whence also we are accustomed to co-arrange Core with Ceres as with a precedaneous cause) and the convertive triad, conformably to the third monad. Hence likewise we establish the peculiar cause of this triad in the demiurgus. For all the triads of the ruling Gods, are suspended from the demiurgic monad, and the progression to all of them is from this. One of them however, he constitutes in conjunction with his father; another in conjunction with the vivific Goddess; and another from the fountain in himself. For in the all-perfect demiurgus there are many fountains, which exist prior to all the second and third generations. For there the fountain of ideas subsists, according to which he adorns the universe, fashions the several particulars in it with forms and reasons, and arranges, and leads them into bound and morphe. For the fountain of souls likewise, and the fountain of all the intellectual Gods which proceed from him, are there. For he possesses a royal soul, and a royal intellect, according to the power of cause, as Socrates says in the *Philebus*. For there also the fontal sun subsists. Hence Timæus, after the generation of the seven bodies, and their position into total circulations, says, that the demiurgus enkindled that light which we now call the sun in the second of the revolutions from the earth, as affording an hypostasis to the sun from his own essence. For that which enkindles the whole sun, produces it, and constitutes that which is enkindled.

The demiurgus therefore, possessing, and comprehending in himself the solar fountain, generates likewise in conjunction with the principles and rulers of wholes, solar powers, and the triad of solar Gods, through which all things are elevated, perfected, and filled with intellectual goods; from one[†] monad indeed, participating unpolluted light, and intelligible harmony, but from the remaining two, efficacious power, acme, and demiurgic perfection. How therefore, does Plato deliver to us these divine orders, and where does he indicate concerning them? Here then, he comprehends the whole triad through one name, in the same manner as he does the triad prior to it. And as there he manifests the whole genus of the vivific principles by the name of Core, so likewise in these, he denominates the whole triad Apolloniacal. But he indicates the multitude in this triad by the many powers of this God.

In the first place therefore, let us survey how Plato, in the same manner as Orpheus, considers the sun to be in a certain respect the same as Apollo, and how he venerates the communion of these Gods. For Orpheus clearly says that the sun is the same with Apollo, and asserts this (as I may say) through the whole of his poetry. But the Athenian guest indicates this through the union of these divinities, constructing a common temple to Apollo and the sun, and at one time making mention of both, but at another, of one only, in consequence of their subsisting according to one union. But he says as follows: "Every year after the conversions of the sun from summer to winter, it is requisite that the whole city should assemble in the temple common to the sun and Apollo, consecrating three of the citizens to the God." In these words therefore, speaking in common about both these divinities, that it is fit there should be a temple of Apollo and the sun, into which it is necessary the whole city should assemble, after the summer solstice, he discourses in what follows about both, as if they were one, adding, that three of the citizens should be consecrated to the God; thus recurring from the division to the union of both. But elsewhere, he latently indicates the communion of them with each other. And again, in what follows, at one time he says that the citizens [consecrated to the God] should offer common first fruits to the sun and Apollo, but at another to the sun alone, in consequence of Apollo being in the sun. According to Plato therefore, there is a kindred conjunction of these divinities, a communion of powers, and an ineffable union.

Socrates also in the Cratylus, proposing to discover the essence of Apollo from his appellation, ascends to the simplicity of his hyparxis, to his power of unfolding truth into light, and to his intellect which is the cause of knowledge, thus sufficiently indicating to us the unmultiplied, simple, and uniform nature of the God. But in the [6th

---

[†] The word μιας is omitted in the original.

book of the] *Republic*, arranging the sun analogous to *The Good*, and sensible light, to the light proceeding from *The Good* to the intelligible, and calling the light which is present to the intelligible from *The Good*, truth, connecting likewise intellect and the intelligible with each other, he evidently collects together these two series, I mean the Apolloniacal and the solar. For each of these is analogous to *The Good*.[†] But sensible light, and intellectual truth, are analogous to superessential light. And these three lights are successive to each other, *viz*. the divine, the intellectual, and sensible light; the last indeed pervading to sensibles from the visible sun; but the second extending from Apollo to intellectuals; and the first, from *The Good* to intelligibles.

Again therefore, these Gods are demonstrated to be connascent with each other, according to their analogy to *The Good*. But together with union, they have also a separation adapted to them. Hence by poets inspired by Phœbus, the different generative causes and fountains of them are celebrated, from which being allotted their hypostasis, they are separated from each other. But they are likewise celebrated by these poets, as mutually connascent and united, and are praised by the appellations of each other. For the sun vehemently rejoices, to be celebrated in hymns as Apollo. And Apollo when he is invoked as the sun, benevolently causes the light of truth to shine forth. If therefore, the hyparxes of these divinities are united to, and subsist together with each other, but many powers of Apollo are delivered to us by Plato himself, and are happily allotted an appropriate theory, it is certainly proper to collect from these by a reasoning process, the solar progressions. But I say these things, looking to Socrates in the Cratylus, and his conceptions through images, which are there delivered, of the Apolloniacal powers. For the name of this God being one, unfolds all his powers, to the lovers of the contemplation of truth. This therefore is a very illustrious indication of the Apolloniacal peculiarity, *viz*. to collect multitude into one, to comprehend number in unity, to produce many things from one, and through intellectual simplicity to convolve to himself all the variety of secondary natures, and by one hyparxis to unite in one, multiform essences and powers. This Socrates says happens to the name Apollo, it being sufficient to signify in one, the various and different powers of the God, so that receiving his last image, and the most obscure representation from him, it is assimilated to his unific, and collective hyparxis, and contributes to our recollection of the Apolloniacal peculiarity. This one name therefore, possesses occultly

---

[†] For $των\ αγαθων$, it is necessary to read $τω\ αγαθω$.

many indications of the powers of the God. And by this simplicity indeed, which is exempt from multitude, the truth which the God through prophesy unfolds to secondary natures, is presented to our view. For the simple is the same with the true. But by the representation [in his name] of dissolution and liberation, the purifying and undefiled nature of the God is signified, and also his power which is the saviour of wholes. By his emission of arrows, his power is indicated which is subversive of every thing inordinate, confused, and incommensurate, through a cause which is the source of the jaculation of arrows. And by his revolution, the harmonious motion of wholes, and the symphony which coalesces in itself, and binds all things, are indicated. Referring therefore, these four powers of the God to forms adapted to the powers, we may thus accommodate them to the solar monads. Hence the first of these monads is enunciative of truth and the intellectual light which subsists occultly in the Gods themselves. But the second is subversive of every thing confused, and exterminative of all disorder. And the third renders all things commensurate and friendly to each other, through harmonic reasons. An undefiled however, and most pure cause presides over these monads, illuminating all things with perfection, and a subsistence according to nature, and expelling the contraries to these.

Of the solar triad, therefore, the first monad, indeed, unfolds intellectual light, and announces it to all secondary natures, fills all things with total truth, and elevates them to the intellect of the Gods. And this we say is the employment of the prophetic power of Apollo, *viz.* to lead forth into light the truth comprehended in divine natures, and to perfect that which is unknown to secondary natures. But the second and third monads, emit efficacious and demiurgic acme, in order to the production of wholes, and perfect energy, according to which they adorn indeed every thing sensible, but exterminate the inordinate and indefinite from the universe. And one of these monads is analogous to the production in wholes through music, and to the harmonious providence of things that are moved. But another is analogous to the power which is subversive of all disorder, and of the confusion and tumult which are contrary to form, and to the arrangement of wholes. And the remaining monad which supplies all things with an unenvying and exuberant communication of what is beautiful, which extends the beneficial, and imparts true blessedness, closes indeed the solar principles, but guards its triple progression. In a similar manner also, it illuminates ascending natures, with the perfect and intellectual measure of a happy life, presiding in the sun analogous to the purifying and Pœonian powers of the king Apollo.

From what is written likewise in the *Republic* concerning the sun, we may be able to collect the same things by a reasoning process. For Socrates there gives to it a transcendency exempt from every thing generated, and says that it is established above things which are borne along in a sensible nature; just as *The Good* is perfectly exempt from intelligibles. He likewise says that the sun generates sense, that which is sensible, and generated natures, just as *The Good* produces essence and true being, and is antecedently the cause of intellect and intelligibles. If, therefore, this sensible world is generated and generation, as Timæus says, and a divine generated† nature, as it is asserted in the *Republic*, but the sun is beyond generation, as Socrates affirms, and in short, is allotted an essence different from sensibles, it is perfectly evident that it is allotted a supermundane order in the world, and exhibits an unbegotten transcendency in generated‡ natures, and an intellectual dignity in sensibles. Hence, Timæus also delivers a twofold progression of the sun from the demiurgus, one indeed being co-arranged with the other planets, but the other exempt, supernatural, and unknown. For the demiurgus, when producing the seven bodies of the planets, and placing them in their proper circulations, at the same time constitutes the sun with the other planets arranging the moon the first from the earth, but the sun in the second circulation; and after these, he enkindles a light in the solar sphere, similar to none of the others; nor does he receive this light from the subject matter, but himself produces and generates it from himself, and extends as it were from certain adyta to mundane natures, a symbol of intellectual essences, and unfolds to the universe that which is arcane in the Gods that are above the world. Hence also the sun when he [first] appeared, astonished the [mundane] Gods, and all of them were desirous to dance round him, and to be filled with his light. This world likewise is beautiful and solar-form.

As we have said, therefore, from the fabrication [of the universe,] in the *Timæus*, the sun is demonstrated to possess this order beyond sensibles, and to be allotted an essence above every thing which is generated, but every thing in the world receives from him, perfection and essence. Hence also, Socrates in the *Republic* calls the sun the

---

† For θειον νοητον, it is necessary to read θειον γεννητον; every perpetually circulating body being thus denominated by Plato.

‡ For νοητοις here, it is necessary to read γεννητοις.

offspring of *The Good*, the demiurgus of a generated nature, and the author of all mundane light. These things, therefore, we must likewise understand analogously about the ruling order of the God; for they are thence communicated to this visible sun. And on this account, here also, the sun is allotted an exempt transcendency with respect to the Gods in the world, because he possesses a precedaneous hypostasis among the leaders and rulers of wholes.

Farther still, in those Gods likewise, the first effective cause of light subsists, generating those supermundane and intellectual rays, through which souls, and all the more excellent genera obtain an elevating progression. With these Gods also, there is the demiurgic duad which produces both simple and composite natures, those that are of a more ruling, and those that are of an inferior order. And in short, this demiurgic duad governs the twofold co-ordinations of the world. Hence those who are wise in divine concerns call this primary cause of light, and the demiurgic duad hands, as being efficacious, motive, and fabricative of wholes. But they establish them to be twofold, the one indeed being dexter, but the other sinister; which things also Timæus admits to be primarily in the celestial periods, and says that this division is derived from the first demiurgus. If, therefore, the demiurgic monad constituted the solar order prior to the world, why is it wonderful that in that order he should establish this division according to the right and left? For Socrates also calls the motive powers of the Parcæ hands, and says that the eldest of the three moves the universe with both her hands; so that we must not refuse to transfer the name of hands to divine concerns. Moreover, will not likewise the last of the solar principles according to Plato be that from which the interpreters of divine concerns say, a happy life, and unpolluted fruits are derived to wholes? Since he calls the sun the offspring of *The Good*, and this essentially pertains to it. For it is evident that as the good extends felicity to all beings, thus also the sun extends to mundane natures measures of felicity adapted to each, and gives completion to this through similitudes, and a tendency to the whole demiurgus. Hence also I think, felicity is said to consist in an assimilation to divinity. And felicity pertains to all the Gods in the world, according to the one ruling cause of them. For thence perfection and blessedness flow upon all things.

CHAPTER XIII

And thus much, following Plato, we have collected by a reasoning process, concerning these particulars. We shall add, however, to what has been said, the theory pertaining to the unpolluted Gods, among the ruling divinities. For Plato also gives us an opportunity of mentioning these, since it is necessary that the rulers and leaders of wholes should subsist analogous to the intellectual kings, though they make their progression in conjunction with division and a separation into parts. For as they imitate the paternal, generative, and convertive powers of the intellectual kings, thus also it is necessary that they should receive the immutable monads in themselves, according to the ruling peculiarity, and establish over their own progressions secondary causes of a guardian characteristic. And the mystic tradition indeed of Orpheus, makes mention of these more clearly. But Plato being persuaded by the mysteries, and by what is performed in them, indicates concerning these unpolluted Gods. And in the *Laws* indeed he reminds us of the inflation of the pipe by the Corybantes, which represses every inordinate and tumultuous motion. But in the *Euthydemus*, he makes mention of the collocation on a throne, which is performed in the Corybantic mysteries; just as in other dialogues he makes mention of the Curetic order, speaking of the armed sports of the Curetes. For they are said to surround and to dance round the demiurgus of wholes, when he was unfolded into light from Rhea. In the intellectual Gods, therefore, the first Curetic order is allotted its hypostasis. But the order of the Corybantes which precedes Core, (*i.e.* Proserpine) and guards her on all sides, as the theology says, is analogous to the Curetes in the intellectual order. If, however, you are willing to speak according to Platonic custom, because these divinities preside over purity, and preserve the Curetic order undefiled, and also preserve immutability in their generations, and stability in their progressions† into the worlds, on this account they were called Corybantes. For το κορον, *to koron*, is every where significant of purity, as Socrates says in the Cratylus; since also you may say, that our mistress Core was no otherwise denominated than from purity, and an unpolluted life. But in consequence of her alliance to this order, she produces twofold guardian triads, one indeed in conjunction with her father, but the other herself, by and from herself, imitating in this respect the whole vivific Goddess. For she constitutes the first Curetes.

Every where, therefore, the guardian and undefiled order is thus denominated by the Grecian theology. Above, however, it is more simple and impartible; but beneath, among the ruling Gods, it presents itself to the view with division and variety. Hence the Corybantes require the Minerval monad, and in a particular manner they are in

---

† For περιοδοις, it is necessary to read προδοις.

want of the third Minerval monad, which unites their progression, sustains their armed motion, and in short, converts them to their proper principles. Moreover, this number the triad, is adapted to these guardian powers, as being perfect, and uniformly comprehending the beginning, middle, and end of secondary natures; for everything which guards, hastens on all sides to comprehend that which is guarded. The triad also preserves the essences, powers, and energies of secondary natures, firm and unmoved. In the intellectual Gods indeed the three [unpolluted] monads, were divided about the three fathers; but here the triad is said to guard Core on all sides, since she also has pre-established triple monads in herself, as we before observed. All these monads, therefore, are preserved immutable through the guardianship of the unpolluted Gods, both in abiding and proceeding. And what else besides this guardian genus of Gods is fit to be co-arranged with prolific powers? For this co-arrangement is necessary, in order that these guardian deities may sustain all the progressions of these powers, and the multiplications in their generations, and may manifestly render their motions immutably established in themselves. And on this account indeed the Gods fill all things with themselves, and generate all things, and do not depart from any thing either of first or last natures. But by being in themselves, they are present to all things, and filling themselves, they fill all secondary natures. And neither does their inflexibility remain unprolific, nor does their fecundity, receive any thing from subordinate natures, but prolific abundance, and immutable power, are in them connascently conjoined. These things have been briefly asserted concerning the undefiled deity, who is co-arranged with the ruling Gods, both by Plato, and the Grecian theologists.

CHAPTER XIV

Again, resuming [the same subject,] let us discuss in common such things as Parmenides delivers to us concerning the whole order of Gods that are called assimilative rulers and leaders. For it is necessary, as we have before observed, to refer the whole divided theory [respecting the Gods] to the common and one mystic doctrine of Parmenides. For there we shall find the connexion of the divine orders, and their common powers delivered to us by Plato in a continued series. The same and the different, therefore, define for us the peculiarity of the demiurgic order. And according to these, we have unfolded in what has been before said, the paternal and prolific cause of the demiurgus, his unpolluted fountain, and the separative power in him, conformably to which he divides his own kingdom from that of Saturn. Since, however, the whole order of the assimilative Gods, is suspended from the demiurgic monad, subsists about, is converted to, and perfected by it, it is indeed necessary to refer the signs of this order to the demiurgic signs, and to give to the former a well-ordered generation proceeding in measures from the latter. For thus the coherence of the divine genera with each other, will become more apparent, and the evolution into light of secondary from more ancient natures, will through these very things become perfectly known to us.

What, therefore, are the peculiarities of this order, which is celebrated as of a ruling and leading nature by others,† but is demonstrated by arguments to be of an assimilative nature? Every thing then which is assimilative, imparts the communication of similitude, and of communion with paradigms to all‡ the beings that are assimilated by it. Together with the similar, however, it produces and commingles the dissimilar; since in the images [of the similar] the genus of similitude is not naturally adapted to be present, separate from its contrary. If, therefore, this order of Gods assimilates sensibles to intellectuals, and produces all things posterior to itself according to an imitation of causes, it is indeed the first-effective cause of similitude to natures posterior to itself. But if it is the cause of this, it is also of the dissimilitude which is co-ordinate with similitude. For it is necessary that all things which participate of the similar, should also participate of the dissimilar. And this order of Gods indeed imparts the similar in a greater degree than the dissimilar to the progeny that are more proximate to their principles; but it constitutes the essence of things that proceed farther from their principles, according to dissimilitude rather than similitude.

For, in short, similitude will have in itself an hypostasis analogous to the paternal causes, and to the causes which convert to principles. But the hypostasis of dissimilitude is analogous to prolific causes, and to those that preside over multitude and division. For similitude indeed proceeds analogous to intelligible bound,§ but dissimilitude to intelligible infinity. Hence the former is collective, but the latter separative of progressions. Since, however, every divine nature begins its own energy from itself, and though its energy is directed to

---

† For υπ' αλληλων, it is necessary to read υπ' αλλων.

‡ For πασης, it is necessary to read πασι.

§ For παρα τι, it is necessary to read περατι.

secondary natures, and it imparts its own peculiarity to things subordinate, yet it establishes and defines itself according to that energy, prior to other things; - this being the case, that which supplies other things with the participation of the similar[†] and the dissimilar, from itself, will entirely possess in itself this similitude and dissimilitude. It is also mingled from both these, though here similitude is emitted in a greater degree, and there dissimilitude. For generative are united to paternal causes, and unpolluted causes to those that hasten to proceed to every thing. Twofold co-ordinations likewise of the divine genera, are connected with each other, energize together with, and subsist in each other. For the genus of the ruling Gods, is similar and dissimilar to itself, and to other things. But being similar and dissimilar to itself, it conjoins itself[‡] to, and separates itself from its principles, preserving the proper boundaries of progression. That, however, which is similar and dissimilar to other things, converts and congregates other things to itself, and separates them from itself. Such, therefore, are the peculiarities of these Gods.

But that the similar and the dissimilar proceed from the demiurgic monad, and the signs which there pre-exist, into this order, Parmenides sufficiently demonstrates to us. For the demiurgic same and different, are the antecedently-existing causes, as he says, of the similitude and dissimilitude in this order. Since, however, though this order of Gods is the summit of the partible genera, and of genera which energize partibly, yet it has a total transcendency with respect to them, in order that being in continuity with the total orders of the Gods, its progression may not be separately allotted its generation from divided causes, but that each of the opposites, as it were, may proceed from the whole demiurgus. For the similar is from same and different, and the dissimilar receives its hypostasis from both these; and thus each participates of the whole demiurgic monad. And this is an indication of total[§] hyparxis, *viz.* to refer each of the parts that are, as it were, different, to the whole. Sameness, therefore, and difference generate similitude; but the one indeed paternally, and the other in an unpolluted manner; and the one generatively, but the other separately. And again, each constitutes dissimilitude in a manner appropriate to itself.

[†] It is necessary here to supply the word ομοιου.

[‡] For εαυτῳ, it is necessary to read εαυτο.

[§] For υλικης, it is necessary to read ολικης.

And thus the genera of the assimilative Gods are varied, subsisting as paternal, generative, and collective of wholes. For they are allotted their evolution into light, doubled according to pre-existent causes. And the demiurgic duad energizing through each of the causes that are pre-established in him, makes a progression from each into secondary natures. The whole conclusions, likewise, are dyadic, (or pertaining to the duad) but they are comprehended by the demiurgic tetrad in pre-arranged boundaries. And the multitude of the assimilative progressions is convolved to union, by the simplicity of the intellectual genera.

Each also of the progressions, has indeed one progression supernatural and unknown to the multitude, but the other apparent and known to all. I mean, for instance, that the similar, so far as it is constituted by difference, has a progression from thence difficult to be known; but that so far as it proceeds from sameness, it exhibits a manifest reason of cause. After the same manner, dissimilitude has difference for the manifest principle of its proper hyparxis; but sameness, for its principle difficult to be known. Hence also Parmenides beginning from things unknown to the multitude, and which are alone apparent to science and intellect, ends in things which are known to all men, and are effable. For in the Gods themselves, the ineffable precedes the effable. And the latent and unknown mode of their hypostasis, precedes that which is known according to progression. And thus much concerning these Gods from the *Parmenides* of Plato.

CHAPTER XV

Making, however, another beginning, let us discuss the orders that follow successively. Since the partial orders of the Gods, therefore, are divided in a threefold manner, according to the all-perfect measure of the triad, proceeding supernally from the first intelligibles, as far as to the last of things, measuring and defining all things as the Oracles say, - the ruling Gods, indeed, are allotted the first and highest rank [among the partial orders,] making their progression proximately after the intellectual order, elevating secondary natures and conjoining them with the demiurgus of wholes, unfolding all impartible and united intellectual goods to things subordinate, and connecting and containing exemptly, their essence and perfection. But the Gods who give completion to the sensible world are allotted the last order, and close the end of the divine progression. These divide the universe, and obtain perpetual allotments and receptacles in it, and through these weave one and the best polity of the world. Between these mundane Gods, however, who are our rulers and saviours, and the supermundane leaders, those Gods subsist who preside over the separable and at the same time inseparable order of sensibles, and define according to this their proper progression, being at one and the same time exempt from the Gods in the universe, and co-arranged with them. And they are expanded, indeed, above the allotment which is adequate to the divided parts of the world, and supernally ascend into many numbers of the mundane Gods; but they make a progression sub-ordinate to the government which extends to all things and to wholes.

For in short, being the media between the supermundane and mundane Gods, they in a certain respect communicate with both, and have an indissoluble communion with both, being mundane, and at the same time supermundane according to order. And above indeed, they are united by the ruling leaders, but beneath, they are produced into multitude by the junior Gods, as Timæus says. For they ride on the mundane Gods, and are in an undefiled manner established on their summits; but they are suspended from the supermundane Gods, and subsist about them. They are also more united than the former; but are more multiplied than the latter. And they divide indeed, the whole monads of the supermundane Gods, into perfect numbers; but they collect the multitudes and the numbers of the mundane Gods into united bounds, converting these Gods to their exempt principles, but calling forth the Gods that are above the world into the generation and providential care of sensible natures, and immutably preserving in themselves the middle form of empire. For the middle bonds give completion to all the genera of the Gods. Thus in intelligibles, between the intelligible and occult order, and the paradigmatic triad, and all-perfect multitude, the intelligible centre subsists, being parturient indeed, with multitude and the first (forms,) but vanquished by the uniform comprehension of the first order. Again, in intelligibles and intellectuals, the connective genus extending from the middle to all the extremes, conjoins and binds all their essences, powers and providential energies.

After the same manner therefore, in these orders also, *viz.* in the kings exempt from, and in those that are co-arranged with the universe, those Gods that emit in themselves uniformly the peculiarities of both these kings, afford a communication to them with each other. Whence also it belongs to them to transport first to second natures, to convert second to first natures, to unite both by an indissoluble connexion, and to guard the whole order in the world. The immutable, therefore, the inflexible, the indissoluble in providential energies, dominion over wholes, the administration of many partible allotments of the Gods at once, and the elevating to supermundane perfection many of their progressions and orders, pertain to these Gods. Hence, we are accustomed to celebrate this genus of Gods as *liberated*, in consequence of being freed from all division according to parts;† as *supercelestial*, in consequence of proximately establishing itself above the Gods in the heavens; as *undefiled*, in consequence of not verging to subordinate natures, nor dissolving its exempt transcendency by a providential attention to the world; as *elevating*, in consequence of extending the mundane Gods to the intellectual and intelligible place of survey; and as *perfect*, in consequence of illuminating all the celestials with the measures of perfection. Since therefore, this order is in continuity with the assimilative rulers, but is arranged prior to the mundane Gods, it is indeed proper to evince that the theology pertaining to it‡ is suspended from the doctrine concerning the ruling Gods, and at the same time affords from itself the principles of the conceptions about the sensible Gods.

CHAPTER XVI

The intelligible king§ therefore, of all intellectuals, luminously emitting from himself the first causes, and which measure wholes, according to the all-perfect triad in himself, defines all wholes as far as to the last of things, and triples the progressions of the Gods from himself, so as to generate indeed three orders, but refer each of them to one monad, and an intelligible transcendency. On this account he constitutes three collective, three connective, and three perfective causes of all intellectuals; extending the triadic light to all things, and imparting by illumination the perfect in the progressions of its proper offspring, to the beginnings, middles, and ends of all separated natures. But again, the demiurgus and father, imitating his father and grandfather,* to the

---

† It is necessary to substitute καυ for το.

‡ Instead of περι αυτων, it is necessary to read περι αυτην.

§ *i.e.* Phanes, or in Platonic language animal itself, subsisting at the extremity of the intelligible order.

* *i.e.* Imitating Saturn and Phanes.

latter of whom he extends his total intelligence, being the same in intellectuals, as he is in intelligibles, and terminating the genus of the intellectual fathers, in the same manner as his grandfather closes the paternal profundity of intelligibles, produces from himself three orders of Gods. And as the total progressions were divided from his grandfather triadically, so the partial progressions are perfected on account of him, according to the triad. Hence, there are also three orders from the demiurgus; but they proceed according to the end adapted to each. And one of them indeed, is supermundane alone; another is mundane; and another is in a certain respect the middle of both. They are likewise allotted the triple proximately from the paternal cause; but each derives the peculiarity of hyparxis from definite principles, and a diminution proceeding according to measures. For they have neither an hypostasis of equal dignity, as mathematical monads have in the triad, nor a disorderly difference of dignity, but they receive the difference of a subordinate essence, and arrangement in their generation from the first causes. And thus, the ruling Gods indeed, are allotted the highest order in the partial progressions, and the exempt cause of the proceeding natures. But the liberated Gods are allotted the second order, being arranged indeed under the ruling, but riding on the mundane Gods. And the mundane Gods are allotted the third order, being elevated through the liberated, but united by the ruling, to the intellectual Gods. In what manner however, the Gods in the world and all the mundane genera participate of the ruling Gods, we have already shown.

But each of the mundane genera enjoy the energy of the liberated governors of the universe, according to a measure adapted to each, and especially such as are able to follow the powers of these Gods. For in the Gods themselves, we may perceive a twofold energy, the one indeed, being co-arranged with the subjects of their providential care, but the other being exempt and separate. According therefore, to the first of these energies, the mundane Gods govern sensibles, and convolve, and convert them to themselves; but according to the other, they follow the liberated Gods, and together with them are elevated to an intelligible nature. And on this account, the Elean guest, makes the periods of the whole world, and of each of the Gods in it to be twofold. For, he says, that the sun, and each of the heavenly bodies, subsist according to both these circulations, *viz.* the intellectual and the mundane; or, if you are willing so to speak, according to the power which is motive of secondary natures, and the power which ascends in conjunction with the liberated Gods.

Moreover, he says, that our souls, and all the natures that have a life separate from bodies, at one time live according to that elevating progression, and at another according to the mundane; and now indeed we proceed from youth to old age, since we have departed from a flourishing and undefiled life, and are borne to earth, and generation; but then on the contrary, we proceeded from old age to youth. On which account, we were led round to a flourishing, intellectual, and liberated form of energy. Hence also, the corporeal-formed nature [with which we are connected,] was gradually obliterated, and whatever causes us to tend downward, and renders us inseparable from the universe. But an incorporeal, and immaterial nature shone forth, and was filled with the Gods who are the leaders of a life of this kind.

If also, you are willing, we may collect the same thing by a reasoning process, from what is written in the *Phædrus*. Socrates, therefore, says in that dialogue, that the soul which is perfect and winged, revolves on high, and governs the whole world; and that this will be the case with our soul, when it arrives at the summit of a happy life. But this is in a much greater degree present with the genera superior to us, and with the Gods themselves. For our souls obtain this end, and this true blessedness, through the Gods. For whence do you think, and from what other causes, is a disencumbered energy, and which has dominion over wholes, imparted to us, and to the genera in the world more excellent than us, but from the liberated Gods? For each of the mundane Gods obtains the administration of its allotment, and of the proper series over which it rules, and which it constitutes about itself, according to the will of the father. For the demiurgus arranges under the several mundane Gods, the herds of dæmons, and partial souls, as Timæus says. But to energize through the whole world, is a supernatural good, and the peculiarity of the exempt government of the supercelestial Gods. Hence, from these this good is imparted to the mundane Gods, and to our souls. Or how can that which is partial extend its proper energy to the whole? And how departing from its own divided peculiarity, can it change its life? For that which directs its energy to the universe, withdraws itself from an energy which is arranged in a part. We must not therefore say, that this divine good is by any means present to mundane natures from any other source than these Gods, who establish their kingdom proximately above the world. As, therefore, the progression to all things through similitude, and the conversion according to similitude to causes, are imparted from the assimilative rulers to the celestial Gods, to the more excellent genera, and to us, thus also, that which is liberated from partial natures, which is disencumbered and which tends spontaneously to many energies, is an impression derived from the liberated rulers. And thus much concerning the providence of these rulers which pervades to all things, and the goods which they impart to subordinate natures. But we shall add to what has been before said, the peculiarity of their essence, according to which they are allotted this order.

CHAPTER XVII

From the intellectual[†] Gods, therefore, [*i.e.* from the assimilative rulers] an immaterial and divine intellect is suspended. But a separate and total intellect is an intellect of this kind. Hence also these Gods are called intellectual. For according to their hyparxes, they are beyond essence and multitude; but according to the participations of them which receive the illumination of a progression of this kind, they are called assimilative. For because they have intellectual hypostases, and perfect powers, since intellect is the last of their participants, and the intellectual peculiarity defines their whole essence,- hence they are allotted this appellation. Of the mundane Gods, indeed, an intellectual nature participates primarily, an undefiled soul also participates of them, and that portion of the world together with which they render the whole world, an intellectual and divine animal, emitting the splendour of themselves as far as to bodies, and imparting to these a vestige of their own peculiarity. It is necessary, therefore, that the orders which are between both these, should rejoice in certain additions, by which they are more multitudinous than the intellectual Gods, and in progressions into participants; but that they should be more singular and simple than the mundane Gods. For the diminutions of the divine essences multiply the receptacles that are suspended from them. Hence, together with the intellectual peculiarity, these Gods assume the psychical power, in order that by the incorporeal nature, they may have the supermundane [property,] but by the psychical, they may be more manifold than the intellectual Gods.

For again, considering the affair in another way, since soul presents itself to the view, and the one fountain of whole souls, in pure [intellectuals,] and constitutes all things in conjunction with the

---

[†] The Greek scholiast observes on this part of the text of Proclus as follows: "By the *intellectual*, Proclus means the *ruling* Gods; but by an immaterial and separate intellect the whole demiurgus. And by *essence* he means a partial hypostasis, such as that of soul, of a dæmon, and the intellect which is co-ordinate to partial souls.

demiurgus, is it not necessary that the supermundane Gods should participate of the psychical peculiarity? For the Gods that are divided about the world, are not filled with the unical soul without a medium, but through other more total media, which do not proceed out of the monad, [*i.e.* out of Juno, or the crater,] and possess an eternal life. From thence, therefore, that is, from the crater of souls, the presence of soul is derived to the ruling and liberated Gods. For the demiurgus Jupiter also, as Socrates says in the *Philebus*, possessing in himself a royal soul, and a royal intellect, according to the reason of cause, and generating according to the whole of himself those Gods that are of a ruling characteristic among the supermundane and mundane divinities, entirely likewise imparts the intellectual and the psychical peculiarity. But the supermundane Gods indeed, being primarily unfolded into light, participate more of an intellectual essence. Hence also, the psychical peculiarity is in them occultly. But the Gods who are allotted the middle order, cause the psychical peculiarity, indeed, to shine forth, yet subsisting with a more abundant separation [than in the supermundane Gods.] The mundane Gods, however, perfectly unfold the psychical peculiarity into light; since intellect also, was indeed occultly in the first intellectuals, but exhibits a forerunning light in the middle, and shines forth in the last intellectuals. And the supermundane Gods, indeed, being perfectly [supermundane] derive the power of soul from the intellectual[†] crater, or the royal soul in the demiurgus; but they pre-establish in themselves another monad of the divided psychical genera. The liberated however, now communicating in essence with the mundane Gods, have the psychical peculiarity from a twofold source, *i.e.* from the fountain of total animations, and from the assimilative principle. And in the last place, the mundane Gods receive the illuminations of all the divinities prior to them. Hence also, they rule over the universe, imitating the liberated Gods, adorn sublunary natures with forms, and assimilate them to intellectual paradigms, imitating the ruling Gods. They likewise pour forth the whole of the life which is inseparable [from body,] from the one fountain of souls, establishing it as an image [of the life which is separate from a corporeal nature] and conjoin themselves to this fountain.

In short, all the genera[‡] being mingled by the demiurgus in the fountain of souls, in order to the generation of the different ranks of

---

[†] For $νοητου$ here, it is necessary to read $νοερου$.

[‡] *viz.* The genera of being, essence, sameness, difference, motion and permanency.

souls, some of these ranks have one thing, but others a different thing at hand. And in some indeed, the essential has dominion over the remaining genera; in others sameness; and in others difference. But those souls that are connascent with the assimilative Gods, have† their whole hypostasis according to essence. Hence they are near to an intellectual hyparxis, and are allotted in the genera of souls, an intelligible and occult transcendency. But those‡ that are co-arranged with the liberated Gods, characterize their proper progression, according to sameness. Hence also, they are consubsistent with the Gods that bind together and congregate the supermundane and mundane Gods. And those souls that are co-divided with the mundane Gods, define the essence of themselves according to difference: and on this account also, the demiurgus, in constituting the soul of the universe, is said to co-adapt difference to other souls by force.

Moreover, the separation into parts in these, the union through harmony, and the energy according to time are effected through the illuminations of difference. But [in the souls] above these essence and sameness subsist, with which there are eternal life, and a union of powers. And thus much concerning these particulars.

From what has been said, however, we may collect by a reasoning process, that intellect, essence, and intellectual life, are suspended from the liberated Gods. In them also soul, and the nature of the super-celestial souls shine with a forerunning light. For they are established above the celestial Gods who ride in bodies, just as the celestial Gods are exempt from the sublunary divinities, and from those who are allotted the government of matter. If, however, the genus of the liberated Gods is of this kind, they are very properly said to belong to the partial orders, in the same manner as the Gods prior to them. But they indeed are more total, because the psychical peculiarity was in them occultly. But the liberated Gods have that which is partial in providential energies more apparent because the psychical power also in these is more manifest, just as the mundane Gods who now preside over partial allotments, perfectly unfold into light the psychical essence. The whole, however, and impartible genera of the Gods shine forth as far as to the intellectual hypostasis. For intellect according to its own nature is impartible.

---

† For εσχατον, it is necessary to read εχουσιν.

‡ For εν δε, it is necessary to read αι δε.

The liberated leaders, therefore, being such as we have shown them to be, let us survey the multiform orders of them adapted to this order. Some of them, therefore, we call *transporters*, and these are such as unfold to secondary natures, the progressions of the assimilative genera. But others are *elevators*, who draw upward the mundane orders, to a separate energy. Others are *colligators*, who administer equally the communion of the extremes. Others are *undefiled*, and these are such as entirely obliterate matter, and impart by illumination the disencumbered to the providential energies of secondary natures. Others are *perfective*, and these are such as are the suppliers of perfection to mundane natures. And others are *prolific*, who multiply the progressions of subordinate essences. For according to these, and far more numerous powers, incomprehensible by our conceptions, they preside over the Gods in the world, and give completion to the divine genera which subsist between the Gods that are exempt, and those that are co-arranged with the parts of the universe.

Moreover, we must assign to them energies in symphony with their powers, *viz.* such energies as are disencumbered, every where apparent, amputating every thing material, and corporeal-formed, emitting an idea undefiled, without contact, and incorporeal, and converting all secondary natures to themselves, and extending them to intellectual light. And farther still, we must ascribe to them energies that unfold the exempt principles of the universe, and also energies more excellent than these, which draw upward to the intellectual Gods, and others still more elevated which conjoin themselves with the intellectual Gods, and exhibit an essence uncoloured, unfigured, and without contact. Again, according to another mode, [we must admit] that some of their energies operate about the secondary Gods, and are collectors of their divine unities to a union prior to the world. But others operate about the mundane intellects, and extend the intellections of them from co-ordinate intelligibles to such as are first, and exempt from the universe. Others again, are elevators of souls to the one fountain of them. And some of their energies, indeed, are the leaders of divine souls themselves; but others preside over the genera that are more excellent than us. And others convolve the multitude of intelligible [souls[†]] to an undefiled life. For being as it were certain leaders of herds, they ascend supernally into all the natures of the world, and as dæmon Gods, they proximately rule over Gods, and are the leaders of the progression to the intelligible, to some in one, and to others in a different way, according to the order

---

[†] By intelligible souls, we must understand partial, but undefiled souls.

which is adapted to the elevated natures. For every thing [mundane] participates of the liberated Gods. But the participation is different. For it is either according to the divine, dæmoniacal, and partible, or according to the uniform, intellectual, and psychical. For all things, as I may say, are allotted a separate[†] life, a disencumbered energy, a supernatural providence, and a common prefecture, from this order of Gods. Let the common definition, therefore, of the liberated Gods, be such as this.

CHAPTER XVIII

In the next place it follows that we should unfold the theory of Plato, first, that which may be obtained in other dialogues, and afterwards, the all-perfect doctrine concerning these Gods, which is to be found in the *Parmenides*. In the *Phædrus* therefore, Socrates energizing enthusiastically, and expanding his intellect to the whole connexion of the divine orders, and not only mystically surveying the mundane progressions of them, but also their indescribable and blessed visions, and discursive energies above[‡] the world, divides indeed, in a threefold manner, all the separate hypostases in the world, from the subjects of their government. And he calls the first of these hypostases divine; but the middle dæmoniacal; and he gives completion to the last from our souls. He also suspends partial souls [such as ours] from dæmons. Hence he denominates them co-attendants, and extends them through dæmons as media, to the divine empire. But he suspends the dæmoniacal orders from the mundane Gods. For dæmons are the attendants of these. He refers however, these whole divine principalities, the dæmoniacal herds, and choirs of partial souls, to the liberated order; and he says that the triadic army of mundane souls is elevated under this order, to the intellectual and intelligible Gods, together at the same time with their first causes.

Here therefore, he defines according to the measure of the dodecad (*i.e.* the number twelve) all the liberated Gods, though the multitude of them is incomprehensible, and not to be numbered by human conceptions; and though none of those theologists that have written any thing concerning them, have been able to define their whole number, in the same manner as they have the ruling multitude (*i.e.* the multitude of

---

[†] For χωρικον, it is necessary to read χωριστον.

[‡] Instead of περι τον κοσμον, it is necessary to read υπερ τον κοσμον.

supermundane Gods,) or the multitude of the intellectual, or intelligible Gods. Plato however, apprehended that the number of the dodecad is adapted to the liberated Gods, as being all-perfect, composed from the first numbers, and completed from things perfect; and he comprehends in this measure all the progressions† of these Gods. For he refers all the genera and peculiarities of them to this dodecad, and defines them according to it. But again dividing the dodecad into two monads and one decad; he suspends all [mundane natures] from the two monads, but delivers to us each of these energizing on the monad posterior to itself, according to its own hyparxis. And one of these monads indeed, he calls Jovian, but he denominates the other Vesta. He likewise makes mention of other more partial principalities, and which give completion to the aforesaid decad, such as those of Apollo, Mars, and Venus. And he suspends indeed, the prophetic form of life from the Apolloniacal principality; but the amatory from the principality of Venus; and the divisive, from that of Mars; for hence the most total and first genera of lives are derived; just as when he introduces into the world souls recently fashioned, he says that some preside over one, and others over another form of life. And it appears to me, that as Timæus makes the division of souls, at one time supermundane, but at another mundane, for he distributes souls equal in number to the stars, and disseminates one into the moon, another into the earth, and others into the other instruments of time; after the same manner also Socrates prearranges twofold rulers and leaders of them; proximately indeed the mundane Gods, but in a still higher rank than these, the liberated Gods.

As we have said however, the twelve Gods convolve every mundane genus, whether it be divine, or dæmoniacal, to the vision of intelligibles, and perfect their separate energy. They likewise comprehend in themselves all the supercelestial genera, so that whether there be a paternal genus of the liberated Gods, or a vivific, or an undefiled and guardian genus, they are comprehended in this number. For this number must not be surveyed as if it was such as twelve is in units; for number in the Gods is not of this kind; but it must be beheld in the peculiarity of hyparxis. For as the duad in the Gods presides over prolific power,‡ and the triad, over the first perfection, thus also the dodecad [in the Gods,] is a symbol of all-perfect progression. For since these Gods close the end of the powers that are unapparent and exempt

---

† For περιοδους, it is necessary to read προοδους.

‡ For δυαδος, it is necessary to read δυναμεως.

from the world, and ride on the celestial Gods, according to each of these, the dodecad pertains to them, *viz.* it belongs to them as terminating the all-perfect in the progression of the supermundane, and as presiding over the celestial Gods. For they impart to the latter a distribution from themselves into the dodecad, and especially guard them in this number. The ruling dodecad therefore, was all-perfectly supermundane; but the celestial, is evidently mundane only; and the dodecad of the liberated rulers contains the communion of the extremes, and binds the order posterior, to that which is prior to itself. And on this account indeed, the liberated Gods are perfective of the mundane Gods, and lead them upward. But they are proximately suspended from the ruling Gods, are emitted from them, and administer the indissoluble connexion of both. [*i.e.* of the supermundane and mundane Gods.]

CHAPTER XIX

That we may not however present the reader with our conceptions, but may unfold to the utmost of our power the theory of Plato, to the lovers of the contemplation of truth, let us consider by ourselves, where those leaders must be arranged, which Socrates celebrates in the *Phædrus*, and with whom it is fit to connumerate, and with what orders of Gods, it is proper to co-arrange the great ruler of those leaders, who drives a winged chariot. For it is necessary either to give to him an intellectual, or an assimilative, or a liberated, or a mundane order. For these are the decrements accompanying the progression of the great God Jupiter. If however, he is the intellectual Jupiter, whom we have denominated the demiurgus of the universe, and have made Plato bear testimony to our assertion, how is he the leader of the above mentioned dodecad? And how is he divided oppositely to the principality of Vesta? For the demiurgic monad closes indeed, the intellectual breadth, but is exempt from all other numbers, and unco-ordinated with all [the monads of other numbers.] For it neither was, nor is lawful for effects to have an hypostasis opposed in division to their causes. It is not therefore proper to make twelve leaders of wholes, but to make the number of causes to be one, as Timæus says. Moreover, Jupiter the demiurgus is exempt[†] from the universe, as being himself the author of the apparent order of things. But the first of the twelve leaders, is said by Socrates to drive a winged chariot in the heavens. How therefore, can he who is connected with the world, and who approximates to the Gods in the heavens, be

---

[†] For εξηρτηται, it is necessary to read εξηρηται.

considered as the same with him who is exempt from all [mundane natures,] and who abides, as Timæus says, in his own accustomed manner?

Farther still, this Jupiter indeed, presides over a philosophic life, and souls [that follow him] perpetually lead this life. But another God presides over the prophetic, amatory, and poetic life. The demiurgus of wholes, however, contains in himself the paradigms of all lives; and as he uniformly comprehends the essence of souls, after the same manner also, he comprehends all the different mutations of their lives. He is not, therefore, divisibly the cause of the lives in the soul, but pre-establishes according to one demiurgic cause, all the periods of souls, all the variety, and all the measures of life. And as the mundane sun is not the cause of some things, but the demiurgus of others, but of whatever the sun is the author, the demiurgus is in a greater degree the fabricator, and precedaneous cause, - thus also in the lives of souls, it is not proper to refer the cause to the demiurgus in a divided manner. For the demiurgic monad, presides as the impartible, common, and one cause of all lives; but the divisions according to lives, and the different paradigms of mundane natures, pertain to the Gods posterior to him.

If, however, some one should think that we ought to abandon this hypothesis, but that we should assert this Jupiter, and the other leaders to be mundane, where must we arrange the Gods that follow him? For Socrates says, "that the army of Gods and dæmons divided into eleven parts, follows Jupiter." For there are more comprehensive and partial orders of Gods in the universe than these, and some of them have the relation of leaders, but others of followers. The magnitude, however of the principality celebrated by Socrates, does not manifest to us a transcendency co-arranged with, but exempt from mundane natures. For in incorporeal causes, *the great*, imparts a peculiarity of this kind to those to whom it is present. And as Love being not simply called a dæmon by Diotima, but a *great* dæmon, is demonstrated to be expanded above all dæmons, and is a god, but is not arranged in the genus of dæmons, thus also Jupiter, being celebrated as the *great* leader, not as the mundane leader of mundane natures, but as exempt from, and transcending the mundane order, is allotted this appellation. But if Jupiter is exempt from the Gods in the world, it is necessary that the other leaders also should have an essence antecedent to those that follow Jupiter. For all of them are allotted a ruling dignity. But if the other leaders are arranged as mundane, and Jupiter alone is a leader beyond these, again we must transfer the whole principality from the dodecad, to the Jovian monad. It is necessary, however, to attribute a ruling power to all of them, and to preserve to Jupiter the principal authority among them.

It remains, therefore, that a principality such as this of the Gods, must either be that of the assimilative Gods, or of those that are allotted a liberated dominion in the universe, as we say it must. If, however, we should admit it to belong to the assimilative orders, it will be the leader of a demiurgic triad, but not of the dodecad which is now celebrated. The Jupiter, therefore, who is among the assimilative Gods, and whom we have before unfolded, is the first of the sons of Saturn. For these sons, as Socrates says in the *Gorgias*, divide the whole kingdom of Saturn. And the first of them indeed is the author of first, the second of middle, and the third of last natures. The division, therefore, of mundane natures being threefold, the first of the sons of Saturn may be called the leader of the triadic division, and the multitude proximately suspended from him will be the first of the triadic division in the universe. But the leader of the twelve Gods, presides over an army distributed into eleven parts. Hence[†] the one defines his proper dominion in the thirds of wholes, but the other in the twelfths. And according to the power of comprehension, one of them defines his principality conformably to the triad, but the other according to the endecad [or the number eleven.] By no means, therefore, is each of these allotted the same order. The demiurgus, therefore, and saviour Jupiter is unco-arranged with all these. But the assimilative Jupiter is the leader of the division of wholes into a triad. And the mundane Jupiter is among the number of leaders that follow, and not of those that are exempt. The Jupiter, however, who is celebrated by Socrates in the *Phædrus*, is co-arranged with the other leaders, and presides over those that are disposed in an orderly manner according to eleven parts, and not over those that receive a tripartite division; and he is also exempt from all mundane natures on account of the magnitude of his ruling transcendency. Hence he is different from all the above-mentioned orders, and exhibits in no one of them the peculiarity which is now presented to our view.

It remains, therefore, that we should connumerate him with the liberated Gods, in order that he may be proximate to the mundane Gods; and on this account he is said to be in the heavens, and to be exempt from the mundane divinities. On this account, likewise, he is celebrated as *great*. For frequently media present themselves to our view, from the extremes being surveyed according to mixture. Since

---

† For ουτε, it is necessary to read ουκουν.

therefore, Jupiter is said to drive a winged chariot in the heavens, and is denominated great, he is in a certain respect co-arranged with the celestial Gods, and is exempt from them. But he who is at one and the same time co-arranged with the Gods in the universe, among whom the celestial Jupiter is allotted the highest dignity, and is exempt from them, ranks among the liberated Gods, if in what has been before said, we have rightly determined. Hence, of the Gods, some are exempt from the universe; but others give completion to it; and others are at one and the same time allotted a co-arranged, and an exempt transcendency. This great leader in the heavens therefore Jupiter, is liberated and supercelestial, and the whole dodecad shines forth in this order of Gods. For there is one all-perfect and divine number, to which the twelve leaders give completion. So that it is necessary the whole number should be placed in this order of Gods, but we must not call in a divided manner some of the leading and ruling Gods mundane, and others supermundane. But if the first of them is supermundane, the rest also will after the same manner establish themselves above the Gods in the world. Each also is the leader of an appropriate multitude, and is surrounded with a great number† of Gods and dæmons. But partial souls rank among the last of their followers. For they are co-divided with dæmons, and divine natures, and participate of the liberated principality of the Gods, as far as they are able. For, as Socrates says, "that which is willing and able always follows the Gods." Through these things therefore, we have reminded the reader, that the twelve leaders of wholes celebrated by Socrates in the *Phædrus*, belong to the liberated Gods.

CHAPTER XX

In the next place, let us show whence they derive the whole of this number. It is necessary therefore, that they should have their hypostasis from the Gods prior to them; since the progression to the assimilative Gods was from the intellectual fathers, and to the intellectual fathers supernally from the intelligible and at the same time intellectual Gods, just as to these the progression was from the first intelligibles. For since the order of the assimilative rulers is prior to that of the liberated Gods; as is also the triad of the intellectual kings; or rather the demiurgic monad establishing in itself the all-perfect measure of the division of wholes into the triad, - this being the case we must survey the causes of

---

† For οχετον, I read οχλον.

the generation† of the liberated Gods according to both these, *viz.* according to the demiurgic measure, and the genera of the assimilative Gods. For the different orders of them are imparted from these two.

Moreover, if we remember what has been before observed, we gave a fourfold division to the middle progressions of the assimilative Gods. And we said, that some of them are paternal, others prolific, others of an elevating, and others of a guardian nature. Since therefore, the demiurgic monad divides progressions into first, middle, and last, in the same manner as the intelligible father prior to it, but the Gods posterior to this monad, emit the rivers of themselves tetradically to secondary natures, - this being the case, the dodecad of liberated Gods presents itself to our view, above indeed proceeding according to the triad, but beneath being quadruply multiplied. Hence, of the genera which give completion to it, some indeed, are allotted the demiurgic and paternal triadically; others, the generative and vivific triadically; others, the elevating peculiarity triadically; and others after the same manner the undefiled and guardian characteristic. For all their peculiarities are derived from the multitude of the assimilative Gods. But the division of them into first, middle and last, proceeds from the demiurgic cause. And thus much concerning the number of the liberated Gods, whence, and how it is generated.

CHAPTER XXI

Since therefore, as we have before observed, there are twelve leaders of all the mundane Gods, of all dæmons, and farther still, of such partial souls as are able to be extended to the intelligible, again in this dodecad, the mighty Jupiter and Vesta are allotted the more ruling order. But the principality of the rest is co-arranged with these, and has a secondary dignity. And Jupiter indeed, being neither the intellect of the universe, as some say he is, nor the intellect in the sun, nor in short, any one of mundane intellects or souls, but being expanded above all these, and pre-existing among the liberated Gods, elevates the choir of Gods, and of the genera superior to us that follow him, and imparts paternal goodness to the multitude converted to him. But he is the leader of all the other numbers that terminate under the twelve Gods. Again however, Vesta indeed governs an appropriate multitude, but she neither has the order of the first soul, nor is that which is called the earth in the universe. But prior to these, she is allotted a ruling power among the supercelestial

---

† For την απογεννησιν, it is necessary to read της απογεννησεως.

Gods. She imparts however, her own peculiarity to the numbers of the other leaders, in the same manner as Jupiter. For the leaders that are suspended from the decad, participate also of these two monads.

Jupiter however, being indeed the cause of motion is the leader to all things of a progression to the intelligible. But Vesta illuminates all things with stable† and inflexible power; though Jupiter also abiding in himself, is thus elevated to the intelligible place of survey; and Vesta on account of an inflexible and undefiled permanency in herself, is conjoined to the first causes. The emission however of a different peculiarity, affords the difference of dominion. For since there are twofold conversions in the Gods (for all things are converted to themselves and to their principles) each form of conversion indeed, was impartibly in king Saturn. For according to Parmenides he is demonstrated to be in himself, and in another. And the latter indeed, pertains to a conversion to a more excellent nature, but the former implies a conversion to himself. In the secondary however, and more partial Gods, both these forms shine forth in a divided manner. And Vesta indeed, imparts to the mundane Gods an undefiled establishment in themselves; but Jupiter imparts to them an elevating motion to first natures. For Vesta belongs to the undefiled, but Jupiter to the paternal series; but they are divided by a subsistence in self, and a subsistence in another, as we have before observed. It must be said therefore, that every thing stable and immutable, and which possesses an invariable sameness of subsistence, arrives to all mundane natures from the supercelestial Vesta, and that on this account all the poles are immovable, and the axes about which the circulations of the spheres convolve themselves. It must also be said, that the wholenesses of the circulations are firmly established, that the earth abides immovably in the middle, and that the centres have an unshaken permanency [from this supercelestial Vesta.]

Again therefore, it must be admitted that all motions, separate energies, and the conversions of secondary to first natures, are derived to wholes from Jupiter. For the intellectual orders are not only united to co-ordinate intelligibles, but also to such as are exempt, on account of the elevating progression of Jupiter. And divine souls following the mighty Jupiter are extended as far as to the first causes. The attendants of these also are collected together with the Gods, in consequence of being suspended from the paternal government of Jupiter. But again, with respect to all the remaining leaders, each presides over his proper series,

---

† For γονιμον, it is necessary to read μονιμον.

and imparts from himself his peculiarity to the whole multitude [suspended from him.] And one of them indeed, imparts as far as to the last of things an unfolding, another, a prolific, and another, an immutable peculiarity, being themselves allotted a supercelestial order, and drawing upward a numerous army of partible Gods. Hence Socrates also at one and the same time denominates them rulers, says that they have an arrangement, and that their energy is directed to secondary natures, according to the order in which they are placed. Each, however, of the other ruling Gods who are ranked in the number of the twelve, is a leader according to the order in which he is arranged. The ruling and leading peculiarity, therefore, alone, pertains to the supermundane Gods. But to be arranged, and that which is arranged itself by itself, pertain to the mundane Gods. For these are they who participate of order, and who are allotted order according to participation. Both these peculiarities, however, pertain to the liberated Gods. For they are rulers and leaders, as being in continuity with the ruling [supermundane] Gods, and they are arranged and participate of order, as being proximate to the mundane Gods. But being the middle of both, they connect the whole progressions of them according to one intellectual bond. Farther still, as presiding indeed over the ruling order in the heavens, they come into contact with the mundane Gods, and as being in themselves, and extended to the intelligible, they are allotted a transcendency separate from the universe, and exempt from their participants. Thus much, therefore, may suffice concerning the first division of these Gods. Since, however, we have before observed that their progression is tetradic and triadic, we shall concisely define[†] the peculiarities of the arranged triads.

CHAPTER XXII

These, therefore, being arranged according to triads, as we have said, of the demiurgic triad, indeed, Jupiter is allotted the highest order, supernally from intellect governing souls and bodies, and as Socrates says, taking care of all things. But Neptune here also gives completion to the middle of the demiurgic [triad], and especially governs the psychical order. For this God is the cause of motion, and of all generation. But soul is the first of generated natures, and is essentially motion. And Vulcan inspires the nature of bodies, and fabricates all the mundane seats of the Gods. Again, of the guardian and immutable triad,

---

[†] For αφαιρησωμεθα, it is necessary to read αφορισμεθα.

the first indeed is Vesta, because she preserves the very being of things, and an undefiled essence. For Socrates in the Cratylus gives to her the highest order, as connectedly containing the summits of wholes. But Minerva preserves middle lives inflexible, through intellection, and a self-energizing life, sustaining them from [the incursions of] of matter. And Mars illuminates corporeal-formed natures with power, and an infrangible[†] strength, as Socrates says in the Cratylus. Hence he is perfected by Minerva, and participates of a more intellectual inspiration, as the poetry [of Orpheus] says, and of a life separate from generated natures.

Moreover, of the vivific triad, Ceres is the chief, entirely generating all mundane life, *viz.* the intellectual, the psychical, and that which is inseparable from body. But Juno contains the middle of the triad, and imparts the generation of soul. For the intellectual goddess emits from herself all the progressions of the other psychical genera. And Diana is allotted the end of the triad, moving all natural reasons into energy, and perfecting the imperfection[‡] of matter. Hence theologists, and Socrates in the Theætetus, call her *Lochia*, (or the power that presides over births) as being the inspective guardian of psychical progression and generation. Of the remaining triad, therefore, the anagogic, or elevating, Hermes indeed is the supplier of philosophy, and through this elevates souls, and by the dialectic powers, sends upward both total and partial souls to the good itself. But Venus is the first-effective cause of the amatory inspiration which pervades through wholes, and familiarizes to the beautiful the lives that are elevated by her. And Apollo perfects and converts all things through music, convolving, as Socrates says [in the Cratylus], and through harmony and rhythm attracting to intellectual truth, and the light which is there.

We say, however, in common respecting all of them, that establishing themselves above the mundane Gods, they contain all the choir of the liberated Gods. And souls indeed are suspended from them, but intellectual souls, and such as are as it were powers generative of souls. Hence Socrates also gives to them chariots. For Jupiter is said to drive a winged chariot, and the other Gods after the same manner as Jupiter use secondary vehicles. But what else can we say these are than supermundane souls, on which they ride, and which are intellectual indeed, but the sources of partibility and division, from which mundane

---

[†] For αρρητον, it is necessary to read αρρηκτον.

[‡] For αυτοτελες, it is necessary to read ατελες.

souls are allotted their hypostasis; a more abundant separation, and a greater number of parts appearing in them, in consequence of their being adapted to be bound through analogy? In the liberated Gods, therefore, the psychical peculiarity unites itself to intellect. Hence also, Jupiter is said to drive a winged chariot, without division, in consequence of this chariot being intellectual, and not departing from an immaterial and divine intellect. But in the mundane Gods, divisions of horses and charioteers are delivered. [For Socrates says in the *Phædrus*], "All the horses, therefore, and chariots of the Gods are good, and consist of such things as are good." Hence an energy according to time first shines forth in the mundane Gods, where there is a more abundant separation of powers. But in the liberated Gods, time is always with eternity, and partibility with union. For they are the principles of souls, and the causes of mundane natures, and are as it were intellectual seeds abiding in the intellectual comprehensions of themselves. And thus much concerning these things.

CHAPTER XXIII

I wish, however, to show from other writings of Plato what the peculiarity is which he exhibits to us of the liberated order. In the *Republic*, therefore, teaching us the order of the universe which pervades through the mundane wholes, supernally from the inerratic sphere, and which governs the elections of human life that are different at different times, this life also varying the measure of justice adapted to it, he refers the first-effective cause of this order to a monad and triad exempt from [the mundane] wholes. And to the monad indeed, he gives the power of dominion, extending the authority of it to all heaven, its empire being at one and the same time impartibly present to all things, governing all things indivisibly, and according to one energy, and moving wholes by the lowest powers of itself. Giving also to the triad a progression from the monad, he distributes from it into the universe a partible energy and production. For that which is simple and united in exempt providence, is educed into multitude through secondary inspection. Thus, therefore, the one cause of multitude possesses a greater authority, but the distributed cause appears to be more proximate to its effects. For all the variety of powers in the world, the infinity of motions, and the multiform difference of reasons, [*i.e.* of productive principles] are convolved under the triad of the Fates. But again this triad is extended to the one monad which is prior to the three Fates, and which Socrates denominates Necessity, not as ruling over wholes by violence, nor as obliterating the self-motive nature of our life, nor as deprived of intellect and the most excellent knowledge, but as comprehending all things intellectually, and introducing bound to things indefinite, and order to things inordinate. And farther still, he thus denominates it, as causing all things to be obedient to itself, and extending them to good, as subjecting them to demiurgic sacred laws, as guarding all things within the world, and as comprehending all things in the universe in a circle, and leaving nothing deprived of the justice pertaining to it, nor suffering it, besides this, to fly from the divine law.

Since, therefore, we give a twofold division to the causes of the order of the world, and we admit one of the causes to be monadic, but the other triadic, and we acknowledge that the monad is productive of the triad, being persuaded by Plato, and since we have shown that the triad is the offspring of the monad, let us see in what order it is possible to arrange each of these. For wishing to learn this, we have undertaken the present discussion concerning them. The monad, therefore, which, as we have said, Socrates calls Necessity, is perfectly exempt from mundane natures, and by the last of her powers imparts motion to all heaven, neither being converted to it, nor energizing about it, but imparting an orderly circulation to the world, by her very essence, and by being firmly established. For [Socrates says] that the spindle is moved on the knees of Necessity; but that she herself having royally established herself on a throne near to the universe, governs the heavens in a silent path. But the triad is now in a certain respect co-arranged with the circulations of the heavens, convolves them with hands, and energizes about them, and no longer causes them to revolve by its very being alone [in the same manner as the monad]. For the triad is the cause of the order and circulations of the universe, by producing and performing a certain thing; though in this also there is a different energy. For Lachesis indeed moves with both her hands; but each of the remaining Parcæ, with one hand only. This however we shall again discuss. But it is obvious to every one, that of this production which subsists according to the monad, and the triad proceeding from it, it must be granted that the monad is established in a more ancient order of Gods, but the triad in an inferior order.

We say, therefore, that Necessity who is called the mother of the Parcæ, first subsists in the intellectual Gods, analogous to the intelligible and intellectual monad of Adrastia; and that thence being unfolded into light in the ruling orders, she generates this triad of the Parcæ. For that which is total in providence, energy, and the convolution of wholes by the very being itself of that which convolves them, are indications of intellectual transcendency. To extend, likewise, impartibly production to all things, is co-equalized with demiurgic dominion. And this Goddess appears to me to illuminate all the progeny of the demiurgus with an ineffable guard. As likewise he is the generator of wholes impartibly, thus too Necessity guards inflexibly all things in herself, and comprehends them monadically, preserving indissoluble the order which proceeds from the demiurgus into the world. Necessity, therefore, being allotted such an authority and kingdom in wholes, the triad of the Parcæ rules over the universe in a liberated manner. For it comes into contact with the heavens, and for a time relinquishes the contact, as Socrates says. And through contact indeed, it is co-arranged with the bodies that are moved, and is connascent with them; but through a retention of energies, it is without contact, is separate from the things governed, and is exempt from them. Being, however, at one and the same time allotted both these peculiarities, it exists in the liberated Gods. For to touch, and not to touch, to move and not to move, as the fable relates, are not according to a part in the Gods, but are co-existent, and subsist with each other at once. For divine natures do not change their energies according to time, nor like partial souls, do they at one time energize separately, and at another providentially attend to secondary natures; but abiding in themselves they are every where present, and being present to all things, they do not depart from the watch-tower of themselves. At one and the same time, therefore, the being without contact, and the coming into contact with the celestial periods, are present with the Parcæ, and they also comprehend that which is exempt and liberated from sensibles, according to one peculiarity, and that which is co-arranged with, and allied to them. And on this account, they possess a liberated order with reference to the whole heaven.

If, however, there is also a mundane triad of the Parcæ, and a providence proximate to the subjects of their government, it is not wonderful. For of Jupiter, and Juno, Apollo and Minerva, there are common progressions and co-arrangements, after the supercelestial allotment, and together with the mundane Gods. For powers which give completion to the last order of the Gods, approximate to the universe from all the liberated Gods. But Socrates, celebrating the liberated and supermundane kingdoms of the Parcæ, has represented them to us as touching and not touching the whole circulations, dividing the limitation† of their peculiarities, by mutation according to time. For to relinquish [the contact] for a time, affords a representation of a

---

† For περιφορας, I read περιγραφας.

temporal mutation of energies. This, however, pertains to the concealment which is adapted to divine fables. For fables introducing generations of things unbegotten, compositions of things simple, and distributions of things impartible, obumbrate under many veils the truth of things. If, however, as fables call the transition from cause to existence, generation, denominate the causal comprehension of composite in simple natures, composition itself, and say that the division of secondary about first natures, is the distribution of the latter into parts, - thus also, if we do not apprehend according to time, the alternately coming into contact with, and being separated from things that are moved, conformably to the apparent meaning of the fable, but according to the different peculiarities of the Parcæ,[†] and an hypostasis mingled from the extremes, we shall be most near to the conception of Plato. Here, therefore, let us terminate this, which does not require much discussion at present.

But let us consider the order of the Parcæ by itself. For of these, some think that Lachesis should be arranged as the first, but others as the last of the three. And of the remaining two, some give a prior arrangement to Atropos, and place her in the order of a monad, but others to Clotho. Since, however, Plato in the *Laws* clearly says, that Lachesis is the first, Clotho the second, and Atropos the third, I think that what is said in the *Republic* should be referred to this definite order in them, and that we should not make any innovation by following the mutable opinions of interpreters. Socrates, therefore, says, that Lachesis sings the past, but Clotho the present, and Atropos the future; here also in a similar manner using an order of division conformably to their energies. And to Lachesis indeed he gives predominance, and a uniform dominion over the rest. But he gives to Clotho a dominion subordinate to that of Lachesis, but more comprehensive than the kingdom of Atropos. And to Atropos he attributes the third kingdom, which is comprehended by the others, and is arranged under them. The multitude, therefore, are ignorant that Socrates uses the parts of time as symbols of the comprehension according to cause. For the past was once the future, and the present, but the future[‡] is not yet the past, but has the whole of its essence in existing in some after time. We must assume, therefore, the triple causes analogous to these three parts of time; and say that the cause which is the most perfect, and the most comprehensive of the

---

[†] For μερων, it is necessary to read Μοιρων.

[‡] In the original το δε μελλον is omitted.

others, sings the past, as the cause of the others, and the source of their energy. For the past is comprehensive of the future and the present. But the second cause is the present,† which partly comprehends, and is partly comprehended. For this prior to its being the present was the future. And the third cause, and which is comprehended by both the others, is the future. For this requires the present and the past, the one unfolding it, but the other bounding its progression. Lachesis, therefore, is the first-effective cause, comprehending the other causes in herself; but each of the remaining Parcæ is comprehended by her. And Clotho indeed is allotted a superior, but Atropos an inferior order. And on this account, Lachesis indeed moves with both her hands, as giving completion in a greater and more total manner to those things which are effected by them more partially. But Clotho turns the spindle with her right, and Atropos with her left hand, so far as the former indeed is the primary leader of the energies, but the latter follows, and governs all things in conjunction with the former. For in mortal animals, the right hand is the principle of motion; and in wholes, the motion to the right is comprehensive of the motion to the left hand. On this account, therefore, the triad of the Fates, in the *Laws* and in the *Republic*, is divided by Plato according to the same order, into first, middle, and last.

And not only in the before mentioned passages, but also at the end of the fable, in which he leads the soul to the mortal place, and to a polity the work of generation under the dæmon allotted to it as a ruler, supernally from the heavens, and the summit of the universe, he arranges souls under Lachesis as the first, under Clotho as the second, and under Atropos as the third. And after these, when they become perfectly situated under the throne of Necessity, he leads them to the plain of Oblivion, and the river of Negligence. It is necessary, therefore, either to disturb the descent of souls, and subvert the continuity of remission, which the prefecture of the governing dæmon affords to souls, or to assign to Lachesis a rank more elevated than that of the other Parcæ; but to give to Clotho the second, and to Atropos after the same manner the third rank. For the progression into generation beginning from more perfect natures, and subsiding according to a tendency to an earthly nature, originates indeed from Lachesis, but ends in Atropos.

Farther still, the lots, and the paradigms of lives, are extended to souls from the knees of Lachesis, through the prophet as a medium. And as the fable before said that the whole spindle is turned on the knees of

---

† For τα παραγοντα, it is necessary to read τα παροντα.

Necessity, thus also it suspends the providence about partial souls from the knees of Lachesis, who moves the universe perpetually with her hands, as with more elevated powers, but in her knees possesses subordinately the causes of the psychical periods. Hence the prophet in a remarkable manner celebrates this daughter of the Goddess: "This is the speech of the virgin Lachesis, the daughter of Necessity." But again, Clotho is said to weave things consequent to the elections made by souls, and to distribute to each of them an appropriate destiny. And after her, Atropos imparts to the webs the immutable and the definite, giving completion to the end of the canons of the Fates, and to the order which extends from the universe to us. If, therefore, Lachesis energizes in souls prior to their election, and after their choice is made, defines all the periods of them in the realms of generation, by the most beautiful boundaries; but the other Parcæ after the election made by souls, allot them what is convenient, and connect their lives with the order of the universe, does it not appear that Lachesis precedes Clotho and Atropos, and that they follow her, and together with her give completion to their appropriate providence? Lachesis, therefore, appears to possess the second dignity of a mother with respect to the other Parcæ, and to be a certain monad co-arranged with them, just as Necessity in an exempt manner comprehends the powers of all of them. But the other Parcæ are proximately indeed perfected under Lachesis, but still higher than her, under Necessity. Such, therefore, is the order of them according to the narration of Plato.

The symbols, however, which the fable attributes to them, magnificently celebrate their kingdoms. For their walking on the [celestial] circles, signifies their exempt and separate dominion. But their sitting on thrones, and not on the circles themselves, as the Sirens do, indicates that the receptacles which are primarily illuminated by them, are established above the celestial bodies. For a throne is the vehicle and receptacle of those that are seated on it. And all the participants of the participable Gods, are placed under them like vehicles, and the [participable] Gods are eternally established in, ride on, and energize through them. But the Fates being seated at equal distances from each other, manifest the orderly separation of them, their remission proceeding according to analogy, and the distribution supernally derived to them from their mother. For from thence, that which is arranged in progression, and that which is according to desert in energies, are imparted to the Fates.

Moreover, the having a crown on their heads, signifies that their summits are surrounded with a divine light, and that they are adorned by prolific and undefiled causes, through which also they fill the heavens with generative power, and immutable purity. But their being invested with white garments evinces that all their externally emitted reasons, and the lives which they propose to themselves, are intellectual and luciform, and full of divine splendour. And the garments indeed appear to indicate the essences which participate of the Fates; but the thrones, the receptacles in the first firmaments. For with us also, garments are proximately connected with our bodies; but vehicles are apprehended to be more remote from us. This, however, is assumed from another theology, from which we are instructed in the orders that are above the inerratic sphere. But the assertion that one of the Fates sings the past, another the present, and the third the future, evinces that all their externally proceeding energies are elegant and intellectual, and full of harmony. For the Fates perfect the songs of the Sirens, and the very orderly and elegant motions of the heavens, and fill all things with their hymns; calling forth indeed the production of their mother into the universe, through intellectual hymns, but converting all things to themselves through the harmonious motion of wholes. All these particulars, however, sufficiently demonstrate to us the perfect, undefiled, and supercelestial order of the Fates.

CHAPTER XXIV

It remains, therefore, for us to adduce the *Parmenides* as a witness of the doctrine concerning these gods. For Plato in that dialogue most clearly delivers the one peculiarity of them. For after the progression of the assimilative orders, in which the similar and dissimilar shine forth to the view from intellectual sameness and difference, at one time indeed according to analogy, but at another according to a generation which is different [from that of the other orders], and difficult to be surveyed, he demonstrates that *The One* touches and does not touch,[†] both itself and other things. For all the divine genera after the demiurgic monad double their energies. For they are naturally adapted to energize both towards themselves, and other things posterior to themselves, rejoicing in progressions, being subservient to the providence of secondary natures, through the will of their father, and calling forth his supernatural, impartible, and all-perfect production, and communicating the streams of it to secondary natures. Does not, therefore, this contact and division with things subordinate, represent to us the liberated

---

[†] In the original ουχ απτομενον is omitted.

peculiarity? For to touch, is an indication of alliance with us, and of a co-arranged providence. But again, not to touch, is an indication of a transcendency exempt and separate from mundane natures. In what has been before said, therefore, we have demonstrated that a thing of this kind pertains to the genus of the liberated Gods, who at one and the same time come into contact with celestial natures, and are expanded above them, and proceed to all things with an unrestrained energy, and free from all habitude. On this account also, we have placed the Fates in the supercelestial order. For Socrates says that they touch the [celestial] circulations; and in the Cratylus he asserts that the mundane Core (or Proserpine) who associates with Pluto, and administers the whole of generation, comes into contact with a mutable essence, and that through this contact she is called Pherephatta.

Farther still, in the *Phædo*, teaching us what the mode of the cathartic life of souls is, he says "that the soul when it does not associate with the body, comes into contact with [true] being." Through all these particulars, therefore, he indicates that contact is the work of an inseparable providence, and of a co-arranged administration; but that the negation of contact is the business of a prefecture, separate, unrestrained, and exempt from the subjects of government. *The One*, therefore, which touches and does not touch other things, is conjoined with other things, and established above them. Hence, at one and the same time it is allotted the power of things established above the world, and of mundane natures. For being in the middle of both, it comprehends in one the divided peculiarities of the extremes. And moreover, it touches, and does not touch itself prior to other things; because there are in it multitude, a separation of wholeness, and the parts of wholeness, and a union collective of all the multitude. For if it has proceeded from its principles, and if it energizes partibly, it is various and multiform. For every progression diminishes indeed, the powers of the proceeding natures, but increases the multitude which is in them, and if it has not entirely proceeded, the uniform nature of its essence shines forth to the view, at one and the same time, with the multitude it contains. This genus of Gods, therefore, is co-arranged with the mundane Gods, and transcends the subjects of its government. It is also liberated, being separated from things which are perfectly divided. Hence, if it is one and multitude, producing indeed into secondary natures the many rivers of the fountains, but surpassing partible allotments, it will at one and the same time touch and not touch itself. On account of its separate union indeed, it is not in want of contact; but on account of its progression into multitude, it touches itself. "For it comprehends many things in itself, and touches itself, so far as it is in itself," says Parmenides. In short, so far as it is without contact, it is separate; but so far as it proceeds from itself, and is again established in itself, it touches itself. And so far indeed, as it is in other things, it comes into contact with other things; but so far as it is unco-arranged with others, and so far as it has not a co-ordinate number in them, it is separated from them. At one and the same time therefore, this genus of Gods is uniform and multiplied, and is uniformly varied. It also abides and proceeds, and is participated by more imperfect natures, and is imparticipable, existing prior to them. All these particulars, however, are the elements of the supercelestial order, presenting to our view an hypostasis mingled from perfectly divided peculiarities. And thus much concerning the essence and hyparxis of these Gods, which Parmenides exhibits to us in the above citation.

It is necessary, however, to assume from the things placed before us, the causes of the generation of these Gods. Since it is demonstrated, therefore, that these divinities are according to union itself beyond all partible separation, and contact, they will have their progression from *The One*. For union is thence derived to all things, from the first unity, which is exempt from all multitude, and all division. But in consequence of their having pre-assumed the power of touching themselves, according to a subsistence in self they derive their existence from the unpolluted Gods. For the subsistence in self in the first of the intellectual fathers, was the symbol of a cause inflexible, and which immutably sustains multitude from secondary natures. If, therefore, this one touches itself, on account of a subsistence in self, it establishes multitude in *The One*, and contains parts in wholeness, on account of undefiled power in progression. And in the intellectual fathers, indeed, a subsistence in self primarily shines forth to the view, and comprehends contact causally, as was demonstrated to us through the first hypothesis. But in the liberated Gods, a subsistence in self is according to participation. Contact, however, is in this one according to essence, and is consubsistent with the multitude it contains.

Farther still, [*The One*] being in other things touches other things; but not being co-arranged with them according to any common number, it is separated from them. By this, therefore, Parmenides appears indeed to form his reasoning from a subsistence in another; since that *The One* touches itself, was before demonstrated, through a subsistence in itself. It is, however, wonderful that a subsistence in another is, in the first progression,† superior to a subsistence in self, but in the participation of the liberated Gods is subordinate to a subsistence in self. For we say, that for a thing to come into contact, and be co-arranged with other things, is in every respect more imperfect than for it to convert multitude to itself. We must, therefore, say that the liberated Gods have their progression from the demiurgic and the assimilative order. Hence Parmenides does not say that *The One* is in another thing, but in other things. But other things are primarily suspended from the [demiurgic] monad; but secondarily from the assimilative Gods. The liberated Gods, therefore, from thence receive their subsistence in others. For the demiurgic one being same and different, imparts to them sameness and union exemptly. But the assimilative one illuminates them with a separate similitude. But *The One* of the liberated Gods subsists now with others, so far as it is co-arranged with them, and proximately presides over them. Again, however, because it differs from the mundane unities, it is allotted the whole of its appropriate number exempt from others. And thus other things participating of no number which is common with this one, cannot proximately participate of it. Hence the progression to the liberated Gods, is from the first causes, and from causes that are arranged near to them. For their progression is from *The One*; since as *The One* is exempt from intelligibles, thus also the liberated Gods are exempt from sensibles. And their progression is likewise from the undefiled order. For they have not the disencumbered from any other source than that of immutable power, and the demiurgic cause. Being likewise generated from the assimilative Gods, they receive a communion with other things, and from themselves they are established above others. For they establish their appropriate number above the subsistence of other things. And thus much concerning these Gods may be assumed from the *Parmenides*. But we have elsewhere accurately explained the several particulars relating to them, and there is no occasion to write the same things in the present treatise [as we have there written].

---

† For περιοδῳ, it is necessary to read προδῳ.

BOOK VII

CHAPTER I

The mundane Gods, or those divinities who give completion to the sensible world, are assigned the last order of deific progression, as we are informed by Proclus in the preceding book. They also divide the universe, and obtain perpetual allotments and receptacles in it, and through these weave one and the best polity of the universe. Each of the mundane genera likewise enjoy the energy of the liberated governors of the universe, according to a measure adapted to each, and especially such as are able to follow the powers of these Gods. For in the Gods themselves we may perceive a twofold energy, the one indeed being co-arranged with the subjects of their providential care, but the other being exempt and separate. According, therefore, to the first of these energies, the mundane Gods govern sensibles, and convolve and convert them to themselves; but according to the other, they follow the liberated Gods, and together with them are elevated to an intelligible nature. The mundane Gods also perfectly unfold the psychical peculiarity into light; and receive the illuminations of all the divinities prior to them. Hence too, they rule over the universe imitating the liberated Gods, adorn sublunary natures with forms, and assimilate them to intellectual paradigms, imitating the ruling Gods. They likewise pour forth the whole of the life which is inseparable from body, from the one fountain of souls, establishing it as an image of the life which is separate from a corporeal nature, and unite themselves to this fountain.

Again, the world is said by Plato in the *Timæus* to be the image of the eternal, *i.e.* of the intelligible Gods. For it is filled from them with deity, and the progressions into it of the mundane Gods, are as it were certain rivers and illuminations of the intelligible Gods. These progressions also the world receives, not only according to the celestial part of it, but according to the whole of itself. For in the air, the earth and sea, there are advents of terrestrial, aquatic, and aerial Gods. Hence the world is throughout filled with deity; and on this account is according to the whole of itself the image of the intelligible Gods. Not that it receives indeed these Gods themselves; for images do not receive the exempt essences of the total Gods; but illuminations poured from thence on the secondary orders, to the reception of which they are commensurate.

Farther still, of the mundane Gods, some are the causes of the existence of the world; others animate it; others again harmonize it thus composed of different natures; and others, lastly, guard and preserve it when harmonically arranged. And since these orders are four, and each consists of things first, middle and last, it is necessary that the disposers of these should be twelve. Hence Jupiter, Neptune, and Vulcan, fabricate the world; Ceres, Juno and Diana animate it; Mercury, Venus, and Apollo harmonize it; and lastly, Vesta, Minerva, and Mars, preside over it with a guardian power. But the truth of this may be seen in statues as in enigmas. For Apollo harmonizes the lyre; Pallas is invested with arms; and Venus is naked; since harmony generates beauty, and beauty is not concealed in objects of sensible inspection. Since, however, these Gods primarily possess the world, it is necessary to consider the other mundane Gods as subsisting in these; as Bacchus in Jupiter, Esculapius in Apollo, and the Graces in Venus. We may likewise, behold the spheres with which they are connected; *viz.* Vesta with earth, Neptune with water, Juno with air, and Vulcan with fire. But the six superior Gods we denominate from general custom. For Apollo and Diana are assumed for the sun and moon; but the orb of Saturn is attributed to Ceres; æther to Pallas; and heaven is common to them all. And thus much concerning the mundane Gods in general, the sources of their progression, their orders, powers, and spheres.†

CHAPTER II

The division, however, of the mundane Gods is into the celestial and sublunary. And of the celestial, the divinity of the inerratic sphere has the relation of a monad to the divinities of the planets. But the triad under this monad consists of Saturn, Jupiter, and Mars; of which the first is the cause of connected comprehension, the second of symmetry, and the third of division and separation. And again, with respect to the sublunary deities, the moon ranks as a monad, being the cause of all generation and corruption. But the triad under it, consists of the divinities who preside over the elements of air, water and earth. Between these are the planets that revolve with an equal velocity. And of these, the sun indeed unfolds truth into light, Venus beauty, and Mercury the symmetry of reasons or productive principles, conformably to the analogy of the three monads mentioned by Plato in the *Philebus*, as subsisting in the vestibule of *The Good*. It may also be said that the moon is the cause of nature to the mortal genera, being the visible image of the fontal nature existing in the goddess Rhea. But the sun is the

---

† Vid. Sallust. *de Diis et Mundo*, Cap 6 [TTS vol. IV, p. 9.]

fabricator of all the senses, because he is the author of seeing and of being seen. Mercury is the cause of the motions of the phantasy; for the sun gives subsistence to the essence of the phantasy, so far as it is the same with sense. But Venus is the cause of the appetites of that irrational part of the soul which is called desire; and Mars, of those irascible motions which are conformable to nature. Jupiter also, is the common cause of all vital, and Saturn of all gnostic powers. For all the irrational forms may be divided into these. The causes, therefore, of these, are antecedently comprehended in the celestial Gods, and in the spheres with which they are connected.

The allotments also of the mundane Gods are conformable to the divisions of the universe. But the universe is divided by demiurgic numbers, *viz.* by the duad, triad, tetrad, pentad, hebdomad, and dodecad. For after the one fabrication of things by the demiurgus, the division of the universe into two parts, heaven and generation (or the sublunary region), gives subsistence to twofold allotments, the celestial and the sublunary. After this, the triad divides the universe, to which Homer alludes when he says that Neptune is allotted the hoary deep, Jupiter, the extended heavens, and Pluto, the subterranean darkness. But after the triple distribution, the tetradic follows, which gives a fourfold arrangement to the elements in the universe, as the Pythagoreans say, viz. the celestial and the ethereal, above the earth and under the earth. The universe also receives a division into five parts. For the world is one and quintuple, and is appropriately divided by celestial, empyreal, aerial, aquatic and terrestrial figures and presiding Gods. After this follows its division into seven parts. For the heptad beginning supernally from the inerratic sphere, pervades through all the elements. And in the last place is the division of the universe by the dodecad, *viz.* into the sphere of the fixed stars, the spheres of the seven planets, and the spheres of the four elements.

Moreover, the allotment of angels and dæmons is co-suspended from the divine allotments, but has a more various distribution. For one divine allotment comprehends in itself many angelic, and a still greater number of dæmoniacal allotments; since every angel rules over many dæmons, and every angelic allotment is surrounded with numerous dæmoniacal allotments. For what a monad is in the Gods, that a tribe is among dæmons. Here, therefore, instead of the triad we must assume three compositions, and instead of the tetrad or dodecad, four or twelve choirs following their respective leaders. And thus we shall always preserve the higher allotments. For as in essences, powers and energies, progressions generate multitude; thus also in allotments, such as are first, have a precedency in power, but are diminished in multitude, as being nearer to the one father of the universe, and the whole and one providence which extends to all things. But secondary allotments, have a diminution of power, but an increase of multitude. And thus much concerning allotments in general.

Since, however, according to a division of the universe into two parts, we have distributed allotments into the celestial and sublunary, there can be no doubt what the former are, and whether they possess an invariable sameness of subsistence. But the sublunary allotments are deservedly a subject of admiration, whether they are said to be perpetual or not. For since all things in generation are continually changing and flowing, how can the allotments of the providential rulers of them be said to be perpetual? For things in generation are not perpetual. But if their allotments are not perpetual, how is it possible to suppose that divine government can subsist differently at different times? For an allotment is neither a certain separate energy of the Gods, so that sublunary natures changing, we might say that it is exempt and remains immutable, nor is it that which is governed alone, so that no absurdity would follow from admitting that an allotment is in a flowing condition, and is conversant with all-various mutations; but it is a providential inspection, and unrestrained government of divinity over sublunary concerns. Such being the doubts with which this subject is attended, the following appears to be the only solution of the difficulty.

We must say then, that it is not proper to consider all the natures that are in generation and generation itself, as alone consisting of things mutable and flowing, but that there is also something immutable in these, and which is naturally adapted to remain perpetually the same. For the interval which receives and comprehends in itself all the parts of the world, and which has an arrangement through all bodies, is immoveable, lest being moved it should require another place, and thus should proceed from one receptacle to another ad infinitum. The etherial vehicles also of divine souls with which they are circularly invested, and which imitate the lives in the heavens, have a perpetual essence, and are eternally suspended from these divine souls themselves, being full of prolific powers, and performing a circular motion, according to a certain secondary revolution of the celestial orbs. And in the third place the wholeness (ολοτης) of the elements has a permanent subsistence, though the parts are all-variously corrupted. For it is necessary that every form in the universe should be never failing, in order that the universe may be perfect, and that being generated from an immoveable cause, it may be immoveable in its essence. But every wholeness is a form; or rather it is that which it is said to be through the participation of one all-perfect form.

And here we may see the orderly progression of the nature of bodies. For the interval of the universe is immoveable according to every kind of motion. But the vehicles of divine souls alone receive a mutation according to place; for such a motion as this, is most remote from essential mutation. And the wholeness of the elements admits in its parts the other motions of bodies, but the whole remains perfectly immutable. The celestial allotments also which proximately divide the interval of the universe, co-distribute likewise the heavens themselves. But those in the sublunary region, are primarily indeed allotted the parts which are in the interval of the universe, but afterwards they make a distribution according to the definite vehicles of souls. And in the third place, they remain perpetually the same according to the total parts of generation. The allotments of the Gods therefore do not change, nor do they subsist differently at different times; for they have not their subsistence proximately in that which may be changed.

How therefore do the illuminations of the Gods accede to these? How are the dissolutions of sacred rites effected? And how is the same place at different times under the influence of different spirits? May it not be said, that since the Gods have perpetual allotments, and divide the earth according to divine numbers, similarly to the sections of the heavens, the parts of the earth also are illuminated, so far as they participate of aptitude. But the circulation of the heavenly bodies, through the figures which they possess produce this aptitude; divine illumination at the same time imparting a power more excellent than the nature which is present to these parts of the earth. This aptitude is also effected by nature herself as a whole inserting divine impressions in each of the illuminated parts, through which they spontaneously participate of the Gods. For as these parts depend on the Gods, nature inserts in such of them, as are different, different images of the divinities. Times too co-operate in producing this aptitude, according to which other things also are governed; the proper temperature of the air; and in short, every thing by which we are surrounded contributes to the increase and diminution of this aptitude. When therefore conformably to a concurrence of these many causes, an aptitude to the participation of the Gods is ingenerated in some one of the natures which are disposed to be changed, then a certain divinity is unfolded into light, which prior to this was concealed through the inaptitude of the recipients; possessing indeed his appropriate allotment eternally, and always extending the participation of himself, similarly to illuminations from the sun, but not being always participated by sublunary natures, in consequence of their inaptitude to such participation. For as with respect to partial souls such as ours, which at different times embrace different lives, some of them indeed, choose lives accommodated to their appropriate Gods, but others foreign lives, through oblivion of the divinities to whom they belong; thus also with respect to sacred places, some are adapted to the power which there receives its allotment, but others are suspended from a different order. And on this account, as the Athenian guest in Plato says, some places are more fortunate, but others more unfortunate.

The divine Iamblichus however, doubts how the Gods are said to be allotted certain places according to definite times, as by Plato in the *Timæus*, Minerva is said to have been first allotted the guardianship of Athens, and afterwards of Sais. For if their allotment commenced from a certain time, it will also at a certain time cease. For every thing which is measured by time is of this kind. And farther still was the place which at a certain time they are allotted, without a presiding deity prior to this allotment, or was it under the government of other Gods? For if it was without a presiding deity, how is it to be admitted that a certain part of the universe was once entirely destitute of divinity? How can any place remain without the guardianship of superior beings? And, if any place is sufficient to the preservation of itself, how does it afterwards become the allotment of some one of the Gods? But if it should be said that it is afterwards under the government of another God, of whom it becomes this allotment, this also is absurd. For the second God does not divulse the government and allotment of the former, nor do the Gods alternately occupy the places of each other, nor dæmons change their allotments. Such being the doubts on this subject, he solves them by saying that the allotments of the Gods remain perpetually unchanged, but that the participants of them, at one time indeed enjoy the beneficent influence of the presiding powers, but at another are deprived of it. He adds that these are the mutations measured by time, which sacred institutes frequently call the birth-day of the Gods.[†]

CHAPTER III

In the next place, it is necessary to observe of the mundane Gods that they do not obtain the rank which they hold in the universe from any habitude or arrangement towards bodies; for they are all of them

---

[†] Vid. Procl. in Tim. 45A.

essentially liberated from body, unrestrained in their energies, and have no proximity or alliance to a corporeal nature. For bodies are ministrant to them, and are subservient to the generation of mutable essences. Hence they are not in bodies, but rule over them externally; so that they are not changed together with them. Farther still, they impart from themselves to bodies, every good which they are capable of receiving, but do not in return receive any thing from bodies; and consequently they do not receive certain peculiarities from them. For if indeed they had a subsistence like the habits of bodies, or like material forms, or were corporeal after any other manner, it might perhaps be possible for them to be transmuted together with the differences of bodies. But if they antecedently subsist separate from bodies, and are essentially unmingled with them, what reasonable distinction can they derive from a corporeal nature? To which may be added, that such a hypothesis makes bodies to be better than the divine genera, if they afford a seat to more excellent causes, and essentially insert in them characteristic peculiarities. He therefore, who co-arranges the allotments and distributions of the governors with the governed, will evidently ascribe authority and dominion to better natures. For because the presiding powers possess such peculiarities, on this account they chose such an allotment, and give it essentially a specific distinction; but the allotment itself is not assimilated to the nature of the recipient.

With respect indeed to partial souls such as ours it is requisite to admit that such as is the life which it emitted before it was inserted in a human body, such also will be the organic body with which it is connected, and such will be the nature consequent to it, and which receives from the soul a more perfect life. But with respect to the natures superior to man, and which have dominion as wholes, it must be admitted, that inferior are produced in more excellent natures, bodies in incorporeal essences, and fabrications in the fabricators of them, and that being circularly comprehended in them, they are governed according to invariable rectitude. The circulations therefore of the celestial orbs are primarily inserted in the celestial circulations of the etherial soul, in which they are perpetually inherent. And the souls of the spheres being extended to the intellect which they participate, are perfectly comprehended by, and are primarily generated in it. Intellect also, both that which is partial, and that which is universal, are comprehended in the more excellent genera. Since therefore secondary natures are always converted to such as are first, and superior natures as paradigms are the leaders of those that are subordinate, both essence and form are derived from more excellent beings to those of an inferior rank, and the latter are primarily produced in the former, so as to derive from them order and measure, and the properties by which they are characterised; while on the contrary such properties do not flow from subordinate natures to such as have a precedency and a greater dignity of essence.

In short, neither are the Gods held in subjection by certain parts of the world, nor are terrestrial natures destitute of their all-preserving influence; but superior powers at the same time that they comprehend all things in themselves, are not comprehended by any thing. And terrestrial natures having their very being in the plenitudes of the Gods, when they become adapted to divine participation, immediately prior to their own proper essence, manifestly possess the Gods which latently pre-subsisted in it.[†]

Farther still, divinity whether it is allotted certain portions of the universe, such as the heavens or the earth, or sacred cities and regions, or certain groves and sacred statues, illuminates all these externally, *viz.* without any alliance to the things themselves, in the same manner as the sun externally enlightens all things with its rays; except that in the latter instance, the illuminating cause is locally, but in the former is impassively, unextendedly, and in short incorporeally external. As therefore, the solar light comprehends in itself the illuminated objects, thus also the power of the Gods, externally comprehends its participants. And as light is present with the air, without being essentially mingled with it; which is evident from no light remaining in the air, when once the illuminating source has departed, though heat is present with it when that which heated is entirely withdrawn; thus also the light of the Gods illuminates in a separate manner, and being firmly established in itself, pervades totally through all things. Indeed, this visible light of the sun, is one, continued, and is every where the same whole, so that it is not possible for any part of it to be separated and cut off from the rest, nor to inclose it on all sides, nor divulse it from its source. After the same manner therefore, the whole world being partible, is divided about the one impartible light of the Gods. But this light is one and every where the same whole, and is impartibly present to all the natures that are able to partake of it. It likewise fills all things through an all-perfect power, and bounds in itself wholes, by a certain infinite causal transcendency; is every where united to itself, and conjoins the terminations with the beginnings of things. But all heaven and the world imitating this light, is circularly convolved, is united to

---

[†] Vid. Iamblich. *de Mysteriis*, sect I, 8, 29 [TTS vol. XVII, p. 32]

itself, conducts the elements in their circular motion, causes all things to be in, and tend to each other, and ends to have juxtaposition with their principles, and produces one connexion and consent of wholes with wholes.

He therefore who surveys this visible image of the Gods (the world) thus united in itself, will be ashamed to have a different opinion of the Gods the causes of it, and to introduce in them divisions, obstructions, and corporeal circumscriptions. For if there is no ratio, no habitude of symmetry, no communion of essence, no connexion either according to power or energy, between the adorning cause and adorned effect; if this be the case, in the former there is neither a certain extension according to interval, nor any local comprehension, or any partible interception, nor any other similar innate equalization in the manner in which the Gods are present. For in things which are of a kindred nature either according to essence or power, or which are in a certain respect similar in species, or homogeneous, a certain mutual comprehension or retention may be perceived; but what coercion, or transition through the universe, or partible circumscription, or local comprehension, or any thing else of the like kind can there be in natures perfectly exempt from the whole of things? For the participants indeed of the divinities are such, that some of them participate etherially, others aerially, and others aquatically of a divine nature. And this the ancients perceiving, employed in their divine operations, adaptations and invocations, conformably to a division of this kind. And thus much concerning the distribution of the Gods in the world.[†]

CHAPTER IV

If, however, the mundane as well as the supermundane Gods are incorporeal, it may be asked how the visible celestial orbs can be Gods? To this we reply, that the celestial Gods are not comprehended by bodies, but that they contain bodies in their divine lives and energies; that they are not converted to body, but that the body which is suspended from their essence is converted to a divine cause; and that body is no impediment to their intellectual and incorporeal perfection, and is not the cause of any molestation to them by its intervention. Hence it does not require an abundant care and attention, but spontaneously and after a certain manner self-motively follows the divinities with which it is connected, nor being in want of any

---

[†] Vid. Iamblich. *de Mysteriis*, sect I, 9 [TTS vol. XVII, p. 33]

manuduction, but by its elevation to the one of the Gods, is also itself uniformly raised by itself.

Indeed, a celestial body is allied in the most eminent degree to the incorporeal essence of the Gods. For as the latter is characterized by unity, so the former is simple. As that is impartible, this is indivisible. And as that is immutable, this after a similar manner is unchanged in quality. If also it is admitted that the energies of the Gods are uniform, this body likewise has one circulation. Besides this, it imitates the sameness of the Gods, by its perpetual and invariable motion according to, and towards the same things, conformably to one reason and order. It likewise imitates the divine life of the Gods by the life which is connascent with the etherial bodies. Hence, neither is a celestial body so constituted as if composed of contrary and different natures, as is the case with our bodies; nor does the soul of the celestial Gods so coalesce with the body suspended from it, as to form one animal from the two; but the animals of these divinities are perfectly similar and united to the Gods from whom they depend; and are throughout whole, uniform, and free from all composition. For more excellent natures always subsisting with invariable sameness in themselves, but inferior being suspended from the dominion of superior beings, yet so as never to draw down this dominion to themselves, wholes likewise being collected into one order and one perfection, and after a certain manner all things in the celestial Gods being incorporeal and throughout divine, because the divine form universally predominates in them, - this being the case, one total essence in the nature of these divinities every where prevails. And thus the visible celestial orbs are all of them Gods, and are after a certain manner incorporeal.†

If, therefore, these divinities as being incorporeal, intellectual, and united, ride as it were in the celestial spheres, they have their origin in the intelligible world, and there intellectually perceiving the divine forms of themselves, they govern the whole of heaven according to one infinite energy. And if being present to the heavens in a separate manner, they lead its perpetual circulations by their will alone, they are themselves unmingled with a sensible nature, and are consubsistent with the intelligible Gods. Indeed, the celestial orbs, those visible statues as it were of the Gods, are generated from, and subsist about, the intelligible Gods, and being thus generated are established in them, and have the image elevated to them which from them also receives its perfection. The divine intellectual forms also which are present to the visible bodies

---

† Vid. Iamblich. *de Mysteriis*, sect I, 17. [TTS vol. XVII, p. 42]

of the Gods, have a subsistence prior to them in a separate manner; but the unmingled and supercelestial intelligible paradigms of them, abide in themselves, containing all things simultaneously in one, according to the eternal transcendency of their nature.

Hence there is one common indivisible bond of them according to intellectual energies. There is also the same bond between them according to the common participations of forms, since there is nothing to intercept them, nor any intervening medium. Indeed, an immaterial and incorporeal essence, being neither separated by places nor subjects, nor defined by any divisible circumscriptions of parts, immediately coalesces in sameness; and the elevation of wholes to *The One*, and the universal dominion of *The One*, collects the communion of the mundane Gods with the divinities that pre-subsist in the intelligible world.

Farther still, the intellectual conversion of secondary to first natures, and the gift of the same essence and power from the primary to the secondary Gods connects their congress into an indissoluble one. In things of different essences indeed, such as soul and body, and in things of different species, such as material forms, and those natures which in any other way are separated from each other, the connascent union is adventitious, being derived from supernal causes, and lost in certain definite periods of time. But the higher we ascend, to the sameness of first causes, both according to form and according to essence, and the more we raise ourselves from parts to wholes, by so much the more shall we discover and survey that union which is eternal, precedaneous and more principal, and which contains about and in itself difference and multitude.

Since, however, the order of all the Gods consists in union, and the first and second genera of them, and the multitude which germinates about them coexist in unity; since also every thing in them is characterized by *The One*; hence the beginning, middle, and end of their essence consubsists according to *The One*. It is not proper, therefore, to enquire whence unity extends to all things in them; for their very being, whatever it may be, consists in *The One*. And secondary genera indeed remain with invariable sameness in *The One* of the first genera. But the latter impart from themselves union to the former; while all of them possess in each other the communion of an indissoluble connexion.

From this cause, therefore, the perfectly incorporeal Gods, are united to the sensible Gods who are connected with bodies. For the visible Gods themselves are external to bodies, and on this account are in the intelligible world. And the intelligible Gods on account of their infinite union comprehend in themselves the apparent divinities; while in the mean time both these are established according to a common union and one energy. In a similar manner, this likewise is the illustrious prerogative of a deific cause and orderly distribution, that the same union of all things pervades from on high as far as to the end of the divine order. And thus much concerning the contact of the sensible with the intelligible Gods.[†]

CHAPTER V

What has been above delivered concerning the mundane Gods is perfectly conformable to the doctrine of Plato, as delivered by him in the *Timæus*, in the speech[‡] of the demiurgus to the junior Gods. For it is there said, "When, therefore, all such Gods as visibly revolve, and all such as become apparent when they please, were generated, he who fabricated this universe thus addressed them: Gods of Gods, of whom I am the demiurgus and father, whatever is generated by me is indissoluble, such being my will in its fabrication. Indeed every thing which is bound is dissoluble; but to be willing to dissolve that which is beautifully harmonized and well composed is the property of an evil nature. Hence, so far as you are generated, you are not immortal, nor in every respect indissoluble, yet you shall never be dissolved, nor become subject to the fatality of death; my will being a much greater and more excellent bond than the vital connectives with which you were bound at the commencement of your generation. Learn now, therefore, what I say to you indicating my desire. Three genera of mortals yet remain to be produced. Without the generation of these, therefore, the universe will be imperfect; for it will not contain every kind of animal in its spacious extent. But it ought to contain them, that it may be sufficiently perfect. Yet if these are generated and participate of life through me they will become equal to the Gods. That mortal natures, therefore, may subsist, and that the universe may be truly all, convert yourselves according to your nature to the fabrication of animals, imitating the power which I employed in your generation. And whatever among these is of such a nature as to deserve the same appellation with immortals, which is called divine, obtains sovereignty in them, and willingly pursues justice and reverences you, - of this I

[†] Vid. Iamblich. *de Mysteriis*, sect I, 19. [TTS vol. XVII, p. 42]

[‡] See the 5th book of this work, in which this speech is admirably discussed by Proclus, though not so fully as in these extracts.

myself will deliver the seed and beginning. It is your business to accomplish the rest; to weave together the mortal and immortal nature; by this mean fabricating and generating animals, causing them to increase by supplying them with nutriment, and receiving them back again when dissolved by corruption."

As the commentary of Proclus on this speech most admirably unfolds its recondite meaning, and is at the same time replete with the most interesting information respecting the mundane Gods, I shall give the following extracts from it, in which the most magnificent exuberance of diction if combined with the greatest fecundity and scientific accuracy of conception.

"The scope of this speech (says Proclus) is to insert demiurgic power and providence in the mundane genera of Gods, to lead them forth to the generation of the remaining kinds of animals, and to place them over mortals, analogously to the father of wholes over the one orderly distribution of the universe. For it is necessary that some things should be primarily generated by the demiurgic monad, and others through other media; the Demiurgus, indeed, producing all things from himself, at once and eternally, but the things produced in order, and first proceeding from him, producing together with him the natures posterior to themselves. Thus, for instance, the celestial produce sublunary Gods, and these generate mortal animals; the Demiurgus at the same time fabricating these in conjunction with the celestial and sublunary divinities. For in speaking he understands all things, and by understanding all things he also makes the mortal genera of animals; these requiring another proximate generating cause, so far as they are mortal, and through this receiving a progression into being. But the character of the words is enthusiastic, shining with intellectual intuitions, pure and venerable as being perfected by the father of the Gods, differing from and transcending human conceptions, delicate and at the same time terrific, full of grace and beauty - at once concise and perfectly accurate. Plato, therefore, particularly studies these things in the imitations of divine speeches; as he also evinces in the *Republic*, when he represents the Muses speaking sublimely, and the prophet ascending to a lofty seat. He also adorns both these speeches with conciseness and venerableness, employing the accurate powers of colons, directly shadowing forth divine intellections through such a form of words. But in the words before us he omits no transcendency either of the grand and robust in the sentences and the names adapted to these devices, or of magnitude in the conceptions and the figures which give completion to this idea. Besides this, also, much distinction and purity, the unfolding of truth, and the illustrious prerogatives of beauty, are mingled with the idea of magnitude, this being especially adapted to the subject things, to the speaker, and to the hearers. For the objects of this speech are, the perfection of the universe, an assimilation to all-perfect animal [*i.e.* to its paradigm], and the generation of all mortal animals; the maker of all things, at the same time, pre-subsisting and adorning all things through exempt transcendency; but the secondary fabricators adding what was wanting to the formation of the universe. All, therefore, being great and divine, as well the persons as the things, and shining with beauty and a distinction from each other, Plato has employed words adapted to the form of the speech.

"Homer, also, when energizing enthusiastically, represents Jupiter speaking, converting to himself the twofold co-ordinations of Gods; becoming himself, as it were, the centre of all the divine genera in the world, and making all things obedient to his intellection. But at one time he conjoins the multitude of Gods with himself without a medium, and at another through Themis as the medium.

> But Jove to Themis gives command to call
> The Gods to council.

"This Goddess pervading every-where collects the divine number, and converts it to the demiurgic monad. For the Gods are both separate from mundane affairs, and eternally provide for all things, being at the same time exempt from them through the highest transcendency, and extending their providence every-where. For their unmingled nature is not without providential energy, nor is their providence mingled with matter. Through transcendency of power they are not filled with the subjects of their government, and through beneficent will, they make all things similar to themselves; in permanently abiding, proceeding, and in being separated from all things, being similarly present to all things. Since, therefore, the Gods that govern the world, and the dæmons the attendants of these, receive after this manner unmingled purity, and providential administration from their father; at one time he converts them to himself without a medium, and illuminates them with a separate, unmingled, and pure form of life. Whence also I think he orders them to be separated from all things, to remain exempt in Olympus, and neither convert themselves to Greeks nor Barbarians; which is the just the same as to say, that they must transcend the twofold orders of mundane natures, and abide immutably in undefiled intellection. But at another time he converts them to a providential attention to secondary natures, through Themis, and calls upon them to direct the mundane battle, and excites different Gods to different works. These divinities, therefore, especially require the assistance of Themis, who contains in herself the divine laws, according to which providence is intimately connected with wholes. Homer, therefore, divinely delivers twofold speeches, accompanying the twofold energies of Jupiter; but Plato, through this one speech, comprehends those twofold modes of discourse. For the Demiurgus renders the Gods unmingled with secondary natures, and causes them to provide for, and give existence to, mortals. But he orders them to fabricate in imitation of himself: and in an injunction of this kind, both these are comprehended, *viz.* the unmingled through the imitation of the father, for he is separate, being exempt from mundane wholes; but providential energy, through the command to fabricate, nourish, and increase mortal natures. Or rather, we may survey both in each; for in imitating the demiurgus, they provide for secondary natures, as he does for the immortals; and in fabricating they are separate from the things fabricated. For every demiurgic cause is exempt from the things generated by it; but that which is mingled with and filled from them is imbecil and inefficacious, and is unable to adorn and fabricate them. And thus much in common respecting the whole of the speech.

"Let us then, in the first place, consider what we are to understand by "Gods of Gods," and what power it possesses: for that this invocation is collective and convertive of multitude to its monad, that it calls upwards the natures which have proceeded to the one fabrication of them, and inserts a boundary and divine measure in them, is clear to those who are not entirely unacquainted with such-like discourses. But how those that are allotted the world by their father are called Gods of Gods, and according to what conception, cannot easily be indicated to the many; for there is an unfolding of one divine intelligence in these names." Proclus then proceeds to relate the explanations given by others of these words; which having rejected as erroneous, he very properly, in my opinion, adopts the following, which is that of his preceptor, the great Syrianus. "All the mundane Gods are not simply Gods, but they are wholly Gods which participate: for there is in them that which is separate, unapparent, and supermundane, and also that which is the apparent image of them, and has an orderly establishment in the world. And that, indeed, which is unapparent in them is primarily a God, this being undistributed and one: but this vehicle which is suspended from their unapparent essence is secondarily a God. For if, with respect to us, man is twofold, one inward, according to the soul, the other apparent, which we see, much more must both these be asserted of the mundane Gods; since divinity also is twofold, one unapparent and the other apparent. This being the case, we must say, that "Gods of Gods" is addressed to all the mundane divinities, in whom there is a connection of unapparent with apparent Gods: for they are Gods that participate. In short, since twofold orders are produced by the Demiurgus, some being supermundane, and others mundane, and some being without, and others with participation [of body], if the Demiurgus now addressed the supermundane orders, he would have alone said to them, "Gods:" for they are without participation [*i.e.* without the participation of body], are separate and unapparent:- but since the speech is to the mundane Gods, he calls them Gods of Gods, as being participated by other apparent divinities. In these also dæmons are comprehended; for they also are Gods, as to their order with respect to the Gods, whose peculiarity they indivisibly participate. Thus also Plato, in the *Phædrus*, when he calls the twelve Gods the leaders of dæmons, at the same time denominates all the attendants of the divinities Gods, adding, 'and this is the life of the Gods.' All these, therefore, are Gods of Gods, as possessing the apparent connected with the unapparent, and the mundane with the supermundane.

CHAPTER VI

And thus much concerning the whole conception of the speech. It is necessary, however, since we have said the words are demiurgic or fabricative, that they should be received in a manner adapted to demiurgic providence. But if these words are intellectual conceptions, and the intellectual conceptions themselves are productions, what shall we say the demiurgus effects in the multitude of mundane Gods by the first words of his speech? Is it not evident we must say that this energy of his is deific? For this one divine intellectual conception which is the first and most simple proceeding from the demiurgus, deifies all the recipients of it, and makes them demiurgic Gods, participated Gods, and Gods unapparent, and at the same time apparent. For this, as has been said, is the meaning of "Gods of Gods." For the term Gods is not alone adapted to them; since they are not alone unapparent; nor the word Gods twice enunciated, as if some one should say Gods and Gods; for every bond of this kind is artificial, and foreign from divine union.

It is also necessary to observe that every mundane God has an animal suspended from him, according to which he is denominated mundane. He has likewise a divine soul, which rules over its depending vehicle; and an immaterial and separate intellect, according to which he is united to the intelligible, in order that he may imitate the world in which all these are contained. And by the animal suspended from him, he is indeed a part of the sensible universe; but by intellect he belongs to an intelligible essence; and by soul he conjoins the impartible life which is in him, with the life that is divisible about body. Such a composition, however, being triple in each mundane God, neither does Plato here deliver the demiurgus speaking to intellects; for intellects subsist in unproceeding union with the divine intellect, and are entirely unbegotten; but soul is the first of generated natures, and a little after the demiurgus addresses these when he says, "since ye are generated." Nor does he represent the demiurgus as speaking only to the animals which are suspended from the souls of these Gods; for they pertain to corporeal natures, and are not adapted to enjoy the one demiurgic intelligence, without a medium. Nor yet does he represent him as speaking to souls by themselves; for they are entirely immortal; but the Gods whom he now addresses are said by him not[†] to be in every respect immortal. If therefore it be requisite for me to say what appears to me to be the truth, the words of the demiurgus are addressed to the composite from soul and animal, *viz.* to the animal which is divine, and partakes of a soul. For intellect does not know the demiurgic will through reason, but through intelligence, or in other words, through intellectual vision; nor through conversion, but through a union with that intellect which ranks as a whole, as being itself intellect, and as it were of the same colour with it. But soul as being reason, and not intellect itself, requires appropriately to its essence the energy of reason, and a rational conversion to the intelligible.[‡] To these, therefore, as being essentially rational, and as being essentialized in reasons, the demiurgic speech proceeds. And it is adapted to them in a twofold respect; first, as being participated by bodies; for they are Gods of those Gods; and secondly, as participating of intellects; for they are Gods of [*viz.* derived from] intellects which are also Gods. And they participate of intellects, and are participable by bodies. Hence the assertions that they are generated, and that they are not entirely immortal, and every thing else in the speech, are appropriately adapted to them, so far as they have a certain co-ordination and connexion with mundane natures, and so far as they are participated by them. But the mandates "learn

---

[†] For μεν ειναι το παμπαν αθανατους in the original, it is necessary to read μη ειναι κ.τ.λ..

[‡] Instead of νοητον, it is requisite to read νοητῳ.

and generate," and every thing else of this kind which is more divine than generated natures, are adapted to them as intellectual essences.

Let us in the next place attend to the meaning of the words, "Of whom I am the demiurgus and father, whatever is generated by me is indissoluble, such being my will in its fabrication." Plato then appears to give a triple division to the energy of the one demiurgus in his production of the junior Gods, *viz.* division into the deific, into that which imparts connexion and into that which supplies a similitude to animal itself. For the address of the demiurgus evinces those to be Gods that proceed from him. But the assertions respecting the indissoluble and dissoluble, by defining the measure of a medium between these, impart a distribution and connexion commensurate to the order of the mundane Gods. And the words calling on them to the fabrication of mortal natures, cause them to be the sources of perfection to the universe, and the fabricators of secondary animals, conformably to the imitation of the paradigm. But through these three energies the demiurgus elevates his offspring to all the intelligible Gods, and establishes them in the intelligible triads. In the one being indeed, [or the summit of these triads] through the first of these energies; for that is primarily deified, in which *The One* is deity, but *being* is the first participant of it. For *The One Itself* is alone deity, without habitude to any thing, and is not participable; but *the one being* in which there is the first participation is God of God. And being is deity as the summit of all things; but *The One* of it is deity as proceeding from *The One* itself, which is primarily God. But through the second of these energies the demiurgus establishes his offspring in the second of the intelligible triads, *i.e.* in eternity itself. For eternity is the cause of this indissoluble permanency to every thing which continues perpetually undissolved. Hence all mundane natures are bound according to the demiurgic will, and have something of the indissoluble through the participation of him; the natures which are primarily indissoluble being different from these, and those that are truly immortal subsisting for his sake. And he establishes them in all-perfect animal [or the third of the intelligible triads] through the third of these energies. For to this the vivific assimilates the mundane Gods, and inserts in them the paradigms of animals which they generate. And this, indeed, will be one scope of generation, the converting and perfecting the proceeding multitude of the Gods. But after the one there will be a triple design, which establishes them in the three intelligible orders.

This second demiurgic intelligence, therefore, after the first which is deific, illuminates the mundane Gods with a firm establishment, an immutable power, and an eternal essence, through which the whole world, and all the divine allotments subsist always the same, participating through the father of an immutable nature and undecaying power. For every thing which is generated from an immoveable cause, is indissoluble and immutable; but all the progeny of a moveable cause are moveable. Hence among mundane natures, such as proceed from the demiurgic cause alone, in consequence of being generated according to an invariable sameness are permanent, and are exempt from every mutable and variable essence. But such as proceed both from this cause, and from other moveable principles, are indeed immutable so far as they proceed from the demiurgus, but mutable so far as they proceed from the latter. For those natures which the demiurgus alone generates, these he fabricates immutable and indissoluble, both according to their own nature, and according to his power and will. For he imparts to them a guardian and preserving power, and he connects their essence in a manner transcendent and exempt. For all things are preserved in a twofold respect, from the power which he contains, and from his providential goodness, which is truly able and willing to preserve every thing which may be lawfully perpetually saved. The most divine of visible natures therefore, are, as we have said, from their own nature indissoluble; but they are likewise so from the demiurgic power which pervades through all things, and eternally connects them. For this power is the guard and the divine law which connectedly contains all things. But a still greater and more principal cause than these is the demiurgic will which employs this power in its productions. For what is superior to goodness, or what bond is more perfect than this, which imparts by illumination union, connects an eternal essence, and is the bound and measure of all things; to which also the demiurgus now refers the cause of immutable power, saying, "such being my will in its fabrication." For he established his own will as a guard over his own proper works, as that which gives union, connexion and measure to the whole of things.

Who the demiurgus, however, is, and who father is, has been unfolded by us before, and will be now also concisely shown. There are then these four; father alone; maker alone; father and maker; maker and father. And father indeed is æther [or bound] being the first procession from *The One*. Father and maker is the divinity who subsists according to the intelligible paradigm [at the extremity of the intelligible order,] and whom Orpheus says, the blessed Gods call Phanes Protogonus. But maker and father is Jupiter, who is now called by himself the demiurgus, but whom the Orphic writers would call the father of works. And maker alone, is the cause of partible fabrication,[†] as the same writers would say. To father alone, therefore, all intelligible, intellectual, supermundane and mundane natures are in subjection. To father and maker, all intellectual, supermundane, and mundane natures are subordinate. To maker and father who is an intellectual deity, supermundane and mundane natures are subservient. But to maker alone, mundane natures alone are in subjection. And all these particulars we learn from the narration of Orpheus; for according to each peculiarity of the four there is a subject multitude of Gods.

CHAPTER VII

In the next place, the demiurgus says: "Every thing, therefore, which is bound is dissoluble, but to be willing to dissolve that which is beautifully harmonized and well composed, is the province of an evil nature." It is requisite then to consider how the dissoluble and indissoluble are asserted of the Gods, and to conjoin proper modes of solution with appropriate bonds. For every thing is not bound after a similar manner, nor is that which is bound in one way, dissolved in different ways. But that which is in a certain respect bound, has also its dissolution according to this mode. That which is in every respect bound, is likewise in every respect dissolved. And that which is bound by itself is also by itself dissolved. But that which is bound by something different from itself, has also on that its dissolution depending. That likewise which is bound in time, is also dissolved according to time. But that which is allotted a perpetual bond, must also be said to be perpetually dissolved. For in short, dissolution is conjoined with every bond. For a bond is not union without multitude; since *The One* does not require a bond. Nor is it an assemblage of many and different things, no longer preserving their characteristic peculiarities. For a thing of this kind is confusion; and that which results from them is one thing, consisting of things corrupted together, but does not become bound. For it is necessary that things that are bound should remain as they are, but not be bound when corrupted. Hence a bond then alone takes place, when there are many things, and which are preserved, having one power connective and collective of them, whether this power be corporeal or incorporeal. If this, however, be the case, things that are bound are united through the bond, and separated, because each preserves its own proper nature.

[†] This divinity is Vulcan.

Every where, therefore, as we have said, a bond has also dissolution connected with it. Bonds, however, and their dissolutions differ in subsisting in a certain respect, and simply, from themselves, and from others, according to time, and perpetually. For in these their differences consist. We must not, therefore, wonder if the same thing is both dissoluble and indissoluble; and if it is in a certain respect indissoluble, and in a certain respect dissoluble. So that the works of the father, if they are indeed indissoluble, are so, as not to be dissolved according to time. But they are dissoluble, as having together with a bond, a separation of the simple things of which they consist, according to the definite causes of things that are bound, existing in him that binds. For as that which is self-subsistent is said to be so in a twofold respect, one, as supplying all things from itself alone, but another, as subsisting indeed from itself, and also from another which is the cause of it, thus also the indissoluble is so, from another,[†] and from itself; just as that which is moved is twofold, and subsists in a similar manner.

To these two modes, however, two modes of dissolution are also opposed; *viz.* that which is dissoluble from another and from itself is opposed to that which is indissoluble from another and from itself. And this, indeed, is dissoluble in itself, as consisting of things that are separate. But in consequence of having in something else prior to itself the causes of its subsistence, by this cause, and according to this mode alone it becomes dissoluble. Again, that which is simply dissoluble in a twofold respect, and which contains in itself the cause of its dissolution, and also receives it from another, is opposed to that which is simply indissoluble in a twofold respect, from itself and from another. These, therefore, are four in number, *viz.* that which is simply indissoluble from another and from itself. And again, that which is indissoluble after a certain manner in a twofold respect; that which is dissoluble after a certain manner in a twofold respect; and that which is dissoluble simply from itself, and from another.[‡] Of these four, however, the first pertains to intelligibles; for they are indissoluble, as being entirely simple, and receiving no composition or dissolution whatever. But the fourth belongs to mortal natures, which are dissoluble from themselves and from others, as consisting of many things, and being composed by their causes in such a way, as to be at a

---

[†] παρ' ετερου is omitted in the original.

[‡] The words και λυτον απλως παρ' εαυτου και παρ' ετερου, are omitted in the original.

certain time dissolved. And the middles pertain to the mundane Gods; for the second and the third of these four concur with them. For after a certain manner, these as being the works of the father are indissoluble; and they are saved from themselves and through his will. And again, they are in a certain respect dissoluble, because they are bound by him; and he contains the productive principle of those simple natures from which they are composed. Every thing, therefore, which is bound is dissoluble; and this is also the case with the works of the father. For these are, all bodies, the composition of animals, and the number of participated souls. But intellects which ride as it were in souls as in a vehicle, cannot be called the works of the father; for they were not generated, but were unfolded into light in an unbegotten manner, as if fashioned within the adyta of his essence, and not proceeding out of them. For there are no paradigms of these, but of middle and last natures; since soul is the first of images. But the wholes such as animals, the participants of soul and intellect, and generated natures, derive their subsistence from intellectual paradigms, of which animal itself is the comprehending cause.

Bodies, therefore, are bound through analogy; for this is the most beautiful bond of them. But animals are bound with animated bonds. And souls which contain something of a partible nature are bound by media, [*viz.* by geometrical, arithmetical and harmonical ratios;] for Plato calls these and all the productive principles of which the soul consists, bonds. Hence the indissoluble in the mundane Gods subsists according to nature; for each of them is generated indissoluble; such being the works of the father through the power, which he contains. They are also indissoluble from the demiurgic will, since they are of a composite nature, and possess the indissoluble with a bond. But there is likewise in a certain respect a dissolution of them, so far as they consist of things of a simple nature, of which the father contains in himself the definite causes. At one and the same time, therefore, they are indissoluble and dissoluble. They are not, however, so indissoluble as the intelligible; for that is indissoluble through transcendency of simplicity. But these are at the same time indissoluble and dissoluble, as consisting of simple natures, and as being perpetually bound. For all the natures that are bound being dissoluble, such as are perpetual, possessing through the whole of time, beauty from the intelligible, divine union, and demiurgic harmony, are indissoluble. But mortal natures are dissoluble alone, because they are connected with the deformity and inaptitude of matter. And the former indeed are beautifully harmonised through the union inserted in them by their harmonizing cause; but this is not the case with the latter, on account of the multitude of causes which no longer insert in them a similar union;† for their union is dissipated through the multitude which is mingled in their composition; so that they are very properly allotted a remitted‡ harmony.

Hence, every thing which is bound is dissoluble. But one thing is thus dissoluble and indissoluble, and another is dissoluble only, just as the intelligible is alone indissoluble. Why, therefore, is that which is primarily bound at one and the same time dissoluble and indissoluble? Because it is *beautifully* harmonized, and is *well* composed. For from being *well* composed it obtains union; since *goodness* is unific. But from the intelligible it obtains the *beautifully*; for from thence beauty is derived. And from fabricating power it obtains *harmony*; for this is the cause of the Muses, and is the source of harmonical arrangement to mundane natures. Hence we again have the three causes, the final through the *well*, the paradigmatic through the *beautifully*; and the demiurgic through the *harmonized*.§ But it is necessary that a composition of this kind, harmonized by the one fabricating power, filled with divine beauty, and obtaining a boniform union, should be indissoluble; for the demiurgus says, that to dissolve it is the province of an evil nature.

Moreover, prior to this Plato had said, that the universe is indissoluble except by him by whom it was bound. If, however, it is entirely impossible for the universe to be dissolved by any other, but the father alone is able to dissolve it, and it is impossible for him to effect this, for it is the province of an evil nature, - it is impossible for the universe to be dissolved. For either he must dissolve it, or some other. But if some other, who is it that is able to offer violence to the demiurgus? For it is impossible that a dissolution of it should be effected, except by him that bound it. But if he dissolves it, how being good, can he dissolve that which is beautifully harmonized and well composed. For that which is subversive of these, is productive of evil; just as that which is subversive of evil is allotted a beneficent nature. Hence, there is an equal necessity that the demiurgus should be depraved, if it be lawful so

---

† For ενδοσιν, it is necessary to read ενωσιν.

‡ Κεχαρασμενην is erroneously printed for κεχαλασμενην.

§ After την παραδειγματικην it is necessary to supply the words δια του καλως, την δημιουργικην, which are wanting in the original.

to speak, or that this world should be dissolved, [*viz.* each of these is equally impossible.] Such, therefore, is the necessity which Plato assigns to the incorruptibility of the universe. Hence, that Plato gives the indissoluble to the composition of the mundane Gods, he clearly manifests when he orders them to bind mortal natures, not with those indissoluble bonds with which they are connected. For if the connective bonds of these Gods are indissoluble, they themselves must be essentially indissoluble. Here, however, he says that they are not in every respect indissoluble. It is evident, therefore, from both these assertions, that they are indissoluble, and at the same time dissoluble,[†] and that they are not in every respect indissoluble, in consequence of their being appropriately bound. But if these things are true, there is every necessity that the dissolution of them should be very different from that which we call corruption. For that which is dissoluble after such a manner as the corruptible, not being indissoluble, is so far from being not in every respect indissoluble, that it is in every respect dissoluble. Hence it is not proper to say that the mundane Gods are of themselves corruptible, but remain incorruptible through the will of the father; but we ought to say that they are in their own nature[‡] incorruptible.

CHAPTER VIII

In the next place let us attend to the meaning of the following part of the speech of the demiurgus to the mundane Gods, as beautifully unfolded by Proclus: "Hence so far as you are generated, you are not immortal, nor in every respect indissoluble, yet you shall never be dissolved, nor become subject to the fatality of death; my will being a much greater and more excellent bond than the vital connectives with which you were bound at the commencement of your generation." Since all the mundane Gods to whom these words are addressed consist of divine souls, and animals suspended from them, or in other words, since they are participated souls, and since the demiurgus denominates them indissoluble and at the same time dissoluble, in the way above explained, he now wishes to collect in one point of view, and into one truth, all that he had said separately about them. For at one and the same time he takes away from them the immortal and the indissoluble, and again confers these on them through a subversion of their opposites.

[†] The words και λυτοι are omitted in the original.

[‡] For αυτου φυσιν, it is necessary to read αυτων φυσιν.

For media are allotted this nature, not receiving the nature of the extremes, and appearing to comprehend the whole of both. Just as if some one should call the soul impartible and at the same time partible, as consisting of both, and neither impartible, nor partible, as being different from the extremes. For see how a middle of this kind may be surveyed in the mundane Gods.

That is principally and primarily called immortal, which supplies itself with immortality; since that also is primarily being which is being from itself; intellect which is intellect from itself; and one which is from itself one. For every where that which primarily possesses any thing is such from itself; since if it were not so from itself but from another, that other would be primarily, either intellect, or life, or *The One*, or something else; and either this would be primarily so, or if there is nothing primarily, the ascent will be to infinity. Thus therefore, that is truly immortal, which is immortal from itself, and which imparts to itself immortality. But that which is neither vital according to the whole of itself, nor self-subsistent, nor possesses immortality from itself, is not primarily immortal. Hence as that which is secondarily being is not being, so that which is secondarily immortal is not immortal, yet it is not mortal; for this is entirely a defection or departure from the immortal, neither possessing a connascent life, nor infinite power. For these three are in a successive order: That which possesses from itself infinite life; that which receives infinite life from another; and that which neither from itself nor another exhibits the infinity of life. And the first indeed, is immortal; the second is not immortal; the third is mortal; and the mean is adapted to the mundane Gods. For they neither have the immortal from themselves, so far as they derive it from that which is truly and primarily immortal, and so far as bodies are suspended from them; nor have they a finite life; but they are filled indeed from the eternal Gods, and produce mortal natures. For the second fabrication is connected with the first, proceeds about it, is governed by it, and refers to it the production of the mortal genera.

Again, with respect to the indissoluble, that which is principally and primarily so is simple and free from all composition. For where there is no composition what representation can there be of dissolution? But that is secondarily indissoluble, which is indissoluble with a bond; which is at the same time dissoluble in consequence of proceeding from divided causes. For it is not simply dissoluble, but dissoluble by its cause. For that which is bound prior to all time, is alone bound according to cause; but that which is alone causally bound, is alone causally dissolved. And the third from that which is properly indissoluble is that which was indissoluble for a certain time; because the first indeed, is properly indissoluble in conjunction with simplicity; but the second is subordinately so, together with composition: and the third, falling off from both, is in its own nature dissoluble.

Neither therefore, are the mundane Gods entirely indissoluble; for this pertains to the most simple natures. Nor are they dissoluble according to time; for the composition of them proceeds from the demiurgic union. As therefore in the cause union precedes things of a simple nature, after the same manner here also, a bond precedes dissolution; for it is more excellent, and the resemblance of a more divine power. And this is seen in souls; for there were bonds and media in them, as has been before observed in the generation of the soul. It is also seen in bodies; for analogy is a bond. And likewise in animals; for being bound with animated bonds they become animals. Hence, the immortal and the indissoluble, do not entirely pertain to the mundane Gods; yet at the same time they do pertain to them. And because they are not in every respect present with them nor in such a manner as in intelligibles, immortality must be taken from them. For in the *Banquet* also, Plato does not think fit to call Love immortal, yet he does not denominate it mortal; but asserts it to be something between both these. For there is a great extent of the mortal and immortal, and they are bound together by many media. It appears likewise, with respect to the immortal, that one kind of it is common to all the beings that differ from a mortal nature,[†] and which consists in not being deprived of the life which it possesses. According to this sense of the word, Plato says that the demiurgus is the cause of immortal natures, but the junior Gods, of such as are mortal. But another kind of the immortal is the peculiarity of intelligibles, being eternally so. And another belongs to the mundane Gods, which is an immortality perpetually rising into existence, and having its subsistence in always becoming to be. Hence, it may be said that the immortal and mortal are oppositely divided without a medium, if the common signification of the immortal is assumed; and that they are not opposed to each other without a medium, if that which is primarily immortal is considered; and this is that which *is* always immortal. For the medium between this and the mortal, is that which is always *becoming to be* immortal. But that which is properly immortal possesses the whole of its life in eternity. That however which has its life evolved through the whole of time, and has not always one and the same indivisible life, this possesses an immortality coextended with the

---

[†] Instead of του μη θνητου, it is necessary to read του θνητου.

flux of generation, but is not immortal according to the stability of being. And again, the medium between the immortality of the mundane Gods and that of partial souls, is that which has a life always rising into existence, and which ascends and descends in intellectual energy, so as to be nearer to mortal natures, leaving indeed a more excellent intellection, but transferring itself into one that is subordinate, and again recurring to its pristine condition without oblivion. And of these, the former indeed, is the peculiarity of the mundane Gods; but the latter, of dæmons the attendants on these Gods. But if the nature which remains is filled with oblivion in descending, becomes most proximate to mortals, entirely destroys the true life which it contains, and alone possesses the essential life, - such an immortality as this belongs to partial souls. Hence, the demiurgus in his speech calls the immortality in these homonymous to that of the immortals. If however, there is any nature after these which casts aside its essential life, this is alone[†] mortal. Hence, the primarily immortal and the mortal are the extremes. But the immortality of the mundane Gods, and that of partial souls, are the sub-extremes. And the immortality which is truly the medium between these, is that of dæmons. Hence too, dæmons are in reality entirely of a middle nature.

CHAPTER IX

After this, the demiurgus sublimely addresses the mundane Gods in the following words: "Learn now therefore what I say to you indicating my desire." The first address to the mundane Gods, says Proclus, was deific of or deified the auditors; for it evinced all of them to be Gods, and to be participated by the bodies in which they ride. For these very bodies also are Gods, as being the statues [as it were] of Gods; since Plato likewise calls the earth the first and most ancient of the Gods within the heavens. But these deified bodies are participants of the Gods truly so called, from which they are suspended, and which are prior to generation. For these bodies have, as we have observed, generation. But the second address to the mundane Gods, inserted in them an eternal power, through the participation of an indissoluble connexion. And the present words fill them with divine, and demiurgic conceptions, proceeding supernally from intelligible animal [the paradigm of the universe.] For the being instructed in the fabrication of animals, so far as it is mathesis or learning, is adapted to soul. But these words fill the

---

[†] The original has erroneously μονας instead of μονον.

multitude of Gods with the demiurgic intelligence of all the forms that are contained in intelligible animal. And through the word *now* indeed, the *eternal* is after a manner indicated; through the word *what* the united, and convolved; through *I say*, that which proceeds into multitude, and is disseminated about the many Gods; and through *indication* a plenitude derived from intelligible and unapparent causes is signified. For we only *indicate* in things unapparent to the multitude. But through all the words together it is evident that the demiurgus establishes himself analogous to intelligible intellect, and fills the mundane number of Gods with intellectual conceptions. Farther still, these words convert this multitude to the one demiurgic intelligence, and prior to a providential attention to secondary natures, illuminate it with unmingled purity, and stable intellection. For as the demiurgus makes by energizing intellectually, and generates from inward, externally proceeding energy, thus also he wishes the mundane Gods first to learn and understand the will of their father, and thus afterwards to imitate his power.

In the next place, the demiurgus says, "Three genera of mortals yet remain to be produced. Without the generation of these therefore, the universe will be imperfect; for it will not contain every kind of animal in its spacious extent. But it ought to contain them that it may be sufficiently perfect. Yet if these are generated and participate of life through me they will become equal to the Gods." On these words Proclus observes: The most total, first, and most divine of ideas, not only give subsistence to such mundane natures as are perpetual, in an exempt manner, but likewise to all mortal natures, according to one united cause. For the idea of winged natures which is there is the paradigm of all winged animals whatever; the idea of the aquatic, of all aquatic; and the idea of the pedestrial, of all pedestrial animals. But the progressions of intelligibles into the intellectual orders, become the sources of division to united ideas, produce into multitude total causes, and unfold the definite principles of multiform natures. For there is no longer in intelligibles one intellectual cause of all aerial animals; since there is not a separate intellection of perpetual animals of this kind; nor one intellectual cause of aquatic, nor in a similar manner of terrestrial animals; but the power of difference [in the intellectual order] minutely distributes the whole into parts, and monads into numbers. Hence the causes of divine animals, according to which the demiurgus gives subsistence to the orders of Gods and dæmons that produce generation, exist in him separate from the causes of mortal natures, according to which he calls on the junior Gods to generate mortal animals. For the demiurgus precedes the generative energy of these Gods, and makes by merely saying that a thing is to be made. For the words of the father are demiurgic intellections, and his intellections are creations; but a proximate making is adapted to the multitude of Gods. And again you see how the order of effective and generative causes in unfolded into light. For the choir of mundane Gods produces indeed mortal animals, but in conjunction with motion and mutation.† And the demiurgus also produces them but by speaking, *viz.* by intellection. For he speaks indeed, intellectually perceiving, and immovably and intellectually. Animal itself also produces them; for it contains the one cause of all winged, of all aquatic, and of all terrestrial animals. But it produces them with silence, by its very essence and intelligibly. For the demiurgic speech receives indeed the paternal silence, but the intellectual production, the intelligible cause, and the generation which subsists according to energizing, the providence according to existence. Motion also receives the demiurgic words, but the orderly distribution which is mingled with a sensible nature, receives the intellectual energy. For the fabrications which exist at the extremity of things require a producing cause of this kind. Every thing therefore which is mutable, which is changed in quality, which is generated and corruptible, is generated from a cause, immoveable indeed according to essence, but moved according to energy. For the motion which is there separated from essence, here produces an essence which is moved. Hence, because that which makes, makes both according to essence and according to energy, both which are as it were woven together, mutation of essence thence derives its progression. Mortal natures therefore require moveable causes, and those that are very mutable, many such causes. For it is impossible that they should remain only-begotten; since the mortal genera would not have an existence.

It is necessary however, that the mortal nature should exist, in the first place, in order that every thing may have a subsistence which is capable of being generated, *viz.* both perpetual beings, and those which at a certain time cease to exist. For beyond these is that which in no respect whatever is. In the next place this is necessary, in order that divine natures and being may not be the last of things; since that which is generative of any thing is more excellent and more divine than the thing which it generates. And in the third place it is necessary in order that the world may not be imperfect, not comprehending every thing the

---

† For μετα βουλης, I read μεταβολης. For the mundane Gods are in no part of the *Timæus* represented in consulting about the fabrication of things.

causes of which are contained in animal itself. For the ideas which are there, are the causes of every thing whether divine or mortal. Hence Orpheus says that the vivific cause[†] of partible natures, while she remained on high weaving the order of celestials, was a nymph, as being undefiled, and in consequence of this connected with Jupiter, and abiding in her appropriate manners; but that proceeding from her proper habitation, she left her webs unfinished, was ravished, having been ravished was married, and being married generated, in order that she might animate things which have an adventitious life. For the unfinished state of her webs indicates, I think, that the universe is imperfect or unfinished as far as to perpetual animals. Hence Plato says, that the one demiurgus calls on the many demiurgi to weave together the mortal and immortal natures, after a manner reminding us that the addition of the mortal genera is the perfection of the textorial life of the universe, and also exciting our recollection of the divine Orphic fable, and affording us interpretative causes of the unfinished webs [of Proserpine].

The divine number therefore, has its proper boundary and end, and is perfect. But it is also necessary that the mortal nature should exist, and have an appropriate limit; and this triply, aerially, aquatically and terrestrially. For celestially, is impossible, because the summit, and the first genus of every order is undefiled and perpetual, in consequence of being assimilated to the cause which is prior to it. As therefore, the first of intellectuals is intelligible, and the first of angels is a God, thus also the first of sensibles is perpetual and divine.

When however the demiurgus says, "Yet if these are generated and participate of life through me they will become equal to the Gods," he confirms what has been before asserted, that every thing which is produced by an immoveable cause is unbegotten and immutable; but that every thing which is produced indeed by an immoveable cause, yet through the medium of a cause that is moved, is partly unbegotten, and partly mutable. For from the immoveable cause indeed it receives unity, but from the moveable cause multitude. And from the former it derives being and form, but from the latter individuality, and a flowing existence; through which the form or species is preserved, but the individual is destroyed.

[†] *i.e.* Proserpine.

CHAPTER X

After this, the demiurgus says, "That mortal natures therefore may subsist, and that the universe may be truly all, convert yourselves according to nature to the fabrication of animals, imitating the power which I employed in your generation." A twofold scope of fabrication, says Proclus, is here delivered, one indeed providential, but the other assimilative; the one being more proximate, but the other more total. For to fabricate for the sake of giving subsistence to mortal natures, indicates providence, and the perfection[†] of power. For all superplentitude of power is prolific of other things subordinate to itself. But to fabricate for the sake of giving completion to the universe, indicates an energy according to assimilative power, in order that this universe may be rendered similar to all-perfect animal, in consequence of being adorned with all the numbers of divine and mortal animals. For if all things were immortal, the most divine[‡] of sensible natures would be unprolific. And if the universe was not filled with all the forms of life, it would not be perfect, nor sufficiently similar to all-perfect animal. That neither of these defects therefore might happen, the first demiurgus excites the second fabrication supernally from his own exalted place of survey. He also pours on the mundane Gods vivific and demiurgic power, through which they generate from themselves secondary essences, fill them with life, and give them a specific distinction. For the peculiarity of vivific deity is to vivify, but of demiurgic deity to be productive of form. The expression therefore "*convert yourselves*" is of an exciting nature, and is similar to the mandate of Jupiter to the Gods in Homer,

> Haste, to the Greek and Trojan hosts descend.[§]

For as that calls them to the war of generation, so this in Plato excites them to the fabrication of mortals, which they effect through motion. And this indeed is accomplished by all the mundane Gods, but especially by the governors of the world [or the planets], and in the most eminent degree by the sovereign sun. For the demiurgus gave him dominion

---

[†] For τελειοτατα, it is necessary to read τελειοτητα.

[‡] For τα θειοτα, it is necessary to read τα θειοτατα.

[§] Iliad xx 24.

over wholes, fabricated him as a guardian, and ordered him, as Orpheus says,

> . . . . O'er all to rule.

The words likewise, "according to nature," bound their fabrication according to measure and the good: and besides this, spread under them all physical production as an instrument to their energies. This therefore which is subservient to their will they move and govern. And in the third place, these words define their subsistence as media; for it pertains to the middle to fabricate the extremes according to nature. For things which sometimes have an existence are suspended from those that are perpetual according to time; and the latter are suspended from eternal entities. And primary natures indeed are generative of media; but these are productive of such beings as are last in the series of things. The word "*yourselves*" also which denotes manual operation, excites the divine lives themselves to fabrication. Nor ought we to wonder whence demiurgic power is derived to divine souls, this being the peculiarity of the superessential Gods. For as Orpheus, placing an intellectual essence in Jupiter, renders it demiurgic, thus also Plato producing words from the father, evinces that the souls which rank as wholes are divine and demiurgic. Nor must we doubt why of mundane natures† some are immortal, but others mortal, since all of them are generated according to intelligible causes; for some of them proceed from one, but others from another proximate producing cause. And it is necessary to look to these, and not to paradigms alone. Nor must we investigate ideas of Socrates, Plato, or of any thing that ranks as a particular. For the demiurgus divides mortal animals according to genera, and stops at total intellections; and through these comprehends every thing of a partial nature. For as the demiurgus makes that which is material immaterially, and that which is generated ingenerably, thus also he produces mortal natures immortally.‡ For he makes these indeed, but through the junior Gods; since prior to their making, he made by intellection alone. Nor must we deny that mortal natures subsist also divinely, and not mortally only. For the things which the demiurgus now extends in his speech are hypostases or subsisting natures about the junior or mundane Gods, which the heavens primarily receive; and according to which the Gods fabricate the mortal genera. For the monads of every mortal-formed life

---

† Instead of δια τινων εγκοσμιων, it is necessary to read δια τι των εγκοσμιων.

‡ αθανατως is omitted in the original.

proceed into the heavens from the intelligible forms. But from these monads which are divine, all the multitude of material animals is generated. For if we adopt these conceptions, we shall accord with Plato, and shall not wander from the nature of things.

Again, when the demiurgus says, "*Imitating the power which I employed about your generation,*" we must understand by this that an assimilation to the one exempt fabrication of things, and a conversion to it, is the highest end of the second fabrication. For it is necessary that self-motive should follow immoveable natures, and such as are very mutable, such as are always moved, and that there should be perpetually a series of secondary beings assimilated to those that are prior to them. Since however there was a divine will and a divine power in the demiurgus, he unfolds his will to the mundane Gods through *learning*; and through this perfects their demiurgic will. But he unfolds his power to them through this *imitation*, according to which he orders them to imitate the power of the one demiurgus, conformably to which they were generated by him. For by saying that which he wills, he imparts to them will; and by saying that which he is able to effect, he supplies them with power. And in the last place he demonstrates them to be secondary fabricators imitators of their father. Whether, therefore, there is a mundane power, or an efficacious energy of dæmons, or a fortitude and supernatural strength of heroes, to all this the demiurgus gives subsistence, and imparts it to those that give completion to the whole of the second fabrication. For the first power is in him, and the monad of demiurgic powers. Since, however, he is also intellect and father, all things will be in him, *viz.* father, the power of the father, and the paternal intellect. Hence Plato was not ignorant of this division; and on this account the demiurgus as being father, calls power his power. This also he manifests by adding, "*which I employed about your generation.*" For the father is the cause of this in conjunction with power; just as father here in conjunction with the female is the cause of the propagation of the human species. [For power is of a feminine characteristic.]

CHAPTER XI

And thus much for the development of such particulars in the speech of the demiurgus as relate to the junior or mundane Gods. Others, however, no less important respecting the fabrication of these Gods remain to be collected from another part of the *Timæus*; and which accompanied with the admirable elucidations of Proclus are as follow:

After the demiurgus had instructed souls in all that was necessary to their well being, and had disseminated some of them into the earth, others into the moon, and others into the remaining different instruments of time, Plato adds: "But after this semination he delivered to the junior Gods the province of fabricating mortal bodies, and generating whatever else remained necessary to the human soul; and gave them dominion over every thing consequent to their fabrications." Who the junior Gods are, says Proclus, must now be shown; for that the mundane Gods are thus denominated is evident. But it seems they are thus called by Plato, either from a comparison with the more ancient dignity of the unapparent [i.e. the intellectual] fabrication, and with the transcendency of the power in it, and the perfection of intellectual vision. For that which is more intellectual is with the Gods more ancient.

"But Jove was born the first, and more he knows," says Homer. Or they are thus denominated, because they always make generation to be new; and when it becomes old and imbecil through its subject nature, again recall it to a subsistence according to nature by their motions, sending into it effluxions of all-various productive principles and powers, and thus render it perpetually new. Or, they are thus called, because having intellectual essences suspended from them, they eternally energize with the acme of intellectual vigor. For as the poets say, Hebe pours out their wine, and they drink nectar, and survey the whole sensible world. Employing, therefore, immutable and undeviating intellections, they fill all things with their demiurgic providence. Or they have this appellation, because Curetic deity is present with them. [or deity belonging to the order of the Curetes,] illuminating their intellectual conceptions with purity, their motion with inflexibility, and supplying the whole of them with rigid power, through which they govern all things without departing from the characteristics of their nature. Or, which is the truest reason of all the preceding, they are thus denominated, because the monad of them is called the *recent* God. For theologists give this appellation to Bacchus, who is the monad of all the second fabrication. For Jupiter established him the king of all the mundane Gods, and distributed to him the first honours. On this account also, theologists are accustomed to call the sun *a recent God*, and Heraclitus says, that the sun is *a diurnal youth*, as participating of Dionysiacal power. Or, for a reason most appropriate to Platonic principles, they are thus denominated, because bodies which have generation are suspended from them; and the essence of these is not allotted a subsistence in eternity, but in the whole of time. They are junior, therefore, not as once beginning to exist, but as being always generated, and as we have before observed, subsisting in becoming to be, or perpetually rising into existence. For every thing which is generated has not the whole of what it possesses present at once, nor a simultaneous infinity, but an infinity which is perpetually supplying. Thus, therefore, they are called junior, as having a subsistence co-extended with time, and always advancing into existence, and as possessing a renovated immortality.

Again, the delivery of the first fabrication is a communication and generation of demiurgic powers, exempt from every thing which the second fabrication produces proximately, a progression of production from the unapparent into the apparent, and a division of uniform power into the multiplied government of the world. But the formation of bodies assimilates the junior Gods to the unapparent fabrication. For that was the cause of bodies that rank as wholes, just as they are the causes of partial bodies, at the same time exhibiting a diminution of power. For of the body of which they are the makers and formers, the demiurgus also is the cause; but they are the formers of partial bodies, which are bodies endued with certain qualities. Hence body indeed is simply unbegotten as from time, and incorruptible as was also the opinion of Aristotle. "For," says he, "there would be a vacuum if body could be generated, external[†] to the body of the universe." But this *particular* body is corruptible, as being of a partial nature; for the *wholes* of the elements derived their subsistence from *total* fabrication. The accession, however, of the human soul which remained[‡] to be generated, assimilates the mundane Gods to the paternal power. For it is the province of a father to generate life; since the first father, and every father is the cause of life; the intelligible father, indeed, of intelligible, but the intellectual of intellectual, and the supermundane of supermundane life. And hence, the mundane Gods who generate corporeal life are fathers. The fabrication, however, adapted to these Gods, produces the nature of partial animals. For this partial animal which is suspended from the immortal soul, consists of soul and body. But the *dominion* which the demiurgus gave the junior Gods, excites their providential inspection, their connective power, and their guardian comprehensions. For without these, the bodies that are fashioned, and the mortal form of life, would rapidly vanish into non-entity. Prior,

---

[†] For εξ ου σωματος, it is necessary to read εξω σωματος.

[‡] For λοπης, it is requisite to read λοιπης.

therefore, to the generation of these, the demiurgus made their ruling Gods to be the guardians and saviours of them. In the junior Gods, therefore, there are demiurgic powers, according to which they invest generated natures with forms; vivific powers, according to which they give subsistence to a secondary life; and perfective powers, through which they give completion to what is deficient in generation. There are also many other powers in them besides these, which are inexplicable by our conceptions.

CHAPTER XII

After this, Plato adds, "He likewise commanded them to govern as much as possible in the best and most beautiful manner the mortal animal, that it might not become the cause of evil to itself." On these words Proclus observes: Of all that the one demiurgus delivers to the junior Gods, it must be admitted that there are three most beautiful boundaries, the boniform will of him that delivers, the perfect power of the recipients, and the symmetry of both these with each other. Of the demiurgic production, however, of the junior Gods themselves, three elements and these the greatest must be again surveyed, a reduction to the good, a conversion to intelligible beauty, and a liberated power sufficient to rule over all the subjects of its government. For as Phanes,[†] himself the demiurgus of wholes, rendered the whole world as much as possible the most beautiful and the best, thus also he was willing that the second fabricators should govern the mortal animal in a way the most beautiful and the best; pouring on them indeed from intelligibles, beauty, but filling them with that boniform power and will, which he himself possessing fabricated the whole world. For thus generation also will participate of beauty and goodness, as far as it is naturally adapted to such participation, if the Gods by whom it is connected and contained, adorn it, who are themselves transcendently decorated with beauty and good.

If, however, the second demiurgi have such a nature as this, nothing evil or preternatural is generated from the celestial Gods; nor is it proper to divide the Gods in the heavens after this manner, as many do, *viz.* into the beneficent and malignant; for being Gods this is impossible. But the mortal animal is the cause of evil to itself. For neither disease,

---

[†] *i.e.* Jupiter, who is so called in this place by Proclus, because he contains in himself by participation, the Phanes or Protogonus who is the paradigm of the universe.

nor poverty,† nor any thing else of this kind is evil; but the depravity of the soul, intemperance, timidity, and every vice. Of these things, however, we are the causes to ourselves. For though being impelled by others to these vices we are badly affected, yet again it is through ourselves; since we have the power of associating with the good, and separating ourselves from the bad. According to Plato, therefore, we must not think that of the Gods some are malignant and others beneficent, but we must admit that all of them are the sources to mortals of all the good which they are able to receive; and that things which are truly evils are not produced, but are only signified by them, as we have before observed. For they extend terrific appearances and signs to those who are able to see and read the letters in the universe, which the framers of mortal natures during their revolutions write by their configurations. And though some one should derive a certain evil from the motions of the celestial Gods, so as to become timid or intemperate, yet they operate in one way, and their influences are participated by souls in another. For the efflux of intellect, says Plotinus, becomes craft in him who receives the efflux badly; the gift of an elegant life becomes intemperance through a similar cause; and in short, while they produce beneficently, their gifts are participated by terrestrial natures, after a contrary manner. Hence the givers who bestow beneficently are not to be accused as the authors of evil, but the recipients who pervert their gifts by their own inaptitudes. Thus also Jupiter in Homer blames souls as in vain accusing the Gods, while they themselves are the causes of evils. For the Gods are the sources of good, and the suppliers of intellect and life, but are not the causes of any evil; since even a partial nature is not the cause of evil to its offspring. What, therefore, ought we to think concerning the Gods themselves? Is it not, that they are much more the causes of good to their productions; since with them there is power, with them there is a self-perfect nature, with them there is universal goodness, to all which evil is contrary. For in its own nature it is powerless, imperfect, and without measure.

In the next place Plato says, "At the same time he who orderly disposed all these particulars, remained in his own accustomed manner." And Proclus observes, that Plato every where after having employed many words, summarily comprehends the multitude of them in the conclusion. For he knew that in the Demiurgus, one intellectual perception comprehends the multitude of intellectual conceptions; that one power connects many powers; and that a uniform cause collects into

---

† For πονηρια, it is necessary to read πενια.

one union divided causes. Hence the words [prior to these], "Having, therefore, instructed souls in all these particulars," and the words before us, "He who orderly disposed all these particulars," lead the distinct energy of the Demiurgus to an united cause. Farther still, the word *all* manifests that which is consummated from all its appropriate boundaries. But the words *orderly disposed*, indicate the order pervading through all beings, which the Demiurgus introduced to the mundane Gods, and to partial souls; demonstrating the former to be demiurgi, but inscribing in the latter the laws of Fate. Moreover, the word *remained*, does not manifest station, and inflexible intellection, but *an establishment*[†] *in the one*. For according to this, he is exempt from wholes, and is separated from the beings that intellectually perceive him. But this establishment itself is eternal, and always invariably permanent. These things, therefore, are also indicated by the words *accustomed* and *manner*; the one exhibiting sameness of permanency; but the other the peculiarity of the demiurgic stability. For *manner* is indicative of peculiarity; since connective is different from immutable, and both these from demiurgic permanency.

CHAPTER XIII

"But in consequence of his abiding," says Plato, "as soon as his children understood the order of their father, they became obedient to it." When the Demiurgus speaks, says Proclus, then the junior Gods have the order of hearers. When he intellectually perceives, then they learn; for learning is dianoetic. When he abides according to union itself, then his children intellectually perceive. For they always receive from him an inferior order. And as filled indeed from him, they preserve the analogy of hearers with reference to him; but as evolving his one power, they are analogous to learners. For he who learns evolves the intellect of his preceptor. As being deified, however, by him, they have the analogy of those that perceive intellectually. For intellect becomes deific, by its contact[‡] with *The One*. The father, therefore, abiding, his children very properly intellectually perceive. For they are intellects participated by divine souls, that ride in the vehicles of undefiled bodies. But they intellectually perceive the order of the father pre-subsisting in him prior to the arranged effects, according to which order he became all things.

[†] For ιδρυαν, it is necessary to read ιδρυσιν.

[‡] σαφη is erroneously printed for αφη.

504

Mortal natures, therefore, were fashioned and animated by the demiurgic intellection alone. But the junior Gods unfold his total production, through their own manifest fabrication; being filled from the demiurgic monad.

In the last place, Plato adds, "And receiving the immortal principle of mortal animal, in imitation of their artificer, they borrowed from the world the parts of fire and earth, water and air, as things which they should restore back again; and conglutinated the received parts together, but not with the same indissoluble bonds by which they were connected." On these words Proclus admirably comments as follows: Plato indicates to us, the separation of the second from the first fabrication, through many words and steps.† For if the Demiurgus orderly disposes, but the junior Gods are obedient to his mandates, the former by merely commanding is the cause of generated natures, but the latter being excited by the Demiurgus, receive from thence the boundary of the whole of their fabrication. And if, indeed, he abides in himself, but they are moved about him, it is evident that he is eternally the cause of things which subsist in time, but that they being filled from him energize according to the whole of time. And if he perfectly establishes himself in his own accustomed manner, but they proceeding from him, unfold into light this united and ineffable disposition of himself, they derive from him secondary measures of fabrication.

Moreover, he is said to have a paternal dignity, but they are denominated his children, as expressing his prolific power, and his single goodness. And he indeed, is celebrated as delivering from his exalted abode the principles of fabrication; but they are celebrated as receiving the immortal principle contributing to the orderly distribution of mortals. He is said to have the fountain of the vivification of perpetual natures; but they are the causes of the subsistence of mortal-formed animals. And he indeed extends himself as a paradigm to the many Gods; but they are said to imitate the demiurgic intellect. He is said to produce the whole world, and the plenitudes of it; but they are said to borrow parts from the fabrications of their father, in order to the completion of their proper works. And he indeed employs all incorporeal powers; but they also employ such as are corporeal. He gives subsistence to indissoluble bonds; but they to such as are dissoluble. And he, indeed, is said to insert a union more ancient than the natures which it unites; but they are said to introduce an adventitious union, and which is of an origin posterior to this, to the

---

† For καὶ βαθεων, it is necessary to read καὶ βαθμων.

beings that consist of many contrary natures. And he is said to produce all things impartibly; but they with division, minutely distributing the subsistence of mortal natures into small and invisible nails. From these things, therefore, the separation of the two fabrications may be assumed; but the union and contact of them may be surveyed from the words before us. For here a contact is effected of the second with the first fabrication; of apparent with unapparent, and of divided with monadic production.

Hence it is necessary that the lowest part of the first and unapparent fabrication, should coalesce with the summit of the second. For thus also the heavens are conjoined with generation [or the sublunary region] the lowest of the celestial bodies exhibiting the principle of mutation; but the summit of the essence of sublunary natures, being moved in conjunction with the heavens. Hence too, here also the rational soul is conjoined with the mortal form of life; *viz.* the lowest and most partial of the productions of the father, with the highest of the natures generated by the junior Gods. For they, indeed, as being certain fathers produce lives; but as fabricators, bodies. And they imitate indeed Vulcan by the fabrication of bodies; but Juno by vivification. But through both these they imitate the whole Demiurgus. For he is maker and father; but they fashion bodies by borrowing parts from wholes. For every where parts derive their composition from wholes. When, however, the wholes are incorporeal, they remain undiminished by the subsistence of the parts; but when they are corporeal, the parts that are generated from them diminish the wholes. Hence an ablation always taking place, but the parts always remaining, the wholes perish. And thus generation will no longer exist, and the works of the first fabrication will all vanish through the second, which it is not lawful to assert. That nothing of this kind, therefore, may take place in the universe, the composite parts are again dissolved, in order to fill up their wholes. And the generation of one thing is the corruption of another; but the corruption of one thing is the generation of another; in order that generation and corruption may always remain. For if generation existed only once, it would at a certain time stop, in consequence of consisting of finite things, and these being consumed. But these perishing corruption also would stop, all things being destroyed. Hence if it is necessary that one of these should exist, the other also will exist. Every thing, therefore, which is generated from the second fabrication is a composite and dissoluble, and deriving its composition from time, will also in time be again dissolved. The junior Gods, therefore, are very properly said to borrow parts which are again to be restored to their wholes. But they borrow them from the universe.[†] For that which they borrow is fire, earth, water and air; and they again restore them to the universe.[‡] The father, therefore, wishes the wholes to remain which he generated and arranged. And thus much concerning all the fabrication of the junior Gods.

CHAPTER XIV

Having, therefore, thus largely presented to the reader what pertains to the mundane Gods in general, it is now requisite to descend to particulars, and to discuss separately the peculiarities of the celestial, and those of the sublunary Gods. The order of the celestial Gods then consisting of the fixed stars and the planets, the sphere in which the former are placed has the relation of a monad, as we have before observed, to the starry deities which that sphere contains. For the first of the four ideas in the paradigm of the universe being an exempt monad, the multitude of the stars proceeding from it is comprehended by a co-ordinate monad, which is the inerratic sphere. This sphere is called by Plato in the *Timæus* a true world, because it is more properly a world than the sublunary region, which always requires a foreign arrangement, and is conversant with unceasing mutation. It is also a world thus variegated with stars, as expressing intellectual variety, and receiving from thence as it were in the whole of itself the uniform flowers with which the intellectual world is surrounded, and which imitate the beauty of the celestial paradigms. But Plato very accurately says, that the Demiurgus gave this sphere a circular *distribution* about the whole of the heavens. For to *distribute* and *to distribute in a circle*, is adapted to this sphere; since the former signifies intellectual distribution, but the latter demiurgic order. Hence theologists[§] establish Eumonia in the inerratic sphere, who separates the multitude it contains, and always preserves each of the stars in its proper order. Hence also celebrating Vulcan as the maker of the heavens, they conjoin with him Aglaia, as causing all heaven to be splendid through the variety of the stars. And again, of the Seasons, they place Dice or Justice over the planetary region, as bringing in a circular order the inequability of the

---

[†] For παρρος, it is necessary to read παντος.

[‡] Here also for πατρι, it is necessary to read παντι.

[§] Vid. Proclus in Tim. 275E. [TTS vol. XVI, p. 831]

motions of the planets to an equability according to reason; but of the Graces, Thalia, as causing their lives to be ever-flourishing. And in the sublunary region, they establish Irene or peace, as conciliating the war of the elements; but of the Graces Euphrosune, as conferring on every thing a facility of natural energy.

But the planets are called the Governors of the world, (κοσμοκρατορες) and are allotted a total power. As the inerratic sphere too, has a number of starry animals, so each of the planets is the leader of a multitude of animals, or of certain other things of this kind. Hence the doubt may be solved, why the one sphere of the fixed stars comprehends a multitude of stars, but each of the planetary spheres convolves only one star. For it must be said, that in the former case the sphere indeed is a monad, comprehending in itself an appropriate multitude, and is sufficient to the comprehension of a mundane multitude which ranks as the first. But in the latter case, the governing power is twofold, *viz.* the sphere, and each of the governors of the world, who is a monad co-arranged with multitude. The sphere itself, however, is a leader, a co-arranged monad and a wholeness; (ολοτης) but each of the governors of the world is a leader and a monad, but is not a wholeness. Indeed, subordinate natures require a greater number of leaders, and a multitude in each of the spheres unapparent on account of diminution. But in the sublunary region, the orders which are the leaders of the genera in each of the elements are still more numerous than those of the planets, as we learn from the Grecian theogony.

In each of the planetary spheres, therefore, there is a number of satellites analogous to the choir of the fixed stars, subsisting with proper circulations of their own. The revolution also of these satellites is similar to that of the planets which they follow; and this according to Plato is a spiral revolution. With respect, likewise, to these satellites, the first in order about every planet are Gods; after these dæmons revolve in lucid orbicular bodies; and these are followed by partial souls such as ours. That in each of the planetary spheres, however, there is a multitude co-ordinate to each may be inferred from the extremes. For if the inerratic sphere has a multitude co-ordinate to itself, and earth is with respect to terrestrial animals what the inerratic sphere is to such as are celestial, it is necessary that every *wholeness* should entirely possess certain partial animals co-ordinate to itself, through which also the spheres derive the appellation of *wholenesses*.† But the natures situated in the middle are concealed from our sense, while in the mean time those contained in the extremes are apparent, - one kind through their transcendently luminous essence, and the other through their alliance to ourselves. If also partial souls are disseminated about these spheres, some indeed about the sun, but others about the moon, and others about each of the remaining spheres; and if prior to souls, there are dæmons giving completion to the herds of which they are the leaders; it is evident that it is beautifully said, that *each of the spheres is a world*. And this is conformable to the doctrines of theologists,‡ when they teach us that there are Gods in every sphere prior to dæmons, the government of some receiving its perfection under that of others. As for instance, with respect to our queen the moon, that she contains the Goddess Hecate, and Diana; and with respect to the sovereign sun, and the Gods which he contains, theologists celebrate Bacchus as subsisting there

>The sun's assessor, who with watchful eye
>Inspects the sacred pole.

They also celebrate Jupiter as seated there, Osiris, and a solar Pan, as likewise other divinities, of which the books of theologists and theurgists are full. From all which it is evident how true it is that each of the planets is the prefect of many Gods, who give completion to its proper circulation.§

---

† These ολοτητες, according to the Platonic philosophy, have so far as they are wholes, a perpetual subsistence, and are the spheres of the fixed stars, the spheres of the planets, the sphere of air, the globe on which we live, and the ocean. See more on this subject in my *Dissertation on the Philosophy of Aristotle*.

‡ Vid Procl. in Tim. p. 257B and 279E. [TTS vol. XVI, p. 778 & 843]

§ Hence, we may perceive at one view, as I have elsewhere observed, why the sun in the Orphic hymns is called Jupiter, why Apollo is called Pan, and Bacchus the Sun; and why the moon seems to be the same with Rhea, Ceres, Proserpine, Juno, Venus, etc. For from this theory it follows, that every sphere contains a Jupiter, Neptune, Vulcan, Vesta, Minerva, Mars, Ceres, Juno, Diana, Mercury, Venus, Apollo, and in short, every deity, - each sphere at the same time conferring on these Gods the peculiar characteristics of its nature; so that for instance, in the sun they possess a solar property; in the moon a lunar one; and so the rest.

This theory too is one of the grand keys to the theology of the Greeks; as it shows why one God is so often celebrated by the appellations of another; an ignorance of the cause of which led Macrobius to think that all the Gods were nothing more than the

CHAPTER XV

Owing to the loss of a seventh book *On the Theology of Plato*, written by Proclus, copious information respecting the peculiarities of all the celestial Gods is unfortunately not to be obtained. All that can be procured, however, on this subject, and which I have diligently collected from Platonic writings, I shall now present to the philosophic reader, beginning in the first place with the moon. This divinity then has the relation of nature and of a mother with respect to generation, or the sublunary region. For all things are convolved and co-increased by her when she increases; but are diminished when she diminishes. This Goddess, too, benevolently leads into light the unapparent productive principles of nature. She likewise gives perfection to souls through a life according to virtue; but imparts to mortal animals a restitution to form.

Next to the moon is Mercury, who is the cause of symmetry to all mundane natures, having the relation of reason to things in generation. For all symmetry proceeds according to one ratio, and according to number of which this God is the giver. This deity, too, is the inspective guardian of *gymnastic* exercises; and hence *hermæ*, or carved statues of Mercury were placed in the Palæstræ; of *music*, and hence he is honoured as the lyrist (λυραιος) among the celestial constellations; and of *disciplines*, because the invention of geometry, reasoning and discourse is referred to this God. He presides, therefore, over every species of discipline, leading us to an intelligible essence from this mortal abode, governing the different herds of souls, and dispersing the sleep and oblivion with which they are oppressed. He is likewise the supplier of recollection, the end of which is a genuine intellectual apprehension of divine natures. Hence, among the Athenians, certain images of these things were preserved; grammar having a reference to dialectic discipline; playing on the harp pertaining to music; and wrestling to gymnastic, in which those youths that were well born were instructed.

In the next place follows Venus, who is the cause of beauty to generated natures, which is an imitation of intelligible beauty. This goddess also is the source of the union of form with matter; connecting and comprehending the powers of all the elements; and her principal employment consists in beautifully illuminating the order, harmony, and communion of all mundane concerns. She likewise governs all the co-ordinations in the celestial world and the earth, binds them to each

---

different powers of the sun, and has been one great source of the idle conjecture of the moderns about the divinities of the ancients.

other, and perfects their generative progressions through a kindred conjunction. And she unites and leads into communion the Hermaic production which has a remitted subsistence, and is in subjection to the solar fabrication.

The next celestial divinity in order after Venus is the sovereign Sun, whose essence and dignity are so great, according to the theology of Plato, as to possess a supermundane prerogative among mundane natures. This Plato indicates in the *Timæus*, when speaking of the sun he says: "In order that these circles might possess a certain manifest measure of slowness and swiftness with reference to each other, and that the motion of the eight circulations might be conspicuous, the divinity enkindled a light which we now denominate the sun, in the second revolution from the earth; that the heavens might become eminently apparent to all things, and that such animals might participate of number as are adapted to its participation, receiving numerical information from the revolution of a nature similar and the same." On these words Proclus admirably comments as follows:[†] Plato here delivers the one ruling cause of the generation of apparent time. For as the Demiurgus gives subsistence to unapparent time, thus also the sun to the time which is apparent, and which measures the motion of bodies. For through light he leads into visibility every temporal interval, gives bound to all periods, and exhibits measures of restoration to a pristine state. Deservedly, therefore, is the sun a manifest measure, as especially unfolding the progression[‡] of time according to number, into the universe. For it has a more accurate period than that of the five planets, its motions being less anomalous than theirs; and also than that of the moon, by always terminating at the same point, its progressions to the north and the south. But if it has a more accurate period, it is deservedly a measure of measures, and from itself bounds[§] the periodic measures of the other planets, and the swiftness of their motions with reference to each other. It also in a greater degree imitates the perpetual permanency of eternity, by always revolving after the same manner. In this way, therefore, it differs from the planets.

After another manner, likewise, the sun is a more manifest measure than the measure of the inerratic sphere. For though this sphere has a

---

[†] Vid. Procl. in Tim. IV, 263E. [TTS vol. XVI, p. 797]

[‡] For περιοδον, it is necessary to read προοδον.

[§] For γνωριζειν, it is necessary to read οριζει.

certain appropriate measure, a proper interval, and one immutable number of its peculiar motion, yet the solar light causes this measure and all the evolution of apparent time to be manifest and known. Hence Plato says, "In order that there might be a certain manifest measure." For though there is a certain measure in the other planets, yet it is not clear and manifest. But the sun unfolds into light both other intelligibles and time. You must not however on this account say that the solar light was generated for the sake of measurement. For how is it possible that wholes should subsist for the sake of parts; governing natures for the sake of the governed; and perpetual for the sake of corruptible natures? But we should rather say that light possessing an evolving power unfolds total time, and calls forth its supermundane monad, and one measure into the measurement of the periods of bodies. And this makes time to be, as it were, sensible. Hence, it is the light of the sun which causes every thing that is moved to have a clear and manifest measure. And this indeed is its whole good. After wholes, however, it likewise benefits parts in a secondary degree. For it imparts the generation of number, and measure to the natures which are adapted to participate of these. For irrational beings indeed are destitute of these; but the genera of dæmons who follow the periods of the Gods, and men become partakers of them. The supply of good, therefore, through the solar light, beginning supernally from wholes, descends as far as to parts. And if beginning from visible natures, you are willing to speak of such as are invisible, the light of the sun gives splendour to the whole world, causes a corporeal-formed nature to be divine, and wholly filled through the whole of itself with life. But it leads souls through undefiled light, imparts to them a pure and elevating power, and governs the world by its rays. And it likewise fills souls with empyrean fruits. For the order of the sun is supernally derived from supermundane natures. Hence Plato does not here fabricate the solar light, but says that the Demiurgus enkindled it, as giving subsistence from his own essence to this sphere, and emitting from the solar fountain a life extended into interval and continually renewed. *And this also is asserted by theologists concerning the supermundane firmaments.*

On this account, it appears to me that Plato delivers a twofold generation of the sun; one indeed in conjunction with the seven governors of the world, when he fashions the bodies of them, and inserts them in their circulations; but the other according to the enkindling of light, through which he imparts to the sun supermundane power. For it is one thing to generate the bulk of the sun itself by itself, and another in conjunction with a ruling characteristic, through which the sun is called the king of every visible nature, and is established analogous to the one fountain of good. For as this fountain being better than the intelligible essence, illuminates both intellect and the intelligible, thus also the sun being better than a visible nature, illuminates both that which is visible and sight. But if the sun is beyond a visible essence, it will have a supermundane nature. For the world is visible and tangible, and has a body. Hence, we must survey the sun in a twofold respect; *viz.* as one of the seven planets, and as the leader of wholes; and as mundane and supermundane, according to the latter of which he splendidly emits a divine light. For in the same manner as *The Good* luminously emits truth which deifies the intelligible and intellectual orders; as Phanes in Orpheus sends forth intelligible light which fills with intelligence all the intellectual Gods; and as Jupiter enkindles an intellectual and demiurgic light in all the supermundane Gods; thus also the sun illuminates every thing visible through this undefiled light. The illuminating cause too is always in an order superior to the illuminated natures. For neither is *The Good* intelligible, nor Phanes intellectual, nor Jupiter supermundane. In consequence of this reasoning, therefore, the sun being supermundane emits the fountains of light. And according to the most mystic doctrines, the wholeness of the sun is in the supermundane orders; for in them there is a solar world, and a total light, as the Chaldæan oracles[†] assert, and which I am persuaded is true.

That the stars, however, and the whole of the heavens receive their light from the sun may easily be perceived. For that which is common in many things derives its subsistence from one cause; and in one way indeed from an exempt, but in another from a co-arranged cause. But this cause is that which primarily participates of that form. The primary participant, however, is that in which either primarily or especially this form exists. If, therefore, light especially subsists in the sun, this will be the first light; and from this that which is in other things will be derived.

[†] According to the Chaldaic dogmas, as explained by Psellus [see TTS VII], there are seven corporeal worlds, one empyrean and the first; after this three etherial; and then three material worlds, *viz.* the inerratic sphere, the seven planetary spheres, and the sublunary region. They also assert that there are two solar worlds; one which is subservient to the etherial profundity; the other zonaic, being one of the seven spheres.

CHAPTER XVI

Conformably, also, to this doctrine of Plato concerning the sun, the emperor Julian sublimely theologizes about this divinity in his very elegant oration to him,[†] from which the following is an extract. The apparent and splendid orbicular sun is the cause of well-being to sensible natures. And whatever we have asserted as flowing from the mighty intellectual sun among the intellectual Gods,[‡] the same perfections the apparent sun communicates to apparent forms; the truth of which will be clearly evinced by contemplating invisible natures from the objects of sensible inspection. And in the first place, is not light the incorporeal and divine form of that which is diaphanous in energy? But whatever that which is diaphanous may be, which is subjected to all the elements, and is their proximate form, it is certain that it is neither corporeal nor mixed, nor does it display any of the peculiar qualities of body. Hence, you cannot affirm that heat is one of its properties, nor its contrary cold; you can neither ascribe to it hardness nor softness, nor any other tangible difference; nor attribute taste or smell as peculiarities of its essence. For a nature of this kind, which is called forth into energy by the interposition of light, is alone subject to the power of sight. But light is the form of a diaphanous essence which resembles that common matter the subject of bodies, through which it is every where diffused; and rays are the summit, and as it were flower of light, which is an incorporeal nature. According to the opinion of the Phœnicians, however, who are skilled in divine science and wisdom, the universally-diffused splendour of light is the unmingled energy of an intellect perfectly pure. And this doctrine will be found agreeable to reason, when we consider that since light is incorporeal, its fountain cannot be body, but the pure energy of intellect, illuminating in its proper habitation the middle region of the heavens: and from this exalted situation scattering its light, it fills all the celestial orbs with powerful vigour, and illuminates the universe with divine and incorruptible light.

Whatever, likewise, we first perceive by the sight, is nothing but a mere name of honourable labour, unless it receives the ruling assistance of light. For how can any thing be visible, unless, like matter, it is moved to the artificer that it may receive the supervening investments of form? Just as gold in a state of simple fusion is indeed gold, but is

---

[†] TTS vol. IV.

[‡] *Viz.* The supermundane Gods.

not a statue or an image till the artificer invests it with form. In a similar manner all naturally visible objects cease to be apparent, unless light is present with the perceiver. Hence, since it confers vision on the perceiver, and visibility on the objects of perception, it perfects two natures in energy, sight and that which is visible. Perfections, however, are form and essence; though perhaps an assertion of this kind is more subtle than is suited to our present purpose.

Of this, however, all men are persuaded, both the scientific and the illiterate, philosophers and the learned, that day and night are fabricated by the power of this rising and setting divinity; and that he manifestly changes and convolves the world. But to which of the other stars does a province of this kind belong? Do we not, therefore, derive conviction from hence, that the unapparent and divine race of intellectual Gods,[†] above the heavens, are replenished from the sun with boniform powers; to whose authority the whole choir of the stars submits; and whose nod generation, which he governs by his providence, attentively obeys? For the planets, indeed, dancing round him as their king, harmoniously revolve in a circle, with definite intervals, about his orb; producing certain stable energies, and advancing backwards and forwards; terms by which the skilful in the spheric theory signify such like phænomena of the stars. To which we may add, as manifest to every one, that the light of the moon is augmented or diminished according to her distance from the sun.

Is it not then highly probable that the orderly disposition of the intellectual Gods, which is more ancient than that of bodies, is analogous to the mundane arrangement? Hence we infer his *perfective* power from the whole phænomena, because he gives vision to visive natures; for he perfects these by his light. But we collect his *demiurgic* and *prolific* power from the mutation of the universe; and his *capacity of collecting all things into one*, from the properties of motion conspiring into union and consent; and *middle position*, from his own central situation. Lastly, we infer his *royal establishment among the intellectual Gods*, from his middle order between the planets. For if we perceived these, or as many other properties, belonging to any other of the apparent Gods, we should not ascribe the principality among them to the sun.

[†] It must be carefully observed, however, that this is only true of the Gods characteristically called supermundane. For it does not apply to the Gods who are *primarily* intellectual, since they are above the supermundane order, to which the sun and Apollo belong.

515

Again, that we may consider this affair in a different mode, since there is one demiurgus of the universe, but many demiurgic Gods, who revolve round the heavens, it is proper to place in the midst of these the mundane administration of the sun. Besides, the fertile power of life is copious and redundant in intelligibles, and the world is full of the same prolific life. Hence it is evident that the fertile life of the sovereign sun is a medium between the two, as the mundane phænomena perpetually evince. For with respect to forms, some he perfects, and others he fabricates; some he adorns, and others he excites; nor is any thing capable of advancing into light and generation without the demiurgic power of the sun. Add too, that if we attend to the unmingled, pure and immaterial essence of intelligibles, to which nothing extrinsical flows, and nothing foreign adheres, but which is full of its own appropriate simplicity, and afterwards consider the defecated nature of that pure and divine body which is conversant with mundane bodies revolving in an orb, and which is free from all elementary mixture, we shall find that the splendid and incorruptible essence of the royal sun, is a medium between the immaterial purity of intelligibles and that which in sensibles is unmingled and remote from generation and corruption.

The greatest argument, however, for the truth of this is derived from hence, that the light which flows from the sun upon the earth will not suffer itself to be mingled with any thing; nor is it polluted by any sordid nature, or by any contagion; but it abides every where pure, undefiled, and impassive. Again, if we consider not only immaterial and intelligible forms, but such as are sensible, subsisting in matter, the middle intellectual situation of forms about the mighty sun will be no less certain and clear. For these afford continual assistance to forms merged in matter; so that they could neither exist, nor preserve themselves in existence, unless this beneficent deity co-operated with their essence. In short, is he not the cause of the separation of forms and the concretion of matter? From whom we not only possess the power of understanding his nature, but from whom our eyes are endued with the faculty of sight? For the distribution of rays throughout the world, and union of light, exhibit the demiurgic separation of the artificer.

Again, the solar orb is moved in the starless, which is far higher than the inerratic sphere. Hence, he is not the middle of the planets, but of the three worlds, according to the mystic hypotheses;[†] if it be proper to call them hypotheses, and not rather dogmas; confining the appellation of hypotheses to the doctrine of the sphere. For the truth of the former is testified by men who audibly received this information from Gods, or mighty dæmons; but the latter is founded on the probability arising from the agreement of the phænomena. But besides those which I have mentioned, there is an innumerable multitude of celestial Gods, perceived by such as do not contemplate the heavens indolently and after the manner of brutes. As the sun quadruply divides these three worlds, on account of the communion of the zodiac with each, so he again divides the zodiac into twelve powers of Gods, and each of these into three others, so that thirty-six are produced in the whole. Hence, as it appears to me, a triple benefit of the Graces proceeds to us from the heavens, I mean from those circles which the God quadruply dividing produces in consequence of this, a quadripartite beauty and elegance of seasons and times. But the Graces also imitate a circle in their resemblances on the earth. Add too, that Bacchus is the source of joy, who is said to obtain a common kingdom with the sun. But why should I here mention the epithet Horus, or other names of the Gods, all of which correspond with the divinity of the sun? Mankind, indeed, may conceive the excellence of the God from his operations; since he perfects the heavens with intellectual goods, and renders them partakers of intelligible beauty. For as he originates from this beauty, he applies himself both wholly and by parts, to the distribution of good.

In the last place, as the sun is the source of our existence, so likewise of the aliment by which that existence is supported. And, indeed, he confers on us more divine advantages peculiar to souls; for he loosens these from the bands of a corporeal nature, reduces them to the kindred essence of divinity, and assigns them the subtile and firm texture of divine splendour, as a vehicle in which they may safely descend to the realms of generation. And these benefits of the God have been celebrated by others according to their desert, and require the assistance of faith more than the evidence of demonstration.

[†] That is, according to the Chaldean oracles, the sun is the middle of the empyrean, etherial, and material worlds, the two last of which, as I have observed in a former note, receive a triple division.

CHAPTER XVII

From the MS. Scholia likewise of Proclus on the *Cratylus* of Plato, we derive the following very important information concerning Apollo; in which the principal powers of the God are unfolded by him with his usual magnificence of diction, and divine fecundity of conception. Socrates, therefore, in the *Cratylus* says, "that there is no other name [than that of Apollo] which can more harmonize with the four powers of this God, because it touches upon them all, and evinces in a certain respect his *harmonic, prophetic, medicinal*, and *arrow-darting skill*." And shortly after he adds, "that the name is so composed that it touches upon all the powers of the God, *viz*. his *simplicity, perpetual jaculation, purifying*, and *joint-revolving nature*." On these words Proclus observes, that very rationally after Proserpine, Plato analyzes Apollo. For there is a great communion between the Coric and the Apolloniacal series; since the former is the unity of the middle triad of the supermundane Gods, and emits from herself vivific powers; but the latter converts the solar principles to one union; and the solar principles are allotted a subsistence immediately after the vivific. Hence, according to Orpheus, when Ceres delivered up the government to Proserpine, she thus admonished her:

Αυταρ Απολλωνος θαλερον λεχος εισαναβασα,
Τεξεται αγλαα τεκνα πυριφλεγεθοντα προσωποις.[†]

That is,

But next Apollo's florid bed ascend;
For thus the God fam'd offspring shall beget,
Refulgent with the beams of glowing fire.

But how could this be the case, unless there was a considerable degree of communion between these divinities?

It is necessary however, to know thus much concerning Apollo, that according to the first and most natural conception, his name signifies the cause of union, and that power which collects multitude into one; and this mode of speculation concerning his name harmonizes with all the orders of the God. But Socrates alone considers his more partial powers: for the multitude of the powers of Apollo are not to be comprehended, nor described by us. For when will man who is merely rational, be able to comprehend not only all the peculiarities of Apollo, but all those of

---

[†] These verses are not in Gesner's collection of the Orphic fragments.

any other God? Theologists indeed deliver to us a great multitude of Apolloniacal peculiarities; but Socrates now only mentions four of them. For the world is as it were a decad, being filled from all productive principles, receiving all things in itself, and being converted to the proper principle of the decad, of which the tetrad proximately contains the cause, but in an exempt manner the monad. And the former without separation and occultly, but the latter with separation; just as Apollo proximately unites the multitude of mundane natures, but the demiurgic intellect exemptly. Why then does Socrates use an order of this kind? For beginning from the *medicinal* power of the god, and proceeding through his *prophetic* and *arrow-darting* powers, he ends in his *harmonic* power. We reply, that all the energies of this god, are in all the orders of beings, beginning from on high and proceeding as far as to the last of things; but different energies appear to have more or less dominion in different orders. Thus for instance the *medicinal* power of Apollo is most apparent in the sublunary region, for

> There slaughter, rage, and countless ills beside,
> Disease, decay, and rottenness reside.†

And as these are moved in an inordinate manner, they require to be restored from a condition contrary, into one agreeable to nature, and from incommensuration and manifold division, into symmetry and union.

But the *prophetic* energy of the god is most apparent in the heavens; for there his enunciative power shines forth, unfolding intelligible good to celestial natures, and on this account he revolves together with the sun, with whom he participates the same intellect in common; since the sun also illuminates whatever the heavens contain, and extends a unifying power to all their parts. But his *arrow-darting* energy mostly prevails among the *liberated* gods; for there ruling over the wholes which the universe contains, he excites their motions by his rays, which are always assimilated to arrows, extirpates every thing inordinate, and fills all things with demiurgic gifts. And though he has a separate and exempt subsistence, he reaches all things by his energies.

Again, his *harmonic* power is more predominant in the *ruling supermundane* order; for it is this divinity who harmonizing the universe, establishes about himself according to one union the choir of the Muses,

---

† These lines from Empedocles are as follow in the original:

Ενθα κοτος τε φονος τε και αλλων εθνεα κηρων,
Αυχμηραι τε νοσοι, και σηψιες, εργα τε ρευστα.

and produces by this mean as a certain Theurgist says "*the harmony of exulting light.*" Apollo therefore as we have shown is *harmonic*, and this is likewise the case with the other Apollos which are contained in the earth and the other spheres; but this power appears in some places more, and in others less. These powers too subsist in the god himself in an united manner, and exempt from other natures, but in those attendants of the Gods who are superior to us, divisibly, and according to participation; for there is a great multitude of medicinal, prophetic, harmonic, and arrow-darting angels, dæmons, and heroes, suspended from Apollo, who distribute in a partial manner the uniform powers of the god.

But it is necessary to consider each of these powers according to one definite characteristic; as for instance, his *harmonic* power, according to its binding together separated multitude; his *prophetic* power according to the enunciative; his *arrow-darting* power, according to its being subvertive of an inordinate nature; and his *medicinal* power according to its perfective energy. We should likewise speculate these characteristics differently in Gods, angels, dæmons, heroes, men, animals, and plants; for the powers of the Gods extend from on high to the last of things, and at the same time appear in an accommodated manner in each; and the telestic (*i.e.* mystic) art endeavours through sympathy to conjoin these ultimate participants with the Gods. But in all these orders we must carefully observe, that this God is the cause of union to multiplied natures: for his *medicinal* power, which takes away the *multiform* nature of disease, imparts *uniform* health; since health is symmetry and a subsistence according to nature, but that which is contrary to nature is multifarious. Thus too, his *prophetic* power, which unfolds the simplicity of truth, takes away the variety of that which is false; but his *arrow-darting* power, which exterminates every thing furious and wild, but prepares that which is orderly and gentle to exercise dominion, vindicates to itself unity, and exterminates a disordered nature tending to multitude; and his *musical* power, through rhythm and harmony, places a bond, friendship and union in *wholes*, and subdues the contraries to these.

And all these powers indeed, subsist primarily, in an exempt manner, and uniformly in Jupiter the demiurgus of wholes, but secondarily and separately in Apollo. Hence Apollo is not the same with the demiurgic intellect; for this comprehends these powers totally and paternally, but Apollo with subjection, imitating his father; since all the energies and powers of secondary Gods, are comprehended in the demiurgus according to cause. And the demiurgus fabricates and adorns the universe according to all these powers, and in a collected manner; but the other deities which proceed from him, co-operate with their father according to different powers.

Purification however being seen not only in the medicinal, but also in the prophetic art evinces, that the cathartic power of Apollo comprehends the two powers: for it illustrates the world with the glittering splendours of light, and purifies all material immoderation by pæonian energies; which physicians and prophets among us imitating, the former purify bodies, and the latter through sulphureous preparations render themselves and their associates pure. For, as *Timæus* says, the Gods purify the universe, either by fire or water; and prophets also in this respect imitate the Gods. In the most sacred of the mysteries too, purifications are employed prior to initiation into them, in order to take away every thing foreign from the proposed sacred mystery. We may likewise add, that the referring multiform purifications to the one cathartic power of the Gods, is adapted to him. For Apollo every where unites and elevates multitude to *The One*, and uniformly comprehends all the modes of purification; purifying all heaven, generation, and all mundane lives, and separating partial souls from the grossness of matter. Hence the theurgist who is the leader of the mysteries of this God begins from purifications and sprinklings:

Αυτος δ' εν πρωτοις ιερευς πυρος εργα κυβερνων,
Κυματι ραινεσθω παγερω βαρυηχετος αλμης.

i.e. "The priest in the first place governing the works of fire, must sprinkle with the cold water of the loud-sounding sea," as the Oracle says concerning him. But the assertion that the God presides over simplicity according to knowledge, and unfolds truth into light, presents him to our view as analogous to *The Good*, which Socrates celebrates in the *Republic*; in which place he calls the sun the progeny of *The Good*, and says that the former is analogous to the latter. Apollo therefore being the source of union, and this to the mundane Gods, is arranged analogous to *The Good*; and through *truth*, he unfolds to us his similitude to it, if it be lawful so to speak. For *the simple* is a manifestation of *The One*, and the truth which subsists according to knowledge is a luminous representation of superessential truth, which first proceeds from *The Good*. But *the perpetually prevailing might of the God in the jaculation of arrows*, evinces his dominion which vanquishes every thing in the world. For on high from the supercelestial order, he scatters the rivers of Jupiter, and pours his rays on the whole world: for his arrows obscurely signify his rays. Again, the assertion that he presides over music, represents to us that this God is the cause of all harmony, both unapparent and apparent, through his ruling supermundane powers, according to which he generates together with Mnesmosyne and Jupiter, the Muses. But he orderly disposes every thing sensible by his *demiurgic powers*, which the sons of *theurgists* denominate *hands*; since the energy of the harmony of sounds is suspended from the motion of the hands. He likewise orderly disposes souls and bodies through harmonic reasons, using their different powers as if they were sounds; and he moves all things harmoniously and rhythmically by his demiurgic motions. The whole of the celestial order too, and motion, exhibit the harmonious work of the God; on which account also, partial souls are no otherwise perfected than through an harmonic similitude to the universe, and abandoning the dissonance arising from generation; for then they obtain the most excellent life, which is proposed to them by the God.

CHAPTER XVIII

As the Muses derive their subsistence from Apollo, and are perpetually united to him, it is necessary to consider the nature of these divinities in the next place, and the good which they confer on the universe in conjunction with their leader Apollo. Plato therefore in the *Cratylus* says "That the name of the Muses, and universally that of music, was derived, as it seems, from μωσθαι, *to inquire*, and from investigation and philosophy." On which Proclus in his MS. Scholia on that dialogue observes as follows:

"From discoursing about king Apollo, Plato proceeds to the Muses, and the name of music; for Apollo is celebrated as Musagetes, or the leader of the Muses. And he indeed is a monad with respect to the harmony of the world; but the choir of the Muses is the monad of all the number of the ennead (*i.e.* nine): From both likewise the whole world is bound in indissoluble bonds, and is one and all-perfect, through the communications of these divinities; possessing the former through the Apolloniacal monad, but its all-perfect subsistence through the number of the Muses. For the number nine which is generated from the first perfect number (that is 3) is, through similitude and sameness, accommodated to the multiform causes of the mundane order and harmony; all these causes at the same time being collected into one summit for the purpose of producing one consummate perfection. For the Muses generate the variety of reasons with which the world is replete; but Apollo comprehends in union all the multitude of these. And the Muses give subsistence to the harmony of soul; but Apollo is the leader of intellectual and impartible harmony. The Muses distribute the phænomena according to harmonical reasons; but Apollo comprehends unapparent and separate harmony. And though both give subsistence to the same things, yet the Muses effect this according to number, but Apollo according to union. And the Muses indeed distribute the unity of Apollo; but Apollo unites harmonic multitude, which he also converts and comprehends. For the multitude of the Muses proceeds from the essence of *Musagetes*, which is both separate, and subsists according to the nature of *The One*; and their number evolves the one and primary cause of the harmony of the universe.

That such being the etymology of the name of the Muses, since Plato calls philosophy the greatest music, as causing our psychical powers to be moved harmoniously, in symphony with real beings, and in conformity to the orderly motions of the celestial orbs; and since the investigation of our own essence and that of the universe leads us to this harmony, through a conversion to ourselves and more excellent natures, - hence also we denominate the Muses from investigation. For Musagetes himself unfolds truth to souls, according to one intellectual simplicity; but the Muses perfect our various energies elevating them to an intellectual unity. For investigations have the relation of matter, with reference to the end from invention; just as multitude with respect to *The One*, and variety with respect to simplicity. We know therefore, that the Muses impart to souls the investigation of truth, to bodies the multitude of powers, and that they are every where the sources of the variety of harmonies.

In the fable likewise in the *Phædrus* about the grass-hoppers Plato speaks of the four Muses, Terpsichore, Erato, Calliope, and Urania, as follows: "It is said the race of the grasshoppers received this gift from the Muses, that they should never want nutriment, but should continue singing without meat or drink till they died; and that after death they should depart to the Muses, and inform them what Muse was honoured by some particular person among us. Hence that by acquainting Terpsichore with those who reverence her in the dance, they render her propitious to such. By informing Erato of her votaries, they render her favourable in amatory concerns; and the rest in a similar manner, according to the species of veneration belonging to each. But that they announce to the most ancient Calliope, and after her to Urania, those who have lived in the exercise of philosophy, and have cultivated the music over which they preside; these Muses more than all the rest being conversant with the heavens, and with both divine and human discourse; and sending forth the most beautiful voice."

On what Plato here says of these Muses, Hermeas in his MS. Commentary On the *Phædrus*, makes the following beautiful remarks: "Dancing here must not be understood literally, as if Terpsichore was propitious to those who engage in that kind of dancing which is the object of sense; for this would be ridiculous. We must say therefore, that there are divine dances; in the first place, the dance of the Gods; and in the second place, that of divine souls. In the third place, the revolution of the celestial divinities, *viz.* of the seven planets, and the inerratic sphere, is called a dance. In the fourth place, those who are initiated in the mysteries perform a certain dance. And in the last place, the whole life of a philosopher is a dance. Who then are those that honour the Goddess in the dance? Not those who dance well, but those who live well through the whole of the present existence, elegantly arranging their life, and dancing in symphony with the universe. Again, Erato is denominated from Love, and from making the works of Love, lovely; for she co-operates with Love. But Calliope is denominated from the eye; and Urania presides over astronomy. Through these two Goddesses we preserve our rational part from being in subjection to the irrational nature. For through sight surveying the order of the celestial Gods, we properly arrange our irrational part. And farther still, through rhythms, philosophy, and hearing, we elegantly dispose that which we contain of the disorderly and void of rhythm."

CHAPTER XIX

The triad of celestial Gods immediately above the sun consists of Mars, Jupiter, and Saturn, of which the first who is the source of division and motion, perpetually separates, nourishes and excites the contrarieties of the universe, that the world may exist perfect and entire from all its parts. He requires, however, the assistance of Venus, that he may insert order and harmony into things contrary and discordant. But Jupiter is the cause of a royal and political life, and is the supplier of a ruling prudence and a practical and adorning intellect. And Saturn is the source of intellect, in consequence of being an intellectual deity, and ascending as far as to the first cause. Hence, as there is nothing disordered and novel in intellect, Saturn is represented as an old man, and as slow in his motion: and on this account, astrologers says, that such as have Saturn well situated in their nativity are endued with intellect.

Plato in the *Timæus* delivers to us the manner in which each of these seven divinities becomes an animal, and is suspended from a more divine soul, and what kind of perfection it affords to the universe. For he says,

"When therefore, each of the natures necessary to a joint fabrication of time had arrived at a local motion adapted to its condition, and their bodies became animals through the connecting power of vital bonds, they then learned their prescribed order." For each of them, says Proclus, is allotted an appropriate life and motion. For since the demiurgic sacred law distributes to every mortal nature that which is adapted to it, and co-arranges every thing with a view to the blessedness of the universe, what ought we to say concerning the governors of the world? Ought we not to assert that they have received from their father, every thing appropriate and every good; and that shining with the splendours of beauty, they not only fabricate the generation of time in conjunction with the father, but also lead and govern the whole world? For by thus speaking of them we shall speak rightly. In addition to these things likewise, we ought to assert, that they not only receive the beautiful and the good from the demiurgic monad, but also that being self-motive, they impart these to themselves; and that from themselves the giving of good originates. Plato indeed, indicating this says, "that each of them *arrives* (αφικεσθαι) at a local motion, adapted to its condition," as defining from itself the measure of the life, the order, and the motion which it is allotted in the universe.

Since, however, each of the seven bodies has a twofold life, the one inseparable, but the other separable; and the one indeed intellectual, and in a ruling manner established in itself, but the other divided about body, which it connects and moves; according to the latter indeed, it is an animal, but according to the former a God. Plato, therefore, distinguishing both these, and rightly conceiving that a divine and intellectual soul, and which does not depart from intelligibles, is one thing, but another, the animal which is suspended from it, possesses life from, and is the image of it says, "that their bodies became animals through the connecting power of vital bonds, and that they then learned their prescribed order." For a divine soul learns indeed the demiurgic will, understands the works of the father, and fabricates in conjunction with him mundane natures; and this, through intellectually perceiving him, and being filled from him with divine powers. For it is not possible for either intellect or soul to provide for wholes in an exempt manner, in any other way than by the participation of deity, and through a deific life. The words, therefore, "a joint fabrication of time," manifest that they are allotted a secondary power in the generation of it; in consequence of their father possessing a primary power. For he, indeed, generated the wholeness of time; but these divinities co-operate with him in the production of the parts of which time consists. For the periods of these are the parts of the whole of time; just as they also were generated parts of the world.

But the animated body is an animal bound with vital bonds, possessing life from the soul which it receives according to the demiurgic allotments. For if with us also, the animal is different from the man, and the visible Socrates is one thing, but the true another, much more are the true sun and the true Jupiter different from the visible orbs of these divinities, and not composites of body and soul. Conformably to this Socrates in the *Phædrus* says, "that we do not sufficiently understand that a God is an immortal animal, possessing indeed a soul and a body, connascent through the whole of time." Indeed the unity in each of these divinities, and the ineffable participation of the fountain of all the numbers characterised by unity, form that which is primarily a God. But the intellect which connects each of these deities stably, uniformly, and invariably, is secondarily a God. And the soul which is filled from intellect, and evolves the one comprehension of it, is a God in the third place. And the first indeed of these is truly a God; the second is most divine; and the third is itself also divine, but illuminates the animal with which it is connected with the peculiarity of deity; according to which this likewise is divine, being bound with animated bonds, which may be said to be vivific, demiurgic and indissoluble bonds, as Plato himself afterwards asserts. For the whole of the divine bodies, are bound in souls, are comprehended by and established in them; the *being bound* indeed indicating the stable and immutable comprehension of bodies in souls, and their undisjoined communion with them. Such therefore being the nature of divine bodies, they fabricate time in conjunction with the demiurgus, call forth its one and unapparent power, and impart a progression to it into the world, which unfolds many temporal measures.

CHAPTER XX

The celestial Gods therefore, according to Plato subsisting after this manner, and the unity in each of them ineffably proceeding from the fountain of good, it is evident that they are all of them beneficent, and after a similar manner the causes of good. The bodies also which are suspended from their divine souls possess indescribable powers, some indeed being firmly established in the divine bodies themselves, but others proceeding from them into the nature of the world and into the world itself, descending in an orderly manner through the whole of generation, and without impediment extending as far as to particulars. With respect to the powers therefore, which remain in the divine celestial bodies themselves, there can be no doubt but that they are all similar; hence those powers remain to be considered which are sent to this terrestrial region, and are mingled with generation.

These then descend after the same manner for the safety of the universe, and connect with invariable sameness the whole of generation. They are likewise impassive and immutable, though they arrive at that which is mutable and passive. Generation indeed, being multiform, and consisting of things of a different nature, it receives the unity and simplicity of these Gods through its appropriate contrariety and division, in a hostile and partible manner. It likewise receives that which is impassive passively: and in short it participates of these Gods according to its own nature, and not according to their power. Hence, as that which is generated participates of being according to a flux of existence; and body participates of an incorporeal nature corporeally; thus also the natural and material substances which are in generation, participate of the immaterial and etherial bodies which are above nature and generation, in a confused and disorderly manner. Those therefore are absurd who attribute colour, figure and contact to intelligible forms, because the participants of them are coloured, figured and tangible; and they are no less absurd who ascribe evil to the celestial bodies, because the participants of them are sometimes evil. For there could be no participation, if the participant was not different from that which it participates. But if that which is participated is received in something different from itself, this something different, is in terrestrial places that which is evil and disorderly.

This participation therefore, becomes the cause of the abundant difference in secondary natures, and also the mixture of material with immaterial influences. To which may be added likewise, as another cause, that what is imparted in one way, is received after another in these inferior realms. Thus for instance, the influence of Saturn is connective, but that of Mars motive. In these material realms however, the passive receptacle of generation, receives the former according to congelation and frigidity; but the latter according to immoderate heat. Hence, corruption and the privation of symmetry are to be ascribed to the alterant, material and passive nature of the recipients.

Farther still, the imbecility of material and terrestrial places, not being able to receive the genuine power and most pure life of the etherial natures, ascribes its own defects to first causes. Just as if some one being weak in his body, and not able to bear the vivifying heat of the sun, should falsely dare to say, influenced by his own infirmities, that the sun is not advantageous to health and life. A thing of this kind likewise, may take place in the harmony and temperament of the universe, I mean, that the same things which are salutary to the whole, through the perfection of the recipients and things received, may be noxious to the parts through their partible privation of symmetry. In the motion of the universe therefore, all the circulations preserve the whole world after a similar manner, though frequently one certain part is injured by another; just as in a dance, where the order of the whole choir is still preserved, though a foot or a finger may happen to be hurt. Again, to be corrupted, and to be changed, are affections connascent with particulars. But it is not proper to accuse on this account wholes and first causes, either as containing these in themselves, or as if these proceeded from them into these inferior realms. And thus it appears, that neither the celestial Gods themselves, nor their gifts are productive of evil.[†]

CHAPTER XXI

And thus much concerning the planetary deities, who were called by the ancients, the governors of the world. In the next place therefore, let us direct our attention to what Plato and his best interpreter Proclus have transmitted to us concerning Minerva, who as a mundane divinity is connected with ether, and has also an allotment in the celestial regions. Plato then in the *Timæus* describes this Goddess as both a lover of war, and a lover of wisdom; for he says that she is philopolemic and philosophic. As she every where however exerts this twofold power, according to her intellectual, supermundane, and mundane subsistence, I shall present the reader with the whole of what Proclus says[‡] respecting these two powers of the goddess, in his commentary on that part of the *Timæus* where she is celebrated by Plato.

In the demiurgus and father, says he, of the whole world, many orders of Gods that have the form of *The One* present themselves to the view. And these are of a guardian, or demiurgic, or elevating, or connective, or perfective characteristic. But the undefiled and untamed deity Minerva, is one of the first intellectual unities subsisting in the demiurgus, according to which he himself remains firm and immutable, and all things proceeding from him participate of inflexible power; and through which he intellectually perceives every thing, and is separate in an exempt manner from all beings. All theologists therefore, call this

---

[†] Vid. Iamblich. de Myst. lib i, 18. [TTS vol. XVII, p. 43 f]

[‡] In Tim. lib i, 51C. [TTS vol. XV, p. 157]

divinity Minerva, as being brought forth indeed from the summit of her father, and abiding in him, being a demiurgic, separate, and immaterial intelligence. Hence Socrates in the *Cratylus*, celebrates her as *theonoe* (θεονοη) or *deific intellection*. But as, in conjunction with other divinities sustaining all things in the one demiurgus, and arranging wholes, together with her father; - through the first of these, they denominate her philosophic, but through the second philopolemic. For she who according to the form of one connectedly-contains all the paternal wisdom is a philosopher. And she who invariably rules over all contrariety, may be properly called a lover of war. Hence Orpheus speaking of her birth says, that Jupiter generated her from his head,

> With armour shining like a brazen flower.

Since however, it was necessary that she should proceed into second and third orders, she appears in the order to which Proserpine belongs, according to the undefiled heptad; but she generates every virtue from herself, and elevating powers, and illuminates secondary natures with intellect, and an undefiled life. Hence she is called *Core Tritogenes*. She likewise appears among the liberated Gods, uniting the lunar order with intellectual and demiurgic light, causing the productions of those divinities to be undefiled, and demonstrating the one unity of them to be unmingled with their depending powers. She also appears in the heavens and the sublunary region; and according to the united gift of herself, imparts the cause both of the philosophic and the philopolemic power. For her inflexibility is intellectual, and her separate wisdom is pure and unmingled with secondary natures; and the one characteristic peculiarity of Minerval providence, extends as far as to the last orders. For since wherever there are partial souls that resemble her divinity, they exert an admirable prudence, and exhibit an unconquerable strength, what ought we to say of her attendant choirs[†] of dæmons or divine, mundane, liberated, and ruling orders? For all these receive as from a fountain the twofold peculiarity of this Goddess. Hence also the divine poet [Homer] indicating both these powers of Minerva, in conjunction with fabulous devices says,

> The radiant veil her sacred fingers wove,
> Floats in rich waves, and spreads the court of Jove.
> Her father's warlike robe her limbs invest.[‡]

[†] For χορευτων, it is necessary to read χορων των.

[‡] *Iliad* viii.

In which verses by the veil which she wove, and to which she gave subsistence by her intellections, her intellectual wisdom is signified. But by the warlike robe of Jupiter we must understand her demiurgic providence, which immutably takes care of mundane natures, and prepares more divine beings always to have dominion in the world. Hence also, I think Homer represents her as an associate in battle with the Greeks against the Barbarians; just as Plato here relates that she was an associate with the Greeks against the inhabitants of the Atlantic island; in order that every where more intellectual and divine natures may rule over such as are most irrational and vile. For Mars also is a friend to war and contrarieties, but with a separation and division more adapted to the things themselves. Minerva however, connects contrariety, and illuminates the subjects of her government with union. Hence likewise she is said to be philopolemic. For,

> Strife, fighting, war, she always loves.

And she is a friend to war indeed, because she is allotted the summit of separation; but she is a lover of contrarieties, because these are in a certain respect congregated through this goddess, in consequence of better natures having dominion. On this account likewise, the ancients co-arranged Victory with Minerva.

If therefore, these things are rightly asserted, she is philosophic indeed, as being demiurgic intelligence, and as separate and immaterial wisdom. Hence also, she is called Metis by the Gods. But she is philopolemic, as connecting the contrarieties in wholes, and as an untamed and inflexible deity. On this account likewise, she preserves Bacchus undefiled, but vanquishes the giants in conjunction with her father. She too alone shakes the ægis, without waiting for the mandate of Jupiter. She also hurls the javelin,

> Shook by her arm, the massy javelin bends,
> Huge, ponderous, strong! that when her fury burns
> Whole ranks of heroes tames and overturns.[†]

Again, she is *Phosphoros*, as every way extending intellectual light; the *Saviour*, as establishing every partial intellect in the total intellections of her father; *Ergane*, or the artificer, as presiding over demiurgic works. Hence the theologist Orpheus says, that the father produced her,

> That she the queen might be of mighty works.

[†] *Iliad* viii.

But she is *Calliergos*, or the beautiful fabricator, as connecting by beauty all the works of the father; a *Virgin*, as exerting an undefiled and unmingled purity; and *Aigiochos*, or ægis-bearing, as moving the whole of fate, and being the leader of its productions.

With respect to the spear and shield with which this Goddess, in the statues of her, is represented as armed, Iamblichus, as we are informed by Proclus, explains these in a most divinely-inspired manner as follows: Since every divine nature ought to act and not to suffer; in order that by operating it may not have the inefficacious which is similar to matter, but by not suffering, it may not have that efficacy which resembles material natures, that produce accompanied with passion, - that it may have neither of these, he asserts that shields are powers, through which a divine nature remains impassive and pure, surrounding itself with an infrangible guard. But spears are powers, according to which it proceeds without contact through all things, operates in all things, amputating a material nature, and giving assistance to every generation-producing form. These powers, however, are first seen about Minerva. Hence also in the statues of her she is armed with a spear and shield. For she vanquishes every thing, and according to theologists, remains inflexibly, and uncontaminated in her father. But these things are seen in a secondary degree in the Minerval powers, both in such as a whole, and such as are partial. For as the Jovian and demiurgic multitudes imitate their monads; and as the prophetic and Apolloniacal multitudes participate of the characteristic peculiarity of Apollo; thus also the Minerval number adumbrates the uncontaminated and unmingled nature of Minerva. And they are seen ultimately in Minerval souls. For in these also the shield is the untamed and inflexible power of reason; but the spear is that which is incisive of matter, and which liberates souls from the perturbations arising from dæmons or destiny.

With respect to the mundane allotment also of this Goddess who proceeds supernally from intellectual causes to the earth, Proclus observes, (in Tim. 43D) that she primarily subsists in her father; but secondarily in the supermundane Gods; that her third progression is in the twelve liberated rulers; and that after this, she unfolds into light a liberated authority in the heavens. In one way indeed in the inerratic sphere; for there also, a certain allotment of this Goddess is expanded; whether it be the place about the ram, or that about the virgin, or whether it be some one of the northern stars, as the Electra which is there is by certain persons asserted to be. But she unfolds this power in another way in the sun. For there also an admirable power, and a Minerval order, fabricates wholes, according to theologists, in conjunction with the sun. And again, in another way in the moon, being the monad of the triad[†] which is there. But in another way in the earth, according to the similitude of the allotments of the earth to the celestial distributions. And lastly, she unfolds this liberated authority differently in different parts of the earth, according to the peculiarities of providential energy. This being the case, it is by no means wonderful that one deity, Minerva, is said by Plato to have been allotted Athens, and Saïs in Egypt. For it must not be supposed, that because partial souls are not naturally adapted to inhabit two bodies at once, this is also impossible to the Gods. But there is a participation of the same divine power according to different places, yet in the one power there is also multitude. And by this place, indeed, it is participated in one way; but by other places in a different way. And in some sameness is more abundant, but in others difference.

In another part, likewise, of the same admirable work (30C) Proclus observes of this Goddess, that it is manifest from the Greeks, that her dominion extends from on high as far as to the last of things; for they say she was generated from the summit or head of Jupiter. But the Egyptians relate that this inscription was written in the adytum of the Goddess. *I am the things that are, that will be, and that have been. No one has ever laid open the garment by which I am concealed. The fruit which I brought forth was the sun.*[‡] The Goddess, therefore, being demiurgic, and at the same time apparent and unapparent, has an allotment in the heavens, and illuminates generation with forms. For of the signs of the zodiac, the ram is ascribed to the Goddess, and the equinoctial circle itself, where especially a power motive of the universe is established. And thus much concerning the philopolemic and philosophic Goddess Minerva.

CHAPTER XXII

Let us in the next place direct our attention to that great mundane divinity the earth, and consider what it is, whence it proceeds, and how it is said by Plato in the *Timæus* to be our nurse, and the most ancient

---

[†] This triad consists of Minerva, Diana, and Proserpine.

[‡] The former part of this inscription is to be found in Plutarch's treatise of Isis and Osiris; but the latter part, viz. *the fruit which I brought forth was the sun*, is only to be found in the above Commentary of Proclus. The original is, ον εγω καρπον ετεκον ηλιος εγενετο.

and first of the Gods within the heavens, deriving our information about this Goddess also from Proclus, (in Tim. 280A). Earth then proceeds primarily from the intelligible earth which comprehends all the intelligible orders of the Gods, and is eternally established in the father.[†] It also proceeds from the intellectual Earth which is co-arranged with Heaven, and all the productions of which it receives. For being analogous to these, it also abides perpetually as in the centre of the heavens, and being contained, on all sides by them, is full of generative power, and demiurgic perfection. The true earth, therefore, is neither this corporeal-formed and gross bulk; for it will not be the most ancient of the Gods from its bulk, nor the first of the Gods that are arranged within the heavens; nor is it the soul of this body; for it would not be, as Plato says it is, extended about the pole of the universe, since not the soul, but the body of the earth is a thing of this kind; but if it be necessary to speak what is most true concerning it, it is an animal consisting of a divine soul, and a living body. Hence the whole is, as Plato says, an animal. For there are in it an immaterial and separate intellect; a divine soul dancing round this intellect; an etherial body proximately suspended from its informing soul; and in the last place, this visible bulk, which is on all sides inspired with life by the vehicle[‡] of this soul, with which also being filled, it generates and nourishes all-various animals. For some animals[§] are rooted in it, but others about it. And this likewise, Aristotle perceiving, was ashamed not to give to the earth a natural life. For whence is it that plants while they remain in the earth live, but when divulsed from it die, unless this earthly mass was full of life? It is necessary, also, to assume universally, that wholes are animated prior to parts. For it would be ridiculous that man indeed should participate of a rational soul and of intellect, but that no soul should be assigned to the earth and the air, supernally riding in [as it were] and governing the elements, and preserving them in their proper boundaries. For wholes, as Theophrastus says, would have less authority than parts, and perpetual than corruptible natures, if they were destitute of soul. Hence, it is necessary to grant that a soul and an intellect are in the earth; the former causing it to be prolific, but the latter connectedly-containing it in the middle of the universe.

[†] *viz.* In *ether* or *bound*, the summit of the intelligible triad.

[‡] Instead of σχηματος here, it is necessary to read οχηματος.

[§] For according to Plato, plants also, as having life, are animals.

Earth herself, therefore, being a divine animal, is also a plenitude of intellectual and psychical essences, and of immaterial powers. For if a partial soul has besides a material body an immaterial vehicle, what ought we to think of a soul so divine as that of the earth? Is it not, that by a much greater priority visible bodies are suspended from this soul through other vehicles as media, and that through these, the visible bodies are able to receive the illuminations of soul? Such then being the nature of earth herself, she is said to be our nurse; in the first place, indeed, as possessing a power in a certain respect equivalent to Heaven. For as that comprehends in itself divine animals, thus also earth is seen to contain terrestrial animals. But in the second place, she is our nurse, as inspiring our lives from her own proper life. For she not only produces fruits, and nourishes our bodies through these, but she also fills our souls with the illuminations of herself. For being a divine animal, and generating us who are partial animals, through her own body indeed she nourishes and connectedly-contains our bulk; but from her own soul perfects ours. By her own intellect, likewise, she excites the intellect which is in us; and thus according to the whole of herself becomes the nurse of our whole composition. On this account it appears to me that Plato calls her our nurse, indicating by this her intellectual nutritive energy. For if she is our nurse, but we are truly souls and intellects, according to these especially, she will be the perfector of our essence, moving and exciting our intellectual part. But being a divine animal, and comprehending in herself many partial animals, she is said by Plato to be conglobed about the pole which is extended through the universe; because she is contained and compressed about its axis. For the axis also is the pole. And the pole is thus now denominated, because the universe revolves about it. Because, however, the pole [properly so called] is impartible, but the axis is a pole with interval, just as if some one should say that a line is a flowing point, -on this account, the pole is said by Plato to be extended through the universe, as entirely pervading through the centre of the earth.

But we must survey the poles as powers that give stability to the universe, exciting indeed the whole bulk of it to intelligible love, and impartibly connecting that which is partible, and unitedly and without interval that which is extended by interval. Hence, also, Plato in the *Republic*, makes the spindle of Lachesis of adamant, indicating, as we have said, their inflexible and untamed power. And we must consider the axis, as that one divinity which collects the centres of the universe, which is connective of the whole world, and motive of the divine circulations; and as that about which wholes dance and are convolved, and as sustaining all heaven, being on this account denominated Atlas, as possessing an immutable and unwearied energy. The word τεταμενον also, or *extended*, used here by Plato, indicates that this one power is Titannic, guarding the circulations of wholes. But if, as the divine Iamblichus says, we understand by the pole extended through the universe, the heavens, neither thus shall we wander from the conception of Plato. For, as Plato says in the *Cratylus*, those who are skilled in astronomy call the heavens the pole, as harmoniously revolving. According to this conception, therefore, you may call heaven the pole extended through the universe, as being incurvated through the whole of itself, in consequence of being without an angle. For after this manner the superficies of a circle is extended. About this, however, earth is conglobed, not locally, but through a desire of becoming assimilated to it, converging to the middle, in order that as heaven is moved about the centre, so she by tending to the centre, may become similar to that which is essentially spherical, being herself as much as possible conglobed. Hence she is compressed about the heaven in such a way as to be wholly extended about it.

According to each of these conceptions, therefore, Plato delivers the cause through which earth is contained in the middle. For the axis is a power connective of the earth; and the earth is on all sides compressed by the circulation of the heaven, and is collected together into the centre of the universe. Earth, therefore, being such, Timæus afterwards clearly shows what utility she affords to the universe; for he calls her the guardian and artificer of day and night. And indeed that she is the maker of night, is evident. For she produces a conical shadow; and her magnitude and figure, are the causes of the dimension and quality of the figure of this shadow. But after what manner is she likewise the fabricator of day? Or does she not produce this day which is conjoined with night? For about her the risings and settings of the sun are surveyed. And that Plato assumes this day which is convolved with night, is evident from his arranging the former under the latter; as also prior to this, when he says, night therefore and day were thus generated. Earth, therefore, is the fabricator of both these, producing both in conjunction with the sun; the sun indeed being in a greater degree the cause of day, but the earth of night.

Being, however, the fabricator, she is also the guardian of them, preserving their boundaries and contrariety with reference to each other, and also their augmentations and diminutions, according to a certain analogy. Hence, some denominate her Isis, as equalizing the inequality, and bringing to an analogy the increase and decrease of both day and night. But others looking to her prolific power call her Ceres, as Plotinus, who denominates the intellect of the earth Vesta, but the soul of it Ceres. We, however, say that the first causes of these divinities are intellectual, ruling[†] and liberated; but that from these causes illuminations and powers extend to the earth. Hence there is a terrestrial Ceres and Vesta, and a terrestrial Isis, in the same manner as there is a terrestrial Jupiter, and a terrestrial Hermes; these terrene deities being arranged about the one divinity of the earth; just as a multitude of celestial Gods proceeds about the one divinity of the heavens. For there are progressions and terminations of all the celestial Gods into the earth; and all things are in her terrestrially, which are contained in the heavens celestially. For the intellectual earth receives the paternal powers of heaven, and contains all things after a generative manner. Thus, therefore, we say that there is a terrestrial Bacchus, and a terrestrial Apollo, who is the source of prophetic[‡] waters in many parts of the earth, and of openings which predict future events. But the Pæonian[§] and judicial powers which proceed into it, render other places of it of a purifying or medicinal nature. All the other powers of the earth, however, it is impossible to enumerate. For divine powers are indeed inexplicable. But the orders of angels and dæmons that follow these powers are still more numerous, and are circularly allotted the whole earth, and dance round its one divinity, its one intellect, and one soul.

CHAPTER XXIII

It remains in the next place, that we should survey how the earth is said to be the most ancient, and the first of the Gods within the heavens. For this will be taken literally by those who are accustomed to look only to its material, gross and dark bulk. But we indeed grant them that there is something of such a kind in the bulk of the earth as they say there is; but we think it proper that they should likewise look to the other goods of the earth, through which it surpasses the prerogatives of the other elements, *viz.* its stability, its generative power, its concord with the heavens, and its position in the centre of the

---

[†] For δαιμονικας here, it is necessary to read ηγεμονικας.

[‡] παντικα is evidently printed in the original for μαντικα.

[§] For αιωνιοι, it is evidently necessary to read in this place παιωνιοι.

universe. For the centre has great power in the universe, as being connective of every circulation. Hence also the Pythagoreans call the centre the tower of Jupiter, in consequence of containing in itself a demiurgic guard. We shall likewise remind our opponents of the Platonic hypothesis concerning the earth, mentioned by Socrates in the *Phædo*, where he says that the place of our abode is hollow and dark, and bound by the sea; but that there is another true earth, containing the receptacles of the Gods, and possessing a beauty resembling that of the heavens. We ought not, therefore, to wonder if now the earth is said to be the most ancient and the first of the Gods within the heavens, since she possesses so great an altitude, and such a surpassing beauty, and as Socrates afterwards says, was fashioned by the Demiurgus resembling a sphere covered with twelve skins, just as the heaven is similar to a dodecahedron. We must likewise understand that the Demiurgus gave to the earth alone among the elements to have all the elements separately, causing her to be wholly a world, variegated analogous to the heavens. For she contains a river of fire, of air, and of water, and of another earth, which has the same relation to her which she has to the universe, as Socrates says in the *Phædo*. But if this be the case, she very much transcends the other elements as imitating the heavens, and possessing every thing in herself terrestrially, which is celestially contained in the heavens.

To this also we may add, that the Demiurgus produced these two elements the first, earth and fire; but the others for the sake of these, in order that they might have the ratio of bonds with respect to them. And that the four elements are both in the heavens, and in the sublunary region; but in the former, indeed, according to a fiery characteristic, since fire there predominates, as Plato says, but in the latter according to a terrestrial peculiarity. For the profundity of air, and the bulk of water are spread round the earth, and possess much of an earthly property, on which account they are in their own nature dark. In the heavens, therefore, there is a predominance of fire, but in the sublunary region of earth. Since, however, generation is connascently conjoined with the heavens, the end of the latter is earth, so far as earth is in the heavens, but the beginning of generation is fire, considered as subsisting in generation. For it is usual to call the moon earth, as having the same ratio to the sun, which earth has to fire. "But [the Demiurgus] says Orpheus, fabricated another infinite earth, which the immortals call *Selene*, but terrestrials *Mene*." And it is usual to denominate the summit of generation fire, which Aristotle also does, when he calls ether fire. In another place, however, he does not think it proper to call ether fire, but fiery-formed. Hence, the end of the heavens is not entirely destitute of mutation, in consequence of its propinquity to generation; but the beginning of generation is moved in a circle imitating the heavens.

Farther still, this likewise must be considered, that we ought not to judge of the dignity of things from places, but from powers and essence. By what peculiarities, therefore, are we to form a judgment of transcendencies? But what others than those which the divine orders exhibit? For transcendency truly so called is with the Gods. From the divine orders, therefore, we must assume *the monadic, the stable, the all-perfect, the prolific, the connective, the perfective, the every-way extended, the vivific, the adorning, the assimilative,* and *the comprehending* power. For these are the peculiarities of all the divine orders. According to all these however, the earth surpasses the other elements, so that she may justly be called the most ancient, and the first of the Gods.

Again, a twofold nature of things may be surveyed, the one indeed according to progression, which always makes things that have a secondary arrangement subordinate to those that are prior to them; but the other according to conversion, which conjoins extremes to primary natures through similitude, and produces one circle of the whole generation. Since also the world is spherical, but a figure of this kind is the peculiarity of things that subsist according to conversion, earth likewise must be conjoined in it to the heavens, through one circle, and one similitude. For thus also the centre is most similar to the poles. For the heavens indeed entirely comprehend wholes, being moved about the poles; but the earth is allotted permanency in the centre. For it is appropriate to generation that the immoveable should be more ancient than that which is moved. Hence, according to all these conceptions it may be said, that earth as co-ordinate with heaven, is the most ancient of the Gods within the heavens. For she is within them, as being on all sides comprehended by them. For as the demiurgus fashioned the whole of a corporeal nature within the soul of the world, thus also he fabricated earth within the heavens, as compressed and contained by them, and in conjunction with them fabricating wholes.

She has, however, so far as she is *the first* of the Gods, an indication of transcendency according to essence; but so far as she is *the most ancient*, she exhibits to our view the divinity which she is allotted. For how is it possible not to admit that she is allotted a great portion in the world, and is very honourable, in whom there are the tower of Jupiter, and the progression of Saturn? For not only Tartarus, which is the extremity of the earth, is on all sides comprehended by Saturn, and the Saturnian power, but also whatever else may be conceived subordinate to this. For Homer says that this is connectedly-contained through the sub-tartarean Gods. Not that he arranges Gods beyond Tartarus, as the words indicate; but that Tartarus itself is on all sides comprehended by them.

Farther still, we may survey the analogy which earth has to the intellectual earth. For as the latter comprehends and gives subsistence to perfective, guardian, and Titannic orders of Gods, of which the Orphic theologies are full, so likewise the former possesses various powers. And as a nurse indeed she imitates the perfective order, according to which the Athenians also are accustomed to call her κουροτροφος, or *the nourisher of youth*, and ανησιδωρα, or *scattering gifts*, as producing and nourishing plants and animals. But as a guard she imitates the guardian, and as conglobed about the pole which is extended (τεταμενη) through the universe, the *Titannic* order. Since, however, the intellectual earth prior to other divinities generated Aigle and the Hesperian Erithya, thus also our earth is the fabricator of day and night. And the analogy of the latter to the former is evident.

In the last place, Proclus adds, if also you are willing after another manner to understand that she is the first and most ancient of the Gods, as deriving her subsistence from the first and most ancient causes, this reason also will be attended with probability, since first causes proceed by their energies to the utmost extent of things; and besides this, the last of things frequently preserve the analogy of such as are first, as possessing their order from them alone. Hence, every way the assertion of Plato is true, whether you are willing to look to the bulk of the earth, or to the powers which she contains. And thus much from Proclus, concerning that great mundane divinity, the earth, who in the language of Theophrastus[†] is the common Vesta of Gods and men; and on whose fertile surface reclining, says he, as on the soft bosom of a mother or a nurse, we ought to celebrate her divinity with hymns, and incline to her with filial affection, as to the source of our existence.

CHAPTER XXIV

Having thus amply discussed the theory pertaining to the celestial Gods, it is necessary in the next place, that we should direct our attention to the sublunary deities, who are denominated γενεσιουργοι, or *the fabricators of generation*. Plato in the *Timæus* calls these Gods

---

[†] Apud. Porphyr. de Abstin. [TTS vol. II.]

dæmons, because they are so with reference to the celestial Gods. For they are suspended from them, and together with them providentially attend to their appropriate allotments. Conformably to this, also, in the *Banquet* he calls Love a dæmon, as being the attendant of Venus, and as proceeding from the God Porus, who is truly the source of abundance; though in the *Phædrus* he admits Love to be a God, as with reference to the life of which he is the leader. What Plato, therefore, says of these Gods in the *Timæus* is as follows: "But to speak concerning the other dæmons, and to know their generation, is a task beyond our ability to perform. It is, therefore, necessary in this case to believe in ancient men; who being the progeny of the Gods, as they themselves assert, must have a clear knowledge of their parents. It is impossible, therefore, not to believe in the children of the Gods, though they should speak without probable and necessary arguments; but as they declare that their narrations are about affairs to which they are naturally allied, it is proper that complying with the law, we should assent to their tradition. In this manner then, according to them, the generation of these Gods is to be described. That Ocean and Tethys were the progeny of Heaven and Earth. That from hence Phorcys, Saturn, and Rhea, and such as subsist together with these, were produced. That from Saturn and Rhea, Jupiter, Juno, and all such as we know are called the brethren of these descended. And lastly others, which are reported to be the progeny of these."

Proclus, in his usual admirable manner, copiously elucidates these words of Plato, and in his comment fully unfolds the theory of the sublunary Gods. But unfortunately there are many chasms in some of the most important parts of his elucidations, which no critical acumen, nor sagacious conjecture, can fully supply. I shall endeavour, however, to extract from his commentary, in the best manner I am able, all the information on this subject which can at present be derived from this invaluable work, occasionally attempting to restore the sense, where from the mutilated state of the original it is wanting.

Plato then, intending now to speak of the sublunary Gods, says, that the discourse about them is admirable, and beyond our ability to perform, if we intend to discover the generation of them, and promulgate it to others. For what he before said of the demiurgus, that it is difficult to discover him, and impossible to speak of him to all men, this he now says of the sublunary Gods, that to know and to speak of the generation of them, surpasses our ability. What, therefore, does Plato mean by this mode of indication? For as he has delivered so many and such admirable things concerning all heaven, and the intelligible paradigm, how is it that he says, that to speak of the Gods who are the fabricators of the generation, is a task beyond our ability to perform? Perhaps it is because many physiologists considered these sublunary elements to be inanimate natures casually borne along, and destitute of providential care. For they acknowledged that the celestial bodies, on account of their orderly motions, participate of intellect and the Gods; but they left generation, as being very mutable and indefinite, deprived of providential inspection. In order, therefore, that we might not be affected in the same manner as they were, he antecedently celebrates and proclaims the generation of the sublunary Gods to be divine and intellectual, requiring no such mode of indication in speaking of the celestial Gods. Perhaps also it may be said, that souls more swiftly forget things nearer to themselves, but have a greater remembrance of superior principles. For they in a greater degree operate upon them through transcendency of power, and appear through energy to be present with them. The same thing also happens with respect to our sight. For though we do not see many things that are situated on the earth, yet at the same time we appear to see the inerratic sphere, and the stars themselves, because they illuminate our sight with their light. The eye of the soul, therefore, becomes in a greater degree oblivious of, and blind to, more proximate than to higher and more divine principles. Thus, all religions and sects acknowledge that there is a first principle of things, and all men invoke God as their helper; but all do not believe that there are Gods posterior to this principle, and that a providential energy proceeds from them into the universe. For *The One* is seen by them in a clearer manner than multitude. Others, again, believe indeed that there are Gods, but after the Gods, admitting the dæmoniacal genus, they are ignorant of the heroic order. And in short, this is the greatest work of science, subtilly to distinguish the media and the progressions of beings. If, therefore, we rightly assert these things, Plato, when speaking of the celestial Gods, very properly indicates nothing of the difficulty of the subject; but when speaking of the sublunary Gods, says that it surpasses our ability. For the discussion of these is more difficult, because we cannot collect any thing about them from apparent objects, but it alone requires a divinely-inspired energy, and intellectual projection. And thus much concerning this doubt.

Again, though we have assigned a reason why Plato calls the sublunary Gods dæmons, we may likewise say according to another conception, that in the celestial regions there are dæmons, and in the sublunary

Gods; but that in the former the genus is indeed divine,† though dæmons also are generated according to it;‡ and that in the latter the whole multitude are dæmons. For there indeed, the divine peculiarity, but here the dæmoniacal predominates, to which some alone looking, have divided the divine and the dæmoniacal, according to the heavens and generation. They ought however, to have arranged both in both; but in the former indeed the divine nature, and in the latter the dæmoniacal predominates; though in the former there is also the divine peculiarity. For if the whole world is a blessed God, no one of the parts which give completion to it is destitute of divinity, and providential inspection. But if all things participate of deity and providence, the world is allotted a divine nature. And if this be the case, appropriate orders of Gods preside over its different parts. For if the heavens through souls and intellects as media participate of one soul, and one intellect, what ought we to think of these sublunary elements? How is it possible, that these should not in a much greater degree participate through certain middle divine orders, of the one deity of the world?

Farther still, it would also be absurd that the telestic art (or the art pertaining to mystic ceremonies) should establish on the earth places fitted for oracles, and statues of the Gods, and through certain symbols should cause things generated from a partial and corruptible matter, to become adapted to the participation of deity, to be moved by him, and to predict future events; but that the demiurgus of wholes, should not place over the whole elements which are the incorruptible plenitudes of the world, divine souls, intellects and Gods. For whether was he unwilling? But how could he be unwilling, since he wished to make all things similar to himself? Was he then unable? But what could hinder him? For we see that this is possible from telestic works. But if he was both willing and able, it is evident that he gave subsistence to Gods, who have allotments in, and are the inspective guardians of generation. Since however the genus of dæmons is every where an attendant on the Gods, there are also dæmons who are the fabricators of generation; some of whom indeed rule over the whole elements, but others are the guardians of climates, others are the rulers of nations, others of cities, others of certain families, and others are the guardians of individuals. For the guardianship of dæmons extends as far as to the most extreme division.

---

† It is necessary here to supply the word θειον.

‡ It is requisite to read κατ' εκεινον, instead of κατ' εκεινην.

CHAPTER XXV

Having therefore solved the problem pertaining to the essence, let us in the next place consider the order of the sublunary Gods, and the meaning of the subsequent words of Plato. For let them be Gods, and let them be called dæmons for the cause above assigned, where must we arrange them? Must it be, as we have before said, under the moon, or prior to the celestial† Gods? For this may appear to be proper for these two reasons; one indeed, because Plato indicates that he ascends to a greater order, by saying that it exceeds our ability to speak concerning them, having already spoken concerning the celestial Gods; but the other, because he follows in what he says, those who have delivered to us Theogonies. For they prior to the world and the demiurgus, delivered these generations of Gods proceeding from Heaven and Earth. In answer to this query however, we must say, that he produces them after the celestial Gods, and through this from Heaven and Earth. For on this account he said that Earth was the most ancient of the Gods within the Heaven, because from this and Heaven, he was about to produce the other Gods which the heavens contain. This we demonstrate from the demiurgus addressing his speech to these Gods, and to all the rest, as being produced by him within the universe. Why, however, Plato says that he follows the Theogony, and why he shall omit to speak concerning the sublunary deities, we must refer to his having no clear indications of the subsistence of these from the phænomena, as he had of the celestial divinities, from the order of their periods, which is adapted to the government of Gods. It exceeds the province therefore of physiology to speak of beings, concerning whom natural effects afford us no stable belief. Hence Plato says, as a physiologist, that it surpasses his ability to speak of these.

If, however, he says that he follows those who are divinely inspired, but they speaking concerning the supercelestial Gods, he adopts a similar Theogony, though discoursing of the sub-celestial divinities, we must not consider this as wonderful. For he knew that all the orders of the Gods, proceed as far as to the last of things, from the arrangement which is the principle of their progression, every where generating series from themselves analogous to the superior deities from which they proceed. Hence, though the orders of these Gods which are celebrated by theologists, are above the world, yet they subsist also in the sensible universe. And as this visible heaven is allied to that which is

---

† The word ουρανιων is omitted in the original.

supermundane, so likewise our earth is allied to the earth which is there, and the orders subsisting from the one to the orders proceeding from the other. From these things too, this also may be assumed, that according to Plato as well as according to other theologists, first natures as they proceed, produce things subordinate in conjunction with the causes of themselves. For these sublunary Gods proceeding from the demiurgus, are also said to be generated from Heaven and Earth that first proceed from him. The demiurgus therefore says to all of them that they ought to fabricate mortal natures, imitating his† power about their generation. Hence all of them proceed from one producing cause, though those of a secondary order proceed likewise from the Gods that are prior to them. It follows therefore from this, that not every thing which is produced by the junior Gods is mortal, since some of these proceed from other junior Gods; but the contrary alone is true, that every thing mortal is generated by these divinities. And again, it follows from this, that the junior Gods produce some things according to the immoveable, but others according to the moveable hyparxes of themselves. For they would not be the causes of immortals, if they produced all things according to moveable hyparxes; if it be true that every thing which subsists from a moveable cause, is essentially mutable.

Again, when Plato says, "It is therefore necessary to believe in ancient men, who being the progeny of the Gods as they themselves assert, must have a clear knowledge of their parents; for it is impossible not to believe in the children of the Gods, though they should speak without probable and necessary arguments," we may collect from this, that he who simply believes in things which seem difficult to be known, and which are of a dubious nature, runs in the paths of abundance, recurring to divine knowledge, and deific intelligence, through which all things become apparent and known. For all things are contained in the Gods. But that which antecedently comprehends all things, is likewise able to fill other things with the knowledge of itself. Hence, Timæus here sends us to theologists, and to the generation of the Gods celebrated by them. Who therefore are they, and what is their knowledge? They indeed are the progeny of the Gods, and clearly know their progenitors; being the progeny and children of the Gods, as preserving the form of their presiding deity according to the present life. For Apolloniacal souls, in consequence of chusing a prophetic, or telestic life, are called the children and progeny of Apollo; children indeed, so far as they are souls pertaining to this God, and adapted to this series; but progeny because

---

† It is obviously necessary here for εαυτων to read εαυτου.

they demonstrate their present life to be conformable to these characteristics of the God. All souls therefore, are the children of the Gods; but all do not know their presiding God. Such however, as have this knowledge and chuse a similar life, are called the children and progeny† of the Gods. Hence Plato adds, "as they say," for they unfold the order from which they came. Thus the Sibyl‡ as soon as she was born, uttered oracles; and Hercules appeared at his birth with demiurgic symbols. But souls of this kind convert themselves to their progenitors, and are filled from them with deific knowledge. Their knowledge however, is enthusiastic, being conjoined to deity through divine light, and exempt from all other knowledge, both that which is probable, and that which is demonstrative. For the former is conversant with nature, and the universal in particulars; but the latter with an incorporeal essence, and the objects of science. Divinely-inspired knowledge however, alone, is conjoined with the Gods themselves.

Timæus, or in other words Plato, afterwards adds: "But as they declare that their narrations are about affairs, to which they are naturally allied, it is proper that complying with the law, we should assent to their tradition." From these words, he who considers them accurately may assume many things, such as that divinely-inspired knowledge is perfected through familiarity with and alliance to the Gods. For the sun is seen through solar-form light, and divinity becomes apparent through divine illumination. It may likewise be inferred that the divine law defines the orders of the Gods which the divinely-inspired conceptions of the ancients unfold, according to which also souls energizing, though not enthusiastically, are persuaded by those that enthusiastically energize. Complying with this law, Timæus in the beginning of this dialogue says that he shall invoke the Gods and Goddesses. From these words also we may infer, that all the kingdoms both in the heavens and the sublunary region, are adorned and distributed in order, according to the first and intellectual principles; and that all of them are every where according to the analogous. Likewise that the order of things precedes our conceptions. But it is Pythagoric to follow the Orphic genealogies. For the science concerning the Gods proceeded from the Orphic tradition

---

† εγγονοι is omitted in the original.

‡ This is doubtless the Sybil, of whom Proclus also observes (in Tim. p 325) "that proceeding into light, she knew her own order, and manifested that she came from the Gods, saying I am the medium between Gods and men." ειδε γαρ τοι Σιβυλλα προελθουσα εις φως, και την ταξιν εαυτης, και ως εκ θεων ηκει δεδηλωκεν, ειμι δ' εγω μεση τε θεων ειπουσα μεση τ' ἀνθρωπων.

through Pythagoras, to the Greeks, as Pythagoras himself says in the *Sacred Discourse*.

CHAPTER XXVI

Again then, following Proclus, we say that the theory of the sublunary is immediately connected with that of the celestial Gods; and in consequence of being suspended from it, possesses the perfect and the scientific. For the generation-producing choir of Gods, follows the Gods in the heavens, and in imitation of the celestial circle, convolves also the circle in generation. For secondary follow the natures prior to them, according to an indivisible and united progression. Because however, the divinities that govern generation, subsist immediately from the celestial Gods, on this account also they are converted to them according to one undisjoined union; just as the celestial are converted to the supercelestial deities, from whom they were proximately generated; but the supercelestial to the intellectual, by whom they were adorned and distributed; and again the intellectual to the intelligible Gods, from whom they were ineffably unfolded into light, and who indescribably and occultly comprehend all things.

Of the whole of this truly golden chain therefore, the summit is indeed the genus of the intelligible Gods, but the end is that of the sublunary deities, who govern[†] generation in an unbegotten, and nature in a supernatural manner, to which the demiurgic intellect now gives subsistence; the dominion of the Gods extending supernally from the heavens, as far as to the last of things. Of these sublunary deities however, it is necessary to observe in the first place, that all of them preserve the generative and perfective energy of their generating cause, and also his demiurgic and stable productive power. They likewise receive measures, boundaries, and order from their father. And such things as he governs exemptly and totally, they being divided according to allotments, fabricate, generate, and perfect. Some of them also are proximate to the celestial Gods; but others proceed to a greater distance from them. Hence, some preserve the idea of these Gods, so far as it can be preserved in the sublunary order; but others are established according to their appropriate power. For of every order, the summit is analogous to the order prior to it. Thus the summit of intelligibles is unity; of intellectuals is intelligible; of the supermundane order, is intellectual; and of the mundane order, supermundane. And some of the

---

† For επιπορευοντων, it is necessary to read επιτροπευοντων.

sublunary Gods indeed, are in a greater degree united to the demiurgic monad; but others are more distant from it. Hence, some being analogous to it, are the leaders of the whole of this series; but others have a more partial similitude to it. For the father established in every order powers analogous to him in their arrangement; since in all the divine orders a certain cause pre-subsists analogous to *The Good*.

Conformably to these causes which are thus analogous to the ineffable principle of things, and which with reference to it are called monads, the sublunary Gods proceed, and adorn and distribute generation in a becoming manner. And some indeed, give completion to this, but others to some other will of their father. For some complete his connective, others his prolific, others his motive, others his guardian will, and others, some other will of the demiurgus pertaining to the wholes in the sublunary region. And some of them have dominion over souls, others over dæmons, and others over Gods. All of them however are intellectual according to essence, but mundane according to allotment. They are also perfective and powerful, governing generation in an unbegotten manner, beings deprived of intellect, intellectually, and inanimate natures, vitally. For they adorn all things according to their own essence, and not according to the imbecility of the recipients. But Plato is evidently of opinion that these Gods use certain other bodies more simple and perpetual that these elements by saying, that they appear when they please and become visible to us. That he likewise gives them souls is manifest from his saying that every mundane God is conjoined to bodies through soul. For he then first called the world itself a God, when he had established a soul in it. And again that he suspends intellects from them, through which their souls are intellectual, and are immediately converted to the demiurgus, is evident from the speech of the demiurgus to them.

If likewise it is requisite that the whole world should be perfect, it is necessary that together with the divine genera we should conceive that the dæmoniacal order was generated prior to our souls, and which receives a triple division, *viz.* into angels, dæmons properly so called, and heroes. For the whole of this order fills up the middle space between Gods and men; because there is an all-perfect separation or interval between our concerns, and those of the Gods. For the latter are eternal, but the former are frail and mortal. And the former indeed are satisfied with the enjoyment of intellect in energy partially; but the latter ascend into total intellects themselves. On this account, there is a triad which conjoins our concerns with the Gods, and which proceeds analogous to the three principal causes of things; though Plato is accustomed to call the whole of this triad dæmoniacal. For the angelic is analogous to being, or the intelligible which is first unfolded into light from the ineffable and occult fountain of beings. Hence also, it unfolds the Gods themselves, and announces that which is occult in their essence. But the dæmoniacal is analogous to infinite life. On which account it proceeds every where according to many orders, and is of a multiform nature. And the heroic is analogous to intellect and conversion. Hence also, it is the inspective guardian of purification, and is the supplier of a magnificent and elevated life. Farther still, the angelic indeed proceeds according to the intellectual life of the demiurgus. Hence it also is essentially intellectual, and interprets, and transmits a divine intellect to secondary natures. But the dæmoniacal proceeds according to the demiurgic providence of wholes, governs nature, and rightly gives completion to the order of the whole world. And the heroic again, proceeds according to the convertive providence of all these. Hence, this genus likewise is elevated, raises souls on high, and is the cause of a grand and vigorous energy.

Such therefore being the nature of these triple genera, they are suspended from the Gods; some indeed from the celestial Gods, but others from the divinities who are the inspective guardians of generation. And about every God there is an appropriate number of angels, heroes and dæmons. For every God is the leader of a multitude which receives his characteristic form. Hence of the celestial Gods, the angels, dæmons and heroes are celestial; but of the fabricators of generations, they have a generation-producing characteristic. Of the elevating Gods, they have an elevating property: but of the demiurgic, a demiurgic; of the vivific, a vivific property. And so of the rest. And again, among the elevating Gods, of those that are of a Saturnian characteristic, the angels, dæmons, and heroes are Saturnian; but of those that are Solar, they are Solar. Among the vivific Gods likewise of those that are Lunar, the ministrant powers are Lunar; but of the Aphrodisiacal, or those that have the characteristic of Venus, they are Aphrodisiacal. For they bear the names of the Gods from whom they are suspended, as being in connected continuity with them, and receiving one and the same idea with an appropriate subjection. Nor is this wonderful, since partial souls also, when they know their patron and leading Gods, call themselves by their names. Or whence were the Esculapiuses, the Bacchuses, and the Dioscuri denominated, who being men of a heroic character, took the names of the deities from whom they descended?† As therefore, of the celestial, so likewise of the Gods who are the fabricators of generation, it is necessary to survey about each of them, a co-ordinate angelical, dæmoniacal, and heroical multitude; and that the number suspended from them retains the appellation of its producing monad. Hence, there is a celestial God, angel and hero; and the like is also true of the earth.‡ In a similar manner we must say that Ocean and Tethys proceed into all the orders; and conformably to this the other Gods. For there is likewise a Jovian, a Junonian, and a Saturnian multitude, which is called by the same appellation of life. Nor is there any absurdity, in calling man both the intelligible and the sensible man; though in these, there is a much greater separation and interval.§ And thus much in common concerning the Gods and dæmons who are the fabricators of generation.

CHAPTER XXVII

It now remains to show what conceptions we ought to have of the Gods mentioned by Plato in the passage before cited from the *Timæus*. For of the ancients, some referred what is said about them to fables, others to the fathers of cities, others to guardian powers, others to ethical explanations, and others to souls. These, however, are sufficiently confuted by the divine Iamblichus, who demonstrates that they wander from the meaning of Plato, and from the truth of things. After this manner, therefore, we must say, that Timæus being a Pythagorean, follows the Pythagorean principles. But these are the Orphic traditions. For what Orpheus delivered mystically through arcane narrations, these Pythagoras learned, being initiated by Aglaophemus in the mystic wisdom which Orpheus derived from his mother Calliope. For these things Pythagoras says in the *Sacred Discourse*. What then are the Orphic traditions, since we are of opinion that the doctrine of Timæus about the Gods should be referred to these? They are as follow: Orpheus delivered the kingdoms of the Gods who

---

† Some of the moderns, from being profoundly ignorant of this circumstance, have stupidly supposed that the Gods of the ancients were nothing more than dead men deified; taking for their guides on this important subject, mere historians, philologists and rhetoricians, instead of philosophers.

‡ For $\epsilon\pi\iota\ \tau\eta\varsigma$, it is necessary to read $\epsilon\pi\iota\ \gamma\eta\varsigma$.

§ For $\alpha\pi o\kappa\alpha\tau\alpha\sigma\tau\alpha\sigma\epsilon\omega\varsigma$, it is requisite to read $\alpha\pi o\sigma\tau\alpha\sigma\epsilon\omega\varsigma$.

preside over wholes, according to a perfect number, *viz.* Phanes, Night, Heaven, Saturn, Jupiter, Bacchus. For Phanes is the first that bears a sceptre, and the first king is the celebrated Ericapæus. But the second is Night, who receives the sceptre from her father [Phanes]. The third is Heaven, who receives it from Night. The fourth is Saturn, who, as they say, offered violence to his father. The fifth is Jupiter, who subdued his father. And after him, the sixth is Bacchus. All these kings, therefore, beginning supernally from the intelligible and intellectual Gods, proceed through the middle orders, and into the world, that they may adorn mundane affairs. For Phanes is not only in intelligibles, but also in intellectuals, in the demiurgic, and in the supermundane order; and in a similar manner, Heaven and Night. For the peculiarities of them proceed through all the middle orders. And with respect to the mighty Saturn, is he not arranged prior to Jupiter, and does he not after the Jovian kingdom, divide the Bacchic fabrication in conjunction with the other Titans? And this indeed, he effects in one way in the heavens, and in another in the sublunary region; in one way in the inerratic sphere, and in another among the planets. And in a similar manner Jupiter and Bacchus. *These things, therefore, are clearly asserted by the ancients.*

If, however we are right in these assertions, these divinities have every where an analogous subsistence; and he who wishes to survey the progressions of them into the heavens, or the sublunary region, should look to the first and principal causes of their kingdoms. For from thence, and according to them, their generation is derived. Some, therefore, say, that Plato omits to investigate the Gods who are analogous to the two kings in the heavens, I mean Phanes and Night. For it is necessary to place them in a superior order, and not among the mundane Gods; because prior to the world, they are the leaders of the intellectual Gods, being eternally established in the adytum, as Orpheus says of Phanes, who by the word adytum, signifies their occult and immanifest order. Whether, therefore, we refer the circulation of same and different, mentioned by Plato in this dialogue, to the analogy of these, as male and female, or paternal and generative, we shall not wander from the truth. Or whether we refer the sun and moon, as opposed to each other among the planets, to the same analogy, we shall not err. For the sun indeed through his light preserves a similitude to Phanes, but the moon to Night. Jupiter, or the demiurgus, in the intellectual, is analogous to Phanes in the intelligible order. And the vivific crater Juno is analogous to Night, who produces all life in conjunction with Phanes from unapparent causes; just as Juno is parturient with, and emits into light, all the soul contained in the world.

For it is better to conceive both these as prior to the world; and to arrange the demiurgus himself as analogous to Phanes; since he is said to be assimilated to him according to the production of wholes; but to arrange the power conjoined with Jupiter, (*i.e.* Juno) and which is generative of wholes, to Night, who produces all things from the father Phanes. After these, however, we must consider the remaining, as analogous to the intellectual kingdoms.

If, likewise, it should be asked why Plato does not mention the kingdoms of Phanes and Night, to whom we have said Jupiter and Juno are analogous? It may be readily answered, that the tradition of Orpheus contains these; on which account Plato celebrates the kingdom of Heaven and Earth as the first, the Greeks being more accustomed to this than to the Orphic traditions; as he himself says in the *Cratylus*, where he particularly mentions the Theogony of Hesiod, and recurs as far as to this kingdom according to that poet. Beginning, therefore, from this Theogony as more known, and assuming Heaven and Earth as the first kingdoms above the world, he produces the visible Heaven and Earth analogous to those in the intellectual order, and celebrates the latter as the most ancient of the Gods within the former. From these also, he begins the Theogony of the sublunary Gods. These things, however, if divinity pleases, will be manifest from what follows. At present we shall only add, that it is requisite to survey all these names divinely or dæmoniacally, and according to the allotments of these divinities in the four elements. For this ennead is in ether and water, in earth and in air, all-variously, according to the divine, and also according to the dæmonical peculiarity. And again, these names are to be surveyed aquatically and aerially, and likewise in the earth terrestrially, in order that all of them may be every where, according to an all-various mode of subsistence. For there are many modes of providence divine and dæmoniacal, and many allotments according to the division of the elements.

CHAPTER XXVIII

Let us, therefore, now return to the words of Plato. In the first place then he says that Ocean and Tethys were the progeny of Heaven and Earth. And here we may observe, that as this whole world is ample and various, as adumbrating the intellectual order of forms, it contains these two extremities in itself, Earth and Heaven; the latter having the relation of a father, but the former of a mother. On this account Plato calls Earth the most ancient of the Gods within the heavens, in order that conformably to this he might say, that Earth is the mother of all that Heaven is the father; at the same time evincing that partial causes are not only subordinate to their progeny, as Poverty, in the *Banquet* of Plato to Love, but are likewise superior to them, as alone receiving the offspring proceeding from the fathers. These two extremities, therefore, must be conceived in the world, Heaven as the father, and Earth as the mother of her common progeny. For all the rest terminate in these, some giving completion to the celestial number, but others to the wholeness of Earth. After the same manner, likewise, in each of the elements of the world, these two principles, Heaven and Earth, must be admitted, subsisting aerially indeed in air, but aquatically in water, and terrestrially in earth; and according to all the above-mentioned modes; in order that each may be a perfect world, adorned and distributed from analogous† principles. For if man is said to be a microcosm, is it not necessary that each of the elements by a much greater priority should contain in itself appropriately all that the world contains totally? Hence, it appears to me that Plato immediately after speaking about Heaven and Earth, delivers the theory of these Gods, beginning from those two divinities; for the other divinities proceed analogous to Heaven and Earth. These two divinities, however, are totally the causes of all the Gods that are now produced. And these divinities that are the progeny of Heaven and Earth, are analogous to the whole of each. These two, likewise, as we have before observed, are in each of the elements, aerially, or aquatically, or terrestrially. For Heaven is in Earth, and Earth in Heaven.[7] And here, indeed, Heaven subsists terrestrially, but there Earth celestially. For Orpheus calls the moon celestial earth.‡ Nor is it proper to wonder that this should be the case. For we may survey the same things every where, according to the analogous, in intelligibles, in intellectuals, in the supermundane order, in the heavens, and in generation, conformably to the proper order of each.

With respect, however, to each of these divinities, some of the interpreters of Plato understand by Earth, this solid bulk which is the object of sensible inspection; others as that which has an arrangement analogous to matter, and is supposed to exist prior to generated natures; others, as intelligible matter; others, as the power of intellect; others, as

---

† In the original αλογων is erroneously printed for αναλογων.

‡ Instead of και γαρ ουρανιαν και την σεληνην Ορφευς προσηγορευσεν, the sense requires we should read και γαρ ουρανιαν γην την σεληνην, κ.λ.

life; others, as an incorporeal form inseparable from earth; others conceive it to be soul; and others intellect. In a similar manner with respect to Heaven, some suppose it to be the visible heavens; others, the motion about the middle of the universe; others, power aptly proceeding in conjunction with motion; others, that which possesses intellect; others, a pure and separate intellect; others, the nature of circulation; others, soul; and others, intellect. I know, likewise, that the divine Iamblichus understands by Earth, every thing stable and firm, according to the essence of the mundane Gods, and which according to energy and a perpetual circulation, comprehends more excellent powers and total lives. But by Heaven, he understands the total and perfect energy proceeding from the demiurgus, which is full of appropriate power, and subsists about the demiurgus, as being the boundary of itself and of wholes. I know, likewise, that the admirable Theodorus establishes both these powers in the life which subsists according to habitude.

In order, however, that we may avoid erroneous opinions, and may adhere to the most pure conceptions of Iamblichus, and the traditions of Syrianus, it is necessary in the first place to recollect, that Plato is now speaking of the sublunary Gods, that all of them are every where, and that they proceed according to the analogy of the intelligible and intellectual kings. And in the second place we must say, that as the first Heaven is the boundary of and connectedly contains the intellectual Gods, containing the measure which proceeds from *The Good*[†] and the intelligible Gods, into the intellectual orders, after the same manner the Heaven which is now mentioned by Plato, is the boundary and container of the Gods that are the fabricators of generation, comprehending in one bound the demiurgic measure, and also that which proceeds from the celestial Gods to those divinities that are allotted the realms of generation, and connecting them with the celestial government of the Gods. For as the demiurgus is to *The Good Itself*, so is the one divinity of this Heaven, to the intellectual Heaven. Hence, as there, measure and bound proceeds from *The Good* through Heaven to all the intellectual Gods, so likewise here a bound arrives to the Gods the fabricators of generation and to the more excellent genera [*viz.* to angels, dæmons and heroes] from the demiurgus, and the summit of the mundane Gods; *viz.* through the connectedly-containing medium of this

---

[†] For εκ τ' αυτου, it is necessary to read εκ τ' αγαθου.

Heaven.† For the every-where proceeding Heaven is allotted this order; in one procession of things indeed, unitedly and occultly; but in another manifestly and separately. For in one order, it introduces bound to souls; in another to the works of nature; and in another in a different manner to other things. And in air indeed, it effects this primarily; but in the aquatic orders secondarily; and in earth, and terrestrial works, in an ultimate degree. But there are also complications of these. For the divine mode of subsistence, and also the dæmoniacal are different in the air, and in the earth. For in one place, the mode is the same in different orders; but in another the mode is different in one allotment. And thus much concerning the power of Heaven.

CHAPTER XXIX

In the next place, directing our attention to Earth, we shall derive the whole of the theory concerning her from her first evolution into light. She first becomes manifest, therefore, in the middle triads‡ of the intellectual Gods, together with Heaven who connectedly contains the whole intellectual order. She likewise proceeds analogous to the intelligible Earth, which we find to be the first of the intelligible§ triads. And as ranking in the vivific orders, she is assimilated to the first infinity. But she is the receiving bosom of the generative deity of Heaven, and the middle centre of his paternal goodness. She also reigns together with him, and is the power of him who ranks as a father. The Earth, however, which is analogous to her, and presides in the sublunary regions, is as it were the prolific power of the Heaven pertaining to the realms of generation, unfolding into light his paternal, definitive, measuring and containing providence, which prolifically extends to all things. She likewise generates all the sublunary infinity;* just as Heaven who belongs to the co-ordination of bound, introduces termination and end to secondary natures. Bound, therefore, and end define the hyparxis of every thing according to which Gods and dæmons, souls and bodies

---

† Instead of λεγω δη τοις του Ουρανου τουδε συνοχικης μεσοτητος, it is requisite to read λεγω δια της του Ουρανου, κ.λ.

‡ For τριαδην, it is necessary to read τριαδαις.

§ For νοερων, read νοητων.

* For αποριαν, read απειριαν.

are connected and made to be one, imitating the one unity of wholes, or in other words, the ineffable principle of things; but infinity multiplies the powers of every being. For there is much bound in all sublunary natures, and likewise much infinity, which through divinity, and after the Gods extends to all things. We have, therefore, these two orders, which are generative of the divine or dæmoniacal progressions, in all the sublunary genera and elements; and one kingdom of them in the same manner as in the intellectual orders.

From these, however, a second duad proceeds, Ocean and Tethys, this generation not being effected by copulation, nor by any conjunction of things separated, nor by division, nor according to a certain abscission, for all these are foreign from the Gods; but they are accomplished according to one union and indivisible conjunction of powers. And this union theologists are accustomed to call marriage. For marriage, as the theologist Orpheus says, is appropriate to this order. For he calls Earth the first Nymph, and the union of her with Heaven the first marriage; since there is no marriage in the divinities that are in the most eminent degree united. Hence there is no marriage between Phanes and Night, who are intelligibly united to each other. And marriage appears on this account to be adapted to the Heaven and Earth which we are at present considering, so far as they adumbrate the intellectual Heaven and Earth; which the sacred laws of the Athenians likewise knowing, ordered that the marriages of Heaven and Earth should be celebrated, as preparatory to initiation into the mysteries. Directing their attention to these also, in the Eleusinian mysteries looking upward to the heavens, they exclaimed, O son! but looking downward to the earth, O parent! According to this union, therefore, in conjunction with separation, Heaven and Earth produce through their goodness Ocean and Tethys. Or rather, they do not immediately produce these, but prior to these two monads, two triads, and duple hebdomads, among which are Ocean and Tethys. And the monads indeed, together with the triads, remain with the father. But of the hebdomads, Ocean, together with Tethys, abide, and at the same time proceed. All the rest, however, proceed into another order of Gods. And this indeed is the mode of their subsistence in the intellectual order. But here, Plato entirely omits the causes that abide in the father, but delivers to us those that proceed and at the same time abide, because his intention is to speak of the Gods that are the fabricators of generation. To these, however, progression, motion, and difference, are adapted, and a co-arrangement of the male with the female; in order that there may be generation, that matter may be adorned with forms, and that difference may be combined with sameness. Hence Plato commences from the duad, proceeds through it, and again returns to it. For the duad is adapted to material natures, as well as difference, on account of the division of forms about matter. Having mentioned a duad, likewise, he begins from Earth; for this is more adapted to things pertaining to generation.

With respect to these two divinities, however, Ocean and Tethys, who abide in their causes and at the same time proceed from them, some say that Ocean is a corporeal essence, others, that it is a swiftly pervading nature; others, that it is the motion of a humid essence; others, that it is ether, through the velocity of its motion; and others, that it is the intelligible profundity itself of life. The divine Iamblichus, however, defines it to be the middle motive divine cause, which middle souls, lives, and intellections, efficacious natures, and those elements that are pneumatic, such as air and fire, first participate. And with respect to Tethys, some say that it is a humid essence; others, that it is a very-mutable nature; and others, that it is the hilarity of the universe. But the divine Iamblichus asserts it to be a productive power, possessing in energizing an efficacious establishment, the stable intellections of which, souls, natures, and powers participate, and which is likewise participated by certain solid receptacles, either of earth or water, which prepare a seat for the elements.

We, however, again assuming our principles, say, that the causes of these are indeed in the intellectual Gods, and that they are likewise in the sensible universe. For Ocean every where distinguishes first from second orders, in consequence of which poets do not improperly call it the boundary of the earth. But the Ocean which is now the subject of discussion, is the cause of motion, progression, and power; inserting in intellectual lives indeed, acme, and prolific abundance; but in souls, celerity and vigour, in their energies, and purity in their generations; and in bodies facility of motion. And in the Gods indeed it imparts a motive and providential cause; but in angels an unfolding and intellectual celerity and vigour. Again, in dæmons it is the supplier of efficacious power; but in heroes, of a magnificent and flourishing life. It likewise subsists in each of the elements, according to its characteristic peculiarity. Hence, the aerial Ocean is the cause of all the mutation of aerial natures, and of the circle of the meteors, as also Aristotle says. But the aquatic Ocean gives subsistence to fertility, facility of motion, and all-various powers. For according to the poets,

> From this all seas, and every river flow.

And the terrestrial ocean is the producing cause of generative perfection, of the separation of forms, and of generation and corruption. Whether also there are certain terrestrial orders, vivific and demiurgic, it is the source of their distinction; or whether there are powers connective of the productive principles of the earth, and the inspective guardians of generation, - these also it excites and multiplies, and calls into motion.

With respect to Tethys, as the name indeed evinces, she is the most ancient, and the progenitor, of the Gods, in the same manner as it is fit to acknowledge of the mother Rhea. For theologists denominate another Goddess prior to her, Maia. Thus, Orpheus,

> Maia, of Gods supreme, immortal Night,
> What mean you, say?

But according to the etymology of Plato, she is a certain fontal deity. For the undefiled and pure, and that which percolates are signified through her name. For since Ocean produces all things, and is the source of all motions, whence also it is called the generation of the Gods, Tethys separates the unical cause of his motions into primary and secondary motions. Hence Plato says, that she derives her appellation from *leaping* and *percolating*. For these are separative names, in the same manner, as he says in the *Sophista*, (το ξαινειν και κερκιζειν) to card, and to separate threads in weaving with a shuttle. Ocean, therefore, generating all motion collectively, whether divine, or intellectual, or psychical, or physical, Tethys separating both internal and external motions, is so called from causing material motions to leap and be percolated from such as are immaterial. Hence, the separating characteristic is adapted to the female, and the unical[†] to the male. Plato, therefore, would assert such peculiarities as these, of Ocean and Tethys, and does assert them in the *Cratylus*. But according to the divine Iamblichus, Tethys must be defined to be the supplier of position and firm establishment. From all that has been said, however, it may be summarily asserted that Tethys is the cause of permanency, and a firm establishment of things in herself, separating them from the motions that proceed externally.

In short, Ocean is the cause of all motion, intellectual, psychical, and physical to all secondary natures; but Tethys is the cause of all the separation of the streams proceeding from Ocean, imparting to each a proper purity in the motion adapted to it by nature; through which each, though it may move itself, or though it may move other things,

---

[†] For ενιαυτον here, it is necessary to read ενιαιον.

yet moves in a transcendent manner. But theologists manifest that Ocean is the supplier of all motion, when they say that he sends forth ten streams, nine of which proceed into the sea; because it is necessary, that of motions nine should be corporeal, but that there should be one alone of the essence which is separate from bodies, as we are informed by Plato in the *Laws*.[†] Such divine natures, therefore, as the mighty Ocean generates, these he excites to motion, and renders them efficacious. But Tethys distinguishes these, preserving generative causes pure from their progeny, and establishing them in energies more ancient than those that proceed into the external world. And thus much concerning each of these divinities, Ocean and Tethys.

Since, however, as we have said, the generation of these, is from the prior divinities, Heaven and Earth, but is not effected either by a copulation such as that which is in sensibles, nor according to such a union as that of Night and Phanes in intelligibles, it very properly follows that their progeny are separated from each other, analogously to their parents, and that each receives a similitude to both. For Ocean indeed, as being the male, is assimilated to the paternal cause, Heaven; but as the supplier of motion to the maternal cause, Earth, who is the cause of progressions. And Tethys indeed, as the female is assimilated to the prolific cause; but as producing a firm establishment[‡] of her progeny in their proper lives, she is assimilated to the fabricating cause. For the male is analogous to the monadic; but the female to the dyadic. And the stable is adapted to the former; but the motive to the latter. A duad, therefore, proceeding from a duad, and being assimilated according to the whole of itself to the duad which is generative of it, defines and distinguishes the causes of itself, and all the number posterior to itself; in order that every where we may ascribe that which defines and separates, to the order of Ocean and Tethys.

[†] Plato in the 10th book of the *Laws*, distinguishes the genus of motions into ten species, *viz.* circulation about an immoveable centre, local transition, condensation, rarefaction, increase, decrease, generation, corruption, mutation or alteration, produced in another by another, and a mutation produced from a thing itself, both in itself, and in another. This last is the motion of an essence separate from bodies, and is the motion of soul.

[‡] For γονιμον, it is necessary to read μονιμον.

CHAPTER XXX

In the next place Plato says, "that from Ocean and Tethys, Phorcys, Saturn, and Rhea, and such as subsist together with these were produced;" the theory of which divinities is as follows. In the former progeny, a duad generative and motive, was produced from a terminating and definitive duad; *viz.* Ocean and Tethys, from Heaven and Earth; but in the second progeny, a multitude converted to its causes through the triad, is generated from the duad; indicating likewise an all-perfect progression. For this multitude also is divided, into the analogous to bound, and the co-ordinate to infinity. For the triad is the bound in this multitude; but the nameless number is the infinity in it. And of the triad itself, likewise, one thing is analogous to the monad and bound, but another to the duad and infinity. And in the former progression, indeed, the progeny alone proceeded according to bound and the intellectual; but in this there is also a mixture of the indefinite. But after the boundary from the triad, Plato adds, "And such as subsist together with these," indicating the entire progression and separation of these triple orders; so that the progeny of this progression is triadic through the peculiarity of conversion, and dyadic through the intervention of the infinite and indefinite.

Since, however, these differ according to their intellectual causes, in the same manner as the before-mentioned orders; but in them Ocean and Tethys were said to be the brethren, and not the fathers[†] of Saturn and Rhea; for the progression to these was from Heaven and Earth, and all the Titannic order is thence derived; let us see on what account Plato here gives subsistence to Phorcys, Saturn and Rhea, from Ocean and Tethys. For he may appear to say this not conformably to the Orphic principles. For "Earth lately bore from Heaven, as the theologist says, seven pure beautiful virgins with rolling eyes, and seven sons that were kings, with fine long hair. And the daughters indeed were Themis, and the joyful Tethys, Mnemosyne with thick-curled hair, and the blessed Rhea. She likewise bore Dione having a very-graceful form, and Phœbe, and Thea the mother of king Jupiter. But the venerable Earth brought forth those celestial youths, who are called by the appellation of Titans, because they revenged the mighty starry Heaven. And she also bore Cæus, the great Cræus, and the strong Phorcys, and likewise Saturn, and Ocean, Hyperion and Japetus." These things then having been written by the theologist prior to Plato, how is it that Timæus produces Saturn

---

[†] πατρος is erroneously printed instead of πατερες.

and Rhea, from Ocean and Tethys? In answer to this, as we have before arranged Ocean and Tethys above Saturn and Rhea, as being the media between these and the fathers, and guardians of the boundaries of both, as it is usual to celebrate them; we must say in the first place, indeed, that it is not wonderful that the same divinities should be brothers, and yet through transcendency of dignity should be called the fathers of certain Gods. For such things as are first, when they proceed from their causes, produce in conjunction with those causes, the natures posterior to themselves. Thus all souls indeed are sisters, according to one demiurgic cause, and according to the vivific principle and fountain from which they proceed; at the same time divine souls produce partial souls together with the demiurgus and vivific causes, in consequence of first proceeding into light, and abiding in their wholeness, receiving the power of fabricating natures similar to themselves. Besides, in the Gods themselves, all the offspring of Saturn are brethren, according to the one generative monad by which they were produced; yet at the same time Jupiter is called father, in the divine poet Homer, both by Juno and Neptune. So that it is not at all wonderful, if Ocean and Tethys are called both brethren and fathers of Saturn and Rhea; in consequence of preserving as among brethren the paternal peculiarity. In the first place, therefore, the doubt may after this manner be solved.

In the next place, it may be said, that of the divine Titannic hebdomads, Ocean indeed both abides and proceeds, uniting himself to his father, and not departing from his kingdom. But all the rest rejoicing in progression, are said to have given completion to the will of Earth, but to have assaulted their father, dividing themselves from his kingdom, and proceeding into another order. Or rather, of all the celestial genera, some alone abide in their principles, as the two first triads. For, as soon as Heaven understood that they had an implacable heart, and a lawless nature, he hurled them into Tartarus, the profundity of the earth, [says Orpheus]. He concealed them, therefore, in the unapparent, through transcendency of power. But others both abide in, and proceed from, their principles, as Ocean and Tethys. For when the other Titans proceeded to assault their father Heaven, Ocean prohibited them from obeying the mandates of their mother, being dubious of their rectitude. He, therefore, abides, and at the same time proceeds, together with Tethys; for she is conjoined with him according to the first progeny. But the other Titans are induced to separation and progression. And the leader of these is the mighty Saturn, as the theologist says; though he evinces that Saturn is superior to Ocean, by saying, that Saturn himself received the celestial Olympus, and that there being throned he reigns over the Titans; but that Ocean obtained all the middle allotment. For he says, that he dwells in the divine streams which are posterior to Olympus, and that he environs the Heaven which is there, and not the highest Heaven, but as the fable says, that which fell from Olympus, and was there arranged.†

Ocean and Tethys, therefore, so far as they abide, and are united to Heaven, produce in conjunction with him the kingdom of Saturn and Rhea; and so far as they are established in the first power of their mother, so far they produce Phorcys in conjunction with her.‡ For she produces him together with Nereus and Thaumas,§ from being mingled through love with the sea. For Phorcys is not celestial, but Ocean, as is evident from the *Theogony.** And so far as Tethys is full of Earth, so far being as it were a certain Earth, she may be said to produce this Phorcys in conjunction with Ocean; so far as Ocean also comprehends the intelligible in himself. Hence Tethys, so far as she is Earth according to participation, and Ocean so far as he is causally the sea, give subsistence in conjunction with Saturn and Rhea to this God. If, however, any arguments should demonstrate that in the intellectual order Saturn is above Ocean, or Rhea above Tethys, it must be said that this arrangement is indeed there; for in that order the causes of intellection are superior to those of motion; but that here on the contrary, all things are in mutation and a flowing condition, so that here Ocean is very properly prior to Saturn, since it is the fountain of motion, and Tethys is prior to Rhea. Hence, after another manner, the doubt may be thus solved.

---

† As this is a remarkably curious Orphic fragment, and it is not to be found in Gesner's collection of the Orphic remains, I shall give the original for the sake of the learned reader. Και τοι γε οτι ο Κρονος υπερτερος εστι του Οκεανου, δεδηλωκεν ο θεολογος παλιν λεγων· τον μεν Κρονον ουτον καταλαμβανειν τον ουρανιον Ολυμπον, κҳκει θρονισθεντα, βασιλευειν των Τιτανων· τον δε Οκεανον την ληξιν απασαν την μεσην· ναιειν γαρ αυτον εν τοις θεσπεσιοις ρειθροις τοις μετα τον Ολυμπον, και τον εκει περιεπειν Ουρανον, αλλ' ου τον ακροτατον, ως δε φησιν ο μυθος, τον εμπεσοντα του Ουλυμπου, και εκει τεταγμενον. (Procl. in Tim. 296.)

‡ For μετ' αυτου, it is necessary to read μετ' αυτης.

§ For Θαυμαντα, it is requisite to read Θαυμαντος; and for ποντον, ποντῳ.

* The original here is evidently erroneous; for it is, ου γαρ εστιν ο φορκυς ουρανιδης αλλα ο φορκυς, ως εστι δηλον εκ της θεογονιας. For αλλα ο φορκυς, therefore, I read αλλα ο Ωκεανος; Ocean, according to the *Theogony* of Hesiod, being the progeny of Heaven and Earth.

That we may speak, however, about each of these Gods, Theodorus refers souls that subsist in habitude to these divinities, and arranges them as presiding over the three divisions of the world. And Phorcys indeed, he arranges in the starless sphere, as moving the lation of the universe. He ought, however, to persuade us that Plato was acquainted with a certain starless sphere, and afterwards, that he thus arranged Phorcys in this sphere. But he places Saturn over the motions of the stars, because time[†] is from these, and the generations and corruptions of things. And he places Rhea over the material part of the world, because by materiality she has a redundancy with respect to the divinities prior to herself. But the divine Iamblichus arranges them in the three spheres between the heavens and the earth. For some of the sublunary deities give a twofold division to the sublunary region, but these divide it in a three-fold manner. And Phorcys indeed, according to him, presides over the whole[‡] of a humid essence, containing all of it impartibly. But Rhea is a divinity connective of flowing and aerial-formed spirits. And Saturn governs the highest and most attenuated sphere of ether, having a middle arrangement according to Plato; because the middle and the centre in incorporeal essences, have a greater authority than the powers situated about the middle. We, indeed, admire this intellectual explanation of Iamblichus; but we think it proper to survey these Gods every where, both in all the elements, and all orders. For thus we shall behold that which is common in them, and which extends to all things. And we say, indeed, that Phorcys is the inspective guardian of every spermatic essence, and of physical, and as it were spermatic productive principles, as being pregnant with, and the cause of generation. For there are spermatic productive principles in each of the elements; and different orders of Gods and dæmons preside over them, all which Plato comprehends through Phorcys. But king Saturn divides forms and productive principles, and produces more total into more partial powers. Hence he is not only an animal but pedestrious, aquatic and a bird. And he is not only pedestrious, but likewise man and horse. For the productive principles in him are more partial than in the celestial deities. Among the intellectual Gods, therefore, he is allotted this power, *viz.* to multiply and divide intelligibles. Hence, he is the leader of the Titans, as being especially characterized by the dividing peculiarity.

[†] Κρονος is erroneously printed for χρονος.

[‡] For της υγρας υλης ουσιας, I read της υγρας ολης ουσιας.

Again, we say that Rhea receives the unapparent powers of king Saturn, leads them forth to secondary natures, and excites the paternal powers to the fabrication of visible objects. For thus also, her first order is moved, is filled with power and life, and produces into that which is apparent, the causes that abide in Saturn. Hence Saturn is every where the supplier of intellectual forms; Rhea is the cause of all souls, and of every kind of life; and Phorcys is prolific with physical productive principles. Since however another number of Gods pertains to the kingdom of these, and which Saturn and Rhea comprehend, on this account Plato adds, "and such as subsist together with these." For he not only through this comprehends dæmons, as some say, but both the angelic and the dæmoniacal Saturn have with themselves a multitude, the one angelic, but the other dæmoniacal. And the multitude which is in the Gods is divine; that which is in the air is aerial; and in a similar manner in the other elements, and in the other more excellent genera arranged under these Gods.

By the words also "such as subsist together with these," Plato appears to signify the remaining Titans, *viz.* Cæus and Hyperion, Creus, Japetus, and likewise the remaining Titanidæ, *viz.* Phœbe, Theia, Mnemosyne, Themis, and Dione, with whom Saturn and Rhea proceeded into light. Also, those that proceeded together with Phorcys, *viz.* Nereus and Thaumas, the most motive Eurybia, and those who especially contain and connect the whole of generation. Moreover, it is worth while to observe that it is not proper to discuss accurately the arrangement in these divinities, and whether Saturn or Phorcys is the superior deity; for they are united and similar to each other. But if it be requisite to make a division, it is better to adopt the arrangement of the divine Iamblichus, *viz.* that Saturn is a monad; but Rhea a certain duad calling forth the powers that are in Saturn; and that Phorcys gives perfection to their progression.

CHAPTER XXXI

It now remains that we direct our attention to the other kings, who produce the apparent sublunary order of things; for such is the arrangement which they are allotted. Plato adds therefore, "That from Saturn and Rhea, Jupiter, Juno, and all such as we know are called the brethren of these descended." This is the third progression of the Gods who are the fabricators of generation, but the fourth order, closing as a tetrad the nomination of the leading Gods. For the tetrad is comprehensive of the divine orders. But as a duad this progression is assimilated to the first kingdom; because that as well as this is dyadic. There are, however, present with it, the all-perfect according to progression, and the uncircumscribed according to number. But Plato here not only adds the words "*such as,*" as in the progression prior to it, but likewise the word "*all,*" that he may indicate the progression of them to every thing. For we use the term το οσαν *such as* in speaking of things united, but the term το παντας *all*, in speaking of things now divided and multiplied. The total (το ολικον) likewise pertains to this progression. For the Gods which are denominated in it, and those that proceed every where together with them, are characterized according to this form of fabrication. For all demiurgi are total. Who therefore are they, and what kind of order do they possess?

The divine Iamblichus then asserts that Jupiter is the perfector of all generation; but that Juno is the cause of power, connexion, plenitude and life to all things; and that the brethren of them are those that communicate with them in the fabrication of generation, being also themselves intellects, and receiving a completion according to a perfection and power similar to them. But Theodorus, again dividing the life which animates the total in habitude, and forming it as he is accustomed to do into triads, calls Jupiter the power that governs the upper region as far as to the air; but Juno the power who is allotted the aerial part of the world; and the brethren of them those that give completion to the remaining parts. For Jupiter is the essential of the soul that subsists in a material habit, because there is nothing more vital than essence. But Juno is the intellectual part of such a soul, because the natures on the earth are governed by the productive principles proceeding from the air. And the other number is the psychical distributed into particulars.

We, however, consequently† to what has been before asserted, say, that according to Plato there are many orders of Jupiter. For one is the demiurgus, as it is written in the *Cratylus*; another, is the first of the Saturnian triad, as it is asserted in the *Gorgias*; another is the liberated, as it is delivered in the *Phædrus*; and another is the celestial, whether in the inerratic sphere, or among the planets. Moreover, as the first Jupiter produced into the visible fabrication the power of his father, which was concealed in the unapparent, being excited‡ to this by his mother Rhea; after the same manner the Jupiter delivered here, who is the fabricator

---

† The words ημεις δε επομενως are omitted in the original.

‡ For διανοηθεις, it is necessary to read διακινηθεις.

of generation, causes the unapparent divisions and separations of forms made by Saturn to become apparent; but Rhea calls them forth, into motion and generation; and Phorcys inserts them in matter, produces sensible natures, and adorns the visible essence, in order that there may not only be divisions of productive principles in natures and in souls, and in intellectual essences prior to these, but likewise in sensibles. For this is the peculiarity of fabrication. And if it be requisite to speak what appears to me to be the truth, Saturn indeed produces intellectual sections, but Rhea such as are psychical, and Phorcys such as are physical. For all spermatic productive principles are under nature. But Jupiter adorning sensible and visible sections, gives a specific distinction to such beings in the sublunary region as are totally vital, and causes them to be moved. Since, however, these sensible forms which are generated and perfected, are multiformly evolved, being moved and changed according to all-various evolutions, on this account, the queen Juno is conjoined with Jupiter, giving perfection to this motion of visible natures, and to the evolution of forms. Hence fables represent her as at one time sending mania to certain persons, but ordering others to undergo severe labours, in order that through intellect being present with all things, and partial souls energizing divinely both theoretically and practically, every progression, and all the generation of the sublunary region may obtain complete perfection.

Such, therefore, being the nature of this duad, there are also other demiurgic powers which triply divide the apparent† world of generation; one of these being allotted the government of air; another, that of water; and another that of earth, conformably to demiurgic allotments. Hence they are said to be the brothers of these, because they also preside over the visible fabrication. And farther still, there are others the progeny of these; which is the last progression of the divinities mentioned in this place by Plato. Hence, they are delivered anonymously; Plato by this indicating the diminution of it as far as to the last division: For as in the Gods that are above the world, the partible proceeds from the total fabrication, and the series of kings terminates in this; after the same manner also among the sublunary Gods, the progeny of Jupiter proceed from the Jovian order; among which progeny, likewise, is the choir of partible fabrication. For the above-mentioned demiurgi producing sensibles totally, it is necessary that those deities should have a subsistence who distribute different powers and peculiarities to different natures, and divide the sublunary generation into multitude. Hence

---

† For $\alpha\phi\alpha\nu\eta$ here it is necessary to read $\epsilon\mu\phi\alpha\nu\eta$.

Plato alone denominates them *others*, and does not employ the expressions *such as*, and *all*, because they associate with all-various diversity.

With respect, therefore, to this ennead of Gods, Heaven terminates, Earth corroborates, and Ocean moves all generation. But Tethys establishes every thing in its proper motion; intellectual essences in intellectual; middle essences in psychical; and such as are corporeal in physical motion; Ocean at the same time collectively moving all things. Saturn alone divides intellectually; Rhea vivifies; Phorcys distributes spermatic productive principles; Jupiter perfects things apparent from such as are unapparent; and Juno evolves according to the all-various mutations of visible natures. And thus through this ennead all the sublunary world derives its completion, and is fitly arranged; divinely indeed from the Gods, but angelically, as we say, from angels, and dæmoniacally from dæmons; the Gods indeed subsisting about bodies, souls and intellects; but angels exhibiting their providence about souls and bodies; and dæmons being distributed about the fabrication of nature, and the providential care of bodies. But again, the number of the ennead is adapted to generation. For it proceeds from the monad as far as to the extremities without retrogression;[8] which is the peculiarity of generation. For reasons (*i.e.* productive principles) fall into matter, and are unable to convert themselves to the principles of their existence. Moreover, the duad is triadic; for three dyadic orders were assumed; *viz.* Heaven and Earth; Ocean and Tethys; Jupiter and Juno. And this last duad ranks as the fourth progression, because prior to it, is the triad Phorcys, Saturn, and Rhea; which manifests the complication here, of the perfect and the imperfect, and of bound with infinity. For all celestial natures are definite, and as Aristotle says, are always in the end. But things in generation proceed† from the imperfect to the perfect, and receive the same boundary indefinitely. Besides this, the tetrad arising from the generation of these divinities is adapted to the orders of the fabricators of the sublunary region; in order that they may contain multitude unitedly, and the partible impartibly; and also to the natures that exist in generation. For the sublunary elements are four; the seasons according to which generation is evolved are four; and the centres are four. And in short, there is an abundant dominion of the tetrad in generation.

Why, however, it may be said, does Plato comprehend all the multitude of the Gods that fabricate generation, in this ennead? I

---

† For εστι, it is requisite to read προεισι.

answer, because this ennead gives completion to all the fabrication of generation. For in the sublunary realms there are bodies and natures, souls, and intellects, and this both totally and partially. And all these are in both respects in each of the elements. This ennead in each of the elements, is as follows, *viz.* total and partial bodies, total and partial natures, total and partial souls, and total and partial intellects, and the monad which contains these, *viz.* the elementary sphere itself; because wholes and parts are consubsistent with each other. Heaven and Earth, however, generate the unapparent essences of these, *i.e.* of wholes and parts, the former indeed according to union, but the latter according to multiplication. And the former according to bound, but the latter according to infinity; being the leaders of essence to all things. But Ocean and Tethys give perfection to both the common and divided motion of them. There is, however, a different motion of different things, *viz.* of total intellect, of total soul, and of total nature; and in a similar manner in such of these as are partial. The sublunary wholes, therefore, being thus adorned and distributed, Saturn, indeed, divides partial from total natures, but intellectually; Rhea, calls forth this division from intellectuals, into all-various progressions,[†] as far as to the last forms of life, being a vivific deity; but Phorcys produces the Titannic separation, to physical productive principles. After these three, are the fathers of composite natures. And Jupiter indeed, adorns sensibles totally, according to an imitation of Heaven. For the Jupiter in the intellectual order, proceeds analogous to the intellectual Heaven, in the royal series. But Juno moves wholes, fills them with powers, and evolves, according to every progression. And the Gods posterior to these fabricate the partial works of sensibles, some according to one, but others according to another peculiarity, either demiurgic, or vivific, or perfective, or connective, being evolved and dividing themselves, as far as to the last of things, analogously to the Saturnian order. For the dividing peculiarity originates from the Saturnian dominion.

CHAPTER XXXII

In the last place, let us consider why Plato denominates the sublunary deities, "such as become apparent when they please." Shall we say it is because these material elements are hurled forth before them as veils[‡] of the splendour of the etherial vehicles which are proximately

---

[†] προοδους is omitted in the original.

[‡] In the original it is παραπετα instead of παραπετασματα.

suspended from them? For it is evident that being mundane they must also necessarily have a mundane starry vehicle. The light of them, however, shines forth to the view, when they are about to benefit the places that receive their illumination. But if Plato says that they become visible when they please, it is necessary that this appearance of them should either be an evolution into light of the incorporeal powers which they contain, or of the bodies which are entirely spread under them. But if it is an evolution of their incorporeal powers, this is also common to the visible Gods. For they are not always apparent by their incorporeal powers, but only sometimes, and when they please. It is not proper, therefore, to divide the sublunary oppositely to the visible Gods, according to that which is common to both, but so far as they have entirely something peculiar. But if they produce a luminous evolution of certain bodies when they please, they must necessarily use other bodies prior to these material elements; and which then become visible to us, when it seems fit to the powers that use them. Hence, other bodies more divine than such as are apparent, are spread under the invisible Gods; and according to these, they are said to be, and are mundane. Through these also as media, they ride in and govern these elements. For they impart to them as much of themselves as they are able to receive, and contain the forms and the natures of them in their powers. For since no one of these is an object of sense, and it is necessary that the vehicles of rational souls should be things of this kind, it is evident that they must use other vehicles prior to these visible bodies.

With respect, however, to all the Gods that govern generation, we must not say that they have an essence mingled with matter, as the Stoics assert they have. For nothing which verges to matter is able to govern with intellect and wisdom, nor is properly a producing cause, but an organ of something else. Nor must we say that they have an essence unmingled with matter, but powers and energies mingled with it, as Numenius and his followers assert. For the energies of the Gods concur with their essences, and their inward subsist prior to their externally proceeding energies; since a partial soul also prior to the life which is inserted in the animal suspended from it, contains a more principal life in itself; and prior to the externally proceeding motion, through which it moves other things, it is moved with a motion converted to itself. The sublunary Gods, therefore, are entirely unmingled with matter; adorning indeed things mingled in an unmingled, and things generated, in an unbegotten manner. They likewise contain partibles impartibly, are the causes of life, the suppliers of intellect, the replenishers of power, the givers of soul, the primary leaders of all good, and the sources of order, providence, and the best administration. They also give subsistence to more excellent animals about themselves, are the leaders of angels, the rulers of dæmons, and the prefects of heroes; governing through this triple army the whole of generation. If, therefore, we assert that the appropriate order of these divinities about generation is the basis and seat of the total Gods, we shall speak rightly. And we shall likewise not err in asserting that they convolve the end of the divine decrement to the beginning. Such then being the nature of these divinities, Plato indeed looking to the Gods that are both intelligible and intellectual, and to those that are properly called intellectual, surveyed four progressions of them in common. But they also contain powers derived from the supermundane Gods; whether they proceed from the twelve leaders, or from certain other deities.

From the celestial choir of Gods likewise, a certain order proceeds into generation, which, as the divine Iamblichus says, is doubled in its progression. For from the twenty-one leaders, forty-two governments of Gods who are the fabricators of generation, are derived, according to each elementary allotment. But from the thirty-six decadarchs,[†] seventy-two sublunary rulers proceed; and in a similar manner other Gods; being the double of the celestial Gods in multitude, but falling short of them in power. It is likewise necessary to survey their triple progressions, their quintuple divisions, and their divine generation according to the hebdomad. For they receive an orderly distribution in a threefold, fivefold, and sevenfold manner analogous to the whole world; in order that each of the elements may be a world, and may be truly an imitation of the universe. Such, therefore, is the concise doctrine concerning the sublunary Gods, according to twofold essences, lives, and allotments; just as Plato also makes the ruling progeny of them to be dyadic.

CHAPTER XXXIII

Having therefore discussed the theory pertaining to the celestial and sublunary Gods, it now remains that we ascend to the summit or monad of all the mundane Gods, Bacchus, in whose divinity they all subsist and are rooted, similarly to the fixed stars in the inerratic sphere. For after

---

[†] These thirty-six decadarchs are the divinities alluded to by the Emperor Julian in his *Oration to the Sun*, when he says, "that the Sun divides the zodiac into twelve powers of Gods, and each of these into three others, so that thirty-six are produced in the whole." [See TTS vol. IV, p. 66.]

this manner, every monad analogously contains its co-ordinate multitude.

Bacchus therefore, is the mundane intellect, from which the soul and body of the world are suspended. With respect however, to intellect it is necessary to observe that one kind is imparticipable and total; another is participable indeed but essentially so; and a third is participable, and subsists as a habit. All intellects unconnected with soul belong to the first kind. The mundane intellect, and the intellects of all the mundane Gods and beneficent dæmons, rank in the second division. And to the third class such intellects as ours belong. This deity also is the monad of the Titans, or ultimate fabricators of things, by whom he is said in divine fables to have been torn in pieces; because the mundane soul which participates of this divinity, and is on this account intellectual, is participated by the Titans, and through them distributed into every part of the universe. Plato in the *Cratylus* says of this divinity "that he is the giver of wine; and that οινος *wine* may most justly be denominated οιονους because it is accustomed to deprive those of intellect who possessed it before." On which words Proclus in his MS Scholia on that dialogue observes as follows: "The young man Cratylus appears to inquire about our sovereign master Bacchus, as if it were about things of small importance, and on this account he is silenced by Socrates.†" And he does not indeed pay attention to the occult, but only to the last and mundane progressions of the Gods. These indeed, the wise man venerates, though as he says, they are sports, through these Gods [Bacchus and Venus] being lovers of sport. For as he says of the terminations of the other Gods, that they are terrible, and that they avenge and punish, and thus give perfection to souls; as for instance, that Justice follows Jupiter, the avenger of the divine law, and that this divinity is benevolent to those whose manners are orderly, and who live according to intellect, but that she is baneful to those who mingle their life with insolence and ignorance, till she has entirely subverted them, their houses and cities; - in like manner, he venerates the terminations of Bacchus and Venus, which produce γλυκυθυμια *sweetness of sensation*; every where purifying our conceptions concerning the Gods, and preparing us to understand that all things look to the best end, whatever it may be. For because the terminations of these divinities strengthen the infirmity of the mortal nature, and alleviate corporeal molestation, on this account the Gods the causes of these things, are φιλοπαιγμονες lovers of sport. Hence, of statues, they make some of them laughing

---

† This is implied by Socrates telling him that he inquires about *great* things.

and dancing, and exhibiting relaxation, but others austere, astonishing, and terrible to the view, analogously to the mundane allotments of the Gods.

But theologists frequently call Bacchus *wine*, from the last of his gifts, as for instance, Orpheus,

Οινου παντα μελη κοσμῳ λαβε, και μοι ενεικε.

i.e. "Take all the members of *Wine* [that are distributed] in the world, and bring them to me." If however the God is thus denominated, certainly his first and middle energies will be thus called, as well as his last; so that Socrates now looking to this calls the God διδοινυσας beginning from wine, which as we have said manifests all the powers of Bacchus. Thus also in the *Phædrus*, Socrates calls Love in common *great*, both that which is divine, and that which is a lover of body. By this epithet *wine* therefore, we must understand that the peculiarity of a partial intellect, is in common presented to our view. For the word οιουν *such as*, is nothing else than intellectual form separated from a total intellect, and in consequence of this becoming participated, *particular* and *alone*. For an all-perfect intellect is all things, and energizes according to all things with invariable sameness: but a partial and participated intellect, is indeed all things, but this according to one form, such as a solar, lunar, or mercurial form. This therefore, the peculiarity of which is to be separated from the rest, wine indicates, signifying an intellect *such as* and *particular*. (σημαινων τον οιον και τινα νουν)

Since, therefore, every partial fabrication is suspended from the Dionysiacal or Bacchic monad, which distributes participated mundane intellects from total intellect, (or that intellect which ranks as a whole) many souls from one soul, and all sensible forms from their proper wholenesses; on this account theologists call both this God and all his fabrications *wine*. For all these are the progeny of intellect. And some things participate of the partial distribution of intellect in a more distant, but others in a nearer degree. Wine therefore energizes in things analogous to its subsistence in them; in body indeed, after the manner of an image, according to a false opinion and imagination; but in intellectual natures, according to an intellectual energy and fabrication. For in the laceration of Bacchus by the Titans, the *heart* of the God is said to have alone remained undistributed, *i.e. the indivisible* or impartible *essence of intellect*.

With respect to the mundane soul which is the immediate participant of this Bacchic intellect, the composition of it is most accurately delivered by Plato in the *Timæus*, and admirably unfolded by Proclus in his Commentaries on that dialogue. For full information therefore on this subject I refer the reader to those works; and shall only summarily observe at present that there are five genera of being, from which all things after the first being are composed; *viz. essence, permanency, motion, sameness,* and *difference*. For every thing must possess *essence*; must *abide* in its cause, from which also it must *proceed*, and to which it must be *converted*; must be the *same* with itself and certain other natures, and at the same time different from others, and distinguished in itself. But Plato for the sake of brevity, assumes only three of these in the composition of the mundane soul, *viz. essence, sameness, and difference*; for the other two must necessarily subsist in conjunction with these. When therefore Plato says, "that from an essence impartible, and always subsisting according to sameness of being, and from a nature divisible about bodies, the demiurgus mingled from both a third form of essence, having a middle subsistence between the two," - by the impartible essence he means intellect, and by the nature which is divisible about bodies, a corporeal life. Hence the mundane soul is a medium between the mundane intellect, and the whole of that corporeal life which the world participates. We must not however suppose that when the soul is said to be mingled from these two, the indivisible and divisible natures are consumed in the mixture, as is the case when corporeal substances are mingled together; but we must understand that the soul is of a middle nature between these, so as to be different from each, and yet a participant of each. In short, the intellect participated by soul, is called by Plato impartible; but the nature which is divisible about bodies is the corporeal-formed life proceeding from the mundane soul, and which has the relation of splendour to it. For intellect is analogous to the sun; soul, to the light proceeding from the sun; and a divisible life to the splendour proceeding from light.

Proclus observes on the above cited words of Plato, that they are conformable to the Orphic traditions. "For," says he,[†] "Orpheus does not predicate the impartible of every intelligible or intellectual order, but according to him there are certain natures superior to this appellation, in the same manner as others are superior to other names. For king and father are not adapted to all the divine orders. Where, therefore, according to Orpheus, shall we first survey the impartible, in order that we may understand the divine conception of Plato? Orpheus therefore establishes one demiurgus of every divisible fabrication, analogous to the one father who generates the total fabrication, and from him produces

---

[†] In Tim. 184C.

the whole intellectual mundane multitude, the number of souls, and corporeal compositions. And this one demiurgus indeed (*i.e.* Bacchus) generates all these unitedly; but the Gods that surround him, divide and separate his fabrications. Orpheus however says that all his other fabrications were distributed into parts by the Gods whose characteristic is of a dividing nature; but that his heart alone was preserved impartible, through the providence of Minerva. For since he gives subsistence to intellects, souls and bodies; but souls and bodies indeed, receive in themselves an abundant division and distribution into parts, intellect remaining united and indivisible, being all things in one, and comprehending total intelligibles in one intellection; - this being the case, he says that the intellectual essence alone, and the intellectual number was saved entire by Minerva. For says he,

The intellectual heart alone was left,

directly calling it intellectual.

"If therefore the impartible heart is intellectual, it will evidently be intellect and an intellectual number; not indeed every intellect, but the mundane; for this is the impartible heart, since the divided God was also the fabricator of this. Orpheus therefore calls the impartible essence of Bacchus intellect. But he denominates the life which is divisible about body, which is physical, and pregnant with seeds, the genitals of the God. And he says that Diana who presides over all the generation in nature, and is the midwife of physical productive principles, extends these genitals, distributing as far to subterranean natures, the prolific power of the God. But all the remaining body of Bacchus was, he says, the psychical essence, this also being divided into seven parts. For they divided all the seven parts of the boy, says the theologist, speaking of the Titans; just as Timæus divides the soul into seven parts. And perhaps Timæus, when he says that soul is extended through the whole world, will remind the followers of Orpheus of the Titanic division, through which soul is not only spread round the universe like a veil, but is also extended through it. Very properly therefore, does Plato call the essence which is proximately above soul, an impartible essence. And in short, he thus denominates the intellect which is participated by soul, following the Orphic fables, and wishing to be as it were an interpreter of what is said in the mysteries." And thus much concerning Bacchus, or the monad of the mundane Gods.

CHAPTER XXXIV

In the next place let us direct our attention to the *Parmenides* of Plato, and see how in that most theological dialogue the mundane Gods are characterized. In the first hypothesis therefore of that dialogue, in which all the divine orders are denied of *The One*, Parmenides characterizes the mundane Gods by the equal and the unequal as follows: "But since *The One* is such, it will neither be equal nor unequal either to itself or to another. How so? If it were equal, indeed, it would be of the same measures with that to which it is equal. Certainly. But that which is greater or less than the things with which it is commensurate, will possess more measures than the less quantities, but fewer than the greater. Certainly. But to those to which it is incommensurable, with respect to the one part, it will consist of less; and with respect to the other of greater measures. How should it not? Is it not therefore impossible that a thing which does not participate of same should either be of the same measures, or admit any thing in any respect the same? It is impossible. It will therefore neither be equal to itself nor to another, if it does not consist of the same measures. It does not appear that it will. But if it consists of more or fewer measures, it will be of as many parts as there are measures; and so again, it will no longer be *The One*, but as many as there are measures. Right. But if it should be of one measure, it would become equal to that measure. It has, however, appeared that *The One* cannot be equal to any thing. It has appeared so. *The One*, therefore, neither participates of one measure, nor of many, nor of a few; nor (since it in no respect participates of *same*) can it ever, as it appears, be equal to itself or to another, nor again greater or less either than itself or another. It is in every respect so."

As the commentary of Proclus on the second hypothesis of the *Parmenides*, in which the equal and the unequal are affirmed of *The One*, is lost, and in which I have no doubt, the properties of the mundane Gods were most fully unfolded, I shall present the reader with the following extract from his commentary on the above passage in the *Parmenides* of Plato. The peculiarity of the mundane Gods is the equal and the unequal, the former of these indicating their fullness, and their receiving neither any addition nor ablation; (for such is that which is equal to itself, always preserving the same boundary); but the latter, the multitude of their powers, and the excess and defect which they contain. For in these, divisions, variety of powers, differences of progressions, analogies, and bonds through these, are, according to ancient theologists, especially allotted a place. Hence, Timæus also constitutes souls through analogy, the causes of which must necessarily pre-subsist in the Gods that proximately preside over souls. And as all analogies subsist from equality, Plato very properly indicates the peculiarity of these divinities by the equal and the unequal. But he now rightly frames the demonstrations of the negations of the equal and the unequal from *sameness and the many*, and not from *the similar and the dissimilar*, though immediately before he spoke of these. For every mundane deity proceeds from the demiurgic monad, and the first multitude which he denies of *The One*.

Of this then we must be entirely persuaded, that the things of which demonstrations consist are the preceding causes of the particulars about which Parmenides discourses; so that *the equal* and *the unequal*, so far as they proceed from *The One*, and subsist through *sameness* and *the many*, so far through these they are denied of *The One*. Hence, Plato thus begins his discussion of them:- "But since it (*viz. The One*) is such," *i.e.* not as we have just now demonstrated, but as was formerly shown, that it neither receives *same* nor *different*, and is *without multitude*, - being such, it is neither equal nor unequal, neither to itself, nor to others. For again, there are here twofold conclusions, in the same manner as concerning the similar and the dissimilar, and the same and the different. But that *the equal* and *the unequal* are suspended from the twofold co-ordinations of divine natures is not immanifest. For *the equal* is arranged under *the similar*, and *the same, subsistence in another, the round, and the whole*; but *the unequal*, under *the dissimilar, the different, subsistence in itself, the straight*, and *the possession of parts*. And again, of these the former are suspended from *bound*, but the latter from infinity. Plato also appears to produce the discourse through certain oppositions, as it were, that he may show that *The One* is above all opposition. For *The One* cannot be the worse of the two opposites, since this would be absurd; nor can it be the better of the two, since in this case it would not be the cause of all things. For the better opposite is not the cause of the worse, but in a certain respect communicates with it, without being properly its cause. For neither does sameness give subsistence to difference, nor permanency to motion; but comprehension and union pervade from the better to the worse.

It is, however, by no means wonderful that the demonstrations of *the equal* and *the unequal*, which are here assumed as symbols of mundane deity, should be adapted to physical and mathematical equals, to the equals in the reasons of soul, and to those in intellectual forms. For it is necessary that demonstrations in all these negations should begin supernally, and should extend through all secondary natures, that they may show that *The One* of the Gods is exempt from intellectual, psychical, mathematical, and physical forms. All such axioms, therefore, as are now assumed concerning things equal and unequal, must be adapted to this order of Gods. Hence, as it contains many powers, some of which are co-ordinate with each other, and extend themselves to the self-perfect and *The Good*, but others differ according to transcendency and subjection - the former must be said to be characterized by *equality*, but the latter by *inequality*. For *The Good* is the measure of every thing: and hence such things as are united by the same good are measured by the same measure, and are equal to each other. But things which are unco-ordinated with each other make their progression according to the unequal.

Since, however, of things unequal, some are commensurate and others incommensurate, it is evident that these also must be adapted to divine natures. Hence commensuration must be referred to those Gods, through whom secondary natures are mingled with those prior to them, and participate of the whole of more excellent beings. For thus, in things commensurate, the less is willing to have a common measure with the greater, the same thing measuring the whole of each. But incommensuration must be ascribed to those divinities from whom things subordinate, through the exempt transcendency of more excellent natures, participate of them in a certain respect, but are incapable through their subjection of being conjoined with the whole of them. For the communion proceeding from first to partial and multifarious natures is incommensurate to the latter. If, indeed, *the equal* and *the unequal* are symbols of the mundane Gods, *the commensurate* and *the incommensurate* are here very properly introduced. For in things incorporeal and immaterial this opposition has no place, all things being there effable; but where there is a material subject, and a mixture of form and something formless, there an opposition of commensuration very properly subsists. Hence, as the mundane Gods are proximately connective of souls and bodies, form and matter, a division appears in them, according to *the equal* and *the unequal*.

CHAPTER XXXV

After the mundane Gods, the scientific order of discussion requires that we should consider divine souls, and the triple genera of natures more excellent than man, *viz.* angels, dæmons, and heroes. Previous, however, to this, that I may as much as possible unfold to the reader the whole of the Platonic theory about the Gods, I shall present him with a development of the nature of certain other divinities mentioned by Plato; and which, owing to the loss of the seventh book of Proclus, and of other theological works of the most genuine Platonists, cannot at this remote and barren period be scientifically classed.

In the first place then, I shall present the reader with what Plato says in the *Phædrus* of Boreas and Orithya, the Centaurs, Chimæras, Gorgons, Pegasuses, Typhons, Achelous, and the Nymphs, accompanied with the elucidations of Ammonius Hermeas. "Phædr. Inform me, Socrates, whether this is not the place in which Boreas is reported to have ravished Orithya from Ilissus. Soc. It is reported so indeed. Phædr. Was it not just here then? for the brooks hereabouts appear to be grateful to the view, pure and transparent, and very well adapted to the sports of virgins. Soc. It was not, but two or three stadia lower down, where we meet with the temple of Diana, and in that very place there is a certain altar sacred to Boreas. Phædr. I did not perfectly know this. But tell me by Jupiter, Socrates, are you persuaded that this fabulous narration is true? Soc. If I should not believe in it, as is the case with the wise, I should not be absurd: and afterwards, speaking sophistically, I should say that the wind Boreas hurled from the neighbouring rocks Orithya, sporting with Pharmacia; and that she dying in consequence of this, was said to have been ravished by Boreas, or from the hill of Mars. There is also another report, that she was not ravished from this place, but from that. But for my own part, Phædrus, I consider interpretations of this kind as pleasant enough, but at the same time, as the province of a man vehemently curious and laborious, and not entirely happy; and this for no other reason, than because after such an explanation, it is necessary for him to collect the shape of the Centaurs, and Chimæra. And besides this, a crowd of Gorgons and Pegasuses will pour upon him for an exposition of this kind, and of certain other prodigious natures, immense both in multitude and novelty. All which, if any one, not believing in their literal meaning, should draw to a probable sense, employing for this purpose a certain rustic wisdom, he will stand in need of most abundant leisure. With respect to myself, indeed, I have not leisure for such an undertaking; and this because I am not yet able, according to the Delphic precept, to know myself. But it appears to me to be ridiculous, while I am yet ignorant of this, to speculate things foreign from the knowledge of myself. Hence, bidding farewell to these, and being persuaded in the opinion which I have just now mentioned respecting them, I do not contemplate these, but myself, considering whether I am not a wild beast, possessing more folds than Typhon, and far more raging and fierce; or whether I am a more mild and simple animal, naturally participating of a certain divine and modest condition. But are we not, my friend, in the midst of our discourse arrived at our destined seat? And is not yonder the oak to which you were to lead us? Phædr. That indeed is it. Soc. By Juno, a beautiful retreat. For the plane-tree very widely spreads its shady branches, and is remarkably tall; and the height and opacity of the willow, are perfectly beautiful, being now in the vigour of its vegetation, and, on this account, filling all the place with the most agreeable odour. Add too, that a most pleasant fountain of extreme cool water flows under the plane-tree, as may be inferred from its effect on our feet, and which appears to be sacred to certain Nymphs, and to Achelous, from the virgins and statues with which it is adorned."

On this very beautiful passage, Hermeas comments as follows: The Athenians established a temple of Rural Diana, because this Goddess is the inspective guardian of every thing rural, and represses every thing rustic and uncultivated. But the altars and temples of the Gods signify their allotments; as you may also call this mundane body, or apparent solar orb, the altar and temple of the sun, and of the soul of the sun.

With respect to the fable, a twofold solution may be given of it; one from history, more ethical, but the other transferring us to wholes. And the former of these is as follows: Orithya was the daughter of Erectheus, and the priestess of Boreas; for each of the winds has a presiding deity, which the telestic art, or the art pertaining to sacred mysteries, religiously cultivates. To this Orithya, then, the God was so very propitious, that he sent the north wind for the safety of the country; and besides this, he is said to have assisted the Athenians in their naval battles. Orithya, therefore, becoming enthusiastic, being possessed by her proper God Boreas, and no longer energizing as a human being (for animals cease to energize according to their own peculiarities when possessed by superior causes) died under the inspiring influence, and thus was said to have been ravished by Boreas. And this is the more ethical explanation of the fable.

But the second, which transfers the narration to wholes, is as follows, and does not entirely subvert the former: for divine fables often employ transactions and histories in subserviency to the discipline of wholes. They say, then, that Erectheus is the God that rules over the three elements, air, water, and earth. Sometimes, however, he is considered as alone the ruler of the earth, and sometimes as the presiding deity of Attica alone. Of this deity, Orithya is the daughter. And she is the prolific power of the earth, which is indeed co-extended with the word *Erectheus*, as the unfolding of the name signifies. For it is *the prolific power of the earth flourishing and restored according to the seasons*. But Boreas is the providence of the Gods supernally illuminating secondary natures; for the providence of the Gods in the world is signified by Boreas, because this divinity blows from lofty places. But the elevating power of the Gods is signified by the south wind, because this wind blows from low to lofty places; and besides this, things situated towards the south are more divine. The providence of the Gods, therefore, causes the prolific power of the earth, or of the Attic land, to ascend, and proceed into the apparent.

Orithya, also, may be said to be a soul[†] aspiring after things above, from ορουω and θειω, according to the Attic custom of adding a letter at the end of a word, which letter is here an ω. Such a soul, therefore, is ravished by Boreas supernally blowing. But if Orithya was hurled from a precipice, this also is appropriate. For such a soul dies a philosophic, not receiving a physical death, and abandons a *proairetic*,[‡] at the same time that she lives a physical life. And philosophy, according to Socrates in the *Phædo*, is nothing else than a meditation of death.

According to some, however, Socrates in what he here says about Orithya and Boreas does not admit the explanation of fables. But it is evident that he frequently does admit and employ fables. Now, indeed, he blames those explanations which make fables to be nothing more than certain histories, and unfold them into material causes, airs, and earth, and winds, which do not revert to true beings, nor harmonize with divine concerns. Hence, Socrates now says, If unfolding this fable I should recur to physical causes, and should assert that the wind Boreas, blowing vehemently, hurled Orithya as she was playing from the rock, and thus dying she was said to have been ravished by Boreas, - should I not speak absurdly? For this explanation which is adopted by the *wise*, *viz.* by those who are employed in physical speculations, is meagre and conjectural; since it does not recur to true beings, but to natures, and winds, airs and vortices, as he also says in the *Phædo*. He rejects, therefore, these naturalists, and those who thus explain this fable, as falling into the indefinite and infinite, and not recurring to soul, intellect, and the Gods. But when Socrates says that he considers such interpretations as the province of a man *very curious and laborious, and*

[†] This is according to the psychical mode of interpreting fables. See my translation of Sallust *On the Gods and the World*. [TTS vol. IV.]

[‡] This is a life pertaining to her own will; for the soul in this case gives herself up to the will of divinity.

not entirely happy, these words indicate the being conversant with things sensible and material. And the Centaurs, Chimæras, Gorgons, and Pegasuses, are powers which preside over a material nature, and the region about the earth.†

When Socrates also says, that he is not yet able to know himself, his meaning may be, either that he does not yet know himself as pure soul itself, but that as being in body he knows himself; or that he does not yet know himself, as he is known by divinity. For if ever any man knew himself, this was certainly the case with Socrates.

When likewise he says, "I do not contemplate these, but myself;" this is because he who knows himself knows all things. For in consequence of the soul being παμμορφον αγαλμα an omniform image, he beholds all things in himself. But by Typhon here we must understand that power which presides over the confused and disordered in the universe, or in other words over the last procession of things. The term *manifold*, therefore, in this place, must not be applied to the God Typhon, but to that over which he presides, as being in its own nature moved in a confused, disordered, and manifold manner. For it is usual with fables to refer the properties of the objects of providential care to the providing powers themselves.

Farther still, Socrates mentions Juno, as generating and adorning the beauty of the mundane fabrication; and hence she is said to have received the Cestus from Venus. But Achelous is the deity who presides over the much-honoured power of water. For by this mighty river, the God who is the inspective guardian of potable water is manifested. And Nymphs are Goddesses who preside over regeneration, and are ministrant to Bacchus the offspring of Semele. But this Bacchus supplies the regeneration of the whole sensible world.

I shall only add, that Nymphs according to Servius on the first Æneid are distributed into three classes. But Nymphs belonging to mountains are called Oreades; to woods, Dryades; those that are born with woods, Hamadryades; those that belong to fountains, Napæ, or Naiades; and those that belong to the sea, Nereides.

---

† For an account of divine fables, and specimens of the mode in which they ought to be explained, see my Introduction to the second Book of the *Republic*, in Vol. I [TTS vol. IX] of my translation of Plato.

CHAPTER XXXVI

Again, the following divinities are also mentioned by Plato in different parts of his works. In the first place, Pan, at the end of the *Phædrus*; to which divinity Socrates addresses the following admirable prayer: "O beloved Pan, and all ye other Gods, who are residents of this place, grant that I may become beautiful within, and that whatever I possess externally may be friendly to my inward attainments! Grant also, that I may consider the wise man as one who abounds in wealth; and that I may enjoy that portion of gold, which no other than a prudent man is able either to bear, or properly manage!" In this prayer, by Pan and the other Gods, we must understand local deities under the moon. But Pan is denominated as it were *all*, because he possesses the most ample sway in the order of local Gods. For as the supermundane Gods are referred to Jupiter, and the celestial to Bacchus, so all the sublunary local Gods and dæmons are referred to Pan.

In the next place, Tartarus is mentioned by Plato in the *Phædo*, as one of the greatest chasms of the earth; and of which, says he, Homer[†] thus speaks:

> Far, very far, where under earth is found
> A gulf, of every depth, the most profound.

But Tartarus, says Olympiodorus, is the extremity of the universe, and subsists oppositely to Olympus. It is also a deity, the inspective guardian of that which is last in every order. Hence, there is a celestial Tartarus, in which Heaven concealed his offspring; a Saturnian Tartarus, in which likewise Saturn concealed his offspring; and also a Jovian of this kind, which is demiurgic.

Again, the characteristic peculiarity of Prometheus, as mentioned by Plato in the *Gorgias*, is thus unfolded by Olympiodorus in his MS. Scholia on that dialogue; Prometheus is the inspective guardian of the descent of rational souls. For to exert a *providential energy* is the employment of the rational soul, and, prior to any thing else, to know itself. Irrational natures indeed perceive through percussion, and prior to impulsion know nothing; but the rational nature is able, prior to information from another, to know what is useful. Hence, *Epimetheus* is the inspective guardian of the irrational soul, because it knows through percussion, and not prior to it. Prometheus, therefore, is that power which presides over the descent of rational souls. But *fire*

[†] *Iliad* lib. viii.

signifies the rational soul itself; because, as fire tends upwards, so the rational soul pursues things on high. But you will say, why is this fire said to have been stolen? Because that which is stolen is transferred from its proper place to one that is foreign. Hence, since the rational soul is sent from its proper place of abode on high, to earth, as to a foreign region, on this account the fire is said to be stolen. But why was it concealed in a reed? Because a reed is full of cavities, and therefore signifies the flowing body in which the soul is carried. But why was the fire stolen contrary to the will of Jupiter? Again, the fable speaks as a fable. For both Prometheus and Jupiter are willing that the soul should abide on high; but as it is requisite that she should descend, the fable fabricates particulars accommodated to the persons. And it represents indeed the superior character, which is Jupiter, as unwilling; for he wishes the soul always to abide on high. But the inferior character, Prometheus, obliges her to descend: Jupiter, therefore, ordered Pandora to be made. And what else is this than *the irrational soul*, which is of a feminine characteristic? For as it was necessary that the soul should descend to these lower regions, but being incorporeal and divine, it was impossible for her to be conjoined with body without a medium, hence she becomes united with it through the irrational soul. But this irrational soul was called Pandora, because each of the Gods bestowed on it some particular gift. And this signifies that the illuminations which terrestrial natures receive take place through the celestial bodies.†

Again, in the *Phædo*, mention is made by Plato of Cadmus, who, according to Olympiodorus, is the sublunary world, as being Dionysiacal, on which account Harmonia or Harmony is united to the God, and also as being the father of the four Bacchuses. The four elements likewise he informs us are said to be Dionysiacal, *viz. fire* to be *Semele*; *earth, Agave*, tearing in pieces her own offspring; *water, Ino*; and lastly, *air, Autonoe*. There is great beauty in conjoining Harmony, the daughter of Venus and Mars, with Cadmus. For Venus, as we have before observed, is the cause of all the harmony and analogy in the universe, and beautifully illuminates the order and communion of all mundane concerns. But Mars excites the contrarieties of the universe, that the world may exist perfect and entire from all its parts. The

---

† For the irrational soul is an *immaterial body*, or in other words, *vitalized extension*, such as the mathematical bodies which we frame in the phantasy; and the celestial bodies are of this kind.

progeny, therefore, of these two divinities must be the *concordant discord*, or *harmony* of the sublunary world.

Farther still, the Sirens are mentioned by Plato, both in the 10th book of the *Republic*, and in the *Cratylus*. And Proclus, in the 6th book of this work, has explained the meaning of what Plato says of them in the former of those dialogues. But in his MS. Scholia on the *Cratylus* he says, "The divine Plato knew that there are three kinds of Sirens; the *celestial*, which is under the government of Jupiter; *that which produces generation*, and is under the government of Neptune; and that which is *cathartic*, and is under the government of Pluto. It is common to all these, to incline all things through an harmonic motion to their ruling Gods. Hence, when the soul is in the heavens, the Sirens are desirous of uniting it to the divine life which flourishes there. But it is proper that souls living in generation should sail beyond them, like the Homeric Ulysses, that they may not be allured by generation, of which the sea is an image. And when souls are in Hades, the Sirens are desirous of uniting them through intellectual conceptions to Pluto. So that Plato knew that in the kingdom of Hades there are Gods, dæmons, and souls, who dance as it were round Pluto, allured by the Sirens that dwell there."

CHAPTER XXXVII

In the next place, let us direct our attention to Plato's theological conceptions of Nature, Fate, and Fortune. From the *Timæus*, therefore, it appears that Plato does not consider either matter, or material form, or body, or natural powers, as worthy to be called Nature, though it has been thus denominated by others. Nor does he think proper to call Nature soul; but establishing its essence between soul and corporeal powers, he considers it as inferior to the former through its being divided about bodies, and its incapacity of conversion to itself, but as surpassing the latter through containing the productive principles, and generating and vivifying every part of the visible world. For Nature verges towards bodies, and is inseparable from their fluctuating empire. But soul is separate from body, is established in herself, and subsists both from herself and another; from another, that is, from intellect through participation; and from herself, on account of not verging to body, but abiding in her own essence, and at the same time illuminating the obscure nature of matter with a secondary life. Nature, therefore, is the last of the causes which fabricate this corporeal and sensible world; bounds the progressions of incorporeal essences, and is full of reasons and powers through which she governs mundane affairs. And she is a Goddess indeed considered as deified, and not according to the primary signification of the word; for divine bodies are also called Gods, as being the statues or images of the Gods. But she governs the whole world by her powers; by her summit comprehending the heavens, but through heaven governing generation. And she every where weaves partial natures in amicable conjunction with wholes.

Nature, however, thus subsisting, she proceeds from the vivific Goddess Rhea; (for "immense Nature," says the Chaldean oracle, "is suspended from the shoulders of the Goddess;") from whom all life is derived, both that which is intellectual, and that which is inseparable from the subjects of its government. But Nature being from thence suspended, she pervades through and inspires all things without impediment. Hence, the most inanimate beings participate of a certain soul, and corruptible natures remain perpetually in the world, being connected and comprehended by the causes of forms which she contains. And those indeed who call Nature demiurgic art, if they mean by this the Nature which abides in the demiurgus himself, they do not speak rightly; but if they mean that which proceeds from him, their conception is accurate. For art must be considered as having a three-fold subsistence; one, that which does not proceed out of the artist; the second, that which proceeds indeed, but is converted to him; and the third, that which has now proceeded, and has its subsistence in something else. The art, therefore, which is in the demiurgus, abides indeed in him; but the intellectual soul is art, yet at the same time both abiding and proceeding. And Nature is art, alone proceeding into something different from herself. Hence, she is said to be the organ of the Gods, not deprived of life, nor alter-motive alone, but having in a certain respect, a self-motive power, in consequence of energizing from herself. For the organs of the Gods are essentialized in efficacious powers, are vital, and concur with their energies. And thus much concerning Nature according to the conceptions of Plato, as unfolded by Proclus.

In the next place with respect to Fate, in the fable in the *Politicus*, Plato says, that "Fate and connate desire convolve the world, when it is considered by itself as a corporeal nature, without the intellectual Gods." And in the *Timæus* he represents the demiurgus exhibiting to souls the nature of the universe, and announcing to them the laws of Fate. On which Proclus admirably comments as follows: It must not be said, that Fate is a partial nature, as some of the Peripatetics assert it is; as for instance, Alexander; for such a nature is imbecil and not perpetual. For from common conceptions, we pre-assume that the power of Fate is something very great and stable. Nor must it be said, that it is the order of the mundane periods, as Aristotle asserts it to be, who denominates the increase which is contrary to order *preterfatal*, as if order and Fate were the same. For the cause of order is one thing, but order itself is another. Nor is it soul subsisting in habitude, as Theodorus says; for such a form of life in wholes is not a principle. Nor is it simply Nature, as Porphyry says it is. For many things which are supernatural, and out of the dominion of Nature are produced by Fate, such as nobility, renown, and wealth. For where is it seen that physical motions become the cause of these? Nor is it the intellect of the universe, as again Aristotle says in a certain place, if the treatise *On the World* was written by him. For intellect produces every thing which it produces at once, and is not at all in want of an administration which proceeds according to a certain period, and a continued and well-ordered series of things. But the chain, the order, the periodic production of many causes constitute the peculiarity of Fate.

If, however, it be requisite to comprehend the whole form of it concisely, we must say, that the subject matter as it were of it is Nature herself, but considered as deified, and filled with divine, intellectual, and psychical illuminations. For the order of Gods called the presidents of destiny, (των μοιρηγετων καλουμενων) and the genera that are more excellent than man terminate in Nature. For these impart powers from themselves to the one life of Nature; and the demiurgus of wholes collects and unites all these gifts, and demonstrates them to be one power. For if visible bodies [*i.e.* the celestial bodies], are filled with divine[†] powers, Nature, is by a much greater priority divine. And if the whole visible world is one, much more is the whole essence of Fate one, and derives from many causes the completion of its composition. For being suspended from the providence of the Gods, and from demiurgic goodness, it is united and governed by it, being a productive principle subsisting from productive principles, one multiform power, a divine life, and an order of things that have a prior arrangement. Hence, the ancients looking to this its various and multiform nature, were led to form different opinions concerning it. And some indeed said that it is a Goddess, on account of that which is divine in it; others, that it is a dæmon, on account of the efficacious and at the same time multiform nature of its production; others, that it is intellect, because a certain participation of intellect reaches it; but others, that it is order, so

---

[†] It is necessary here to supply the word θειων.

that every thing which has an arrangement is invisibly comprehended by it. Plato, however, alone surveyed the essence of it, asserting indeed that it is Nature, but Nature suspended from the demiurgus. For how could the demiurgus exhibit Nature to souls, otherwise than by containing the principle of it in himself? And how could he announce to them the laws of Fate, after exhibiting to them the Nature of the universe, except by constituting Nature as the one power that comprehends these laws?

Farther still, in the *Politicus*, Plato more clearly suspends the second life of the universe from Fate, after the departure of the one dæmon that governed it, and the many dæmons that were the followers of that one. Hence, he separates all the providential care of these powers from the universe, and alone leaves it the government according to Fate; the world, indeed, always possessing both these, but the fable separating the first from the second. For he says, "that Fate and connate desire convolve the world," just as the Chaldæan oracles say, "that unwearied Nature rules over the worlds and works, and draws downward in order that the heavens may run an eternal course; and that the other periods of the sun, the moon, the seasons, night and day may be accomplished." Thus, therefore, Plato also says, that the second period of the world is convolved by Fate, and not the first and intellectual period, all but clearly asserting that Fate is the power which proximately moves the sensible world, and is suspended from the invisible providence of the Gods. For establishing Necessity the mother of the Fates prior to these, he represents her in the *Republic* convolving† the world on her knees. And if it be requisite to give my opinion, Plato arranges these three causes of order successive to each other, *viz.* Adrastia, Necessity, and Fate; the first being intellectual, the second supermundane, and the third mundane. For the demiurgus as Orpheus says, was nourished indeed by Adrastia, but associated with Necessity, and generated Fate. And as Adrastia was comprehensive of divine institutions,‡ and the collector of all-various laws, thus also Fate is comprehensive of all the mundane laws, which the demiurgus now inscribes in souls, that he may lead them in conjunction with wholes, and may define what is adapted to them according to the different elections of lives. Hence, a vicious life tends to that which is dark and atheistical, but a pious life leads the soul to the heavens to which she is also conducted by wholes; because each

---

† For τρεφει here, it is necessary to read στρεφει.

‡ For δεσμων here read θεσμων.

of these lives is full of the laws of Fate; and souls lead themselves, as Plotinus says, thither where the law that is in them announces. For this is the peculiarity of the providence of the Gods, to conduct inwardly the subjects for which it provides. And why is it wonderful that this should be the case, since Nature also inserting material and corporeal-formed powers in bodies, moves them through these powers; earth indeed through gravity, but fire through levity. In a much greater degree, therefore, do the Gods move souls through the powers which they disseminate in them. Hence, if they lead souls according to the laws of Fate, these laws also subsist in souls. And they pre-exist indeed intellectually in the demiurgus; for the divine law is established with him. But they exist in divine souls; for according to these laws they govern the universe. And they are participated by partial souls; for through these they conduct themselves to an appropriate place, themselves moving themselves. And through deliberate choice, indeed, they act erroneously and with rectitude; but through law they distribute to themselves an order adapted to their former conduct.

In the last place with respect to Fortune, it is necessary to observe that Plato does not assert as the Stoics do, that the worthy man has no need of the assistance of this divinity; but he is of opinion that the energies of our reasoning power, since according to their external progression they are complicated with corporeal energies, require the inspiration of good Fortune, in order that they may be prosperous and benefit others. Hence in the *Timæus* and the *Parmenides*, the persons of the dialogues are represented as meeting together through a certain good Fortune. And in the *Laws* he says, that God, and after God, Fortune and Time govern all human affairs. "Fortune, therefore," says Proclus,[†] "and her gifts, are not things destitute of design and indefinite; but she is a power collective of many dispersed causes, and which adorns things disordered, and gives completion to the allotments assigned to every thing from the universe." According to Sallust in his elegant treatise *On the Gods and the World*,[‡] "Fortune must be considered as a power of the Gods, disposing things differing from each other, and happening contrary to expectation, to beneficent purposes." He adds, "On this account it is proper that cities should celebrate this Goddess in common; since every city is composed of different particulars. But this Goddess holds her

---

[†] In Tim. 59D.

[‡] See TTS vol. IV.

dominion in sublunary concerns, since every thing fortuitous is excluded from the regions above the moon."

In conformity to this, Simplicius also, in his Commentary On the *Physics* of Aristotle,[†] admirably observes concerning Fortune as follows: "The power of Fortune particularly disposes in an orderly manner the sublunary part of the universe, in which contingencies subsist, and which being essentially disordered, Fortune, in conjunction with other primary causes, directs, places in order, and governs. Hence she is represented guiding a rudder, because she governs things sailing on the sea of generation. Her rudder too is fixed on a globe, because she directs that which is unstable in generation. In her other hand, she holds the horn of Amalthea, which is full of fruits, because she is the cause of obtaining all divine fruits. And on this account, we venerate the fortunes of cities and houses, and of each individual; because being very remote from divine union, we are in danger of being deprived of its participation, and require in order to obtain it the assistance of the Goddess Fortune, and of those natures[‡] superior to the human who possess the characteristic of this divinity. Indeed, every fortune is good; for every attainment respects something good, nor does any thing evil subsist from divinity. But of things that are good, some are precedaneous, and others are of a punishing or revenging characteristic, which we are accustomed to call evils. Hence we speak of two Fortunes, one of which we denominate GOOD, and which is the cause of our obtaining precedaneous goods, but the other EVIL, which prepares us to receive punishment or revenge." And thus much concerning Fortune.

CHAPTER XXXVIII

It remains that we should consider in the next place, what Time, Day and Night, Month and Year are, so far as they are deities, according to the theology of Plato; the Commentaries of Proclus on the *Timæus* fortunately presenting us with much valuable information respecting the nature of these divinities. The speculation also of Time in this place will be very appropriate, as immediately after, the discussion of divine souls, angels, dæmons and heroes will naturally follow, with whose essence Time is intimately and inseparably connected. Plato therefore in the

---

[†] Lib. ii, p. 81.

[‡] *i.e.* Angels, dæmons, and heroes.

Timæus says, "that while the demiurgus was adorning and distributing the universe, he at the same time formed an eternal image flowing according to number, of eternity abiding in one; and which receives from us the appellation of time. But besides this he fabricated the generation of days and nights, and months and years, which had no subsistence prior to the universe, but which together with it rose into existence. And all these indeed, are the proper parts of Time." Proclus[†] in commenting on what Plato here says about Time, after having shown that it is neither any thing belonging to motion, nor an attendant on the energy of soul, nor, in short, the offspring of soul, investigates what it is in the following admirable manner:

"Perhaps," says he, "it is not sufficient to say that it is the measure of mundane natures, nor to enumerate the goods of which it is the cause, but to the utmost of our power we should endeavour to apprehend its peculiarity. May we not therefore say, since its essence is most excellent, perfective of soul, and present to all things, that it is an intellect not only abiding but also subsisting in motion? Abiding indeed according to its inward energy, and by which it is truly eternal, but being moved according to its externally proceeding energy, by which it becomes the boundary of all transition. For eternity possessing permanency, both according to its inward energy, and that which it exerts to things eternal, Time being assimilated to it, according to the former of these energies, becomes separated from it according to the latter, abiding and being moved. And as with respect to the essence of the soul, we say that it is intelligible and at the same time generated, partible, and at the same time impartible, and are no otherwise able to apprehend its middle nature than by employing after a manner opposites, what wonder is there if, perceiving the nature of Time to be partly immoveable, and partly subsisting in motion, we, or rather not we, but prior to us, the philosopher, through *the eternal*, should indicate its intellectual monad abiding in sameness, and through *the moveable* its externally proceeding energy, which is participated by soul and the whole world? For we must not think that the expression *the eternal* simply indicates that Time is the image of eternity; for if this were the case, what would have hindered Plato from directly saying that it is the *image*, and not the *eternal image* of eternity? But he was willing to indicate this very thing, that time has an eternal nature, but not in such a manner as animal itself [the paradigm of the universe] is said to be eternal. For that is eternal both in essence and energy; but Time is

---

[†] Lib. iv, 246B - 247B.

partly eternal, and partly, by its external gift, moveable. Hence theurgists call it eternal; and Plato very properly denominates it not *only* so. For one thing is *alone* moveable, both essentially and according to the participants of it, being *alone* the cause of motion, as soul, and hence it *alone* moves itself and other things; but another thing is *alone* immoveable, preserving itself without transition, and being the cause to other things of a perpetual subsistence after the same manner, and to moveable natures through soul. It is necessary therefore, that the medium between these two extremes should be that which, both according to its own nature, and the gifts which it imparts to others, is immoveable and at the same time moveable, essentially immoveable indeed, but moved in its participants. A thing however of this kind is Time.

"Hence Time is truly, so far as it is considered in itself, immoveable; but so far as it is in its participants, it is moveable, and subsists together with them, unfolding itself unto them. It is therefore, eternal, and a monad and centre essentially, and according to its own abiding energy; but it is at the same time, continuous, and number, and a circle, according to its proceeding and being participated. Hence, it is a certain proceeding intellect, established indeed in eternity, and on this account is said to be eternal. For it would not otherwise contribute to the assimilation of mundane natures to more perfect paradigms, unless it were itself previously suspended from them. But it proceeds and abundantly flows into the things which are guarded by it. Whence I think the chief of theurgists celebrate Time as a God, as Julian in the seventh book of the Zones, and venerate it by those names, through which it is unfolded in its participants, causing some things to be older, and others to be younger, and leading all things in a circle. Time therefore, possessing a certain intellectual nature, circularly leads according to number, both its other participants and souls. For Time is eternal, not in essence only, but also in its inward energy; but so far as it is participated by externals, it is alone moveable, coextending and harmonizing with them the gift which it imparts. But every soul is transitively moved, both according to its inward and external energies, by the latter of which it moves bodies. And it appears to me that those who thus denominated Time χρονος had this conception of its nature, and were therefore willing to call it as it were χορευοντος νους, an intellect moving in measure; but dividing the words, perhaps for the sake of concealment, they called it χρονος. Perhaps too, they gave it this appellation because it abides and is at the same time moved in measure; by one part of itself abiding, and by the other proceeding with measured motion. By the conjunction therefore of both these, they signify the wonderful and demiurgic nature of this God. And it appears, that as the demiurgus being intellectual began from intellect to adorn the universe, so Time being itself supermundane, began from soul to impart perfection. For that Time is not only mundane, but by a much greater priority supermundane, is evident; since as eternity is to animal itself, the paradigm of the universe, so is Time to the world, which is animated and illuminated by intellect, and wholly an image of animal itself, in the same manner as Time of eternity." And thus much concerning Time, according to its first subsistence, and considered as a God.

With respect to Day and Night, according to their more principal subsistence, they are demiurgic measures of Time, exciting and convolving all the apparent and unapparent life and motion, and orderly distribution of the inerratic sphere. For these are the true parts of Time, are present after the same manner to all things, and comprehend the primary cause of apparent day and night, each of these having a different subsistence in apparent time; to which also Timæus looking reminds us how time was generated together with the world. Hence he says in the plural number *nights* and *days*, and also *months* and *years*. But these are obvious to all men. For the unapparent causes of these have a uniform subsistence prior to things multiplied, and which circulate infinitely. Things immoveable also subsist prior to such as are moved, and intellectual natures are prior to sensibles. Such therefore, must be our conceptions of Night and Day according to their first subsistence.

By Month we must understand that truly divine temporal measure which convolves the lunar sphere, and every termination of the circulation about the zodiac. But Year is that which perfects and connects the whole of middle fabrication, according to which the Sun is seen possessing the greatest strength, and measuring all things in conjunction with Time. For neither Day nor Night, nor Month is without the Sun, nor much more Year, nor any other mundane nature. I do not here speak according to the apparent fabrication of things alone; for the apparent Sun is the cause of these measures; but also according to that fabrication which is unapparent. For, ascending higher, we shall find that the more true Sun[†] measures all things in conjunction with Time, being itself in reality Time of Time, according to the Chaldæan oracle concerning it. For that Plato not only knew these apparent parts of Time, but also those divine parts to which these are homonymous, is evident from the 10th book of his *Laws*. For he

---

[†] *Viz.* the Sun considered as subsisting in the supermundane order of Gods.

there asserts that we call Hours and Months divine, as having the same divine lives, and divine intellects presiding over them, as the universe. Let these therefore be the parts of Time, of which some are accommodated to the inerratic Gods, others to the Gods that revolve about the poles of the oblique circle, and others to other Gods, or attendants of the Gods, or to mortal animals, or the more sublime or more abject parts of the universe.

Farther still, concerning Night and Day, Plato afterwards says, "that through these, the period of one most wise circulation [*i.e.* the circulation of the inerratic sphere] was produced;" on which Proclus observes as follows: "It may be doubted how Plato calls Night and Day the measure of the circulation of this sphere. For this measure is every where, originating supernally from the one intelligible cause of the universe, and the first paradigm; but in the sublunary region it is the space of day and night. In answer to this, it must be said that the temporal interval which first subsists in the circulation of the inerratic sphere, and the solar light are productive of the *nycthemeron* or space of day and night. From the last of things therefore, and which are known to us, the whole measure is defined. For this *nycthemeron* is one thing, but another that which subsists in unapparent time. And the former is the image and ultimate termination of the latter. For there are many orders of Night and Day, intelligible and intellectual, supermundane, celestial and sublunary, as we are taught by the Orphic theology. And some of these indeed, are prior to fabrication; but others are comprehended in it; and others proceed from it. Some also are unapparent, but others are apparent. For with respect likewise to Month and Year, one order of these is unapparent, measures, connectedly contains, and gives perfection to the intellectual and corporeal periods of the sun and moon; but another is apparent, which terminates and is the measure of the solar revolution. Thus too in the other Gods, the unapparent Saturnian number is one thing, and the apparent another. And in a similar manner the unapparent and apparent Martial, Jovian and Mercurial numbers differ from each other. For with respect to Month and Year, each of these being one according to each period, and always the same, is a certain God, immovably bounding the measure of motion. For whence have the periods always an invariable sameness, except from a certain immoveable cause? And whence do they derive the difference of their restitutions to their pristine state, except from different immoveable causes? Whence also the unceasing, and the again and again to infinity, except from the infinite powers they contain? But Plato considering all this series as temporal, arranges it under one and that the first Time, which defines the periodic time of a perpetually circulating body, and is, as we have before observed, true number. From these invisible causes however, we must conceive the visible periodic times are derived, proceeding from them according to that which is numbered, since they are able both to number and generate them. And in all these astronomy beautifully instructs us, doxastically apprehending the number of the periodic restitutions of each; and making comparisons of the ratios of the periods to each other; such as that the Saturnian period, is the double and a half of the period of Jupiter, and in a similar manner of the rest. For though their restitutions differ, yet they have a ratio to each other. Sacred rumour also venerates the unapparent causes of these, proclaiming the divine names of Night and Day, and also the causes that constitute, and the invocations, and self-manifestations of Month and Year. Hence, they are not to be surveyed superficially, but as having a subsistence in divine hyparxes. And these the laws of sacred institutions, and the oracles of Apollo ordered to be worshipped and honoured by statues and sacrifices, as histories inform us. When these also are reverenced, mankind are supplied with the benefits arising from the periods of the Seasons, and of the other divinities in a similar manner; but a preternatural disposition of every thing about the earth, is the consequence of the worship of these being neglected."† Plato likewise in the *Laws* proclaims that all these are Gods, *viz.* the Seasons, Years and Months, in the same manner as the stars and the sun; and we do not introduce any thing new by thinking it proper to direct our attention to the unapparent powers of these prior to those that are apparent." And thus much concerning Time, Day and Night, Month and Year, considered according to their first subsistence, by which they are Gods.

CHAPTER XXXIX

After the Gods, it is necessary in the next place to consider the order of divine souls, who are deified by always participating of the Gods. This order, Plato in the *Parmenides* denies of *The One* as follows: "Does it appear that *The One* can be either older or younger, or be of the same

---

† "But we will certainly do whatsoever thing goeth forth out of our own mouth, to burn incense unto the queen of heaven, and to pour out drink offerings unto her, as we have done, we, and our fathers, our kings, and our princes, in the cities of Judah, and in the streets of Jerusalem: for then *had we plenty of victuals, and were well, and saw no evil.* But since we left off to burn incense to the queen of heaven, and to pour out drink offerings unto her, *we have wanted all things,* and have been consumed by the sword and by the famine." Jeremiah, Chap. xliv, 17, 18.

age? What should hinder? If it had in any respect the same age, either with itself, or with another, it would participate equally of time and similitude, which we have nevertheless asserted *The One* does not participate. We have asserted so. And this also we have said, that it neither participates of dissimilitude nor inequality. Entirely so. How therefore being such, can it either be older or younger than any thing, or possess the same age with any thing? It can in no respect. *The One* therefore, will neither be younger nor older, nor will it be of the same age, either with itself or with another. It does not appear that it will. Will it not therefore, be impossible that *The One* should be at all in time, if it be such? Or, is it not necessary that, if any thing is in time, it should always become older than itself? It is necessary. But is not that which is older, always older than the younger? What then? Hence that which is becoming to be older than itself, is at the same time becoming to be younger than itself, if it is about to have that through which it may become older. How do you say? Thus: It is requisite that nothing should subsist in *becoming* to be different from another, when it *is* already different, but that it should *be* now different from that which *is* different, *have been* from that which *was*, and *will be* from that which *is to be hereafter*. But from that which is *becoming to be* different, it ought neither to *have been*, nor to *be hereafter*, nor *to be*, but to subsist in *becoming to be* different, and no otherwise. It is necessary. But the older differs from the younger, and no other. Certainly. Hence, that which is *becoming to be* older than itself, must necessarily at the same time subsist in *becoming to be* younger than itself. It seems so. But likewise it ought not to subsist in *becoming to be* in a longer time than itself, nor yet in a shorter; but in a time equal to itself it should subsist in *becoming to be*, should *be*, *have been*, and *be hereafter*. For these are necessary. It is necessary, therefore, as it appears, that such things as are in time, and participate an affection of this kind, should each one possess the same age with itself, and should subsist in becoming to be both older and younger than itself. It seems so. But no one of these passions belongs to *The One*. None. Neither, therefore, is time present with it, nor does it subsist in any time. It does not indeed according to the decisions of reason."

Plato having proceeded, says Proclus, as far as to the mundane Gods, always taking away things in a consequent order from *The One*, through the middle genera, or, to speak more clearly, the negations always producing things secondary, through such as are proximate to *The One*, from the exempt cause of wholes, he is now about to separate from *The One* the divine essence itself, which first participates of the Gods, and receives their progression into the world; or, to speak more accurately, he is now about to produce this essence from the ineffable fountain of all beings. For, as every thing which has being derives its subsistence from the monad of beings, both *true being*, and that which is assimilated to it, which of itself indeed is not, but through its communion with true being receives an obscure representation of being; in like manner from the one unity of every deity, the peculiarity of which, if it be lawful to speak, is to deify all things according to a certain exempt and ineffable transcendency, every divine number subsists, or rather proceeds, and every deified order of things. The design, therefore, as we have before observed, of what is now said, is to show that *The One* is exempt from, and therefore produces this essence.

And here we may see how Parmenides subverts their hypothesis who contend that the first cause is soul, or any thing else of this kind, and this by showing that *The One* does not participate of time. For it is impossible that a nature which is exempt from time should be soul; since every soul participates of time, and uses periods which are measured by time. *The One* also is better than, and is beyond intellect, because every intellect is both moved and permanent; but it is demonstrated that *The One* neither stands still, nor is moved. Hence through these things, the three hypostases which rank as principles, *viz. The One, intellect*, and *soul*, become known to us. But that *The One* is perfectly exempt from time, Parmenides demonstrates by showing in the first place, that it is neither older nor younger, nor of the same age with itself, nor with any other. For every thing which participates of time necessarily participates of these; so that by showing that *The One* is exempt from these which happen to every thing that participates of time, he also shows that *The One* has no connexion with time. This, however, is incredible to the many, and appeared so to the physiologists prior to Plato, who thought that all things were comprehended in time, and that, if there is any thing perpetual, it is infinite time, but that there is not any thing which time does not measure. For, as they were of opinion that all things are in place, in consequence of thinking that all things are bodies, and that nothing is incorporeal, so they thought that all things subsist in time, and are in motion, and that nothing is immoveable; for the conception of bodies introduces with itself place, but motion time. As, therefore, it was demonstrated that *The One* is not in place, because it is not in another, and on this account is incorporeal, - in like manner through these arguments it is also shown that neither is it in time, and on this account that it is not soul, nor any thing else which requires and participates of time, either according to essence or according to energy.

And here it is well worthy our observation that Parmenides no longer stops at the dyad as in the former conclusions, but triadically enumerates the peculiarities of this order, viz. *the older, the younger,* and *the possession of the same age,* though he might have said dyadically, *of an equal age,* and *of an unequal age,* as there *the equal* and *the unequal.* But there indeed having previously introduced the dyad, he passes from the division of the unequal to the triadic distribution; but here he begins from the triad. For there union precedes multitude, and the whole the parts; but in this order of things multitude is most apparent, and a division into parts, as Timæus says, whom Parmenides, in what is now said imitating, begins indeed from the triad, but proceeds as far as to the hexad. For, *the older* and *the younger,* and *the possession of the same age,* are doubled, being divided into *itself* and *relation to another.* That the triad, indeed, and the hexad are adapted to this order is not immanifest. For the triple nature of soul, consisting of *essence, same* and *different,* and its triple power, which receives its completion from the charioteer and the two horses, as we learn from the *Phædrus,*† evince its alliance with the triad; and its essence being combined from both these shows its natural alliance with the hexad.

It is likewise necessary to observe, that as the discourse is about divine souls who are deified by always participating of the Gods, Time according to its first subsistence pertains to these souls, - not that which proceeds into the apparent, but that which is liberated, and without habitude; and this is the Time which is now denied of *The One.* All the periods of souls, their harmonious motions about the intelligible, and their circulations, are measured by this Time. For it has a supernal origin, imitates eternity, and connects, evolves, and perfects every motion, whether vital, or pertaining to soul, or in whatever other manner it may be said to subsist. This Time also is indeed essentially an intellect, as we have before observed; but it is the cause to divine souls, of their harmonic and infinite motion about the intelligible,

---

† In this dialogue, Plato assimilates the intimate form of the soul to a winged chariot and charioteer, drawn by two horses; and says, "That all the horses and chariots of the Gods are good, and composed of things that are good." In which passage, by the chariots of the Gods are to be understood all the inward discursive powers of their souls, which pursue the intelligence of all things, and can at the same time equally contemplate and provide for inferior creatures. But the horses signify the efficacy and motive vigour of these powers. And the wings are elevating powers, which particularly belong to the charioteer, or intellect.

through which these likewise are led to *the older* and to *the same age*: and this in a twofold respect. For *the older* in these *with respect to themselves* takes place, so far as with their more excellent powers they enjoy in a greater degree the infinity of Time, and participate it more abundantly. For they are not filled with similar perfection from more divine natures, according to all their powers, but with some more, and with others less. But that is said to be older which participates more of time. That which is older is these divine souls *with respect to other things* is effected, so far as some of these receive the whole measure of Time, and the whole of its extension proceeding to souls, but others are measured by more partial periods. Those therefore are older, whose period is more total, and is extended to a longer time. They may also be said to be *older and at the same time younger with respect to themselves*, by becoming *hoary* as it were above, through extending themselves to the whole power of Time, but juvenile *beneath*, by enjoying Time more partially. But, *as with respect to others*, they may be said to be *older and at the same time younger* according to a diminution of energy. For that which has its circulation measured by a less period is younger than that whose circulation is measured by a more extended period.

Again, among things co-ordinate, that which has the same participation and the same measure of perfection with others may be said to be of *the same age with itself and others*. But every divine soul, though its own period is measured according to one Time, and that of the body which is suspended from it according to another, yet it has an equal restitution to the same condition; itself always according to its own Time, and its body also according to its time. Hence, again, it is of the same age with itself and its body, according to the analogous. By thus interpreting what is now said of *The One*, we shall accord with Plato in the *Timæus*, who there evinces that Time is the measure of every transitive life, and who says that soul is the origin of a divine and wise life through the whole of time. And we shall also accord with his assertion in the *Phædrus*, that souls see true being through Time, because they perceive temporally and not eternally.

Farther still, Plato here demonstrates that *The One* is neither older nor younger than itself, or another. For it was necessary to show that *The One* is beyond every divine soul, prior to other souls, in the same manner as it is demonstrated to be prior to true beings, and to be the cause of all things. Hence, since it is the cause of every divine soul, so far as these derive their subsistence as well as all beings from the divine unities, with great propriety is it necessary to show that *The One* is beyond the order of deified souls. For these souls so far as they are intellectual have intellect for their cause; so far as they are essences they originate from being; and so far as they have the form of unity, they are derived from *The One*; receiving their subsistence from this, so far as each is a multitude consisting of certain unities, and of these as elements.

Again, that which participates of time is twofold, the one proceeding, as it were, in a right line, and beginning from one thing, and ending in another; but the other proceeding circularly, and having its motion from the same to the same, to which both the beginning and the end are the same, and the motion is unceasing, every thing in it being both beginning and end. That, therefore, which energizes circularly, participates of time periodically: and so far as it departs from the beginning it becomes older, but so far as it approaches to the end it becomes younger. For becoming nearer the end, it becomes nearer to its proper beginning. But that which becomes nearer to its beginning becomes younger. Hence, that which circularly approaches to the end becomes younger, the same also according to the same becoming older; for that which approximates to its end proceeds to that which is older. That to which the beginning therefore is one thing, and the end another, to this the younger is different from the older; but that to which the beginning and the end are the same, is in no respect older than younger, but as Plato says, at the same time becomes younger and older than itself. Every thing, therefore, which participates of time, if it becomes both older and younger than itself, is circularly moved. But divine souls are of this kind: for they participate of time, and the time of their proper motion is periodical.

CHAPTER XL

Having in the preceding chapters presented the reader from the most genuine sources, with all the information that can at present be obtained concerning the mundane Gods, the order of scientific theology requires that those perpetual attendants of the Gods, denominated angels, dæmons and heroes, should be in the next place considered. As all these ministrant powers however, are frequently called by one name dæmons, and as Love is denominated by Plato a great dæmon, and contains in himself the paradigm of the whole dæmoniacal series, it is necessary that the development of the nature of Love should precede the discussion of the peculiarities of dæmons. The following admirable account therefore of this mighty divinity, by Proclus the Coryphæus of all true philosophers, is extracted from his MS. Commentary on the *First Alcibiades* of Plato.

There are different properties of different Gods. For some are the fabricators of wholes, of the form of beings, and of their essential ornament. But others are the suppliers of life, and are the sources of its various genera. Others again preserve the unchangeable order, and guard the indissoluble connexion of things. And others lastly, who are allotted a different power, preserve all things by their beneficent energies. In like manner every amatory order is the cause to all things of conversion to divine beauty, leading back, conjoining, and establishing all secondary natures in the beautiful, replenishing them from thence, and irradiating all things with the gifts of its light. On this account it is asserted in the *Banquet* of Plato that Love is a great dæmon, because Love first demonstrates in itself a power of this kind, and is the medium between the object of desire and the desiring nature, and is the cause of the conversion of subsequent to prior natures. The whole amatory series therefore, being established in the vestibule of the cause of beauty, calls upwards all things to this cause, and forms a middle progression between the object of Love and the natures which are recalled by Love. Hence it pre-establishes in itself the paradigm of the whole dæmoniacal order, obtaining the same middle situation among the Gods as dæmons between divine and mortal natures. Since therefore, every amatory series possesses this property among the Gods, we must consider its uniform and occult summit as ineffably established in the first orders of the Gods, and conjoined with the first and intelligible beauty; its middle process as shining forth among the supermundane Gods, with an intellectual condition; its third progression as possessing an exempt power among the liberated Gods; and its fourth as multifariously distributed about the world, producing many orders and powers from itself, and distributing gifts of this kind to the different parts of the world.

But after the unific and first principle of Love, and after the tripartite essence perfected from thence, a various multitude of Loves shines forth with divine light, from whence the choirs of angels are filled with Love; and the herds of dæmons full of this God attend on the Gods who are recalled to intelligible beauty. Add too, that the army of heroes, together with dæmons and angels, are agitated about the participation of the beautiful with divine bacchanalian fury. Lastly, all things are excited, revive and flourish through the influx of the beautiful. But the souls of such men as receive an inspiration of this kind, and are naturally allied to the God, assiduously move about beauty, and fall into the realms of generation, for the purpose of benefiting more imperfect souls, and providing for those natures which require to be saved. The

Gods indeed, and the attendants on the Gods, abiding in their proper habits, benefit all following natures, and convert them to themselves; but the souls of men descending, and touching on the coasts of generation, imitate the beneficent providence of the Gods. As, therefore, souls established according to some other God descend with purity into the regions of mortality, and benefit souls that revolve in it; and some indeed benefit more imperfect souls by prophecy, others by mystic ceremonies, and others by divine medicinal skill; -thus also souls that chuse an amatory life, are moved about the deity who presides over beautiful natures, for the purpose of taking care of well-born souls. But from apparent beauty they are led back to divine beauty, and together with themselves elevate those who are the objects of their love. And this also divine Love primarily effects in intelligibles. For he unites himself to the object of love, extends to it the participants of his power, and inserts in all things one bond, and one indissoluble friendship with each other, and with the beautiful itself. Souls therefore possessed with Love, and participating the inspiration thence derived, in consequence of using an undefiled vehicle, are led from apparent to intelligible beauty, and make this the end of their energy. Likewise enkindling a light in more imperfect souls, they also lead these back to a divine nature, and are divinely agitated together with them about the fountain of all-perfect beauty.

But such souls as from a perverse education fall from the gift which is thence derived, yet are allotted an amatory nature, these, through their ignorance of true beauty, are busily employed about that which is material and divisible, at which also they are astonished in consequence of not knowing the passion which they suffer. Hence, they abandon every thing divine, and gradually decline into impiety and the darkness of matter. They appear indeed to hasten to a union with the beautiful, in the same manner as perfectly amatory souls; but they are ignorant of the union, and tend to a dissipated condition of life, and to matter, which Plato calls the sea of dissimilitude. They are also conjoined with the base itself, and material privation of form. For where are material natures able to pervade through each other? Or where is apparent beauty, pure and genuine, being thus mingled with matter, and replete with the deformity of its subject? Some souls therefore genuinely participate the gifts of Love, and by others these gifts are perverted. For as according to Plotinus the defluxion of intellect produces craft, and an erroneous participation of wisdom sophistry, so likewise the illumination of Love when it meets with a depraved recipient, produces a tyrannic and intemperate life.

CHAPTER XLI

In another part, likewise, of the same admirable Commentary, Proclus presents us, as he says, with some of the more arcane assertions concerning Love; and these are as follow:

Love is neither to be placed in the first, nor among the last of beings. Not in the first, because the object of Love is superior to Love: nor yet among the last, because the lover participates of Love. It is requisite, therefore, that love should be established between the object of Love and the lover, and that it should be posterior to the beautiful, but prior to every nature endued with love. Where then does it first subsist? How does it extend itself through the universe, and with what monads does it leap forth?

There are three hypostases, therefore, among the intelligible and occult Gods. And the first, indeed, is characterized by *The Good*, understanding *the good itself*, and residing in that place where according to the oracle the paternal monad abides. But the second is characterized by wisdom, where the first intelligence flourishes. And the third by the beautiful, where, as Timæus says, the most beautiful of intelligibles abides. There are, however, three monads according to these intelligible causes, subsisting uniformly and causally in intelligibles, but first unfolding themselves into light in the ineffable order of the Gods,[†] I mean Faith, Truth, and Love. And Faith indeed establishes all things in good; but Truth unfolds all the knowledge in beings; and lastly, Love converts all things, and congregates them into the nature of the beautiful. This triad, indeed, thence proceeds through all the orders of the Gods, and imparts to all things, by its light, a union with intelligible itself. It also unfolds itself differently in different orders, every where combining its powers with the peculiarities of the Gods. And among some it subsists ineffably, incomprehensibly, and unifically; but among others, as the cause of connecting and binding; and among others, as endued with a perfective and forming power. Here again, it subsists intellectually and paternally; but there in a manner entirely motive, vivific, and effective. Here, as governing and assimilating; there in a liberated and undefiled manner; and elsewhere according to a multiplied and dividing mode. Love, therefore, supernally descends from intelligibles to mundane natures, calling all things upwards to divine beauty. Truth also proceeds through all things, illuminating all things

---

[†] *i.e.* In the summit of that order which is called intelligible and at the same time intellectual.

with knowledge. And lastly, Faith proceeds through the universe, establishing all things unically in good. Hence the Chaldæan oracles assert that all things are governed by, and abide in, these. And on this account they order Theurgists to conjoin themselves to divinity through this triad. Intelligibles themselves, indeed, do not require the amatory medium, on account of their ineffable union. But where there is a union and separation of beings, there also Love abides. For it is the binder and conciliator of natures posterior and prior to itself; but the converter of subsequent into prior, and the elevating and perfecting cause of imperfect natures.

The Chaldæan oracles, therefore, speak of Love as binding, and residing in all things: and hence, if it connects all things, it also copulates us with the governments of dæmons. But Diotima in the *Banquet*, calls Love a great dæmon, because it every where fills up the medium between desiring and desirable natures. And indeed that which is the object of Love vindicates to itself the first order; but that which loves is in the third order from the beloved object. Lastly, Love usurps a middle situation between each, congregating and collecting together that which desires and that which is desired, and filling subordinate from better natures. But among the intelligible and occult Gods, it unites intelligible intellect to the first and secret beauty by a certain life better than intelligence. Hence, the theologist of the Greeks [Orpheus], calls this Love, blind; for he says,

> In his breast feeding, eyeless, rapid Love.†

But in natures posterior to intelligibles, it imparts by illumination an indissoluble bond to all things perfected by itself; for a bond is a certain union, but accompanied with much separation. On this account the Chaldæan oracles are accustomed to call the fire of this Love a copulator. For proceeding from intelligible intellect, it binds all following natures to each other, and to itself. Hence, it conjoins all the Gods with intelligible beauty, and dæmons with Gods; but it conjoins us both with Gods and dæmons. In the Gods indeed it has a primary subsistence; in dæmons a secondary one; and in partial souls a subsistence through a certain third procession from principles. Again, in the Gods it subsists above essence; for every genus of Gods is superessential. But in dæmons it subsists according to essence; and in souls according to illumination. And this triple order appears similar to the triple power of intellect. For one intellect subsists as imparticipable,

---

† ποιμαινων πραπεδεσσιν ανομματον ωκυν ερωτα.

being exempt from all partial genera; but another as participated, of which also the souls of the Gods participate as of a better nature; and another is from this ingenerated in souls, and which is indeed their perfection. And these three distinctions of intellect Timæus himself indicates. Hence, that Love which subsists in the Gods must be considered as analogous to imparticipable intellect; for this is exempt from all the beings which receive and are illuminated by its nature. But dæmoniacal Love is analogous to participated intellect; for this is essential and is perfected from itself, in the same manner as participated intellect is proximately resident in souls. And the third Love is analogous to intellect which subsists as a habit, and which inserts an illumination in souls. Nor is it unjustly that we consider Love as coordinate with this intellectual difference; for in intelligible intellect it possesses its first and occult subsistence. And if it thence leaps forth, it is also established there according to cause. It likewise appears to me that Plato finding that intelligible intellect was called by Orpheus both Love and a great dæmon, was himself pleased to celebrate Love in a similar manner. Very properly, therefore, does Diotima call it a great Dæmon. And Socrates conjoins the discourse about Love with that concerning dæmons. For as every thing dæmoniacal is suspended from the amatory medium, so likewise the discourse concerning a dæmoniacal nature is conjoined with that concerning Love, and is allied to it. For Love is a medium between the object of Love and the lover; and a dæmon is a medium between man and divinity.

CHAPTER XLII

The nature of dæmons, therefore, remains in the next place to be more fully disclosed; for the reader has been already presented with some very important information concerning them, in the discussion of the sublunary Gods. As there is no vacuum then in corporeal, so neither in incorporeal natures. Hence, between divine essences which are the first of things, and partial essences such as ours, which are nothing more than the dregs of the rational nature, there must necessarily be a middle rank of beings, in order that divinity may be connected with man, and that the progression of things may form an entire whole, suspended like the golden chain of Homer from the summit of Olympus. This middle rank of beings, considered according to a twofold division, consists of dæmons and heroes, the latter of which is proximate to partial souls such as ours, and the former to divine natures, just as air and water subsist between fire and earth. Hence, whatever is ineffable and occult in the Gods, dæmons and heroes express and unfold. They likewise conciliate all things, and are the sources of the harmonic consent and sympathy of all things with each other. They transmit divine gifts to us, and equally carry back ours to the divinities. But the characteristics of divine natures are unity, permanency in themselves, a subsistence as an immoveable cause of motion, transcendent providence, and which possesses nothing in common with the subjects of their providential energies. And these characteristics are preserved in them according to essence, power and energy. On the other hand, the characteristics of partial souls are, a declination to multitude and motion, a conjunction with the Gods, an aptitude to receive something from other natures, and to mingle together all things in itself, and through itself. And these characteristics they also possess according to essence, power and energy. Such then being the peculiarities of the two extremes, we shall find that those of dæmons are to contain in themselves the gifts of divine natures, in a more inferior manner indeed than the Gods, but yet so as to comprehend the conditions of subordinate natures, under the idea of a divine essence. In other words, the prerogatives of deity characterize and absorb as it were by their powerful light, whatever dæmons possess peculiar to inferior beings. Hence, they are multiplied indeed but unitedly; mingled, but yet so that the unmingled predominates; and are moved, but with stablity. On the contrary, heroes possess unity, identity, permanency, and every excellence, under the condition of multitude, motion, and mixture; *viz.* the prerogatives of subordinate predominate in these over the characteristics of superior natures, yet so as never to induce a cessation of energy about, or oblivion of, divinity. In short, dæmons and heroes are composed of the properties of the two extremes - Gods and partial souls; but in dæmons there is more of the divine, and in heroes more of the human nature.

Having premised thus much, I shall next present the reader with all the information I have been able to collect from the most genuine Platonists, and especially from Proclus, on the nature of this middle order of beings. In the first place, therefore, what follows on this subject is derived from the MS. Commentary of Proclus On the *First Alcibiades*, in which extract also the nature of the dæmon of Socrates is unfolded, about which modern wit has been so much puzzled, and so egregiously mistaken.

Let us now speak first, concerning dæmons in general; secondly, concerning those that are allotted us in common; and thirdly, concerning the dæmon of Socrates. For it is always requisite that demonstrations should begin from things more universal, and proceed from these as far as to individuals. For this mode of proceeding is natural, and is more adapted to science. Dæmons, therefore, deriving their first subsistence from the vivific Goddess [Juno], and flowing from thence as from a certain fountain, are allotted an essence characterized by soul. This essence in those of a superior order is more intellectual, and more perfect according to hyparxis; in those of a middle order it is more rational; and in those which rank in the third degree, and which subsist at the extremity of the dæmoniacal order, it is various, more irrational, and more material. Possessing, therefore, an essence of this kind, they are distributed in conjunction with the Gods, as being allotted a power ministrant to deity. Hence, they are in one way subservient to the liberated Gods, who are the leaders of wholes prior to the world; and in another to the mundane Gods, who proximately preside over the parts of the universe. For there is one division of dæmons according to the twelve supercelestial Gods, and another according to all the peculiarities of the mundane Gods. For every mundane God is the leader of a certain dæmoniacal order, to which he proximately imparts his power; *viz.* if he is a demiurgic God, he imparts a demiurgic power; if immutable, an undefiled power; if telesiurgic, a perfective power. And about each of the divinities, there is an innumerable multitude of dæmons, and which are dignified with the same appellations as their leading Gods. Hence, they rejoice when they are called by the names of Jupiter, Apollo, and Hermes, etc. as expressing the peculiarity of their proper deities. And from these, mortal natures also participate of divine influxions. And thus animals and plants are fabricated, bearing the images of different Gods; dæmons proximately imparting to these the representations of their leaders. But the Gods in an exempt manner supernally preside over dæmons; and through this last natures sympathize with such as are first. For the representations of first are seen in last natures; and the causes of things that are last are comprehended in primary beings. The middle genera, too, of dæmons give completion to wholes, the communion of which they bind and connect; participating indeed of the Gods, but participated by mortal natures. He, therefore, will not err who asserts that the mundane artificer established the centres of the order of the universe in dæmons; since Diotima also assigns them this order, *viz.* that of binding together divine and mortal natures, of deducing supernal streams, elevating all secondary natures to the Gods, and giving completion to wholes through the connexion of a medium.

Hence, we must not assent to their doctrine, who say that dæmons are the souls of men that have changed the present life. For it is not proper to consider a dæmoniacal nature *according to habitude*, as the same with a nature essentially dæmoniacal; nor to assert that the perpetual medium of all mundane natures consists from a life conversant with multiform mutations. For a dæmoniacal guard subsists always the same, connecting the mundane wholes. But soul does not always thus retain its own order, as Socrates says in the *Republic*; since at different times it chooses different lives. Nor do we praise those who make certain of the Gods to be dæmons, such as the erratic Gods, [*i.e.* the planets] according to Amelius. But we are persuaded by Plato, who calls the Gods the rulers of the universe, but subjects to them the herds of dæmons. And we shall every where preserve the doctrine of Diotima, who assigns the middle order, between all divine and mortal natures, to a dæmoniacal essence. Let this then be the conception respecting the whole of the dæmoniacal order in common.

CHAPTER XLIII

In the next place, let us speak concerning the dæmons, who are allotted the superintendence of mankind. For of these dæmons, which, as we have said, rank in the middle order, the first and highest are divine dæmons, and who often appear as Gods, through their transcendent similitude to the divinities. For, in short, that which is first in every order preserves the form of the nature prior to itself. Thus, the first intellect is a God, and the most ancient of souls is intellectual. Hence, the highest genus of dæmons, as being proximate to the Gods, is uniform and divine. The next to these in order are those dæmons who participate of an intellectual peculiarity, and preside over the ascent and descent of souls, and who unfold into light and deliver to all things the productions of the Gods. The third are those who distribute the productions of divine souls to secondary natures, and complete the bond of those that receive effluxions from thence. The fourth are those that transmit the efficacious powers of whole natures to things generated and corrupted, and who inspire partial natures with life, order, reasons, and the all-various perfect operations which things mortal are able to effect. The fifth are corporeal, and bind together the extremes in bodies. For, how can perpetual accord with corruptible bodies, and efficients with effects, except through this medium? For it is this ultimate nature which has dominion over corporeal goods, and provides for all natural prerogatives. The sixth in order are those that revolve about matter, connect the powers which descend from celestial to sublunary matter, perpetually guard this matter, and defend the shadowy representation of forms which it contains.

Dæmons, therefore, as Diotima also says, being many and all-various, the highest of them conjoin souls proceeding from their father to their leading Gods. For every God, as we have said, is the leader in the first place of dæmons, and in the next of partial souls. For the demiurgus disseminated these, as Timæus says, into the sun and moon, and the other instruments of time. These divine dæmons, therefore, are those which are essentially allotted to souls, and conjoin them to their proper leaders. And every soul, though it revolves together with its leading deity, requires a dæmon of this kind. But dæmons of the second rank preside over the ascensions and descensions of souls; and from these the souls of the multitude derive their elections. For the most perfect souls, who are conversant with generation in an undefiled manner, as they choose a life conformable to their presiding God, so they live according to a divine dæmon, who conjoined them to their proper deity when they dwelt on high. Hence, the Egyptian priest admired Plotinus, as being governed by a divine dæmon. To souls, therefore, who live as those that shortly return to the intelligible world whence they came, the supernal is the same with the dæmon which attends them here. But to imperfect souls the essential is different from the dæmon that attends them at their birth.

If these things then are rightly asserted, we must not assent to those who make our rational soul a dæmon. For a dæmon is different from man, as Diotima says, who places dæmons between Gods and men, and as Socrates also evinces, when he divides a dæmoniacal oppositely to the human nature. "For," says he, "not a human but a dæmoniacal obstacle detains me." But man is a soul using the body as an instrument. A dæmon, therefore, is not the same with the rational soul.

This also is evident from Plato in the *Timæus*, where he says that intellect has in us the relation of a dæmon. But this is only true as far as pertains to analogy. For a dæmon according to essence is different from a dæmon according to analogy. For in many instances, that which proximately presides, subsisting in the order of a dæmon with respect to that which is inferior, is called a dæmon. Thus Jupiter in Orpheus calls his father Saturn an illustrious dæmon; and Plato in the *Timæus* calls those Gods who proximately preside over, and orderly distribute the realms of generation, dæmons. "For," says he, "to speak concerning other dæmons, and to know their generation, exceeds the ability of human nature." But a dæmon according to analogy is that which proximately presides over any thing, though it should be a God, or though it should be some one of the natures posterior to the Gods. And the soul that through similitude to the dæmoniacal genus produces energies more wonderful than those which belong to human nature, and which suspends the whole of its life from dæmons, is a dæmon κατα σχεσιν, according to habitude, *i.e.* proximity or alliance. Thus, as it appears to me, Socrates in the *Republic* calls those dæmons, who have lived well, and who in consequence of this are transferred to a better condition of being, and to more holy places. But an essential dæmon is neither called a dæmon through habitude to secondary natures, nor through an assimilation to something different from itself; but is allotted this peculiarity from himself, and is defined by a certain hyparxis, by appropriate powers, and by different modes of energies. In short, the rational soul is called in the *Timæus* the dæmon of the animal; but we investigate the dæmon of man, and not of the animal; that which governs the rational soul itself, and not its instrument; and that which leads the soul to its judges, after the dissolution of the animal, as Socrates says in the *Phædo*. For when the animal is no more, the dæmon which the soul was allotted while connected with the body, conducts it to its judge. For, if the soul possesses that dæmon while living in the body, which is said to lead it to judgment after death, this dæmon must be the dæmon of the man, and not of the animal alone. To which we may add, that beginning from on high, it governs the whole of our composition.

Nor again, dismissing the rational soul, must it be said that a dæmon is that which energizes in the soul: as for instance, that in those who live according to reason, reason is the dæmon; in those that live according to anger, the irascible part; and in those that live according to desire, the epithymetic or desiring part. Nor must it be said that the nature which proximately presides over that which energizes in our life, is a dæmon: as for instance, that reason is the dæmon of the irascible, and anger of those that live according to desire. For, in the first place, to assert that dæmons are parts of our soul, is to admire human life in an improper degree, and oppose the division of Socrates in the *Republic*, who after Gods and dæmons places the heroic and human race, and blames the poets for introducing in their poems heroes in no respect better than men, but subject to similar passions. By this accusation, therefore, it is plain that Socrates was very far from thinking that dæmons, who are of a sublimer order than heroes, are to be ranked among the parts and powers of the soul. For from this doctrine it will follow that things essentially more excellent give completion to such as are subordinate. And in the second place, from this hypothesis, mutations of lives would also introduce multiform mutations of dæmons. For the avaricious character is frequently changed into an ambitious life, this again into a life which is formed by right opinion, and this last into a scientific life. The dæmon, therefore, will vary according to these changes; for the energizing part will be different at different times. If, therefore, either this energizing part itself is a dæmon, or that part which has an arrangement prior to it, dæmons will be changed together with the mutation of human life, and the same person will have many dæmons in one life; which is of all things the most impossible. For the soul never changes in one life the government of its dæmon; but it is the same dæmon which presides over us till we are brought before the judges of our conduct, as also Socrates asserts in the *Phædo*.

Again, those who consider a partial intellect, or that intellect which subsists at the extremity of the intellectual order, as the same with the dæmon which is assigned to man, appear to me to confound the intellectual peculiarity with the dæmoniacal essence. For all dæmons subsist in the extent of souls, and rank as the next in order to divine souls. But the intellectual order is different from that of soul, and is neither allotted the same essence, nor power, nor energy.

Further still, this also may be said, that souls enjoy intellect then only when they convert themselves to it, receive its light, and conjoin their own with intellectual energy; but they experience the presiding care of a dæmoniacal nature through the whole of life, and in every thing which proceeds from fate and providence. For it is the dæmon that governs the whole of our life, and that fulfils the elections which we made prior to generation, together with the gifts of fate, and of those Gods that preside over fate. It is likewise the dæmon that supplies and measures the illuminations from providence. And as souls indeed, we are suspended from intellect, but as souls using the body we require the aid of a dæmon. Hence, Plato in the *Phædrus* calls intellect the governor of the soul; but he every where calls a dæmon the inspector and guardian of mankind. And no one who considers the affair rightly, will find any other one and proximate providence of every thing pertaining to us, besides that of a dæmon. For intellect, as we have said, is participated by the rational soul, but not by the body; and nature is participated by the body, but not by the dianoetic part. And further still, the rational soul rules over anger and desire, but it has no dominion over fortuitous events. But the dæmon alone moves, governs, and orderly disposes all our affairs. For he gives perfection to reason, measures the passions, inspires nature, connects the body, supplies things fortuitous, accomplishes the decrees of fate, and imparts the gifts of providence. In short, he is the king of every thing in and about us, and is the pilot of the whole of our life. And thus much concerning our allotted dæmons.

CHAPTER XLIV

In the next place, with respect to the dæmon of Socrates, these three things are to be particularly considered. First, that he not only ranks as a dæmon, but also as a God. For in the *First Alcibiades* Socrates clearly says, "I have long been of opinion that the God did not as yet direct me to hold any conversation with you." He calls the same power therefore a dæmon and a God. And in the *Apology* he more clearly evinces that this dæmon is allotted a divine transcendency, considered as ranking in a dæmoniacal order. And this is what we before said, that the dæmons of divine souls, and who make choice of an intellectual and elevating life, are divine, transcending the whole of a dæmoniacal genus, and being the first participants of the Gods. For, as is a dæmon among Gods, such also is a God among dæmons. Among the divinities however the hyparxis is divine; but in dæmons on the contrary, the peculiarity of their essence is dæmoniacal, but the analogy which they bear to divinity evinces their essence to be godlike. For on account of their transcendency with respect to other dæmons they frequently appear as Gods. With great propriety therefore, does Socrates call his dæmon a God; for he belonged to the first and highest dæmons. Hence Socrates was most perfect, being governed by such a presiding power, and conducting himself by the will of such a leader and guardian of his life. This then was one of the illustrious prerogatives of the dæmon of Socrates. The second was this: that Socrates perceived a certain voice proceeding from his dæmon. For this is asserted by him in the *Theætetus* and in the *Phædrus*. This voice also is the signal from the dæmon, which he speaks of in the *Theages*. And again in the *Phædrus*, when he was about to pass over the river, he experienced the accustomed signal from the dæmon. What then, does Socrates indicate by these assertions, and what was the voice through which he says the dæmon signified to him his will?

In the first place, we must say that Socrates, through his dianoetic power, and his science of things, enjoyed the inspiration of his dæmon, who continually recalled him to divine love. In the second place, in the affairs of life, Socrates supernally directed his providential attention to more imperfect souls. And according to the energy of his dæmon, he received the light proceeding from thence, neither in his dianoetic part alone, nor in his doxastic powers, but also in his spirit, the illumination of the dæmon suddenly diffusing itself through the whole of his life, and now moving sense itself. For it is evident that reason, imagination, and sense, enjoy the same energy differently; and that each of our inward parts is passive to, and is moved by the dæmon in a peculiar manner. The voice therefore, did not act upon Socrates externally with passivity; but the dæmoniacal inspiration, proceeding inwardly through his whole soul, and diffusing itself as far as to the organs of sense, became at last a voice, which was rather recognized by consciousness than by sense. For such are the illuminations of good dæmons and the Gods.

In the third place, let us consider the peculiarity of the dæmon of Socrates; for it never exhorted, but perpetually recalled him. This also must be again referred to the Socratic life. For it is not a property common to our allotted dæmons, but was the characteristic of the guardian of Socrates. We must say therefore, that the beneficent and philanthropic disposition of Socrates, and his great promptitude with respect to the communication of good, did not require the exhortation of the dæmon. For he was impelled from himself, and was ready at all times to impart to all men the most excellent life. But since many of those that came to him were unadapted to the pursuit of virtue and the science of wholes, his governing good dæmon restrained him from a providential care of such as these. Just as a good charioteer alone restrains the impetus of a horse naturally well adapted for the race, but does not stimulate him, in consequence of his being excited to motion from himself, and not requiring the spur, but the bridle. And hence Socrates, from his great readiness to benefit those with whom he conversed, rather required a recalling than an exciting dæmon. For the inaptitude of auditors, which is for the most part concealed from human sagacity, requires a dæmoniacal discrimination; and the knowledge of favourable opportunities can by this alone be accurately announced to us. Socrates therefore being naturally impelled to good, alone required to be recalled in his unseasonable impulses.

But farther still, it may be said, that of dæmons, some are allotted a purifying and undefiled power; others a perfective; and others a demiurgic power. And in short, they are divided according to the characteristic peculiarities of the Gods, and the powers under which they are arranged. Each likewise, according to his hyparxis, incites the object of his providential care to a blessed life; some of them moving us to an attention to inferior concerns; and others restraining us from action, and an energy verging to externals. It appears therefore, that the dæmon of Socrates being allotted this peculiarity, *viz.* cathartic, and the source of an undefiled life, and being arranged under this power of Apollo, and uniformly presiding over the whole of purification, separated also Socrates from too much commerce with the vulgar, and a life extending itself into multitude. But it led him into the depths of his soul, and an energy undefiled by subordinate natures. And hence it never exhorted, but perpetually recalled him. For, what else is to recall, than to withdraw him from the multitude to inward energy? And of what is this the peculiarity except of purification? Indeed, it appears to me, that as Orpheus places the Apolloniacal monad over king Bacchus, which recalls him from a progression into Titannic multitude, and a desertion of his royal throne, in like manner the dæmon of Socrates conducted him to an intellectual place of survey, and restrained his association with the multitude. For the dæmon is analogous to Apollo, being his attendant, but the intellect of Socrates to Bacchus; for our intellect is the progeny of the power of this divinity.

CHAPTER XLV

From the MS. Scholia also of Proclus on the *Cratylus*, we derive the following important information concerning this order of beings who connect the divine and human nature together. Of the genera posterior to the Gods, and which are indeed their perpetual attendants, but produce in conjunction with them mundane fabrications from on high, as far as to the last of things; - of these genera, some unfold generation into light; others are transporters of union; others of power; and others call forth the knowledge of the Gods, and an intellectual essence. But of these, some are called angelic, by those that are skilful in divine concerns, in consequence of being established according to the hyparxis itself of the Gods, and making that which is uniform in their nature commensurate with things of a secondary rank. Hence, the angelic tribe is *boniform*, as unfolding into light the occult *goodness* of the Gods. Others among these are called by theologists dæmoniacal, as binding the middle of all things, and as distributing divine power, and producing it as far as to the last of things. For δαισαι is μερισαι. But this genus possesses abundance of power, and is multifarious, as giving subsistence to those last dæmons who are material, who draw down souls, and proceed to the most partial and material form of energy. Others again, are denominated by them heroic, who lead human souls on high through love, and who are the suppliers of an intellectual life, of magnitude of operation, and transcendency of wisdom. In short, they are allotted a convertive order and providence, and an alliance to a divine intellect, to which they also convert secondary natures. Hence, they are allotted this appellation, as being able to *raise* and *extend* souls to the Gods. (ως αιρειν και ανατεινειν τας ψυχας επι θεους δυναμενα)

These triple genera posterior to, are indeed, always suspended from the Gods, but they are divided from each other. And some of them are essentially intellectual; others are essentialized in rational souls; and others subsist in irrational and phantastic lives, *i.e.* in lives characterized by imagination. It is also evident that such of them as are intellectual, are allotted a prudence or wisdom transcending that of human nature, and which is eternally conjoined with the objects of their intellection. But such of them as are rational, energize discursively according to prudence. And the irrational kind are destitute of prudence. For they dwell in matter, and the darkest parts of the universe. They also bind souls to image-producing bosoms, (και συνδει τας ψυχας τοις ειδωλοποιοις κολποις) and strangle such as are brought into that region, until they have suffered the punishment which is their due. These three genera therefore, which are more excellent than us, Socrates now calls dæmons. And thus much concerning these triple genera, according to Proclus.

Again, with respect to dæmons properly so called, there are three species of them according to the Platonic theology; the first of which is rational only, and the last is irrational only; but the middle species is partly rational and partly irrational. And again, of these the first is perfectly beneficent, but many among the other two species are malevolent and noxious to mankind: not indeed essentially malevolent (for there is nothing in the universe, the ample abode of all-bountiful Jove, essentially evil), but only so from the office which they are destined to perform. For nothing which operates naturally, operates as to itself evilly. But the Platonic Hermeas in his MS. Commentary on the *Phædrus*, and on that part of it in which Plato says, "There are indeed, other evils besides these, but a certain dæmon immediately mingles pleasure with most of them," admirably observes respecting dæmons as follows: "The distribution of good and evil originates from the dæmoniacal genus. For every genus transcending that of dæmons, uniformly possesses good. There are therefore, certain genera of dæmons, some of which adorn and administer certain parts of the world; but others certain species of animals. Hence, the dæmon who is the inspective guardian of life, hastens souls into that condition which he himself is allotted; as for instance, into injustice or intemperance, and continually mingles pleasure in them as a snare. But there are other dæmons transcending these, who are the punishers of souls, converting them to a more perfect and elevated life. And the first of these it is necessary to avoid; but the second sort we should render propitious. There are other dæmons however, more excellent than these, who distribute good in an uniform manner."

Farther still, Plato in the *Phædo*, says, "that the dæmon of each person, which was allotted to him while living, endeavours to lead each to a certain place, where it is necessary that all of them being collected together, after they have been judged, should proceed to Hades, together with their leader, who is ordered to conduct them from hence thither. But there receiving the allotments proper to their condition, and abiding for a necessary time, another leader brings them back hither again, in many and long periods of time." Olympiodorus in his MS. Commentary on that dialogue, observes on this passage as follows:

"Since there are in the universe, things which subsist differently at different times, and since there are also natures which are conjoined with the superessential unities, it is necessary that there should be a certain middle genus, which is neither immediately suspended from deity, nor subsists differently at different times according to better and worse, but which is always perfect, and does not depart from its proper virtue; and is immutable indeed but is not conjoined with the superessential. The whole of this genus is dæmoniacal. There are also different genera of dæmons; for they are arranged under the mundane Gods. The highest of these subsists according to *The One* of the Gods, which is called an unific and divine genus of dæmons. The next according to the intellect which is suspended from Deity, and is called intellectual. The third subsists according to soul, and is called rational. The fourth according to nature, and is denominated physical. The fifth according to body, and is called corporeal-formed. And the sixth according to matter, and this is denominated material. Or after another manner it may be said, that some of these are celestial, others ethereal, others aerial, others aquatic, others terrestrial, and others subterranean. With respect also to this division, it is evident that it is derived from the parts of the universe. But irrational dæmons originate from the aerial governors, whence also the [Chaldean] Oracle says,

$$\eta\epsilon\rho\iota\omega\nu\ \epsilon\lambda\alpha\tau\eta\rho\alpha\ \kappa\upsilon\nu\omega\nu\ \chi\theta\omicron\nu\iota\omega\nu\ \tau\epsilon\ \kappa\alpha\iota\ \upsilon\gamma\rho\omega\nu.$$

i.e. "being the charioteer of the aerial, terrestrial and aquatic dogs." Our guardian dæmons, however, belong to that order of dæmons which is arranged under the Gods that preside over the ascent and descent of souls."

Olympiodorus further observes, "that the dæmon endeavours to lead the soul as exciting its conceptions and imaginations, at the same time, however, yielding to the self-motive power of the soul. But in consequence of the dæmon exciting, one soul follows voluntarily, another violently, and another according to a mode subsisting between these. There is also one dæmon who leads the soul to its judges from the present life; another who is ministrant to the judges, giving completion, as it were, to the sentence which is passed; and a third who is allotted the guardianship of life."

In the next place, with respect to irrational dæmons, it remains to investigate how they subsist. For if they derive their subsistence from the junior Gods, how, since these are the fathers of mortal natures, are these dæmons immortal? But if from the demiurgus how are they irrational? For he is the father of things in conjunction with intellect. This doubt is beautifully solved by Proclus as follows: irrational dæmons derive their subsistence from the junior Gods, yet are not on this account mortal, since of these Gods some generate others. And perhaps the generated Gods are called by Plato, in the *Timæus*, dæmons, because those that are truly dæmons are produced by the junior Gods. But they likewise proceed from the one demiurgus. For as Timæus says, he is the cause of all immortal natures. If, however, the demiurgus imparts intellect to all things, there is also in irrational dæmons an ultimate vestige of the intellectual peculiarity, so far as they have a facility of imagination; for this is the last echo as it were of intellect. And on this account the phantasy is not improperly called by others passive intellect.

Lastly, after essential heroes, an order of souls follows, who proximately govern the affairs of men, and are dæmoniacal according to habitude or alliance, but not essentially. These souls likewise are the perpetual attendants of the Gods, but they have not an essence *wholly* superior to man. Of this kind, as we are informed by Proclus in his MS. Scholia on the *Cratylus*, are the Nymphs that sympathize with waters, Pans with the feet of goats and the like. They also differ from those powers that are essentially of a dæmoniacal characteristic in this, that they assume a variety of shapes (each of the others immutably preserving one form) are subject to various passions, and are the causes of every kind of deception to mankind. Proclus likewise observes, that the Minerva which so often appeared to Ulysses and Telemachus belonged to this order of souls.

CHAPTER XLVI

After the triple genera that are the perpetual attendants of the Gods, those human souls follow that are of an heroic characteristic, are undefiled, associating with generation, and abandoning their proper order but for a little time. For the souls that descend and are defiled with vice, are very remote from those that abide on high with immaculate purity. The media, therefore, between these, are the souls that descend indeed, but without defilement; since it is not lawful for the contrary to take place, *viz.* to be defiled with vice, and yet to abide on high. For evil is not in the Gods, but in the regions of mortality, and material affairs. The first genus of souls, therefore, is divine. For every where, that which is the recipient of deity has a ruling and leading order, in essences, in intellects, in souls and in bodies. But the second genus of souls is always conjoined to the Gods, in order that through this those that sometimes depart from, may again be recalled to them. The third genus is that which descends indeed into generation, but descends with purity, exchanges a more divine life for one of a subordinate nature, but is exempt from vice, and liberated from the dominion of the passions. For this genus exists in continuity with that which always abides on high, and is always undefiled. And the fourth and last genus is that of the souls of the bulk of mankind, which wanders abundantly, descends as far as to Tartarus, and is again excited from thence. It likewise evolves all-various forms of life, uses a variety of manners, is under the influence of different passions at different times, and assumes the forms of dæmons, men, and irrational animals. At the same time, however, it is corrected and amended by Justice, recurs from earth to heaven, and is led round from matter to intellect, but according to certain orderly periods of wholes.

Plotinus beautifully alludes to this undefiled genus of human souls in the 9th book of his 5th *Ennead*,[†] On Intellect, Ideas, and Being, as follows: "Since all men from their birth employ sense prior to intellect, and are necessarily first conversant with sensibles, some proceeding no farther pass through life, considering these as the first and last of things, and apprehending that whatever is painful among these is evil, and whatever is pleasant is good; thus thinking it sufficient to pursue the one and avoid the other. Those too, among them, who pretend to a greater share of reason than others, esteem this to be wisdom, being affected in a manner similar to more heavy birds, who, collecting many things from the earth, and being oppressed with the weight, are unable to fly on high, though they have received wings for this purpose from nature. But others are in a small degree elevated from things subordinate, the more excellent part of the soul recalling them from pleasure to a more

---

† TTS Vol. III, p. 313 *et seq.*

worthy pursuit. As they are, however, unable to look on high, and as not possessing any thing else which can afford them rest, they betake themselves together with the name of virtue to actions and the election of things inferior, from which they at first endeavoured to raise themselves, though in vain. *In the third class is the race of divine men,* who through a more excellent power, and with piercing eyes, acutely perceive supernal light, to the vision of which they raise themselves above the clouds and darkness as it were of this lower world, and there abiding despise every thing in these regions of sense; being no otherwise delighted with the place which is truly and properly their own, than he who after many wanderings is at length restored to his lawful country."

These undefiled souls are called by the author of the *Golden Verses,* "terrestrial dæmons," because, as Hierocles observes, they are by nature men, but by habitude dæmons, and possess a scientific knowledge of divinity. For since all men are terrestrial, as ranking in the third degree of rational beings, but all are not skilful (δαημονων) and wise, the author of the verses very properly calls wise men both terrestrial and dæmons conjointly. For neither are all men wise, nor are all the beings that are wise, men. But the illustrious heroes[†] and the immortal Gods, being naturally more excellent than men, are wise and good. The verses therefore exhort us to reverence those men who are co-arranged with the divine genera, and who (according to habitude) are equal to angels and dæmons, and are similar to the illustrious heroes.

Plato, in the *Cratylus,* calls these undefiled souls both dæmons and heroes, and speaks of them as follows: "Soc. Do you not know who those dæmons are which Hesiod speaks of? Herm. I do not. Soc. And are you ignorant that he says the golden race of men was first generated? Herm. This I know. Soc. He says, therefore, that after this race was concealed by Fate, it produced dæmons denominated holy, terrestrial, good, expellers of evil, and guardians of mortal men. Herm. But what then? Soc. I think, indeed, that he calls it a golden race, not as naturally consisting of gold, but as being beautiful and good. I infer this, however, from his denominating our race an iron one. Herm. You speak the truth. Soc. Do you not therefore think, that if any one of the present times should appear to be good, Hesiod would say he belonged to the golden race? Herm. It is probable he would. Soc. But are the good any other than such as are [intellectually] prudent? Herm. They

---

[†] The author of these verses comprehends the triple genera that are more excellent than man, *viz.* angels, dæmons and heroes, under the appellation of illustrious heroes.

are not. Soc. On this account, therefore, as it appears to me, more than any other he calls them dæmons, because they were *prudent* and *learned* (δαημονες). And in our ancient tongue this very name is to be found. Hence both he and many other poets, speak in a becoming manner, when they say that a good man after death will receive a mighty destiny and renown, and will become a *dæmon*, according to the surname of prudence. I therefore assert the same, that every good man is *learned* and *skilful*; that he is dæmoniacal both while living and when dead; and that he is properly denominated a dæmon. Herm. And I also, Socrates, seem to myself to agree with you perfectly in this particular. But what does the name hero signify? Soc. This is by no means difficult to understand. For this name is very little different from its original, evincing that its generation is derived from love. Herm. How is this? Soc. Do you not know that heroes are demigods? Herm. What then? Soc. All of them were doubtless generated either from the love of a God towards a mortal maid, or from the love of a man towards a Goddess. If, therefore, you consider this matter according to the ancient Attic tongue, you will more clearly understand the truth of this derivation. For it will be evident to you that the word hero is derived from love, with a trifling mutation for the sake of the name."

The meaning of Plato in this passage, and also the characteristic properties of terrestrial heroes are beautifully unfolded by Proclus as follows, in his very rare and invaluable MS. Scholia on the *Cratylus*. "Every where the extremities of a prior, are conjoined with the summits of a secondary order. Thus for instance, our master Hermes (ο δεσποτης ημων Ερμης) being an archangelic monad, is celebrated as a God. But Plato calls the whole extent between Gods and men dæmons. And they indeed, are dæmons by nature. Those dæmons, however, that are now mentioned, together with the demigods heroes, are not dæmons and heroes by nature, for they do not always follow the Gods; but they are only so from habitude, being souls who naturally deliver themselves to generation, such as was the great Hercules, and others of the like kind. But the peculiarity of heroic souls is magnitude of operation, elevation and magnificence. Such heroes also it is necessary to honour, and to perform funeral rites to their memory, conformably to the exhortation of the Athenian guest in the *Laws*. This heroic genus of souls, therefore, does not always follow the Gods, but is undefiled, and more intellectual than other souls. And it descends indeed for the benefit of the life of men, as partaking of a destiny inclining downwards; but it has much of an elevated nature, and which is properly liberated from matter. Hence souls of this kind are easily led back to the intelligible world, in which they live for many periods; while on the contrary, the more irrational kind of souls, are either never led back, or this is accomplished with great difficulty, or continues for a very inconsiderable period of time.

Each of the Gods indeed is perfectly exempt from secondary natures, and the first and more total of dæmons are likewise established above a habitude of this kind. They employ, however, terrestrial and partial spirits in the generations of some of the human race, not physically mingling with mortals, but moving nature, perfecting its power, expanding the path of generation, and removing all impediments. Fables, therefore, through the similitude of appellation conceal the things themselves. For spirits of this kind are similarly denominated with the Gods, the leading causes of their series. Hence they say, either that Gods have connexion with women, or men with Goddesses. But if they were willing to speak plainly and clearly, they would say that Venus, Mars, Thetis, and the other divinities, produce their respective series, beginning from on high, as far as to the last of things; each of which series comprehends in itself many essences differing from each other; such as the angelical, dæmoniacal, heroical, nymphical, and the like. The lowest powers, therefore, of these orders, have much communion with the human race; for the extremities of first are connascent with the summits of secondary natures. And they contribute to our other natural operations, and to the production of our species. On this account it is frequently seen that from the mixture of these powers with men heroes are generated, who appear to possess a certain prerogative above human nature. Not only a dæmoniacal genus, however, of this kind, physically sympathizes with men, but a different genus sympathizes with other animals, as Nymphs with trees, others with fountains, and others with stags, or serpents.

But how is it that at one time the Gods are said to have connexion with mortal females, and at another time mortal females with the Gods? We reply, that the communion of Gods with Goddesses gives subsistence to Gods or dæmons eternally; but heroic souls having a twofold form of life, *viz. doxastic* and *dianoetic*, the former of which is called by Plato in the *Timæus the circle of difference*, and the latter, *the circle of sameness*, and which are characterized by the properties of *male* and *female*;- hence these souls at one time exhibit a deiform power, by energizing according to the masculine prerogative of their nature, or *the circle of sameness*, and at another time according to their feminine prerogative, or *the circle of difference*; yet so as that according to both these energies they act with rectitude, and without merging themselves in the darkness of body.

They likewise know the natures prior to their own, and exercise a providential care over inferior concerns, without at the same time having that propensity to such concerns which is found in the bulk of mankind. But the souls which act erroneously according to the energies of both these circles, or which, in other words, neither exhibit accurate specimens of practical, nor of intellectual virtue - these differ in no respect from *gregarious* souls, or the herd of mankind, with whom the circle of sameness is fettered, and the circle of difference sustains all-various fractions and distortions.

As it is impossible therefore, that these heroic souls can act with equal vigour and perfection, according to both these circles at once, since this is the province of natures more divine than the human, it is necessary that they should sometimes descend and energize principally according to their doxastic part, and sometimes according to their more intellectual part. Hence, one of these circles must energize naturally, and the other be hindered from its proper energy. On this account heroes are called *demigods*, as having only one of their circles illuminated by the Gods. Such of these therefore, as have the circle of sameness unfettered, as are excited to an intellectual life, and are moved about it according to a deific energy, - these are said to have a God for their father, and a mortal for their mother, through a defect with respect to the doxastic form of life. But such, on the contrary, as energize without impediment according to the circle of difference, who act with becoming rectitude in practical affairs, and at the same time *enthusiastically*, or in other words, under the inspiring influence of divinity, - these are said to have a mortal for their father, and a Goddess for their mother. In short, rectitude of energy in each of these circles is to be ascribed to a divine cause.† Hence when the circle of sameness has dominion, the divine cause of illumination is said to be masculine and paternal; but when the circle of difference predominates, it is said to be maternal. Hence too, Achilles in Homer acts with rectitude in practical affairs,‡ and at the same time exhibits specimens of magnificent, vehement, and divinely-inspired energy, as being the son of a Goddess. And such is his

---

† It must be carefully observed, that this divine cause illuminates, investigates, and excites these circles in the most unrestrained and impassive manner, without destroying freedom of energy in the circles themselves, or causing any partial affection, sympathy or tendency in illuminating deity.

‡ See a more masterly defence of the character of Achilles as a hero in my translation of Proclus's noble apology for Homer, in the first Volume of my Plato. [TTS vol. IX.]

attachment to practical virtue, that even when in Hades, he desires a union with body, that he may assist his father. While on the contrary, Minos and Rhadamanthus, who were heroes illuminated by Jupiter, raised themselves from generation to true being, and meddled with mortal concerns no further than absolute necessity required.

In the last place Proclus adds, that heroes are very properly denominated from Love, since Love is a great dæmon: and from the cooperation of dæmons heroes are produced. To which may also be added, that Love originated from Plenty as the more excellent cause, and from Poverty as the recipient and the worse cause; and heroes are analogously produced from different genera.

Plato who was one of these heroes or demigods, was the offspring of Apollo in the way above explained by Proclus, as we are informed by Olympiodorus in his life of him. For he says, "It is reported that an Apolloniacal spectre had connection with Perictione the mother of Plato, and that appearing in the night to Aristo the father of Plato, it commanded him not to sleep with Perictione during the time of her pregnancy - which mandate Aristo obeyed." The like account of the divine origin of Plato is also given by Apuleius in his treatise on the dogmas of Plato, and by Plutarch in the 8th book of his *Symoposiacs*. Epimenides likewise, Eudoxus and Xenocrates asserted that Apollo becoming connected with Parthenis the mother of Pythagoras, and causing her to be pregnant, had in consequence of this predicted concerning Pythagoras by his priest.[†] And thus much concerning those undefiled souls who were called by the ancients terrestrial dæmons, heroes and demigods, and who descended into the regions of mortality for the benevolent purpose of benefiting those apostate souls, who are elegantly called by Empedocles,

Heaven's exiles straying from the orb of light.

CHAPTER XLVII

The triple genera that are the perpetual attendants of the Gods, and which have been unfolded in the preceding chapters, are indicated by the following division of time, in the first hypothesis of the *Parmenides*; from which division *The One* is shown to be exempt: "Do not the terms *it was, it has been, it did become*, seem to signify the participation of the time past? Certainly. And do not the terms *it will be, it may become*,

---

[†] Vid. Iamblich. de vita Pythag. cap. 2. [TTS vol. XVII]

and *it will be generated*, signify that which is about to be hereafter? Certainly. But are not the terms *it is*, and *it is becoming to be*, marks of the present time? Entirely so. If then *The One* participates in no respect of any time, it neither ever *was*, nor *has been* nor *did become*. Nor is it *now generated*, nor is *becoming to be*, nor *is*, nor *may become* hereafter, nor *will be generated*, nor *will be*. It is most true."

The commentary of Proclus on this passage is as follows: "This division of time accords with the multitude of the divine genera, which are suspended from divine souls, *viz*. with angels, dæmons, and heroes. And in the first place, this division proceeds to them supernally, according to a triadic distribution into the *present, past*, and *future*; and in the next place, according to a distribution into nine, each of these three being again subdivided into three. For the monad of souls is united to the one whole of time, but this is participated secondarily by the multitude of souls. And of this multitude, those participate of this whole *totally*, that subsist according to *the past*, or *the present*, or *the future*; but those participate of it *partially*, that are essentialized according to the differences of these. For to each of the wholes a multitude is co-ordinated, divided into things first, middle, and last. For a certain multitude subsists in conjunction with that which is established conformably to *the past*, the *summit* of which is according to *the was*, but the *middle* according to *it has been*, and the *end* according to *it did become*. With that also which is established according to *the present*, there is another multitude, the *principal* part of which is characterized by *the is*, the *middle* by *it is generated*, and the *end* by *it is becoming to be*. And there is another triad with that which subsists according to *the future*, the *most elevated* part of which is characterized by *the will be*, that which ranks in the *middle* by *it may become*, and the *end* by *it will be generated*. And thus there will be three triads proximately suspended from these three totalities, but all these are suspended from their monad.

All these orders, likewise, which are distributed according to the parts of time, energize according to the whole of time; this whole containing in itself triple powers, one of which is *perfective* of all motion, the second *connects* and *guards* things which are governed by it, and the third *unfolds* divine natures into light. For, as all such things are not eternal, are led round in a circle, the wholeness or the monad of time, perfects and connects their essence, and discloses to them the united infinity of eternity, evolving the contracted multitude which subsists in eternal natures; whence also this apparent time, as Timæus says, unfolds to us the measures of divine periods, perfects sensibles, and guards things which are generated in their proper numbers. Time, therefore, possesses triple powers prior to souls, *viz. the perfective, the connective,* and *the unfolding,* according to a similitude to eternity. For eternity, possessing a middle order in intelligibles, *perfects* the order posterior to itself, supplying it with union, but *unfolds into light* that which is prior to itself, producing into multitude its ineffable union, and *connects* the middle bond of intelligibles, and guards all things intransitively through its power. Time, therefore, receiving supernally the triple powers of eternity, imparts them to souls. Eternity, however, possesses this triad unitedly; but time both unitedly and distributively; and souls distributively alone. Hence, of souls, some are characterized according to one, and others according to another power of time; some imitating its *unfolding*, others its *perfective* and others its *connective* power. Thus also with respect to the Fates, some of these being adapted to give completion and perfection to things, are said to sing the past, always indeed energizing, and always singing, their songs being intellections, and fabricative energies about the world: for the past is the source of *completion.* Others again of these are adapted to *connect* things *present*; for they guard the essence and the generation of these. And others are adapted to *unfold the future*; for they lead into essence and to an end that which as yet is not.

We may also say, since there is an order of souls more excellent than ours divided into such as are first, such as are middle, and such as are last, the most total of these are adapted to *the past.* For as this comprehends in itself the present and the future, so these souls comprehend in themselves the rest. But souls of a middle rank are adapted to *the present* for this was once *future,* but is not yet *the past.* As, therefore, *the present* contains in itself *the future,* so these middle souls comprehend those posterior, but are comprehended in those prior to themselves. And souls of the third order correspond to *the future.* For this does not proceed through *the present,* nor has become *the past,* but is *the future* alone; just as these third souls are of themselves alone, but through falling into a more partial subsistence, are by no means comprehensive of others. For they convolve the boundary according to a triadic division of the genera posterior to the Gods.

The whole of the first triad, therefore, has *the once*, for this is the peculiarity of *the past*, and of completion; but it is divided into *the was, it was generated*, and *it did become*. Again, therefore, of these three, *the was* signifies the summit of the triad, bounded according to hyparxis itself; but *it was generated,* signifies an at-once-collected perfection; and *it did become* an extension in being perfected; these things being imitations of intelligibles. For *the was* is an imitation of *being, it was generated*, of *eternity*, and *it did become* of that which is *primarily eternal*. For *being* is derived to all things from the first of these; a subsistence at once as *all*, and a *whole* from the second; and an *extension into multitude* from the third.

CHAPTER XLVIII

Having, therefore, unfolded to the reader the orders and characteristic properties of the mundane Gods, and of the triple genera that are perpetually suspended from them, I shall in the next place present him with what Plato says, in celebration of the divinity of the World, the great monad which comprehends all these, so far as the whole of it is a God, consisting of a superessential unity derived from the ineffable principle of all things, a divine intellect, a divine soul, and a deified body. In the *Timæus* then, Plato celebrates the world as a deity in the following manner: "When, therefore, that God who is an eternally reasoning divinity cogitated about the God who at a certain time would exist, he fabricated his body smooth and equable, and every way from the middle equal and whole, and perfect from the composition of perfect bodies. But placing soul in the middle of the world, he extended it through the whole; and besides this, externally surrounded the body of the universe with soul. And causing circle to revolve in a circle, he established heaven (*i.e.* the world) one, only, solitary nature, able through virtue to converse with itself, indigent of nothing external, and sufficiently known and friendly to itself. And on all these accounts the world was generated by him, a blessed God. The first part of this extract, as far as to the word "perfect bodies," is admirably elucidated by Proclus as follows:

What is here said, imitating the one intellect which comprehends the intellection of wholes in one, collects all things into sameness, and refers to one summit all the fabrication of the corporeal system. It is necessary, therefore, that we should recall to our memory what has been already asserted. It has been said then, that the elements through analogy rendered all things in concord with each other. That the universe was generated a whole consisting of wholes. That it is spherical and smooth, and has itself a knowledge of itself, and a motion in itself. Hence, it is evident that the whole world is assimilated to [its paradigm] all-perfect animal. But the orderly distribution according to the wholes which it contains proceeds analogous to its second and third causes. And the number of its elements indeed, and the unifying bond of them through analogy, corresponds to the essence which is without colour, without figure, and without contact;[†] for number is there. The first wholeness of the world which adorns all things, and which consists of the wholes of the elements proceeds analogous to the intellectual wholeness.[‡] Its sphericity is analogous to intellectual figure.[§] Its sufficiency, intellectual motion, and sameness of convolution, are analogous to the God who absorbs all his offspring in himself.[*] Its animation corresponds to its vivific cause [Rhea]. And its possession of intellect is analogous to the demiurgic intellect; though from this all things proceed, and from the natures prior to it, different things being analogous to different causes. And the more excellent natures indeed are the causes of all that proceeds from secondary principles; but secondary principles are the causes of less numerous and less excellent effects. For with respect to the demiurgus himself, so far as he is *intellectual*, he produces all things intellectual; but so far as he is *being*, he is the father of all bodies and of every thing incorporeal; and so far as he is a God, he also gives subsistence to matter itself. In what is now said, therefore, Plato makes a summary repetition of every thing which the universe derives from the intellectual Gods. And thus much concerning the whole theory.

Let us survey, however, more particularly the truth of what is now said. When, therefore, Plato calls the demiurgus, "an eternally reasoning being," he makes the essence and at the same time the intellection of him through which the world is perpetual, to be eternal. It is requisite, likewise, to observe how he arranges the demiurgus among beings that always exist, assigning to him an eternal order; so that he will not be soul. For in the *Laws* Plato says that soul is immortal indeed, and indestructible, but is not eternal. Hence, it appears that every one who fancies soul is the demiurgus, is ignorant of the difference between the eternal and the indestructible. But *reasoning* is significant of distributed or divided fabrication. And the words, "who at a certain time would exist," do not indicate a temporal beginning, as Atticus imagined they did, but an essence conjoined with time. For Plato says in this dialogue, "that time was generated together with the universe," and the world is

---

[†] And this essence, as is shown in the 4th book, subsists at the summit of the intelligible and at the same time intellectual order.

[‡] This forms the middle of the above-mentioned order.

[§] This forms the extremity of that order.

[*] *Viz.* to Saturn, who subsists at the summit of the intellectual order.

temporal, and time is mundane. For time and the world are consubsistent with each other, and co-produced from the one fabrication of things. And a *temporal ever*, may be said to be *at a certain time*, when compared with that which is eternal, just as that which is *generatively being*, is *non-being*, when compared with that which is *intelligibly being*. Though the world, therefore, exists through the whole of time, yet its being consists in *becoming to be*, and is in a part of time. But this is the ποτε or the *at a certain time*, mentioned by Plato, and is not a simultaneous subsistence in all time, but is always *at a certain time*. For the eternal is always in the whole of eternity; but the temporal in a certain time, is always differently in a different time. Hence, the world, as with reference to an *eternally* existing God, is very properly called a God, who at *a certain time* would exist. For the former is sensible with reference to the latter, who is intellectual. That which is sensible, therefore, is *always generated*, but *is* at a certain time. For it possesses existence partibly, and is perpetually advancing into being from that which always is. For since, as we have before observed, it derives from something else an infinite power of existing, and that which it possesses is finite, but it is perpetual by always receiving, the ability of existing infinitely, being numbered in that which is finite, it is evident that it is at a certain time; from *a certain time* always possessing existence; and in consequence of that which is imparted to it never ceasing, always becoming to be;[†] but in its own nature existing at a certain time, and having, as Plato says in the *Politicus*, a renovated immortality. For subsisting in rising into existence, the whole of it does not at once participate of the whole of being, but again and again, not existing without an extension of being. Unless, perhaps, the expression *at a certain time*, signifies the *whole* of time. For the evolution of time, as with reference to an *eternal infinity* is ποτε a certain time. And the whole of time has the same ratio to eternity, that a part of time the ποτε has to the whole.

If, also, you are willing, it may be said after another manner, that Plato denominates the world "a God that at a certain time would exist," since he has now fashioned a corporeal nature, and given subsistence to intellect, but not yet to soul, because the world also as a God will have a subsistence in the course of his narration. For divinity produces at once both parts and the whole, but language divides things that are consubsistent, generates things that are unbegotten, and distributes

---

[†] Instead of και δια το μη λεγειν, το διδον αει γινομενος, it is necessary to read δια το μη ληγειν το διδον, αει γινουενος.

eternal natures according to time. The God, therefore, that at a certain time would exist, is that which is fashioned in the narration of Plato, and according to which there are division and composition. For this, also, the Pythagoric Timæus himself indicates to those who are able to understand him, when he says in his treatise [*On the soul of the world*], "Before heaven (*i.e.* the world) was generated in words, there were idea and matter, and God the demiurgus." For he clearly manifests that he fashions in words the generation of the world.

When Plato, likewise, says that the demiurgus fabricated the body of the world smooth and equable, this manifests the one comprehension in the world, and its supreme aptitude to the participation of a divine soul. But the words, "every way from the middle equal," exhibit the peculiarity of a spherical figure; for this is every way equally distant according to all intervals. And the words "whole and perfect from the composition of perfect bodies, "give to the world a consummate similitude to all-perfect animal; for that was in all things perfect; and also to the demiurgus himself. For as he is the father of fathers, and the supreme of rulers, so the world is the most perfect of perfect natures, and the most total of wholes. You may also say, that Plato calls the world smooth, as not being in want of any motive, or nutritive, or sensitive organs; for this had just before been demonstrated by him. But that it is every way equal from the middle, as having a spherical figure. And that it is whole and perfect, as being all-perfect, and leaving nothing external to itself; for this is properly a whole and perfect. It likewise consists of perfect bodies, as being composed of the four elements. But Plato calls it in the singular number a body, as being only-begotten. And thus beginning from the only-begotten, and proceeding as far as to perfection, he again returns to it through the above-mentioned words, imitating the progression of the world from its paradigm, and its perfect conversion to it.

CHAPTER XLIX

In the next place, let us direct our attention to the words, "But placing soul in the middle of the world, he extended it through the whole; and besides this, externally surrounded the body of the universe with soul." Divinity, says Proclus, at once and eternally produces all things. For according to his very being, and according to the eternal intellection of wholes, he generates all things from himself, supermundane and mundane beings, intellects, souls, natures, bodies, and matter itself. And indeed, an at-once-collected subsistence in a greater degree belongs to the demiurgic progeny, than to the solar illumination; though in this the whole light proceeds simultaneously with the sun. But it is evident that the sun imitating the father of the universe through visible fabrication is inferior to eternal and invisible production. All things, therefore, as we have said, being produced from the invisible fabrication at once and eternally, at the same time, the order of the effects is likewise preserved. For all things proceed collectively together with their own proper order. For in the producing cause, there was also an eternal intellection, and order prior to the things that were arranged. Hence, though all things proceed at once from one cause, yet some have a first, and others a diminished dignity. For some things proceed in a greater, but others in a less degree. And some are co-arranged with the demiurgus according to union, others according to contact, and others according to participation. For intellect is able to be connascent with intellect through union; but soul is naturally adapted to be conjoined with intellect; and bodies participate of it only, just as things in the profundity of the earth participate of the splendour of the sun. All these, therefore, subsisting in the world, *viz.* intellect, soul, and body, and all these being produced at once, and at the same time, there being an order in these proceeding from the demiurgus, language at one time beginning supernally according to progression, ends at the boundaries of fabrication, but at another time being incited† from things last, according to conversion, recurs to the summits of the universe, conformably to things themselves. For all things proceed, and are converted to the cause and principle from which they proceeded; in so doing exhibiting a certain demiurgic circle.

Plato, however, delivered to us the order of the plenitudes (πληρωματων)‡ of the world, according to progression, in what he before said, when the demiurgus placing intellect in soul, and soul in body fabricated§ the universe, but in the present passage, he unfolds to us the order according to conversion. And in the first place, he assumes two contraries in the universe, adds two media to these, and unites them through analogy. Afterwards giving completion to the world, by rendering it a whole of wholes, he surrounds it with an intellectual [*i.e.* with a spherical] figure, gives it the power of participating a divine life,

---

† For ορωμενος here, it is necessary to read ορμωμενος.

‡ Wholes whether corporeal or incorporeal are thus denominated.

§ For συνεκτεινατο, it is necessary to read συνετεκταινετο.

and a motion imitating intellect.† Always, likewise, causing the world to be more perfect by the additions, he introduces soul into it as her proper place of abode, and fills as things with life, but different things with a different life. He also inserts intellect in soul, and through this conjoins her with her fountain. For the soul of the universe participating of intellect, is connected with intelligibles themselves. And thus he ends at the principle from which the mundane intellect, soul and the body of the world proceed. For giving a three-fold division to the universe, *viz.* into intellect, soul, and body, he discusses in the first place the two latter which are subordinate. For such is the mode according to conversion. And he terminates indeed the discussion of the body of the world, having unfolded its essence, its figure, and its motion. But the theory of soul is connected with this, just as the body itself of the world is suspended from a divine soul.

With respect, however, to the position of soul in the middle of the universe, it is differently explained by the different interpreters of Plato. For some call the centre of the earth the middle, but others the moon, as being the isthmus of generated and divine natures. Others again say that the sun is the middle, as being established in the place of a heart [in the world], others the inerratic sphere, others the equinoctial, as bounding the breadth of the universe, and others the zodiac. And some indeed place the governing principle in the centre of the universe, others in the moon, others in the sun, others in the equinoctial, and others in the zodiac. And the power of the centre testifies in favour of the first of these, since it is connective of every circulation; the motion of the moon, in favour of the second, since it variously changes generation; the vivific heat of the sun, in favour of the third; the facility of the motion of the equinoctial circle, of the fourth; and in favour of the fifth, the circulation of the stars about the zodiac. Porphyry, however, and Iamblichus, oppose all these interpretations, and reprobate them as understanding the middle in a way accompanied with interval, and enclosing in a certain part the soul of the whole world, which is every where similarly present, which rules over all things, and leads all things by its own motions. Of these divine men, however, Porphyry assuming the soul to be the soul of the universe, interprets the *middle* according to the psychical essence; for soul is the middle of intelligibles and sensibles. This interpretation, however, does not appear to say any thing as with reference to the words of Plato. But if we assume this, that the universe derives its completion from intellect, soul and body,

---

† *i.e.* a circular motion.

and that it is a psychical and intellectual animal, we shall find in this system that soul is the middle. This, therefore, Plato had before asserted; and now he will appear to say nothing else, than that the soul of the world is extended through the universe, being allotted a middle order in it. But the philosopher Iamblichus thinks that by *soul* we should understand the exempt, supermundane, and liberated soul, and which has dominion over all things. For according to him, Plato does not here speak of the mundane soul, but of the soul which is not participated by body, and which is arranged as a monad above all mundane souls. For the first soul is of this kind, and the *middle* is asserted of this, as being similarly present to all things, because it does not belong to any body, has no manner of habitude whatever, similarly animates all things, and is equally distant from all things. For it is not distant from some things in a less, and from others in a greater degree, since it is without habitude; but it is alike distant from all things; though all things are not after the same manner distant from it. For in its participants there is the more and the less.

Our leader, however, [Syrianus] more aptly interprets the words of Plato. For the soul of the world has indeed that which is supermundane and exempt from the universe, according to which it is conjoined with intellect, which Plato in the *Phædrus*, and Orpheus in his verses concerning *Ippa*[†] denominate the head or summit of the soul. It has also another multitude of powers proceeding from this monad, divided about the world, and appropriately present to all the parts of the universe. And these subsist in one way indeed about the middle, in another way about the earth, in another about the sun, and in another about each of the spheres. Our leader, therefore, says that all these are comprehended in the present words of Plato who indicates by them, that the soul of the world in one way animates the middle, in another the whole bulk, and that it leaves something else prior to these exempt from the universe.

That we may not, however, carelessly attend to what is here said by Plato, but may offer something demonstrative about the psychical powers, it must be said, that soul by a much greater priority than body is a vital world, and is both one and number. And by the one indeed, it is better than every form of habitude; but by the multitude it rules over the different parts of the universe. For in its guardian powers it contains the centre; since from thence the whole sphere is governed, to

---

[†] Proclus elsewhere informs us in these Commentaries, that the soul of the world is called by Orpheus *Ippa*.

which also it converges. Farther still, every thing turbulent in the world is impelled to the middle, and requires a divine guard, which is able to arrange it, and detain it in its proper boundaries. Hence also, theologists terminate the progressions of the highest Gods in that place; and the Pythagoreans call the middle either the tower or the prison of Jupiter. But in its stable and at the same time vivific powers, it contains the sphere of the earth. In its perfective and generative powers, the sphere of water. In its connective and motive powers it comprehends the air. In its undefiled powers, fire. And in its intellectual powers, the whole heaven. In these powers, likewise, it in one way contains the lunar, in another the solar, and in another the inerratic sphere.

Such therefore, being the animation of the world, or its participation of soul, Plato, as it is usual with him, beginning according to conversion from things that are last, first imparts soul to the middle, afterwards to the universe, and in the third place leaves something of soul external to the universe. For as he gave subsistence to body prior to soul, and to parts prior to wholes, thus also he imparts soul to the world, beginning from things that have an ultimate existence. When Plato therefore delivered the order of the plenitudes of the world according to progression, beginning supernally, he placed intellect in soul, and soul in body. But here where he delivers the order according to conversion, he first animates the middle, and afterwards the universe itself. For the river of vivification proceeds as far as to the centre; as the Chaldæan oracles also assert, when speaking about the middle of the five centres, which from on high passes entirely to the opposite part, through the centre of the earth. For they say: "And another fifth middle fiery centre, where a life-bearing fire descends as far as to the material rivers." Hence Plato beginning from those things in which animation ends, recurs to the whole vivification, and prior to this surveys the exempt power of the soul. We must not therefore place the ruling part of the soul in the centre; for this is exempt from the universe; but a certain power of it which guards the whole order of the world. For nothing else in the universe has so much the power of entirely subverting the whole of things, as the centre and the power of the centre, about which the universe with measured motion harmoniously revolves. Hence it appears to me that Plato divinely says that the demiurgus placed *soul* and not *the soul* in the middle of the universe. For these differ from each other, because the latter establishes the whole soul in the centre, but the former a certain power of it, and a different power in different parts.

The philosopher himself however, shortly after, when speaking of the animation itself of the world says, "But the soul being extended from the middle to the very extremities of the universe, and investing it externally in a circle, gave rise to the divine commencement of an unceasing and wise life through the whole of time." For the words "to be every way extended from the middle," have the same meaning as "to be extended from the middle to the very extremities of the universe." But in the latter, the soul herself illuminates from herself the centre of the universe and the whole sphere of it by her powers; while in the former, the demiurgus is the cause of the animation, himself introducing the soul into the universe as into her proper place of abode. For the same thing is effected by both, but demiurgically indeed and intellectually by the cause, and self-motively by soul. Now however, the philosopher delivers the bond which proceeds from fabrication alone. For we particularly refer wholes and such things as are good to a divine cause; but we consider partial natures, and such things as are not good, to be unworthy of divine fabrication; and we suspend them from other proximate causes, though these also, as it is frequently said, subsist from divinity. Since therefore both a divine and a partial soul have communication with bodies, the former indeed subsisting according to boniform will, and not departing from intelligible progressions is deific; but the latter which takes place through a defluxion of the wings of the soul, or through audacity, or flight, is atheistical, though the former is complicated with the self-motive energy, and the latter with providential care. But in the one a subsistence according to deity is apparent through the presence of divinity; and in the other, a subsistence from soul, through the representation of aberration.

CHAPTER L

In the next place Timæus, or rather Plato adds, "And causing circle to revolve in a circle, he established heaven (*i.e.* the world) one, only, solitary nature;" on which Proclus observes as follows: The philosopher Porphyry well interprets the meaning of circle revolving in a circle. For it is possible, says he, for that which is not a circle to be moved in a circle, as a stone when whirled round; and also for a circle to be moved not in a circle, as a wheel when rolled along. But it is the peculiarity of the world, that being circular it is moved in a circle, through harmoniously revolving about the centre. In a still greater degree however, the divine Iamblichus well interprets the meaning of these words. For he says that the circle is twofold, the one being psychical, but the other corporeal, and that the latter is moved in the former. For this is conformable to what has been before said, and accords with what is afterwards asserted. For Plato himself shortly after moves the corporeal nature according to the psychical circle, and renders the twofold circulations analogous to the periods in the soul.

Moreover, to comprehend the whole blessedness of the world in three appellations, it most appropriate to that which subsists according to a triple cause, *viz.* the final, the paradigmatic, and the demiurgic. For of the appellations themselves, the first of them, *viz. one*, is assumed from the final cause; for *The One* is the same with *The Good*. But the second, *viz. only*, is assumed from the paradigmatic cause. For the *only* begotten and *onlyness* (μονωσις) were, prior to the universe, in all-perfect animal. And the third, *viz.* the *solitary*, is assumed from the demiurgic cause. For the ability of using itself, and through itself governing the world, proceeds from the demiurgic goodness. The world therefore is *one*, so far as it is united, and is converted to *The One*. But it is *only*, so far as it participates of the intelligible, and comprehends all things in itself. And it is *solitary*, so far as it is similar to its father, and is able to save itself. From the three however, it appears that it is a God. For *The One*, the *perfect*, and the *self-sufficient*, are the elements of deity. Hence, the world receiving these, is also itself a God; being *one* indeed, according to hyparxis; but *alone*, according to a perfection which derives its completion from all sensible natures; and *solitary*, through being sufficient to itself. For those that lead a solitary life, being converted to themselves, have the hopes of salvation in themselves. And that this is the meaning of the term *solitary*, will be evident from the following words of Plato: "Able through virtue to converse with itself, indigent of nothing external, and sufficiently known and friendly to itself." For in these words, he clearly manifests what the solitariness in which he ascribes to the world, and that he denominates that being solitary, who looks to himself, to that with which he is furnished, and to his own proper measure. For those that live in solitary places, are the saviours of themselves, so far as respects human causes. The universe therefore is likewise after this manner solitary, as being sufficient to itself, and preserving itself, not through a diminution, but from an exuberance of power; for self-sufficiency is here indicated; and as he says, through virtue. For he alone among partial animals [such as we are] who possesses virtue is able to associate with, and love himself with a parental affection. But the vicious man looking to his inward baseness, is indignant with himself and with his own essence, is astonished with externals, and pursues an association with others, in consequence of his inability to behold himself. On the contrary, the worthy man perceiving himself beautiful rejoices and is delighted, and producing in himself beautiful conceptions, gladly embraces an association with himself. For we are naturally domesticated to the beautiful, but hastily withdraw ourselves from deformity. Hence, if the world possesses virtue adapted to itself, in its intellectual and psychical essence, and in the perfection of its animal nature, looking to itself, it loves itself, and is present with, and sufficient to itself.

It is proper therefore to assert these things to those who place intelligibles external to intellect. For how can that which tends to other things, and as being deficient is indigent of externals, be blessed? Hence, if the world is through virtue converted to itself, must not intellect do this in a much greater degree? Intellect therefore intellectually perceives itself. And this is among the number of things immediately known. This also deserves to be remarked, that Plato when he gives animation to the world, directly imparts virtue to it. For the participation of soul is immediately accompanied with the fullness of virtue, in the being which subsists according to nature; since the one cause of the virtues, is also co-arranged with the fountain of souls, and the progression of this fountain is conjoined with the progression of soul. For with respect to virtue, one indeed is unical, primary and all-perfect; but another subsists in the ruling supermundane Gods; another in the liberated Gods; and another is mundane, through which the whole world possesses undefiled intelligence, an undeviating life, an energy converted to itself, and a purity unmingled with the animals which it contains. From this virtue therefore, the world becomes known and friendly to itself. For knowledge precedes familiarity.

Since the universe also is intellectual, an animal, and a God, so far indeed, as it is intellectual, it becomes known to itself; but so far as it is a God, it is friendly to itself. For union is more perfect than knowledge. If therefore, the universe is known to itself, it is intellectual; for that which is primarily known to itself is intellect. And if it is friendly to itself, it is united. But that which is united is deified; for *The One* which is an intellect is a God. Again therefore, you have virtue, a knowledge of, and a friendship with itself, in the world; the first of these proceeding into it from soul; the second from intellect; and the third from deity. Hence Plato very properly adds, that on account of these things, the world was generated by the demiurgus a blessed God; for the presence of soul, the participation of intellect, and the reception of union, render the universe a God. And the blessed God which he now mentions is the God "who at a certain time would exist," animated, endued with intellect, and united. Union however is present with it according to the bond of analogy; but much more from the one soul and the one intellect which it participates. For through these, greater bonds, and a more excellent union proceeded into the universe. And still beyond these unions, divine friendship, and the supply of good, contain and connect the whole world. For the bond which proceeds from intellect and soul is strong, as Orpheus also says; but the union of the golden chain [*i.e.* of the deific series] is still greater, and is the cause of greater good to all things.

Moreover, felicity must likewise be assumed in a way adapted to the universe. For since it is suspended from the paternal intellect and the whole fabrication of things, and since it lives conformably to these causes, it is consequently happy ($ευδαιμων$)† from them. For the demiurgus also is denominated a dæmon by Plato in the *Politicus*, and a great dæmon by Orpheus when he says,

> One the great dæmon and the lord of all.‡

He therefore who lives according to the will of the father, and preserves the intellectual nature which was imparted to him from thence immutable is happy, and blessed. The first, and the all-perfect form of felicity likewise, is that of the world. The second is that of the mundane Gods, whom Plato in the *Phædrus* calls happy Gods, following the mighty Jupiter. The third is that of the genera superior to us [*viz.* the felicity of angels, dæmons, and heroes]. For there is one virtue of angels, another of dæmons, and another of the heroic genera: and the form of felicity is triple being different according to each genus. The fourth form of felicity is that which subsists in the undefiled souls, who make blameless descents [into the realms of generation,] and exert an inflexible and untamed life. The fifth is that of partial souls [such as ours]; and this is multiform. For the soul which is an attendant on the moon, is not similarly happy with the soul that is suspended from the solar order; but as the form of life is different, so likewise perfection is defined by different measures. And the last form of felicity is that which is seen in irrational animals. For every thing which obtains a perfection adapted to it according to nature, is happy. For through its proper perfection, it is conjoined to its proper dæmon, and partakes of his providential care. The forms of felicity therefore, being so many, the first and highest must be placed in the world, and which also is now

---

† *i.e.* Having a good dæmon.

‡ Instead of $εις δαιμων εγενετο μεγας αρχος απο παντων$, it is requisite to read $εις δαιμων γενετο μεγας αρχος απαντων$.

mentioned by Plato. We must not however wonder that he immediately calls the world a God, from its participation of soul. For every thing is deified through that which is proximately prior to it; the corporeal world indeed through soul; but soul through intellect, as the Athenian guest also says; and intellect through *The One*. Hence, intellect is divine, but not a God. *The One* however is no longer a God through any thing else, but is primarily a God; just as intellect is primarily gnostic, as soul is primarily self-motive, and as body is primarily in place.

CHAPTER LI

In the last place, I shall present the reader with what Plato says in the *Timæus* about the name of the world, and add to it the elucidations of Proclus; for thus every thing pertaining to the mundane Gods, and their great recipient the universe will have been amply, and I trust satisfactorily discussed. Plato therefore says on this subject: "We shall denominate the universe, *heaven*, or *the world*, or any other appellation in which it may especially rejoice." These names, says Proclus, were attended with much ambiguity with the ancients. For some alone called the sublunary region κοσμος *kosmos, the world*, and the region above it ουρανος *ouranos, heaven*; but others called *heaven* a part of *the world*. And some indeed, considered the moon as the boundary of *heaven*; but others denominated the summits of generation *heaven*. Thus Homer,

> Extended heaven in ether and the clouds
> Fell to the lot of Jove.

Hence Plato very properly prior to the whole theory speaks definitively concerning these names, denominating the universe *heaven* and *the world*. And he calls it *heaven* indeed, as perceiving the things above, contemplating the intelligible, and participating an intellectual essence; but *the world*, as always being filled and adorned by true beings. He likewise denominates it *heaven* as being converted to the principles of its existence; but *the world* as proceeding from them. For it was generated by true beings, and is converted to them. As however, of statues which are established by the telestic (or mystic) art, some things are apparent[†] in them, but others are inwardly concealed, which are symbolical[‡] of

---

[†] For αφανη here, it is necessary to read εμφανη.

[‡] For συμβολικης των θεων παρουσιας, it is requisite to read συμβολικα της των, κ.λ.

the presence of the Gods, and are known to the mystic framers of them alone; after the same manner the universe being the statue of the intelligible world, and perfected by the father, has some things apparent which are indications of its divinity, but others unapparent, which are the marks, seals, or impressions of the participation of true being,[†] which it received from the father who gave it perfection; in order that through these it may be eternally rooted in real essence. The appellations also *heaven* and *the world* are names significant of the apparent powers in the universe; the latter indeed, so far as they proceed from the intelligible, but the former, as far as they are converted to it.

It is necessary however, to know that the divine name of the abiding power of the universe, and which is a symbol of the demiurgic seal, according to which also it subsists in unproceeding union with real being, is ineffable, and not vocal, and is known to the Gods themselves. For there are appropriate names in every order of things; divine indeed, in the Gods; but dianoetic in the subjects of the discursive power of reason; and doxastic in the objects of opinion. And this also Plato asserts in the *Cratylus*, assenting to Homer who places one kind of names of the same things in the Gods, and another kind in the opinions of men, as

> Gods call it Xanthus, but Scamander men.

And

> Chalcis its name with those of heavenly birth,
> But call'd Cymindis by the sons of earth.

And in a similar manner in many other names. For as the knowledge of the Gods is of one kind, but that of partial souls of another, so names in the former are different from those in the latter. Divine names however, unfold the whole essence of the things named; but those of men only effect this partially. Plato therefore knowing that this pre-existed in the world, omits to mention what the divine and ineffable name of it is which is different from the apparent, and with great caution speaks of it as a symbol of the divine impression which the world contains. For the words, "or by any other appellation in which it may especially rejoice," are a latent hymn of the mundane name so far as it is allotted an unspeakable and divine essence, in order that it may be co-ordinate to that which is signified by him. Hence also, divine mundane names are delivered by theurgists; some being called by them

---

[†] After του οντως here, it is requisite to supply οντος.

ineffable, but others effable; and some of them being the names of the unapparent powers in the world, but others, of the visible elements from which it derives its completion. Plato therefore, here delivers both the apparent and the unapparent name of the world, the former indeed, dyadically, but the latter monadically; for the words, "or by any other," are significant of oneness. And *the ineffable name* indeed of the universe, is indicative of its abiding in its father; the name *world*, of its progression; and *heaven*, of its regression. But through the three, you have the final cause, on account of which it is full of good, abiding indeed ineffably, but proceeding perfectly, and returning to *The Good*, as to the pre-existing object of desire.

Additional Notes

1. *Being likewise a partaker of the dialectic of Plato.* (See page 54.) The dialectic of Plato is very different from the dialectic which is conversant with opinion, and is accurately investigated in the *Topics* of Aristotle. For the business of this first of sciences, is to employ definitions, divisions, analyzations, and demonstrations, as primary sciences in the investigation of causes; imitating the progression of beings from the first principle of things, and their continual conversion to it, as the ultimate object of desire. "But there are three energies," says Proclus (in MS. Comment. in Parmenid. lib. i), "of this most scientific method, the first of which is adapted to youth, and is useful for the purpose of rousing their intellect, which is, as it were, in a dormant state. For it is a true exercise of the soul in the speculation of things, leading forth through opposite positions the essential impression of ideas which it contains, and considering not only the divine path, as it were, which conducts to truth, but exploring whether the deviations from it contain any thing worthy of belief; and lastly, stimulating the all-various conceptions of the soul. But the second energy takes place when intellect rests from its former investigations, as becoming most familiar with the speculation of beings, and beholds truth itself firmly established on a pure and holy foundation. And this energy, according to Socrates, by a progression through ideas, evolves the whole of an intelligible nature, till it arrives at that which is first; and this by analysing, defining, demonstrating and dividing, proceeding upwards and downwards, till, having entirely investigated the nature of intelligibles, it raises itself to a nature superior to beings. But the soul being perfectly established in this nature, as in her paternal port, no longer tends to a more excellent object of desire, as she has now arrived at the end of her search. And you may say that what is delivered in the *Phædrus* and *Sophista* is the employment of this energy, giving a twofold division to some, and a fourfold to other operations of the dialectic art. Hence it is assigned to such as philosophise purely, and no longer require preparatory exercise, but nourish the intellect of their soul in pure intellection. But the third energy purifies from twofold ignorance, when its reasons are employed upon men full of opinion; and this is spoken of in the *Sophista*." So that the dialectic energy is triple, either subsisting through opposite arguments, or alone unfolding truth, or alone confuting falsehood. See admirable specimens of this master science in the notes to my Plato, Vol 3 [TTS vol. XI].

2. *And thus much concerning divine names.* (See page 125.) In addition to what is here said, Proclus admirably remarks on this subject as follows, in his MS. Scholia on the *Cratylus* of Plato.

Since, however, the present discourse is about divine names, it is necessary to speak a little concerning them. And in the first place, let us speak concerning the names which are occultly established in the Gods themselves; since some of the ancients said that these originated from the more excellent genera,[†] but that the Gods are established beyond a signification of this kind; but others admitted that names are in the Gods themselves, and in those Gods that are allotted the highest order.

The Gods, therefore, possess an hyparxis uniform and ineffable, a power generative of wholes, and an intellect perfect and full of conceptions; and they give subsistence to all things according to this triad. Hence it is necessary that the participations of those divinities who are of a more elevated order, and who are arranged nearer to *The Good*, should proceed triadically through all things to which they give subsistence. It is also necessary that among these, those participations should be more ineffable, which are defined according to the *hyparxes* of the first Gods; but that those should be more apparent, and more divided, which are illuminated according to the *intellect* of exempt causes; and that those participations which are between these, should be such as are the effluxions of *prolific powers*. For the fathers of wholes giving subsistence to all things, have disseminated in all things vestiges, and impressions of their own triadic hypostasis; since nature also inserts in bodies an exciting principle ($\epsilon\nu\alpha\nu\sigma\mu\alpha$) derived from her proper idiom through which she moves bodies, and governs them as by a rudder. And the demiurgus has established in the universe an image of his own monadic transcendency, through which he governs the world, holding a rudder, as Plato says, like a pilot. It is proper to think therefore, that these rudders and this helm of the universe, in which the demiurgus being seated orderly disposes the world, are nothing else than a symbol of the whole fabrication of things, to us indeed difficult of comprehension, but to the Gods themselves known and manifest. And why is it requisite to speak concerning these things, since of the ineffable cause of all, who is beyond intelligibles, there is an impression in every being, and even as far as to the last of things, through which all things are suspended from him, some more remotely, and others more near, according to the clearness and obscurity of the impression which they contain. This it is which moves all things to the desire of good, and imparts to beings this inextinguishable love. And this impression is indeed unknown: for it pervades as far as to things which are incapable of knowledge. It is also more excellent than life; for it is present with things inanimate: and has not an intellectual power; since it lies in things destitute of intellectual energy. As nature therefore, the demiurgic monad, and the father himself who is exempt from all things, have disseminated

---

[†] *viz.* angels, dæmons and heroes.

in things posterior, impressions of their respective peculiarities, and through these convert all things to themselves, in like manner all the Gods impart to their progeny, symbols of their cause, and through these establish all things in themselves. The impressions, therefore, of the hyparxis of the higher order of Gods, which are disseminated in secondary natures are ineffable and unknown, and their efficacious and motive energy surpasses all intelligence. And of this kind are the characters of light, through which the Gods unfold themselves to their progeny; these characters subsist unically in the Gods themselves, but shining forth to the view in the genera more excellent than man, and presenting themselves to us divisibly, and accompanied with form. Hence the Gods[†] exhort "To understand the fore-running form of light." For subsisting on high without form, it becomes invested with form through its progression; and there being established occultly and uniformly, it becomes apparent to us through motion, from the Gods themselves; possessing indeed an efficacious energy, through a divine cause, but becoming figured, through the essence by which it is received.

Again, the impressions which are illuminated from powers, are in a certain respect media between things ineffable and effable, and pervade through all the middle genera. For it is not possible for the primary gifts of the Gods to arrive to us, without the more excellent genera (*i.e.* angels, dæmons and heroes) previously participating the illuminations which thence proceed. But these illuminations subsisting appropriately in each of their participants, and co-ordinately in all things, unfold the powers that give them subsistence. Of this kind are the symbols of the Gods, which are indeed uniform in the more elevated orders, but multiform in those that are subordinate; and which the theurgic art imitating exhibits through inarticulate evocations ($\alpha\delta\iota\alpha\rho\theta\rho\omega\tau\omega\nu$ $\epsilon\kappa\phi\omega\nu\eta\sigma\epsilon\omega\nu$).

The impressions which rank as the third in order, which pervade from intellectual essences to all peculiarities, and proceed as far as to us, are divine names, through which the Gods are invoked, and by which they are celebrated, being unfolded into light by the Gods themselves, and reverting to them, and producing to human knowledge as much of the Gods as is apparent. For through these we are able to signify something to each other, and to converse with ourselves about the Gods. Different nations however, participate differently of these, as for instance the Egyptians according to their native tongue, receiving names of this kind from the Gods; but the Chaldeans and Indians in a different manner, according to their proper tongue; and in a similar manner the Greeks according to their dialect. Though a certain divinity therefore may be called by the Greeks Briareus, but differently by the Chaldeans, we must nevertheless admit that each of these names is the progeny of the Gods, and that it signifies the same essence. But if some names are more and other less efficacious, it is not wonderful; since of things which are known

---

[†] Proclus here alludes to one of the Chaldean Oracles. [See TTS vol. VII, page 45.]

to us, such as are dæmoniacal and angelic are more efficacious; and in short of things denominated the names of such as are nearer are more perfect than the names of those that are more remote.

Not every genus of the Gods however, can be denominated. For Parmenides evinces that the God who is beyond all things is ineffable. "For," says he, "he can neither be denominated, nor spoken of." And of the intelligible Gods the first genera, which are conjoined with *The One Itself*, and are called occult, have much of the unknown and ineffable. For that which is perfectly apparent and effable, cannot be conjoined with the perfectly ineffable, but it is requisite that the progression of intelligibles, should be terminated in this order; in which there is the first effable,[†] and that which is called by proper names. For the first forms are there, and the intellectual nature of intelligibles there shines forth to the view. But all natures prior to this being silent and occult, are only known by intelligence.[‡] Hence the whole of the telestic art energizing theurgically ascends as far as to this order. Orpheus also says, that this is first called by a name by the other Gods; for the light proceeding from it is known to and denominated by the intellectual orders. But he thus spake,

μητιν σπερμα φεροντα θεων, κλυτον οντε φανητα,
πρωτογονον μακαρες καλεον κατα μακρον Ολημπον.

i.e. "Metis bearing the seed of the Gods, whom the Gods about lofty Olympus call the illustrious Phanes Protogonus." In the Gods however nomination is united with intellectual conception, and both are present with them through the participation of the light which the mighty Phanes emits to all things. But in our soul these two are divided from each other; and intellectual conception is one thing, and name another: and the one has the order of an image, but the other of a paradigm. In the middle genera there is indeed a separation, but there is also a union of the intellective and onomastic energy. The transportive name (διαπορθμιον ονομα) of *Iynxes*[§] (ιγγυων) which is said to sustain all the fountains, appears to me to signify a thing of this kind. Such also is the appellation *teletarchic* (το τελεταρχικον) which some one of the Gods[*] says, "leaps into the worlds, through the rapid reproof of the father." ιοσμοις ενθρωσκειν κραιπνην δια πατρος ενιπην. For all these things are occultly with

---

[†] The first effable subsists in the God Phanes, or the extremity of the intelligible order.

[‡] See this explained in the notes on my translation of the *Parmenides* of Plato.

[§] The *Iynx, Synoches, and Telearches* of the Chaldeans, compose that divine order, which is called by Proclus *intelligible and at the same time intellectual*, and is unfolded by him in the fourth book.

[*] This is one of the Chaldean oracles. [See TTS vol. VII]

the Gods, but are unfolded according to second and third progressions, and to men that are allied to the Gods.

There is therefore a certain abiding name in the Gods, through which the subordinate invoke the superior, as Orpheus says of Phanes, or through which the superior denominate the subordinate, as Jupiter in Plato gives names to the unapparent periods of souls.[†] For fathers define the energies of their offspring, and the offspring know their producing causes through the intellectual impressions which they bear. Such then are the first names which are unfolded from the Gods and which through the middle genera end in the rational essence.

There are however other names of a second and third rank; and these are such as partial souls have produced, at one time energizing enthusiastically about the Gods, and at another time energizing according to science; either conjoining their own intelligence with divine light, and thence deriving perfection; or committing the fabrication of names to the rational power. For thus artists, such as geometricians, physicians and rhetoricians give names to the things the peculiarities of which they understand. Thus too poets inspired by Phœbus (των ποιητων οι φοιβοληπτοι) ascribe many names to the Gods, and to human names give a division opposite to these; receiving the former from enthusiastic energy and the latter from science and opinion; concerning which Socrates now says Homer indicates, referring some names to the Gods and others to men.

3. *So that language when conversant with that which is ineffable, being subverted about itself, has no cessation and opposes itself.* (See page 166.) Damascius likewise, in a wonderfully sublime manner speaks of the immense principle of the universe, conformably to what is now said by Proclus, in his excellent MS. treatise περι αρχων, or *Concerning Principles*; and the following is an epitome of what he says on this subject.

"Our soul prophesies that the principle which is beyond all things that can in any respect be conceived, is unco-ordinated with all things. Neither therefore, must it be called principle, nor cause, nor that which is first, nor prior to all things, nor beyond all things. By no means therefore, must we celebrate it as all things, nor in short, is it to be celebrated, nor called into memory. For whatever we conceive or consider, is either something belonging to all things, or is all things, though analyzing we should ascend to that which is most simple, and which is the most comprehensive of all things, being as it were, the ultimate circumference, not of beings, but of non-beings. For of beings, that which has an united subsistence, and is perfectly without separation, is the extremity, since every being is mingled from elements which are either bound and infinity, or the progeny of these. But *The One* is simply

---

[†] See the *Timæus*.

the last boundary of *the many*. For we cannot conceive any thing more simple than that which is perfectly *one*; which if we denominate the principle and cause, the first, and the most simple, these and all other things are there only according to *The One*. But we not being able to contract our conceptions into profound union, are divided about it, and predicate of *The One* the distributed multitude which is ourselves; unless we despise these appellations also, because *the many* cannot be adapted to *The One*. Hence it can neither be known nor named; for, if it could, it would in this respect be many. Or, these things also will be contained in it, according to *The One*. For the nature of *The One* is all-receptive, or rather all-producing, and there is not any thing whatever which *The One* is not. Hence all things are as it were evolved from it. It is therefore, properly cause, and the first, the end and the last, the defensive enclosure of all things, and the one nature of all things; not that nature which is in things, and which proceeds from *The One*, but that which is prior to them, which is the most impartible summit of all things whatever, and the greatest comprehension of all things which in any respect are said to have a being.

"But if *The One* is the cause of all things, and is comprehensive of all things, what ascent will there be for us beyond this also? For we do not strive in vain, extending ourselves to that which is nothing. For that which is not even *one*, *is* not according to the most just mode of speaking. Whence then do we conceive that there is something beyond *The One*? For *the many* require nothing else than *The One*. And hence *The One* alone is the cause of *the many*. Hence also *The One* is entirely cause, because it is necessary that the cause of *the many* should alone be *The One*. For it cannot be nothing; since nothing is the cause of nothing. Nor can it be *the many*: for so far as many they are unco-ordinated; and *the many* will not be one cause. But if there are many causes, they will not be causes of each other, through being unco-ordinated, and through a progression in a circle, the same things being causes and the things caused. Each therefore, will be the cause of itself, and thus there will be no cause of the many. Hence it is necessary that *The One* should be the cause of *the many*, and which is also the cause of their co-ordination: for there is a certain conspiring co-ordination, and a union with each other.

"If, therefore, some one thus doubting should say that *The One* is a sufficient principle, and should add as the summit that we have not any conception or suspicion more simple than that of *The One*, and should therefore ask how we can suspect any thing beyond the last suspicion and conception we are able to frame; - if some one should thus speak, we must pardon the doubt. For a speculation of this kind is it seems inaccessible and immense: at the same time however, from things more known to us we must extend the ineffable parturitions of our soul, to the ineffable co-sensation of this sublime truth. For as that which subsists without is in every respect more honourable than that which subsists with habitude, and the unco-ordinated than the co-ordinated, as the theoretic than the political life, and Saturn for instance than Jupiter, being than forms, and *The One* than *the many* of which *The One* is the principle; so in short, that which transcends every thing of this kind is more honourable than all causes and principles, and is not to be considered as subsisting in any co-arrangement and habitude; since *The One* is naturally prior to *the many*, that which is most simple to things composite, and that which is most comprehensive to the things which it comprehends. So that if you are willing thus to speak, *the first* is beyond all such opposition, not only that which is in things co-ordinate, but even that which takes place from its subsistence as the first. *The One* therefore, and the united are posterior to the first: for these causally contain multitude as numerous[†] as that which is unfolded from them. *The One* however, is no less one, if indeed it is not more so, because separate multitude is posterior to and not in it; and the united is no less united because it contracted in one things separated prior to separation. Each of these therefore, is all things, whether according to co-ordination, or according to its own nature. But all things cannot be things first, nor the principle. Nor yet one of them alone, because this one will be at the same time all things, according to *The One*: but we shall not yet have discovered that which is beyond all things. To which we may also add, *The One* is the summit of *the many*, as the cause of the things proceeding from it. We may likewise say that we form a conception of *The One* according to a purified suspicion extended to that which is most simple and most comprehensive. But that which is most venerable, must necessarily be incomprehensible by all conceptions and suspicions; since also in other things, that which always soars beyond our conceptions is more honourable than that which is more obvious: so that what flies from all our suspicions will be most honourable. But if this be the case it is *nothing*. Let however nothing be twofold, one better than *The One*, the other posterior to sensibles. If also, we strive in vain in asserting these things, striving in vain is likewise twofold; the one falling into the ineffable, the other into that which is in no respect whatever has any subsistence. For *this* also is ineffable, as Plato says, but according to the worse, but *that* according to the better. If too, we search for a certain advantage arising from it, this is the most necessary advantage of all others, that all things thence proceed as from an adytum, from the ineffable, and in an ineffable manner. For neither do they proceed as *The One* produces *the many*, nor as *the united* things *separated*, but as the ineffable similarly produces all things, ineffably. But if in asserting these things concerning it, that it is no one of all things, that it is incomprehensible, we subvert what we say, it is proper to know that these are the names and words of our parturitions, daring anxiously to explore it, and which standing in the vestibules of the adytum, announce indeed nothing pertaining to the ineffable, but signify the manner in which we are affected about it, our doubts and disappointment; nor yet this clearly, but through indications to such as are

---

[†] It must however be carefully observed that multitude when it subsists causally, subsists without that distinction and separation which it possesses when unfolded; and that in *The One* it has no distinction whatever. For *The One* is all things prior to the all.

able to understand these investigations. We also see that our parturitions suffer these things about *The One*, and that in a similar manner they are solicitous and subverted. For, *The One* says Plato, if it *is*, is not *The One*. But if it is not, no assertion can be adapted to it; so that neither can there be a negation of it, nor can any name be given to it; for neither is a name simple. Nor is there any opinion nor science of it; for neither are these simple. So that *The One* is in every respect unknown and ineffable.

"What then? Shall we investigate something else beyond the ineffable? Or, perhaps indeed, Plato leads us ineffably through *The One* as a medium, to the ineffable beyond *The One*, which is now the subject of discussion; and this by an ablation of *The One*, in the same manner as he leads us to *The One* by an ablation of other things. For, that he gives to *The One* a certain position is evident from his *Sophista*, where he demonstrates that it subsists prior to being, itself by itself. But if, having ascended as far as to *The One*, he is silent, this also is becoming in Plato to be perfectly silent, after the manner of the ancients concerning things in every respect unspeakable; for the discourse was indeed most dangerous, in consequence of falling on idiotical ears. Indeed, when discoursing concerning that which in no respect has any subsistence, he subverts his assertions, and is fearful of falling into the sea of dissimilitude, or, rather of unsubsisting void. But if demonstrations do not accord with *The One*, it is by no means wonderful; for they are human and divisible, and more composite than is fit. Indeed, they are not even adapted to being, since they are formal, or rather, they are neither adapted to forms nor essences. Or, is it not Plato himself, who in his epistles[†] evinces that we have nothing which is significant of form, no type nor name, nor discourse, nor opinion, nor science? For it is intellect alone which can apprehend ideas by its projecting energies, which we cannot possess while busily engaged in discourse. If therefore we even energize intellectually, since in this case our intellection is characterized by form, we shall not accord with *the united* and with being. And if at any time we are able to project a contracted intelligence, even this is unadapted and discordant with *The One*. If, also, we energize according to the most profoundly united intelligence, and through this occultly perceive *The One Itself*, yet even this is expanded only as far as to *The One*, if there is a knowledge of *The One*; for this we have not yet determined. At the same time however, let us now apply ourselves to the discussion of things of such great importance, through indications and suspicions, being purified with respect to unusual conceptions, and led through analogies and negations, despising what we possess with respect to these, and advancing from things more ignoble with us to things more honourable.

"Shall we therefore say, that the nature which we now investigate as the first, is so perfectly ineffable, that it must not even be admitted concerning it that it is thus ineffable; but that *The One* is ineffable, as flying from all composition

---

[†] See the 7th *Epistle* of Plato.

of words and names, and all distinction of that which is known from that which knows, and is to be apprehended in a manner the most simple and comprehensive, and that it is not one alone as the characteristic of one, but as *one all things,* and *one prior to all things,* and not one which is something belonging to all things? These indeed, are the parturitions of the soul, and are thus purified with respect to *the simply one,* and that which is truly the one cause of all things. But, in short, we thus form a conception of *The One* which we contain as the summit or flower of our essence, as being more proximate and allied to us, and more prompt to such a suspicion of that which nearly leaves all things behind it. But from some particular thing which is made the subject of hypothesis, the transition is easy to that which is simply supposed, though we should in no respect accede to it, but being carried in that which is most simple in us, should form a suspicion concerning that which is prior to all things. *The One* therefore, is thus effable, and thus ineffable, but that which is beyond it is to be honoured in the most perfect silence, and prior to this, by the most perfect ignorance† which despises all knowledge.

"Let us therefore, now consider, in the second place, how it is said to be perfectly unknown. For if this be true, how do we assert all these things concerning it? For we do not elucidate by much discussion about things of which we are ignorant. But if it is in reality unco-ordinated with all things, and without habitude to all things, and is nothing of all things, nor even *The One Itself,* these very things are the natures of it. Besides, with respect to its being unknown, we either know that it is unknown, or we are ignorant of this. But if the latter, how do we say that it is perfectly unknown? And if we know this, in this respect therefore, it is known. Or shall we say that it is known, that the unknown is unknown? We cannot therefore deny one thing of another, not knowing that which is the subject of the negation; nor can we say that it is not this or that, when we can in no respect reach it. How therefore can we deny of that of which we are perfectly ignorant the things which we know? For this is just as if some one who was blind from his birth should assert that heat is not in colour. Or perhaps indeed, he also will justly say, that colour is not hot. For he knows this by the touch; but he knows nothing of colour, except that it is not tangible; for he knows that he does not know it. Such a knowledge indeed, is not a knowledge of colour, but of his own ignorance. And we also when we say that the first is unknown, do not announce any thing of it, but we confess the manner in which we are affected about it. For the non-perception of the blind man is not in the colour, nor yet his blindness, but in him. The ignorance therefore of that of which we are ignorant is in us. For the knowledge of that which is known, is in him that

---

† As that which is below all knowledge is an ignorance worse than knowledge, so the silence in which our ascent to the ineffable terminates is preceded by an ignorance superior to all knowledge. Let it however, be carefully remembered, that such an ignorance is only to be obtained after the most scientific and intellectual energies.

knows, and not in the thing known. But if knowledge is in that which is known being as it were the splendour of it, so some one should say ignorance is in that which is unknown, being as it were the darkness of it, or obscurity, according to which it is unknown by, and is unapparent to all things, - he who says this is ignorant, that as blindness is a privation, so likewise all ignorance, and that as is the invisible, so that of which we are ignorant, and which is unknown. In other things therefore, the privation of this or that leaves something else. For that which is incorporeal, though invisible, yet is intelligible; and that which is not intelligible by a certain intelligence, leaves at the same time something else. But if we take away every conception and suspicion, this also we must say is perfectly unknown by us, about which we close every eye. Nor must we assert any thing of it, as we do of the intelligible, that it is not adapted to be seen by the eyes, or as we do of *The One*, that it is not naturally adapted to be understood by an essential and abundant intellect: for it imparts nothing by which it can be apprehended, nothing which can lead to a suspicion of its nature. For neither do we only say that it is unknown, that being something else it may naturally possess the unknown, but we do not think fit to predicate of it either *being*, or *The One*, or *all things*, or *the principle of all things*, or in short, *any thing*. Neither therefore, are these things the nature of it, *viz. the nothing, the being beyond all things, supercausal subsistence, and the unco-ordinated with all things;* but these are only ablations of things posterior to it. How, therefore, do we speak concerning it? Shall we say, that knowing these posterior things, we despise them with respect to the position, if I may so speak, of that which is in every respect ineffable? For as that which is beyond some particular knowledge is better than that which is apprehended by such knowledge, so that which is beyond all suspicion must necessarily be most venerable; not that it is known to be so, but possessing the most venerable as in us, and as the consequence of the manner in which we are affected about it. We also call this a prodigy, from its being entirely incomprehensible by our conceptions: for it is through analogy, if that which in a certain respect is unknown, according to a more excellent subsistence, is superior to that which is in every respect known. Hence that which is in every respect unknown according to a more excellent subsistence, must necessarily be acknowledged to be supreme, though it indeed has neither the supreme, nor the most excellent, nor the most venerable; for these things are our confessions about that, which entirely flies from all our conceptions and suspicions. For by this very assertion, that we can form no suspicion of it, we acknowledge that it is most wonderful; since if we should suspect any thing concerning it, we must also investigate something else prior to this suspicion, and either proceed to infinity in our search, or stop at that which is perfectly ineffable. Can we therefore, demonstrate any thing concerning it? And is that demonstrable which we do not think fit to consider as a thing whose subsistence we can even suspect? Or, when we assert these things, do we not indeed demonstrate *concerning* it, but not *it*? For neither does it contain the demonstrable, nor any thing else. What then? Do we not opine concerning it these things which we now assert? But if there is an opinion of it, it is also the object of opinion. Or shall we say we opine that it is not these things? For Aristotle also says that there is true opinion. If therefore, the opinion is true, the thing likewise is to which opinion being adapted becomes true. For, in consequence of the thing subsisting, the opinion also is true. Though indeed, how will that be true which is perfectly unknown? Or shall we say this is true, that it is not these things, and that it is not known? Is it therefore truly false, that it is these things, and that it is known? Or shall we say that these things are to be referred to privations, and to that which in a certain respect is not, in which there may be a falling from the hypostasis of form? Just as we call the absence of light darkness. For, light not existing, neither is there any darkness. But to that which is never and in no respect being, nothing among beings can, as Plato says, accede. Neither, therefore, is it non-being, nor, in short, privation; and even the expression *never in no respect* (το μηδαμη μηδαμως) is incapable of signifying its nature. For this expression is being, and *signification* is something belonging to beings. Likewise, though we should opine that it is not in any respect, yet at the same time, since it thus becomes the object of opinion, it belongs to beings. Hence, Plato very properly calls that which never and in no respect is, ineffable and incapable of being opined, and this according to the worse than the effable and opinion, in the same manner as we say the supreme is according to that which is better than these. What then, do we not think, and are we not persuaded that the supreme thus subsists? Or, as we have often said, do not these things express the manner in which we are affected about it? But we possess in ourselves this opinion, which is therefore empty, as is the opinion of a vacuum, and the infinite. As therefore, we form a phantastic and fictitious opinion of these though they are not, as if they were, just as we opine the sun to be no larger than a sphere whose diameter is but a foot, though this far from being the case; - so if we opine any thing concerning that which never and in no respect is, or concerning that of which we write these things, the opinion is our own, and the vain attempt is in us, in apprehending which we think that we apprehend the supreme. It is, however, nothing pertaining to us, so much does it transcend our conceptions. How therefore, do we demonstrate that there is such an ignorance in us concerning it? And how do we say that it is unknown? We reply in one word, because we always find that what is above knowledge is more honourable; so that what is above all knowledge, if it were to be found, would be found to be most honourable. But it is sufficient to the demonstration that it cannot be found. We also say that it is above all things; because if it were any thing known, it would rank among all things; and there would be something common to it with all things, *viz.* the being known. But there is one co-ordination of things in which there is something common; so that in consequence of this, it will subsist together with all things. Hence it is necessary that it should be unknown.

"In the third place, the unknown is inherent in beings as well as the known, though they are relatively inherent at the same time. As, therefore, we say that the same thing is relatively large and small, so likewise we say, that a thing is known and unknown with reference to different things. And as the same thing, by participating of the two forms, the great and the small, is at the same time both great and small, so that which at the same time participates of the known and the unknown is both these. Thus, the intelligible is unknown to sense, but is known to intellect. For the more excellent will not be privation, the inferior at the same time being form; since every absence, and a privation of this kind, is either in matter, or in soul; but all things are present in intellect, and still more in a certain respect in the intelligible. Unless indeed, we denominate privation according to a more excellent subsistence, as we say that is not form which is above form; and that is not being which is superessential; and that is nothing which is truly unknown, according to a transcendency which surpasses all things. If, therefore, *The One* is the last known of things which are in any respect whatever known or suspected, that which is beyond *The One* is primarily and perfectly unknown; which also is so unknown, that neither has it an unknown nature, nor can we accede to it as to the unknown, but it is even unknown to us whether it is unknown. For there is an all-perfect ignorance about it, nor can we know it, neither as known nor unknown. Hence, we are on all sides subverted, in consequence of not being able to reach it in any respect, because it is not even one thing, or rather, it is not that which is not even one thing. Hence it is that which in no respect whatever has any subsistence; or it is even beyond this, since this is a negation of being, and that which is not even one thing is a negation of *The One*. But that which is not one thing, or in other words, that which is nothing, is a void, and a falling from all things. We do not however thus conceive concerning the ineffable. Or shall we say that *nothing* is twofold, the one being beyond, and the other below, all things? For *The One* also is twofold, *this* being the extreme, as *The One* of matter, and *that* the first, as that which is more ancient than being. So that with respect to *nothing* also, *this* will be as that which is not even the last one, but *that* as neither being the first one. In this way therefore, that which is unknown and ineffable is twofold, *this*, as not even possessing the last suspicion of subsistence, and *that*, as not even being the first of things. Must we therefore, consider it as that which is unknown to us? Or this indeed is nothing paradoxical: for it will be unknown even to much-honoured intellect, if it be lawful so to speak. For every intellect looks to the intelligible; and the intelligible is either *form* or *being*. But may not divine knowledge know it; and may it not be known to this superessentially? This knowledge, however, applies itself to *The One*, but that which we are now investigating is beyond *The One*. In short, if it also is known, in conjunction with others, it will also be something belonging to all things; for it will be common to it with others to be known, and thus far it will be co-ordinated with others. Further still, if it is known, divine knowledge will comprehend it. It will therefore define it. Every boundary however, ascends ultimately as far as to *The One*; but *that* is beyond *The One*. It is therefore perfectly incomprehensible and invisible, and consequently is not to be apprehended by any kind of knowledge. To which we may add, that knowledge is of things which may be known as beings, or as having a subsistence, or as participating of *The One*. But this is beyond all these. Further still, *The One* also appears to be unknown, if it is necessary that what is known should be one thing, and that which knows another, though both should be in the same thing. So that *the truly one* will not know itself; for it does not possess a certain duplicity. There will not therefore be in it that which knows, and that which is known. Hence, neither will a God, considered according to *The One Itself* alone, and as being conjoined with *The One*, be united with that which is simple, according to duplicity. For how can the double be conjoined with the simple? But if he knows *The One* by *The One*, that which knows, and also that which is known will be *one*, and in each the nature of *The One* will be shown, subsisting alone, and being *one*. So that he will not be conjoined as different with that which is different, or as that which is gnostic with that which is known, since this very thing is one alone; so that neither will he be conjoined according to knowledge. Much more therefore, is that which is not even *The One* unknown. But if *The One* is the last thing known, we know nothing of that which is beyond *The One*; so that the present rhapsody is vain. Or shall we say we know that these things are unworthy to be asserted, if it be lawful so to speak, of the first hypothesis [in the *Parmenides* of Plato,] since, not yet knowing even intelligible forms, we despise the images which subsist in us of their eternal and impartible nature; since these images are partible, and multifariously mutable. Again, being ignorant of the contracted subsistence of intelligible species and genera, but possessing an image of this, which is a contraction of the genera and species in us, we suspect that being itself resembles this contraction, but is at the same time something more excellent; and this must be especially the case with that which has an united subsistence. But now we are ignorant of *The One*, not contracting, but expanding all things to it; and in us simplicity itself consists, with relation to the all which we contain, but is very far from coming into contact with the all-perfect nature of *The One*. For *the one and the simple* in our nature, are in the smallest degree that which they are said to be, except that they are a sign or indication of the nature which is there. Thus also assuming in intellect every thing which can be in any respect known or suspected, we think fit to ascribe it as far as to *The One;* if it be requisite to speak of things unspeakable, and to conceive things which are inconceivable. At the same time also, we think fit to make that the subject of hypothesis, which cannot be compared, and is unco-ordinated with all things, and which is so exempt that neither in reality does it possess the exempt. For that which is exempt is always exempt from something, and is not in every respect exempt, as possessing habitude to that from which it is exempt, and in short, preceding in a certain co-ordination. If, therefore, we intend to make that which is truly exempt the subject of hypothesis, we must not even suppose it to be exempt. For, accurately speaking, its proper name will not be verified when ascribed to *the exempt;* since in this case it would at the same time be co-ordinated; so that it is necessary even to deny this of it.

Likewise, negation is a certain sentence, and that which is denied is a certain thing: but that of which we are now endeavouring to speak is not any thing. Neither therefore, can it be denied, nor spoken of, nor be in any way known: so that neither is it possible to deny the negation; but that which appears to us to be a demonstration of what we say, is a perfect subversion of language and conception. What end therefore, will there be of the discourse, except the most profound silence, and an acknowledgement that we know nothing of that which it is not lawful, since impossible, to lead into knowledge?"

In another part, near the beginning of the same admirable work, he remarks that *The One* in every thing is the more true thing itself. "Thus for instance, *The One* of man [or the summit and flower of his nature,] is the more true man, that of soul is the more true soul, and that of body the more true body. Thus also *The One* of the sun, and *The One* of the moon, are the more true sun and moon." After which he observes as follows: "Neither *The One*, nor *all things* accords with the nature of *The One*. For these are opposed to each other, and distribute our conceptions. For, if we look to the simple and *The One*, we destroy its immensely great perfection; and if we conceive all things subsisting together, we abolish *The One* and *the simple*. But this is because we are divided, and look to divided peculiarities. At the same time however, aspiring after the knowledge of it, we connect all things together, that we may thus be able to apprehend this mighty nature. But fearing the introduction of all multitudes, or contracting the peculiar nature of *The One*, and rejoicing in that which is simple and the first in speaking of the most ancient principle, we thus introduce *The One Itself* as a symbol of simplicity; since we likewise introduce *all things* as a symbol of the comprehension of all things. But that which is above or prior to both we can neither conceive nor denominate. And why is it wonderful that we should suffer these things about it, since the distinct knowledge of it is unical, which we cannot perceive? Other things too of this kind we suffer about *being*. For endeavouring to perceive *being*, we dismiss it, but run round the elements of it, bound and infinity. But if we form a more true conception of it, that it is an united plenitude of all things, in this case the conception of *all things* draws us down to multitude, and the conception of *the united* abolishes that of all things. Neither however is this yet wonderful. For with respect to forms also, when we wish to survey any one of these, we run round the elements of it, and, striving to perceive its unity, we obliterate its elements. At the same time however, every form is one and many; not indeed partly one, and partly many, but the whole of it is through the whole a thing of this kind. Not being able, therefore, to apprehend this collectively, we rejoice in acceding to it with a distribution of our conceptions. But always adhering in our secret, like those who climb clinging with their hands and feet, to things which extend us to a more impartible nature, we obtain in a certain respect a co-sensation in the distribution of that which is uniform. We despise therefore this, with respect to the collected apprehension of it, which we cannot obtain, unless a certain vestige of collected intelligence in our nature is agitated. And this is the light of truth, which is suddenly enkindled, as if from the collision of fire stones. For our greatest conceptions, when exercised with each other, verge to a uniform and simple summit as their end, like the extremities of lines in a circle hastening to the centre. And though even thus they subsist indeed with distribution, yet a certain vestige of the knowledge of form which we contain is pre-excited; just as the equal tendency of all the lines in a circle to terminate in the middle affords a certain obscure representation of the centre. After the same manner also we ascend to being, in the first place, by understanding every form which falls upon us as distributed, not only as impartible, but also as united, and this by confounding, if it be proper so to speak, the multitude in each. In the next place, we must collect every thing separated together, and take away the circumscriptions, just as if making many streams of water to be one collection of water, except that we must not understand that which is united from all things, as one collection of water, but we must conceive that which is prior to all things, as the form of water prior to divided streams of water. Thus therefore, we must expand ourselves to *The One*, first collecting and afterwards dismissing what we have collected, for the super-expanded transcendency of *The One*. Ascending therefore, shall we meet with it as that which is known? Or, wishing to meet with it as such shall we arrive at the unknown? Or may we not say that each of these is true? For we meet with it afar off as that which is known, and when we are united to it from afar, passing beyond that in our nature which is gnostic of *The One*, then are we brought to be one, that is, to be unknown instead of being gnostic. This contact therefore, as of one with one, is above knowledge, but the other is as of that which is gnostic with that which is known. As however, the crooked is known by the straight, so we form a conjecture of the unknown by the known. And this indeed is a mode of knowledge. *The One* therefore, is so far known, that it does not admit of an approximating knowledge, but appears afar off as known, and imparts a gnostic indication of itself. Unlike other things however, the nearer we approach to it, it is not the more, but on the contrary, less known; knowledge being dissolved by *The One* into ignorance, since as we have before observed, where there is knowledge, there also is separation. But separation approaching to *The One* is inclosed in union; so that knowledge also is refunded into ignorance. Thus too, the analogy of Plato requires. For first we endeavour to see the sun, and we do indeed see it afar off; but by how much the nearer we approach to it, by so much the less do we see it; and at length we neither see other things, nor it, the eye becoming spontaneously dazzled by its light. Is therefore *The One* in its proper nature unknown, though there is something else unknown besides *The One?* *The One* indeed wills to be by itself, but with no other; but the unknown beyond *The One* is perfectly ineffable, which we acknowledge we neither know, nor are ignorant of, but which has about itself super-ignorance. Hence by proximity to this *The One Itself* is darkened: for being very near to the immense principle, if it be lawful so to speak, it remains as it were in the adytum of that truly mystic silence. On this account, Plato in speaking of it finds all his assertions subverted: for it is near to the subversion of every thing, which takes place about the first. It differs from it however in this, that it is *one* simply, and that according to *The One* it is also at the same time all things. But the first is above *The One* and *all things*, being more simple than either of these."

4. *And Plotinus, exhibiting in a most divinely inspired manner, the peculiarity of eternity, according to the theology of Plato, defines it to be infinite life, at once unfolding into light the whole of itself, and its own being.* (See page 209.) The 7th book of the 3rd Ennead of Plotinus[†] is concerning Eternity, and the following beautiful extract from it contains the definition of eternity alluded to by Proclus.

"Perhaps we ought to conceive of eternity, as a certain one collected from many; viz. either as one intelligence or one nature, whether consequent to things in the intelligible world, or existing together with it, or beheld as situated in the depths of its essence. All these, I say, reduced into eternity as one, which is also many, and is endued with a various capacity. Indeed, he who beholds a various capacity, when he considers it as a subject denominates it essence; but so far as he perceives life, he denominates it motion; and afterwards permanency, considered as abiding in a manner entirely the same. He will likewise behold difference and sameness, so far as they are many, bound in one. So that he who contracts the difference, subsisting in things which are many, into one life alone, and contemplates an unceasing sameness of energy, never passing its intelligence or life, from one thing into another, but ever abiding in the same manner in itself far remote from all interval; he I say, who beholds all these, contemplates eternity, viewing life ever possessing a present whole, where all things abide together in sameness, without the order of first and last, and are comprehended in an indivisible bound. Where all things are collected into one, as into a point, not yet proceeding into a linear flux, but abiding in sameness, that is, in itself, in an ever present *now*; because nothing of its nature is past, nothing in it is future; but what it is, it always is. Hence eternity is not a subject, but that which beams as it were from its subject, according to the possession of an ever present identity; promising itself that its ever abiding nature, will never be changed. For what should happen to this in future which it is not at present? Since it is a perfect and present plenitude of all things. Nor can the term was, the appellation of time past, belong to eternity. For what can that be, which *was* present with its nature, and is *past*? It is in like manner independent of all connection with futurity. And hence eternity is that which neither *was* nor *will be*, but alone *is*, which it possesses in a stable manner; because it is neither changed into a future, nor altered from a past duration. So that the eternity which we are now

---

[†] TTS vol. III, p. 263.

investigating, is life total and full, abiding in its essence about being itself; and is every where without interval and one.

"Hence, eternity is something especially venerable, and a God, as inherent intelligence affirms. But intelligence likewise dictates, that eternity is the same with that God whom we denominate being and life. And it may with the greatest propriety be said, that eternity is a deity shining and unfolding himself in intelligible light, such as he is in his essence; in an essence, I say, perfectly unchangeable and the same, and thus firmly abiding in an unceasing energy of life. Nor ought any one to wonder that we speak of eternity, as consisting of many things. For every thing which abides in the intelligible world, is called many, on account of its infinite power; since infinite there receives its denomination, because it never falls off from the consummate intellectual plenitude of its nature. And indeed, it is particularly called after this manner, because it loses nothing of its own. And if any one should describe eternity, as life already infinite because universal, and because it never deserts the integrity of its nature; (since it cannot be diminished by the past, nor increased by the future, because it is a perfect whole) - if any one should thus describe eternity, he will approach very near to its true definition. For what is afterwards added, that it is a perfect whole, and loses nothing of its integrity, is only a certain exposition of the definition which affirms it to be infinite life. But because a nature of this kind, thus all-beautiful and eternal, abides about *The One Itself*, emanating and in no respect departing from it, but ever abiding about and in it, and living with it in indissoluble union; hence it is said by Plato, not rashly, but in a manner truly beautiful and profound, that *eternity abides in one*. So that he not only reduces that which eternity contains into one; but the life of being in like manner reduces itself, about *The One Itself*. This then is what we investigate, and that is eternity, which thus abides. For that which is the energy of life abiding from itself, and residing in the depths of unity, without any deception, either in essence or life, is without all controversy eternity. Since *truly to be, is never not to be*, and to possess no diversity of being. But when in discoursing on eternity, we use the term *ever;* and also when we say it is not sometimes being, and sometimes non-being, we must consider these appellations as adopted only for the purpose of explanation. For the term *ever* is not perhaps principally assumed, but is employed, in order to show an incorruptible and never-failing nature."

5. *Let us in the next place speak in common about all the intelligible triads, etc.* (See page 229.) For the further information of the reader on this most profound subject the intelligible triad, the following observations are added, being an extract from the Introduction to my translation of the *Parmenides* of Plato.

As the first cause then is *The One*, and this is the same with *The Good*, the universality of things must form a whole, the best and the most profoundly united in all its parts which can possibly be conceived: for *the first good* must be the cause of the greatest good, that is, the whole of things; and as goodness is union, the best production must be that which is most united. But as there is a difference in things, and some are more excellent than others, and this in proportion to their proximity to the first cause, a profound union can no otherwise take place than by the extremity of a superior order coalescing through intimate alliance with the summit of the proximately inferior. Hence the first of bodies, though they are essentially corporeal, yet κατα σχεσιν, through *habitude* or *alliance*, are most vital, or lives. The highest of souls are after this manner intellects, and the first of beings are gods. For as *being* is the highest of things after *the first cause*, its first subsistence must be according to a superessential characteristic.

Now that which is superessential, considered as participated by the highest or *true being*, constitutes that which is called *intelligible*. So that every true being depending on the gods is a *divine intelligible*. It is *divine* indeed, as that which is deified; but it is *intelligible*, as the object of desire to intellect, as perfective and connective of its nature, and as the plenitude of *being* itself. But in the first being life and intellect subsist according to cause: for every thing subsists either according to cause, or according to *hyparxis*, or according to *participation*. That is, every thing may be considered either as subsisting occultly in its cause, or openly in its own order (or according to what it is,) or as participated by something else. The first of these is analogous to light when viewed subsisting in its fountain the sun; the second to the light immediately proceeding from the sun; and the third to the splendour communicated to other natures by this light.

The first procession therefore from the first cause, will be the intelligible triad, consisting of *being*, *life*, and *intellect*, which are the three highest things after the first god, and of which *being* is prior to *life*, and *life* to *intellect*. For whatever partakes of life partakes also of being: but the contrary is not true, and therefore being is above life; since it is the characteristic of higher natures to extend their communications beyond such as are subordinate. But *life* is prior to *intellect*, because all intellectual natures are vital, but all vital natures are not intellectual. But in this intelligible triad, on account of its superessential characteristic, all things may be considered as subsisting according to cause; and consequently number here has not a proper subsistence, but is involved in unproceeding union, and absorbed in superessential light. Hence, when it is called a triad, we must not suppose that any *essential distinction* takes place, but must consider this appellation as expressive of its ineffable perfection. For as it is the nearest of all things to *The One*, its union must be transcendently profound and ineffably occult.

All the gods indeed considered according to their unities are all in all, and are at the same time united with the first god like rays to light, or lines to a centre. And hence they are all established in the first cause (as Proclus beautifully observes) like the roots of trees in the earth; so that they are all as much as possible superessential, just as trees are eminently of an earthly nature, without at the same time being earth itself: for the nature of the earth as being a whole, or subsisting according to the eternal, is different from the partial natures which it produces. The intelligible triad, therefore, from its being wholly of a superessential idiom, must possess an inconceivable profundity of union, both with itself and its cause, so as to subsist wholly according *to the united*, το ηνωμενον; and hence it appears to the eye of pure intellect, as one simple indivisible splendour beaming from an unknown and inaccessible fire.

He then who is able, by opening the greatest eye of the soul, to see that perfectly which subsists without distinction, will behold the simplicity of the intelligible triad subsisting in a manner so transcendent as to be apprehended only by a superintellectual energy, and a deific union of the perceiver with this most arcane object of perception. But since in our present state it is impossible to behold an object so astonishingly lucid with a perfect and steady vision, we must be content, as Damascius well observes,[†] with a far distant, scarcely attainable, and most obscure glimpse; or with difficulty apprehending a trace of this light, like a sudden coruscation bursting on our sight. Such then is the pre-eminence of the intelligible order, to which on account of the infirmity of our mental eye, we assign a triple division, beholding in our phantasy as in a mirror a luminous triad, beaming from a uniform light; just, says Damascius, as the uniform colour of the sun appears in a cloud which possesses three catoptric intervals, through the various coloured nature of the rainbow.

But when we view this order in a distributed way, or as possessing distinction in order to accommodate its all-perfect mode of subsistence to our imperfect conceptions, it is necessary to give the triad itself a triple division. For we have said that it consists of *being, life*, and *intellect*. But in *being* we may view life and intellect, according to cause; in *life* being according to participation, and intellect according to cause; and in *intellect* both being and life according to participation; while at the same time in reality the whole is profoundly one, and contains all things occultly, or according to cause. But when viewed in this divided manner, each triad is said in the Chaldaic theology to consist of *father, power*, and *intellect; father* being the same with *hyparxis, unity, summit*, or *that which is superessential; power* being a certain pouring forth, or infinity of *The One*[‡] (or the summit); and on this account, says Damascius, it is present with *father*, as a diffused with an abiding one, and as pouring itself forth into a true chaos: but *intellect*, that is *paternal intellect*, subsisting according to a conversion to the paternal one; a conversion transcending all other conversions, as being neither gnostic, nor vital, nor essential, but an indistinct surpassing energy, which is union rather than conversion.

[†] Vid. Excerpts ex Damascio, a Wolfio, p. 232

[‡] Let the reader be careful to remember that *The One* of the gods is their superessential characteristic.

Such then is the intelligible triad, considered according to an all-perfect distribution, in accommodation to the imbecility of our mental eye. But if we are desirous, after having bid adieu to corporeal vision, and the fascinating but delusive forms of the phantasy, which Calypso-like, detain us in exile from our fathers' land: after having through a long and laborious dialectic wandering gained our paternal port, and purified ourselves from the baneful rout of the passions, those domestic foes of the soul; if after all this we are desirous of gaining a glimpse of the surpassing simplicity and ineffable union of this occult and astonishing light, we must crowd all our conceptions together into the most profound indivisibility, and, opening the greatest eye of the soul, entreat this all-comprehending deity to approach: for then, preceded by unadorned Beauty, silently walking on the extremities of her shining feet, he will suddenly from his awful sanctuary rise to our view.

But after such a vision, what can language announce concerning this transcendent object? That it is perfectly indistinct and void of number. "And," as Damascius[†] beautifully observes, "since this is the case, we should consider whether it is proper to call *this* which belongs to it *simplicity* απλοτης; *something else, multiplicity* πολλοτης and *something besides this, universality* παντοτης. For that which is intelligible is *one, many, all,* that we may triply explain a nature which is one. But how can one nature be *one* and *many*? Because *many* is the infinite power of *The One*. But how can it be *one* and *all*? Because *all* is the every way extended energy of *The One*. Nor yet is it to be called an energy, as if it was an extension of power to that which is external; nor power, as an extension of hyparxis abiding within, but again, it is necessary to call them three instead of one: for one appellation, as we have often testified, is by no means sufficient for an explanation of this order. And are all things then here indistinct? But how can this be easy to understand? For we have said that there are three principles consequent to each other, *viz. father, power,* and *paternal intellect. But these in reality are neither one, nor three, nor one and at the same time three.*[‡] But it is necessary that we should explain these by names and conceptions of this kind, through our penury in what is adapted to their nature, or rather through our desire of expressing something proper on the occasion. For as we denominate this triad *one,* and *many,* and *all,* and *father, power,* and *paternal intellect,* and again *bound, infinite,* and *mixed* - so likewise we call it a *monad,* and *the indefinite duad,* and *a triad,* and a paternal nature composed from both these. And as in consequence of purifying our conceptions we reject the former appellations, as incapable of harmonizing with the things themselves, we should likewise reject the latter on the same account."

[†] Vid. Excerpts, p. 228.

[‡] Αλλ' αυται μεν ουκ εισι κατα αληθειαν, ουτε μιαν, ουτε τρεις, ουτε μια αμα και τρεις.

But in order to convince the reader that this doctrine of the intelligible triad is not a fiction devised by the latter Platonists, I shall present him with the following translation from Damascius (περι αρχων) *Concerning Principles*,[†] in which the agreement of all the ancient theologists concerning this triad is most admirably evinced.

"The theology contained in the Orphic rhapsodies concerning the intelligible Gods is as follows: *Time* is symbolically placed for the one principle of the universe; but *æther* and *chaos*, for the two posterior to this one; and *being*, simply considered, is represented under the symbol of an egg. And this is the first triad of the intelligible Gods. But for the perfection of the second triad, they establish either a conceiving and a conceived egg as a God, or a white garment, or a cloud: because from them Phanes leaps forth into light. For indeed they philosophize variously concerning the middle triad. But Phanes here represents intellect. But conceiving him over and above this, as father and power, contributes nothing to Orpheus. But they call the third triad Metis as *intellect*,[‡] Ericapæus as *power*, and Phanes as *father*. But sometimes[§] the middle triad is considered according to the three-shaped God, while conceived in the egg; for the middle always represents each of the extremes; as in this instance, where the egg and the three-shaped God subsist together. And here you may perceive that the egg is that which is united; but that the three-shaped and really multiform God is the separating and discriminating cause of that which is intelligible. Likewise the middle triad subsists according to the egg, as yet united; but the third[*] according to the God who separates and distributes the whole intelligible order. And this is the common and familiar Orphic theology. But that delivered by Hieronymus and Hellanicus is as follows. According to them *water* and *matter* were the first productions, from which earth was secretly drawn forth: so that water and earth are established as the two first principles; the latter of these having a *dispersed* subsistence; but the former conglutinating and connecting the latter. But they are silent concerning the principle prior to these two, as being ineffable: for as there are no illuminations about him, his arcane and ineffable nature is from hence sufficiently evinced. But the third principle posterior to these two, *water* and *earth*, and which is generated from them, is *a dragon*, naturally endued with the heads of a bull and a lion, but in the middle having the countenance of the God himself. They add likewise that he has wings on his shoulders, and that he is called *undecaying Time*, and *Hercules;* that *Necessity* resides with him, which is

---

[†] Vid. Wolfii Anecdot. Græc. tom. iii p. 252.

[‡] ως νουν is omitted in the original.

[§] μηποτε is erroneously printed instead of ποτι.

[*] το τριτον is I conceive erroneously omitted in the original.

the same as *Nature*, and incorporeal *Adrastia*, which is extended throughout the universe, whose limits she binds in amicable conjunction. But as it appears to me, they denominate this third principle as established according to essence; and assert, besides this, that it subsists as male and female, for the purpose of exhibiting the generative causes of all things.

"But I likewise find in the Orphic rhapsodies, that neglecting the two first principles, together with the one principle who is delivered in silence, the third principle, posterior to the two, is established by the theology as the original; because this first of all possesses something effable and commensurate to human discourse. For in the former hypothesis, the highly reverenced and undecaying *Time*, the father of æther and chaos, was the principle: but in this *Time* is neglected, and the principle becomes *a dragon*. It likewise calls triple æther, moist; and Chaos, infinite; and Erebus, cloudy and dark; delivering this second triad analogous to the first; this being potential, as that was paternal. Hence the third procession of this triad is dark Erebus: its paternal and summit æther, not according to a simple but intellectual subsistence: but its middle infinite chaos, considered as a progeny or procession, and among these parturient, because from these the third intelligible triad proceeds. What then is the third intelligible triad? I answer, the egg; the duad of the natures of male and female which it contains, and the multitude of all-various seeds, residing in the middle of this triad: And the third among these is an incorporeal God, bearing golden wings on his shoulders; but in his inward parts naturally possessing the heads of bulls, upon which heads a mighty dragon appears, invested with the all-various forms of wild-beasts. This last then must be considered as the *intellect* of the triad; but the middle progeny, which are *many* as well as *two*, correspond to *power*, and the egg itself is *the paternal principle* of the third triad: but the third God of this third triad, this theology celebrates as *Protogonus*, and calls him *Jupiter*, the disposer of all things and of the whole world; and on this account denominates him *Pan*. And such is the information which this theology affords us, concerning the genealogy of the intelligible principles of things.

But in the writings of the Peripatetic Eudemus, containing the *Theology* of Orpheus, the whole intelligible order is passed over in silence, as being every way ineffable and unknown, and incapable of verbal enunciation. Eudemus therefore commences his genealogy from *Night*, from which also Homer begins: though Eudemus is far from making the Homeric genealogy consistent and connected, for he asserts that Homer begins from Ocean and Tethys. It is however apparent, that *Night* is according to Homer the greatest divinity, since she is reverenced even by Jupiter himself. For the poet says of Jupiter - "that he feared lest he should act in a manner displeasing to swift *Night.*" So that Homer begins his genealogy of the gods from *Night*. But it appears to me that Hesiod, when he asserts that Chaos was first generated, signifies by Chaos the incomprehensible and perfectly united nature of that which is intelligible: but that he produces earth[†] the first from thence, as a certain principle of the whole procession of the Gods. Unless perhaps Chaos is the second of the two principles: but Earth,[‡] Tartarus, and Love, form the triple intelligible. So that *Love* is to be placed for the third monad of the intelligible order, considered according to its convertive nature; for it is thus denominated by Orpheus in his rhapsodies. But *Earth* for the first, as being first established in a certain firm and essential station. But *Tartarus* for the middle, as in a certain respect exciting and moving forms into distribution. But Acusilaus appears to me to establish *Chaos* for the first principle, as entirely unknown; and after this, two principles, *Erebus* as male, and *Night* as female; placing the latter for *infinity*, but the former for *bound*. But from the mixture of these, he says that *Æther*, *Love* and *Counsel* are generated, forming three intelligible hypostases. And he places *Æther* as the summit; but *Love* in the middle, according to its naturally middle subsistence; but *Metis* or *Counsel* as the third, and the same as highly-reverenced intellect. And, according to the history of Eudemus, from these he produces a great number of other Gods. But Epimenides establishes *Air* and *Night* as the two first principles; manifestly reverencing in silence the one principle prior to these two. But from air and night *Tartarus* is generated, forming as it appears to me the third principle, as a certain mixed temperature from the two. And thus mixture is called by some an intelligible medium, because it extends itself to both the summit and the end. But from the mixture of the extremes with each other, an egg is generated, which is truly an intelligible animal: and from this again another progeny proceeds. But according to Pherecydes Syrius, the three first principles are a *Perpetually-abiding Vital Nature, Time*,[§] and *an Earthly Nature:* one of these subsisting, as

---

[†] Tην is printed instead of Γην.

[‡] As the whole of the Grecian theology is the progeny of the mystic traditions of Orpheus, it is evident that the Gods which Hesiod celebrates by the epithets of *Earth*, *Heaven*, etc. cannot be the visible *Heaven* and *Earth*; for Plato in the *Cratylus*, following the Orphic doctrine concerning the Gods, as we have evinced in our notes on that dialogue, plainly shows, in explaining the name of Jupiter, that this divinity is the artificer of the sensible universe; and consequently *Saturn*, *Heaven*, *Earth*, etc. are much superior to the mundane deities. Indeed if this be not admitted, the *Theogony* of Hesiod must be perfectly absurd and inexplicable. For why does he call Jupiter, agreeably to Homer (πατηρ ανδρων τε θεων τε), "*father of Gods and men?*" Shall we say that he means literally that Jupiter is the father of *all* the Gods? But this is impossible; for he delivers the generation of Gods who are the parents of Jupiter. He can therefore only mean that Jupiter is the parent of all the mundane Gods: and his *Theogony*, when considered according to this exposition, will be found to be beautifully consistent, accurate and sublime. I only add, that την is again erroneously printed in the *Excerpts* of Wolfius for γην.

[§] χθονον is printed for χρονον.

I conceive, prior to the other two. But he asserts that *Time* generates from the progeny of itself, *Fire, Spirit* and *Water:* which signify, as it appears to me, the triple nature of that which is intelligible. But from these, distributed into five profound recesses, a numerous progeny of Gods is constituted, which he calls *five-times animated* (πεντεμψυχος) and which is perhaps the same as if he had said πεντεκοσμος, or *a five-fold world*. But we may probably discourse on this subject at some other opportunity. And thus much may suffice at present concerning the hypotheses derived from the Grecian fables, which are both many and various.

But with respect to the theology of the Barbarians, the Babylonians seem to pass over in silence the one principle of the universe. But they establish two principles, Tauthe and Apasoon. And they consider Apasoon as the husband of Tauthe, whom they denominate the mother of the Gods; from whom an only-begotten son *Mooumis* was produced: which, as it appears to me, is no other than the intelligible world deduced from two principles.[†] But from these another procession is derived, *Dache* and *Dachus*. And likewise a third from these, *Kissare* and *Assoorus*. And from these again three deities are produced, *Anus, Illinus*, and *Aus*. But from *Aus* and *Dache* a son called Belus is produced, who they say is the demiurgus of the world. But with respect to the Magi, and all the Arion race, as we are informed by Eudemus, some of them call all the intelligible and united world *Place*, and some of them *Time:* from which *a good divinity* and *an evil daemon* are distributed; *Light* and *Darkness* subsisting prior to these, according to the assertions of others. However, both the one and the other, after an undistributed nature, consider that nature as having a subsistence which distributes the two-fold co-ordination of better natures: one of which co-ordinations *Orosmades* presides over, and the other *Arimanius*. But the Sidonians, according to the same historian, place before all things, *Time, Desire,* and *cloudy Darkness*. And they assert that from the mingling of *Desire* and *Darkness* as two principles, *Air* and *a gentle Wind* were produced: *Air* evincing the summit of the intelligible triad; but *the gentle Wind* raised and proceeding from this, the vital prototype of the intelligible. And again that from both these the bird *Otus*, similar to a night raven, was produced; representing, as it appears to me, intelligible intellect. But as we find (without the assistance of Eudemus) the Phœnician mythology, according to Mochus, places *Æther* and *Air* as the two first principles, from which the intelligible god *Oulomus* was produced; who, as it appears to me, is the summit of the intelligible order. But from this god (yet proceeding together with him) they assert that *Chousorus* was produced, being the first unfolding procession. And after this *an egg* succeeds; which I think must be called intelligible intellect. But the unfolding *Chousorus* is intelligible power, because this is the first nature which distributes an undistributed subsistence; unless perhaps after the two principles *Æther* and *Air*, the summit is *One Wind:* but the middle *Two Winds,*

[†] That is, from *bound* and *infinite*.

the *south-west* and the *south;* for in a certain respect they place these prior to *Oulomus.* But *Oulomus* himself is intelligible intellect: and unfolding *Chousorus*[†] the first order after the intelligible series. But the *egg itself* is heaven; from the bursting of which into two parts, the sections are said to have become heaven and earth. But with respect to the Egyptians, nothing accurately is related of them by Eudemus: we have, however, by means of some Egyptian philosophers resident among us, been instructed in the occult truth of their theological doctrine. According to these philosophers then, the Egyptians in certain discourses celebrate *an unknown Darkness* as the one principle of the universe, and this *thrice pronounced as such:* but for the two principles after the first they place *Water* and *Sand,* according to Heraiscus; but according to the more ancient writer Asclepiades, *Sand* and *Water;* from which and after which the first *Kamephis* is generated. But after this *a second,* and from this again *a third;* by all which, the whole intelligible distribution is accomplished. For thus Asclepiades determines. But the more modern Heraiscus says that the Egyptians, denominating the third Kamephis from his father and grandfather, assert that he is *the Sun;* which doubtless signifies in this case intelligible intellect. But a more accurate knowledge of these affairs must be received from the above-mentioned authors themselves. It must however be observed, that with the Egyptians there are many distributions of things according to union; because they unfold an intelligible nature into characteristics, or peculiarities of many gods, as may be learned from such as are desirous of consulting their writings on this subject."

Thus far Damascius; from which curious and interesting relation the reader may not only perceive at one view the agreement of the ancient theologists with each other in celebrating the intelligible triad, and venerating in silence the ineffable principle of things, but may likewise see that the Christian trinity is essentially different from this triad, because according to Plato and the ancient theologists, the first cause is not a part of any triad, or order of things. Consonant too with the above relation is the doctrine of the Chaldeans concerning the intelligible order, as delivered by Johannes Picus, in his *Conclusions according to the opinion of the Chaldean Theologists.*[‡] "The intelligible co-ordinations (says he) is not in the intellectual co-ordinations, as Amasis the Egyptian asserts, but is above every intellectual hierarchy, imparticipably concealed in the abyss of the first unity, and under the obscurity of the first darkness." Co-ordinatio intelligibilis non est in intellectuali co-ordinatione, ut dixit Amasis Egyptius, sed est super omnem intellectualem hierarchium, in abysso primæ unitatis, et sub caligine primarum tenebrarum imparticipaliter abscondita.

[†] χουσωρος should be read instead of χουσωρου.

[‡] Vid. Piei Opera, tom. 1. p. 54.

But from this triad it may be demonstrated, that all the processions of the Gods may be comprehended in six orders, viz. the *intelligible order*, the *intelligible and at the same time intellectual*, the *intellectual*, the *super-mundane*, the *liberated*, and the *mundane*. †233 For the *intelligible*, as we have already observed, must hold the first rank, and must consist of *being, life*, and *intellect;* i.e. must *abide, proceed*, and *return;* at the same time that it is characterised, or subsists principally according to *permanent being*. But in the next place that which is both *intelligible* and *intellectual* succeeds, which must likewise be triple, but must principally subsist according to *life* or *intelligence*. And in the third place the *intellectual* order must succeed, which is *triply convertive*. But as in consequence of the existence of the sensible world, it is necessary that there should be some demiurgic cause of its existence, this cause can only be found in *intellect*, and in the last hypostasis of the *intellectual triad*. For all forms in this hypostasis subsist according to all-various and perfect divisions; and forms can only fabricate when they have a perfect intellectual separation from each other. But since *fabrication* is nothing more than *procession*, the demiurgus will be to the posterior orders of Gods what *The One* is to the orders prior to the *demiurgus*; and consequently he will be that secondarily which the first cause of all is primarily. Hence his first production will be an order of Gods analogous to the *intelligible order*, and which is denominated *super-mundane*. After this he must produce an order of Gods similar to the *intelligible* and *intellectual* order, and which are denominated *liberated* Gods. And in the last place, a procession correspondent to the *intellectual order*, and which can be no other than the mundane Gods. For the demiurgus is chiefly characterised according to diversity, and is allotted the boundary of all universal hypostases.

All these orders, as is shown by Proclus in this work, are unfolded by Plato in the conclusions of the second hypothesis of the *Parmenides*; and this in a manner perfectly conformable to the Chaldaic theology. In proof of this I refer the reader to my collection of Chaldean oracles, in the *Old Monthly Magazine*.‡

6. *It is difficult to discover the fabricator and father of this universe, and when found, it is impossible to speak of him to all men.* (See page 332.)

The following admirable development by Proclus of the difficulty of discovering the maker of the universe, is extracted from 91E - 93A of his Commentaries on the *Timæus* of Plato.

---

† i.e. θεοι νοητοι, νοητοι και νοεροι, νοεροι, υπερκοσμιοι, απολυτοι sive υπερουρανιοι, et εγκοσμιοι.

‡ See TTS vol. VII.

"Father and fabricator differ from each other, so far as the former is the cause of matter,[†] but the latter of the world and order, and in short, of the formal cause; and so far indeed, as the former is the supplier of being and union, but the latter of powers and a multiform essence; and so far as the one stably contains all things in himself, but the other is the cause of progression and generation: and so far as the former signifies ineffable and divine providence, but the latter an abundant communication of productive principles. Porphyry however says, that father is he who generates the universe from himself, but fabricator he who receives the matter of it from another. Hence Aristo indeed, is said to be the *father* of Plato, but the builder of a house is the *maker* or fabricator of it, as not himself generating the matter of which it consists. If however, this is true, there was no occasion to call the demiurgus father, because according to Timæus, he does not give subsistence to matter. Is not the demiurgus therefore, rather the fabricator as producing form? For we call all these makers who produce any thing from a non-existent state into existence. But so far as the demiurgus produces that which he produces, in conjunction with life, he is father. For fathers are the causes of animals, and of certain living beings, and impart seed together with life. And thus much concerning this particular.

"But *this universe* signifies indeed, the corporeal masses, and the whole spheres [of which it consists] and the plenitudes of each. It also signifies the vital and intellectual powers, which ride as it were in the corporeal masses. It also comprehends all the mundane causes[‡] and the whole divinity of the world, about which the number of the mundane Gods proceeds; likewise, the one divinity, the divine soul, and the whole bulk of the world, together with the divine, intellectual, psychical, and corporeal-formed number that is conjoined with the world. For every monad has a multitude co-ordinate to itself. All these therefore must be assumed for *the universe*; since it signifies all these. Perhaps likewise the addition of the pronoun *this*, is significant of the universe being in a certain respect sensible and partial. For the intelligible universe is not *this*, because it is comprehensive of *all intellectual forms*. But the term *this* is adapted to the visible universe which is allotted a sensible and material nature. It is difficult therefore, as Plato says, to discover the demiurgus of this universe. For since with respect to discovery, one kind proceeds scientifically from such things as are first,[§] but another journeys on from things of a secondary nature, according to reminiscence; the discovery from such things as are first may be said to be difficult, because the invention of the intermediate

---

[†] For ολης here, it is necessary to read υλης, because matter according to Plato proceeds from the father Phanes, or animal itself, and not from the demiurgus.

[‡] For αυτους, it is necessary to read αιτιας.

[§] *Viz.* From axioms and definitions.

powers, pertains to the highest theory. But the discovery from such things as are secondary, is nearly more difficult than the former. For if we intend from these to survey the essence of the demiurgus, and his other powers, it is necessary that we should have beheld all the nature of the things generated by him, all the visible parts of the world, and the unapparent natural powers which it contains, according to which the sympathy and antipathy of the parts in the world subsist. Prior to these also, we must have surveyed the stable physical reasons, and natures themselves, both the more total and the more partial,[†] and again, the immaterial and material, the divine and the dæmoniacal, and the natures of mortal animals. And farther still, the genera which are under life, the perpetual and the mortal, the undefiled and the material, such as are wholes, and such as are parts, the rational and the irrational, and the prerogatives which are superior to ours, through which every thing between the Gods and the mortal nature are bound together. We must likewise have beheld the all-various souls, the different numbers of Gods according to the different parts of the universe, and the ineffable and effable impressions of the world through which it is conjoined with the father. For he who without having seen these is impelled to the survey of the demiurgus, is more imperfect than is requisite to the intellectual perception of the father. But it is not lawful for any thing imperfect to be conjoined with that which is all-perfect.

"Moreover, it is necessary,[‡] that the soul becoming an intellectual world, and being assimilated as much as possible to the whole intelligible world, should introduce herself to the maker of the universe; and from this introduction, should in a certain respect become familiar with him through a continued intellectual energy. For uninterrupted energy about any thing, calls forth and resuscitates our [dormant] ideas. But through this familiarity, becoming stationed at the door of the father, it is necessary, that we should be united to him. For discovery is this, to meet him, to be united to him, to associate alone with the alone, and to see him himself, the soul hastily withdrawing herself from every other energy to him. For then she is present with her father, banquets together with him on the truth of real being, and in pure splendour is purely initiated in entire and stable visions. Such therefore is the discovery of the father, not that which is doxastic; for this is dubious, and not very remote from the irrational life. Neither is it scientific; for this is syllogistic and composite, and does not come into contact with the intellectual essence of the intellectual demiurgus. But it is that which subsists according to intellectual vision itself, a contact with the intelligible, and a union with the demiurgic intellect. For this may properly be denominated difficult, either as hard to obtain, presenting itself to souls after every evolution of life; or as the true labour of souls. For after the wandering about generation, after purification,

---

[†] μερικωτερας is omitted in the original.

[‡] For δη here, it is requisite to read δει.

and the light of science, intellectual energy and the intellect which is in us shine forth, placing the soul in the father as in a port, purely establishing her in demiurgic intellections, and conjoining light with light, not such as that of science, but more beautiful, more intellectual, and partaking more of the nature of *The One* than this. For this is the paternal port,[†] and the discovery of the father, *viz.* an undefiled union with him.

"But to say *that when found it is impossible to speak of him to all men*,[‡]2 perhaps indicates the custom of the Pythagoreans, who had arcane assertions about divine natures, and did not divulge them to all men. For as the Elean guest says, the eyes of the multitude are not strong enough to look to truth. Perhaps also this may be said which is much more venerable, that it is impossible for him who has discovered the maker and father of the universe to speak of him to certain persons such as he has seen him. For the discovery was not made by the soul speaking, but closing her eyes, and being converted[§] to the divine light. Nor was it made by her being moved with her own proper motion, but through being silent with a silence which leads the way [to union]. For since the essence of other things is not naturally adapted to be spoken of, either through a name, or through definition, or through science, but is seen through intellection alone, as Plato says in his Epistles, in what other way can it be possible to discover the essence of the demiurgus, than by intellectual energy? And how when having thus found it, is it possible to tell what is seen, and explain it to others, through nouns and verbs? For the evolution which is conversant with composition, cannot exhibit a uniform and simple nature. What then, some one may say, do we not assert many things about the demiurgus, and about the other Gods, and even of *The One Itself*? To this we reply, we speak indeed *about* them, but we do not speak *of each of them itself*. And we are able indeed to speak *scientifically* of them, but not *intellectually*.

[†] Proclus here alludes to the fabulous wanderings of Ulysses in the *Odyssey*. For Homer by these occultly indicates the life of a man who passes in a regular manner from a sensible to an intellectual life, and who being thoroughly purified by the exercise of the cathartic virtues, is at length able to energize according to the intuitive perception of intellect, and thus after becoming reunited to Penelope or Philosophy, meets with and embraces his father. This appears also to have been the opinion of the Pythagorean Numenius, as we are informed by Porphyry in his treatise *De Antro Nympharum*. [TTS vol. II] "For he thought that the person of Ulysses in the *Odyssey* represented to us a man who passes in a regular manner over the dark and stormy sea of generation; and thus at length arrives at that region (*i.e.* the intellectual region) where tempests and seas are unknown, and finds a nation
Who ne'er knew salt, or heard the billows roar.

[‡] For μηδε ευροντα δυνατα ειναι λεγειν, it is necessary to read, μηδε ευροντα εις απαντας δυνατον, κ.λ.

[§] For απεστραμμενης, it is requisite to read επιστραμμενης.

For this, as we have before observed, is to discover them. But if the discovery is a silence of the soul, how can speech flowing through the mouth, be sufficient to lead that which is discovered into light?"

The following extract from the *Manuscript Scholia of* PROCLUS *On the Cratylus of Plato*, are added on account of their great importance; and that the reader may be furnished with all the information on the recondite theology of Greece, that it was in my power to obtain.

This manuscript is so rare that, if I am not mistaken, no copy of it is to be found in any of the colleges either of Oxford or Cambridge. My copy of it is a transcript of that which is now in the possession of MR HEBER of Oxford.

The reader, however, must be careful to remember that the design of Plato in the Cratylus was to unfold those peculiarities only of the Gods that are apparent in their names.

"That Jupiter is not *said to be*, but *is* the father of those who genuinely preserve the proper form of life, such as Hercules and the Dioscuri; but of those who are never at any time able to convert themselves to a divine nature, he never *is*, nor *is said to be* the father. Such therefore as having been partakers of a certain energy above human nature, have again fallen into *the sea of dissimilitude*,[†] and for honour among men have embraced error towards the Gods, - of these Jupiter is *said to be* the father.

"That the paternal cause originates supernally from intelligible and occult gods; for there the first fathers of wholes subsist; but it proceeds through all the intellectual Gods into the demiurgic order. For Timæus celebrates this order as at the same time *fabricative* and *paternal*; since he calls Jupiter the *demiurgus* and *father*. The fathers however who are superior to the one fabrication are called Gods of Gods, but the demiurgus is the father of Gods and men. Farther still, Jupiter is said to be *peculiarly* the father of some, as of Hercules, who immutably preserve a Jovian and ruling life during their converse with the realms of generation. Jupiter therefore, is triply father, of Gods, partial souls, and of souls that embrace an intellectual and Jovian life. The intellectual order of the Gods therefore, is supernally bounded by the king[‡] of the total divine genera, and who has a paternal transcendency with respect to all the intellectual Gods. This king according to Orpheus is called by the blessed immortals that dwell on lofty Olympus Phanes Protogonus. But this order proceeds through the three Nights, and the celestial orders, into the Titanic or saturnian series, where it first separates itself from the fathers and changes the kingdom of the

---

† Plato in the *Politicus* thus calls the realms of generation, *i.e.* the whole of a visible nature.

‡ That is, intelligible intellect, the extremity of the intelligible order.

Synoches,† for a distributive government of wholes, and unfolds every demiurgic genus of the Gods, from all the above-mentioned ruling and royal causes, but proximately from Saturn the leader of the Titanic orders. Prior however to other fabricators (δημιοιργοι) it unfolds Jupiter, who is allotted the unical strength of the whole demiurgic series, and who produces and gives subsistence to all unapparent and apparent natures. And he is indeed intellectual according to the order in which he ranks, but he produces the species and genera of beings into the order of sensibles. He is likewise filled with the Gods above himself, but imparts from himself a progression into being to all mundane natures. Hence Orpheus represents him fabricating every celestial race, making the sun and moon and the other starry Gods, together with the sublunary elements, and diversifying the latter with forms which before had a disordered subsistence. He likewise represents him presiding over the Gods who are distributed about the whole world, and who are suspended from him; and in the character of a legislator assigning distributions of providence in the universe according to desert to all the mundane Gods.‡ Homer too, following Orpheus, celebrates him as the common father of Gods and men, as leader and king, and as the supreme of rulers. He also says that all the multitude of mundane Gods is collected about him, abides in and is perfected by him. For all the mundane Gods are converted to Jupiter through Themis,

Ζευς δε Θεμιστα κελευσε Θεους, αγορην δε καλεσσαι
. . . . ηδ' αρα παντη
φοιτησασα κελευσε Διος προς δωμα νεεσθαι.

i.e. 'But Jupiter orders Themis to call the Gods to council; and she directing her course every where commands them to go to the house of Jupiter.'§ All of them therefore are excited according to the one will of Jupiter, and become διος ενδον,* *within Jupiter*, as the poet says. Jupiter too again separates them within himself, according to two co-ordinations, and excites them to providential

---

† That is, the divinities who compose the middle order of Gods, which is denominated intelligible and at the same time intellectual.

‡ As what is here said from Orpheus concerning Jupiter is very remarkable, and is no where else to be found, I give the original for the sake of the learned reader. διο και Ορφευς δημιουργουντα μεν αυτον την ουρανιαν πασαν γενεαν παραδιδωσι, και ηλιον ποιουντα και σεληνην, και τους αλλους αστρωους θεους· δημιουργουντα δε τα υποσεληνην στοιχεια, και διακρινοντα τοις ειδεσιν ατακτως εχοντα προτερον· σειρας δ' εφισταντα θεων περι ολον τον κοσμον εις αυτον ανηρτημενας, και διαθεσμοθετουντα πασι τοις εγκοσμιοις θεοις κατ' αξιαν διανομας της εν τω παντι προνοιας.

§ *Iliad* XX v. 4.

* See the 14th line.

energies about secondary natures; he at the same time as Timæus says, abiding after his accustomed manner:

ως εφατο κρονιδης πολεμον δ' αλιαστον εγερεν.

i.e. 'this spoke Saturnian Jupiter, and excited inevitable war.'[†] Jupiter however is separate and exempt from all mundane natures; whence also the most total and leading of the other Gods, though they appear to have in a certain respect equal authority with Jupiter, through a progression from the same causes, yet call him father. For both Neptune and Juno celebrate him by this appellation. And though Juno speaks to him as one who is of the same order,

και γαρ εγω θεος ειμι· γενος δε μοι ενθεν σοι,
και με πρεσβυτατην τεκετο κρονος αγκυλομητις,

i.e. 'For I also am a divinity, and Saturn, of inflected counsel, endowed me with the greatest dignity, when he begot me:'[‡]
"And though Neptune says

τρεις γαρ τ' εκ κρονου ειμεν αδελφεοι, ους τεκε Ρειν,
Ζευς και εγω, τριτατος δ' Αϊδης ενεροισιν ανασσων,

i.e. 'For we are three brothers from Saturn, whom Rhea bore, Jupiter and I, and the third is Pluto, who governs the infernal realms:'[§]
"Yet Jupiter is called father by both these divinities; and this because he comprehends in himself the one and impartible cause of all fabrication; is prior to Saturnian triad;[*] connectedly contains the three fathers; and comprehends on all sides the vivification of Juno. Hence, at the same time that this goddess gives animation to the universe, he also together with other Gods gives subsistence to souls. Very properly therefore do we say that the demiurgus in the *Timæus* is the mighty Jupiter. For he it is who produces mundane intellects and souls, who adorns all bodies with figures and numbers, and inserts in them one union, and an indissoluble friendship and bond. For Night also in Orpheus advises Jupiter to employ things of this kind in the fabrication of the universe.

[†] Ibid 32.

[‡] *Iliad* IV v. 58.

[§] *Iliad* XV v. 187.

[*] For the Saturnian triad belongs to that order of Gods which is called supermundane, and which immediately subsists after the intellectual order; so that the Jupiter who ranks at the summit of this triad is different from and inferior to the demiurgus.

αυταρ επην δεσμον κρατερον περι πασι τανυσσης

i.e. But when your power around the whole has spread
A strong coercive bond. -

The proximate bond indeed of mundane natures is that which subsists through analogy; but the more perfect bond is derived from intellect and soul. Hence Timæus calls the communion of the elements through analogy, and the indissoluble union from life, a bond. For he says animals were generated bound with animated bonds. But a more venerable bond than these subsists from the demiurgic will. "For my will," says Jupiter in the *Timæus*, "is a greater and more principal bond, etc."

Firmly adhering therefore to this conception respecting the mighty Jupiter, *viz.* that he is the demiurgus and father of the universe, that he is an all-perfect imparticipable intellect,[†] and that he fills all things both with other goods, and with life, let us survey how from names Socrates unfolds the mystic truth concerning this divinity. Timæus then says that it is difficult to know the essence of the demiurgus, and Socrates now says that it is not easy to understand his name, which manifests his power and energy.

That our soul knows partibly the impartible nature of the energy of the Gods, and that which is characterised by unity in this energy, in a multiplied manner: and this especially takes place about the demiurgus who expands intellectual forms, and calls forth intelligible causes, and evolves them to the fabrication of the universe. For Parmenides characterises him by sameness and difference. According to Homer two tubs are placed near him; and the most mystic tradition, and the oracles of the Gods say that the duad is seated with him. For thus they speak: "He possesses both; containing intelligibles in intellect, but introducing sense to the worlds."[‡] These oracles likewise call him *twice beyond*, and *twice there* (δις επεκεινα και δις εκει). And in short they celebrate him through the duad. For the demiurgus comprehends in himself unitedly every thing *prolific*,[§] and which gives subsistence to mundane natures. Very properly therefore is his name twofold, of which δια manifests *the cause through which*, and this is paternal goodness; but ζηνα signifies *vivification*, the first cause of which in the universe the demiurgus unically comprehends. The former too, is a symbol of the Saturnian and paternal series; but the latter of the vivific and maternal Rhea. So far likewise as Jupiter receives the whole of Saturn, he gives subsistence to a triple essence, the impartible, the partible, and that which subsists between these; but according to the Rhea which he contains in himself, he scatters as from a fountain, intellectual, psychical, and corporeal

---

[†] That is, he is not an intellect consubsistent with soul.

[‡] See page 31 TTS vol. VII.

[§] And the duad considered as a divine form or idea is the source of fecundity.

life. But by his demiurgic powers and energies, he gives a formal subsistence to these and separates them from forms of a prior order, and from each other. He is also the ruler and king of all things: and is exempt from the three demiurgi. For they, as Socrates says in the Gorgias, divide the kingdom of their father; but Jupiter the demiurgus at once, without division reigns over the three, and unically governs them.

He is therefore the cause of the paternal triad, and of all fabrication; but he connectedly contains the three demiurgi. And he is a *king* indeed, as being coordinated with the fathers; but a *ruler*, as being proximately established above the demiurgic triad, and comprehending the uniform cause of it. Plato therefore by considering his name in two ways evinces that images receive partibly the unical causes of paradigms, and that this is adapted to him who establishes the intellectual duad in himself. For he gives subsistence to twofold orders, the celestial, and the supercelestial; whence also the theologist Orpheus says, that his sceptre consists of four and twenty measures; as ruling over a twofold twelve.[†]

That the soul of the world gives life to alter-motive natures; for to these it becomes the fountain and principle of motion, as Plato says in the *Phædrus* and *Laws*. But the demiurgus simply imparts to all things life divine, intellectual, psychical, and that which is divisible about bodies. No one however should think that the Gods in their generations of secondary natures are diminished; or that they sustain a division of their proper essence in giving subsistence to things subordinate; or that they expose their progeny to the view, externally to themselves, in the same manner as the causes of mortal offspring. Nor in short, must we suppose that they generate with motion or mutation, but that abiding in themselves, they produce by their very essence posterior natures, comprehend on all sides their progeny, and supernally perfect the productions and energies of their offspring. Nor again when it is said that gods are the sons of more total Gods, must it be supposed that they are disjoined from more ancient causes, and are cut off from a union with them; or that they receive the peculiarity of their hyparxis through motion, and an indefiniteness converting itself to bound. For there is nothing irrational and without measure, in the natures superior to us. But we must conceive that their progressions are effected through similitude; and that there is one communion of essence, and an indivisible continuity of powers and energies, between the sons of Gods and their fathers; all those Gods that rank in the second order, being established in such as are more ancient; and the more ancient imparting much of perfection, vigour, and efficacious production to the subordinate. And after this manner

---

[†] *i.e.* The twelve Gods who first subsist in the *liberated* or supercelestial order and who are divided into four triads, and the twelve mundane Gods, Jupiter, Neptune, Vulcan; Vesta, Minerva, Mars; Ceres, Juno, Diana; and Mercury, Venus, Apollo. The first of these triads is *fabricative*; the second *defensive*; the third *vivific*; and the fourth *anagogic or elevating*, as is shown by Proclus in the sixth book of his Theology.

we must understand that Jupiter is said to be the son of Saturn. For Jupiter being the demiurgic intellect proceeds from another intellect, superior and more uniform, which increases indeed its proper intellections, but converts the multitude of them to union; and multiplies its intellectual powers, but elevates their all-various evolutions to impartible sameness. Jupiter therefore proximately establishing a communion with this divinity, and being filled from him with total intellectual good, is very properly said to be the son of Saturn, both in hymns and in invocations, as unfolding into light that which is occult, expanding that which is contracted, and dividing that which is impartible in the Saturnian monad; and as emitting a second more partial kingdom, instead of that which is more total, a demiurgic instead of a paternal dominion, and an empire which proceeds every where instead of that which stably abides in itself.

Why does Socrates apprehend the name of king Saturn to be *υβριστικον insolent*, and looking to what does he assert this? We reply that according to the poets *satiety* (κορος) is the cause of *insolence;* for they thus denominate immoderation and repletion; and they say that *Satiety* brought forth *Insolence* (υβριν φασιν τικει κορος). He therefore who looks without attention to the name of Saturn, will consider it as signifying *insolence*. For to him who suddenly hears it, it manifests satiety and repletion. Why therefore, since a name of this kind is expressive of insolence, do we not pass it over in silence, as not being auspicious and adapted to the Gods? May we not say that the royal series† of the Gods, beginning from Phanes and ending in Bacchus, and producing the same sceptre supernally as far as to the last kingdom, Saturn being allotted the fourth royal order; appears according to the fabulous pretext,

---

† This royal series consists of Phanes, Night, Heaven, Saturn, Jupiter, Bacchus. "Ancient theologists, says Syrianus (in his commentary on the 14th book of Aristotle's *Metaphysics*) assert that Night and Heaven reigned, and prior to these the mighty father of Night and Heaven, who distributed the world to Gods and mortals, and who first possessed royal authority, the illustrious Ericapæus.

τοιον ελων διενειμε θεοις, θνητοισι δε κοσμον
ου πρωτος βασιλευε περικλυτος ηρικεπαιος,

Night succeeded Ericapæus, in the hands of whom she has a sceptre:

σκεπτρον εχ ους· εν χερσιν ηρικεπαιου·

To Night, Heaven succeeded, who first reigned over the Gods after mother Night.

ος πρωτος βασιλευς θεων μετα μητερα νυκτα.

Chaos transcends the habitude of sovereign dominion: and, with respect to Jupiter, the oracles given to him by Night, manifestly call him not the first, but the fifth immortal king of the Gods.

αθανατον βασιλεα θεων πεμπτον γενεσθαι.

According to these theologists therefore, that principle which is most eminently the first, is *The One* or *The Good*, after which according to Pythagoras, are these two principles Æther and Chaos, which are superior to the possession of sovereign dominion. In the next place succeed the first and occult genera of the Gods, in which first shines forth the father and king of all wholes, and whom on this account they call *Phanes.*"

differently from the other kings, to have received the sceptre insolently from Heaven, and to have given it to Jupiter? For Night receives the sceptre from Phanes; Heaven derives from Night, the dominion over wholes; and Bacchus who is the last king of the Gods receives the kingdom from Jupiter. For the father (Jupiter) establishes him in the royal throne, puts into his hand the sceptre, and makes him the king of all the mundane Gods. "Hear me ye Gods, I place over you a king."

κλυτε θεοι τον δ' υμμιν βασιλεα τιθημι.

says Jupiter to the junior Gods. But Saturn alone perfectly deprives Heaven of the kingdom, and concedes dominion to Jupiter, cutting and being cut off as the fable says. Plato therefore seeing this succession, which in Saturn is called by theologists *insolent* (υβριστικη) thought it worth while to mention the appearance of insolence in the name; that from this he might evince the name is adapted to the God, and that it bears an image of the insolence which is ascribed to him in fables. At the same time he teaches us to refer mythical devices to the truth concerning the Gods, and the apparent absurdity which they contain, to scientific conceptions.

That *the great* when ascribed to the Gods, must not be considered as belonging to interval, but as subsisting intellectually, and according to the power of cause, but not according to partible transcendency. But why does Plato now call Saturn διανοια the dianoetic part of the soul? May we not say, that it is because he looks to the multitude of intellectual conceptions in him, the orders of intelligibles, and the evolution of forms which he contains; since also in the *Timæus*, he represents the demiurgic intellect as reasoning, and making the world, dianoetically energizing: and this in consequence of looking to his partible and divided intellections, according to which he fabricates not only wholes but parts. When Saturn, however, is called intellect, Jupiter has the order of the dianoetic part: and when again, Saturn is called the dianoetic part, we must say that he is so called according to analogy with reference to a certain other intellect of a higher order. Whether therefore you are willing to speak of intelligible and occult intellect, or of that which unfolds into light (εκφαντορικος νους) or of that which connectedly contains (συνεκτικος νους) or of that which imparts perfection,† (τελεσιουργος νους) Saturn will be as the dianoetic part to all these. For he produces united intellection into multitude, and fills himself wholly with excited intelligibles. Whence also, he is said to be the leader of the Titanic race, and the source of all-various separation and diversifying power. And perhaps Plato here primarily delivers twofold interpretations of the name of the Titans, which Iamblichus and Amelius

---

† Of these intellects the first is Phanes, the second Heaven, the third Earth, and the fourth the Subcelestial Arch which is celebrated in the *Phædrus*, viz. νους νοητος ο Φανης, εκφαντορικος νους ο Ουρανος, συνεκτικος νους η γη, τελεσιουργος δε νους η υπ' ουρανιος αψις.

afterwards adopted. For the one interprets this name from the Titans extending their powers to all things; but the other from *something insectile* (παρα το τι ατομον) because the division and separation of wholes into parts receives its beginning from the Titans. Socrates therefore now indicates both these interpretations, by asserting of the king of the Titans that he is a *certain great dianoetic power*. For the term *great* is a symbol of power pervading to all things; but the term *a certain*, of power proceeding to the most partial natures.

That the name Saturn is now triply analysed; of which the first asserting this God to be the plenitude of intellectual good, and to be the satiety of a divine intellect, from its conveying an image of the satiety and repletion which are reprobated by the many, is ejected as insolent. The second also which exhibits the imperfect and the puerile, is in like manner rejected. But the third, which celebrates this God as full of purity, and as the leader of undefiled intelligence, and an undeviating life, is approved. For king Saturn is intellect, and the supplier of all intellectual life; but he is an intellect exempt from co-ordination with sensibles, immaterial and separate, and converted to himself. He likewise converts his progeny and after producing them into light again embosoms and firmly establishes them in himself. For the demiurgus of the universe, though it is a divine intellect, yet he orderly arranges sensibles, and provides for subordinate natures. But the mighty Saturn is essentialized in separate intellections, and which transcend wholes. "For the fire which is beyond the first, says the Chaldean Oracle, does not incline its power downwards." But the demiurgus is suspended and proceeds from Saturn, being himself an intellect subsisting about an immaterial intellect, energizing about it as the intelligible, and producing that which is occult in it, into the apparent. For the maker of the world is an intellect of intellect. And it appears to me, that as Saturn is the summit of those Gods, that are properly called intellectual, he is intellect, as with reference to the intelligible genus of Gods. For all the intellectual adhere to the intelligible genus of Gods, and are conjoined with them through intellections. "Ye who understand the supermundane paternal profundity," says the hymn to them. But Saturn is intelligible, with reference to all the intellectual Gods. *Purity* therefore indicates this impartible and imparticipable transcendency of Saturn. For the not coming into contact with matter, the impartible, and an exemption from habitude, are signified by purity. Such indeed is the transcendency of this God with respect to all co-ordination with things subordinate, and such his undefiled union with the intelligible, that he does not require a Curetic guard, like Rhea, Jupiter and Proserpine. For all these, through their progressions into secondary natures, require the immutable defence of the Curetes. But Saturn being firmly established in himself, and hastily withdrawing himself from all subordinate natures is established above the guardianship of the Curetes. He contains however, the cause of these uniformly in himself. For this purity, and the undefiled which he possesses, give subsistence to all the progressions of the Curetes. Hence in the Oracles, he is said to comprehend the first fountain of the Amilicti, and to ride on all the others. "The intellect of the father riding on attenuated rulers, they become refulgent with the furrows of inflexible and implacable fire."

Νους πατρος αραιοις εποχουμενος ιθυντηρσιν
Ακναμπτου αστραπτουσιν αμειλικτου πυρος ολκοις.

He is therefore *pure intellect*, as giving subsistence to the undefiled order, and as being the leader of the whole intellectual series.

Αυτου γαρ εκθρωσκουσιν αμειλικτοι τε κεραυνοι,
Και πρηστηροδοχοι κολποι παμφεγγεος αλκης.
Πατρογενους Εκατης, και υπεζωκος πυρος ανθος,
Ηδε κραταιον πνευμα πολων πυριων επεκεινα.

i.e. "From him leap forth the implacable thunders, and the prester-capacious bosoms of the all-splendid strength of the father-begotten Hecate, together with the environed flower of fire, and the strong spirit which is beyond the fiery poles."

For he convolves all the hebdomad of the fountains,[†] and gives subsistence to it, from his unical and intelligible summit. For he is, as the Oracles says, αμιστυλλευτος uncut into fragments, uniform, and undistributed, and connectedly contains all the fountains, converting and uniting all of them to himself, and being separate from all things with immaculate purity. Hence he is κορονους, as an immaterial and pure intellect, and as establishing himself in the paternal silence. He is also celebrated as the father of fathers. Saturn therefore is a father, and intelligible, as with reference to the intellectual Gods.

That every intellect either abides, and is then intelligible, as being better than motion; or it is moved, and is then intellectual; or it is both, and is then intelligible, and at the same time intellectual. The first of these is Phanes; the second which is alone moved is Saturn; and the third which is both moved and permanent is Heaven.

That Saturn from his impartible, unical, paternal, and beneficent subsistence in the intellectual orders has been considered by some as the same with the one cause of all things. He is however only analogous to this cause, just as Orpheus calls the first cause *Time* (χρνος) nearly homonymously with Saturn (κρονος). But the Oracles of the Gods characterise this deity by the epithet of *the once*; (τῳ απαξ) calling him *once beyond* (απαξ επεκεινα). For *the once* is allied to *The One*.

That *Heaven* the father of Saturn, is an intellect understanding himself indeed, but united to the first intelligibles; in which he is also firmly established; and connectedly contains all the intellectual orders, by abiding in intelligible union. This God too is *connective*, just as Saturn is of a *separating* idiom; and on this account he is *father*. For connecting precede separating causes; and the

---

[†] That is of the whole intellectual order, which consists of Saturn, Rhea, Jupiter, the three Curetes, and the separating monad Ocean.

intelligible and at the same time intellectual such as are intellectual only. Whence also *Heaven* being the *Synoches* (συνοχευς) of wholes, according to one union gives subsistence to the Titanic series, and prior to this, to other orders of the Gods; some of which abide only in him, which he retains in himself, but others both abide and proceed, which he is said to have concealed, after they were unfolded into light. And after all these he gives subsistence to those divine orders, which proceed into the universe, and are separated from their father. For he produces twofold monads, and triads, and hebdomads equal in number to the monads. These things however will be investigated more fully elsewhere. But this deity is denominated according to the similitude of the apparent Heaven. For each of them compresses and connects all the multitude which it contains, and causes the sympathy and connection of the whole world to be one. For connection is second to unifying power, and proceeds from it. In the *Phædrus* therefore Plato delivers to us the production of all secondary natures by Heaven, and shows us how this divinity leads upwards and convolves all things to the intelligible. He likewise teaches us what its summit is, what the profundity of its whole order, and what the boundary of the whole of its progression. Here therefore investigating the truth of things from names, he declares its energy with respect to things more elevated and simple, and which are arranged nearer to *The One*. He also clearly appears here to consider the order of Heaven, as intelligible and at the same time intellectual. For if it sees things on high, it energizes intellectually, and there is prior to it the intelligible genus of Gods, to which looking it is intellectual; just as it is intelligible to the natures which proceed from it. What then are the things on high which it beholds? Is it not evident that they are, the supercelestial place, an essence without colour, without figure, and without the touch, and all the intelligible extent? An extent comprehending as Plato would say intelligible animals, the one cause of all eternal natures, and the occult principles of these; but as the followers of Orpheus would say, bounded by æther upwards, and by Phanes downwards. For all between these two gives completion to the intelligible order. But Plato now calls this both singularly and plurally; since all things are there united, and at the same time each is separated peculiarly; and this according to the highest union and separation.

With respect to the term μετεωρολογοι, *i.e. those who discourse on sublime affairs,* we must now consider it in a manner adapted to those who choose an anagogic life, who live intellectually, and who do not gravitate to earth, but sublimely tend to a theoretic life. For that which is called Earth there, maternally gives subsistence to such things as Heaven, which is co-ordinate to that Earth, produces paternally. And he who energizes there, may be properly called μετεωρολογος, or, *one who discourses about things on high.* Heaven therefore, being of a *connective* nature, is expanded above the Saturnian orders, and all the intellectual series; and produces from himself all the Titanic race; and prior to this, the perfective and defensive orders: and in short is the leader of every good to the intellectual Gods. Plato therefore, having celebrated Saturn, for his intelligence which is without habitude to mundane natures, and for his life which is converted to his own exalted place of survey, now celebrates Heaven for another more perfect energy. For to be conjoined to more elevated natures is a greater good than to be converted to oneself. Let no one however think, that on this account the above-mentioned energies are distributed in the Gods; as for instance, that there is providence alone, in Jupiter, a conversion alone to himself, in Saturn, and an elevation alone to the intelligible, in Heaven. For Jupiter no otherwise provides for mundane natures than by looking to the intelligible; since as Plato says in the *Timæus*, intellect understanding ideas in animal itself, thought it requisite that as many and such as it there perceived should be contained in the universe; but as Orpheus[†] says with a divinely inspired mouth, "Jupiter swallows his progenitor Phanes, embosoms all his powers, and becomes all things intellectually which Phanes is intelligibly." Saturn also imparts to Jupiter the principles of fabrication, and of providential attention to sensibles, and understanding himself, he becomes united to first intelligibles, and is filled with the goods which are thence derived. Hence also the theologist (Orpheus) says "that he was nursed by Night."[‡] If therefore the intelligible is nutriment, Saturn is replete not only with the intelligibles co-ordinated with him, but also with the highest and occult intellections. Heaven himself also fills all secondary natures with his proper goods, but guards all things by his own most vigorous powers; and the father supernally committed to him the connecting and guarding the causes of eternal animal. But he intellectually perceives himself, and is converted to the intelligibles which he contains; and this his intelligence, Plato in the *Phædrus* calls *circulation*. For as that which is moved in a circle is moved about its own centre, so Heaven energizes about its own intelligible, according to intellectual circulation. But all the Gods subsisting in all, and each possessing all energies, one transcends more in this, and another in a different energy, and each is particularly characterised according to that in which it transcends. Thus Jupiter is characterised by providence, and hence his name is now thus analysed; but Saturn by a conversion to himself, whence also he is *inflected counsel* αγκυλομητις; and Heaven by habitude to things more excellent; from which also he receives his appellation. For his giving subsistence to a pure and the Saturnian intellect, represents his energy to the other part. But as there are many powers in Heaven, such as the connective, guardian, and convertive, you will find that this name is appropriately adapted to all these. For the connective is signified through bounding the intellectual Gods; since the connective bounds the multitude which he contains. The power which guards

---

[†] ως δ' Ορφευς ενθεω στοματι λεγει, και καταπινει τον προγονον αυτου τον φανητα, και εγκολπιζεται πασας αυτου τας δυναμεις ο ζευς, και γινεται νοιρως, οσαπερ ην εκεινος νοητως.

[‡] διο και τρεφεσθαι φησιν αυτον ο θεολογος υπο της νυκτος. "εκ παντων δε κρονον νυξ ετρεφεν ηδ' ατιταλλεν."

wholes subsists through the termination and security of an intellectual essence. And the convertive power subsists through converting seeing, and intellectually energizing natures, to things on high. But all these are adapted to Heaven. For there is no fear that the Gods will be dissipated, and that on this account they require connective causes; or that they will sustain mutation, and that on this account they stand in need of the saving aid of guardian causes; but now Socrates at once manifests all the powers of Heaven, through convertive energy. For this is to behold things on high, to be converted to them, and through this to be connected and defended. And it appears to me that Heaven possesses this idiom according to analogy to the intelligible eternity and the intelligible wholeness. For Timæus particularly characterizes eternity by this, *viz.* by abiding in the one prior to it, and by being established in the summit of intelligibles; and Socrates says that Heaven surveys things on high, *viz.* the supercelestial place, and such things as are comprehended in the god-nourished silence of the fathers (και οσα τη θεοθρεμμονι σιγη περιειληπται των πατερων). As therefore Parmenides signifies each of these orders through *wholeness,* the one through intelligible, and the other through intellectual wholeness, in like manner both Timæus and Socrates characterise them by a conversion to more excellent natures. But the conversion as well as the wholeness is different. For that of eternity is intelligible, on which account Timæus does not say that it looks to its intelligible, but only that it stably abides. But the conversion of Heaven is intellectual, and on this account Socrates says that it sees things on high, and through this converts, guards, and connects all things posterior to itself. Whence also in the *Phædrus,* it is said by the circulation of itself, to lead all things to the supercelestial place, and the summit of the first intelligibles.

That there being three fathers and kings of which Socrates here makes mention, Saturn alone appears to have received the government from his father, and to have transmitted it to Jupiter, by violence. Mythologists therefore celebrate the sections of Heaven and Saturn. But the cause of this is, that Heaven is of the connective, Saturn of the Titanic, and Jupiter of the demiurgic order. Again, the Titanic genus rejoices in separations and differences, progressions and multiplications of powers. Saturn therefore, as a dividing God, separates his kingdom from that of Heaven; but as a pure intellect he is exempt from a fabricative energy proceeding into matter. Hence also the demiurgic genus is again separated from him. Section therefore is on both sides of him. For so far as he is a Titan, he is cut off from the connective causes, but so far as he does not give himself to material fabrication, he is cut off from the demiurgus Jupiter.

That with respect to the supercelestial place to which Heaven extends his intellectual life, some characterise it by ineffable symbols; but others after giving it a name celebrate it as unknown, neither being able to speak of its form, or figure. And proceeding somewhat higher than this, they have been able to manifest the boundary† of the intelligible Gods by name alone. But the natures which are beyond this, they signify through analogy alone, these natures being ineffable and incomprehensible. Since that God who closes the paternal order, is said by the wise to be the only deity among the intelligible Gods, that is denominated: and theurgy ascends as far as to this order. Since therefore the natures prior to Heaven, are allotted such a transcendency of uniform subsistence, that some of them are said to be effable, and at the same time ineffable, known, and at the same time unknown, through their alliance to *The One*, Socrates very properly restrains the discourse about them, in consequence of names not being able to represent their hyparxes; and in short, because it requires a certain wonderful employment, to separate the effable and ineffable, of their hyparxis or power. He accuses therefore his memory, not as disbelieving in the fables, which assert that there are certain more ancient causes beyond Heaven, nor as not thinking it worth while to mention them. For in the *Phædrus* he himself celebrates the supercelestial place. But he says this, because the first of beings cannot become known by the exercise of memory and through phantasy, or opinion, or the dianoetic part. For we are alone naturally adapted to be conjoined to them, with the flower of intellect and the hyparxis of our essence; and through these we receive the sensation of their unknown nature. Socrates therefore says, that what in them is exempt, both from our gnostic and recollective life, is the cause of our inability to give them a name; for they are not naturally adapted to be known through names. Theologists likewise would not remotely signify them, and through the analogy of things apparent to them, if they could be named, and apprehended by knowledge.

That Homer‡ does not ascend beyond the Saturnian order, but evincing that Saturn is the proximate cause of the demiurgus, he calls Jupiter, who is the demiurgus, the son of Saturn. He also calls the divinities co-ordinate with him Juno, Neptune, and Mars; and he denominates Jupiter, the father of men and Gods. But he does not introduce Saturn, as either energising, or saying any thing, but as truly αγκυλομητις in consequence of being converted to himself.

That Orpheus greatly availed himself of the licence of fables, and manifests every thing prior to Heaven by names, as far as to the first cause. He also denominates the ineffable, who transcends the intelligible unities, *Time;* whether because *Time* pre-subsists as the cause of all generation, or because, as delivering the generation of true beings, he thus denominates the ineffable, that he may indicate the order of true beings, and the transcendency of the more total to the more partial; that a subsistence according to Time may be the same with a

---

† That is Phanes, intelligible intellect, or in the language of Plato αυτοζωον *animal* itself.

‡ Homer however appears to have ascended as far as to the goddess Night, or the summit of the intelligible and at the same time intellectual order.

subsistence according to cause; in the same manner as generation with an arranged progression. But Hesiod venerates many of the divine natures in silence, and does not in short name the first. For that what is posterior to the first proceeds from something else, is evident from the verse,
"Chaos of all things was the first produced."
For it is perfectly impossible that it could be produced without a cause; but he does not say what that is which gave subsistence to Chaos. He is silent indeed with respect to both the fathers[†] of intelligibles, the exempt, and the co-ordinate; for they are perfectly ineffable. And with respect to the two co-ordinations, the natures which are co-ordinate with the one, he passes by in silence, but those alone which are co-ordinate with the indefinite duad, he unfolds through genealogy. And on this account Plato now thinks Hesiod deserves to be mentioned, for passing by the natures prior to Heaven, as being ineffable. For this also is indicated concerning them by the Oracles, which likewise add "they possess mystic silence," σιγ' εχε μυστα. And Socrates himself in the *Phædrus*, calls the intellectual perception of them μυησις and εποπτεια, *in which nearly the whole business is ineffable and unknown.*

That Saturn in conjunction with Rhea produced Vesta and Juno who are co-ordinate to the demiurgic causes. For Vesta imparts from herself to the Gods an uninclining permanency, and seat in themselves, and an indissoluble essence. But Juno imparts progression, and a multiplication into things secondary. She is also the vivifying fountain of wholes, and the mother of prolific powers; and on this account she is said to have proceeded together with Jupiter the demiurgus; and through this communion she generates maternally, such things as Jupiter generates paternally. But Vesta abides in herself, possessing an undefiled virginity, and being the cause of sameness to all things. Each of these divinities however together with her own proper perfection, possesses according to participation the power of the other. Hence some say that Vesta is denominated from essence (απο της εστιας) looking to her proper hyparxis. But others looking to her vivific and motive power which she derives from Juno say that she is thus denominated ως ωσεως ουσαν αιτιαν *as being the cause of impulsion.* For all divine natures are in all, and particularly such as are co-ordinate with each other, participate of, and subsist in each other. Each therefore of the demiurgic and vivific orders, participates the form by which it is characterised, from Vesta. The orbs of the planets likewise possess the sameness of their revolutions from her; and the poles and centres are always allotted from her their rest.

That Vesta does not manifest essence, but the abiding and firm establishment of essence in itself; and hence this goddess proceeds into light after the mighty Saturn. For the divinities prior to Saturn have not a subsistence in themselves

---

[†] That is to say *the first cause and bound*, which is called by Orpheus *ether*.

and in another,† but this originates from Saturn. And a subsistence in *self* is the peculiarity of Vesta, but in *another* of Juno.

That the theology of Hesiod from the monad Rhea produces according to things which are more excellent in the co-ordination, Vesta, but according to those which are subordinate Juno; and according to those which subsist between, Ceres. But according to Orpheus, Ceres is in a certain respect the same with the whole of vivification, and in a certain respect is not the same. For on high she is Rhea, but below in conjunction with Jupiter, she is Ceres: for here the things begotten are similar to the begetters, and are nearly the same.

That we ought to receive with caution what is now said concerning effluxions and motions. For Socrates does not descend to the material flowing of Heraclitus; for this is false,‡ and unworthy the dianoetic conceptions of Plato. But since it is lawful to interpret things divine analogously, through appropriate images, Socrates very properly assimilates fontal and Saturnian deities to streams; in so doing jesting and at the same time acting seriously, because good is always derived as it were in streams from on high, to things below. Hence, according to the image of rivers, after the fontal deities, who eternally devolve streams of good, the deities who subsist as principles are celebrated. For after the *fountain* of a river the place where it *begins* to flow is surveyed.

That those divinities who are peculiarly denominated total intellectual gods, of whom the great Saturn is the father, are properly called fontal. For "from him leap forth the implacable thunders," says the oracle concerning Saturn. But concerning the vivific fountain Rhea from which all life, divine, intellectual, psychical and mundane is generated, the Chaldean oracles thus speak,

$$\text{Ρειη τοι νοερων μακαρων πηγη τε ροη τε.}$$
$$\text{Παντων γαρ πρωτη δυναμεις κολποισιν αφραστοις}$$
$$\text{Δεξαμενη, γενεην επι παν προχεει τροχαουσαν.}$$

i.e. "Rhea§ is the fountain and river of the blessed intellectual Gods. For first receiving the powers of all things in her ineffable bosoms, she pours running generation into every thing."

For this divinity gives subsistence to the infinite diffusion of all life, and to all never-failing powers. She likewise moves all things according to the measures of divine motions, and converts them to herself; establishing all things

---

† See this explained in the notes on my translation of the *Parmenides* of Plato.

‡ That is to say, it is false to assert of intellectual and divine natures, that they are in a perpetual flux; for they are eternally stable themselves, and are the sources of stability to other things.

§ Gesner aided by Patricius, has imported these lines among the Orphic fragments, in his edition of the works of Orpheus.

in herself, as being co-ordinate to Saturn. Rhea therefore is so called from causing a perpetual influx of good, and through being the cause of divine *facility*, since the life of the gods is attended with *ease* (θεοι ρεια ζωντες).

That Ocean is the cause to all the Gods of acute and vigorous energy, and bounds the separations of the first, middle, and last orders; converting himself to himself, and to his proper principles, through swiftness of intellect, but moving all things from himself, to energies accommodated to their natures; perfecting their powers, and causing them to have a never-failing subsistence. But Tethys imparts permanency to the natures which are moved by Ocean, and stability to the beings which are excited by him to the generation of secondary natures. She is also the source of purity of essence to those beings who perpetually desire to produce all things; as sustaining every thing in the divine essences which as it were *leaps forth and percolates*. For each of first causes, though it imparts to secondary natures a participation of good, yet at the same time retains with itself that which is undefiled, unmingled and pure from participation. Thus for instance, intellect is filled with life, being, and intelligence, with which also it fills soul; but establishing in itself that which in each of these is genuine and exempt, it also illuminates from itself to beings of a subordinate rank, inferior measures of these goods. And vigour of energy indeed, is present with more ancient natures, through Ocean; but the leaping forth and percolating through Tethys. For every thing which is imparted from superior to subordinate natures, whether it be essence, life, or intelligence, is *percolated*. And such of these as are primary, are established in themselves; but such as are more imperfect, are transferred to things of a subject order. Just as with respect to streams of water, such of them as are nearer their source are purer, but the more remote are more turbid. Both Ocean and Tethys therefore, are fontal Gods, according to their first subsistence. Hence Socrates now calls them the fathers of streams. But they also proceed into other orders of Gods, exhibiting the same powers among the Gods who rank as principles or rulers, among those of a liberated, and those of a celestial characteristic; and appropriately in each of these. Timæus, however, celebrates their sublunary orders, calling them fathers of Saturn and Rhea, but the progeny of Heaven and Earth. But their last processions are their divisible allotments about the earth; both those which are apparent on its surface, and those which under the earth, separate the kingdom of Hades, from the dominion of Neptune.

That Saturn is conjoined both to Rhea and Jupiter, but to the former as father to prolific power, but to the latter, as father to intelligible[†] intellect.

That Ocean is said to have married Tethys, and Jupiter Juno, and the like, as establishing a communion with her, conformably to the generation of subordinate natures. For an according co-arrangement of the Gods, and a connascent co-operation in their productions, is called by theologists *marriage*.

[†] Proclus here means that there is the same analogy between Saturn, Rhea, and Jupiter, as in the intelligible triad, between father, power, and intellect.

That Tethys is denominated from leaping forth and *straining* or *cleansing*, being as it were *Diatethys*, and by taking away the first two syllables *Tethys*.†

That Saturn is the monad of the Titanic order of the Gods, but Jupiter of the demiurgic. This last divinity however is twofold, the one exempt and co-ordinated with Saturn, being a fontal God, and in short ranking with the intellectual fathers, and convolving the extremity of them; but the other being connumerated with the sons of Saturn, and allotted a Saturnian summit and dominion in this triad; concerning which also the Homeric Neptune says,

τρεις γαρ τ' εκ Κρονου ειμεν αδελφεοι, ους τεκε Ρειη.‡

As brother Gods we three from Saturn came,
And Rhea bore us.

And the first Jupiter indeed, as being the demiurgus of wholes, is the king of things first, middle, and last, concerning whom Socrates also had just said, that he is the ruler and king of all things; and life and salvation are imparted to all things through him.

But the ruling Jupiter, who ranks as a principle, and who is co-ordinate with the three sons of Saturn governs the third part of the whole of things, according to that of Homer,

τριχθα δε παντα δεδασται . . . .§

A triple distribution all things own.

He is also the summit of the three, has the same name with the fontal Jupiter, is united to him, and is monadically called Jupiter. But the second is called dyadically, marine Jupiter, and Neptune. And the third is triadically denominated, terrestrial Jupiter, Pluto, and Hades. The first of these also preserves, fabricates, and vivifies summits, but the second, things of a second rank, and the third those of a third order. Hence this last is said to have ravished Proserpine, that together with her he might animate the extremities of the universe.

That the Titanic order dividing itself from the connecting order of Heaven, but having also something in itself abiding, and connascent with the order, Saturn is the leader of the separation, and on this account he both arms others against his father, and receives the scythe* from his mother, through which he

---

† Οτι ωνομασται η Τηθυς παρα το διαττομενον και ηθουμενον, οιον Διατηθυς, και αφαιρεσει των πρωτων δυσσυλλαβων Τηθυς.

‡ Iliad XV 187.

§ Iliad XV 189.

* See the *Theogony* of Hesiod v.176, etc.

divides his own kingdom from that of Heaven. But Ocean is co-ordinated with those that abide†in the manners of the father, and guards the middle of the two orders; so far as a Titan being connumerated with the gods that subsist with Saturn; but so far as rejoicing in a co-ordination with Heaven conjoining himself with the Synoches. For it is fit that he who bounds the first and second orders, should be arranged in the middle of the natures that are bounded. But every where this god is allotted a power of this kind, and separates the genera of the Gods, the Titanic from the connecting (των συνοχικων) and the vivific from the demiurgic. Whence also ancient rumour calls Ocean the God who separates the apparent part of Heaven from the unapparent; and on this account poets say, that the sun and the other stars rise from the ocean. What is now said therefore by Plato comprehends all the Titanic order through these two conjunctions; this order abiding and at the same time proceeding. And through the Saturnian order indeed, it comprehends every thing separated from the fathers; but through that of Ocean, every thing conjoined with the connecting Gods. Or if you had rather so speak, through the Saturnian order, he comprehends every maternal cause, but through the other, every thing subservient to the paternal cause. For the female is the cause of progression and separation, but the male of union and stable permanency.

That of the demiurgic triad‡ which divides the whole world, and distributes the indivisible, one and whole fabrication of the first Jupiter, the summit, and which has the relation of father is Jupiter, who through union with the whole demiurgic intellect having the same appellation with it, is for this reason not mentioned here by Plato. But Neptune is allotted the middle and that which binds together both the extremes; being filled indeed from the essence of Jupiter, but filling Pluto. For of the whole of this triad, Jupiter indeed is the

---

† Proclus here alludes to the following Orphic verses cited by him in his Commentary on the *Timæus*, lib. 5, 296A:

ενθ' ουν τ' ωκεανος μεν, ενι μεγαροισιν εμιμνεν
ορμαινων ποτερωσε νοον τραποι, ηε πατερα
ον γνωση τε βιης, και ατασθαλα λωβησαιτο
συν κρονω, ηδ' αλλοις αδελθοις οι πεπιθοντο
μητρι φιλη, η τους γε λιπων, μενει ενδον εκηλος·
πολλα δε πορφυρων, μενει ημερος εν μεγαροισι
σκυζομενος τη μητρι, κασιγνητοισι δε μαλλον.

i.e. "But Ocean remained within the simple house, considering how he should act, whether he should deprive his father of his strength, and basely injure him, together with Saturn and the rest of his brethren, who were obedient to their dear mother; or whether leaving these, he should stay quietly at home. After much deliberation, he remained quietly at home, being angry with his mother, but more so with his brothers."

‡ That is, of the first triad of the supermundane, which subsists immediately after the intellectual order.

father, but Neptune the power, and Pluto the intellect. And all indeed are in all; but each receives a different character of subsistence. Thus Jupiter subsists according to *being;* but Neptune according to *power,* and Pluto according to *intellect.* And though all these divinities are the causes of the life of all things, yet one is so *essentially,* another *vitally,* and another *intellectually.* Whence also the theologist Orpheus says, that the extremes fabricate in conjunction with Proserpine things first and last; the middle being co-arranged with generative cause from his own allotment, without Proserpine. Hence *violence* is said to have been offered to Proserpine by Jupiter: but she is said to have been *ravished* by Pluto, (διο και φασι την κορην υπο μεν του διος βιαζεσθαι, υπο δε του πλουτωνος αρπαζεσθαι.) But the middle is said to be the cause of motion to all things. Hence also, he is called *earthshaker,* as being the origin of motion. And among those who are allotted the kingdom of Saturn, the middle allotment, and the agile sea (η ευκινητος θαλασσα) are assigned to him. According to every division therefore, the summits are Jovian, the middles belong to Neptune, and the extremes to Pluto. And if you look to the centres, such as the east, that of mid-heaven and the west; if also you divide the whole world, as for instance into the inerratic, planetary and sublunary spheres; - or again, if you divide that which is generated into the fiery, terrestrial, and that which subsists between; or the earth into its summits, middle, and hollow, and subterranean parts, this triad every where distributes the first, middle and last differences of things fabricated in demiurgic boundaries.

That the name Neptune is now triply analysed. For Neptune is the trident-bearer, and the Tritons, and Amphitrite are the familiars of this God. And the first analyzation of his name is from the allotment over which he presides, and from souls coming into generation, in whom the circle of sameness is fettered; since the sea is analogous to generation. But the second is from communion with the first.

αλλα ζευς προτερος γεγονει, και πλειονα ηδει.[†]

But Jove was born the first, and more he knew.
For a Jupiter of this kind, is the proximate intelligible of Neptune. But the third analysis of his name is from his energy in externals. For he is motive of nature, and vivific of things last. He is also the guardian of the earth, and excites it to generation.

That Neptune is an intellectual demiurgic God, who receives souls descending into generation; but Hades is an intellectual demiurgic God, who frees souls from generation. For as our whole period receives a triple division, into a life prior to generation, which is Jovian, into a life in generation which is Neptunian, and into a life posterior to generation which is Plutonian; Pluto, who is characterised by intellect, very properly converts ends to beginnings, effecting a circle without a beginning, and without an end, not only in souls,

---

[†] Hom. *Iliad.*

but also in every fabrication of bodies, and in short, of all periods; - which circle also, he perpetually convolves. Thus for instance, he converts the ends to the beginnings of the souls of the stars, and the convolutions of souls about generation, and the like. And hence Jupiter is the guardian of the life of souls prior to generation.

That some badly analyze the name of Pluto into wealth from the earth, through fruits and metals; but Hades into the invisible, dark and dreadful. These Socrates now reprobates, bringing the two names to the same signification; referring the name of Pluto, as intellect, to the wealth of prudence, but that of Hades to an intellect knowing all things. For this God is a sophist, who purifying souls after death, frees them from generation. For Hades is not, as some improperly explain it, evil: for neither is death evil; though Hades to some appears to be attended with perturbations ($\epsilon\mu\pi\alpha\theta\omega\varsigma$); but it is invisible and better than the apparent; such as is every thing intelligible. Intellect therefore, in every triad of beings, convolves itself to being, and the paternal cause, imitating in its energy the circle.

That men who are lovers of body, badly refer to themselves the passions of the animated nature, and on this account consider death to be dreadful, as being the cause of corruption. The truth however is, that it is much better for man to die, and live in Hades a life according to nature, since a life in conjunction with body is contrary to nature, and is an impediment to intellectual energy. Hence it is necessary to divest ourselves of the fleshly garments with which we are clothed, as Ulysses did of his ragged vestments, and no longer like a wretched mendicant together with the indigence of body, put on our rags. For as the Chaldean Oracle says, "things divine cannot be obtained by those whose intellectual eye is directed to body; but those only can arrive at the possession of them who stript of their garments hasten to the summit."

That Neptune when compared with Jupiter is said to know *many* things; but Hades compared with souls to whom he imparts knowledge is said to know *all* things; though Neptune is more total than Hades.

That as it is necessary to analyse Pluto, not only into the obvious wealth from the earth, but also into the wealth of wisdom, so likewise Ceres must be analysed not only into corporeal nutriment; but beginning from the Gods themselves it is requisite to conceive her to be the supplier of aliment, first to the Gods themselves, afterwards to the natures posterior to the Gods; and in the last place, that the series of this beneficent energy extends as far as to corporeal nutriment. For the characteristic of love shines forth first of all in the Gods: and this is the case with the medicinal and prophetic powers of Apollo, and with those of every other divinity. But nutriment, when considered with reference to the Gods, is the communication of intellectual plenitude from more exalted natures to those of an inferior rank. Gods therefore, are nourished, when they view with the eye of intellect Gods prior to themselves; and when they are perfected and view intelligible beauties, such as justice itself, temperance itself, and the like, as it is said in the *Phædrus*.

That from sportive conceptions about the Gods, it is possible for those to energize entheastically, or according to a divinely inspired energy, who apply themselves to things in a more intellectual manner. Thus for instance, according to the material conceptions of the multitude, Venus derives her origin from foam; and foam corresponds to seed. Hence according to them the pleasure arising from this in coition is Venus. Who however, is so stupid, as not to survey primary and eternal natures, prior to such as are last and corruptible? I will therefore unfold the divine conception respecting Venus.

They say then that the first Venus was produced from twofold causes, the one as that *through which*,[†] co-operating with her progression, as calling forth the prolific power of the father, and imparting it to the intellectual orders; but Heaven as the maker and cause unfolding the goddess into light, from his own generative abundance. For whence could that which congregates different genera, according to one desire of beauty, receive its subsistence except from the *synochical* power of Heaven? From the foam therefore of his own prolific parts thrown into the sea, Heaven produced this goddess, as Orpheus says. But the second Venus, Jupiter produces from his own generative powers, in conjunction with Dione: and this goddess likewise proceeds from foam, after the same manner with the more ancient Venus, as Orpheus evinces. These goddesses therefore differ from each other, according to the causes of their production, their orders and their powers. For she that proceeds from the genitals of Heaven is supermundane, leads upwards to intelligible beauty, is the supplier of an unpolluted life, and separates from generation. But the Venus that proceeds from Dione governs all the co-ordinations in the celestial world and the earth, binds them to each other, and perfects their generative progressions, through a kindred conjunction. These divinities too, are united with each other through a similitude of subsistence: for they both proceed from generative powers; one from that of the connectedly-containing power of Heaven, and the other from Jupiter the demiurgus. But the sea signifies an expanded and circumscribed life; its profundity, the universally-extended progression of such a life; and its foam, the greatest purity of nature, that which is full of prolific light and power, and that which swims upon all life, and is as it were its highest flower.

That according to Orpheus Ceres is the same with Rhea. For he says that subsisting on high in unproceeding union with Saturn, she is *Rhea*, but that by emitting and generating Jupiter, she is *Ceres*. For thus he speaks,

Ρειην το πριν εουσαν, επιε διος επλετο μητηρ
Γεγονε δημητηρ[‡]

[†] This cause is Saturn, who according to the fable cut off the genital parts of Heaven. See the *Theogony* of Hesiod.

[‡] This Orphic fragment is not to be found in Gesner's collection of the Orphic remains.

i.e. The Goddess who was *Rhea,* when she bore Jove became Ceres.

But Hesiod says that Ceres is the daughter of Rhea. It is however evident, that these theologists harmonize; for whether this goddess proceeds from union with Saturn to a secondary order, or whether she is the first progeny of Rhea, she is still the same. Ceres therefore, thus subsisting, and receiving the most ancient and ruling order from the whole vivific Rhea, (της ολης ζωογονου ρεας) and comprehending the middle centres of whole vivification, (της ολης ζωογονιας) she fills all supermundane natures with the rivers of all-perfect life, pouring upon all things vitally, indivisibly, and uniformly.

Prior however to all this, she unfolds to us the demiurgic intellect, (Jupiter) and imparts to him the power of vivifying wholes. For as Saturn supplies her from on high with the cause of being; so Ceres from on high, and from her own prolific bosoms, pours forth vivification to the demiurgus. But possessing herself the middle of all vivific deity, she governs the whole fountains which she contains, and comprehends the one bond of the first and last powers of life. She stably convolves too, and contains all secondary fountains. But she leads forth the uniform causes of prior natures to the generation of others. This goddess too comprehends *Vesta* and *Juno:* in her right hand parts Juno, who pours forth the whole order of souls; but in her left hand parts Vesta, who leads forth all the light of virtue. Hence, Ceres is with great propriety called by Plato,[†] *mother,* and, at the same time the *supplier of aliment.* For, so far as she comprehends in herself the cause of Juno, she is a mother; but as containing Vesta in her essence, she is the supplier of aliment. But the paradigm of this goddess is *Night: for immortal Night is called the nurse of the Gods.* Night however is the cause of aliment intelligibly:[‡] for that which is intelligible is, according to the oracle,[§] the aliment of the intellectual orders of Gods. But Ceres first of all separates the two kinds of aliment in the Gods, as Orpheus says:

    Μησατο γαρ προπολους, και αμφιπολους, και οπαδους·
    Μησατο δ' αμβροσιην, και ερυθρου νεκταρος αρθρον·
    Μησατο δ' αγλαα εργα μελισσαων εριβομβων[*]

i.e. She cares for pow'rs ministrant, whether they
    Or Gods *precede* or *follow,* or *surround:*
    Ambrosia, and *tenacious nectar red*

[†] See p. 599, Vol. V of my Translation of Plato [TTS vol XIII.]

[‡] Because Night subsists at the summit of *the intelligible and at the same time intellectual* order, and is wholly absorbed in the intelligible.

[§] That is, according to one of the Chaldean Oracles.

[*] These verses likewise, are not in Gesner's collection.

Are too the objects of her bounteous care.
Last to the bee her providence extends,
Who gathers honey with resounding hum.

Ceres therefore, our sovereign mistress (δεσποινα) not only generates life, but that which gives perfection to life; and this from supernal natures to such as are last: *for virtue is the perfection of souls*. Hence mothers who are connected with the circulations of time, bring forth their offspring in imitation of this twofold and eternal generation of Ceres. For, at the same time that they send forth their young into the light, they extend to them milk naturally produced as their food.

That the conjunction of the demiurgic intellect with the vivific causes is triple: for it is conjoined with the fountains prior to itself; is present with its kindred co-ordinate natures; and co-energizes with the orders posterior to itself. For it is present with the mother prior to itself, *convertively;* (επιστρεπτικως) with Proserpine posterior to itself, *providentially;* (προνοητικως) and with Juno co-ordinate to itself with an *amatory energy* (ερασμιως). Hence Jupiter is said to be enamoured of Juno,

ως σεο νυν εραμαι

As now I love thee,[†]

And this love indeed is legal, but the other two appear to be illegal. This goddess therefore produces from herself in conjunction with the demiurgus and father all the genera of souls, the supermundane and the mundane, the celestial and sublunary, the divine, angelic, dæmoniacal, and partial. After a certain manner too, she is divided from the demiurgus, but in a certain respect she is united to him: for Jupiter is said, in the *Philebus*, to contain a royal intellect and a royal soul. For he contains uniformly the paternal and maternal cause of the world; and the fountain of souls is said to be in Jupiter; just as again, the intelligence of Jupiter is said to be first participated by Juno. For no other divinity, says Jupiter in Homer, knows my mind prior to Juno. Through this ineffable union therefore of these divinities, the world participates of intellectual souls. They also give subsistence to intellects who are carried in souls, and who together with them give completion to the whole fabrication of things.

That the series of our sovereign mistress Juno, beginning from on high pervades to the last of things; and her allotment in the sublunary region is the air. For *air* is a symbol of *soul*, according to which also soul is called a *spirit;* (πνευμα); just as *fire* is an image of *intellect*, but *water* of *nature*, by which the world is nourished (της κοσμοτροφου φυσεως), through which all nutriment and increase are produced. But *earth* is the image of *body* through its gross and material nature. Hence Homer obscurely signifying this, represents Juno

---

[†] *Iliad* XIV 328.

suspended with two anvils under her feet: for the air is allotted two heavy elements beneath itself.

For

ηλιον δ' ακαμαντα βοωπις ποτνια ηρη
πεμψεν επ' ωκεανοιο ρους

i.e. "Fair-eyed venerable Juno sent the sun to the streams of the ocean," - is from the same conception.

For he calls the thick cloud produced by Juno, the setting of the sun. The assertion likewise that the end of this name will be conjoined with the beginning, if any one frequently repeats the name of the goddess, evinces the conversion of rational souls to her which proceed from her; and that voice is air that is struck. On this account also the voice of rational animals is especially dedicated to this goddess, who made the horse of Achilles to become vocal. But Socrates now delivers these three vivific monads in a consequent order, *viz.* Ceres, Juno, Proserpine; calling the first the mother, the second the sister, and the third the daughter of the demiurgus. All of them however are partakers of the whole of fabrication; the first in an exempt manner and intellectually, the second in a fontal manner and at the same time in a way adapted to a principle (αρχικως) and the third, in a manner adapted to a principle and leader (αρχικως και ηγεμονικως).

Of these goddesses the last possesses triple powers, and impartibly and uniformly comprehends three monads of Gods. But she is called Core (κορη) through the purity of her essence, and her undefiled transcendency in her generations. She also possesses a first, middle and last empire. And according to her summit indeed, she is called Diana by Orpheus; but according to her middle Proserpine; and according to the extremity of the order Minerva. Likewise, according to an hyparxis transcending the other powers of this triple vivific order, the dominion of Hecate is established; but according to a middle power, and which is generative of wholes, that of Soul; and according to intellectual conversion that of virtue.† Core therefore, subsisting on high, and among the supermundane Gods, uniformly extends this triple order of divinities; and together with Jupiter generates Bacchus, who impartibly presides over partible fabrication. But beneath, in conjunction with Pluto, she is particularly beheld according to the middle peculiarity; for it is this which proceeding every where imparts vivification to the last of things. Hence she is called Proserpine, because she especially associates with Pluto, and together with him orderly distributes the extremities of the universe. And according to her extremities indeed, she is said to be a virgin and to remain undefiled: but according to her middle, to be conjoined with Hades, and to beget the Furies

---

† Proclus says this conformably to the theology of the Chaldeans. For according to that theology, the first monad of the vivific triad is *Hecate*, the second *Soul*, and the third *Virtue*.

in the subterranean regions. She therefore is also called Core, but after another manner than the supermundane and ruling Core. For the one is the connective unity of the three vivific principles; but the other is the middle of them, in herself possessing the peculiarities of the extremes. Hence in the Proserpine conjoined with Pluto, you will find the peculiarities of Hecate and Minerva; but these extremes subsist in her occultly, while the idiom of the middle shines forth, and that which is characteristic of ruling soul, which in the supermundane Core was of a *ruling*[†] nature, but here subsists according to a mundane peculiarity.

That Proserpine is denominated, either through judging of forms and separating them from each other, thus obscurely signifying the ablation of slaughter. (δια το κρινειν τα ειδη και χωριζειν αλληλων, ως του φονου την αναιρεσιν αινιττομενον) or through separating souls perfectly from bodies, through a conversion to things on high, which is the most fortunate slaughter and death, to such as are worthy of it. (η δια το χωριζειν τας ψυχας τελεως εκ των σωματων δια της προς τα ανω επιστροφης, οπερ εστιν ευτυχεστατος φονος και θανατος τοις αξιουμενοις τουτου.) But the name φερεφαττα Pherephatta, according to a contact with generation is adapted to Proserpine; but according to wisdom and counsel to Minerva. At the same time however all the appellations by which she is distinguished are adapted to the perfection of soul. On this account also she is called Proserpine, and not the names of the extremes; since that which was ravished by Pluto is the middle; the extremes at the same time being firmly established in themselves, according to which Core is said to remain a virgin.

With respect to our sovereign mistress Diana, Plato delivers three peculiarities of her, the undefiled, the mundane, and the anagogic. And through the first of these indeed, the goddess is said to be a lover of virginity; but through the second, according to which she is perfective of works (τελεσιουργος) she is said to be the inspective guardian of virtue; and through the third she is said to hate the impulses arising from generation. Of these three likewise, the first is especially adapted to the progression of the goddess, according to which she is allotted an hyparxis in the vivific triad of the supermundane Gods; whether we call this deity Hecatic, as Theurgists say, or Diana with Orpheus. For there being established, she is filled with undefiled powers from the Gods called *Amilicti*.[‡] But she looks to the fountain of virtue, and embraces its virginity. For the virginity which is there does not proceed forth, as the Oracle says, but abiding gives subsistence to Diana, and to supermundane virtue, and is exempt from all communion, conjunction and progression, according to generation. Hence Core also, according to the Diana and Minerva which she contains, is said to remain a virgin; but according to the prolific power of Proserpine, she

---

[†] That is, of a supermundane nature; for the *ruling*, are the *supermundane*, Gods.

[‡] That is, the Corybantes.

is said to proceed forth, and to be conjoined with the third demiurgus, and to bring forth as Orpheus says, "nine azure-eyed, flower-producing daughters;"

εννεα θυγατερας γλαυκωπιδας ανθεσιουγους.

since the Diana and the Minerva which she contains preserve their virginity always the same. For the former of these is characterised according to her stability, but the latter according to her convertive energy. But that which is generative is allotted in her a middle order. They say too, that she aspires after virginity, since the form of her is comprehended in the vivific fountain, and she understands fontal virtue, gives subsistence to supermundane and anagogic virtue, and despises all material sexual connexion, though she inspects the fruits arising from it.

She appears also to be averse to the generations and progressions of things, but to introduce perfections to them. And she gives perfection indeed to souls through a life according to virtue; but to mortal animals she imparts a restitution to form. But that there is a great union between Diana, the mundane Hecate, and Core, is evident to those that are in the least degree conversant with the writings of Orpheus; from which it appears that Latona is comprehended in Ceres, and together with Jupiter gives subsistence to Core and the mundane Hecate. To which we may also add that Orpheus[†] calls Diana Hecate. So that it is nothing wonderful, if we should elsewhere call the Diana contained in Core Hecate.

"Again, theologists especially celebrate two powers of our sovereign mistress Minerva, the *defensive*, and the *perfective;* the former preserving the order of wholes undefiled, and unvanquished by matter, and the latter filling all things with intellectual light, and converting them to their cause. And on this account, Plato also in the *Timæus*, analogously celebrates Minerva as *philopolemic* and *philosophic.* But three orders of this Goddess are delivered by theologists; the one fontal and intellectual, according to which she establishes herself in her father Jupiter, and subsists in unproceeding union with him; but the second ranks among the supermundane Gods, according to which she is present with Core, and bounds and converts all the progression of that Goddess to herself. And the third is *liberated,* according to which she perfects and guards the whole world, and circularly invests it with her powers, as with a veil; binding together all the mundane summits, and giving subsistence to all the allotments in the heavens, and to those which proceed into the sublunary region. Now therefore Socrates celebrates her *guardian* power, through the name of *Pallas;* but her *perfective* power through that of *Minerva.* She is the cause therefore of orderly and measured motion, which she first imparts to the Curetic order, and afterwards to the other Gods. For Minerva according to this power is the leader of the Curetes, as Orpheus says, whence also, as well

---

† Η δ' αρα εκατη παιδος μελη αυθι λυπουσα
Αητους ευπλοκαμοιο κορη προσεβησατ' ολυμπον.

as those divinities she is adorned with empyrean arms, through which she represses all disorder, preserves the demiurgic series immoveable, and unfolds dancing through rhythmical motion. She also guards reason as it proceeds from intellect; through this power vanquishing matter. For the visible region, says Timæus, is mingled from intellect and necessity, the latter being obedient to the former, and all material causes being in subjection to the will of the father. It is this goddess therefore, who arranges necessity under the productions of intellect, raises the universe to the participation of Jupiter, excites and establishes it in the port of its father, and eternally guards and defends it. Hence, if the universe is said to be indissoluble, it is this goddess who supplies its permanency; and if it moves in measured motion, through the whole of time, according to one reason and order, she is the source of this supply. She watchfully surveys therefore all the fabrication of her father, and connects and converts it to him; and vanquishes all material indefiniteness. Hence she is called *Victory* and *Health;* the former because she causes intellect to rule over necessity, and form over matter; and the latter, because she preserves the universe perpetually whole, perfect, exempt from age, and free from disease. It is the property therefore of this goddess to elevate and distribute, and through an intellectual dance as it were, to connect, establish, and defend inferior natures in such as are more divine."[†]

7. (See page 551.) This is a very ancient Egyptian doctrine. And hence Kircher in his *Oedipus Egyptiacus* says that he read the following words engraved in a stone near Memphis: *Coelum sursum, coelum deorsum, quod sursum id omne deorsum, hæc cape et beaberis, i.e. Heaven is above and heaven is beneath. Every thing which is above is also beneath. Understand this, and you will be blessed.* Conformably to this also the celebrated Smaragdine Table, which is of such great authority with the Alchemists, and which whether originally written or not by Hermes Trismegistus, is doubtless of great antiquity, says that all that is beneath resembles all that is above. But the Table itself is as follows: Verum sine mendacio, certum et verissimum: quod est inferius, est sicut id quod est superius, et quod est superius, est sicut id, quod est inferius ad perpetrandum miraculum unius rei. Et sicut res omnes fuerunt ab uno mediatione unius, sic omnes res natæ ab hac re adoptatione. Pater ejus est sol, mater ejus luna. Portavit illud ventus in ventre suo. Nutrix ejus terra, pater omnis telesmi totius mundi est hic. Virtus ejus integra est, si vera fuerit in terram. Separabis terram ab igne, subtile a spisso suaviter cum magno ingenio. Ascendit a terra in coelum, iterumque descendit in terram, et recipit vim

---

[†] These admirable Scholia on the *Cratylus* end here, being unfortunately, like most both of the published and unpublished writings of Proclus, incomplete. These very scholia too appear to be nothing more than extracts from a copious commentary of Proclus which is lost.

superiorum et inferiorum. Sic habebis gloriam totius mundi, ideo fugiet à te omnis obscuritas. Hæc est totius fortitudinis fortitudo fortis, quia vincet omnem rem subtilem, omniaque solida penetrabit. Sic mundus creatus est. Hinc erunt adoptationes mirabiles, quarum modus hic est. Itaque vecatus sum Hermes Trismegistus habens tres partes philosophiæ tortius mundi. Completum est quod dixi de opere solis." *i.e.* "It is true without a lie, certain, and most true, that what is beneath is like that which is above, and what is above is like that which is beneath, for the purpose of accomplishing the miracle of one thing. And as all things were from one through the mediation of one, so all things were generated from this thing by adoption [*i.e.* by participation.] The sun is its father, and the moon its mother. The wind carried it in its belly. The earth is its nurse. This is the father of all the perfection of the whole world. Its power is entire when it is converted into earth. You must separate the earth from the fire, the subtil from the thick sweetly with great genius. It ascends from earth to heaven, and again descends to the earth, and receives the power of things superior and inferior. Thus you will have the glory of the whole world, and thus all obscurity will fly from you. This is the strong fortitude of all fortitude, because it vanquishes every subtile thing, and penetrates all solid substances. Thus the world was fabricated. Hence admirable adoptions will take place of which this is the mode. I am therefore called Hermes Trismegistus possessing three parts of the philosophy of the whole world. That which I have said concerning the work of the sun is complete."

8. (See page 565.) The meaning of Proclus in asserting that the ennead proceeds from the monad as far as to the extremities without regression is as follows: The ennead, according to the Pythagoreans, circulates all numbers within itself, and there can be no number beyond it. For the natural progression of numbers is as far as to 9, but after it their retrogression takes place. For 10 becomes as it were again the monad. Thus, if from each of the numbers 10, 11, 12, 13, 14, 15, 16, 17, 18, and 19, the number 9 is subtracted, the numbers that remain will be 1, 2, 3, 4, 5, 6, 7, 8, 9, 10. And vice versa, the progression will receive an increase by the addition of 9. For, if to each of the numbers 1, 2, 3, 4, 5, etc. 9 is added, the numbers produced will be 10, 11, 12, 13, etc. Likewise by subtracting from 20 twice 9, from 30 thrice 9, from 40 four times 9, from 50 five times 9 etc., the numbers 2, 3, 4, 5, 6, etc. will be produced. By taking likewise from 100 eleven times 9, we again return to the monad. And after the same manner we may proceed to infinity. Hence it is not possible there should be any elementary number beyond the ennead. Hence too the Pythagoreans, called it Ocean and the Horizon, because all numbers are comprehended by and revolve within it. On this account likewise, it was called by them Halios, ($\pi\alpha\rho\alpha$ το αλιζειν) and Concord and Perseïa because it congregates all numbers, and collects them into one, and does not permit the conspiration of the numbers beyond it to be dissipated. Vid. Anonym. in opere quod inscripsit τα θεολογουμενα της αριθμητικης.

695

References in the seven books
to the dialogues of Plato.

N.B. The page numbers below include all the references to Timæus and Parmenides, whether Proclus is refering to persons or the dialogues named after them.

Banquet	59, 63, 64, 67, 113, 114, 120, 124, 246, 261, 276, 376, 491, 539, 551, 598, 601.
Cratylus	63, 64, 108, 124, 244, 272, 274, 308-310, 312, 322, 323, 349, 351, 354, 360, 375, 378, 381-383, 391, 413, 415, 419, 423, 424-426, 428, 429, 433, 455, 463, 517, 521, 528, 534, 550, 556, 563, 569, 582, 611, 614, 616, 617, 636.
Critias	348.
Epistles	158, 189.
Euthydemus	433.
First Alcibiades	597, 603, 609.
Gorgias	59, 63-65, 263, 318, 319, 383, 409, 413, 414, 419, 450, 563, 580.
Parmenides	54, 59, 61, 67-72, 75, 77, 81-83, 124, 148-150, 152, 155, 164, 165, 167, 168, 170-173, 178-180, 188, 189, 201, 214-217, 222-232, 255-257, 280-283, 286, 289, 290, 292, 293, 295-297, 321, 365, 384, 385, 387-394, 396, 399, 401, 402, 407, 414, 415, 434, 436, 437, 446, 453, 462, 464, 465, 573, 574, 586, 592, 594, 595, 620.
Philebus	63, 64, 66, 75, 111, 125, 148, 185, 189, 190, 197, 199, 204, 213, 220, 308, 352, 366, 372, 415, 427, 443, 467.
Politicus	60, 63, 106, 226, 315, 318, 319, 335, 342, 357, 375, 415, 583, 585, 625, 634.
Protagoras	59, 63, 65, 355-357, 377.
Republic	61, 63, 65, 71, 98, 103, 110, 113, 120, 145, 149, 150, 152-154, 159, 180, 185, 188, 194, 294, 295, 310, 356, 368, 429, 431, 456, 459, 460, 478, 520, 533, 579, 582, 585, 605, 607.
Sophista	59, 63, 70, 71, 76, 119, 147, 186, 214, 225, 230, 556.
Laws	63, 84, 90, 98, 117, 119, 185, 309, 318, 323, 361, 375, 380, 415, 433, 459, 460, 503, 557, 586, 592, 617, 624
Theages	609